Multimedia Forensics and Security

Chang-Tsun Li
University of Warwick, UK

INFORMATION SCIENCE REFERENCE

Hershey · New York

Acquisitions Editor:	Kristin Klinger
Managing Development Editor:	Kristin Roth
Assistant Managing Development Editor:	Jessica Thompson
Editorial Assistant:	Rebecca Beistline
Senior Managing Editor:	Jennifer Neidig
Managing Editor:	Jamie Snavely
Assistant Managing Editor:	Carole Coulson
Copy Editor:	Holly Powell
Typesetter:	Carole Coulson
Cover Design:	Lisa Tosheff
Printed at:	Yurchak Printing Inc.

Published in the United States of America by
Information Science Reference (an imprint of IGI Global)
701 E. Chocolate Avenue, Suite 200
Hershey PA 17033
Tel: 717-533-8845
Fax: 717-533-8661
E-mail: cust@igi-global.com
Web site: http://www.igi-global.com

and in the United Kingdom by
Information Science Reference (an imprint of IGI Global)
3 Henrietta Street
Covent Garden
London WC2E 8LU
Tel: 44 20 7240 0856
Fax: 44 20 7379 0609
Web site: http://www.eurospanbookstore.com

Library of Congress Cataloging-in-Publication Data

Multimedia forensics and security / Chang-Tsun Li, editor.

   p. cm.

 Includes bibliographical references and index.

 Summary: "This book provides an in-depth treatment of advancements in the emerging field of multimedia forensics and security by tackling challenging issues such as digital watermarking for copyright protection, digital fingerprinting for transaction tracking, and digital camera source identification"--Provided by publisher.

 ISBN 978-1-59904-869-7 (hardcover) -- ISBN 978-1-59904-870-3 (ebook)

 1. Multimedia systems--Security measures. 2. Data encryption (Computer science) 3. Data protection. I. Li, Chang-Tsun.

 QA76.575.M83187 2008

 005.8--dc22

                             2008008467

British Cataloguing in Publication Data
A Cataloguing in Publication record for this book is available from the British Library.

All work contributed to this book set is original material. The views expressed in this book are those of the authors, but not necessarily of the publisher.

List of Reviewers

Andrew Ker
Oxford University, UK

Alain Trémeau
Université Jean Monnet - Bat. E, FRANCE

Natasa Terzija
University of Manchester, UK

Chang-Tsun Li
Univeristy of Warwick, UK

Yinyin Yuan
Univeristy of Warwick, UK

Yue Li
Univeristy of Warwick, UK

Andreas Uhl
Salzburg University, Salzburg, Austria

Zhu Yan
Peiking University, China

Fouad Khelif
Queen's University Belfast, UK

Martin Steinebach
Media Security in IT, Germany

Patrick.Wolf
Media Security in IT, Germany

Maciej Li´skiewicz
Federal Office for Information Security (BSI), Germany

Ulrich Wölfel
Federal Office for Information Security (BSI), Germany

Florent Autrusseau
l'Université de Nantes, FRANCE

Maria Calagna
Universita' La Sapienza, Italy

Hongxia Jin
IBM Almaden Research Center, USA

Hae Yong Kim
Universidade de São Paulo, Brazil

Sergio Pamboukian
Universidade Presbiteriana Mackenzie, Brazil

Shiguo Liang
France Telecom R&D Beijing

Angela Wong
University of Adelaide, Australia

Matthew Sorell
University of Adelaide, Australia

Roberto Caldelli
University of Florence, Italy

Alessandro Piva
University of Florence, Italy

Abdellatif ZAIDI
UCL, Belgium

Yonggang Fu
Jimei University, China

Xingming Sun
Hunan University, China

Yongjian Hu
South China University of Technology, China

Table of Contents

Detailed Table of Contents

Data hiding (DH) is a technique used to embed a sequence of bits in a cover image with small visual deterioration and the means to extract it afterwards. Authentication watermarking (AW) techniques use DHs to insert a particular data into an image, in order to detect later any accidental or malicious alterations in the image, as well as to certify that the image came from the right source. In recent years, some AWs for binary images have been proposed in the literature. The authentication of binary images is necessary in practice, because most scanned and computer-generated document images are binary. This publication describes techniques and theories involved in binary image AW: We describe DH techniques for binary images and analyze which of them are adequate to be used in AWs; analyze the most adequate secret and public-key cryptographic ciphers for the AWs; describe how to spatially localize the alteration in the image (besides detecting it) without compromising the security; present AWs for JBIG2-compressed binary images; present a reversible AW for binary images; and finally present our conclusions and future research.

Since the past decade, multimedia protection technologies have been attracting more and more researchers. Among them, multimedia encryption and watermarking are two typical ones. Multimedia encryption encodes media data into an unintelligible form, which emphasizes on confidentiality protection. Multimedia watermarking embeds information into media data, which can be detected or extracted and used to authenticate the copyright. Traditionally, in multimedia distribution, media data are encrypted and then transmitted, while the copyright information is not considered. As an important application, to trace illegal distributors, the customer information (e.g., customer ID) is embedded into media data, which can trace illegal distributors. In this chapter, the multimedia distribution scheme based on watermarking technology is investigated, which realizes both confidentiality protection and copyright protection. Firstly, some related works, including multimedia encryption and digital watermarking, are introduced. Then, the existing watermarking-based distribution schemes are reviewed and analyzed. Furthermore, the novel scheme is proposed and evaluated. Finally, some open issues are presented.

Chapter III

The chapter illustrates watermarking based on the transform domain. It argues that transform-based watermarking is robust to possible attacks and imperceptible with respect to the quality of the multimedia file we would like to protect. Among those transforms commonly used in communications, we emphasize the use of singular value decomposition (SVD) for digital watermarking; the main advantage of this choice is flexibility of application. In fact, SVD may be applied in several fields where data are organized as matrices, including multimedia and communications. We present a robust SVD-based watermarking scheme for images. According to the detection steps, the watermark can be determined univocally, while other related works present flaws in watermark detection. A case study of our approach refers to the protection of geographical and spatial data in case of the raster representation model of maps.

Chapter IV

This chapter is devoted to the analysis of the collusion attack applied to current digital video watermarking algorithms. In particular, we analyze which are the effects of collusion attacks, with particular attention to the temporal frame averaging (TFA), applied to two basic watermarking systems like spread spectrum (SS) and spread transform dither modulation (STDM). The chapter describes the main drawbacks and advantages in using these two watermarking schemes and, above all, the fundamental issues to be taken into account to grant a certain level of robustness when a collusion attack is carried out by an attacker.

Chapter V

The resistance of watermarking schemes against geometric distortions has been the subject of much research and development effort in the last 10 years. This is due to the fact that even the minor geometric manipulation of the watermarked image can dramatically reduce the ability of the watermark detector to detect the watermark, that is, the watermark detector can lose the synchronization. By this, the watermark synchronization can be defined as a process for finding the location for watermark embedding and detection. A variety of techniques have been proposed to provide partial robustness against geometrical distortions. These techniques can be divided into two groups: techniques that use the original image to recover to synchronization and techniques that do not have the access to the original image content during the synchronization process. This chapter classifies and analyzes techniques and approaches that are currently used in watermarking schemes to recover the synchronization.

Chapter VI

Martin Steinebach, Fraunhofer Institute for Secure Information Technology (SIT), Germany
Patrick Wolf, Fraunhofer Institute for Secure Information Technology (SIT), Germany

Digital watermarking promises to be a mechanism for copyright protection without being a technology for copy prevention. This sometimes makes it hard to convince content owners to use digital watermarking for protecting their content. It is only passive technology adding information into the content to be protected. Therefore some active mechanism is required that completes the protection. This needs to be a search mechanism that localizes potentially watermarked media on the Internet. Only then the passive information embedded in the content can help to fight illegal copies. We discuss strategies and approaches for retrieving watermarks from the Internet with the help of a media search framework. While various Internet domains like HTML pages (the Web), eBay, or FTP are discussed, the focus of this work is on content shared within peer-to-peer networks.

Chapter VII

Fouad Khelifi, The Institute of Electronics Communications and Information Technology
    (ECIT), Queen's University Belfast, UK
Fatih Kurugollu, The Institute of Electronics Communications and Information Technology
    (ECIT), Queen's University Belfast, UK
Ahmed Bouridane, The Institute of Electronics Communications and Information Technology
    (ECIT), Queen's University Belfast, UK

The problem of multiplicative watermark detection in digital images can be viewed as a binary decision where the observation is the possibly watermarked samples that can be thought of as a noisy environment in which a desirable signal, called watermark, may exist. In this chapter, we investigate the optimum watermark detection from the viewpoint of decision theory. Different transform domains are considered with generalized noise models. We study the effect of the watermark strength on both the detector performance and the imperceptibility of the host image. Also, the robustness issue is addressed while considering a number of commonly used attacks.

Chapter VIII

Christopher B. Smith, Southwest Research Institute, USA
Sos S. Agaian, The University of Texas at San Antonio, USA

Modern digital steganography has evolved a number of techniques to embed information near invisibly into digital media. Many of the techniques for information hiding result in a set of changes to the cover image that appear for all intents and purposes to be noise. This chapter presents information for the reader to understand how noise is intentionally and unintentionally used in information hiding. This chapter first reviews a series of noise-like steganography methods. From these techniques the problems faced by the active warden can be posed in a systematic way. Results of using advanced clean image estimation techniques for active-warden-based steganalysis are presented. This chapter is concluded with a discussion of the future of steganography.

Chapter IX

Patrick Le Callet, Polytech'Nantes, University of Nantes, IRCCyN Lab, France
Florent Autrusseau, Polytech'Nantes, University of Nantes, IRCCyN Lab, France
Patrizio Campisi, Università degli Studi Roma TRE, Italy

In watermarking and data hiding context, it may be very useful to have methods checking the invisibility of the inserted data, or at least, checking the objective quality after the mark embedding or after an attack on the watermarked media. Many works exist in the literature dealing with quality assessment, mainly focused on compression application. Nevertheless, visual quality assessment should include special requirements that depend on the application context. This chapter presents an extended review of both subjective and objective quality assessment of images and video in the field of watermarking and data hiding applications.

Chapter X

Maciej Liśkiewicz, Institute of Theoretical Computer Science, University of Lübeck, Germany
Ulrich Wölfel, Federal Office Information Security (BSI), Germany

This chapter provides an overview, based on current research, on theoretical aspects of digital steganography—a relatively new field of computer science that deals with hiding secret data in unsuspicious cover media. We focus on formal analysis of security of steganographic systems from a computational complexity point of view and provide models of secure systems that make realistic assumptions of limited computational resources of involved parties. This allows us to look at steganographic secrecy based on reasonable complexity assumptions similar to the ones commonly accepted in modern cryptography. In this chapter we expand the analyses of stegosystems beyond security aspects that practitioners find difficult to implement (if not impossible to realize), to the question *why* such systems are so difficult to implement and what makes these systems different from practically used ones.

Chapter XI

Christopher B. Smith, Southwest Research Institute, USA
Sos S. Agaian, The University of Texas at San Antonio, USA

Steganalysis is the art and science of detecting hidden information. Modern digital steganography has created techniques to embed information near invisibly into digital media. This chapter explores the idea of exploiting the noise-like qualities of steganography. In particular, the art of steganalysis can be defined as detecting and/or removing a very particular type of noise. This chapter first reviews a series of steganalysis techniques including blind steganalysis and targeted steganalysis methods, *and* highlight how clean image estimation is vital to these techniques. Each technique either implicitly or explicitly uses a clean image model to begin the process of detection. This chapter includes a review of advanced methods of clean image estimation for use in steganalysis. From these ideas of clean image estimation, the problems faced by the passive warden can be posed in a systematic way. This chapter is concluded with a discussion of the future of passive warden steganalysis.

Chapter XII

     Hafiz Malik, University of Michigan–Dearborn, USA
     Rajarathnam Chandramouli, Stevens Institute of Technology, USA
     K. P. Subbalakshmi, Stevens Institute of Technology, USA

In this chapter we provide a detailed overview of the state of the art in steganalysis. Performance of some steganalysis techniques are compared based on critical parameters such as the hidden message detection probability, accuracy of the estimated hidden message length and secret key, and so forth. We also provide an overview of some shareware/freeware steganographic tools. Some open problems in steganalysis are described.

Chapter XIII

     Andrew D. Ker, Oxford University Computing Laboratory, UK

This chapter discusses how to evaluate the effectiveness of steganalysis techniques. In the steganalysis literature, numerous different methods are used to measure detection accuracy, with different authors using incompatible benchmarks. Thus it is difficult to make a fair comparison of competing steganalysis methods. This chapter argues that some of the choices for steganalysis benchmarks are demonstrably poor, either in statistical foundation or by over-valuing irrelevant areas of the performance envelope. Good choices of benchmark are highlighted, and simple statistical techniques demonstrated for evaluating the significance of observed performance differences. It is hoped that this chapter will make practitioners and steganalysis researchers better able to evaluate the quality of steganography detection methods.

Chapter XIV

     Matthew J. Sorell, University of Adelaide, Australia

We propose that the implementation of the JPEG compression algorithm represents a manufacturer and model-series specific means of identification of the source camera of a digital photographic image. Experimental results based on a database of over 5,000 photographs from 27 camera models by 10 brands shows that the choice of JPEG quantisation table, in particular, acts as an effective discriminator between model series with a high level of differentiation. Furthermore, we demonstrate that even after recompression of an image, residual artifacts of double quantisation continue to provide limited means of source camera identification, provided that certain conditions are met. Other common techniques for source camera identification are also introduced, and their strengths and weaknesses are discussed.

This chapter discusses the cryptographic traitor tracing technology that is used to defend against piracy in multimedia content distribution. It talks about different potential pirate attacks in a multimedia content distribution system. It discusses how traitor tracing technologies can be used to defend against those attacks by identifying the attackers involved in the piracy. While traitor tracing has been a long standing cryptographic problem that has attracted extensive research, the main purpose of this chapter is to show how to overcome many practical concerns in order to bring a theoretical solution to practice. Many of these practical concerns have been overlooked in academic research. The author brings first-hand experience on bringing this technology to practice in the context of new industry standard on content protection for next generation high-definition DVDs. The author also hopes to shed new insights on future research directions in this space.

In this chapter we investigate two different techniques for transparent/perceptual encryption of JPEG2000 files or bitstreams in the context of digital right management (DRM) schemes. These methods are efficient in the sense of minimizing the computational costs of encryption. A classical bitstream-based approach employing format-compliant encryption of packet body data is compared to a compression-integrated technique, which uses the concept of secret transform domains, in our case a wavelet packet transform.

Foreword

The advances and convergence of information and communication technology (ICT) and multimedia techniques have brought about unprecedented possibilities and opportunities. The upside is that we benefit from the convenience that these technologies have to offer. Information can be exchanged in various forms of media through far-reaching networks, while multimedia processing techniques facilitate efficient fusion of media with stunning effects, which have already made a profound impact on the ways we communicate, learn, and entertain. However, the downside is that these technologies could also be exploited for malicious purposes such as copyright piracy and document forgery, to name a few. To prevent abuses of the usage of ICT and multimedia techniques, the study of multimedia forensics and security has emerged in recent years as a new interdisciplinary area encompassing aspects of digital cryptography, digital watermarking, data hiding, steganography, and steganalysis. Moreover, multimedia forensic techniques have also opened up a new horizon for helping companies, government, and law enforcement agencies in combating crime and fraudulent activities.

The past decade has seen an exciting development of techniques revolving around the issues of multimedia forensics and security. Although a number of quality books have been published in the literature, the fast-advancing technology in this field entails a constant renewal of systematic and comprehensive accounts of the latest researches and developments. Aiming at serving this purpose, this book contains a collection of informative and stimulating chapters written by knowledgeable experts and covers a wide spectrum of the state-of-the-art techniques for tackling the issues of multimedia forensics and security. Each chapter is a self-contained treatment on one aspect of the broad subject, allowing the readers to follow any order of their liking. The chapters are selected to suit readers of different levels with various interests, making this book an invaluable reference for beginners as well as experts alike.

Professor Anthony TS Ho
Professor and Chair of Multimedia Security,
Director of Postgraduate Research
Department of Computing,
Faculty of Engineering and Physical Sciences,
University of Surrey,
Guildford, Surrey, GU2 7XH
UK

Preface

In the last two decades, the development of information and communication technology (ICT) and multimedia processing techniques has revolutionized the ways we create, exchange, and manipulate information. Most people, if not all, with access to computers and the Internet, can not only share information instantly at insignificant cost, but also creatively produce their own media of various forms, such as text, audio, speech, music, image, and video. This wave of ICT revolution has undoubtedly brought about enormous opportunities for the world economy and exciting possibilities for every sector of the modern societies. Educators are now equipped with *e-tools* to deliver their knowledge and expertise to the remote corners of the world with Internet access. Harnessing these ICT resources, *e-governments* can now provide various aspects of *e-services* to the people. Willingly or reluctantly, directly or indirectly, we are all now immersed in some way in the cyberspace full of *e-opportunities* and *e-possibilities* and permeated with data and information. However, this type of close and strong interweaving poses concerns and threats. When exploited with malign intentions, the same tools provide means for doing harms at a colossal scale. These concerns create anxiety and uncertainty about the reality of the media we deal with.

In response to these issues, the last decade has seen the emergence of the new interdisciplinary field of multimedia forensics and security, which aims at pooling expertise in various areas, such as signal processing, information theory, cryptography, and so forth to combat the abuses of ICT and multimedia techniques. In particular, digital watermarking schemes have been proposed to meet copyright protection needs, for example, ownership identification, copy control, transaction tracking, and to deal with content authentication and integrity verification. Challenged by its competing steganalytical techniques, steganographic methods have been developed and are being constantly improved for data hiding and embedding applications. Multimedia forensic techniques have also been studied and derived for providing evidences to aid with resolving civil and criminal court cases. Added to the excitement of the races between new measures and countermeasures in this new area is the difficulties in striking a balance between conflicting requirements. For example, in the context of digital watermarking, high robustness is usually gained at the expense of high distortion, while, in the context of steganography, low distortion is, most of the times, achieved at the cost of low payload.

This book aims to create a collection of quality chapters on information hiding for multimedia forensics and security contributed by leading experts in the related fields. It embraces a wide variety of aspects of the related subject areas covered in 16 chapters and provides a scientifically and scholarly sound treatment of state-of-the-art techniques to students, researchers, academics, personnel of law enforcement, and IT/multimedia practitioners, who are interested or involved in the study, research, use, design, and development of techniques related to multimedia forensics and security.

This book consists of three main components. The first component, comprised of Chapters I to VII, aims at dissemilating the idea of digital watermarking and its applications to multimedia security in general and copyright protection in particular. The second component, which covers Chapters VIII to XIII, is concerned with the two competing arts of steganography and steganalysis. The third component, comprising Chapters XIV to XVI, deals with methods that harness the techniques of data hiding and cryptography for the applications of multimedia forensics.

Chapter I, *Authentication Watermarkings for Binary Images*, presented by Hae Yong Kim, Sergio Pamboukian, and Paulo Barreto, is concerned with a class of data hiding techniques and the analysis of which of them are suitable for authenticating binary images. Ways of detecting and localising tamper, aiming at revealing the attacker's possible intention, are described. A new irreversible scheme for authenticating JBIG2-compressed binary images and a new reversible algorithm for authenticating general binary images are presented.

In Chapter II, *Secure Multimedia Content Distribution Based on Watermarking Technology*, Shiguo Lian defines the performance requirements of watermarking-based multimedia distribution schemes for multimedia communication applications and reviewed a number of related schemes, with their characteristics and limitations discussed. A new scheme combining fingerprinting and encryption, which realises both confidentiality protection and copyright protection, is then presented to address the issues, such as traitor tracing, robustness, and imperceptibility, surrounding multimedia distribution and to meet the defined requirements.

In Chapter III, *Digital Watermarking in the Transform Domain with Emphasis on SVD*, Maria Calagna first introduces the main mathematical tools, such as discrete cosine transform (DCT), discrete wavelet transform (DWT), and singular value decomposition (SVD) and their applications in digital watermarking and then places emphasis on presenting and comparing related work on SVD watermarking. To overcome the flaws found in the watermark extraction component of some discussed SVD-based schemes, Calagna proposes a new SVD-based scheme for watermarking geographical and spatial images exchanged among a group of GIS users.

In Chapter IV, *Digital Video Watermarking and the Collusion Attack*, Roberto Caldelli and Alessandro Piva present a taxonomy of video watermarking techniques according to data formats and signal processing tools employed for implementation. The idea and types of collusion attacks are then analysed. In particular, the effects of applying temporal frame averaging (TFA) to the watermarking systems implemented with spread spectrum (SS) and spread transform dither modulation (STDM) are studied in great details. This chapter identifies the main advantages and limitations of the SS- and STDM-based schemes in the face of TFA collusion attack.

Chapter V, *A Survey of Current Watermarking Synchronization Techniques*, authored by Natasa Terzija, deals with the synchronization issue of watermark detection under the threat of geometric distortions, such as translation, cropping, rotation, scaling, affine transformation, projective transformation, and so forth. Watermark synchronization has been an active research area in the last 10 years because even a minor geometric distortion of the watermarked image can dramatically reduce the watermark detectors' the ability to detect the presence of the watermark, that is, the watermark detector can lose the *synchronization*. Terija gives an overview of different techniques including image registration techniques, the exhaustive search, periodical sequences, the use of synchronization marks, content-based approaches, and then concludes that the existing techniques can only provide partial robustness against geometrical distortions and more efforts are yet to be made before proper solutions can be put in place.

In Chapter VI, *On the Necessity of Finding Content before Watermark Retrieval—Active Search Strategies for Localizing Watermarked Media on the Internet*, Martin Steinebach and Patrick Wolf state that embedding digital watermark for copyright protection is only a passive protection and, to complete the protection, an active mechanism capable of finding potentially watermarked media that have been distributed is needed before the watermark extraction can actually be carried out to help fight illegal copies. This chapter discusses important issues regarding the search for watermarked content on the Internet and introduces strategies and approaches for retrieving watermarks from the Internet with the help of a media search framework.

In Chapter VII, *Statistical Watermark Detection in the Transform Domain for Digital Images*, Fouad Khelifi, Fatih Kurugollu, and Ahmed Bouridane view the problem of multiplicative watermark detection in digital images as a binary decision where the observation is the possibly watermarked samples that can be thought of as a noisy environment in which a desirable watermark may exist. They investigate optimum watermark detection from the viewpoint of decision theory. Different transform domains are considered with generalized noise models and the effects of the watermark strength on both the detector performance and the imperceptibility of the host image are studied.

Chapter VIII, *On Noise, Steganography, and the Active Warden*, marks the beginning of the second component of this book. In the face of the fact that many data hiding techniques give rise to changes to the cover media that appear to be noise, Christopher Smith and Sos Agaian state in this chapter that steganography can be defined in terms of adding some type of artificial noise and review a series of state-of-the-art, noise-like steganographic schemes. The authors also present information for the reader to understand how noise is unintentionally and intentionally exploited in information hiding and show how passive and active steganalysis can be applied to attack steganographic schemes. Results of using advanced clean image estimation techniques for steganalysis under the active warden scenario are also presented.

Among the many conflicting requirements of digital watermarking and data hiding, visibility (or embedding distortion inflicted on the host media by the marking process) is of significant concern. Chapter IX, *Visibility Control and Quality Assessment of Watermarking and Data Hiding Algorithms*, contributed by Patrick Le Callet and Florent Autrusseau, deals with both the subjective and objective quality assessment of images and video in the context of digital watermarking and data hiding applications. The deficiencies of some quality metrics for data hiding purpose are highlighted. Subjective experimental protocols are conducted. A quality benchmark aiming at identifying the objective metrics among many that best predicts subjective scores is presented.

In Chapter X, *Computational Aspects of Digital Steganography*, Maciej Liśkiewicz and Ulrich Wölfel focus on the formal analysis of the security of steganographic schemes from a computational complexity point of view and provide models of secure schemes that make realistic assumptions of limited computational resources of involved parties. This allows the reader to look at steganographic secrecy based on reasonable complexity assumptions similar to the ones commonly accepted in modern cryptography. The authors expand the analyses of stego-systems beyond security aspects that practitioners find difficult to implement to the tractability aspects, that is, the question *why* such schemes are so difficult to implement and what makes these systems different from practically used ones. These questions concern the maximum achievable security for different steganography scenarios and the limitations in terms of time efficiency associated with stego-systems that achieve the highest levels of security.

In Chapter XI, *On Steganalysis and Clean Image Estimation*, Christopher Smith and Sos Agaian expand on the idea of exploiting the noise-like qualities of steganography and discuss its competing technology of steganalysis, the art and science of detecting hidden information in media. They define the art of steganalysis in terms of detecting and/or removing a particular type of noise and review a series of steganalysis techniques, including blind steganalysis and targeted steganalysis methods, which either implicitly or explicitly use a clean image model to begin the detection of hidden data. From these ideas of clean image estimation, the steganalysis problems faced by the passive warden are formulated as a three-stage process of estimation, feature extraction, and classification (the EFC formulation).

Chapter XII, *Steganalysis: Trends and Challenges*, by Hafiz Malik, R. Chandramouli and K. P. Subbalakshmi provide a detailed overview of the state-of-the-art techniques in steganalysis. The performance of existing steganalysis techniques are compared based on critical parameters such as the hidden message detection probability; the accuracy of the hidden message length and secret key estimates; and the message recovery rate. They also provide an overview of some existing shareware/freeware steganographic tools and highlight the pros and cons of existing steganalysis techniques. The growing gap between recent developments in the steganographic research and the state-of-the-art of steganalysis are also discussed.

Chapter XIII, *Benchmarking Steganalysis*, by Andrew Ker, discusses how to evaluate the effectiveness of steganalysis techniques. In the steganalysis literature, numerous different methods are used to measure detection accuracy, with different authors using incompatible benchmarks. Thus, it is difficult to make a fair comparison of competing steganalysis methods. This chapter argues that some of the choices for steganalysis benchmarks are demonstrably poor, either in statistical foundation or by over-valuing irrelevant areas of the performance envelope. Good choices of benchmarks are highlighted, and simple statistical techniques demonstrated for evaluating the significance of observed performance differences. It is hoped that this chapter will make practitioners and steganalysis researchers better able to evaluate the quality of steganography detection methods.

In the light of the fact that digital photographs are becoming a more common form of evidence used in criminal investigation and civil court of laws, Chapter XIV, *Digital Camera Source Identification Through JPEG Quantisation*, presented by Matthew Sorell, is concerned with the identification of the make, the model series, and the particular source camera of a particular digital photograph. Characteristics of the camera's JPEG coder are exploited to demonstrate the possibility of such identification and the likelihood of detecting sufficient residual characteristics of the original coding even when an image has subsequently been recompressed, allowing the investigator to narrow down the possible camera models of interest in some cases. Three sets of techniques, classified according to the employed data, namely, metadata, bullet scratches/fingerprinting, and manufacturer specific information, for camera identification are discussed.

Chapter XV, *Traitor Tracing for Multimedia Forensics*, authored by Hongxia Jin, reviews potential pirate attacks on multimedia content distribution systems and discusses how traitor tracing techniques can be used to defend against those attacks by tracing the attackers and colluders involved in the piracy. This chapter is also concerned with business scenarios that involve one-way digital content distribution and a large set of receiving users. It shows how to address many overlooked practical concerns and brings first hand experience on bringing this technology to practice in the context of new industry standard on content protection for next generation high-definition DVDs.

In Chapter XVI, *Efficient Transparent JPEG2000 Encryption*, given the fact that many multimedia applications such as TV new broadcasting are designed for the *try and buy* scenario, and thus require security on a much lower level than that of copyright protection applications, Dominik Enge, Thomas Stütz, and Andreas Uhl review several selective or partial encryption schemes and investigate two different techniques for transparent/perceptual encryption of JPEG2000 files or bitstreams in the context of digital right management (DRM) schemes. These methods are efficient in terms of the computational costs of encryption. A classical bitstream-based approach employing format-compliant encryption of packet body data is compared against a compression-integrated technique, which uses the concept of wavelet packet transform.

Chang-Tsun Li received the BS degree in electrical engineering from Chung-Cheng Institute of Technology (CCIT), National Defense University, Taiwan, in 1987, the MS degree in computer science from U. S. Naval Postgraduate School, USA, in 1992, and the PhD degree in computer science from the University of Warwick, UK, in 1998. He was an associate professor of the Department of Electrical Engineering at CCIT during 1999-2002 and a visiting professor of the Department of Computer Science at U.S. Naval Postgraduate School in the second half of 2001. He is currently an associate professor of the Department of Computer Science at the University of Warwick, UK, Editor-in-Chief of the International Journal of Digital Crime and Forensics (IJDCF)and Associate Editor of the International Journal of Applied Systemic Studies (IJASS). He has involved in the organisation of a number of international conferences and workshops and also served as member of the international program committees for several international conferences. His research interests include multimedia security, bioinformatics, image processing, pattern recognition, computer vision and content-based image retrieval.

Acknowledgment

Few books are entirely the unaided efforts of one person and this one is no exception. I would like to thank all the authors of the chapters for their invaluable contributions and enthusiasm in making this book possible. I am also grateful for the reviewers who have contributed their time and expertise in helping the authors improve their chapters. Administrative assistance from the staff at IGI Global has also made the project quite an enjoyable process and was highly appreciated.

Chapter I
Authentication Watermarkings for Binary Images

Hae Yong Kim
Universidade de São Paulo, Brazil

Sergio Vicente Denser Pamboukian
Universidade Presbiteriana Mackenzie, Brazil

Paulo Sérgio Licciardi Messeder Barreto
Universidade de São Paulo, Brazil

ABSTRACT

Data hiding (DH) is a technique used to embed a sequence of bits in a cover image with small visual deterioration and the means to extract it afterwards. Authentication watermarking (AW) techniques use DH to insert particular data into an image, in order to detect later any accidental or malicious alterations in the image, as well as to certify that the image came from the right source. In recent years, some AWs for binary images have been proposed in the literature. The authentication of binary images is necessary in practice, because most scanned and computer-generated document images are binary. This publication describes techniques and theories involved in binary image AW: We describe DH techniques for binary images and analyze which of them are adequate to be used in AWs; analyze the most adequate secret- and public-key cryptographic ciphers for the AWs; describe how to spatially localize the alteration in the image (besides detecting it) without compromising the security; present AWs for JBIG2-compressed binary images; present a reversible AW for binary images; and finally present our conclusions and future research.

INTRODUCTION

This publication describes techniques and theories involved in binary image AW. The authentication of binary images is necessary in practice because most of scanned and computer-generated document images are binary. These documents must be protected against fraudulent alterations and impersonations.

Binary images can be classified as either halftone or non-halftone. Halftone images are binary representations of grayscale images. Halftoning techniques (Knuth, 1987; Roetling & Loce, 1994; Ulichney, 1987) simulate shades of gray by scattering proper amounts of black and white pixels. On the other hand, non-halftone binary images may be composed of characters, drawings, schematics, diagrams, cartoons, equations, and so forth. In many cases, a watermarking algorithm developed for halftone images cannot be applied to non-halftone images and vice versa.

DH or steganography is a technique used to embed a sequence of bits in a cover image with small visual deterioration and the means to extract it afterwards. Most DH techniques in the literature are designed for grayscale and color images and they cannot be directly applied to binary images. Many of continuous-tone DHs modify the least significant bits (Wong, 1998), modify the quantization index (Chen & Wornell, 2001), or modify spectral components of data in a spread-spectrum-like fashion (Cox, Kilian, Leighton, & Shamoon, 1997; Marvel, Boncelet, & Retter, 1999). Many of the continuous-tone DHs makes use of transforms like DCT and wavelet. Unfortunately, none of the previous concepts (least significant bits, quantization indices, and spectral components) are applicable to binary images. Binary images can be viewed as special cases of grayscale images and consequently can be transformed using DCT or wavelet, resulting in continuous-tone images in transform-domain. However, modifying a transform-domain image to insert the hidden data and inverse transforming

it, usually will not yield a binary image. Hence, transforms like DCT and wavelet cannot be used to hide data in binary images. As consequence of the previous reasoning, special DH techniques must be designed specifically for binary images.

A watermark is a signal added to the original cover image that can be extracted later to make an assertion about the image. Digital watermarking techniques can be roughly classified as either *robust watermarks*, or *authentication watermarks*. Robust watermarks are designed to be hard to remove and to resist common image-manipulation procedures. They are useful for copyright and ownership assertion purposes.

AWs use DH techniques to insert the authentication data into an image, in order to detect later any accidental or malicious alterations in the image, as well as to certify that the image came from the right source. AWs can be further classified in two categories: fragile and semi-fragile watermarks.

Fragile watermarks are designed to detect any alteration in the image, even the slightest. They are easily corrupted by any image-processing procedure. However, watermarks for checking image integrity and authenticity can be fragile because if the watermark is removed, the watermark detection algorithm will correctly report the corruption of the image. We stress that fragile AWs are deliberately not robust in any sense. In the literature, there are many AW techniques for continuous-tone images (Barreto & Kim, 1999; Barreto, Kim, & Rijmen, 2002; Holliman & Memon, 2000; Wong, 1998; Yeung & Mintzer, 1997; Zhao & Koch, 1995). It seems to be very difficult to design a really secure AW without making use of the solid cryptography theory and techniques. Indeed, those AWs that were not founded in cryptography theory (Yeung & Mintzer, 1997; Zhao & Koch, 1995) or those that applied cryptographic techniques without the due care (Li, Lou, & Chen, 2000; Wong, 1998) were later shown to be unreliable (Barreto & Kim, 1999; Barreto et al., 2002; Holliman & Memon,

2000). In a cryptography-based AW, the message authentication code (MAC) or the digital signature (DS) of the whole image is computed and inserted into the image itself. However, inserting the MAC/DS alters the image and consequently alters its MAC/DS, invalidating the watermark. This problem can be solved by dividing the cover image Z in two regions Z_1 and Z_2, computing the MAC/DS of Z_2, and inserting it into Z_1. For example, for uncompressed or lossless-compressed gray-scale and color images, usually the least significant bits (LSBs) are cleared, the MAC/DS of the LSB-cleared image is computed and then the code is inserted into the LSBs (Wong, 1998). For JPEG-compressed images, the 8×8 blocks are divided in two groups Z_1 and Z_2, MAC/DS of Z_2 is computed and each bit of the code is inserted in an 8×8 block of Z_1 by, for example, forcing the sum of the DCT coefficient to be odd or even (Marvel, Hartwig, & Boncelet, 2000). In this publication, we describe similar fragile AW techniques for binary images and the associated security issues.

Semi-fragile watermarks, like fragile ones, are designed to check the image integrity and authenticity. However, semi-fragile watermarks try to distinguish harmless alterations (such as lossy compression, brightness/contrast adjusting, etc.) from malicious image forgeries (intended to remove, substitute, or insert objects in the scene). The demarcation line between benign and malicious attacks is tenuous and application-dependent. Consequently, usually semi-fragile AWs are not as secure as cryptography-based fragile AWs.

We are not aware of any semi-fragile AW for binary images. In the literature, there are many semi-fragile watermarks for continuous-tone images (Eggers & Girod, 2001; Fridrich, 1999; Kundur & Hatzinakos, 1998; Lan, Mansour, & Tewfik, 2001; Lin & Chang, 2000; Lin & Chang, 2001; Lin, Podilchuk, & Delp, 2000; Marvel et al., 2000; Yu, Lu, & Liao, 2001). Ekici, Sankur, and Akcay (2004) enumerate eight "permissible"

alterations that a semi-fragile watermarking must withstand:

1. JPEG compression
2. Histogram equalization
3. Sharpening
4. Low-pass filtering
5. Median filtering
6. Additive Gaussian noise
7. Salt-and-pepper noise
8. Random bit error

However, to our knowledge, there are no similar techniques for binary images. This is explicable considering that most of the benign attacks (1, 2, 3, 4, and 6) cannot be applied to binary images. The remaining attacks (5, 7, and 8) can be applied to binary images but they are not so important in practice to deserve designing special semi-fragile watermarkings. Instead, there are practical interests in designing semi-fragile AWs for binary images that resist:

a. Lossy JBIG2 compression
b. Geometric attacks, that is, rotation, scaling, translation, and cropping
c. Print-scan and photocopy

Let us consider the possibilities of developing these semi-fragile AWs:

a. The JBIG2 standard has been developed by the joint bi-level experts group (JBIG) for the efficient lossless and lossy compression of bi-level (black and white) images. It is capable of compressing black and white documents considerably more than the more commonly used CCITT Group 4 TIFF compression. It was incorporated to the well-known PDF format. To our knowledge, there is no semi-fragile watermarking for binary images that resists to different levels of lossy JBIG2 compression. In the *Data Hiding in JBIG2-Compressed Images (DHTCJ)* section, we discuss a DH technique named DHTCJ that embed bits in JBIG2-compressed images (both lossy or lossless). This technique is not semi-fragile, and consequently the hidden bits will be lost if the watermarked image is re-compressed to different compression levels. The hidden bits can be extracted from the bitmap image obtained by uncompressing JBIG2 image.

b. There are many watermarking techniques for continuous-tone images that can resist geometric distortions. For example, Kutter (1998) replicates the same watermark several times at horizontally and vertically shifted locations. The multiple embedding of the watermark results in additional autocorrelation peaks. By analyzing the configuration of the extracted peaks, the affine distortion applied to the image can be determined and inverted. Pereira and Pun (2000) and Pereira, Ruanaidh, Deguillaume, Csurka, Pun (2000), and Lin et al. (2001) present watermarking resistant to geometric distortions based on the logpolar or log-log maps. The technique presented by Kutter (1998) can be applied to halftone binary images. For example, Chun and Ha (2004) insert spatially replicated registration dots to detect the affine distortion in watermarked halftone images. It seems that the logpolar transform cannot be directly applied to halftone images, because discrete halftone dots cannot withstand continuous logpolar transform. There are only a few DH techniques for non-halftone binary images that resist geometric distortions. They can be based on inserting and detecting some synchronization marks (Wu & Liu, 2004) or using document boundaries. Kim and Mayer (2007) present a geometric distortion-resistant DH technique for printed non-halftone binary images based on tiny, hardly visible synchronization dots. However, a watermarking or DH technique that resists geometric attacks is not automatically a semi-fragile AW resistant to geometric distortions. In our opinion, a robust hashing must be somehow integrated to geometric distortion-resistant watermarking to yield geometric distortion-resistant semi-fragile AW. Robust hashing $h(A)$, also called perceptual image hashing or media hashing, is a value that identifies the image A (Schneider & Chang, 1996). Moreover, given two images A and B, the distance D between the hashing must be somehow proportional to the perceptual visual difference of the images A and B. Lu and Hsu (2005) present a robust hashing for continuous-tone image that withstand geometric-distortion. In short, to our knowledge, there is still no geometric distortion-resistant semi-fragile AW for binary images.

c. There are some DH techniques for binary images robust to print-photocopy-scan. Data may be embedded imperceptibly in printed text by altering some measurable property of a font such as position of a character or font size (Brassil, Low, & Maxemchuk, 1999; Maxemchuk & Low, 1997). Bhattacharjya and Ancin (1999) and Borges and Mayer (2007) insert the hidden data by modulating the luminance of the some elements of the binary image (for example, individual characters). These elements are printed in halftone, and the average brightness, standard deviation, or other features are used to extract the hidden bits. Kim and Mayer (2007) print tiny barely visible dots that carry information. The information hidden in these dots survive the photocopy operation. However, a DH that resists print-photocopy-scan is not automatically a semi-fragile AW that resists print-photocopy-scan. We are not aware of any semi-fragile AW for binary images that resists print-photocopy-scan distortion.

This publication discusses only fragile AWs for binary images in digital form, because as we considered previously, semi-fragile AWs are seemingly still in development.

A possible application of AW for binary images is in Internet fax transmission, that is, for legal authentication of documents routed outside the phone network. Let us suppose that Alice wants to send an authenticated binary document to Bob. She watermarks the binary image using her private key and sends it to Bob through an unreliable channel. Bob receives the watermarked document and, using Alice's public key, can verify that Alice signed the document and that it was not modified after watermarking it. Bob sends a copy of the document to Carol, and she also can verify the authenticity and integrity of the document by the same means.

Friedman (1993) introduced the concept of "trustworthy digital camera." In the proposed camera, the image is authenticated as it emerges from the camera. To accomplish this, the camera produces two output files for each captured image: the captured image and an encrypted DS produced by applying the camera's unique private key embedded within the camera's secure microprocessor. Using watermarking, the DS can be embedded into the image. This scheme can be applied to scanners that scan binary documents using the AW techniques presented in this chapter.

The rest of this chapter is organized as follows. In the second section, we describe some DH techniques for binary images. In the third section, we analyze which DH techniques are adequate to be used in binary image AWs. In the fourth section, we analyze the state of the art in cryptography, describing how to get short MACs and DSs without compromising the security. In the fifth section, we describe how to spatially localize the alterations in the watermarked stego-image. In the sixth section, we present an AW for JBIG2-compressed binary images. The creation of secure AWs for compressed binary images is an important practical problem, because uncompressed binary images use to be very large and can be compressed with high compression rates. In the seventh section, we present a reversible DH for binary images and show how to use it as an AW. Reversible DH allows recovering the original cover image exactly (besides allowing to insert a sequence of bits in the image with small visual deterioration and to recover it later). Finally, in the final two sections, we present our conclusions and future research.

DATA HIDING TECHNIQUES FOR BINARY IMAGES

Many papers in the literature describe methods for inserting a sequence of bits in binary and halftone images. They can be divided into three basic classes:

1. **Component-wise:** Change the characteristics of some pixel groups, for example, the thickness of strokes, the position or the area of characters and words, and so forth (Brassil et al., 1999; Maxemchuk & Low, 1997). Unfortunately, the success of this approach depends highly on the type of the cover image.

2. **Pixel-wise:** Change the values of individual pixels. Those pixels can be chosen randomly (Fu & Au, 2000) or according to some visual impact measure (Kim, 2005; Mei, Wong, & Memon, 2001).

3. **Block-wise:** Divide the cover image into blocks and modify some characteristic of each block to hide the data. Some papers suggest changing the parity (or the quantization) of the number of black pixels in each block (Wu & Liu, 2004). Others suggest flipping one specific pixel in the block with m pixels to insert $\lfloor \log_2 (m+1) \rfloor$ bits (Chang, Tseng, & Lin, 2005; Tseng, Chen, & Pan, 2002).

In this section, we present briefly some of the aforementioned DH techniques that will be used to obtain AWs:

Data Hiding by Self-Toggling (DHST, Pixel-Wise)

DHST is probably the simplest DH technique for binary images (Fu & Au, 2000; Kim & Afif, 2004). In DHST, a pseudo-random number generator with a known seed generates a sequence v of pseudo-random non-repeating data-bearing locations within the image. Then one bit is embedded in each data-bearing location by forcing it to be either black or white. To extract the data, the same sequence v is generated and the values of the data-bearing pixels of v are extracted. This technique is adequate primarily for dispersed-dot halftone images. Otherwise, images watermarked by this technique will present salt-and-pepper noise.

Data Hiding by Template Ranking (DHTR, Block-Wise)

In DHTR (Kim & De Queiroz, 2004; Wu & Liu, 2004), the cover image is divided into blocks (say, 8×8). One bit is inserted in each block by forcing the block to have even or odd number of black pixels. If the block already has the desired parity, it is left untouched. Otherwise, toggle the pixel in the block with the lowest visual impact. Figure 1 depicts one of many possible tables with 3×3 patterns in increasing visual impact order of their central pixels. As different blocks may have different quantities of low visibility pixels, it is suggested to *shuffle* the image before embedding data. This shuffling must use a data structure that allows accessing both the shuffled image (to distribute evenly low visible pixels among the blocks) and the original unshuffled image (to allow computing the visual impact of a pixel by

Figure 1. A 3×3 template ranking in increasing visual impact order with symmetrical central pixels. Hatched pixels match either black or white pixels (note that all patterns have hatched central pixels). The score of a given pattern is that of the matching template with the lowest impact. Mirrors, rotations and reverses of each pattern have the same score.

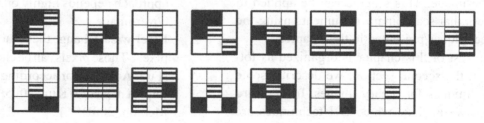

Figure 2. Distribution of candidate pixels to bear data, using 3×3 neighborhoods to evaluate visual impact scores

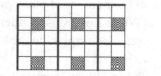

(a) Non-overlapping neighborhoods.

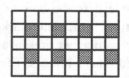

(b) Neighborhoods that do not contain another candidate to bear data.

examining its unshuffled neighborhood). Images watermarked by DHTR usually present high visual quality, because it flips preferentially the pixels with low visual impact.

Data Hiding by Template Ranking with Symmetrical Central Pixels (DHTC, Pixel-Wise)

DHTC is another pixel-based DH technique (Kim, 2005). Here, the sequence v of data-bearing locations is chosen according to some visual impact score, instead of randomly selected as in DHST. The pixels with low visual impact are selected preferentially to bear the data. However, flipping data-bearing pixels may modify the visual scores of the neighboring pixels, and consequently make it impossible to reconstruct v in the data extraction. This problem is solved by: (1) using visual impact scores that do not depend on the value of its central pixel (Figure 1); (2) choosing data-bearing pixels such that their neighborhoods (used to compute the visual scores) do not contain another data-bearing pixel (Figure 2b). In the original paper, the author stated that the data-bearing pixels' neighborhoods should not overlap (Figure 2a); however, we noticed that it is enough that the neighborhoods of data-bearing pixels do not contain another data-bearing pixel (figure 2b), increasing the data embedding capacity. DHTC insertion algorithm is:

1. Let be given a cover image Z and n bits of data to be inserted into Z. Construct the sequence v of candidate pixels to bear data, as explained above.

2. Sort v in increasing order using the visual scores as the primary-key and non-repeating pseudo-random numbers as the secondary-key. The secondary-key prevents from embedding the data mostly in the upper part of the image.

3. Embed n bits of data flipping (if necessary) the n first pixels of v. Those n pixels are called data-bearing pixels.

Mei et al. (2001) present another technique based on similar ideas. The images watermarked by DHTC have high visual quality, because it flips preferentially the pixels with low visual impact.

Chang, Tseng, and Lin's Data Hiding (DHCTL, Block-Wise)

Tseng et al. (2002) present a block-wise DH technique that modifies at most two pixels in a block with m pixels to insert $\lfloor \log_2 (m+1) \rfloor$ bits. Chang et al. (2005) improved this technique to insert the same number of bits by modifying one bit at most. We will explain Chang et al.'s ideas through an example, instead of giving general formulas. Let us suppose that the cover binary image is divided into blocks with 2×4 pixels. In this case, each block can hide 3 bits. The pixels of a block receive *serial numbers* ranging from 001 to 111, as in Figure 3a (some numbers, as 001 in the example, may be repeated). Figure 3b represents the cover block to be watermarked. This block is currently hiding the number $011 \otimes 101 \otimes 111 = 001$ (exclusive-or of the serial numbers of the pixels with value 1). Let us suppose that the number 101 is to be hidden in this block. To modify the hidden

Figure 3. Illustration of DHCTL

001	010	011	100
101	110	111	001

(a) Binary "serial numbers."

0	0	1	0
1	0	1	0

(b) Cover block to watermark.

0	0	1	1
1	0	1	0

(c) Block with hidden 101.

number from 001 to 101, we have to flip the pixel with the serial number $001 \otimes 101 = 100$. Figure 3c depicts the resulting block. A stego-image marked by this technique will present salt-and-pepper noise, because no visual impact was taken into account to choose the flipping pixels.

AUTHENTICATION WATERMARKING FOR BINARY IMAGES

Cryptography-based AWs can be subdivided in three groups:

1. **Keyless:** Keyless AW is useful for detecting unintentional alterations in images. It is a sort of *check-sum*. Cryptographic one-way hashing functions can be used to obtain the integrity index to be inserted in the cover image to certify its integrity.
2. **Secret key:** In a secret-key AW, there must exist a secret key known only by the image generator (say Alice) and the image receiver (say Bob). Alice computes the MAC of the image to be protected using the secret key and inserts it into the image itself. Then, the marked stego-image is transmitted to Bob through an unreliable channel. Bob uses the secret key to verify that the image was not modified after being watermarked by Alice.
3. **Public key:** In a public-key AW, claims of image integrity and authenticity can be settled without disclosing any private information. Alice, the image generator, computes the DS of the image using her private key and inserts it into the image. Only Alice can compute the correct DS, because only she knows her private key. Then, the stego-image is transmitted through an unreliable channel. Anyone that receives the stego-image can verify its authenticity (i.e., whether the image really came from Alice) and integrity (i.e., whether the image was not modified after

being marked by Alice) using the Alice's public key.

An AW scheme (of any of the previous three groups) can either answer only a Boolean response (whether the image contains a valid watermark or not) or insert/extract a logo image (a valid logo will be extracted only if the stego-image is authentic). Introductory books on cryptography, such as Schneier (1996), explain in more detail, concepts like one-way hashing, MAC and DS.

A DH technique can be transformed into an AW computing MAC/DS of the whole image and inserting it into the image itself. However, inserting the MAC/DS alters the image and consequently alters its MAC/DS, invalidating the watermark. This problem can be solved by dividing the cover image Z in two regions Z_1 and Z_2, computing the MAC/DS of Z_2, and inserting it into Z_1. Let us examine how this idea can be applied to the four DH techniques described in the previous section.

Authentication Watermarking by Self-Toggling (AWST)

AWST is obtained applying the previous idea to DHST. In this case, region Z_1 where the MAC/DS will be inserted corresponds to the pixels that belong to the sequence v of data-bearing locations. We describe below the secret-key version of this algorithm that inserts and extracts a logo binary image. The other versions can be derived straightforwardly. Figure 4 illustrates this process.

1. Let Z be a cover binary image to be watermarked and let L be a binary logo. The number of pixels of L must be equal to the length of the chosen one-way hashing function H.
2. Use a pseudo-random number generator with a known seed to generate a sequence v of non-repeating pseudo-random data-bearing locations within the image Z.

3. Let Z_2 be the pixels of Z that do not belong to v, that is, $Z_2 \leftarrow Z \setminus v$. Compute the integrity index $H = H(Z_2)$, exclusive-or H with L, and encrypt the result with the secret key, generating the MAC S.

4. Insert S flipping (if necessary) the pixels of the sequence v, generating the protected stego-image Z'.

The AWST extraction algorithm is:

1. Let Z' be an AWST-marked image. Generate again the sequence of data-bearing pixels v.

2. Let $Z_2' \leftarrow Z' \setminus v$. Compute the integrity index $H = H(Z_2')$.

3. Extract the hidden data from Z' scanning the pixels in v and decrypt it using the secret key, obtaining the decrypted data D.

4. Exclusive-or H with D, obtaining the check image C.

5. If C is equal to the inserted logo image L, the watermark is verified. Otherwise, the stego-image Z' has been modified (or a wrong key has been used).

We suggest using AWCTL (see the *Authentication watermarking derived from Chang, Tseng and Lin's data hiding (AWCTL)* section) instead of AWST, because the former has more data hiding capacity than the latter and an equivalent visual quality.

Authentication Watermarking by Template Ranking (AWTR) and Parity Atacks

AWTR can be directly derived from the corresponding DH technique by dividing the cover image Z in two regions Z_1 and Z_2; computing the MAC/DS of Z_2; and inserting it into Z_1. However, some caution must be taken in transforming a DH scheme into an AW, because although the region Z_2 is well protected (with the security assured by the cryptography theory), the region Z_1 is not. For example, let us take the DH scheme that inserts one bit per connected component, forcing it to have even or odd number of black pixels. A connected component can be forced to have the desired parity by toggling one of its boundary pixels. This scheme can be transformed into an AW using the previously described idea. Yet, a malicious hacker can arbitrarily alter the region Z_1, without being noticed by the AW scheme, as long as the parities of all connected components remain unaltered. For example, a character a in Z_1 region can be changed into an e (or any other character that contains only one connected component) as long as its parity remains unchanged. We refer to this as a *parity attack*. In AWTR, the blocks of Z_1 can be modified, without being detected by the watermark, as long as their parities remain unchanged. To avoid parity attacks, we suggest using AWTC (see the *AW by template ranking with symmetrical central pixels (AWTC)* section) instead of AWTR.

AW by Template Ranking with Symmetrical Central Pixels (AWTC)

Surprisingly, the simple AWST cannot be assaulted by parity attacks. This happens because, in AWST, the number of pixels in Z_1 region is exactly equal to the length of the adopted MAC/DS. All image pixels (except the n pixels that will bear the n bits of the MAC/DS) are taken into account to compute the AS. Consequently, *any* alteration of Z_2 region can be detected because it changes the integrity index of the stego-image, and *any* alteration of Z_1 region can also be detected because it changes the stored MAC/DS. The probability of not detecting an alteration is only 2^{-n} (where n is the length of MAC/DS), which can be neglected.

An image watermarked by AWTR presents high visual quality, but it can be assaulted by parity attacks. On the other hand, an image watermarked by AWST is noisy, but it cannot be assaulted by parity attacks. Is it possible to design

Figure 4. Logo image L (b) was inserted into cover image Z (a) using AWST. Figure (c) depicts the watermarked stego-image. The correct check image C (d) was extracted from the stego-image. When the stego-image was modified (e), a completely random check image was extracted (f).

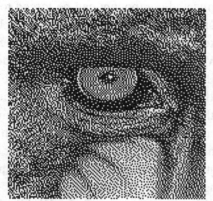

(a) Part of 512×512 cover halftone image Z.

(b) Logo image L (32×32 pixels).

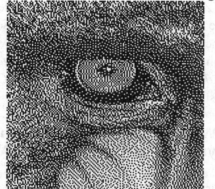

(c) Part of watermarked stego image Z'. 1024 bits were embedded.

(d) Check image C extracted from Z'.

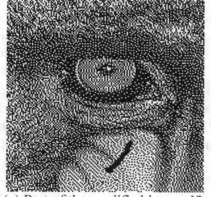

(e) Part of the modified image X'.

(f) Check image C extracted from X'.

an AW with AWTR's visual quality and AWST's security? Fortunately, AWTC (derived directly from DHTC) has high visual quality and is immune to parity attacks. Figure 5 illustrates this technique. A page of a magazine was scanned at 300 dpi (Figure 5a) and watermarked by AWTC with 10240-bits long MAC (much longer than the usual), resulting in Figure 5b. Note in Figure 5c that only low-visibility pixels located at borders of characters were flipped.

Authentication Watermarking Derived from Chang, Tseng and Lin's Data Hiding (AWCTL)

Sometimes, we may not be interested in flipping only low-visibility pixels, for example, to watermarking a dispersed-dot halftone image. In this case, it is possible to use AWST. However, a better technique can be obtained converting DHCTL into an AW. The advantage of AWCTL over AWST is that the MAC/DS can be embedded into the cover image flipping a smaller number of pixels. For example, using blocks with 255 pixels, 1024-bits long MAC/DS can be embedded flipping at most 128 pixels in AWCTL (instead of 1024 bits as in AWST).

AWCTL can be assaulted by parity attack only if $\log_2(m+1)$ is not an integer (m is the number of pixels of a block). Consider Figure 3a, where two pixels have received the same serial number 001. If these two pixels are flipped together, the data hidden in the block will not change. If a hacker flips together any two pixels in a block with the same serial number, this alteration will not be detected by the watermarking scheme. However, if $\log_2(m+1)$ is an integer, there is no set of pixels with the same serial number, and thus this attack becomes impossible.

PUBLIC- AND SECRET-KEY CRYPTOGRAPHY FOR AUTHENTICATION WATERMARKING

The very nature of any watermark requires minimizing the amount of data embedded in the cover image (to avoid deteriorating the quality of the resulting image) and maximizing the processing speed (due to the naturally high number of signatures one must generate and verify in realistic images, especially when spatial localization of alterations is involved). In cryptographic terms, the signatures inserted in a cover image must be as compact as possible, and its processing must be as efficient as feasible.

Figure 5. A page of a magazine scanned at 300 dpi and watermarked by AWTC using an unusually long MAC

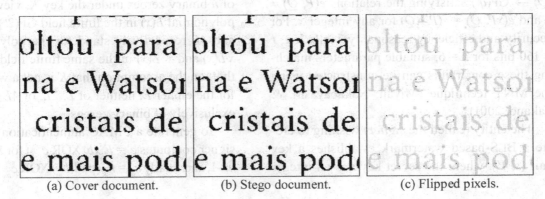

(a) Cover document.   (b) Stego document.   (c) Flipped pixels.

To address these requirements, watermarking schemes usually adopt either public-key DSs like Schnorr (1991), BLS (Boneh, Lynn, & Shacham, 2002), and ZSNS (Zhang, Safavi-Naini, & Susilo, 2004) (the latter two based on the concept of bilinear pairings), or secret-key message authentication codes like CMAC (NIST, 2005) and Galois-Carter-Wegman (McGrew & Viega, 2005) (adopted in existing standards and/or worth of note due to their high performance). Schemes based on the former cryptographic primitives have unique properties like public verifiability (whereby detecting and/or verifying a watermark does not imply revealing private information), while schemes based on the latter are usually much faster (as much as two orders of magnitude).

We now briefly review the BLS and CMAC algorithms, which seem most suitable for watermark-based image authentication.

BLS Signatures

The signature algorithm we now describe makes use of notions from algebraic geometry; the interested reader can refer to Cohen et al. (2005) for a thorough exposition of the concepts involved. BLS signatures adopt as public parameters: an elliptic curve E defined over a finite field $GF(q)$ and the same curve over an extension field $GF(q^k)$; two points $P \in E(GF(q))$ and $Q \in E(GF(q^k))$ of prime order r; a cryptographically secure hash function $H: I \to \langle P \rangle$ where I is the set of all valid images (or image blocks); and a bilinear pairing $e: \langle P \rangle \times \langle Q \rangle \to GF(q^k)$ satisfying the relations $e(P, Q) \neq 1$ and $e(xP, Q) = e(P, xQ)$ for any integer x. For security and efficiency reasons, typically $\log_2 r \approx 160$ bits for $k = 6$; suitable parameters matching these constraints can be constructed using the MNT technique (Miyaji, Nakabayashi, & Takano, 2001).

The entity (called the *signer*) wishing to create a BLS-based watermark establishes a key pair (s, V), where the secret key s is an integer randomly selected in range 1 to r-1, and the public key is the curve point $V = sQ$. To sign an image block $b \in I$, the signer computes $B = H(b)$ and $S = sB$; the signature is the point S. To verify the received signature of a received image block b, any interested party (called the *verifier*) computes $B = H(b)$ and checks that $e(S, Q) = e(B, V)$. This protocol works because, if the received block and signature are authentic, then $e(S, Q) = e(sB, Q) = e(B, sQ) = e(B, V)$. The signature size is only $\log_2 r$, hence typically 160 bits; by comparison, a typical RSA signature for the same security level is 1024-bits long.

CMAC Message Authentication Code

The CMAC message authentication code is defined for an underlying block cipher E accepting a k-bit secret key to encrypt n-bit data blocks. Typically the cipher is either 3DES ($k = 168$ bits and $n = 64$ bits) or AES ($k = 128$, 192 or 256 bits and $n = 128$ bits). We write $E_K(b)$ for the encryption of a data block b under the key K with cipher E. CMAC authentication tags have an arbitrary size t between $n/2$ and n bits, with recommended values $t = 64$ for 3DES and $t = 96$ for AES. Both the signer and the verifier must know the key K. The image to be signed is assumed to be partitioned into blocks $b_1, \ldots, b_m$ according to some conventional ordering, with all blocks except possibly the last one being n bits in length; for convenience, we define a dummy block b_0 consisting of binary zeroes. Let $L = E_K(0^n)$ be the encryption of a string of n binary zeroes under the key K, viewed as a polynomial $L(x)$ in the finite field $GF(2^n)$. Let $2L$ and $4L$ respectively stand for the polynomials $x \cdot L(x)$ and $x^2 \cdot L(x)$ in the same finite field. Notice that, on the assumption that K is not a weak key for the cipher E, neither of L, $2L$, or $4L$ consists exclusively of binary zeroes.

To generate a CMAC authentication tag, the signer computes $c_i = E_K(b_i \text{ XOR } c_{i-1})$ for $i = 1, \ldots, m-1$, and finally $c_m = E_K(\text{pad}(b_m) \text{ XOR } c_{m-1})$ where

$pad(b_m) = b_m$ XOR $2L$ if the length $|b_m|$ of b_m is exactly n, or else $pad(b_m) = (b_m \| 1 \| 0^*)$ XOR $4L$ if $|b_m|$ is strictly smaller than n, where XOR stands for bitwise exclusive-or, $\|$ stands for bit string concatenation, and 0^* denotes a (possible empty) string of binary zeroes long enough to complete an n-bit string (thus in this context the length of 0^* is $n - |b_m| - 1$). The CMAC tag is the value of c_m truncated to the t leftmost bits. To verify a CMAC tag, the verifier repeats this computation for the received image and compares the result with the received tag.

SPATIALLY LOCALIZING THE ALTERATIONS

Watermarks that are capable of not only detecting, but also spatially localizing alterations in stego-images with a previously established resolution are called *topological*. Wong (1998) has proposed a topological scheme that consists of dividing the cover continuous-tone image in blocks, computing MAC/DS of each block, and inserting the result MAC/DS into the least significant bits of the block. Similar ideas can be applied to binary images as well.

However, Wong's (1998) and other topological schemes succumb to a number of attacks, ranging from simple copy-and-paste attacks (whereby individually signed image blocks taken from legitimate images are undetectably copied onto equally sized blocks of other images or different positions in the same images) to the subtler *transplantation attacks* and *advanced birthday attacks*. Only a few proposed watermarking techniques can effectively counter these shortcomings, by introducing either non-deterministic or unbounded context to the generated signatures.

We first examine the principles of the aforementioned attacks, and then we show how to construct topological watermarking schemes that are able to resist them.

Transplantation Attacks

Assume that an authentication scheme adds *locality context* to the signed data, in the sense that the signature of an image region Y depends also on the contents and coordinates of another region X; denote this relation between the regions by $X \to Y$. Also, write $X \sim Y$ if regions X and Y share the same contents (pixel values). Suppose that an opponent obtains two sets S and T of signed regions satisfying the relations:

$$A_S \to U_S \to B_S \to C_{S,}$$
$$A_T \to V_T \to B_T \to C_{T,}$$

where $A_S \sim A_T$, $B_S \sim B_T$, and $C_S \sim C_T$, but $U_S \neq V_T$. If each region carries along its own authentication tag, the pair of regions (U_S, B_S) is undetectably interchangeable with the pair (V_T, B_T), regardless of the signature algorithm being used.

Advanced Birthday Attacks

Let f be a subjective function whose range consists of 2^n distinct values, and suppose that a sequence $(f_1, f_2, \ldots, f_k)$ of values output by f is uniformly distributed at random in the range of f. The probability that two equal values occur in this sequence gets larger than ½ as soon as the sequence length becomes $O(2^{n/2})$. This purely stochastic phenomenon does not depend on the details of f, and is known as the *birthday paradox* (Stinson, 2002).

Assume that the signatures are n bits long, and suppose that a valid message contains three regions satisfying the relations:

$$L \to M \to R.$$

A naïve approach to forge a block M' in place of M would be to collect $O(2^{n/2})$ valid signatures from unrelated blocks (possibly from other images authenticated by the same signer) and to create $O(2^{n/2})$ semantically equivalent variants of M';

by the birthday paradox, with high probability at least one collected signature $s_{M'}$ that fits one of the variants of M'. But since the signature of R depends on the contents of M, its verification will almost certainly fail, not only thwarting this attack but still being capable of locating the forgery with a positional error of just one block. However, a clever attacker can still subvert any such scheme with a somewhat larger effort. Given $O(2^{3n/5})$ collected signatures, the strategy is to create $O(2^{3n/5})$ forged variants of M' and also $O(2^{3n/5})$ forged variants of L', and then to search the database for three signatures $s_{L'}$, $s_{M'}$, s_R that fit the resulting relations:

$$L' \to M' \to R.$$

By the birthday paradox, with high probability at least one such triple exists. Alternatively, the attack could be mounted from a database of $O(2^{n/2})$ collected signatures as in the naïve approach, as long as the forger creates $O(2^{3n/4})$ variants of each of L' and M'.

This attack works whenever the context used in the signatures are limited and deterministic, regardless of the details of the signature algorithm.

Hash Block Chaining (HBC) and Other Schemes

Perhaps the simplest way to thwart the aforementioned attacks against topological watermarks is by adopting *non-deterministic* signatures and extending dependencies of the form $X \to Y$ to $(X, \text{signature}(X)) \to Y$. A signature scheme is said to be non-deterministic if the computation of hash values and generation of signatures depend on one-time private random nonces (Schnorr signatures, for instance, are essentially non-deterministic). Since the modified dependency relation, noted previously, effectively creates a chain of hash values (i.e., the non-deterministic hash of X is included in the computation of the

hash of Y and so on), the resulting scheme is called *hash block chaining* (Barreto et al., 2002), by analogy to the cipher block chaining mode used for data encryption. The image dimensions (M lines and N columns) are also relevant for locating alterations and hence are usually present in the dependency relation, which becomes (M, N, X, signature(X)) $\to Y$.

For binary document images, there may be many entirely white blocks. If these blocks were watermarked, they would be contaminated by salt-and-pepper noise. To avoid this, instead of watermarking them directly, one can adopt a dependency of form (M, N, X, signature(X), k) $\to Y$, where k is the number of white blocks between blocks X and Y.

Few other topological schemes are able to thwart the advanced attacks described previously. It is possible to avoid non-deterministic context by adopting a *t*-ary tree organization of signatures, whereby the individually signed image blocks are grouped into sets of t blocks, each set being individually signed as well; in turn, these sets are grouped into sets of t sets and so on, up to one single set covering the whole image, each intermediate set receiving its own signature (Celik, Sharma, Saber, & Tekalp, 2002b). The advantage of using this method is that, when the image is legitimate, only the upper level signature needs to be verified. The disadvantages are the lack of resolution in alteration localization within a set of blocks (where even the copy-and-paste attack can be mounted) and the larger amount of data that needs to be inserted in the cover image (twice as much for a typical arity of $t = 2$, which minimizes the resolution loss).

DATA HIDING IN JBIG2-COMPRESSED IMAGES (DHTCJ)

The creation and implementation of secure AWs for compressed binary images is an important practical problem, because scanned documents are usually large binary images, which may be stored in compressed formats in order to save the storage space. JBIG2 is an international standard for compressing bi-level images (both lossy and lossless) (Howard, Kossentini, Martins, Forchhammer, & Rucklidge, 1998; International Organization for Standardization [ISO], 1999). In this standard, the image is decomposed in several regions (text, halftone and generic) and each region is compressed using the most appropriate method. In this section, we will describe a DH technique named DHTCJ, derived from DHTC (see the Data hiding by template ranking with symmetrical central pixels (DHTC, pixel-wise) section), that hides data in the text region of JBIG2-compressed binary images (Pamboukian & Kim, 2005). DHST and DHCTL are not adequate to watermark JBIG2 text region because they introduce salt-and-pepper noise, and DHTR is not adequate because of the parity attacks.

A JBIG2 text region is coded using two kinds of segments: (1) *symbol dictionary segment* that contains bitmaps of the characters present in the text region and (2) *text region segment* that describes locations of characters within the text region, with references to the symbol dictionary. Many instances of a character can refer to the same symbol in the dictionary, increasing the compression rate. The compression is lossy if similar instances can refer to a unique symbol in the dictionary, and lossless if only identical instances can refer to a single symbol. The following algorithm embeds information in a JBIG2 text region:

1. Let be given a JBIG2-encoded image Y and n bits of data to be inserted into Y. Decode the text region of Y, obtaining the uncompressed binary image Z.

2. Construct the sequence v of candidate pixels to bear the data and sort it as described in DHTC (see the *Data hiding by template ranking with symmetrical central pixels (DHTC, pixel-wise)* section).

3. Identify in the text region segment the symbols that contain the n first pixels of the sorted sequence v and their references to the symbols to bear the data in the symbol dictionary segment. Note that the number of data bearing symbols (DBSs) can be smaller than n, because each symbol can bear more than one bit.

4. Verify how many times each DBS is referenced in the text region segment. If there is only one reference, the data will be stored in the original symbol. If there is more than one reference, the symbol must be duplicated and inserted at the end of symbol dictionary segment. The data will be inserted in the duplicated symbol, instead of the original. The reference to the symbol in the text region segment should also be modified.

5. Insert n bits of data in the DBSs by flipping, if necessary, the n first pixels of the sorted sequence v.

Special care must be taken to avoid connection or disconnection of the DBSs. To simplify the implementation, we suggest using the template ranking depicted in Figure 6, where only the templates that cannot cause symbol connection or disconnection are listed. DHTCJ data extraction algorithm is straightforward, as well as the derivation of an AW technique. Images watermarked with DHTCJ have pleasant visual quality, as can be seen in Figure 7.

REVERSIBLE DATA-HIDING FOR BINARY IMAGES

Most DH techniques modify and distort the cover image in order to insert the additional information. This distortion is usually small but irreversible. Reversible DH techniques insert the information by modifying the cover image, but enable the exact (lossless) restoration of the original image after extracting the embedded information from the stego-image. Some authors (Awrangjeb & Kankanhalli, 2004; Celik, Sharma, Tekalp, & Saber, 2005; Shi, 2004) classify reversible DHs in two types:

1. Techniques that make use of additive spread spectrum techniques (Fridrich, Goljan, & Du, 2001; Honsinger, Jones, Rabbani, & Stoffel, 2001, see the *Authentication Watermarking for Binary Images* section).

2. Techniques where some portions of the host signal are compressed to provide space to store the net payload data (Awrangjeb & Kankanhalli, 2004; Celik et al., 2005; Celik, Sharma, Tekalp, & Saber, 2002a; Fridrich et al., 2001, see the *Public- and Secret-Key Cryptography for Authentication Watermarking* and *Spatially Localizing the Alterations* sections; Fridrich, Goljan, & Du, 2002; Ni et al., 2004; Tian, 2002, 2003).

Usually the techniques of the first type can hide only a few bits, while the techniques of the second type have more data hiding capacity. This section presents a reversible DH of the second type for binary images, named *reversible data hiding by template ranking with symmetrical central pixels* (RDTC) (Pamboukian & Kim, 2006). Although there are many reversible DH techniques for continuous-tone images, to our knowledge RDTC is the only published reversible DH specifically designed for binary images. It is based on DHTC and uses the Golomb code to compress prediction errors of low visibility pixels to obtain the space to store the hidden data.

In RDTC (as in most reversible DH of the second type) two kinds of information must be embedded in the host image: the compressed data to allow recovering the original image and the net payload data to be hidden. That is, the n data bearing pixels' (DBPs') original values are compressed in order to create space to store the payload data. There are some difficulties to compress the DBPs' original values. Most compression algorithms based on redundancy and dictionaries do not work, because the next bit cannot be predicted based on the previous bits since they correspond to the pixels dispersed throughout the whole image. The solution we found is to compress the prediction errors of DBPs' values, using its neighborhood as the side-information.

We tested two prediction schemes:

1. A pixel can be either of the same color or of the different color than the majority of its spatial neighboring pixels. Let us assume that the first hypothesis is more probable than the second. Let b be the number of black neighbor pixels of a DBP (using 3×3 templates, a DBP has eight neighbor pixels). The prediction is correct (represented by 0) if the original DBP is black and $b>4$, or if it is white and $b\leq4$. Otherwise, the prediction is wrong (represented by 1). If this prediction is reasonable, the predicted value and the true value should be the same with prob-

Figure 6. Set of 3×3 templates designed to be used with DHTCJ, in increasing visual impact order. Only the templates that do not cause symbol connection or disconnection are listed. Hatched pixels match either black or white pixels. The score of a given pattern is that of the matching template with the lowest impact. Mirrors, rotations and reverses of each pattern have the same score.

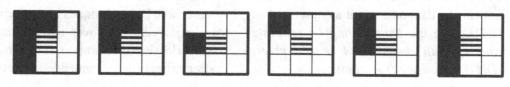

Figure 7. Part of an image scanned at 300 dpi, with 626×240 pixels, 87 symbols instances and water-marked using AWTCJ with 128-bits long MAC

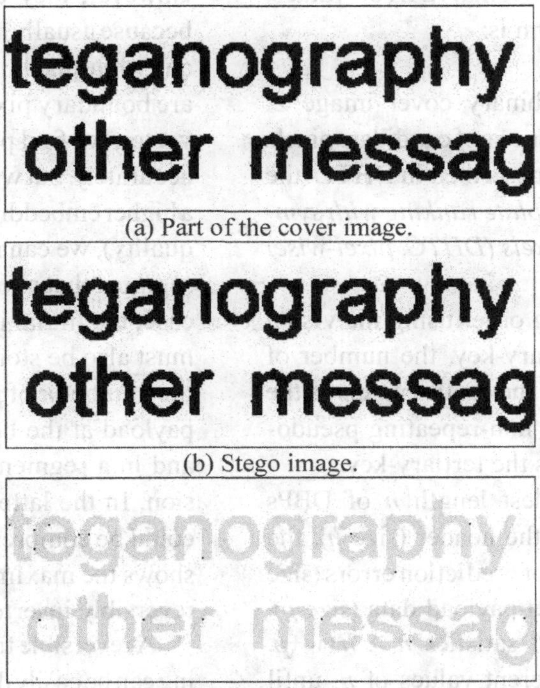

teganography
other messag

(a) Part of the cover image.

teganography
other messag

(b) Stego image.

teganography
other messag

(c) Flipped pixels.

ability higher than 50%. As we store zero when the prediction is correct and one when it is wrong, subsequences of zeroes will be longer (in most cases) than subsequences of ones.

2. We also tested a more elaborate prediction scheme. We constructed a table with 256 elements (all possible configurations of eight neighbor pixels) and, using typical binary images, determined the most probable central pixels' colors, based on the eight neighbors' configurations.

Surprisingly, the two prediction schemes yielded almost the same results. The sequence of prediction errors consists of usually long segments of zeroes separated by usually short segments of ones, because a zero occurs with high probability p and a one occurs with low probability $1-p$. An efficient method to compress this type of information is the Golomb code (Golomb, 1966; Salomon, 2004). The original sequence is first converted in run-lengths of zeroes (sequence of non-negative integers). Then, each integer is compressed by the Golomb code. The Golomb code depends on the choice of an integer parameter $m \geq 2$ and it becomes the best prefix code when

$$m = \left\lceil -\frac{\log_2(1+p)}{\log_2 p} \right\rceil.$$

The reader is referred to Golomb (1966) and Salomon (2004) for more details on the Golomb code.

The stored compressed vector of prediction errors, together with the neighborhoods of DBPs, allows recovering the original DBPs' values. RDTC insertion algorithm is:

1. Let be given the binary cover image Z. Construct the sequence v of candidate pixels for bearing data as described in DHTC (the *Data hiding by template ranking with symmetrical central pixels (DHTC, pixel-wise)* section).

2. Sort v in increasing order using the visual scores as the primary-key, the number of black pixels around the central pixels as the secondary-key and non-repeating pseudo-random numbers as the tertiary-key.

3. Estimate the smallest length n of DBPs capable of storing the header (size h), the compressed vector of prediction errors (size w) and the given net payload data (size p). That is, find n that satisfies $n \geq h+w+p$. Try iteratively different values of n, until obtaining the smallest n that satisfies the inequality.

4. Insert the header (the values of n, w, p and the Golomb code parameter m), the compressed vector of prediction errors and the payload by flipping the central pixels of the first n pieces of the sorted v.

To extract the payload and recover the original image, the sequence v is reconstructed and sorted. Then, the data is extracted from the n first central pixels of v. The compressed vector of prediction errors is uncompressed and used to restore the original image. To obtain AW based on a reversible DH, it is not necessary to compute the MAC/DS of a region of the cover image and store it in another region. Instead, the MAC/DS of the whole image is computed and inserted. The authentication can be verified because it is possible to recover the original image Z and the stored MAC/DS.

We have embedded the data at the beginning of v, because this part has the least visible pixels. However, they cannot be predicted accurately, because usually they have similar number of black and white pixels in their neighborhoods (since they are boundary pixels). As we move forward in the vector, we find pixels that can be predicted more accurately, but with more visual impact. To obtain a higher embedding capacity (sacrificing the visual quality), we can scan the vector v searching for a segment that allows a better compression. In this case, the initial index of the embedded data in v must also be stored in the header. Table 1 shows the number n of needed DBPs to hide 165 bits of payload at the beginning of v (the best quality) and in a segment that allows the best compression. In the latter case, the values of 176 pixels could be compressed to only 11 bits. Table 1 also shows the maximum amount σ of bits that can be reversibly inserted in each image.

A reversible fragile authentication watermarking can be easily derived from RDTC, using secret-key or public/private-key ciphers. Similar reversible authentication techniques for continuous-tone images can be found in many papers on reversible DHs (for example, Dittmann, Katzenbeisser, Schallhart, & Veith, 2004; Fridrich et al., 2001). The public/private-key version of authentication watermarking insertion algorithm is:

1. Given a binary image Z to be authenticated, compute the integrity index of Z using a one-way hashing function $H=H(Z)$. Cryptograph the integrity index H using the private key, obtaining the digital signature S.

2. Insert S into Z using RDTC, obtaining the watermarked stego-image Z'.

The authenticity verification algorithm is:

1. Given a stego-image Z', extract the authentication signature S and decrypted it using the public key, obtaining the extracted integrity index E.

Table 1. Insertion of 128 bits of payload and 37 bits of header in different images, where n is the number of DBPs and w is the size of the compressed DBPs. σ is the maximum amount of bits that can be reversibly inserted.

Image description	Size	Best quality			Best compression			σ
		n	w	n-w	n	w	n-w	
Computer-generated text	1275×1650	336	146	190	176	11	165	401,600
150 dpi scanned text	1275×1650	432	265	167	176	11	165	214,032
300 dpi scanned text	2384×3194	496	325	171	176	11	165	1,543,680

2. Extract the vector of prediction errors, uncompress it and restore the original cover image Z. Recalculate the hashing function, obtaining the check integrity index $C = H(Z)$.
3. If the extracted integrity index E and the check integrity-index C are the same, the image is authentic. Otherwise, the image was modified.

CONCLUSION

As we have seen, it is possible to construct secure topological AW schemes for binary images in digital form, particularly for JBIG2-encoded (lossy of lossless) binary images. Such schemes, based on digital signatures or message authentication codes, can pinpoint alterations in stego-images, and are closely related to DH techniques. In this regard, we have described a reversible DH scheme for authenticating binary images in such a way that the cover image can be entirely recovered.

FUTURE RESEARCH DIRECTIONS

Semi-fragile authentication watermarking for binary images, especially printed binary documents, is an open issue, object of future research. Hardcopy document authentication depends on three components: (1) a data hiding technique that resists print-photocopy-scanning; (2) a perceptual hash that assigns a unique index to visually identical documents (even if these documents contain noise, are rotated, scaled, etc.), (3) and cryptographic algorithms. Among these components, only cryptography is a mature technology. The other two are still undergoing development.

REFERENCES

Awrangjeb, M., & Kankanhalli, M. S. (2004). Lossless watermarking considering the human visual system. *International Workshop on Digital Watermarking 2003* (LNCS 2939, pp. 581-592).

Barreto, P. S. L. M., & Kim, H. Y. (1999). Pitfalls in public key watermarking. In *Proceedings of the Brazilian Symposium on Computer Graphics and Image Processing* (pp. 241-242).

Barreto, P. S. L. M., Kim, H. Y., & Rijmen, V. (2002). Toward a secure public-key blockwise fragile authentication watermarking. *IEE Proceedings Vision, Image and Signal Processing, 149*(2), 57-62.

Bhattacharjya, A. K., & Ancin, H. (1999). Data embedding in text for a copier system. *International Conference on Image Processing, 2*, 245-249.

Boneh, D., Lynn, B., & Shacham, H. (2002). Short signatures from the weil pairing. *Advances in Cryptology—Asiacrypt'2001* (LNCS 2248, pp. 514-532).

Borges, P. V. K., & Mayer, J. (2007). Text luminance modulation for hardcopy watermarking. *Signal Processing, 87*(7), 1754-1771.

Brassil, J. T., Low, S., & Maxemchuk, N. F. (1999, July). Copyright protection for the electronic distribution of text documents. *Proceedings of IEEE, 87*(7), 1181-1196.

Celik, M. U., Sharma, G., Tekalp, A. M., & Saber, E. (2002a). Reversible data hiding. *IEEE International Conference on Image Processing* (Vol. 2, pp. 157-160).

Celik, M. U., Sharma, G., Saber, E., & Tekalp, A. M. (2002b). Hierarchical watermarking for secure image authentication with localization. *IEEE Transactions on Image Processing, 11*(6), 585-595.

Celik, M. U., Sharma, G., Tekalp, A. M., & Saber, E. (2005). Lossless generalized-LSB data embedding. *IEEE Transactions on Image Processing, 14*(2), 253-266.

Chang, C.-C., Tseng, C.-S., & Lin, C.-C. (2005). Hiding data in binary images (LNCS 3439, pp. 338-349).

Chen, B., & Wornell, G. W. (2001). Quantization index modulation: A class of provably good methods for digital watermarking and information embedding. *IEEE Transactions on Information Theory, 47*(4), 1423-1443.

Chun, I. G., & Ha, S. H. (2004). A robust printed image watermarking based on iterative halftoning method. *International Workshop on Digital Watermarking 2003* (LNCS 2939, pp. 200-211).

Cohen, H., Frey, G., Avanzi, R. M., Doche, C., Lange, T., Nguyen, K., et al. (2005). *Handbook of elliptic and hyperelliptic curve cryptography.* Chapman & Hall/CRC.

Cox, I., Kilian, J., Leighton, F. T., & Shamoon, T. (1997). Secure spread spectrum watermarking for multimedia. *IEEE Transactions on Image Processing, 6*(12), 1673-1687.

Dittmann, J., Katzenbeisser, S., Schallhart, C., & Veith, H. (2004). *Provably secure authentication of digital media through invertible watermarks. Cryptology ePrint Archive: Report 2004/293.* Retrieved from http://eprint.iacr.org/2004/293

Eggers, J. J., & Girod, B. (2001). Blind watermarking applied to image authentication. *ICASSP'2001: International Conference on Acoustics, Speech and Signal Processing.* Salt Lake City, UT.

Ekici, O., Sankur, B., & Akcay, M. (2004). A comparative evaluation of semi-fragile watermarking algorithms. *Journal of Electronic Imaging, 13*(1), 209-219.

Fridrich, J. (1999). Methods for tamper detection in digital images. In *Proceedings of the ACM Workshop on Multimedia and Security* (pp. 19-23).

Fridrich, J., Goljan, M., & Du, R. (2001). Invertible authentication. *Proceedings of SPIE Security and Watermarking of Multimedia Contents III* San Jose, CA (Vol. 3971, pp. 197-208).

Fridrich, J., Goljan, M., & Du, R. (2002). Lossless data embedding—New paradigm in digital watermarking. *EURASIP Journal on Applied Signal Processing, 2,* 185-196.

Friedman, G. L. (1993). The trustworthy digital camera: Restoring credibility to the photographic image. *IEEE Transactions on Consumer Electronics, 39*(4), 905-910.

Fu, M. S., & Au, O. C. (2000). Data hiding by smart pair toggling for halftone images. *IEEE International Conference on Acoustics Speech and Signal Processing* (Vol. 4, pp. 2318-2321).

Golomb, S. W. (1966). Run-length encodings. *IEEE Transactions on Information Theory, 12,* 399-401.

Holliman, M., & Memon, N. (2000). Counterfeiting attacks on oblivious block-wise independent invisible watermarking schemes. *IEEE Transactions on Image Processing, 9*(3), 432-441.

Honsinger, C. W., Jones, P. W., Rabbani, M., & Stoffel, J. C. (2001). Lossless recovery of an original image containing embedded data (US Patent #6,278,791).

Howard, P. G., Kossentini, F., Martins, B., Forchhammer, S., & Rucklidge, W. J. (1998). The emerging JBIG2 Standard. *IEEE Transactions on Circuit Systems of Video Technology, 8*(7), 838-848.

International Organization for Standardization (ISO). (1999). *Information technology—Coded representation of picture and audio information—Lossy/lossless coding of bi-level images*. Retrieved from http://www.jpeg.org/public/fcd14492.pdf

Kim, H. Y. (2005). A new public-key authentication watermarking for binary document images resistant to parity attacks. *IEEE International Conference on Image Processing, 2*, 1074-1077.

Kim, H. Y., & Afif, A. (2004). Secure authentication watermarking for halftone and binary images. *International Journal of Imaging Systems and Technology, 14*(4), 147-152.

Kim, H. Y., & De Queiroz, R. L. (2004). Alteration-locating authentication watermarking for binary images. *International Workshop on Digital Watermarking 2004, (Seoul)* (LNCS 3304, pp. 125-136).

Kim, H. Y., & Mayer, J. (2007). Data hiding for binary documents robust to print-scan, photocopy and geometric Distortions. *Proceedings of the Simpósio Bras. Comp. Gráfica e Proc. Imagens*, 105-112.

Knuth, D. E. (1987). Digital halftones by dot diffusion. *ACM Transactions Graph., 6*(4).

Kundur, D., & Hatzinakos, D. (1998). Towards a telltale watermarking technique for tamperproofing. *Proceedings of the IEEE International Conference on Image Processing* (Vol. 2, pp. 409-413).

Kutter, M. (1998). Watermarking resisting to translation, rotation, and scaling. *SPIE Conf. Multimedia Syst. and App.* (Vol. 3528, pp. 423-431).

Lan, T. H., Mansour, M. F., & Tewfik, A. H. (2001). Robust high capacity data embedding. *IEEE International Conference on Acoustics Speech and Signal Processing, 1*, 581-584.

Li, C. T., Lou, D. C., & Chen, T. H. (2000). Image authentication and integrity verification via content-based watermarks and a public key cryptosystem. *IEEE International Conference on Image Processing* (Vol. 3, pp. 694-697).

Lin, C.-Y., & Chang, S.-F. (2000). Semi-fragile watermarking for authenticating JPEG visual content. *Proc. SPIE Int. Soc. Opt. Eng, 3971*, 140-151.

Lin, C.-Y., & Chang, S.-F. (2001). A robust image authentication method distinguishing JPEG compression from malicious manipulation. *IEEE Transactions on Circuits and Systems of Video Technology, 11*(2), 153-168.

Lin, C. Y., Wu, M., Bloom, J. A., Cox, I. J., Miller, M. L., & Lui, Y. M. (2001). Rotation, scale, and translation resilient watermarking for images. *IEEE Transactions on Image Processing, 10*(5), 767-782.

Lin, E., Podilchuk, C., & Delp, E. (2000). Detection of image alterations using semi-fragile watermarks. *Proceedings of the SPIE International Conference on Security and Watermarking of Multimedia Contents II, 3971.*

Lu, C.-S., & Hsu, C.-Y. (2005). Geometric distortion-resilient image hashing scheme and its applications on copy detection and authentication. *Multimedia Systems, 11*(2), 159-173.

Marvel, L. M., Boncelet, C. G., Jr., & Retter, C. T. (1999). Spread spectrum image steganography. *IEEE Transactions on Image Processing, 8*(8), 1075-1083.

Marvel, L. M., Hartwig, G. W., Jr., & Boncelet, C., Jr. (2000). Compression compatible fragile and semifragile tamper detection. *Proceedings of the SPIE International Conference on Security and Watermarking of Multimedia Contents II* (Vol. 3971).

Maxemchuk, N. F., & Low, S. (1997). Marking text documents. *IEEE International Conference on Image Processing* (Vol. 3, pp. 13-17).

McGrew, D. A., & Viega, J. (2005). *The Galois/counter mode of operation (GCM)* (NIST Draft Special Publication 800-38D). Retrieved from http://csrc.nist.gov/CryptoToolkit/modes/proposedmodes/gcm/gcm-revised-spec.pdf

Mei, Q., Wong, E. K., & Memon, N. (2001). Data hiding in binary text documents. *Proceedings of SPIE* (Vol. 4314, pp. 369-375).

Miyaji, A., Nakabayashi, M., & Takano, S. (2001). New explicit conditions of elliptic curve traces for FR-reduction. *IEICE Transactions on Fundamentals, E84-A*(5), 1234-1243.

Ni, Z. C., Shi, Y. Q., Ansari, N., Su, W., Sun, Q. B., & Lin, X. (2004). Robust lossless image data hiding. *IEEE International Conference and Multimedia and Expo 2004* (pp. 2199-2202).

National Institute of Standards and Technology (NIST). (2005). *Recommendation for block cipher modes of operation: The CMAC mode for authentication* (Special Publication 800-38B). Retrieved from http://csrc.nist.gov/CryptoToolkit/modes/800-38_Series_Publications/SP800-38B.pdf

Pamboukian, S. V. D., & Kim, H. Y. (2005). New public-key authentication watermarking for JBIG2 resistant to parity attacks. *International Workshop on Digital Watermarking 2005, (Siena)* (LNCS 3710, pp. 286-298).

Pamboukian, S. V. D., & Kim, H. Y. (2006). Reversible data hiding and reversible authentication watermarking for binary images. In *Proceedings of the Sixth Brazilian Symposium on Information and Computer System Security*. Retrieved from http://www.lps.usp.br/~hae/sbseg2006-rdtc.pdf

Pereira, S., & Pun, T. (2000). Robust template matching for affine resistant image watermarks. *IEEE Transactions on Image Processing, 9*(6), 1123-1129.

Pereira, S., Ruanaidh, J. J. K. O., Deguillaume, F., Csurka, G., & Pun, T. (1999). Template based recovery of fourier-based watermarks using log-polar and log-log maps. *IEEE International Conference Multimedia Comp. Systems, 1,* 870-874.

Roetling, P., & Loce, R. (1994). Digital halftoning. In E. Dougherty (Ed.), *Digital image processing methods.* New York: Marcel Dekker.

Salomon, D. (2004). *Data compression: The complete reference* (3rd ed.). Springer.

Schneider, M., & Chang, S.-F. (1996). A robust content based digital signature for image authentication. *IEEE International Conference on Image Processing* (Vol. 3, pp. 227-230).

Schneier, B. (1996). *Applied cryptography* (2nd ed.). John Wiley & Sons.

Schnorr, C. P. (1991). Efficient signature generation for smart cards. *Journal of Cryptology, 4*(3), 161-174.

Shi, Y. Q. (2004). Reversible data hiding. *International Workshop on Digital Watermarking 2004, (Seoul)* (LNCS 3304, pp. 1-13).

Stinson, D. (2002). *Cryptography: Theory and practice* (2nd ed.). Chapman & Hall/CRC.

Tian, J. (2002). Wavelet-based reversible watermarking for authentication. *Proceedings of the*

SPIE Security and Watermarking of Multimedia Contents IV (Vol. 4675, pp. 679-690).

Tian, J. (2003). Reversible data embedding using difference expansion. *IEEE Transactions on Circuits Systems and Video Technology, 13*(8), 890-896.

Tseng, Y. C., Chen, Y. Y., & Pan, H. K. (2002). A secure data hiding scheme for binary images. *IEEE Transactions on Communications, 50*(8), 1227-1231.

Ulichney, R. (1987). *Digital halftoning*. Cambridge, MA: MIT Press.

Wong, P. W. (1998). A public key watermark for image verification and authentication. *IEEE International Conference on Image Processing* (Vol. 1, pp. 455-459).

Wu, M., & Liu, B. (2004). Data hiding in binary image for authentication and annotation. *IEEE Transactions on Multimedia, 6*(4), 528-538.

Yeung, M. M., & Mintzer, F. (1997). An invisible watermarking technique for image verification. *IEEE International Conference on Image Processing* (Vol. 1, pp. 680-683).

Yu, G. J., Lu, C. S., & Liao, H. Y. M. (2001). Mean-quantization-based fragile watermarking for image authentication. *Optical Engineering, 40*(7), 1396-1408.

Zhang, F., Safavi-Naini, R., & Susilo, W. (2004). An efficient signature scheme from bilinear pairings and its applications. *Practice and Theory in Public Key Cryptography—PKC'2004* (LNCS 2947, pp. 277-290).

Zhao, J., & Koch, E. (1995). Embedding robust labels into images for copyright protection. *International Congress on Intellectual Property Rights, Knowledge and New Technologies* (pp. 242-251).

ADDITIONAL READING

Most of the interesting reading materials were referenced in the main text. The *Authentication Watermarking for Binary Images* and *Public- and Secret-Key Cryptography for Authentication Watermarking* sections use many cryptographic techniques. For readers not familiar with cryptography, we suggest reading Stinson (2002) and Schneier (1996). We suggest reading Barreto et al. (2002), Celik et al. (2002b), and Holliman and Memon (2000) for more details on topological AW. The *Reversible Data-Hiding for Binary Images* section makes use of data compression techniques and Salomon (2004) presents a good introductory text on this subject. In the *Conclusions* section, we said that DH for hardcopy binary documents is an open issue. Probably, future hardcopy DH techniques will make use of the ideas developed for watermarking continuous-tone images resistant to rotation, translation and scaling. Papers (Chun and Ha, 2004; Kutter, 1998; Lin & Chang, 2001; Pereira et al., 1999) are some of the interesting references on this subject.

Chapter II
Secure Multimedia Content Distribution Based on Watermarking Technology

Shiguo Lian
France Telecom Research & Development–Beijing, P.R. China

ABSTRACT

Since the past decade, multimedia protection technologies have been attracting more and more researchers. Among them, multimedia encryption and watermarking are two typical ones. Multimedia encryption encodes media data into an unintelligible form, which emphasizes on confidentiality protection. Multimedia watermarking embeds information into media data, which can be detected or extracted and used to authenticate the copyright. Traditionally, in multimedia distribution, media data are encrypted and then transmitted, while the copyright information is not considered. As an important application, to trace illegal distributors, the customer information (e.g., customer ID) is embedded into media data, which can trace illegal distributors. In this chapter, the multimedia distribution scheme based on watermarking technology is investigated, which realizes both confidentiality protection and copyright protection. Firstly, some related works, including multimedia encryption and digital watermarking, are introduced. Then, the existing watermarking-based distribution schemes are reviewed and analyzed. Furthermore, the novel scheme is proposed and evaluated. Finally, some open issues are presented.

INTRODUCTION

With the development of multimedia technology and network technology, multimedia content becomes more and more popular in our lives. To keep security and privacy, multimedia content protection attracts more and more researchers. Generally, for multimedia data, the confidentiality and copyright are important properties that should be protected (Lin, Eskicioglu, Lagendijk, & Delp, 2005). Among them, confidentiality protection means to make only authorized users access multimedia content, and copyright protection means to verify the ownership of multimedia content. To realize these functionalities, two means have been proposed, that is, digital watermarking and multimedia encryption.

Digital watermarking (Bloom et al., 1999; Hauer & Thiemert, 2004; Moulin & Koetter, 2005) embeds information (also named watermark) into multimedia data by modifying multimedia content slightly, which can also be detected or extracted from multimedia data. According to the visibility of the watermark, digital watermarking can be classified into two types, that is, visible watermarking and invisible watermarking. In visible watermarking, the embedded watermark is visible in multimedia data. In invisible watermarking, the watermark is imperceptible. Digital watermarking can be used for various applications (Cox, Miller, & Bloom, 2002), such as copyright protection, copy protection, transaction tracking, and so on. In copyright protection, the copyright information (e.g., ownership information) is embedded into multimedia content, which can be extracted and used to tell the ownership of the content. In copy protection, the permission information (e.g., copy times) is embedded into multimedia content, which can be modified according to copy operations. For example, if the original embedded copy time is 3, then after one copy operation, the embedded copy time is changed into 2. When the copy time becomes 0, copy operation is forbidden. As an important application, to trace illegal distributors, customer information, for example, customer ID, can be embedded into media data. Thus, each customer receives a slightly different copy, and the contained customer ID can be used to identify the customer. In this chapter, only the traitor tracing property is emphasized, and only the invisible watermarking is used here. In traitor tracing, some properties (Cox et al., 2002) should be satisfied, for example, robustness, imperceptibility, and security. Robustness denotes that the watermark can survive some intentional or unintentional operations, such as general signal

processing (e.g., compression, adding noise, filtering, etc.) or intentional operations (e.g., camera capture, rotation, shifting, translation, etc.). Imperceptibility means that there is no perceptual difference between the watermarked multimedia content and the original content. Security denotes the ability to resist some attackers who forge the watermark or remove the watermark in an unauthorized manner.

Multimedia encryption (Lin et al., 2005; Maniccam & Nikolaos, 2004; Wu & Kuo, 2001) transforms multimedia content into an unintelligible form that can only be recovered by the correct key. Thus, for the authorized customer who has the key, the content can be recovered, while for the unauthorized customer who has no key, he/she can only watch the unintelligible content. As multimedia encryption algorithms, security is the most important requirement. Generally, as an encryption algorithm, it should be secure against such cryptographic attacks (Mollin, 2006) as brute-force attacks, statistical attacks, differential attacks, and so forth. Some detailed information about multimedia encryption will be presented in the second section.

Secure multimedia distribution is a practical application in multimedia communication, which transmits multimedia content from the sender to customers in a secure manner. Generally, both confidentiality protection and copyright protection should be confirmed. Thus, it is reasonable to adopt both multimedia encryption and digital watermarking techniques—for it implements both watermarking and encryption operations. The properties belonging to both watermarking and encryption should be satisfied, which are as follows:

- **Secure against cryptographic attacks.** The encryption algorithm should be secure against such attacks as brute-force attacks, statistical attacks, differential attacks, and so forth.

- **Secure against watermark attackers.** The watermarking algorithm can resist some attackers who forge the watermark or remove the watermark in an unauthorized manner.
- **Robust against intentional or unintentional operations.** The operations include general signal processing (e.g., compression, adding noise, filtering, etc.) and intentional operations (e.g., camera capture, rotation, shifting, translation, etc.).
- **Imperceptibility.** There should be no perceptual difference between the original copy and the watermarked copy.
- **Efficient in implementation.** The fingerprint embedding operation should be efficient in computation or energy consuming.

Until now, some multimedia distribution schemes have been reported. According to the owner who embeds the watermark, the schemes can be classified into three types (Bloom, 2003; Brown, Perkins, & Crowcroft, 1999; Simitopoulos, Zissis, Georgiadis, Emmanouilidis, & Strintzis, 2003): (1) embedding at server side, (2) embedding by relay node, and (3) embedding at customer side. Compared with the former two, the third one moves the embedding operation to the customer side, which makes it suitable for the applications with a large number of customers. However, it is not confirmed whether the customer can steal the media data in the third scheme. To conquer this problem, some works (Anderson & Manifavas, 1997; Kundur & Karthik, 2004; Lemma, Katzenbeisser, Celik, & Veen, 2006; Lian, Liu, Ren, & Wang, 2006; Parnes & Parviainen, 2001) have been proposed that combine decryption process and watermarking process in order to avoid the leakage of media data. These works are named joint fingerprint embedding and decryption (JFD) scheme.

In this chapter, the work related to secure multimedia distribution is presented, the exist-ing watermarking based distribution schemes are reviewed and analyzed, the JFD schemes are proposed and evaluated, and some open issues are presented. The rest of the chapter is arranged as follows. In the second section, the background of secure multimedia distribution is introduced. Watermarking-based distribution schemes are reviewed in the third section. In the fourth section, the JFD scheme based on homogenous operation is presented. The example for video distribution is proposed and evaluated in the fifth section. In the sixth section, some future trends are presented. Finally, the chapter is summarized in the final section.

BACKGROUND

Multimedia Encryption

Because of large volumes in storage, real time operation in access and random error in transmission, multimedia encryption is quite different from binary data encryption. Generally, multimedia encryption has some requirements in security, efficiency, compression ratio, format, and so forth. Firstly, multimedia encryption method's security includes both theoretical security and perceptual security, which is different from text or binary encryption. Secondly, multimedia encryption methods should be efficient in order to satisfy real time applications. Thirdly, a good multimedia encryption method often keeps the compression ratio unchanged. Fourthly, the encryption operation often keeps multimedia format unchanged. Finally, the good encryption method can even support some direct operations on the encrypted stream, such as bit rate change.

Until now, various media encryption schemes have been reported, which can be classified into three types: (1) direct encryption, (2) partial encryption, and (3) compression-combined encryption. Direct encryption method (Lian, Sun, & Wang, 2005a, 2005b; Yi, Tan, Siew, &

Rahman, 2001) encrypts raw data or compressed data with traditional cipher or improved cipher directly. These algorithms are secure, but often cost much time and change data format. Therefore, they are more suitable for data storage than data transmission. Partial encryption method (Ahn, Shim, Jeon, & Choi, 2004; Lian, Liu, Ren, & Wang, 2005c; Shi, King, & Salama, 2006; Tosum & Feng, 2000; Zeng & Lei, 2003) encrypts only parts of multimedia data with traditional ciphers. These algorithms aim to obtain higher efficiency based on the sacrifice of security. For a secure algorithm, the selection of the part to be encrypted should satisfy some principles (Lian, Sun, Zhang, & Wang, 2004a). Compared with direction encryption algorithms, partial encryption algorithms are more suitable for secure multimedia transmission. Compression-combined encryption method (Kankanhalli & Guan, 2002; Lian, Sun, & Wang, 2004b; Wu & Kuo, 2000) incorporates encryption operation into compression and realizes compression and encryption simultaneously. These algorithms are often of high efficiency, while the compression ratio and security are reduced more or less. Thus, these algorithms can be a choice for lightweight media encryption in wireless or mobile network.

Additionally, some typical encryption algorithms are proposed for some special applications. For example, perceptual encryption (Lian, Sun, & Wang, 2004c, 2004d; Torrubia & Mora, 2002) is used for media preview, and visual cryptography (Fu & Au, 2004; Nakajima & Yamaguchi, 2004; Naor & Shamir, 1994) is used for secret communication. Among them, perceptual encryption encrypts media data into degraded copy that is still intelligible. If customers are interested in the media, they may pay for it. This method is based on partial encryption. The difference is to encrypt only the nonsignificant part that should be selected carefully. Differently, visual cryptography uses several images to transmit one image. It is difficult for attackers to determine whether the secret information exists or not.

Digital Fingerprinting

Fingerprinting is a technology used to trace traitors, which embeds users' identification information into media content imperceptibly. Generally, a fingerprinting system is composed of four components: (1) fingerprint generation, (2) fingerprint embedding, (3) collusion attack, and (4) fingerprint detection. Fingerprint generation produces the fingerprint code to be embedded into media content. Fingerprint embedding/detection means to embed or detect the fingerprint code, which is based on watermark embedding/detection (Cox et al., 2002). Thus, fingerprint's robustness against such signal processing operations as recompression, additive noise, filtering, and so forth is determined by the adopted watermark embedding/detection method. Collusion attack is the biggest threat to the fingerprinting system, which means that different customers can combine their copies together through such operation as averaging in order to produce a copy without fingerprint code or forge an unlawful copy containing fingerprint code. The fingerprint generation method secure against collusion attacks is the challenging of fingerprint research.

In collusion attacks, attackers intend to remove the embedded fingerprint by use of the slight difference between different copies. This kind of attack is often classified into two categories (Wu, Trappe, Wang, & Liu, 2004): linear collusion and nonlinear collusion. Among them, linear collusion means to average, plus/subtract, filter, or cut-and-paste the copies, while nonlinear collusion means to take the minimal, maximal, or median pixels in the copies. Generally, five kinds of collusion attacks are considered: (1) averaging attack, (2) min-max attack, (3) negative-correlation attack, (4) zero-correlation attack, and (5) linear combination collusion attack (LCCA) (Wu, 2005).

Some fingerprint generation methods have been proposed to resist collusion attacks, which are able to detect one or more of the colluders. They can be classified into three types: (1) *orthogonal fingerprinting,* (2) *coded fingerprinting,* and (3) *desynchronized fingerprinting.*

Orthogonal fingerprinting. The orthogonal fingerprint is orthogonal to each other (Herrigel, Oruanaidh, Peterson, Pereira, & Pun, 1998; Trappe, Wu, Wang, & Liu, 2003), which keeps the colluded copy still detectable. According to the property of orthogonal sequence, such detection method as correlation detection is still practical although there is some degradation caused by collusion attacks. For example, the algorithm (Herrigel et al., 1998) produces orthogonal fingerprinting for each customer, the fingerprinting is then modulated by the cover video, and correlation detection is used to determine the ownership or colluders. For the colluded copy (averaging two copies), correlation detection obtains a relative small correlation value that is still bigger than the threshold. Thus, the colluders can still be traced. The disadvantage is that the supported customer population is limited by the dimension of the orthogonal vector.

Coded fingerprinting. Fingerprint can be encoded into codeword that can detect the colluders partially or completely. Now, two kinds of encoding methods are often referenced, that is, Boneh-Shaw scheme (Boneh & Shaw, 1998) and the combinatorial design based code (Dinitz & Stinson, 1992; Wang, Wu, Trappe, & Liu, 2005). Boneh-Shaw scheme is based on the marking assumption: only the different bits are changed by colluders, while the same bits can not be changed. By designing the primitive binary code, at least one colluder can be captured out of up to c colluders (c is the number of total colluders). Differently, in a combinatorial design based anti-collusion scheme, the fingerprint acts as a combinatorial codeword. The combinatorial codes, such as AND-ACC (anti-collusion codes) or BIBD (Dinitz & Stinson, 1992), have such property as: each group of colluders' fingerprinting produces a unique codeword that determines all the colluders in the group. These fingerprints support many customers, but are not secure against LCCA (Wu, 2005).

Desynchronized fingerprinting. This kind of fingerprint produces different media copy by desynchronizing media content differently, which makes collusion attacks impractical under the condition of imperceptibility (Celik, Sharma, & Tekalp, 2005; Mao & Mihcak, 2005). Generally, after collusion attack, the colluded copy is degraded and is of no commercial value. The desynchronization operations include random temporal sampling (video frame interpolation, temporal re-sampling, etc.), random spatial sampling (RST operations, random bending, luminance filtering, or parameter smoothing), or random warping. The more the colluders, the greater the degradation is. According to this case, desynchronized fingerprinting makes collusion attacks unpractical, and thus is secure against collusion attacks. However, the desynchronized copy's quality needs to be measured, and the security against resynchronization attack needs to be confirmed.

WATERMARKING-BASED MULTIMEDIA DISTRIBUTION

Considering that fingerprinting technology produces different media copy to different customers, it is easily implemented in a unicast network, while it is difficult in broadcast or multicast networks. The key points to be confirmed are the security and the efficiency. Until now, some distribution schemes based on digital fingerprinting have been proposed, which can be classified into three types, as shown in Figure 1. The first one (Embed Fingerprinting I) (Simitopoulos et al., 2003) embeds the fingerprint and encrypts the fingerprinted media at the server side and decrypts the media content at the customer side. In this scheme, for different customers, the media data should be fingerprinted differently, which increases the server's loading and is not suitable for the applications with large number of customers. The second one (Embed Fingerprinting II) (Brown

Figure 1. Watermarking-based multimedia distribution schemes

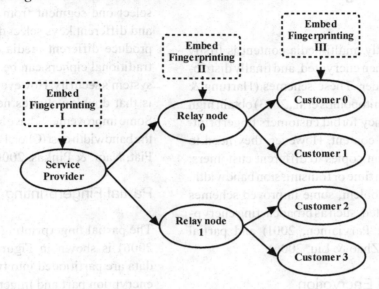

Figure 2. Leakage of multimedia content

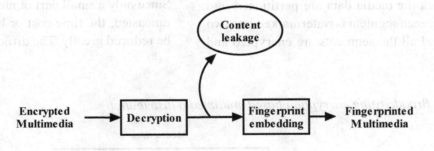

et al., 1999; Judge & Ammar, 2000) embeds the fingerprint and encrypts the fingerprinted media by the relay node and decrypts the media at the customer side. This scheme reduces the server's loading greatly. However, the fingerprinting or encryption operation in relay node makes the network protocol not compliant with the original one. The third one (Embed Fingerprinting III) (Bloom, 2003) encrypts the media data at the server side and decrypts the media and embeds the fingerprint at the customer side. This scheme reduces the server's loading greatly. However, for the decryption and fingerprinting operations are implemented at the customer side, the means to confirm the security is the key problem. To decrypt the media and embed the fingerprint independently is not secure, because the decrypted media data may be leaked out from the gap between the decryption operation and fingerprinting operation, as shown in Figure 2.

Embedding Fingerprint at Sender Side

Straightforwardly, multimedia content is firstly fingerprinted, then encrypted, and finally distributed by the sender. These schemes (Hartung & Girod, 1997; Simitopoulos et al., 2003) obtain high security since they forbid customers fingerprinting multimedia content. However, they need to transmit different copies to different customers, which cost much time or transmission bandwidth. To solve this problem, some improved schemes have been reported, such as broadcasting encryption (Parnes & Parviainen, 2001) and partial fingerprinting (Zhao & Liu, 2006).

Broadcasting Encryption

The broadcasting encryption based method (Parnes & Parviainen, 2001) is shown in Figure 3, in which the media data are partitioned into segments, each segment is watermarked into two copies, and all the segments are encrypted and distributed. At the receiver side, a key is used to select one segment from the couple segments, and different keys select different segments that produce different media copy. In this scheme, traditional ciphers can be used, which keeps the system's security. However, the key disadvantage is that double volumes need to be transmitted. Some improvements have been proposed to reduce the bandwidth cost (Chor, Fiat, & Naor, 1994; Chor, Fiat, Naor, & Pinkas, 2000) in some extent.

Partial Fingerprinting

The partial fingerprinting method (Zhao & Liu, 2006) is shown in Figure 4, in which, media data are partitioned into two parts, for example, encryption part and fingerprinting part. Among them, the former one is encrypted and broadcasted to different customers, while the latter one is fingerprinted and unicasted to each customer. Since only a small part of multimedia content is unicasted, the time cost or bandwidth cost can be reduced greatly. The difficulty is to make the

Figure 3. Broadcasting encryption based multimedia distribution

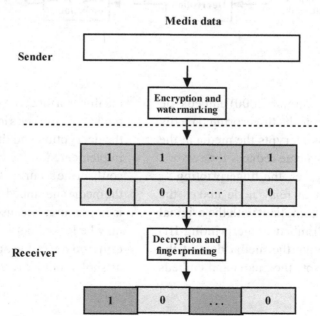

Figure 4. Partial fingerprinting based multimedia distribution

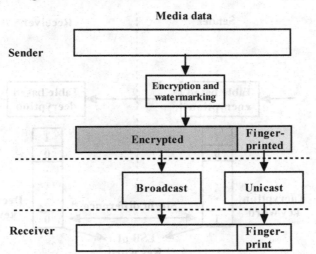

two kinds of communication modes work together simultaneously.

Joint Fingerprint Embedding and Decryption (JFD)

To obtain a trade-off between security and efficiency, some schemes (Anderson & Manifavas, 1997; Kundur & Karthik, 2004; Lemma, et al., 2006; Lian et al., 2006) are proposed to JFD. In these schemes, the fingerprint is embedded into media content during decryption process, which produces the fingerprinted media copy directly, thus avoids the leakage of plain media content and improves the security of embedding fingerprint at the customer side.

Chamleon Method

The Chamleon method (Anderson & Manifavas, 1997) shown in Figure 5 firstly encrypts the media data at the server side, then distributes the media data, and finally decrypts the data by modifying the least significant bits under the control of different decryption key. Here, the encryption and decryption processes use different key tables,

X, Y, and X' denote the original data, encrypted data, and fingerprinted data, respectively. It was reported that the scheme is time efficient and secure against cryptographic attacks. However, for different customers, different key tables should be transmitted, which cost bandwidth. Additionally, the least significant bits are not robust to signal processing, such as recompression, additive noise, filtering, and so forth.

Kundur's Method

The JFD scheme shown in Figure 6 is proposed by Kundur and Karthik (2004). It firstly encrypts the media data partially at the server side, then distributes the data, and finally, decrypts the data by recovering the encrypted parts selectively. The position of the unexplored parts determines the uniqueness of a media copy. Here, the DCT coefficients' signs are encrypted. The scheme is robust to some operations including slight noise, recompression, and filtering, while the imperceptibility can not be confirmed, the encrypted media content is not secure in perception and the security against collusion attacks cannot be confirmed.

Figure 5. Chamleon method for multimedia distribution

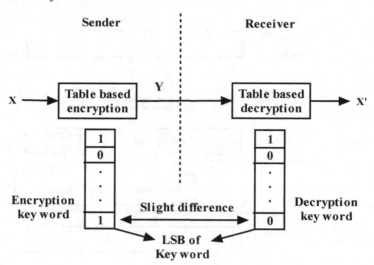

Figure 6. Kundur's method for multimedia distribution

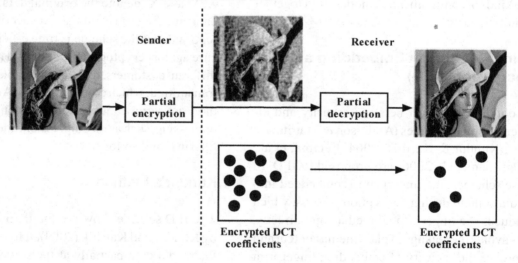

Lian's Method

The scheme shown in Figure 7 is proposed by Lian et al. (2006). It encrypts media data at the server side by encrypting the variable-length code's index and decrypts media data at the customer side by recovering code's index with both decryption and fingerprinting. The scheme is secure against

cryptographic attacks (Maniccam & Nikolaos, 2004), while the robustness against some operations, including recompression, filtering, and adding noise, can not be confirmed.

Lemma's Method

The scheme shown in Figure 8 is proposed by Lemma et al. (2006). It encrypts media data at

Figure 7. Lian's method for multimedia distribution

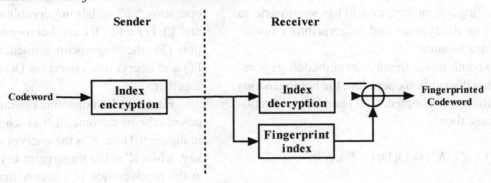

Figure 8. Lemma's method for multimedia distribution

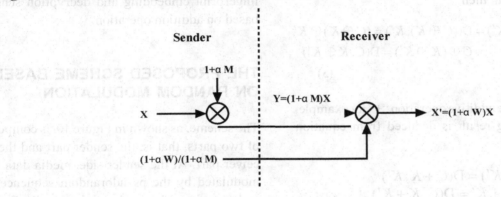

the server side by partial encryption and decrypts media data at the customer side with a new key stream. Here, X, Y, and X' are the original media data, encrypted data, and fingerprinted data, respectively. The encryption key and decryption key are (1+αM) and (1+αW)/(1+αM), respectively. The scheme is robust against signal processing, which benefits from the adopted watermarking algorithms, while the security against cryptographic attacks can not be confirmed. Additionally, the transmission of key stream costs much time and space.

THE PROPOSED JFD SCHEME BASED ON HOMOGENOUS OPERATIONS

Set E() be the encryption operation, D() the decryption operation, F() the fingerprint embedding operation, P the plain media, C the encrypted media, P' the decrypted and fingerprinted media. The general encryption, decryption and fingerprinting operations are defined as,

$$\begin{cases} C = \mathrm{E}(P, K) \\ P' = \mathrm{F}(\mathrm{D}(C, K), K') = \mathrm{F}(P, K') \end{cases} \qquad (1)$$

Here, K is the encryption/decryption key, K' is the fingerprint key, and E() is symmetric to D(). The decryption and fingerprinting operations are isolated.

To combine the fingerprint embedding operation and decryption operation, the homogeneous operations are adopted. If F() and D() are homogeneous, then

$$F(D(C,K),K') = D(D(C,K),K'). \qquad (2)$$

Furthermore, if D() is the operation "$\oplus$" satisfying combinative property, such as addition or multiplication, then

$$D(D(C,K),K') = D((C \oplus K),K') = (C \oplus K) \oplus K'$$
$$= C \oplus (K \oplus K') = D(C,K \oplus K') \qquad (3)$$

Taking the additive operation "+" for example, the following result is deduced from equation (3).

$$D(D(C,K),K') = D(C+K,K')$$
$$= C + K + K' = D(C,K+K'). \qquad (4)$$

According to equation (1)-(3), the following result is deduced.

$$\begin{cases} C = E(P,K) \\ P' = D(C,K \oplus K') = F(P,K') \end{cases} \qquad (5)$$

Here, two conditions are required: 1) D() is the operation "$\oplus$" satisfying combinative property, and 2) F() and D() are homogenous. In equation (5), the fingerprint embedding operation F() and decryption operation D() are combined together.

Based on homogenous operations, the proposed scheme becomes a JFD scheme, as shown in Figure 9. Here, K is the encryption/decryption key, while K' is the fingerprint key and is stored at the receiver side in a secure manner, such as in the trusted computing component.

In the following content, we propose the joint fingerprint embedding and decryption scheme based on addition operation.

THE PROPOSED SCHEME BASED ON RANDOM MODULATION

The scheme, as shown in Figure 10, is composed of two parts, that is, the sender part and the receiver part. At the sender side, media data P is modulated by the pseudorandom sequence S_0, and transformed into the cipher media C. The sequence S_0 is produced by a pseudorandom sequence generator (PSG) under the control of a secret seed K. The encrypted media C is then transmitted to customers. At the receiver side, the media C is demodulated by the pseudorandom

Figure 9. The proposed method for multimedia distribution

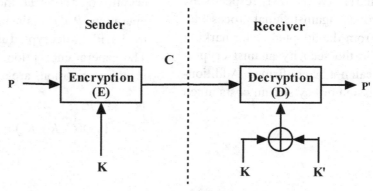

Figure 10. The JFD scheme based on random modulation

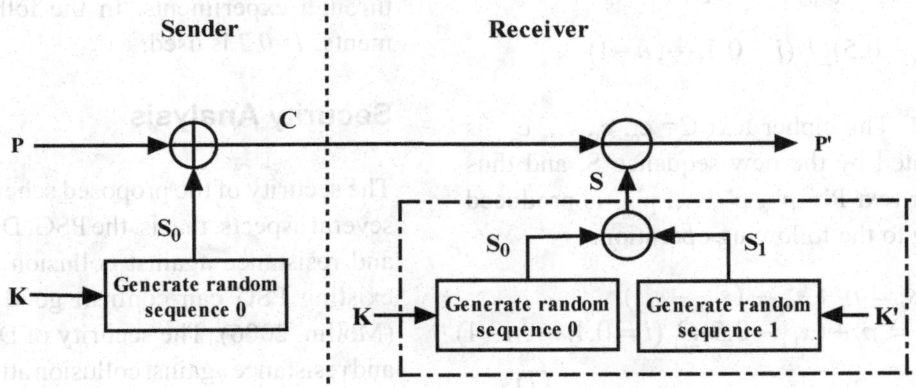

sequence S and transformed into the plain media P'. S is the combination of two sequences, S_0 and S_1. Among them, S_0 is produced by the PSG controlled by the secret seed K, while S_1 is produced by the PSG controlled by a unique customer code K'. The customer code is securely stored at the receiver side.

In the following content, the MPEG2 video distribution scheme based on random modulation will be presented in detail. Here, the DC of each DCT block is encrypted or fingerprinted, similar to the method proposed by Lemma et al. (2006). For the non-DC coefficients, the algorithm is also applied. However, there will be some enlargements in the video file size. If readers are interested, you can try it.

The Encryption Process

The parameter-adjustable PSG is proposed, as shown in Figure 2. It is composed of two steps: pseudorandom sequence generation and sequence modulation.

Step 1. The PSG (Ganz, Park, & Ganz, 1999; Mollin, 2006; Tikkanen, Hannikainen, Hamalainen, & Saarinen, 2000) produces the pseudorandom sequence $X=x_0, x_1, ..., x_{n-1}$ under the control of K. Here, $0 \leq x_i \leq 1$ $(i=0,1,...,n-1)$. The pseudorandom sequence $S_0=s_{0,0}, s_{0,1}, ..., s_{0,n-1}$ is

produced by quantizing X according to quantization factor Q_0 $(0<Q_0 \leq L)$.

$$s_{0,i} = (x_{0,i} - 0.5)Q_0 \ (i=0,1,\cdots,n-1)$$

Step 2. The DCs, $P=p_0, p_1, ..., p_{n-1}$, is modulated by the pseudorandom sequence $S_0=s_{0,0}, s_{0,1}, ..., s_{0,n-1}$. The encrypted DCs, $C=c_0, c_1, ..., c_{n-1}$, is defined as,

$$c_i = p_i + s_{0,i} = p_i +$$
$$(x_{0,i} - 0.5)Q_0 \ (i=0,1,\cdots,n-1) \qquad (6)$$

The Decryption Process

The decryption process is composed of two steps: sequence generation and demodulation operation.

Step 1. The pseudorandom sequence $S_0=s_{0,0}, s_{0,1}, ..., s_{0,n-1}$ is generated with the same method adopted in encryption. Another sequence $S_1=s_{1,0}, s_{1,1}, ..., s_{1,n-1}$ is generated with the same method while different quantization factor. That is $s_{1,i} = (x_{1,i} - 0.5)Q_1 \ (i=0,1,\cdots,n-1)$.

Here, the pseudorandom sequence is produced under the control of the unique customer ID, and Q_1 is another quantization factor. Then, the decryption sequence $S=s_0, s_1, ..., s_{n-1}$ is generated.

$$s_i = s_{0,i} - s_{1,i} = (x_{0,i} - 0.5)Q_0$$

$$- (x_{1,i} - 0.5)Q_1 \quad (i = 0,1,\cdots,n-1)$$

Step 2. The cipher text $C = c_0, c_1, \ldots, c_{n-1}$ is demodulated by the new sequence S, and thus the cipher text $P' = p'_0, p'_1, \ldots, p'_{n-1}$ is produced according to the following operation.

$$p'_i = c_i - s_i = p_i + s_{0,i} - (s_{0,i} - s_{1,i})$$
$$= p_i + s_{1,i} = p_i + (x_{1,i} - 0.5)Q_1 \quad (i = 0,1,\cdots,n-1)$$

$$(7)$$

Seen from equation (7), if $Q_1 = 0$, the decrypted media copy is same to the original copy, $P' = P$. Otherwise, the smaller Q_1 is, the fewer differences between the original copy and the decrypted copy. Generally, the selection of Q_1 depends on both the imperceptibility of the decrypted media data and the robustness of the embedded customer code.

The Tracing Process

To detect which copy has been illegally distributed, the correlation-based detection operation is applied to the media copy. Set $P'_k (k=0,1,\ldots,m-1)$ be the k-th customer's media copy, $S^j_1 (j=0,1,\ldots,m-1)$ the j-th customer's sequence. Thus, the correlation-based detection operation is

$$<P'_k, S^j_1> = \frac{\sum_{i=0}^{n-1} p'_{k,i} s^j_{1,i}}{\sum_{i=0}^{n-1} s^j_{1,i} s^j_{1,i}} = \frac{\sum_{i=0}^{n-1} s^k_{1,i} s^j_{1,i}}{\sum_{i=0}^{n-1} s^j_{1,i} s^j_{1,i}} = <S^k_1, S^j_1>$$

$$(8)$$

For different customer owns different customer ID, the produced pseudorandom sequences are independent from each other. Thus, set the threshold be T, then the customer can be detected by the following method.

$$\begin{cases} k = j, & <S^k_1, S^j_1> \geq T \\ k \neq j, & <S^k_1, S^j_1> < T \end{cases}$$

$$(9)$$

Here, the threshold $T (0<T<1)$ is often selected through experiments. In the following experiments, $T=0.2$ is used.

Security Analysis

The security of the proposed scheme depends on several aspects, that is, the PSG, DCs encryption, and resistance against collusion attacks. Some existing PSG can confirm good performances (Mollin, 2006). The security of DCs encryption and resistance against collusion attacks are evaluated as follows.

Security of DCs Encryption

Encrypting only DC coefficient in each block cannot keep the system secure enough. But, it is a choice for some applications requiring real time operations and low security, for example, wireless broadcasting. In this case, the perceptual security will be emphasized, which keeps the encrypted multimedia data unintelligible. It is investigated that the perceptual security is in relation with the quantization factor Q_0. In experiments, only the luminance block is encrypted, while the chrominance block is left unchanged. As shown in Figure 11, the bigger Q_0 is, the more the multimedia content is degraded. Generally, to keep perceptual security, $Q_0 \geq 90$ is preferred.

Resistance Against Collusion Attacks

Assume N customers $(k, k+1, \ldots, k+N-1)$ attend the collusion attack. In the collusion attack, the N copies $P'_k, P'_{k+1}, \cdots, P'_{k+N-1}$ are averaged, which produces the colluded copy P''. In this case, the colluders can still be detected with a smaller threshold T/N. It can be deduced as follows.

$$<P'', S^j_1> = <\frac{P'_k + P'_{k+1} + \cdots + P'_{k+N-1}}{N}, S^j_1>$$

Figure 11. Encryption results corresponding to different Q_0

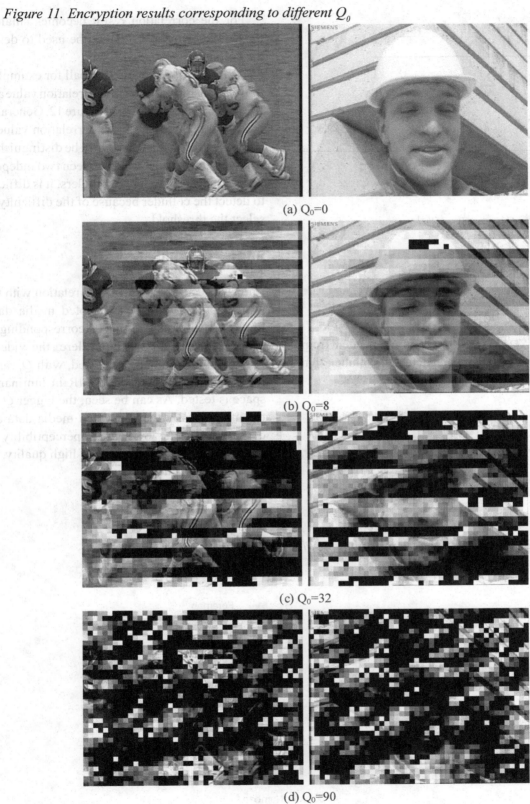

(a) $Q_0=0$

(b) $Q_0=8$

(c) $Q_0=32$

(d) $Q_0=90$

$$= \frac{\sum_{i=0}^{n-1} \dfrac{p'_{k,i} + p'_{k+1,i} + \cdots + p'_{k+N-1,i}}{N} s^j_{1,i}}{\sum_{i=0}^{n-1} s^j_{1,i} s^j_{1,i}}$$

$$= \frac{\dfrac{1}{N}\left[\sum_{i=0}^{n-1} s^k_{1,i} s^j_{1,i} + \sum_{i=0}^{n-1} s^{k+1}_{1,i} s^j_{1,i} + \cdots + \sum_{i=0}^{n-1} s^{k+N-1}_{1,i} s^j_{1,i}\right]}{\sum_{i=0}^{n-1} s^j_{1,i} s^j_{1,i}}$$

$$= \frac{1}{N} < S^k_1, S^j_1 > + \frac{1}{N} < S^{k+1}_1$$

$$, S^j_1 > + \cdots + \frac{1}{N} < S^{k+N-1}_1, S^j_1 >$$

Here, $S^j_1 (j = 0,1,...,m-1)$ is independent from each other. Thus, for each detected colluder, that is, $j=k+1$, the correlation result is

$$< P'', S^j_1 > = \frac{1}{N} < S^{k+1}_1, S^j_1 > = \frac{1}{N} < S^j_1, S^j_1 > \quad (10)$$

For the correlation result becomes smaller, the smaller threshold T/N can be used to detect the colluders.

Taking Foreman and Football for examples, the relationship between the correlation value and colluder number is shown in Figure 12. Generally, if N is no bigger than 4, the correlation value is no smaller than 0.2, that can still be distinguished from the correlation value between two independent sequences. For more colluders, it is difficult to detect the colluder because of the difficulty to select the threshold.

Imperceptibility

The quantization factor Q_l is in relation with the imperceptibility of the decrypted media data. Figure 13 shows some videos corresponding to certain embedding strength. Here, the videos, Foreman and Football, are tested, with Q_l ranging from 4 to 10, and the PSNR in luminance space is tested. As can be seen, the bigger Q_l is, the more greatly the decrypted media data are degraded, and the lower the imperceptibility is. To keep the decrypted image of high quality, Q_l should be kept small.

Figure 12. Relationship between correlation value and colluder number

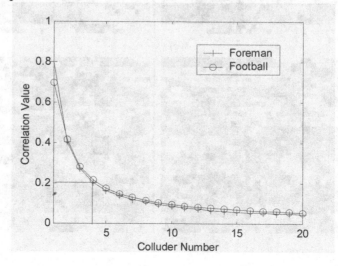

Figure 13. Some decrypted and fingerprinted videos

Figure 14. Robustness against recompression

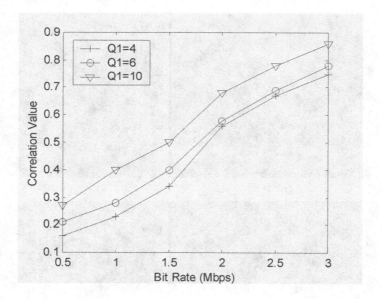

Robustness

The quantization factor Q_1 is in relation with the robustness of the fingerprint. In experiments, the Foreman video is encoded with the bit rate of 3Mbps and then recompressed with lower bit rates. Taking different quantization factor Q_1 for fingerprint embedding, the detected correlation value is tested and shown in Figure 14. As can be seen, for the same bit rate, the bigger Q_1 is, the higher the correlation value is, and the higher the robustness is. Otherwise, the smaller Q_1 is, the smaller the correlation value is, and the smaller the robustness is. To keep it robust against recompression, the big value is selected for Q_1.

CONCLUSION

In this chapter, the multimedia distribution schemes based on watermarking technology are presented and analyzed. Firstly, the performance requirements of watermarking-based multimedia distribution are defined. Then, the existing water-marking-based multimedia distribution schemes are reviewed and compared. Furthermore, the scheme based on homogenous watermarking and encryption operations are proposed and evaluated. Finally, some future trends in this topic are presented. The proposed multimedia distribution scheme joint watermark embedding and decryption, keep the properties of both watermark and encryption unchanged and can realize efficient multimedia distribution. The selection of suitable parameters for the proposed scheme is the future work. It is expected to provide some useful information to researchers or designers who construct or evaluate multimedia distribution schemes.

FUTURE RESEARCH DIRECTIONS

It should be noted that the watermarking-based multimedia distribution is still a new topic, and there are some open issues need to be studied.

Firstly, watermarking algorithms' robustness and security are still not confirmed, which affect the distribution schemes' design. The robustness refers to the resistance against signal processing operations, while the security refers to the resistance against such malicious operations as collusion attacks. These properties confirm that the illegal distributors can be traced.

Secondly, multimedia encryption algorithms' performances are not evaluated thoroughly. To reduce the computational complexity, some partial encryption algorithms are used to encrypt multimedia data. However, there are still no principles for selecting the encryption parts from multimedia data.

Thirdly, some means are required to realize secure key distribution or exchange (Karthik & Hatzinakos, 2007). This depends on the applications environment, such as unicasting network, multicasting network, broadcasting network, or peer-to-peer (p2p) network.

Fourthly, the watermarking based distribution scheme can be combined with existing digital rights management (DRM) systems. Compared with existing DRM systems, the watermarking-based solution owns the special capability of tracing illegal distributors. How to make it compliant with DRM systems is expected to be solved.

Finally, some other research directions are also attractive, such as efficient broadcasting encryption, partial encryption based content distribution, combined encryption and watermarking, and so on.

REFERENCES

Ahn, J., Shim, H., Jeon, B., & Choi, I. (2004). Digital video scrambling method using intra prediction mode. In *PCM2004* (LNCS 3333, pp. 386-393). Springer.

Anderson, R., & Manifavas, C. (1997). Chameleon—A new kind of stream cipher. In *Fast Software Encryption* (LNCS, pp. 107-113). Springer-Verlag.

Bloom, J. (2003). Security and rights management in digital cinema. *Proceedings of IEEE International Conference on Acoustic, Speech and Signal Processing, 4*, 712-715.

Bloom, J. A., Cox, I. J., Kalker, T., Linnartz, J. P., Miller, M. L., & Traw, C. B. (1999). Copy protection for digital video. *Proceedings of IEEE, Special Issue on Identification and Protection of Multimedia Information, 87*(7), 1267-1276.

Boneh, D., & Shaw, J. (1998). Collusion-secure fingerprinting for digital data. *IEEE Transactions on Information Theory, 44*, 1897-1905.

Brown, I., Perkins, C., & Crowcroft, J. (1999). Watercasting: Distributed watermarking of multicast media. In *Proceedings of International Workshop on Networked Group Communication* (LNCS 1736). Springer-Verlag.

Celik, M. U., Sharma, G., & Tekalp, A. M. (2005). Collusion-resilient fingerprinting by random pre-warping. *IEEE Signal Processing Letters*, Preprint.

Chor, B., Fiat, A., & Naor, M. (1994). Tracing traitors. In *Advances in Cryptology, CRYPTO '94* (LNCS 839, pp. 257-270). Springer-Verlag.

Chor, B., Fiat, A., Naor, M., & Pinkas, B. (2000). Tracing traitors. *IEEE Transactions on Information Theory, 46*(3), 893-910.

Cox, I. J., Miller, M. L., & Bloom, J. A. (2002). *Digital watermarking*. San Francisco: Morgan Kaufmann.

Dinitz, J. H., & Stinson, D. R. (1992). *Contemporary design theory: A collection of surveys*. New York: Wiley.

Fu, M. S., & Au, A. C. (2004). Joint visual cryptography and watermarking. In *Proceedings of the International Conference on Multimedia and Expro (ICME2004)* (pp. 975-978).

Ganz, A., Park, S. H., & Ganz, Z. (1999). Experimental measurements and design guidelines for real-time software encryption in multimedia wireless LANs. *Cluster Computing, 2*(1), 35-43.

Hartung, F., & Girod, B. (1997). Digital watermarking of MPEG-2 coded video in the bitstream domain. *Proceedings of the International Conference on Acoustics, Speech and Signal Processing, 4,* 2621-2624.

Hauer, E., & Thiemert, S. (2004). Synchronization techniques to detect MPEG video frames for watermarking retrieval. *Proceedings of the SPIE, Security and Watermarking of Multimedia Contents IV, 5306,* 315-324.

Herrigel, A., Oruanaidh, J., Petersen, H., Pereira, S., & Pun, T. (1998). Secure copyright protection techniques for digital images. In *Second Information Hiding Workshop (IHW)* (LNCS 1525). Springer-Verlag.

Judge, P., & Ammar, M. (2000, June). WHIM: Watermarking multicast video with a hierarchy of intermediaries. In *Proceedings of NOSSDAV 2000.* Chapel Hill, NC.

Kankanhalli, M. S., & Guan, T. T. (2002). Compressed-domain scrambler/descrambler for digital video. *IEEE Transactions on Consumer Electronics, 48*(2), 356-365.

Karthik, K., & Hatzinakos, D. (2007). Decryption key design for joint fingerprinting and decryption in the sign bit plane for multicast content protection. *International Journal of Network Security, 4*(3), 254-265.

Kundur, D., & Karthik, K. (2004). Video fingerprinting and encryption principles for digital rights management. *Proceedings of the IEEE, 92*(6), 918-932.

Lemma, A. N., Katzenbeisser, S., Celik, M. U., & Veen, M. V. (2006). Secure watermark embedding through partial encryption. In *Proceedings of International Workshop on Digital Watermarking (IWDW 2006)* (LNCS 4283, pp. 433-445). Springer.

Lian, S., Liu, Z., Ren, Z., & Wang, H. (2006). Secure distribution scheme for compressed data streams. In *2006 IEEE Conference on Image Processing (ICIP 2006).*

Lian, S., Liu, Z., Ren, Z., & Wang, Z. (2005c). Selective video encryption based on advanced video coding. In *2005 Pacific-Rim Conference on Multimedia (PCM2005)* (LNCS 3768, pp. 281-290).

Lian, S., Sun, J., Zhang, D., & Wang, Z. (2004a). A selective image encryption scheme based on JPEG2000 codec. In *The 2004 Pacific-Rim Conference on Multimedia (PCM2004)* (LNCS 3332, pp. 65-72). Springer.

Lian, S., Sun, J., & Wang, Z. (2004b). A novel image encryption scheme based-on JPEG encoding. In *Proceedings of the Eighth International Conference on Information Visualization (IV)* (pp. 217-220). London.

Lian, S., Sun, J., & Wang, Z. (2004c). Perceptual cryptography on SPIHT compressed images or videos. *The IEEE International Conference on Multimedia and Expro (I) (ICME2004), Taiwan, 3,* 2195-2198.

Lian, S., Sun, J., & Wang, Z. (2004d). Perceptual cryptography on JPEG2000 compressed images or videos. In *The International Conference on Computer and Information Technology (CIT2004)* (pp. 78-83). Wuhan, China.

Lian, S., Sun, J., & Wang, Z. (2005a). Security analysis of a chaos-based image encryption algorithm. *Physica A: Statistical and Theoretical Physics, 351*(2-4), 645-661.

Lian, S., Sun, J., & Wang, Z. (2005b). A block cipher based on a suitable use of the chaotic standard map. *International Journal of Chaos, Solitons and Fractals, 26*(1), 117-129.

Lin, E. I., Eskicioglu, A. M., Lagendijk, R. L., & Delp, E. J. (2005). Advances in digital video content protection. *Proceedings of the IEEE, 93*(1), 171-183.

Maniccam, S. S., & Nikolaos, G. B. (2004). Image and video encryption using SCAN patterns. *Pattern Recognition, 37*(4), 725-737.

Mao, Y., & Mihcak, M. K. (2005). Collusion-resistant international de-synchronization for digital video fingerprinting. In *IEEE Conference on Image Processing.*

Mollin, R. A. (2006). *An introduction to cryptography.* CRC Press.

Moulin, P., & Koetter, R. (2005). Data-hiding codes. *IEEE Proceedings, 93*(12), 2083-2126.

Nakajima, N., & Yamaguchi, Y. (2004). Enhancing registration tolerance of extended visual cryptography for natural images. *Journal of Electronics Imaging, 13*(3), 654-662.

Naor, M., & Shamir, A. (1994). Visual cryptography. In A. De Santis (Ed.), *Advances in Cryptology-Eurocrypt '94* (LNCS 950, pp. 1-12). Berlin, Germany: Springer-Verlag.

Parnes, R., & Parviainen, R. (2001). Large scale distributed watermarking of multicast media through encryption. In *Proceedings of the IFIP International Conference on Communications and Multimedia Security Issues of the New Century.*

Shi, T., King, B., & Salama, P. (2006). Selective encryption for H.264/AVC video coding. *Proceedings of SPIE, Security, Steganography, and Watermarking of Multimedia Contents VIII, 6072,* 607217.

Simitopoulos, D., Zissis, N., Georgiadis, P., Emmanouilidis, V., & Strintzis, M. G. (2003). Encryption and watermarking for the secure distribution of copyrighted MPEG video on DVD.

ACM Multimedia Systems Journal, Special Issue on Multimedia Security, 9(3), 217-227.

Tikkanen, K., Hannikainen, M., Hamalainen, T., & Saarinen, J. (2000). Hardware implementation of the improved WEP and RC4 encryption algorithms for wireless terminals. In *Proceedings of the European Signal Processing Conference* (pp. 2289-2292).

Torrubia, A., & Mora, F. (2002). Perceptual cryptography on MPEG Layer III bit-streams. *IEEE Transactions on Consumer Electronics, 48*(4), 1046-1050.

Tosum, A. S., & Feng, W. (2000). Efficient multi-layer coding and encryption of MPEG video streams. *IEEE International Conference on Multimedia and Expo (I),* 119-122.

Trappe, W., Wu, M., Wang, Z. J., & Liu, K. J. R. (2003). Anti-collusion fingerprinting for multimedia. *IEEE Transactions on Signal Processing, 51,* 1069-1087.

Vleeschouwer, C. D., Delaigle, J. E., & Macq, B. (2001, October). Circular interpretation of histogram for reversible watermarking. In *Proceedings of the IEEE 4th Workshop on Multimedia Signal Processing* (pp. 345-350). France.

Wang, Z. J., Wu, M., Trappe, W., & Liu, K. J. R. (2005). Group-oriented fingerprinting for multimedia forensics. Preprint.

Wu, C., & Kuo, J. C. C. (2000). Fast encryption methods for audiovisual data confidentiality. *Proceedings of SPIE, SPIE International Symposia on Information Technologies 2000, 4209,* 284-295.

Wu, C., & Kuo, J. C. C. (2001). Efficient multimedia encryption via entropy codec design. *Proceedings of SPIE, SPIE International Symposium on Electronic Imaging 2001, 4314,* 128-138.

Wu, M., Trappe, W., Wang, Z. J., & Liu, R. (2004). Collusion-resistant fingerprinting for multimedia. *IEEE Signal Processing Magazine,* 15-27.

Wu, Y. (2005, March 18-23). Linear combination collusion attack and its application on an anti-collusion fingerprinting. IEEE International Conference on Acoustics, Speech, and Signal Processing, 2005. *Proceedings. (ICASSP '05), 2,* 13-16.

Yi, X., Tan, C. H., Siew, C. K., & Rahman, S. M. (2001). Fast encryption for multimedia. *IEEE Transactions on Consumer Electronics, 47*(1), 101-107.

Zeng, W., & Lei, S. (2003). Efficient frequency domain selective scrambling of digital video. *IEEE Transactions on Multimedia, 5*(1), 118-129.

Zhao, H. V., Liu, K. J. R. (2006). Fingerprint multicast in secure video streaming. *IEEE Transactions on Image Processing, 15*(1), 12-29.

ADDITIONAL READING

Aggelos, K., & Moti, Y. (2003). Breaking and repairing asymmetric public-key traitor tracing. In *ACM Digital Rights Management* (pp. 32-50). Berlin, Germany: Springer-Verlag.

Boneh, D., & Franklin, M. (1999). An efficient public key traitor tracing scheme. In *Proceedings of CRYPTO'99* (pp. 338-353). Berlin, Germany: Springer-Verlag.

Chabanne, H., Phan, D. H., & Pointcheva, D. (2005). Public traceability in traitor tracing schemes. In *Advances in Cryptology: EUROCRYPT 2005* (pp. 542-558). Berlin, Germany: Springer.

Craver, S., Memom, N., & Yeo, B. (1998). Resolving rightful ownerships with invisible watermarking techniques: Limitations, attacks, and implications. *IEEE Journal on Selected Areas in Communications, 16*(4), 573-586.

Deguillarme, F., Csurka, G., & Ruanaidh, J. O. (1999). Robust 3D DFT video watermarking. In *Proceedings of SPIE Security and Watermarking of Multimedia Contents* (pp. 113-124). San Jose, CA.

Hartung, F., & Girod, B. (1997). Digital watermarking of MPEG2 coded video in the bitstream domain. In *IEEE International Conference on Acoustic, Speech, and Signal Processing* (pp. 2621-2624). Munich, Germany.

Hartung, F., & Girod, B. (1998). Watermarking of uncompressed and compressed video. *Signal Processing, Special Issue on Copyright Protection and Access Control for Multimedia Services, 66*(3), 283-301.

Hartung, F. H., Su, J. K., & Girod, B. (1999). Spread spectrum watermarking: Malicious attacks and counterattacks. In *Proceedings of SPIE Security and Watermarking of Multimedia Contents* (pp. 147-158). San Jose, CA.

He, S., & Wu, M. (2005). A joint coding and embedding approach to multimedia fingerprinting. *IEEE Transactions on Information Forensics and Security.*

Kurosaua, K., & Desmedt, Y. (1998). Optimum traitor tracing and asymmetric scheme. In *Proceedings of EUROCRYPTO'98* (pp. 145-157). Berlin, Germany: Springer-Verlag.

Kutter, M., Jordan, F., & Ebrahimi, T. (1997). Proposal of a watermarking technique for hiding/retrieving data in compressed and decompressed video (Tech. Rep. No. M2281). ISO/IEC Document, JTCI/SC29/WG11, Stockholm: MPEG4 Meeting.

Lancini, R., Mapelli, F., & Tubaro, S. (2002). A robust video watermarking technique in the spatial domain. In *Proceedings of International Symposium on Video/Image Processing and Multimedia Communications* (pp. 251-256). Zadar, Croatia.

Liu, H. M., Chen, N., & Huang, X. L. (2002). A robust DWT based video watermarking algorithm. In *IEEE International Symposium on Circuits and Systems* (pp. 631-634). Scottsdale, AZ.

Lyuu, Y. D. (2004). *A fully public-key traitor tracing scheme*. Retrieved from http://www.csie.nt u.edu.tw/~lyuu/lyuu.html

Mcgregor, J. P., Yin, Y. L., & Ruby, B. L. (2005). A traitor tracing scheme based on RSA for fast decryption. In *Applied Cryptography and Network Security: Third International Conference* (pp. 56-74). New York.

Piva, A., Caldelli, R., & Rosa, A. D. (2000). A DWT based object watermarking system for MPEG4 video streams. In *2000 International Conference on Image Processing* (pp. 5-8). Vancouver, BC, Canada.

Shan, A., & Salari, E. (2002). Real time digital video watermarking. In *Proceedings of International Conference on Consumer Electronics 2002* (pp. 12-13). Los Angeles.

Shen, K. T., & Chen, L. W. (2002). A new digital watermarking technique for video. In *Recent Advances in Visual Information Systems: 5th International Conference, VISUAL* (pp. 269-275). Hsin Chu, Taiwan.

Simitopoulos, D., Tsaftaris, S. A., & Boulgouris, N. V. (2002). Compressed domain video watermarking of MPEG streams. In *2002 IEEE International Conference on Multimedia and Expo* (pp. 569-572). Lausanne, Switzerland.

Swanson, M. D., & Zhu, B. (1998). Multiresolution scene based video watermarking using perceptual models. *IEEE Journal on Selected Areas in Communications, 16*(4), 540-550.

Teang, W. G., & Tzeng, Z. J. (2001). A public-key traitor tracing scheme with revocation using dynamical shares. In *PKC'2001*.

Vogel, T., & Dittmann, J. (2005). Illustration watermarking: An object-based approach for digital images. *Security, Steganography, and Watermarking of Multimedia Contents 2005*, 578-589.

Voloshynovskiy, S., Pereira, S., & Thierry, P. (2001). Attacks on digital watermarks: Classification, estimation based attacks, and benchmarks. *IEEE Communications Magazine, 39*(8), 118-126.

Wang, Z, Wu, M., Zhao, H., Trappe, W., & Liu, K. J. R. (2005). Collusion resistance of multimedia fingerprinting using orthogonal modulation. *IEEE Transactions on Image Processing, 14*(6), 804-821.

Yan, J. J., & Wu, Y. D. (2004). *An attack on a traitor tracing scheme*. Retrieved from http://www.cl.cam.ac.uk/~jy212/oakland02.pdf

Yu, J. W., Goichiro, H., & Hidek, I. (2001). Efficient asymmetric public-key traitor tracing without trusted agents. In *Proceedings of the CT-RSA 2001* (pp. 392-407). Berlin, Germany: Springer-Verlag.

Zhao, H., Wu, M., Wang, Z., & Liu, K. J. R. (2005). Forensic analysis of nonlinear collusion attacks for multimedia fingerprinting. *IEEE Transactions on Image Processing, 14*(5), 646-661.

Chapter III
Digital Watermarking in the Transform Domain with Emphasis on SVD

Maria Calagna
Dipartimento di Informatica, Universita' di Roma La Sapienza, Italy

ABSTRACT

The chapter illustrates watermarking based on the transform domain. It argues that transform-based watermarking is robust to possible attacks and imperceptible with respect to the quality of the multimedia file we would like to protect. Among those transforms commonly used in communications, we emphasize the use of singular value decomposition (SVD) for digital watermarking. The main advantage of this choice is flexibility of application. In fact, SVD may be applied in several fields where data are organized as matrices, including multimedia and communications. We present a robust SVD-based watermarking scheme for images. According to the detection steps, the watermark can be determined univocally, while other related works present flaws in watermark detection. A case study of our approach refers to the protection of geographical and spatial data in case of the raster representation model of maps.

INTRODUCTION

In recent years digital watermarking has been applied to cope with the main problems of digital spreading of multimedia files: copyright protection, copy protection, proof of ownership, and transaction tracking. *Copyright protection* concerns the possibility to identify the intellectual property on a specific object that could be publicly available to external users. *Copy protection* concerns the prevention of re-distribution of illegal copies of protected objects. This issue is afforded by the adoption of compliant players and compliant recorders; while the former ones are able to play only protected content, the other ones can refuse to create new copies of some content, in the case this action is considered as illegal.

The *proof of ownership* can be used in a court of law in order to assess the ownership rights related to objects. Finally, *transaction tracking* is an emergent research area that is aimed to prevent illegal use of protected objects, by taking into account each transaction event in the digital chain: play, copy, distribution, sale, and so on. In this context, a proper solution to trace user actions is fingerprinting, a process that embeds a distinct watermark in each distributed object.

Watermarking is a technical solution that can be used to address the issue of intellectual rights protection through the embedding of information (watermark) into digital objects (cover). The watermark is a binary string; when it is associated to the cover, it identifies the content univocally. Watermark presence can be identified through detection and extraction procedures that depend on the embedding technique. Multimedia files, including images, video files, and audio files are some examples of possible covers. According to the real-world scenario, watermarking may be classified as *fragile* or *robust*. In a fragile watermarking system the embedded watermark is sensible to changes, then, fragile systems are used for tamper detection. State-of-the-art algorithms are able to identify if changes occur in a digital object and at which locations they occur. On the converse, in a robust watermarking system, the watermark is resistant to class of attacks and the application of stronger ones could destroy the watermark and make the digital content unusable, as well. Definitely, distinguishing properties of watermarking are:

- Imperceptibility
- Robustness

Imperceptibility is related to the quality of the watermarked file. Quality is acceptable if the distortion due to the embedded message is irrelevant for the real-world applications. For example, some broadcast transmissions have poor levels of quality, then the embedded secret message may be imperceptible, even if there are further channel degradations.

The *peak-to-signal-noise-ratio* (PSNR) is a common metric for the difference of quality between two possible images or videos, based on the mean squared error (MSE).

Given two images I_1 and I_2, both of $M \times N$ pixels, the MSE is given by:

$$MSE = \frac{1}{MN} \sum_{i=1}^{M} \sum_{j=1}^{N} \left[I_1(i,j) - I_2(i,j) \right] \quad (1)$$

and the PSNR is computed as:

$$PSNR = 20\log\left(\frac{M\_Intensity}{RMSE} \right) \quad (2)$$

with *M_Intensity* indicating the maximum intensity value in the images and RMSE indicating the squared root of MSE. $I_k(i,j)$ represents the intensity of pixel *(i, j)* in the *k*-th image. The higher the PSNR value between the cover and the watermarked object is, the better the quality the watermarked file is. This metrics give an idea of the quality difference between two images or videos, so the relative values are more relevant than the absolute ones. Thus, by applying the PSNR value, we can consider how the quality difference between two images changes according to the watermarking system in use, or according to the size of the embedded watermark or, alternatively, according to the watermark strength.

The quality level of the watermarked file may be sacrificed for a stronger constraint on the robustness or when there is the need to limit the costs. In a *robust* watermarking system the watermark is still detectable against intentional or non-intentional attacks. The watermark should be neither removed nor distorted. An adversary performs a removal attack if he/she attempts to discover the embedded watermark and may remove it from the watermarked file, while a distortive attack reduces the success of the watermark detection.

In some sense, the watermark provides additional bandwidth that may be used to carry further information. However, watermarking leaves the object size unchanged. In addition, we observe that once the watermark is embedded, the watermark and the object become inseparable, as they undergo the same manipulations.

In this chapter the attention is focused on transform-based watermarking. This approach makes watermarking robust to possible attacks and imperceptible with respect to the quality of the cover. The second section introduces the central topic of current chapter, while the third section illustrates our solution in this field. The

fourth section concludes the chapter and outlines some future directions.

TRANSFORM-BASED WATERMARKING

According to the domain used for embedding, watermarking algorithms are classified in:

*   Spatial-based watermarking
*   Transform-based watermarking

The former embeds the watermark in the spatial values, directly (for example, the pixels intensities of an image), while the latter embeds the watermark in the transform coefficients. Different embedding approaches influence the robustness, the complexity, and the security of watermarking systems. *Spatial-based* watermarking is easy to realize and it has low computational complexity. On the other hand, the longer the watermark is, the more distortions are introduced in the

Figure 1. Watermark embedding in the transform domain

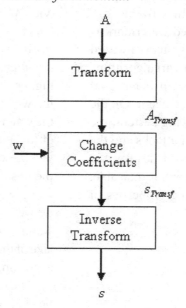

cover. Another drawback is the vulnerability to changes due to common signal processing or lossy compression. *Transform-based* watermarking is more appropriate for real-world applications: the watermark is hidden in the transform coefficients to make it invisible. Many techniques rely on the coefficients properties in order to prevent attacks against the watermarking systems. The embedding process in the transform domain, illustrated in Figure 1, consists of the following steps:

1. The cover-object A is converted in A_{Transf} by applying some transform to A.
2. The secret w is hidden in A_{Transf} by changing the transform coefficients according to some criteria. A key K may be employed in order to add security to the system. The resulting object is s_{Transf}. An additional step is required to use the watermarked object properly;
3. The inverse transform is applied to s_{Transf} that produces the watermarked-object s.

Commonly, the watermark is embedded in a selected part of transform coefficients, excluding those coefficients that are related to the discrete cosine (DC) component. In fact, modifying these coefficients may impact on the overall quality distortion. However, this approach may be a source of security breaches making the watermarked object vulnerable to possible attacks (Si & Li, 2004).

Typical transforms are:

*   Discrete cosine transform (DCT)
*   Discrete wavelet transform (DWT)
*   Discrete Fourier transform (DFT)
*   Singular value decomposition (SVD)

The first three transforms are related to the frequency analysis of digital objects. Their energy compaction and frequency localization allow for more accurate and precise models of the masking properties concerning the imperceptibility and robustness requirements. A relevant property of the DCT and DWT transforms is the possibility to

fully integrate the watermark into the compression scheme. For example, existing solutions for JPEG images, MPEG-2 and MPEG-4 videos embed the watermark in the DCT domain. Likewise, existing solutions for JPEG2000 images embed the watermark in the DWT domain. Images compressed by JPEG2000 are of higher quality than the ones compressed according to the JPEG scheme. The main difference between the approaches is that JPEG compression applies the DCT to blocks, while JPEG2000 applies the DWT by considering the image as a whole: the image is treated as a wave, rather than small sets of discrete pixel values. The orthonormal wavelet transform can be implemented efficiently using a pyramid algorithm that processes the signal by low-pass and high-pass filters and decimates each output by a factor of two. We remind the reader to review the next two sections for a detailed discussion on watermarking based on DCT and DWT transform. Applications of DFT include: correlation, filtering and power spectrum estimation (Phillips & Parr, 1999). Several watermarking solutions are based on Fourier domain. We remind the reader to see the *References* section for further details. Finally, SVD can be used to obtain image coding in terms of n basis images $u_i v_i^T$, which are weighted by the singular values σ_i. It is interesting to use SVD for compression, especially in case of images. The key idea is that this transform captures the best possible basis vectors for the image, rather than using any compatible basis. Important properties of singular values concern their accuracy and sensitivity. In fact, small perturbations in the original matrix lead to small changes in the singular values. SVD-based watermarking is realized on the basis of these properties. We remind the reader to refer to the section on *SVD-Based Watermarking* for related work on this topic.

In the following, we will introduce the main transforms used to represent and process multimedia files and we will discuss some watermarking algorithms based on the transform domain.

DCT-Based Watermarking

The DCT is used to convert a signal in the frequency domain. Basically, a mathematical function f can be represented as the weighted sum of a set of functions $\sum_{i=0}^{N-1} \alpha_i f_i$. The DCT has some connections with the DFT. In the following, the definitions of DFT, DCT, and the corresponding inverse transforms are given.

The DFT of a sequence s of length N is defined as follows:

$$S(k) = F(s) = \sum_{n=0}^{N-1} s(n) \exp\left(\frac{-2in\pi k}{N}\right) \quad (3)$$

The inverse discrete Fourier transform (IDFT) of a sequence S of length N is defined as follows:

$$s(k) = F^{-1}(S) = \sum_{n=0}^{N-1} S(n) \exp\left(\frac{2in\pi k}{N}\right) \quad (4)$$

with $i = \sqrt{-1}$.

The DCT of a sequence s of length N is defined as follows:

$$S(k) = D(s) = \frac{C(k)}{2} \sum_{n=0}^{N} s(n) \cos\left(\frac{(2n+1)\pi k}{2N}\right) \quad (5)$$

where C(u) = 1=p2 if n = 0 and C(n) = 1 otherwise.

The inverse discrete cosine transform (IDCT) of a sequence S of length N is defined as follows:

$$s(k) = D^{-1}(S) = \sum_{n=0}^{N} \frac{C(n)}{2} S(n) \cos\left(\frac{(2n+1)\pi k}{2N}\right) \quad (6)$$

where $C(n) = 1/\sqrt{2}$ if $n = 0$ and $C(n) = 1$ otherwise.

Another useful concept concerns the two-dimensional version of the DCT, as it has applications in images, audio, and video processing. The 2D DCT and 2D IDCT are given by:

$$S(u,v) = D(s) = \frac{2}{N} C(u)C(v) \sum_{x=0}^{N-1} \sum_{y=0}^{N-1} s(x,y) \cos\left(\frac{(2x+1)\pi u}{2N}\right)$$
$$\cos\left(\frac{(2y+1)\pi v}{2N}\right) \quad (7)$$

$$s(x,y) = D^{-1}(s) = \frac{2}{N}$$
$$\sum_{u=0}^{N-1} \sum_{v=0}^{N-1} C(u)C(v)S(u,v) \cos\left(\frac{(2x+1)\pi u}{2N}\right)$$
$$\cos\left(\frac{(2y+1)\pi v}{2N}\right) \quad (8)$$

Among the DCT-based watermarking solutions, we describe the algorithm proposed in Cox, Kilian, Leightont, and Shamoon (1997). Their work is a milestone for robust watermarking systems. The idea is to choose the most perceptually significant elements of the multimedia file as eligible elements for watermark embedding. In this way, watermarking is robust against several kind of attacks, including the lossy compression schemes. Conversely, watermark embedding in the most significant elements may introduce unacceptable distortions in the watermarked file. Distortions may be reduced if frequency-domain techniques are used instead of spatial-domain techniques. However, another issue is to choose the spectrum frequencies to be changed by watermarking. To select high frequencies for watermark embedding makes the approach not robust against common low pass filtering.

The authors use the concept of spread spectrum communication in order to make distortions less noticeable: They consider the frequency domain as a communication channel and the watermark as a signal that is transmitted through it. In spread spectrum communication, a narrow-band signal is transmitted in a larger bandwidth such that the signal energy for each frequency is imperceptible. Similarly, a watermark with high signal-to-noise ratio is spread over a large number of frequencies such that the watermark energy for each frequency is imperceptible. In this way, an adversary may remove the watermark only by adding high amplitude noise to each frequency.

The watermark is embedded in the DCT transform domain with the idea that each DCT coefficient has a perceptual capacity, that is, a quantity measuring the additional information that could be embedded with respect to the imperceptibility requirement.

The watermarking algorithm consists of the following steps:

Input: The image A with $N \times M$ pixels, the watermark W of length n and the watermark strength α.

Output: The watermarked image A'.

- Apply the DCT transform to the original image: $J = DCT(A)$;
- Choose the n greatest DCT coefficients as eligible for watermark embedding;
- Embed the watermark according to one of the following rules:
  - $J'(i) = J(i) + \alpha W(i)$
  - $J'(i) = J(i)(1 + \alpha W(i))$
  - $J'(i) = J(i)(e^{\alpha W(i)})$
- Apply the IDCT in order to produce the watermarked image A', that is: A' = IDCT(J').

The parameter α represents the watermark strength: This parameter is related to the perceptual capacity of each DCT coefficient. Generally,

α may assume the same value for each DCT coefficient, or it may change according to the peculiar perceptual capacity, in order to reduce the distortion introduced by watermarking.

DWT-Based Watermarking

The core of the wavelet transform is the multi-resolution analysis. The idea is to decompose the image space $L^2(R)$ into nesting subspaces $V_m \mid m \in Z$, with the following properties:

1. **Density:** $\bigcup_{m \in Z} V_m = L^2(R)$.
2. **Separability:** $\bigcap_{m \in Z} V_m = 0$.
3. **Scaling:** Given a function $f(t)$ in $L^2(R)$ it holds $f(t) \in V_m$ if $f(2^m t) \in V_0$.
4. **Orthonormality:** The space V_0 associates a scaling function $\varphi(t)$, which generates an orthonormal basis spanning V_0 by translation: $\varphi(t-n) \mid n \in Z$.

Let W_m be the orthogonal complement of $V_m \subset V_{m-1}$. Then, $\oplus W_m = L^2(R)$. By analogy, an orthormal basis $\varphi(t-n) \mid n \in Z$ spans W_0. The basis functions are the translates of the wavelet functions $\varphi(t)$.

The orthonormal wavelet transform can be implemented efficiently using a pyramid algorithm that processes the signal by low-pass and high-pass filters and decimates each output by a factor of two.

As for the watermark embedding in the DWT domain, Ganic and Eskicioglu (2004) propose a hybrid method, which combines the DWT with the SVD transform to realize a robust image watermarking scheme. The idea is to decompose the original image into four frequency bands according to the DWT: *LL, LH, HL, HH* (with *L* and *H* indicating the low-frequency and high-frequency, respectively) and apply the SVD transform to each band, separately. The DWT decomposition may be repeated until the desired resolution is reached.

The watermarking scheme consists of the following steps:

Input: The image A with $N \times M$ pixels and the watermark W of length n.
Output: The watermarked image A'.

- Apply the DWT decomposition to the original image A, thus leading to the frequency bands: LL, LH, HL, HH;
- Apply the SVD transform to each band;
- Apply the SVD transform to the watermark represented as an image;
- Embed the watermark, by adjusting the singular values in the frequency bands λ_i, $i = 1 \cdots n$, with the singular values of the watermark image $\lambda_{wi}, wi = 1 \cdots n$. The embedding rule is: $\lambda_i^* = \lambda_i + \alpha\lambda_{wi}$. Substitute the singular values matrix, containing the updated singular values calculated in the previous step, into the SVD decomposition of each frequency band;
- Apply the inverse DWT (IDWT) transform to produce the watermarked image.

The watermark extraction is possible by reversing the previous steps: the DWT transform is applied to each frequency band and the watermark singular values are computed as:

$$\lambda_{wi} = (\lambda_i^* - \lambda_i)/\alpha.$$

The watermark image is represented as the product of the orthogonal matrices U_w, V_w and the singular values matrix, Σ_w which contains the singular values λ_{wi} as diagonal elements:

$$W = U_w \Sigma_w V_w' \qquad (9)$$

In particular, embedding the watermark in the LL frequency band is robust against typical low-pass filtering, including Gaussian blurring and JPEG compression, while embedding the water-mark in the HH frequency band is robust against typical high-pass filtering, including sharpening and histogram equalization. Then, embedding the watermark in all frequency bands is sufficiently robust to a large class of attacks.

Here, we illustrate a DWT-SVD watermarking scheme. However, a full discussion on SVD transform will be provided in the following section.

SVD-Based Watermarking

Recently, some researchers have used the SVD domain for the watermark embedding. Advantages related to this transform concern the robustness properties of the singular values, as they remain invariant even if they undergo further processing. The SVD is a powerful tool that transforms a generic matrix as a product of three matrices, with interesting properties for several data processing applications. The SVD of a matrix $A^{(m \times n)}$ $(m \leq n)$ is defined as the product of three special matrices: two orthogonal matrices, $U^{(m \times m)}$, $V^{(n \times n)}$ such that $UU^T = VV^T = I$, and a diagonal matrix, $\Sigma = diag(\sigma_1, \sigma_2, \cdots \sigma_m)$, whose main entries $\sigma_i (i = 1 \cdots m)$ are called *singular values*. Singular values are in decreasing order. The columns of U and V are referred as the left and right singular vectors, respectively, of A. In technical terms:

$$A = U\Sigma_w V^T \qquad (10)$$

Singular values play an important role in transforming elements from an m-dimensional vector space into elements of an n-dimensional vector space. A vector x in $\Re^m$ ($\Re^n$) may be expressed in terms of the left (right) singular vectors. The geometrical interpretation of SVD is that this decomposition dilates or contracts some components of x according to the magnitude of corresponding singular values. Given a matrix

A, a singular value and a pair of singular vectors are defined as a non-negative scalar σ and two non-zero vectors u and v, such that:

$$Av = \sigma u \qquad (11)$$

that is, the images under A of the singular vectors $v_1, v_2, \cdots v_m$ are the vectors:

$$\sigma_1 u_1, \sigma_2 u_2, \cdots \sigma_m u_m$$

Equation (11) is equivalent to:

$$A^T u = \sigma v \qquad (12)$$

We remind the author two noticeable properties of SVD, which are at the basis of state-of-the-art watermarking algorithms: *approximation* and *perturbation*.

Approximation. Let the full SVD decomposition of matrix A be given by equation (10). For some $k < r$, with r the rank of the matrix, it is possible to approximate A with A_k:

$$A_k = U_k \Sigma_k V_k^T \qquad (13)$$

where U_k is a $n \times k$ matrix, whose columns are given by the first k left singular of the SVD of A, that is $u_1, u_2, \cdots u_k$ form an orthonormal basis for the range of A and, V_k^T is a $k \times n$ matrix, whose rows are given by the first k right singular vectors of the SVD of A, that is $v_1, v_2, \cdots v_k$ form an orthonormal basis for the kernel of A. $\Sigma_k = diag(\sigma_1, \sigma_2, \cdots \sigma_k)$. Equation (13) represents the best approximation of order k of the original A matrix among all the matrices of order i, with $i < k$. The 2-norm error of the approximation related to equation (13) is equal to σ_{k+1}. The reader is referred to Golub and Van Loan (1996) for proof of this statement. This result is relevant for image compression. In fact, the SVD of an image returns the image coding in terms of n basis images $u_i v_i^T$, which are weighted by the singular values σ_i. It holds that the approximation

of A with the reduced SVD of order k, A_k, is the optimal solution to minimize the Frobenius norm of the error matrix, that is, no other transform has better energy compaction than the reduced SVD of order k. The key idea is that the SVD captures the best possible basis vectors for the image, rather than using any compatible basis. Generally, k is such that $k < r$, where r is the rank of the matrix. Since r is defined as the number of linearly independent columns (rows, respectively), it provides a measure for the redundancy of the matrix.

Perturbation. Important properties of singular values concern their accuracy and sensitivity. Small perturbations in the original matrix lead to small changes in the singular values. Consider a perturbation (δA) to the original matrix A, which produces $(A + \delta A)$ as a result; now, we show the problem of the perturbation analysis by taking into consideration the singular value matrix Σ:

$$\Sigma + \delta\Sigma = U^T (A + \delta A) V \qquad (14)$$

The matrices U and V preserve norms since they are two orthogonal matrices. Thus, it follows that:

$$\|\delta\Sigma\| = \|\delta A\| \qquad (15)$$

Related Work on SVD

SVD is a powerful tool for image processing, especially *image compression* and *image filtering*. Image coding by SVD goes back to the 1970s: Andrews and Patterson (1976) describe the statistical properties of singular values and singular vectors of images. In this work, the SVD by blocks is employed. Experimental results show that singular value mean and variance vary in a large range, which indicates the need for variable bit coding as a function of the singular value index. As for the singular vectors, they are well behaved in their range and tend to have an increasing number of zero-crossings as a function of the singular vectors index.

SVD may be combined with *vector quantization* (*VQ*), which is a low bit-rate compression technique (Chung, Shen, & Chang, 2001; Yang & Lu, 1995). Yang and Lu introduce two methods for image coding: iterative (I) and fast (F) SVD-VQ that lead to different bit-rates. Chung et al. introduce a novel SVD-VQ scheme for information hiding, which produces images with a high level of quality and good compression ratio.

Another interesting property of the SVD is related to the singular values ordering. The higher the singular values are, the more is the energy packed into them. Since the singular values are in decreasing order, it holds that the first singular value of an image contains more information (signal components), while the remaining lower singular values are associated to the noise components. This property is at the basis of image filtering: it is possible to reduce noise in the image by taking into consideration only the first singular values whose magnitude is upon a given threshold. Muti, Bourennane, and Guillaume (2004) discuss the equivalence of SVD and simultaneous row and column *principal components analysis* (*PCA*) and adopt the SVD transform for image filtering. In particular, the SVD transform leads to an image with higher quality. The singular values distribution changes according to the image content. For example, their magnitude covers a large range in the case of a diagonal line, while the energy is concentrated in the very first singular value in the case of a vertical line. This means that the more the principal directions of an image are aligned with the row and column directions, the lower is the number of singular values required to describe image content. Thus, image filtering can be improved by making some image directions to be aligned with row or column directions, that is, by means of image rotation.

Related Work on SVD Watermarking

The adoption of the SVD is very interesting for watermarking purposes. Different proposals of watermarking by SVD exist. In Ganic and Eskicioglu (2004) a combined approach of the SVD and the DWT transform is proposed. The reader may find further details in the section *DWT-Based Watermarking*. In Gorodetski, Popyack, Samoilov, and Skormin (2001), the SVD by blocks is applied for robust data embedding into digital images. Images are subdivided in non-overlapping blocks and the SVD is applied to each one. For each block, the watermark is embedded in the singular values according to two different criteria. The more the singular values are changed the more robust is the technique, with decreasing value of imperceptibility. Experiments are performed on color images. They are represented in the RGB model and the two techniques are applied to each layer of color (R: red, G: green, B: blue) with a good trade-off of data embedding rate.

The SVD may be applied to the whole image or, alternatively, to small blocks of it. In image processing, the analysis of many problems can be simplified substantially by working with block matrices (Jain, 1989). Processing small blocks is suitable in order to capture local variations, which are addressable in a given block and may disappear at a coarser level of representation, such as the whole image. Other advantages of the block-oriented approach include: reduced computation and parallel processing. In Ganic, Zubair, and Eskicioglu (2003), the watermark is embedded by applying the SVD by blocks and to the entire image. Although the watermark is embedded twice, the imperceptibility requirement is satisfied. Moreover, the experiments show that the first approach allows flexibility in data capacity, while applying the SVD to the entire image provides more robustness to the attacks.

Byun, Lee, Tewflk, and Ahn (2002) propose an LSB-based fragile watermarking scheme for image authentication. The SVD is employed to verify the authenticity requirement according to the perturbation analysis of the singular values. Advantages of this scheme are: the detectability of modifications due to traditional attacks, including compression, filtering, and geometric distortions, and the imperceptibility of the watermark, since only a few authentication bits are embedded.

Liu and Tan (2002) and Ozer, Sankur, and Memon (2005) propose a robust watermarking scheme based on SVD. They use a similar approach to embed the watermark in images and audio files, respectively. This technique consists in modifying the singular values of the cover according to the formula: $\sigma_i' = \sigma_i + \alpha w_i$, where σ_i, σ_i' is the i-th singular value in the cover and the watermarked file, respectively, while w_i is the i-th watermark bit to be embedded. However, both the techniques are susceptible to flaws, as we will discuss in the following.

In particular, image watermarking is realized acording to the following steps:

Input: The image A with $N \times M$ pixels, the watermark W of length $N \times M$ and the watermark strength α.

Output: The watermarked image A_w.

- Apply the SVD transform to the original image: $A = U\Sigma V^T$;
- Embed the watermark W into the singular values matrix Σ according to the rule: $\Sigma' = \Sigma + \alpha W$;
- Apply the SVD transform to Σ', that is: $\Sigma' = U_w \Sigma_w V_w^T$;
- Obtain the watermarked image as: $A_w = U\Sigma_w V^T$.

The watermark is extracted by reversing the previous steps, that is:

- Apply the SVD transform to possible counterfeit image $A_w^* = U^* \Sigma_w^* V^{*T}$;
- Compute the temporary matrix $D^* = U_w \Sigma_w^* V_w^T$;
- Extract the watermark as:

$$W = \frac{1}{\alpha}\left(D^* - \Sigma\right).$$

Even if the authors claim that their scheme is robust, there are some weak points in their approach. Firstly, they embed the watermark in the singular values matrix, changing both the diagonal elements (singular values) and the extra-diagonal ones, adding a generic matrix W to a diagonal one. In addition, as shown in Zhang and Li (2005), this watermarking scheme is fundamentally flawed in the extraction steps. An adversary may reveal the presence of any desired watermark in an arbitrary image and then this watermarking scheme cannot be used to protect digital rights. In a few words, the detector considers the image resulting from the product of the singular values matrix of a possible counterfeit image Σ_w^* and the orthogonal matrices U_w, V_w^T that correspond to the SVD of the desired watermark, excluding its diagonal entries. We observe that the orthogonal matrices in the SVD of the image are related to the image details, while the singular values are related to the luminance of the image. Thus, the extracted watermark will be high correlated with the desired one, no matter what the watermark and the counterfeit image are. Suppose the original watermark is W and the desired watermark the adversary is searching for is W', then, according to the detection steps, the presence of the desired watermark W' can be detected in an image with W embedded.

Similarly to the approach used by Liu and Tan (2002), Ozer et al. (2005) describe an audio watermarking scheme that embeds the watermark in the singular values matrix of the spectrogram of the signal. The embedding formula is slightly different.

In the following we illustrate the embedding and the extraction steps.

Input: The audio signal $x(t)$, the watermark W of length $N \times M$ (N: number of frames, M: frame size), the watermark strength α.

Output: The watermarked audio signal $x'(t)$.

- Apply the short-time window Fourier transform (STFT) to the original audio signal $x(t)$ in order to obtain the frequency spectrum A of the signal through short-time windows $g(t)$, that is:

$$A = STFT_x(t, f) = \int x(\tau) g(\tau - t) e^{-j2\pi f t} \, d\tau$$

(16)

- Apply the SVD transform to the matrix A, that is: $A = U \Sigma V^T$;
- Embed the watermark W into the singular values $\sigma(i, j)$ according to the rule:

$$\sigma(i, j)' = \sigma(i, j) + \alpha\beta\sigma(i, j)W(i, j)$$

(17)

where $\beta = 0, 1$ is the polarity of the watermark.

- Apply the SVD transform to the updated matrix Σ', that is: $\Sigma' = U_w \Sigma_w V_w^T$;
- Obtain the watermarked audio signal in the frequency domain as: $A_w = U \Sigma_w V^T$;
- Apply the inverse STFT (ISTFT) to produce the watermarked audio signal in the time domain:

$$x'(t) = A_w g(\tau - t) e^{j2\pi f t} \, dt \, df$$
$$W = U_w \Sigma_w V_w'$$

(18)

Similarly, the detection steps are:

- Apply the SVD transform to possible counterfeit audio signal in the frequency domain, that is:

$$A_w^* = U^* \Sigma_w^* V^{*T};$$

- Compute the temporary matrix:

$$D^* = U_w \Sigma_w^* V_w^T$$

- Extract the watermark as:

$$W = \frac{1}{\alpha} \Sigma^{-1} (D^* - \Sigma)$$

The authors use a different embedding formula that increases the level of robustness of watermarking by weighting the watermark with the singular values of the original signal. However, according to the extraction steps of the watermarking scheme, an adversary may reveal the presence of a desired watermark in an arbitrary audio file, similarly to the flaw encountered in Liu and Tan (2002).

In the novel approach we presented in Calagna, Guo, Mancini, and Jajodia (2006) we experienced that SVD properties illustrated in the previous section may guarantee the robustness of the watermarking scheme. According to our experimental results, our scheme is sufficiently robust against several attacks. Moreover, the computational complexity of our algorithm is reduced as we do not combine the SVD transform with other transforms.

The novelty of our approach consists in considering the input elements of a watermarking system as matrices. Properties of the SVD guarantee the effectiveness of the proposed method. This direction can be further extended to original implementations of watermarking algorithms that can robustly protect intellectual property on digital content. Intuitively, we use the SVD transform in image watermarking since images can be represented as matrices both in the spatial and in the transform domain. The idea is to associate the watermark to the singular values of SVD compression and take into account some well-known properties of SVD (approximation and perturbation). Our approach embeds the watermark in the most significant elements of the cover such that it is more robust to intentional or non-intentional attacks. According to the detection steps, the watermark can be determined univocally, while other related works present flaws in the detection algorithm.

OUR SOLUTION

Within the SPADA@WEB[1] project we developed a semi-blind image watermarking system (Calagna et al., 2006); the knowledge of singular values of the cover image together with the embedded watermark is crucial in the detection phase: the original cover is not required. Every image has associated a set of singular values. However, different images may have the same singular values, then, knowing only this information cannot help an attacker to discover which the original unwatermarked image is. Moreover, knowledge of singular values at the detector is not an issue for the applications we have in mind. These are two key points of our scheme. First of all, our approach is suitable for Internet applications: In this scenario, the original cover could not be available to receivers. Moreover, we developed our scheme for watermarking of geographical and spatial data that can be exchanged by a restricted group of GIS[2] users authorized to have access to this kind of data. According to our scheme, the detector needs only the singular values of the cover image, while the exact representation of the cover features, watermark features, and noise features in statistical means is left for future work.

Our scheme works on a block-by-block basis and makes use of SVD compression to embed the watermark. The watermark is embedded in all the non-zero singular values according to the local features of the cover image so as to balance embedding capacity with distortion. The experimental results show that our scheme is robust, especially with respect to high-pass filtering. To the best of our knowledge the use of the block-based SVD for watermarking applications has not yet been investigated.

The following, the SVD-based watermarking algorithm is presented. This is a novel approach with respect to previous solutions that apply the SVD to the entire image, without considering how singular values vary with different blocks of the same image. Also, embedding the watermark in the most significant singular values of each block makes the watermarking system more robust to possible attacks.

Watermark Embedding

We decide to embed the watermark in the most significant singular values of each block to prevent possible removal attacks, including lossy compression. The model of our watermarking system is discussed in the following.

Let $A^{M \times N}$ be the matrix representation of the original image to be protected by watermarking. Firstly, it is divided in blocks $H_i (i = 1 \cdots B)$, whose size $m \times n$ is small enough to capture the local features. B represents the total number of blocks and is given by:

$$B = \left[\frac{M \times N}{m \times n} \right] \quad (19)$$

The watermark to be embedded into the ith block is represented by the non-zero entries of a diagonal matrix $W_{k_{ri}}$. The watermark is embedded into the first k_{ri} singular values of H_i, and then, the new singular value matrix is used to obtain the watermarked block H'_i. The watermarking embedding consists of the following steps:

1. Choose a proper block size $m \times n$ (M mod $m = N$ mod $n = 0$) and divide the original image, that is represented by the matrix $A^{M \times N}$, into B blocks.
2. For each block H_i $(i = 1 \cdots B)$:
   • Apply the SVD to the matrix H_i and calculate its rank, r_i. According to the rule $\sigma_j = 0$ for $j > r_i$ we represent it as $H_i = U_{ri} \Sigma_{ri} V_{ri}^T$;

- Among the non-zero singular values, select the first k_{ri} which are related to a given percentage of the total sum of singular vales to embed the watermark in the most significant singular values of each block. We may represent the ith block as: $H_i = (H_{k_{ri}} \mid H_{ri-k_{ri}})$, where $H_{k_{ri}}$ is limited to the first k_{ri} singular values and $H_{ri-k_{ri}}$ is related to the remaining singular values in the ith block.

3. The watermark is embedded in the first k_{ri} singular values, as follows:

$$\Sigma'_{k_{ri}} = \Sigma_{k_{ri}} + \alpha \Sigma_{k_{ri}} W_{k_{ri}} \qquad (20)$$

where $\Sigma_{k_{ri}}$ represents the singular values matrix of order and, $\Sigma'_{k_{ri}}$ the updated singular values matrix after the watermarking embedding. The remaining non-zero singular values σ_j $(k_{ri} < j < r_i)$, which are the diagonal entries of $\Sigma_{ri-k_{ri}}$ remain unchanged.

Hence, the reconstructed watermarked block H'_i is represented as:

$$H'_i = (H'_{k_{ri}} \mid H_{ri-k_{ri}}) \qquad (21)$$

where the sub-blocks $H'_{k_{ri}}$ and $H_{ri-k_{ri}}$ are given, respectively, by equations (22) and (23):

$$H'_{k_{ri}} = U_{k_{ri}} \Sigma_{k_{ri}} V^T{}_{k_{ri}} + \alpha U_{k_{ri}} \Sigma_{k_{ri}} W_{k_{ri}} V^T{}_{k_{ri}}$$
$$= H_{k_{ri}} + U_{k_{ri}} \Sigma_{k_{ri}} W_{k_{ri}} V^T{}_{k_{ri}}$$
$$\qquad (22)$$

$$H_{ri-k_{ri}} = U_{ri-k_{ri}} \Sigma_{ri-k_{ri}} V^T{}_{ri-k_{ri}} \qquad (23)$$

In other words, the ith block is reconstructed by updating its first k_r singular values according to step 3 of the watermarking embedding algorithm and updating the sub-blocks of H_i according to the equations (21)-(23).

Thus, the watermarked image is obtained by replacing all the original blocks H_i with these watermarked blocks $H'_{k_{ri}}$.

Watermarking Extraction

In the extraction phase we take into consideration only the singular values σ_j, $j = 1 \cdots k_{ri}$ of each sub-block $H'_{k_{ri}}$, described by equation (22).

Given a possible counterfeit image, whose sub-blocks are indicated with $H'_{k_{ri}}$ and the singular value matrix $\Sigma_{k_{ri}}$ of each sub-block in the cover image, the watermark elements w'_j in each sub-block are extracted according to the following rule:

$$w'_j = \frac{\sigma'_j - \sigma_j}{\alpha \sigma_j} \qquad (24)$$

where w'_j are the diagonal elements of the extracted watermark $W'_{k_{ri}}$ and, σ'_j and σ_j are the singular values of $H'_{k_{ri}}$ and $H_{k_{ri}}$, respectively, for $j = 1 \cdots k_{ri}$.

The extracted watermark elements w'_j are compared to the embedded ones w_j by means of correlation.

Our threat model consists of two main categories of attacks:

- **Removal:** An adversary attempts to discover the embedded watermark and may remove it from the watermarked image;
- **Distortive:** An adversary applies some quality-preserving transformations, including signal processing techniques, to the watermarking image making the watermark undetectable.

We observe that our scheme is robust against both categories of attacks. As for the removal attacks, an adversary is unable to remove the watermark since we assume he/she has no access to the singular values of the cover image.

Figure 2. Aerial picture: Cover (on the left), watermarked image obtained by applying the SVD scheme (on the right)

We remind that the removal attack is the more dangerous, especially in the GIS field, where the digital maps have a great value and they should be protected against malicious attacks.

As for the distortive attacks, Table 1 shows that the attacks included in the Checkmark benchmarking tool (Pereira, Voloshynovskiy, Madueo, Marchand-Maillet, & Pun, 2001) does not alter the embedded watermark, which can be detected correctly.

We applied our scheme to several images. For space reasons, we summarize in this table only the experimental results on the 512×512 aerial grayscale picture, which is illustrated on the left side of Figure 2 together with the watermarked image obtained by applying our SVD scheme (on the right).

We compare our SVD scheme to the Cox et al. (1997) scheme implemented according to the original paper on the spread spectrum algorithm: The watermark is embedded into the 1000 greatest magnitude DCT coefficients (excluding the DC component) of the cover image, with the watermark strength $\alpha = 0.1$. The watermarks are drawn from a Gaussian distribution $N(0; 1)$ in both schemes.

We set the block size $m_i = 8, i = 1 \cdots B$ and the watermark strength $\alpha = 0.3$ in the SVD scheme to obtain an acceptable quality difference between the cover image and the watermarked image as for

the Cox algorithm (in terms of PSNR it is 30 dB for the SVD scheme, 32 dB for the Cox scheme). We observe that by applying our scheme, we may embed a longer watermark in the image with respect to the Cox scheme, without decreasing the quality difference too much.

By our settings, we may embed a watermark of about 8,000 elements in the original image. Embedding 8,000 elements in the Cox et al. (1997) scheme produces images of lower quality, with PSNR = 25.30 dB.

The robustness of the watermarking scheme is evaluated by means of the correlation measure between the extracted watermark from a possible counterfeit image and the embedded watermark. These results are compared to the Cox et al. (1997) watermarking scheme.

For each attack, we obtain different levels of distortion, by changing the corresponding parameter, which is indicated in the second column. The third and fourth columns of Table 1 show the correlation value between the extracted watermark from the attacked image and the embedded one for the Cox et al. (1997) watermarking scheme and our SVD scheme, respectively. The last two columns of the table show the quality difference between the attacked image and the original cover, when the Cox scheme and the

These experiments give evidence that our watermarking scheme is robust against that kind of attacks, including the high-distortive ones, since the measured correlation value is high. Actually, it depends on the specific application if the level of distortion is acceptable or not.

About filtering techniques, we can see that the larger the window size the more distortive the attack is. About the downsampling/upsampling attack, the choice of the first pair of downsample/upsample factor leads to low distortion, while the choice of the second pair lead to a higher distortion. JPEG compression is applied with different quality factors. The lower the quality factor is, the more distortive the attack is. We added white Gaussian noise (AWGN) with different strengths. The higher the strength is, the more distortive the attack is. Our scheme is robust against the contrast enhancement techniques, which improve the visual quality of the image and are considered high frequency preserving (Ganic & Eskicioglu, 2004). They include histogram equalization and intensity adjustment, as well. Finally, we show the robustness of our scheme against the clipping attack. This result is meaningful if we consider that only the 25% of the watermarked image remains after the attack. This portion corresponds to the central block.

To summarize, our scheme is more robust than the Cox et al. (1997) scheme against median filtering, downsampling/upsampling, histogram equalization, intensity adjustment, and clipping attacks, while both the schemes are comparable with respect to other attacks, including the JPEG compression and the addition of white Gaussian noise.

The resulting attacked images have acceptable quality, especially for high-pass filtering, including Gaussian and median filtering, sharpening, contrast enhancement, and clipping. The robustness of watermarking against geometrical attacks, including rotation, translation, and scaling is an open issue. Several authors have discussed on this topic. These attacks represent a threat in the GIS scenario, since they are typical manipulations that can be used to improve map exploration. We

consider this problem by taking into account singular values properties. In fact, it holds:

- **Rotation:** Given a matrix A and its rotated A_r, both have the same singular values;
- **Translation:** Given a matrix A and its translated A_t, both have the same singular values;
- **Scaling:** Given a matrix A and its scaled A_s, if A has the singular values σ_i then A_s has the singular values $\sigma_i \sqrt{L_r L_c}$ with L_r the scaling factor of rows, and L_c the scaling factor of columns. If rows (columns) are mutually scaled, A_s has the singular values $\sigma_i \sqrt{L_r}, \sigma_i \sqrt{L_c}$).

When SVD is applied to the whole image, these properties still hold:

- **Rotation:** Given an image A and its rotated A_r, both have the same singular values;
- **Translation:** Given an image A and its translated A_t, both have the same singular values;
- **Scaling:** Given an image A and its scaled A_s, if A has the singular values σ_i then A_s has the singular values $\sigma_i \sqrt{L_r L_c}$.

If rows (columns) are mutually scaled, A_s has the singular values $\sigma_i \sqrt{L_r}, \sigma_i \sqrt{L_c}$). However, when SVD is applied to the image blocks, this is not true.

The extension of the watermarking algorithm to cope with this kind of problem is left for future work.

CONCLUSION

The chapter illustrates watermarking based on the transform domain. By exploiting intrinsic properties of transform domain, it is possible to design specific watermarking schemes. We emphasize the use of SVD in digital watermarking for its flexibility of application.

Table 1. Robustness of SVD watermarking scheme against attacks

Attack Name	Parameter	Correlation		PSNR (attacked)	
		Cox	SVD	Cox	SVD
Gaussian filter	Window size				
	3	0.95	0.98	25.82	29.00
	5	0.95	0.98	25.80	28.70
Median filter	Window size				
	3	0.65	0.80	24.60	25.50
	5	0.80	0.80	25.00	27.00
	7	0.51	0.60	24.30	26.80
Midpoint filter	Window size				
	3	0.90	0.92	25.70	26.13
	5	0.55	0.60	23.20	24.15
Trimmed mean filter	Window size				
	3	0.95	0.95	27.00	29.18
	5	0.82	0.89	25.86	27.77
Denoising with perceptual denoising(1)	Window size				
	3	0.88	0.90	24.90	24.28
	5	0.76	0.77	24.40	24.67
Denoising with perceptual denoising(2)	Window size				
	3	0.88	0.90	24.41	25.55
	5	0.84	0.87	24.23	25.20
Hard thresholding	Window size				
	3	0.91	0.94	26.20	24.95
	5	0.90	0.93	25.90	25.82
Soft thresholding	Window size				
	3	0.90	0.90	25.97	27.00
	5	0.80	0.83	25.94	27.40
JPEG compression	Quality factor				
	10	0.77	0.78	27.60	29.21
	20	0.83	0.86	29.00	29.25
	30	0.89	0.90	29.22	29.30
	40	0.94	0.95	29.38	29.40
	50	0.95	0.96	29.44	29.43
	60	0.96	0.97	29.74	29.50
	70	0.98	0.98	29.95	29.70
	80	0.99	0.99	29.96	29.75

continued on following page

Table 1. continued

	90	0.99	0.99	29.99	29.97
Downsampling/ Upsampling	*Downsample factor/ Upsample factor*				
	0.75 / 1.33	0.87	0.98	24.01	24.00
	0.50 / 2.00	0.73	0.77	22.97	23.05
AWGN	*Noise strength*				
	2	0.99	0.99	29.80	29.80
	4	0.99	0.99	29.75	29.78
	6	0.96	0.98	28.00	28.00
	8	0.94	0.98	25.58	26.00
	10	0.93	0.97	25.00	25.50
	12	0.91	0.95	24.67	24.50
	14	0.90	0.95	24.03	24.00
	16	0.86	0.92	23.01	23.10
	18	0.82	0.90	22.04	23.00
	20	0.72	0.88	20.56	22.00
Sharpening	*Window size*				
	3	0.77	0.76	22.40	28.50
Histogram equalization	-	0.33	0.65	18.00	20.00
Intensity adjustment	*Intensity values/ Gamma correction*				
	[0, 0.8] → [0, 1] / 1.5	0.65	0.70	21.00	21.15
Clipping	*Clipped portion*				
	75 %	0.31	0.55	9.00	12.78

We presented a robust SVD-based watermarking scheme for images. The idea is to embed more watermark in the high-contrast regions and less watermark in the low-contrast regions of an image. According to the detection steps, the watermark can be determined univocally, while other related works present flaws in the detection algorithm.

A case study of our approach refers to the protection of geographical and spatial data in case of the *raster* representation model of maps. The next section will introduce possible extensions of our scheme.

FUTURE RESEARCH DIRECTIONS

Although we consider image watermarking, we claim that the SVD-based approach can be employed in other multimedia representations, including video and audio content, provided that they are represented as matrices. Moreover, our approach may be extended to other applications, where data to be protected are organized as matrices. The extension of this approach to different applications is left for future work.

As for the application to digital maps, it could be interesting to consider how our approach may be extended to the vector representation model. Moreover, future work concerning this scheme includes the analysis of the watermarking impact on further processing of digital maps (e.g., buffering, classification) and the extension of the scheme to cope with geometrical attacks. These aspects are relevant in the GIS field, any representation model (raster or vector) is used. In fact, a good watermarking scheme should guarantee that original map features may be identifiable clearly after watermarking and, that GIS processing may lead to correct results. Geometrical attacks are of utmost importance for geographical data. However, this remains an open issue. The extension of the SVD-based scheme to cope with this kind of problems is left for future work.

Our scheme can be employed in several applications. The use of SVD in conjunction with other transforms that characterize multimedia files (e.g., DCT, DFT, DWT) seems to be interesting and requires further investigation. In fact, SVD may be applied to the coefficients matrix.

SVD-based watermarking may be extended to other fields where authentication is a relevant issue. Interesting scenarios are: MIMO-OFDM channel estimation (Edfors, Sandell, Van de Beek, Wilson, & Borjesson, 1998; Zamiri-Jafarian & Gulak, 2005) and database protection.

REFERENCES

Andrews, H. C., & Patterson, C. (1976). Singular value decomposition (SVD) image coding. *IEEE Transactions on Communications, 24*(4), 425-432.

Byun, S.-C., Lee, S.-K., Tewflk, H., & Ahn, B.-A. (2002). A SVD-based fragile watermarking scheme for image authentication. In F. A. P. Petitcolas & H. J. Kim (Eds.), *International Workshop on Digital Watermarking* (IWDW '02), Seoul, Korea (pp. 170-178). Berlin/Heidelberg, Germany: Springer.

Cai, L., & Du, S. (2004). Rotation, scale and translation invariant image watermarking using radon transform and Fourier transform. In *Proceedings of the Circuits and Systems Symposium on Emerging Technologies: Frontiers of Mobile and Wireless Communication* (pp. 281-284). IEEE.

Calagna, M., Guo, H., Mancini, L. V., & Jajodia, S. (2006). A robust watermarking system based on SVD compression. In *Proceedings of the Symposium on Applied Computing* (SAC '06) Dijon, France (pp. 1341-1347). New York: ACM Press.

Calagna, M., & Mancini, L. V. (2005). A blind method for digital watermarking attacks. In M. H. Hamza (Ed.), *International Conference on Internet and Multimedia Systems and Applications* (EuroIMSA '05), Grindelwald, Switzerland (pp. 265-270). Calgary, AB, Canada: IASTED/ACTA Press.

Calagna, M., & Mancini, L. V. (2007). Information hiding for spatial and geographical data. In A. Belussi, B. Catania, E. Clementini, & E. Ferrari (Eds.), *Spatial data on the Web—Modeling and management*. Springer.

Chung, K.-L., Shen, C.-H., & Chang, L.-C. (2001). A novel SVD-and VQ-based image hiding scheme. *Pattern Recognition Letters, 22*, 1051-1058.

Cox, I. J., Kilian, J., Leightont, T., & Shamoon, T. (1997). Secure spread spectrum watermarking for multimedia. *IEEE Transactions on Image Processing, 6*(12), 1673-1687.

Edfors, O., Sandell, M., Van de Beek, J.-J., Wilson, S. K., & Borjesson, P. O. (1998). OFDM channel estimation by singular value decomposition. *IEEE Transactions on Communications, 46*(7), 931-939.

Ganic, E., & Eskicioglu, A. M. (2004). Robust DWT-SVD domain image watermarking: Embedding data in all frequencies. In *Proceedings of the Multimedia and Security workshop* (MM&Sec '04), Magdeburg, Germany (pp. 167-174). New York: ACM Press.

Ganic, E., Zubair, N., & Eskicioglu, A. M. (2003). An optimal watermarking scheme based on singular value decomposition. In M. H. Hamza (Ed.), *International Conference on Communication, Network and Information Security* (CNIS '03), Uniondale, NY (pp. 85-90). Calgary, AB, Canada: IASTED/ACTA Press.

Golub, G. H., & Van Loan, C. F. (1996). *Matrix computations* (3rd ed.). Baltimore, MD: Johns Hopkins University Press.

Gorodetski, V. I., Popyack, L. J., Samoilov, V., & Skormin, V. A. (2001). SVD-based approach to transparent embedding data into digital images. In V. I. Gorodetski, V. A. Skormin, & L. J. Popyack (Eds.), *Workshop on information assurance in computer networks: Methods, models, and architectures for network security* (MMM-ACNS '01), St. Petersburg, Russia (LNCS 2052, pp. 263-274). London: Springer-Verlag.

Jain, A. K. (1989). *Fundamentals of digital image processing.* Prentice Hall.

Liu, R., & Tan, T. (2002). An SVD-based watermarking scheme for protecting rightful ownership. *IEEE Transactions on Multimedia, 4*(1), 121-128.

Muti, D., Bourennane, S., & Guillaume, M. (2004). SVD-based image filtering improvement by means of image rotation. In *Proceedings of the International Conference on Acoustics, Speech and Signal Processing* (ICASSP '04), Montreal, Quebec, Canada (pp. 289-292). IEEE Press.

Ozer, H., Sankur, B., & Memon, N. (2005). An SVD-based audio watermarking technique. In *Proceedings of the Workshop on Multimedia and Security* (MM&Sec '05), New York (pp. 51-56). New York: ACM Press.

Pereira, S., Voloshynovskiy, S., Madueo, M., Marchand-Maillet, S., & Pun, T. (2001). Second generation benchmarking and application oriented evaluation. In I. S. Moskowitz (Ed.), International

Workshop on Information Hiding (IWIH '01), Pittsburgh, PA (LNCS 2137, pp. 340-353). London: Springer-Verlag.

Phillips, C. L., & Parr, J. M. (1999). *Signals, systems, and transforms.* Prentice Hall.

Si, H., & Li, C. (2004). Fragile watermarking scheme based on the block-wise dependence in the wavelet domain. In *Proceedings of the Workshop on Multimedia and Security* (MM&Sec '04), Magdeburg, Germany (pp. 214-219). New York: ACM Press.

Solachidis, V., & Pitas, I. (2004). Watermarking polygonal lines using Fourier descriptors. *Computer Graphics and Applications, 24*(3), 44-51.

Yang, J.-F., & Lu, C.-L. (1995). Combined techniques of singular value decomposition and vector quantization for image coding. *IEEE Transactions on Image Processing, 4*(8), 1141-1146.

Zamiri-Jafarian, H., & Gulak, G. (2005). *Iterative MIMO channel SVD estimation. International Conference on Communications* (ICC '05) (pp. 1157-1161). IEEE Press.

Zhang, X.-P., & Li, K. (2005). Comments on "An SVD-based watermarking scheme for protecting rightful ownership." *IEEE Transactions on Multimedia: Correspondence, 7*(1).

ADDITIONAL READING

Arnold, M. (2002). Subjective and objective quality evaluation of watermarked audio tracks. In *Proceedings of the International Conference on Web Delivering of Music* (WEDELMUSIC '02), Darnstadt, Germany (pp. 161-167). IEEE Press.

Arnold, M., Schmucker, M., & Wolthusen, S. D. (2003). *Techniques and applications of digital watermarking and content protection.* Norwood, MA: Artech House.

Barni, M., & Bartolini, F. (2004). *Watermarking systems engineering: Enabling digital asset security and other applications.* New York: Dekkar Press.

Barni, M., Bartolini, F., Cappellini, V., Magli, E., & Olmo, G. (2001). Watermarking techniques for electronic delivery of remote sensing images. In *Proceedings of the International Geoscience and Remote Sensing Symposium* (IGARSS '01), Sidney, Australia. IEEE Press.

Barni, M., Bartolini, F., & Checcacci, N. (2005). Watermarking of MPEG-4 video objects. *IEEE Transactions on Multimedia, 7*(1), 23-32.

Barni, M., Bartolini, F., Magli, E., & Olmo, G. (2002). Watermarking techniques for electronic delivery of remote sensing images. *Optical Engineering: Special Section on Remote Sensing Technology and Applications, 41*(9), 2111-2119.

Bergman, C., & Davidson, J. (2005). Unitary embedding for data hiding with the SVD. In E. J. Delp & P. W. Wong (Eds.), *Proceedings of SPIE: Security, Steganography and Watermarking of Multimedia Contents VII,* San Jose, CA (Vol. 5681, pp. 619-630).

Cox, I., Miller, M., & Bloom, J. (2001). *Digital watermarking.* San Francisco: Morgan Kaufmann.

Fridrich, J., Goljan, M., & Du, R. (2001). Reliable detection of LSB steganography in grayscale and color images. In *Proceedings of the Workshop on Multimedia and Security* (MM&Sec '02) (pp. 27-30). Ottawa, Canada: ACM Press.

Guan, Y. L., & Jin, J. (2001). An objective comparison between spatial and DCT watermarking schemes for MPEG video. In *Proceedings of the International Symposium on Information Technology* (ITCC '01), Las Vegas, NV (pp. 207-211). IEEE Computer Society.

Hou, Z. (2003). Adaptive singular value decomposition in wavelet domain for image denoising.

Journal of Pattern Recognition, 36(8), 1747-1763.

Johnson, N. F., Duric, Z., & Jajodia, S. (2001). *Information hiding steganography and watermarking—Attacks and countermeasures.* Norwell, MA: Kluwer Academic.

Judge, P., & Ammar, M. (2002). WHIM: Watermarking multicast video with a hierarchy of intermediaries. *ACM Computer Networks: The International Journal of Computer and Telecommunications Networking, 39*(6), 699-712.

Judge, P., & Ammar, M. (2003). Security issues and solutions in multicast content distribution: A survey. *IEEE Magazine Network, 17*(1), 30-36.

Kang, K.-P., Choi, Y.-H., & Choi, T.-S. (2004). Real-time video watermarking for MPEG streams. In A. Laganà et al. (Eds.), *International Conference on Computational Science and Its Applications* (ICSSA '04), Assisi, Italy (LNCS 3046, pp. 348-358). Springer.

Lang, A., & Dittmann, J. (2006). Transparency and complexity benchmarking of audio watermarking algorithms issues. In *Proceedings of the Workshop on Multimedia and Security* (MM&Sec '06), Geneva, Switzerland. New York: ACM Press.

Li, L., Pan, Z., Zhang, M., & Ye, K. (2004). Watermarking subdivision surfaces based on addition property of Fourier transform. In S. N. Spencer (Ed.), *International Conference on Computer Graphics and interactive Techniques in Australasia and South East Asia* (GRAPHITE '04), Singapore (pp. 46-49). New York: ACM Press.

Lopez, C. (2002). Watermarking of digital geospatial datasets: A review of technical, legal and copyright issues. *International Journal of Geographical Information Science, 16*(6), 589-607.

Lu, C.-S. (Ed.). (2004). *Multimedia security: Steganography and digital watermarking techniques for protection of intellectual property.* Hershey, PA: Idea Group.

Megias, D., Herrera-Joancomart, J., & Minguillon, J. (2004a). A robust audio watermarking scheme based on MPEG 1 layer 3 compression. In *Proceedings of IFIP Communications and Multimedia Security* (CMS '03), Torino, Italy (LNCS 963, pp. 226-238). Berlin/Heidelberg, Germany: Springer.

Megias, D., Herrera-Joancomart, J., & Minguillon, J. (2004b). An audio watermarking scheme robust against stereo attacks. In *Proceedings of the Workshop on Multimedia and Security* (MM&Sec '04), Magdeburg, Germany (pp. 206-213). New York: ACM Press.

Sikora, T., & Chiariglione, L. (1997). MPEG-4 video and its potential for future multimedia services. In *Proceedings of the International Symposium on Circuits and Systems* (ISCAS '97) Hong Kong (pp. 1468-1471). IEEE Press.

Steinebach, M., Petitcolas, F. A. P., Raynal, F., Dittmann, J., Fontaine, C., Seibel, C., et al. (2001). Stirmark benchmark: Audio watermarking attacks. In *Proceedings of the International Symposium on Information Technology: Coding and Computing* (ITCC '01), Las Vegas, NV (pp. 49-54). IEEE Computer Society.

Terzija, N., & Geisselhardt, W. (2004). Digital image watermarking using complex wavelet transform. In *Proceedings of the Workshop on Multimedia and Security* (MM&Sec '04), Magdeburg, Germany (pp. 193-198). New York: ACM Press.

Yavuz, E., & Telatar, Z. (2006). SVD adapted DCT domain DC subband image watermarking against watermark ambiguity. In B. Gunsel et al. (Eds.), *Workshop on multimedia content representation, classification and security* (MRCS '06) (LNCS 4105, pp. 66-73). Springer.

Zamiri-Jafarian, H., & Gulak, G. (2005). Adaptive channel SVD estimation for MIMO-OFDM systems. *International Conference on Vehicular Technology* (VTC '05) (pp. 552-556). IEEE Press.

ENDNOTES

1. SPADA@WEB is for *Web-based Management and Representation of Spatial and Geographic Data.*
2. GIS is for Geographical Information System.

Chapter IV
Digital Video Watermarking and the Collusion Attack

Robert Caldelli
University of Florence, Italy

Alessandro Piva
University of Florence, Italy

ABSTRACT

This chapter is devoted to the analysis of the collusion attack applied to current digital video watermarking algorithms. In particular, we analyze the effects of collusion attacks, with particular attention to the temporal frame averaging (TFA), applied to two basic watermarking systems like spread spectrum (SS) and spread transform dither modulation (STDM). The chapter describes the main drawbacks and advantages in using these two watermarking schemes and, above all, the fundamental issues to be taken into account to grant a certain level of robustness when a collusion attack is carried out by an attacker.

INTRODUCTION

Digital watermarking technology (Barni & Bartolini, 2004b; Cox, Miller, & Bloom, 2001) allows creators to hide a signal or some information into a digital content (an audio file, a still image, a video sequence, or a combination of the previous), usually named host data, that can be detected or extracted later by means of computing operations to make an assertion about the data. In the beginning the research was mainly devoted to offer a solution to the problem of copyright protection of digital content. In general, watermarking allows creators to provide a communication channel multiplexed into an original content, through which it is possible to transmit some information, depending on the application at hand, from a sender to a receiver.

Figure 1. The proposed model for a digital watermarking system

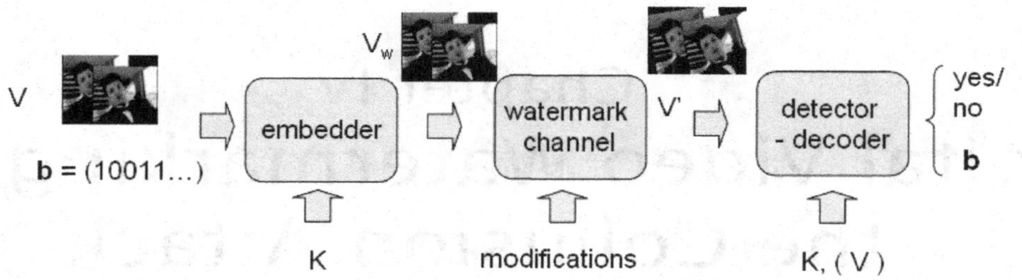

A digital watermarking system can be modeled as described in Figure 1 (Barni & Bartolini, 2004a). The inputs of the system are certain application dependent information, and the original host content is considered to be a video sequence V. The to-be-hidden information is usually represented as a binary string $\mathbf{b} = (b_1, b_2 ...., b_k)$, also referred to as the watermark code. The watermark embedder hides the watermark code $\mathbf{b}$ into the host asset V to produce a watermarked content V_w, usually making use of a secret information K needed to tune some parameters of the embedding process and allow the recovery of the watermark only to authorized users having access to that secret information.

The second element of the model, the watermark channel, takes into account all the processing operations and manipulations, both intentional and non-intentional, that the watermarked content may undergo during its distribution and fruition, so that consequently the watermarked content can be modified into a new version V_m.

The third element of the model is the tool for the recovery of the hidden information from V_m; the extraction of the hidden data may follow two different approaches: the detector can look for the presence of a specific message given to it as input, thus only answering yes or no, or the system (now called decoder) reads the sequence of bits hidden into the watermarked content without knowing it in advance. These two approaches lead to a distinction between *readable* watermarking algorithms, embedding a message that can be read, and *detectable* watermarking algorithms, inserting a code that can only be detected. An additional distinction may be made between systems that need to know the original content V in order to retrieve the hidden information, and those that do not require it. In the latter case we say that the system is *blind*, whereas in the former case it is said to be *non-blind*.

To embed the watermark code into the original content, watermarking techniques apply minor modifications to the host data in a perceptually invisible manner, where the modifications are related to the to-be-hidden data. The hidden information can be retrieved afterwards from the modified content by detecting the presence of these modifications. In general, embedding is achieved by modifying a set of features $\mathbf{f} = (f_1, f_2, ..., f_n)$ representing the host content with a watermark signal $\mathbf{M} = (m_1, m_2, ..., m_n)$ generated from the vector $\mathbf{b}$, according to a proper embedding rule that depends on the particular watermarking scheme, as it will be described in the following.

If we consider the particular case of video watermarking, it has to be pointed out that a video sequence can be considered as a sequence of consecutive and equally time-spaced still images: Video watermarking issue seems thus very similar to the image watermarking one. Actually, there are a lot of papers where an image watermarking system is extended to work with video. However, there are also several differences between images and video, demanding for specific system design. A first important difference is the size of the host data where the watermark has to be hidden: Images are characterized by a limited amount of data (i.e., the number of pixels, or the number of transform domain coefficients), whereas this amount is really higher for video assets. This allows creators to have a less rigid constraint for the achievement of the trade-off between visibility and robustness: since more samples are available, the modifications necessary to embed the hidden information will be less visible, so that there will not be the need to apply complicated models of the human visual system to better hide the watermark. On the other hand, since a really higher amount of data has to be presented to the user, in the case of video sequences there are more demanding constraints on real-time effectiveness of the system. This constraint is even more tight for some particular applications of watermarking, like video-on-demand, where it is not possible to use a watermarking system that works on the uncompressed domain, since the time required for decompression, watermark embedding, and recompression would be too long. Another difference between still images and video is that for the second type of assets, as we will analyze in the following, a number of attacks exist that can not be applied to the still image case, for example, frame averaging or frame swapping.

Classification of Video Watermarking Algorithms

A first distinction can be made between techniques embedding the watermark in the compressed video stream and those embedding the watermark in the raw domain, prior to any compression algorithm possibly applied to the video (Doerr & Dugelay, 2003a).

In a raw domain watermarking algorithm the watermark code is cast directly into the video sequence. Watermark embedding can be performed either in the spatial/temporal domain or a transformed domain (e.g., the discrete cosine transform [DCT] of the discrete Fourier transform [DFT] domain). The choice of the most appropriate category of watermarking algorithm strongly depends on the intended applications, and the requirements it sets to the watermarking system.

To give some general guidelines on the issues to be considered when choosing between raw and compressed domain techniques, we can start by noting that, in many cases, the digital video is stored in a compressed format (e.g., MPEG or H.263). If a raw domain watermarking algorithm is used to embed the watermark code, then the system needs to decompress the video stream, embed the watermark into the uncompressed frame sequence, and compress again the watermarked content to obtain the final watermarked video stream. Watermark detection also needs to be preceded by video decoding. On the contrary, if a compressed domain watermarking algorithm is adopted, it is possible to embed and decode the watermark directly into the compressed bit stream without going through a full decoding, watermarking, and re-encoding process, thus reducing significant complexity and additional time delays.

Compressed domain watermarking systems thus allow for computationally efficient watermark casting and decoding, a characteristic that is of primary importance in many applications, for example, real-time applications. Compressed domain watermarking presents some drawbacks as well. First of all, an additional constraint that the bit rate of the watermarked compressed video stream does not significantly exceed the bit rate of the unwatermarked stream has to be considered. Moreover, this kind of algorithm is sensitive to a number of **attacks** that can be neglected when a raw watermarking scheme is used. One of the most important such attacks is format conversion, for example, NTSC/PAL conversion, MPEG/H.263 transcoding, compression rate conversion, A/D, and D/A conversion.

Another classification of video watermarking systems is distinguished between frame-by-frame and sequence watermarking. In a frame-by-frame watermarking algorithm, the watermark code is embedded into each frame, by considering it as a still image, regardless of the other frames composing the sequence. On the contrary, a sequence watermarking system embeds the code into the whole, or at least a part, of the video stream, involving a set of consecutive frames. Of course, watermark embedding may still operate either in the raw or the compressed domain. Sequence-based algorithms operating in the raw domain, may just design the watermark signal added to the host video in such a way that it spans more than one frame. More sophisticated algorithms may exploit the correlation between subsequent frames, for example, by embedding the watermark in a 3D transformed domain (for example the 3D-DCT or 3D wavelet domains), which takes into account both the spatial and the temporal characteristics of the video sequence. When operating into the compressed domain, it has to be noted that current video compression standards such as MPEG or ITU H.26x standards are based on the same general structure including block based motion compensation, which takes into account temporal correlation of the content, and block-based DCT coding, which takes into account spatial correlation. A video stream contains thus three kinds of bits: header bits, motion vectors, and DCT coefficients. Sequence-based schemes may, then, operate on those parts of the video stream taking into account both the spatial and temporal characteristics of the video, for example, motion vectors or some other information representing all the video sequence like the GOP structure. Alternatively, sequence-oriented watermarking may be achieved by embedding the watermark

into a set of DCT coefficients spanning two or more frames of the video stream.

With regards to possible attacks against sequence watermarking, some new kinds of manipulations have to be taken into account, for example, frame averaging, frame dropping, and frame swapping. At usual frame rates these modifications would possibly not be perceived by the end user, but the watermark synchronization would be lost. Of course these attacks do not constitute a problem with frame-by-frame watermarking algorithms.

Concerning the current chapter, the analysis will be concentrated on raw video watermarking systems that embed the watermark code by considering a video just as a sequence of different still pictures, so that the watermarking procedure is just applied separately to each single video frame. In this framework, it is possible to devise two different approaches: *SS watermarking* and *side-informed watermarking*.

In SS video watermarking, **M** is a pseudo-randomly generated sequence of proper length n, where the components m_i are random variables drawn from a given probability density function (pdf), like a Gaussian of a uniform distribution. This watermarking sequence is added to the video frame with an additive rule as evidenced in the following equation:

$$I_t^{'} = I_t + \alpha M(k),$$

where I_t' and I_t are respectively the watermarked and the original frame (i.e., pixel grey level) at time t, α is the embedding power and $M(k)$ is the embedded watermark (we will assume in the following analysis that the samples follow a normal distribution with zero mean and unit variance) generated with a pseudo-random key k and added to the image. According to the adopted approach, such watermark $M(k)$ can depend on time $(M(k) = M_t(k))$ or can be constant; in the first case, different watermarks are embedded in each frame composing the sequence, in the second situation always the same code is added to the various images belonging to the digital video. Some perceptual considerations can be done to improve invisibility. To extract back the watermark, usually a correlation $C(\cdot)$ is computed as in the sequel:

$$C(I_t^{'}) = \frac{1}{N}\sum_{t=1}^{N} I_t^{'} \cdot M_t(k) = \alpha + \frac{1}{N}\sum_{t=1}^{N} I_t \cdot M_t(k) \approx \alpha,$$

where N represents the number of frames used to perform correlation. If the result is near to α it will be decided that the watermark is present in the video, if it is close to zero the watermark will be assumed to be absent. A decision threshold of $\alpha/2$ is adopted in practice. In both cases, time-varying and constant watermark will lead to the same result for correlation (Doerr & Dugelay, 2004).

In informed schemes the signal embedded within the host data depends on the host data themselves, in opposition to non-informed schemes (i.e., SS) where the embedded signal is unrelated to host data. One well known example of informed embedding method is the STDM approach that belongs to the broader class of quantization index modulation (QIM) watermarking schemes (Chen & Wornell, 2001).

In STDM framework a set of features $f(t) = \{f_1(t), f_2(t) \dots fr(t)\}$ is extracted from the t-th video frame. For instance, $f(t)$ may correspond to the grey levels of randomly chosen pixels from the t-th video frame and the same set of pixels is chosen for all the video frames.

An essential step in STDM watermarking is defining a (secret) direction $s(t)$ which, in general, may depend on t. In the following we will assume that $s(t)$ is a binary zero-mean sequence taking values ± 1 (this choice causes the watermark distortion to be spread uniformly over all the features).

In order to embed the watermark, which we will assume consisting in a single bit b, the correlation between $f(t)$ and $s(t)$ is quantized according to one of two quantizers depending on the to-be-embedded bit value. More precisely, let the two codebooks U_0 and U_1 associated respectively to $b = 0$ and $b = 1$ be defined as:

$$U_0 = \{k\Delta + d, k \in Z\},$$
$$U_1 = \{k\Delta + \Delta/2 + d, k \in Z\},$$

where d is an arbitrary parameter that, once chosen, is equal for each video frame. Let $\rho(t)$ be the correlation between $f(t)$ and $s(t)$, that is,

$$\rho(t) = f(t) \cdot s(t) = \sum_{i=1}^{r} f_i(t)s_i(t)$$

Watermark embedding is achieved by quantizing $\rho(t)$ either with the quantizer Q_0 associated to U_0:

$$Q_0(\rho(t)) = \arg \min_{u_{0,i} \in U_0} |u_{0,i} - \rho(t)|$$

where $u_{0,i}$ are the elements of U_0, or the quantizer associated to U_1:

$$Q_1(\rho(t)) = \arg \min_{u_{1,i} \in U_1} |u_{1,i} - \rho(t)|$$

In practice the watermarked features $f_w(t)$ are obtained by subtracting the projection of $f(t)$ on $s(t)$ from $f(t)$ and by adding a new component along the direction of $s(t)$ resulting in the desired quantized autocorrelation:

$$f_w(t) = f(t) - \rho(t)s(t) + \rho_w(t)s(t)$$

with

$$\rho_w(t) = \begin{cases} Q_0(\rho(t)) & b = 0 \\ Q_1(\rho(t)) & b = 1 \end{cases}$$

To read the watermark, a minimum distance decoder is used:

$$b^* = \arg \min_{b \in \{0,1\}} \min_{u_{b,i} \in U_b} |u_{b,i} - \rho^{'}(t)|$$

where by $\rho'(t)$ we indicate the correlation between the watermarked and possibly attacked features and the spreading vector $s(t)$. If the number of the to-be-embedded bits is $N_b > 1$, the encoding procedure just described is applied for each bit, that is, N_b subsets of features $f_n(t)$ $n = 1....N_b$ are selected, and N_b correlations $\rho_n(t)$ $n = 1....N_b$ are quantized. As a consequence, to embed N_b bits, $r \cdot N_b$ pixels are needed.

Security Requirements in Video Watermarking

When **watermarking** systems were designed, their performances were evaluated by facing them against different hurdles such as how many bits could be embedded in the digital asset (capacity/payload), how good was the perceptual quality of the watermarked object (perceivability), how many and which were the attacks or common processing that system could resist to (robustness), and so on. Not too much consideration has been paid to analyze problems related to **security**, that is, to determine if some lacks existed to allow an attacker to bypass the whole system or to use it in an illegal manner. Only recently the importance of security issues has been brought to the attention of the scientific community (Barni, Bartolini, & Furon, 2003), where by securing the inability by unauthorized users to access the watermarking channel is met (Cayre, Fontaine, & Furon, 2005; Kalker, 2001), and researchers started to give, in some particular cases, an estimate of the effort the hacker should make and also of the means he/she should have at his/her disposal to perform the intended action. Security aspects, though not crucial for some watermarking applications such as database indexing, cataloging, and non-public uses in general, are becoming dramatically important and sometimes determine the effective adoption of a technique for a specific purpose. Applications like copy control, ownership verification, authentication, broadcast monitoring, and

multimedia fingerprinting have to necessarily deal with security, also if it is not so clear, at the moment, in which way and to which extent to deal with these issues.

To give a basic definition of what is intended with the term *security* when talking about watermarking, is quite difficult. In the literature many celebrate phrases that deal with security exist, in particular we would like to cite one of them that is very well-known: the Kerchoff's law (Kerchoff, 1883). It establishes that security cannot be based on algorithm secrecy but on one or more secret keys used by the algorithm itself. Starting from this statement, it is also easy to understand that security must not be studied as a stand-alone problem but is important to take into account some of the main issues that are fundamental to structure in any type of analysis:

- **What is available to the attacker to help the illegal action:** On the basis of which software/hardware devices, multiple watermarked copies, knowledge of the algorithm ,and so on, he/she has access to, he/she is helped in performing the intended action.
- **Which kind of attack procedure the attacker can put in practice:** It refers to the kind of attack among the different ones that are known (and also unknown) the hacker can decide to adopt to circumvent the watermarking algorithm. It will be important to establish which of these attacks will be feasible according to the application at hand and which will be crucial for the specific characteristics of that system.
- **What the attacker wishes to do:** To decode hidden bits, to destroy/alter hidden bits, to make undetected modifications, and so forth.

Many are the attacks that have been proposed in literature under the category of security **attacks**. Among them the sensitivity attack, the

Holliman&Memon attack (Holliman & Memon, 2000), the Craver attack (Craver, Memon, Yeo, & Yeung, 1998) and the collusion attack are the most well-known. In this chapter we would like to focus our attention on the last one because it is a kind of attack that can simply be performed in a real hostile environment (e.g., media distribution over the Internet) where a watermarking system could be asked for working. Collusion attacks require, in general, as it will analyzed in this chapter, a pool of pirates (colluders) who share their resources to break the watermarking system. Collusion in video watermarking has been deeply studied in the last few years (Caldelli, Piva, Barni, & Carboni, 2005; Doerr & Dugelay, 2004; Su, Kundur, & Hatzinakos, 2005a, 2005b; Vinod & Bora, 2006) trying to determine which was the most secure manner to embed a watermark in a framed sequence by relying on the specific features of the video. On the other side, the aspect of video quality obtained after collusion has been taken into account too, so the issue of motion-compensation, before making a collusion, has been later introduced.

In this chapter, after an overview on collusion attacks in video watermarking (see the second section), we will propose a new and specific analysis (see the third section) to make a comparison in terms of robustness between SS and STDM watermarking schemes against collusion attack, in particular when the TFA and its motion compensated version MC-TFA is applied to a video sequence. Two are the typologies of watermarking techniques that have been mainly investigated vs. the collusion attack: first, it has been SS (Cox, Kilian, Leighton, & Shamoon, 1997) and second, the STDM (Chen & Wornell, 2001); here we will study which are the Achilles' heels for both the types of watermarking methods (e.g., repeating the same watermark in all the video frames) and we will provide some solutions.

WHAT IS THE COLLUSION ATTACK?

The collusion attack is an action carried out by a given set of malicious users in possession of a copy of protected content that join together in order to obtain at the end of the attack procedure an unprotected asset. The attack is carried out by properly combining the protected copies of the multimedia documents collected by the colluders, according to the type of content and the kind of adopted protection system.

When the protection is assured by a data hiding algorithm, the collusion usually can take place in one of two different application frameworks: multimedia fingerprinting and ownership verification. In multimedia fingerprinting, a content owner, to protect his/her copyright, embeds a different code into each copy of the content distributed to each customer, in order to be able to trace possible illegal usage of data and discover the source of the leakage of information; in this case, then, each colluder possesses a slightly different copy of the same multimedia content, and the attack consists in averaging all documents they have, trying to produce a new document in which the watermark is no longer present; if the number of averaged documents is large enough, the attack is very effective even without the introduction of perceptually significant degradation between the averaged multimedia document and the original one. In ownership verification, a content owner, to demonstrate he/she is the authorised holder of the distributed content, embeds always the same code, linked to his/her identity, into different watermarked documents before they are distributed to the customers, in such a way that the hidden code can be used to prove ownership in court if someone will infringe on his/her copyrights; in this case, then, each colluder possesses different multimedia documents, with the same hidden code embedded in, so that the attack is carried out by estimating the watermark by means of an average of all the different contents they have (this

Figure 2. TFA attack applied in inter-video collusion: colluders group together owing the same video with different watermarks and apply a TFA collusion attack to obtain an unwatermarked video

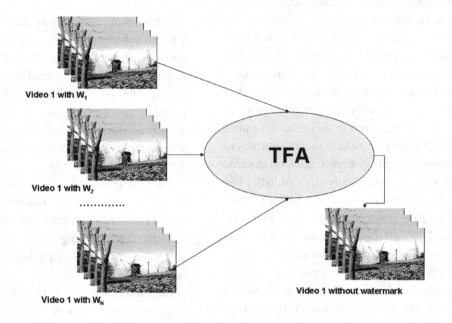

Video 1 with W_1

Video 1 with W_2

....

Video 1 with W_N

Video 1 without watermark

approach is suitable only for data hiding systems in which the hidden watermark does not depend on the host data). Then the estimated watermark can be removed from all the documents hiding it, or even falsely inserted in other ones to generate fake watermarked documents.

In the beginning, research against the collusion attack concerned mainly applications where the multimedia documents were constituted by digital images; in such a case, a possible colluder is obliged to team together with other attackers or, at least, to succeed in collecting a sufficient number of assets to successfully achieve his/her attack. Later, this attack was extended to other kinds of multimedia content like video sequences: in this particular case, the possibility of success of a collusion attack increases, since a video sequence, by one's very nature, is nothing else than a collection of single still images. A single malicious customer in possession of one of few

watermarked video sequences can then combine the single frames composing the video to realize a collusion attack, in order to obtain a set of unwatermarked frames, or to extract the embedded code. In particular, in the case of video content, two kinds of collusion attack can be attempted. The first, usually named ***inter-video*** *collusion*, is the classical attack carried out by resorting to a certain number of different watermarked video sequences, and then requires the cooperation among several malicious users. In Figures 2 and 3 two possible situations are illustrated: in the first one colluders try to erase the watermarks that are embedded in the diverse copies of the same video they own, on the contrary, in the second one, the colluders try to estimate the watermark which is contained in the movies they can share and then subtract it by their watermarked contents to obtain watermark-free copies. The acronyms TFA and WER which appear in Figure 2 and

Figure 3. WER attack applied in inter-video collusion: colluders group together owing different videos with the same watermark and apply a WER collusion attack to obtain a reliable estimate of the watermark so to subtract it by the watermarked contents.and achieve unwatermarked copies

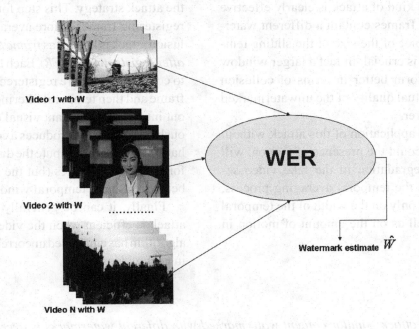

Video 1 with W

Video 2 with W

Video N with W

WER

Watermark estimate $\hat{W}$

Figure 3 state for temporal frame averaging and watermark estimation remodulation, such collusion attacks will be debated in depth in the next subsection.

The second and more interesting collusion attack, video watermarking can suffer, usually called intra-video collusion, refers to the attack performed only by using the frames composing a single video sequence; in this circumstance there is no need for more than one pirate, as the colluder has access to several watermarked frames composing the video sequence; if the length of the video is sufficient to collect a significant number of watermarked frames, the colluder can attempt the attack by himself/herself.

In the sequel, we will focus exclusively on this kind of attack procedure: intra-video collusion.

Intra-Video Collusion: Different Approaches

In intra-video collusion, it is possible to devise diverse manners to act on a video to wash out the watermark, according to the similarity of the content in the video frames, and to the type of embedded watermark. Two of the main approaches to be followed are: try to directly erase the watermark by means of a filtering operation or try to estimate the watermark and then subtract it by the watermarked frames. Both these methodologies can be successful or not on the basis of the watermarking system characteristics.

Temporal Frame Averaging (TFA)

The first one, commonly named *TFA*, known also as frame temporal filtering (FTF), operates by averaging along the time axis several consecutive frames in order to produce a new video sequence where the watermark is no longer readable (see Figure 4); this kind of attack is clearly effective if consecutive frames contain a different watermark. The choice of the size of the sliding temporal window is crucial, in fact a larger window allows to perform better in terms of collusion but the perceptual quality of the unwatermarked content is poorer.

In fact, the application of this attack without taking into account the presence of motion, will introduce a degradation in the fake video sequence due to the temporal averaging process, depending not only on the width of the temporal window as well as on the amount of motion in the sequence.

To avoid this inconvenience which yields to a reduced final quality, the attacker can act differently and can carry out an improvement in the attack strategy. This step forward consists in registering frames before averaging: such a collusion attack is known as *frame temporal filtering after registration (FTFR)*. Each frame, undergone to collusion, is before registered with a reference frame and then temporal filtering is applied without introducing relevant visual distortion. Obviously registration introduces a complexity for the hacker that has to compute the displacement fields for each of the frames (but the reference frame) belonging to the temporal window.

Finally, it can be generally stated that TFA attack is efficient when the video watermarking algorithm has embedded uncorrelated watermarks in each video frame.

Figure 4. TFA attack: similar content watermarked with different watermarks is averaged in order to obtain an unwatermarked version of the content; In this example, the temporal window where the attack is applied is composed by three frames

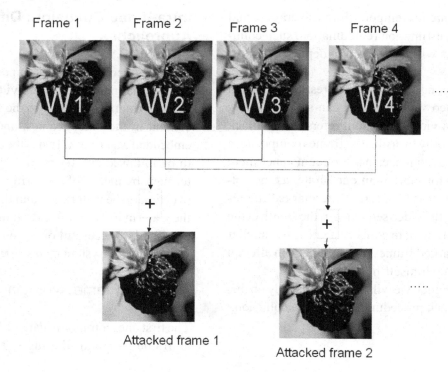

Watermark Estimation Remodulation (WER)

The second kind of **collusion** attack, named WER attack, consists in estimating the watermark and then removing it from the watermarked content (see Figure 5); this attack is effective in the case where the video is composed by a highly varying sequence of frames, each hiding the same watermark.

Usually watermarks are located in high frequencies, watermark estimation can be roughly obtained by a difference between the watermarked content and its low-pass version, then these estimates can be combined together to improve the watermark estimation as in the following equation:

$$\hat{W} = \frac{1}{N_c} \sum_{l=-N_c/2}^{N_c/2} \left(f_w(t+l) - f_{LPw}(t+l) \right)$$

where N_C is the estimation window, and $f_w(t+l)$ and $f_{LPw}(t+l)$ are respectively the watermarked frame and its low-pass version. If the video sequence contains the same watermark in each image this refinement in estimation is pertinent, otherwise, if the watermarks are different, it is useless. The watermark W that has been estimated in this way it is subtracted by each frame of the sequence yielding again, as in the previous case, to an unwatermarked content. Before subtracting the estimated watermark $\hat{W}$ by the watermarked video, it can be remodulated by an appropriate strength factor to improve final perceptual quality.

Obviously, the more accurate the estimation procedure the better the final result; analogously to the case of frame registration, the attacker can put in practice disparate strategies to achieve, in this situation, the aim of a reliable watermark estimate.

Figure 5. WER attack: perceptually different content watermarked with the same watermark are properly processed in order to extract the embedded watermark ; The more uncorrelated are the single frames the more efficient is the estimation process to obtain the embedded watermark

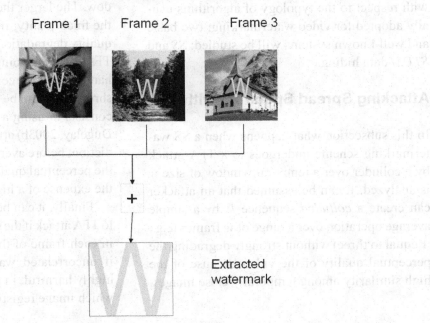

Frame 1   Frame 2   Frame 3

Extracted watermark

Sometimes, N different watermarks are repeated iteratively within the sequence (e.g., the same watermarks within each group of pictures [GOP]), in such a case the attacker has to correctly group the frames, coming from each GOP, to refine the estimate procedure, otherwise if images containing uncorrelated watermarks are coupled, the estimate does not improve. A possible countermeasure for the watermarker could be to randomly choose the watermarks to be embedded, from a set of predefined watermarks.

Finally, it can be assessed that WER attack is very efficient when video watermarking algorithm has embedded correlated watermarks within each video frame and the estimate operation is easier.

THE TFA COLLUSION VS SS AND STDM

In this paragraph the **TFA collusion** attack, which is the most important and easy to apply for a potential hacker against a watermarked digital video, will be analyzed in depth. In particular, such a kind of collusion attack will be considered with respect to the typology of algorithms usually adopted for video watermarking; two basic and well-known systems will be studied: *SS* and *STDM* data hiding.

Attacking Spread Spectrum with TFA

In this subsection what happens when a SS watermarking scheme undergoes to a TFA attack by a colluder over a temporal window of size w is analyzed. It can be assumed that an attacker can create a *colluded* sequence I_t^c by a simple average operation over a range of w frames (e.g., w equal to three) without strongly degrading the perceptual quality of the video because of the high similarity among temporally close images.

In such circumstance the correlation computation $C(\bullet)$ will lead to the following result:

$$C(I_t^c) \approx \frac{\alpha}{wN} \sum_{t=1}^{N} (\sum_{j=-w/2}^{w/2} M_{t+j}(k) \cdot M_t(k)),$$

If the watermark embedded in each frame is the same (i.e., $M_t(k) = M(k)$) all the correlation terms within the summation of index j will be equal to one and the final obtained value is going to be α. On the other hand, if the watermark is temporally different, the summation of index j will have a non-null term only when j is equal to zero, this yields that the total correlation will be α/w. It can be easily understood that in the first case methodology, SS watermarking is not affected by TFA attack but, in the second case, the watermark can be simply removed by using a collusion window of size two.

In addition to the attack effectiveness, the colluder must take into account the final perceptual quality of the attacked sequence, because averaging video frames in dynamic scenes will determine a disturbing effect on the colluded video depending on the size of the collusion window. The larger the collusion window the worst the final quality; if frames are highly static, the quality degradation will not be so important and TFA attack is going to be efficient, on the other hand if sequence contains moving objects another shrewdness can be adopted to improve results. It consists in using a frame registration (Doerr & Dugelay, 2003b) approach, based on motion prediction, before averaging, that allows to improve the perceptual quality of the attacked content, at the expense of a high computational burden.

Finally, it can be assessed that SS is immune to TFA attack if the same watermark is embedded in each frame of the sequence; on the contrary, if uncorrelated watermarks are used, TFA is highly harmful, in particular for static scenes in which image registration can also be omitted by the hacker and the final perceptual quality of the colluded video will be acceptable.

Attacking STDM with TFA

We will assume for the following analysis that the same bit string is embedded in all the frames of the sequence affected by the collusion attack.

When a watermarked video is under a TFA attack, the pirate defines a temporal window of width N_c, setting the number of watermarked frames that will be averaged to create a fake one, then he/she replaces each watermarked frame $f_w(t)$ with an average frame computed as follows:

$$f^C{}_w(t) = \frac{1}{N_c} \sum_{l=-N_c/2}^{N_c/2} f_w(t+l)$$

N_c is chosen depending on the characteristics of the sequence: a wide temporal window size, as previously said, involves a more effective attack, but it can bring an unacceptable loss of quality in the colluded frames, if the sequence is not static.

If the spreading vector is chosen to be constant with t, in decoding phase the STDM decoder correlates $f^C{}_w(t)$ with s and applies the usual decoding rule. Due to linearity, the correlation between the averaged features and s can be calculated as follows:

$$\rho^C(t) = f^C{}_w(t) \cdot s = \frac{1}{N_c} \sum_{l=-N_c/2}^{N_c/2} \rho_w(t+l)$$

That is, the correlation after the TFA attack is the average of the quantized correlation values. It is clearly seen that whether the averaged correlation belongs to the right decoding region or not depends on the particular quantized values $\rho_w(t + l)$, $l = -N_c/2 \dots N_c/2$. Let us consider, for example, the simple case of $N_c = 3$, and let us focus on the

embedding of $b = 0$. We have $\rho_w(t) = k(t)\Delta + d$, $\rho_w(t-1) = k(t-1)\Delta + d$ and $\rho_w(t+1) = k(t+1)\Delta + d$, leading to:

$$\rho^C(t) = \frac{k(t-1) + k(t) + k(t+1)}{3} \Delta + d$$

The decoder will correctly decide for $b = 0$ if and only if $k(t-1)+k(t)+k(t+1)$ is a multiple of 3. This is the case, for example, if $k(t-1) = k(t) = k(t+1)$, but in general there is no assurance that this condition holds.

If spreading vector is not constant with t, decoder still correlates $f^C{}_w(t)$ with $s(t)$ and applies again the decoding rule, but this time $\rho^C(t) \neq f^C{}_w(t) \bullet s(t)$. In fact let us consider, again, case $N_c = 3$, obtaining

$$f^C{}_w(t) \cdot s(t) = \frac{1}{3}(f_w(t-1) \cdot s(t) + f_w(t) \cdot s(t) + f_w(t+1) \cdot s(t))$$

Analyzing each term we obtain:

$$f_w(t) \cdot s(t) = \rho_w(t)$$
$$f_w(t-1) \cdot s(t) \neq \rho_w(t-1)$$
$$f_w(t+1) \cdot s(t) \neq \rho_w(t+1)$$

As can be seen, if spreading vector is not constant with t, the correlation after TFA attack is not the average of the quantized correlation values.

In both cases (i.e., constant and time-variant), STDM robustness against TFA attack cannot be straight-forwardly established like what happened in SS, anyway some further indications to improve robustness of the system can be given. In fact as highlighted in Caldelli et al. (2005), it is possible to achieve a solution by binding all the correlations $\rho(t)$ to be quantized on the same quantized value $-\Delta/4$ or $\Delta/4$ (by choosing $d = \Delta/4$), according respectively to the bit 1 or 0 to be embedded in watermarking. Under this basic assumption, at least in case of *s(t)* constant, we can assure that $\rho^C(t)$ will be quantized, during decoding, on the correct quantizer without jumping on the other one and determining a decoding error. In general, this can be summarized as in the sequel:

$$\sum_{l=-N_c/2}^{N_c/2} k(t+l) = N_c k(t)$$

where, in the case of embedding always the bit *b=1*, *k(t)* is equal to -1 and $\rho_w(t) = -\Delta/4$.

This achievement can be obtained by choosing an ad-hoc couple of values for the parameters *(Δ,r)*, respectively the quantization step and the spreading gain (i.e., the number of used features). We would like to take a high value for *Δ* to get the two quantizer more spatially divided and, conversely, a low value for *r*, to get a strict variance for the correlation *ρ(t)* to be always quantized on the same quantizers -*Δ/4* for *b=1* and *Δ/4* for *b=0*. In fact, by assuming that the features *f(t)* is a set of *r* independent Gaussian random variables, it can be computed that $\sigma_\rho^2 = r \cdot \sigma_f^2$ where σ_ρ^2 states for the variance of the correlation *ρ(t)* and σ_f^2 is the variance of the features. But being proven that exists a direct proportionality between *Δ* and $\sqrt{r}$ and, furthermore, being *r* directly proportional to the document to watermark ratio (DWR) which basically takes into account the perceptual quality of the watermarked content, the values of *r* and *Δ* have to be taken accordingly.

When the spreading vector *s(t)* is not constant with time, all the considerations made so far do not hold anymore, because, during decoding, the watermarked features are now correlated with a different spreading vector with respect to the coding phase, except for those belonging to the frame in the center of the collusion window that will give a right result. All the others results are not predictable and their sum can bring to any kind of output.

Comparison

After this analysis, it can simply be realized that watermarking a video by using a classical SS or a STDM approach to embed a secret message within each frame, without taking into account some other basic considerations, it is not enough. In fact, when dealing with digital video, instead of still images, it is extremely important to be conscious that a potential attacker will have at his/her disposal a huge amount of watermarked data to be used in disparate manners to try to extract information, to obtain a de-watermarked content and so on. Furthermore, if we consider the easiness with which a security attack such as collusion, specifically a TFA attack, can be carried out with no deep knowledge but just averaging frames, it is straightforward to comprehend the importance of knowing the correct settings during the encoding step to avoid or, at least, to drastically reduce this weakness.

In the presented study it has been pointed out that SS approach shows a binary behavior against TFA attack. In fact, immunity can be achieved by simply repeating the same watermark in each frame belonging to the sequence but, on the other hand, if uncorrelated watermarks (i.e., a time-varying watermark) are used, an averaging operation along the time axis deletes any embedded code. So it would be immediate to state that the first solution (i.e., redundant watermarks) is to be chosen but it is interesting to underline that inserting always the same watermark leads to a disturbing persistent pattern, particularly when observing dynamic scenes. Finally, it is proper to say that the approach with time-varying watermarks can also be saved and a certain degree of robustness against TFA attack might be added by binding the choice of the different marks to a restricted finite set of dimension *D* and then, at the detector side, by making correlations over each of the *D* possible watermarks before temporally averaging. This obviously increases the complexity of the whole system.

Because of the concerns of the STDM approach, both with a spreading vector constant and varying with time, diverse considerations have to be made.

We can say that if $s(t)$ is constant with t, using embedding parameters (r, Δ) above a defined threshold computed as previously described, STDM acquires robustness against TFA attack, that is error probability P_e is 0. This is due to the fact that approaching to this condition, more and more correlations $\rho(t)$ are probably quantized on the same values $\pm\Delta/4$. Anyway, it can be experimentally verified that the behavior of P_e depends also, as expected, on dynamic characteristics of the video sequence. If the sequence is highly static, P_e will be very low even for small values of (r, Δ), much below the requested threshold. This is due to the fact that lack of motion assures $f_w(t-1) \approx f_w(t) \approx f_w(t+1)$ and so $\rho_w(t-1) \approx \rho_w(t) \approx \rho_w(t+1)$ regardless of the specific value that it does not need to be necessarily $\Delta/4$.

On the contrary, if $s(t)$ is not constant with t, the previous defined threshold is not valid anymore and STDM system is not robust to TFA attack, that is error probability P_e is greater than 0. Anyway, it can be assessed that a lower P_e is obtained for higher values of parameters (r, Δ), as normally expected, but in this circumstance error probability can not strictly be controlled like the previous case.

CONCLUSION

In this chapter we have analyzed effects of collusion attacks, particularly TFA, when two basic watermarking systems like SS and STDM are used to embed a watermark into a video sequence. Our analysis has highlighted the main drawbacks and advantages in using these two solutions and, above all, the fundamental issues to be taken into account to grant a certain level of robustness when a collusion attack is carried out by an attacker.

FUTURE RESEARCH DIRECTIONS

In this chapter only a general overview on TFA collusion attack has been given particularly with reference to video watermarking through SS and STDM approaches, and obviously many research directions are still open and to be investigated.

Among them, it would be interesting to analyze the behavior of such systems from a perceptual quality point of view. First of all by trying to understand the limits for a colluder (e.g., collusion window, motion estimation) to perform his/her action and secondly, if the set up of the watermarking parameters (e.g., the spreading gain r, the quantization step Δ, the watermark power α) to provide robustness against TFA, determines, and at which extent, a heavy decrement of the quality of the watermarked content. Perceptual aspects, as it often happens in watermarking, can give a help in the design of a secure watermarking strategy.

Another important point to be studied in depth should be the estimate of error probability both for SS and for STDM cases. It would be interesting to theoretically calculate the trends of error rate with respect to the different watermarking parameters and, especially, with regard to various videos with different motion characteristics. Furthermore, it would be of interest to check the correspondence between the experimental results and the expected ones at least in some simple application cases.

Finally, another challenging and unexplored issue to be investigated could be to compare performances of SS and STDM methodologies against WER collusion attack, which, at the moment, has not been studied yet within the watermarking scientific community.

REFERENCES

Barni, M., & Bartolini, F. (2004a). Data hiding for fighting piracy. *IEEE Signal Processing Magazine, 21*(2), 28-39.

Barni, M., & Bartolini, F. (2004b). *Watermarking systems engineering: Enabling digital assets security and other applications.* New York: Marcel Dekker.

Barni, M., Bartolini, F., & Furon, T. (2003). A general framework for robust watermarking security. *Signal Processing, 83*(10), 2069-2084.

Caldelli, R., Piva, A., Barni, M., & Carboni, A. (2005). Effectiveness of ST-DM watermarking against intra-video collusion. In *Proceedings of 4th International Workshop on Digital Watermarking, IWDW 2005,* Siena, Italy (LNCS 3710, pp. 158-170).

Cayre, F., Fontaine, C., & Furon, T. (2005). Watermarking security: Theory and practice. *IEEE Transactions on Signal Processing, 53*(10), 3976-3987.

Chen, B., & Wornell, G. (2001). Quantization index modulation: A class of provably good methods for digital watermarking and information embedding. *IEEE Transactions on Information Theory, 47,* 1423-1443.

Cox, I. J., Kilian, J., Leighton, T., & Shamoon, T. (1997). Secure spread spectrum watermarking for multimedia. *IEEE Transactions on Image Processing, 6,* 1673-1687.

Cox, J., Miller, M. L., & Bloom, J. A. (2001). *Digital watermarking.* San Francisco: Morgan Kaufmann.

Craver, S., Memon, N., Yeo, B., & Yeung, M. (1998). Resolving rightful ownerships with invisible watermarking techniques: Limitations, attacks, and implications. *IEEE Journal on Selected Areas in Communications, 16*(4), 573-586.

Doerr, G., & Dugelay, J.-L. (2003a). A guide tour of video watermarking. *Signal Processing: Image Communication, Special Issue on Technologies for Image Security, 18*(4), 263-282.

Doerr, G., & Dugelay, J. L. (2003b). New intra-video collusion attack using mosaicing. In *Proceedings of IEEE International Conference Multimedia Expo.* (Vol. II, pp. 505-508).

Doerr, G., & Dugelay, J. L. (2004). Security pitfalls of frame-by-frame approaches to video watermarking. *IEEE Transactions on Signal Processing, 52,* 2955-2964.

Holliman, M., & Memon, N. (2000). Counterfeiting attacks on oblivious block-wise independent invisible watermarking schemes. *IEEE Transactions on Image Processing, 9*(3), 432-441.

Kalker, T. (2001). Considerations on watermarking security. In *Proceedings of the IEEE Multimedia Signal Processing MMSP'01 Workshop,* Cannes, France (pp. 201-206).

Kerckhoffs, A. (1883). La cryptographie militaire. *Journal des sciences militaires, IX,* 5-83.

Su, K., Kundur, D., & Hatzinakos, D. (2005a). Spatially localized image-dependent watermarking for statistical invisibility and collusion resistance. *IEEE Transactions on Multimedia, 7,* 52-56.

Su, K., Kundur, D., & Hatzinakos, D. (2005b). Statistical invisibility for collusion-resistant digital video watermarking. *IEEE Transactions on Multimedia, 7,* 43-51.

Vinod, P., & Bora, P. (2006). Motion-compensated inter-frame collusion attack on video watermarking and a countermeasure. *Information Security, IEE Proceedings, 153,* 61-73.

ADDITIONAL READING

Boneh, D., & Shaw, J. (1998). Collusion secure fingerprinting for digital data. *IEEE Transactions on Information Theory, 44*(5), 1897-1905.

Celik, M., Sharma, G., & Tekalp, A. M. (2003). Collusion-resilient fingerprinting using random pre-warping. In *Proceedings of the IEEE International Conference on Image Processing 2003.*

Ergun, F., Kilian, J., & Kumar, R. (1999). A note on the limits of collusion-resistant watermarks. In *Proceedings of Advances in Cryptology, EUROCRYPT' 99* (LNCS 1592, pp. 140-149).

Holliman, M., Macy, W., & Yeung, M. (2000). Robust frame-dependent video watermarking. In *Proceedings of Security and Watermarking of Multimedia Contents II* (Vol. 3971, pp. 186-197).

Kilian, J., Leighton, T., Matheson, L., Shamoon, T., Tarjan, R., & Zane, F. (1998). Resistance of digital watermarks to collusive attacks. In *Proceedings of IEEE International Symposum on Information Theory* (pp. 271-271).

Kirovski, D., & Petitcolas, F. (2002). Replacement attack on arbitrary watermarking systems. In *Proceedings of ACM Workshop on Digital Rights Management 2002.*

Langelaar, G. C., Lagendijk, R. L., & Biemond, J. (1998). Removing spatial spread spectrum watermarks by nonlinear filtering. In *Proceedings of 9th European Signal Processing Conference* (pp. 2281-2284).

Su, K., Kundur, D., & Hatzinakos, D. (2005). Statistical invisibility for collusion-resistant digital video watermarking. *IEEE Transactions on Multimedia, 7*(1), 43-51.

Trappe, W., Wu, M., Wang, Z., & Liu, K. J. R. (2003). Anti-collusion fingerprinting for Multimedia. *IEEE Transactions on Signal Processing, 51*(4), 1069-1087.

Wang, Z. J., Wu, M., Trappe, W., & Liu, K. J. R. (2004). Group-oriented fingerprinting for multimedia forensics. *EURASIP J. Appl. Signal Process, 14,* 2153-2173.

Wang, Z., Wu, M., Zhao, H., Liu, K. J. R., & Trappe, W. (2003). Resistance of orthogonal Gaussian fingerprints to collusion attacks. In *Proceedings of ICASSP2003* (pp. 724-727).

Wu, Y., & Deng, R. (2003). Adaptive collusion attack to a block oriented watermarking scheme. In *Proceedings of International Conference on Information and Communications Security 2003* (LNCS 2836, pp. 238-248).

Wu, M., & Liu, B. (2002). *Multimedia data hiding.* New York: Springer-Verlag.

Wu, M., Trappe, W., Wang, Z. J., & Liu, K. J. R. (2004). Collusion resistant fingerprinting for multimedia. *IEEE Signal Processing Magazine, 21*(2), 15-27.

Zane, F. (2000). Efficient watermark detection and collusion security. In *Proceedings of 4th International Conference on Financial Cryptography* (pp. 21-32).

Zhao, H., Wu, M., Wang, Z., & Liu, K. J. R. (2003). Nonlinear collusion attacks on independent fingerprints for multimedia. In *Proceedings of ICASSP2003* (pp. 664-667).

Zhao, H. V., Wu, M., Wang, Z. J., & Liu, K. J. R. (2005). Forensic analysis of nonlinear collusion on independent multimedia fingerprints. *IEEE Transactions on Image Processing, 14*(5), 646-661.

Chapter V
A Survey of Current Watermarking Synchronization Techniques

Nataša Terzija
The University of Manchester, UK

ABSTRACT

The resistance of watermarking schemes against geometric distortions has been the subject of much research and development effort in the last 10 years. This is due to the fact that even the minor geometric manipulation of the watermarked image can dramatically reduce the ability of the watermark detector to detect the watermark, that is, the watermark detector can lose the synchronization. By this, the watermark synchronization can be defined as a process for finding the location for watermark embedding and detection. A variety of techniques have been proposed to provide partial robustness against geometrical distortions. These techniques can be divided into two groups: (1) techniques that use the original image to recover to synchronization and (2) techniques that do not have the access to the original image content during the synchronization process. This chapter classifies and analyzes techniques and approaches that are currently used in watermarking schemes to recover the synchronization.

INTRODUCTION

Digital watermarking is an approach to solving copyright protection problems of digital information (i.e., audio, video, text, or images). The watermark is embedded in the original image and then extracted to verify the ownership.

The ideal properties of a digital watermark include the invisibility and robustness. The watermarked data should retain the quality of the original one as closely as possible. Robustness refers to the ability to detect the watermark after various types of intentional or unintentional alterations (so called *attacks*). In both cases the watermarking system should be able to detect and extract the watermark after attacks. The best-known watermarking attacks, which may be intentional or unintentional, depending on the application, are: additive noise; filtering; denoising attacks; watermark removal and interference attacks; compressions; statistical averaging; multiple watermarking; geometrical attacks; cropping; random geometric distortions; and printing-scanning.

Various watermarking schemes have been proposed in the present. Unfortunately, up to now there is no algorithm that perfectly fulfils the aforementioned fundamental watermarking requirements: the imperceptibility to the human visual perception and the robustness to any kind of watermarking attacks.

The robustness of the watermark against geometrical attacks is still an open problem in the field of watermarking. Even the minor geometric manipulation of the watermarked image can dramatically reduce the ability of the watermark detector to detect the watermark.

Most previous watermarking algorithms perform weakly against geometric distortions, which desynchronize the location for the embedded watermark. Therefore, the watermark synchronization, which can be defined as a process for finding the location for watermark embedding and detection, is a crucial issue for robust image watermarking.

The effect of geometrical distortions can be better understood by making the analogy between the watermark and any communication system (Cox, Miller, & Bloom, 2001). In a communication system the synchronization between the encoder and decoder is related to the time-synchronization. In a watermarking system the synchronization principle can be applied and it is related to the geometric synchronization. The geometric synchronization refers to the ability of the watermarking detector to perform the watermark detection on the same image part used for the watermark embedding by using the same image coordinates. If the received image is geometrically manipulated the coordinates of the received image will be changed comparing to the coordinates of the original image. As a consequence, the watermark detector will lose the synchronization. Hence, it is required to implement a synchronization recovery technique as a pre-processing step at the decoder side.

A typical geometric distortion affecting an image or a video can be global (rotation, spatial scaling, translation, skew or shear, projective transformation, and change in aspect ratio) or local. We distinguish between global and local geometrical manipulations because the synchronization recovery methods significantly differ. In the first case, there are enough samples to estimate the parameters of the undergone transformation, whereas in the second case, the number of samples is limited since the transformation must be estimated locally.

In this chapter we survey and classify current watermarking techniques (*synchronization* techniques) that provide robustness against geometrical attacks. Roughly, the watermarking schemes dealing with the problem of synchronization can be divided into two groups:

1. Techniques without the access to the original image content (blind synchronization techniques); and
2. Techniques that use the original image content (image registration techniques).

This chapter is organized as follows. Firstly, the geometrical distortion will be classified in the next section. Then, the overview of the existing watermarking techniques which consider the problem of synchronization without access to the original image content will be given in the third section. After that, an image registration technique is described and experimentally tested. At the end the final conclusions will be given.

CLASSIFICATION OF GEOMETRIC DISTORTIONS

There are many different ways to classify the geometrical distortion. Most commonly used classification includes:

1. Translation (cropping),
2. Rotation, scaling, and translation (RTS),
3. Affine transformation,
4. Projective transformation, or
5. Random geometrical distortion (Stirmark attack, see Petiticolas, 2000; Petiticolas, Anderson, & Kuhn, 1998)

Cropping is an important geometric deformation that is seldom discussed. However, as output images cannot include undefined regions, this operation will follow most geometrical deformations. The mathematical expression of the deformation usually does not specify output signal limits.

RTS is very common geometric transformation but it will be discussed here as a part of an affine transformation.

An affine transformation can be expressed as:

$$
\begin{bmatrix} x_{1d} \\ x_{2d} \\ 1 \end{bmatrix} = \mathbf{A}_{ff} \begin{bmatrix} x_1 \\ x_2 \\ 1 \end{bmatrix} \tag{1}
$$

$$
\mathbf{A}_{ff} = \begin{bmatrix} a_{11} & a_{12} & t_{x_1} \\ a_{21} & a_{22} & t_{x_2} \\ 0 & 0 & 1 \end{bmatrix} \tag{2}
$$

where x_1, x_2 are the image coordinates that are transformed to the coordinates x_{1d}, x_{2d} using an affine matrix $\mathbf{A}_{ff}$. The coefficients a_{11}, a_{12}, a_{21}, a_{22} form the linear part of transformation ($\mathbf{A}_{ffL}$); t_{x_1} and t_{x_2} are parameters of translation. The linear part $\mathbf{A}_{ffL}$ of affine matrix $\mathbf{A}_{ff}$ can be expressed as the combination of rotation, scaling, and shearing transformation with the corresponding parameters:

$$
\mathbf{A}_{ffL} = \begin{bmatrix} a_{11} & a_{12} \\ a_{21} & a_{22} \end{bmatrix}
$$

$$
= \begin{bmatrix} \theta cos(\ ) & (\theta sin\ ) \\ -\sin(\theta) & cos(\theta) \end{bmatrix} \begin{bmatrix} S_{x_1} & 0 \\ 0 & S_{x_2} \end{bmatrix} \begin{bmatrix} 1 & Sh \\ 0 & 1 \end{bmatrix} \tag{3}
$$

Each of the parameters of the transformation can be computed:

$$
tan(\theta) = -\frac{a_{21}}{a_{11}} \quad \text{for rotation} \tag{4}
$$

$$
S_{x_1} = \sqrt{a_{11}^2 + a_{21}^2}, S_{x_2} = \frac{\det(\mathbf{A}_{ffL})}{S_{x_1}}
$$

for image scaling $\tag{5}$

$$
Sh = \frac{a_{11}a_{12} + a_{21}a_{22}}{\det(\mathbf{A}_{ffL})}
$$

for shearing $\tag{6}$

Projective transform transforms the spatial coordinates x_1, x_2 into new coordinate system x_1' x_2' defined by the equations:

$$
x_1' = \frac{ax_1 + bx_2 + c}{gx_1 + hx_2 + 1} \tag{7}
$$

$$
x_2' = \frac{dx_1 + ex_2 + f}{gx_1 + hx_2 + 1} \tag{8}
$$

It takes four points, or eight coefficients, to describe this transformation. The coefficients g, h cause nonlinear perspective distortion of the image. If they both equal zero, the projective transform (equations (7) and (8)) becomes linear.

The projective transform can equivalently be described by the (transposed) matrix equations:

$$
x_1' = \frac{u}{w}, \tag{9}
$$

$$x_2' = \frac{v}{w},\tag{10}$$

Where

$$[u\ v\ w] = [x_1\ x_2\ 1]\mathbf{T}\tag{11}$$

and **T** is the 3x3 matrix:

$$\mathbf{T} = \begin{bmatrix} a & d & g \\ b & e & h \\ c & f & 1 \end{bmatrix}\tag{12}$$

Compared with the affine transform, projective transformation cannot be composed as a sequence of translations, shears, scaling, and (optionally) rotations because the projective transform is not linear.

Random geometric distortions. The Stirmark attack has shown remarkable success in removing data embedded by commercially available programs. Stirmark attack introduces first a minor unnoticeable geometric distortion and then the image is slightly stretched, sheared, shifted, bent, and rotated by an unnoticeable random amount. Further, a slight deviation is applied to each pixel,

which is greatest at the centre of the picture and almost null at the border (see Figure 1).

The aim of this attack is that the detector loses the synchronization with the embedded watermark. Figure 1 illustrates the effect of Stirmark attack. An original image (see Figure 1a) is geometrically manipulated applying a geometrical distortion without randomization and given in Figure 1b. After that the same geometrical distortion is applied to the original image, as well as the slightly randomization. In Figure 1c the effect of introduced randomization can be clearly seen at the center part of the grid.

WATERMARKING TECHNIQUES DEALING WITH THE PROBLEM OF SYNCHRONIZATION WITHOUT ACCESS TO THE ORIGINAL IMAGE CONTENT

In the following section a survey of the watermarking techniques claiming resistance to geometrical distortions will be presented. These techniques do not use the original image content. The classification will be organized according to the common approaches. Some techniques can be classified in more than one class because they combine several different approaches.

Figure 1. Random geometric distortion model (a) original image, (b) geometric distortion applied without randomization, and (c) geometric distortion applied with randomization

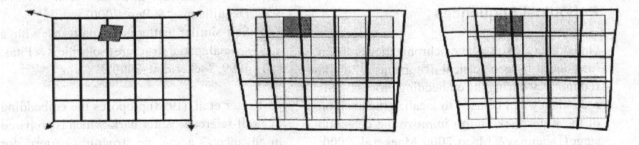

Exhaustive Search

This approach considers all possible geometrical distortions that could take place. After defining a range of likely values for each distortion parameter, every combination of parameters is examined. Each combination of distortion parameters represents a hypothetical distortion that might have been applied to the image after watermark embedding. The inverse transformation is applied to the received image and the watermark detection, too. The embedded watermark is extracted choosing the best detection confidence value (e.g., correlation coefficient), which is beyond the appropriate threshold. The main drawbacks of these approaches are increased computational costs and possibility of false detection. The amount of computation increases with the size of the search space. Therefore these approaches typically use the limited sets of translation, scaling, and rotation parameters.

The false positive occurs when the detector found the watermark in the unwatermarked image. Typically, the detector tests N distorted ersions of the unwatermarked image. If the watermark is found in at least one of these versions, the detector will produce the false positive. The possibility of false watermark detection under exhaustive search is deeply studied (Kalker & Depovere, 1998; Lichtenauer, Setyawan, Kalker, & Lagendijk, 2003; Miller & Bloom, 1999).

In order to decrease the computational costs and to observe more complex transformations, detection procedure can be performed on smaller image regions (Tefas & Pitas, 2000).

Periodical Sequences

One strategy to solve the synchronization problem introduced by geometrical distortions is to add redundancy during the embedding process. This redundancy can be used to localize the position of the watermark and to improve the detection stage (Delannay & Macq, 2000; Maes et al., 2000;

Solachidis & Pitas, 1999). In these approaches the search for synchronization is limited to one repetition period. Hartung and Girod (1999) use the periodical watermark insertion to perform the synchronization. This scheme is designed against Stirmark attack, which introduces small local geometrical distortions. The correlation technique with sliding windows (commonly used in communication in order to recover the synchronization) is implemented. The image is divided into blocks and marks are embedded in these blocks. The technique of sliding window is implemented on image blocks and the correlation between the image block of received image, possibly containing the watermark and the block with the watermark is measured. If the mark is detected in the block the location of the mark in the neighbor block is initialized by the previous location. Another synchronization possibility is provided by the approaches based on self-reference watermarks. The watermark itself is arranged in the special spatial structure, which has desired statistical properties. Based on the watermark design and the watermark statistic used for the estimation the parameters of affine transformation, the following types of self-reference watermark can be distinguished:

- Self-reference watermark based on four times repeated patterns and affine estimation based on autocorrelation function (ACF) (Kutter, 1998)
- Periodic watermarks with any geometry and affine estimation based on the magnitude watermark spectrum (Deguillaume, Voloshynovskiy, & Pun, 2002; Voloshynovskiy, Deguillaume, & Pun, 2000)
- Self-similar patterns or patterns with a special spatial structure (Solachidis & Pitas, 1999; Tsekeridou, 2000)

Kutter et al. (1998) proposes the embedding of a self-reference watermark, which is prepared in advance as a specific structural pattern, for the purpose of calibration. Kutter's reference watermark is composed of nine peaks that are extracted by means of an ACF and used to estimate the effects of geometrical attacks. The main drawbacks of this approach are: increased computational costs due to the computation of six 2-D discrete Fourier transforms (DFT) (used for computation of ACF and the correlation in the translation recovery process) and reduced robustness in the case of lossy compression. To improve the robustness after lossy compression the algorithms based on magnitude spectrum of periodical watermarks are proposed by Voloshynovski et al. (2000). The magnitude spectrum of the estimate watermark is computed. Due to the periodicity of the embedded information the magnitude spectrum showed aligned and regularly spaced peaks. If the affine transformation is applied to the watermarked image, the peaks layout will be rescaled, rotated, or sheared but alignments will be preserved. Actually, it is easy to estimate the affine transformation from these peaks by fitting the alignments and estimating periods. The most important problem with this approach lies in its security: the regular peak grids in the ACF and magnitude spectra are accessible without any knowledge of secure information (typically a key). Key knowledge is necessary only for finding the orientation of the estimated watermark block and decoding of the message. Without key knowledge the watermark block can still be estimated. Embedding the inverted pattern in the watermarked image will completely remove the watermark if the same visual masking is applied that was used for embedding the watermark. This problem has been solved by Delannay and Macq (2002) by removing the periodicity of the watermark with a secret non-periodic modulation signal $s_m(x_1, x_2, k)$:

$$\mathbf{I}'(x_1, x_2) = \mathbf{I}(x_1, x_2)w(x_1, x_2)s_m(x_1, x_2, k)$$

(13)

where $\mathbf{I}'(x_1, x_2)$ is the watermarked image luminance at coordinates (x_1, x_2), $w(x_1, x_2)$ is the tiled watermark pattern and $s_m(x_1, x_2, k)$ is the modulation signal that depends on a secret key k. The function $s_m(x_1, x_2, k)$ must have certain specific properties:

1. The essential property of the used watermark signal is its polarity, therefore, $s(i, j, k)$ must also be a binary function, that is, $s_m(x_1, x_2, k) \in \{1, -1\}$;

2. The result of function $s_m(x_1, x_2, k)$ should be secret. Without knowledge of key k, given only the watermarked image $\mathbf{I}'(x_1, x_2)$, the uncertainty about $s_m(x_1, x_2, k)$ must be maximal;

3. The signal $s_m(x_1, x_2, k)$ has to be always registered with the watermark. However, a possible geometrical distortion cannot be known by the blind detector before-hand. Hence, the only solution is that $s_m(x_1, x_2, k)$ must be a function of both k and the image content;

4. $s_m(x_1, x_2, k)$ has to be approximately the same for the original image, the watermarked image, and the (geometrically) distorted watermarked image. In other words, the modulation signal $s_m(x_1, x_2, k)$ must be calculated using a function that is insensitive to (watermarking) noise, scale, translation, rotation, and shearing (i.e., affine transformation). The algorithm to compute $s_m(x_1, x_2, k)$, presented by Delannay and Macq (2002), satisfies most of the requirements mentioned previously. The authors show the robustness of the modulation function to different kinds of image distortion.

Invariant Domains

The main idea of watermarking in the transform invariant domain is to perform the watermark embedding or detection in the domain invariant to geometrical transformations. One way to achieve this is to apply a Fourier-Mellin transform to the DFT magnitude of the original image spectrum (Lin et al., 2000; Ruanaidh & Pun, 1998).

In Fourier domain magnitude spectrum is insensitive to translation, image scaling produces inverse scaling in frequency domain and image rotation causes the spectrum rotation for the same angle. Transforming the Cartesian coordinates of the Fourier domain in log-polar, image scaling and rotation become the translation. Applying again the Fourier transformation to the log-polar representation of the magnitude spectra, the Fourier-Mellin domain is obtained (see Figure 2). Fourier-Mellin domain is rotation, scale, and translation invariant. The main problem with the implementation of discrete Fourier-Mellin transformation is that the forward and inverse transformations are not straightforward. The logarithmic sampling of the log-polar mapping must be carefully implemented in order to avoid the interpolation errors.

Another possibility to achieve an invariant domain is to apply the log-log mapping of the Fourier spectra (Lin, 1999). Such a representation is insensitive to image cropping, scaling, modification of aspect ratio, but not invariant to rotation.

Synchronization Marks

These approaches use the training signal, also called pilot signals, which have known and easily detectable features. They do not convey payload information. To estimate the distortion at the detector side it is necessary to register correctly the received signal with the original pilot signal. The detection of pilot signals must be robust against the addressed distortions. The pilot signals can be embedded either in the spatial domain (Alghoniemy & Tewfik, 1999; Kutter, Jordan, & Bossen, 1997) or in the frequency domain (Deguillaume, Csurka, Ruanaidh, & Pun, 1999; Herrigel, Ruanaidh, Petersen, Pereira, & Pun, 1998; Pereira & Pun, 2000). The pilot signal that is embedded in the frequency domain is usually called *template*. The template itself does not contain payload information and it is only used to recover the synchronization after the geometrical transformation. A few examples of the templates are presented in Figure 3.

In the template-based approaches it is important to resolve the following problems:

· Where to embed such a template to satisfy the trade-off between the invisibility and robustness. Template points should be embedded as local peaks in its neighborhood.
· How to detect peaks after geometrical attacks possibly followed by lossy compression.
· Design an efficient and fast template matching algorithm for estimation of the parameters of affine transformation (Pereira & Pun, 1999; Pereira, Ruanaidh, Deguillaume, Csurka, & Pun, 1999).

Pereira and Pun (1999) propose the embedding of the template points in the high and middle fre-

Figure 2. Rotation, scale, translation invariant Fourier-Mellin domain

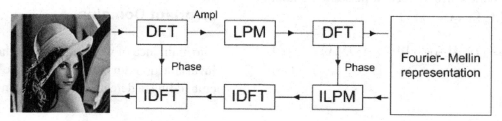

Figure 3. The examples of different templates used in the DFT domain (a) diagonal, (b) circular, and (c) key dependent (random)

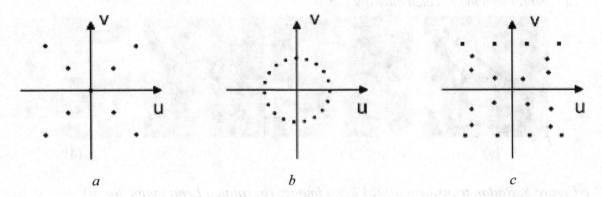

a   b   c

quencies of the DFT spectra in order to satisfy the invisibility and robustness requirements. The embedded template points are uniformly distributed in the DFT spectra and chosen pseudo-randomly. The strength of the template points is determined adaptively as well. The authors found that inserting the points at strength equal to the local average value of DFT points plus three standard deviation yields a good compromise between imperceptibility and robustness. The points are inserted less strongly in the high than in the middle frequencies. Comparison of positions of template points before and after geometric distortion will give us information about the transformation that has been applied. The search for the template points after geometric distortion requires a lot of computational costs. In order to decrease the computational costs Pereira et al. (1999) perform template registration using log-polar and log-log mapping of the DFT spectra. Using the log-polar mapping of DFT spectra provides that scaling and rotations are transformed in translation. Log-log mapping transforms the change of aspect ratio into translation. These properties make the template matching problem tractable however the logarithmic sampling of the log-polar mapping must be carefully handled in order to avoid the interpolation errors. Figure 4 illustrates the effect of a log polar map on the standard Lena image (Figure 4a). Figure 4b shows the log-polar representation of the Lena image. In Figure 4c the inverse log-polar mapping is applied and the difference between the original and reconstructed image is given in Figure 4d. In order to show the difference image better, the intensity values in Figure 4d are rescaled. The effect of interpolation errors can be seen very clearly at the border region of Figure 4c.

Another approach (Terzija & Geisselhardt, 2003) improves the efficiency of the template registration process by using the Radon transform. Radon transform is implemented to the Fourier spectrum in order to detect firstly the angle of image rotation. After that the searching for the template points is performed. Figure 5a shows the Radon transform of the Lena image. The peaks of the Radon transform can be clearly seen at 0° and 90°. Figure 5b shows the Radon transform of the Lena image rotated for 30°. In this case the peaks of the Radon transform are actually shifted for the angle of rotation and can be seen at 30° and 120° (see Figure 5b). By extracting the peaks of the Radon transform from the original and rotated image and by subtracting them the angle of the rotation can be easily calculated.

One of the drawbacks of the template-based approaches is its security. Even if the key-de-

Figure 4. (a) standard Lena image 512 x 512; (b) log-polar mapping of Lena image 452x512; (c) re-constructed Lena image (inverse log-polar transformed image); (d) the difference between the image (a), and (c) with the rescaled intensity values.

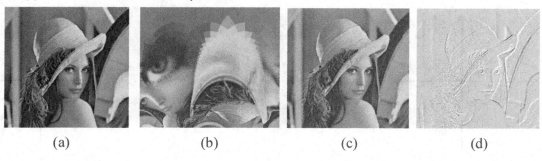

| (a) | (b) | (c) | (d) |

Figure 5. Radon transform of: (a) Lena image; (b) rotated Lena image for 30°

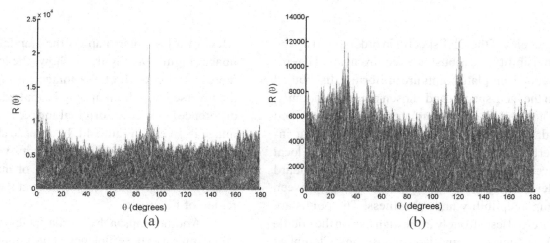

| (a) | (b) |

pendent template is used, an attacker can easily predict the template without key knowledge and remove it. One example of such an attack is template removal attack (Herrigel, Voloshynovskiy, & Rytsar, 2001).

Content-Based Approaches

The content-based approaches also referred to as a *second generation watermarking schemes* (Kutter, Bhattacharjee, & Ebrahimi, 1999) explore the robust image features for building of the reference system for watermark embedding and detection. The main assumption behind it is that the content reference system undergoes the same

geometrical distortions as the watermarked image. In the field of watermarking, the feature points can be used as the reference points for the both the watermark embedding and detection processes. A wide variety of feature point detectors exist in the open literature. Among them the Harris corner detector (Harris & Stephen, 1988) and the Mexican scale interaction method (Marr, 1982) are widely used in designing the watermarking schemes. The group of *scale invariant feature point detectors* (Mikolajczyk & Schmid, 2004), which are robust against transformations such as rotation, scale, translation, illumination changes, or even projective transformation (Lowe, 2004) are promising techniques to be considered in the field of watermarking.

Figure 6. Lena image. Feature points are extracted with: (a) Harris, (b) Harris-Affine corner detector, and (c) SIFT detector

(a)　　　　　　　　　(b)　　　　　　　　　(c)

Figures 6a-6c show the feature points extracted with Harris, Harris-Affine corner detector, and scale invariant feature transform (SIFT) feature point detector, respectively. It can be seen from these figures that each feature point detector gives the different number and locations of the extracted feature points. Depending on the applied watermarking approach, it is more desirable that the feature points have uniform spatial distribution. The next watermarking requirement is that the extracted feature point should be robust against different non-malicious attacks (compressions, filtering, geometrical distortions). Among the listed non-malicious attacks, the most challenging requirement is that the feature points are robust against geometrical distortions. The feature points extracted with Harris corner detector are only robust against rotation transformation.

The properties of the aforementioned feature point detectors are summarized in Table 1. By this, these properties are related to the invariance of the feature points to the geometrical transformations and the affine and projective invariance is only approximately achieved.

The following significant results of application of feature point detectors in the watermarking field are listed as follows:

Nikolaidis and Pitas (1999) use salient spatial features resulting from image segmentation. The first stage of the proposed technique concerns finding segmentation or clustering technique that will provide us with a robust region representation under image processing, in the sense that it will not be seriously affected by usual geometric image manipulations (e.g., rotation, translation, compression, filtering). In order to extract the regions for watermark embedding, they apply an adaptive k-mean clustering technique and retrieve several the largest regions. These regions are approximated by ellipsoids and the bounding rectangle of each region is used for watermark embedding or detection. A drawback of this technique is that image segmentation is strongly dependent on image content and consequently sensitive to attacks that remove the image parts (cropping, or rotation followed by cropping).

Bas, Chassery, & Macq (2002) propose a content-based synchronization approach based on the feature points extracted with the Harris corner detector. Furthermore, in order to decompose the image into a set of disjoint triangles to get the patches for watermark embedding, a *Delaunay tessellation* is applied on the set of extracted feature points. These triangles are used as the location for watermark embedding which is performed in the spatial domain using classical additive watermarking method. If the set of extracted feature points after image distortions is identical with one before distortions Delaunay

Table 1. The properties of the feature point detectors

	Rotation invariance	Scale invariance	Affine invariance	Projective invariance
Harris	yes	no	no	no
Harris-Affine	yes	yes	yes	no
SIFT	yes	yes	yes	yes

tessellation is an efficient method to divide the image in the same manner. Drawbacks of this approach is that the feature points extracted with the Harris corner detector are sensitive to image distortions, that is, Delaunay tessellation of these points is slightly different from Delaunay tessellation applied on the feature points extracted from the original image. Therefore it is difficult to extract the same triangle as one used for the watermark embedding. Consequently, it will reduce the robustness of the watermark detector. The triangles or patches will also not correspond if the image is cropped or if the aspect ratio is changed. In both cases Delaunay tessellation will give different results.

Tang and Hang (2003) use the scale interaction method based on two dimensional Mexican Hat wavelet for the feature points extraction. The scale interaction method determines feature points by identifying the intensity change of the image and it is robust to spatial distortions. Image normalisation (Alghoniemy & Tewfik, 2000) is used as well, because the objects in the normalized image are invariant to geometrical image distortions. They extract the non-overlapped discs of a fixed radius around the feature point and apply image normalization on every disc. The watermark is embedded in the DFT domain of 32x32 image blocks selected from every normalized image disc. This technique is robust against rotation and spatial filtering but it is sensitive to scaling operation. It is not easy efficient to determine the radius of the normalized disc from the rescaled image that should match with the normalized disc from the original image, used for embedding.

This will consequentially reduce the watermark robustness after different scaling operation.

Lee, Kim, and Lee (2006) apply SIFT transform to extract feature points, which are invariant to scaling and translations. The watermark was embedded in the circular region around the feature point using an additive watermarking method in the spatial domain. The radius of the circular region is proportional to the characteristic scale extracted with SIFT. Applying the polar-mapped circular region the rotation invariance is achieved. Problems with this approach arise if the feature points extracted from the distorted image with SIFT are slightly misaligned, while the circular region can not be exactly extracted.

Terzija and Geisselhardt (2006) propose a synchronization technique that computes the parameters of undergone affine transformation which are limited to rotation and scaling. This technique uses a rotation invariant property of the DFT spectra and the scale invariant property of the characteristic scale (Lindeberg, 1998; Mikolajczyk & Schmid, 2001). The characteristic scale is one of the parameters that are extracted with the SIFT detector. The properties of the characteristic scale are deeply studied by Lindeberg. The characteristic scale provides a scale invariant feature for each feature point and it does not depend upon the resolution of the image. In other words if the feature point has characteristic scale s_0 and the corresponding feature point extracted from rescaled image has the characteristic scale s_n, the ratio of the characteristic scales of these two points will give the scaling parameter.

Two template structures embedded in the log

Figure 7. Embedding process

Embedding process:

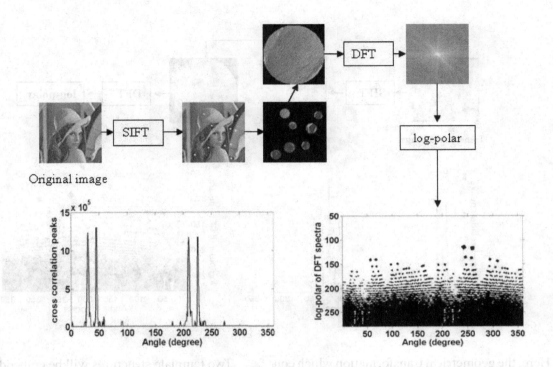

Original image

polar representation of the DFT spectra (bottom right): first one corresponds to the value of characteristic scale $s_0 = 34$ and it is embedded at the angular position of 34°; second template structure has randomly selected value $s_r = 45$ (used to detect rotation) and it is embedded at the angular position of 45°. The corresponding peaks of cross correlation are shown as well (bottom left).

This property was used by Terzija and Geisselhardt (2006) to compute the parameters of scaling in the following way:

1. Let us suppose that we have an original image.
2. Extract the feature points with SIFT detector on original image and for each feature point compute the parameter of characteristic scale s_0.

3. Robustly embed the information about characteristic scale s_0 for each point in the neighborhood of that point.
4. Apply the geometrical transformation (e.g., image scaling) on an image that contains the embedded information.
5. Compute the value of characteristic scale s_n with SIFT for the corresponding point on rescaled image.
6. Extract from the neighborhood of the corresponding point the embedded information s_0.

Using the computed characteristic scale s_n, extracted value for s_0 and taking the ratio of s_n / s_0 will give us exactly the scaling parameter.

This algorithm is slightly modified if additional rotation has been applied. The basic algorithm is presented in Figures 7 and 8.

Figure 8. Extraction process

Extraction process:

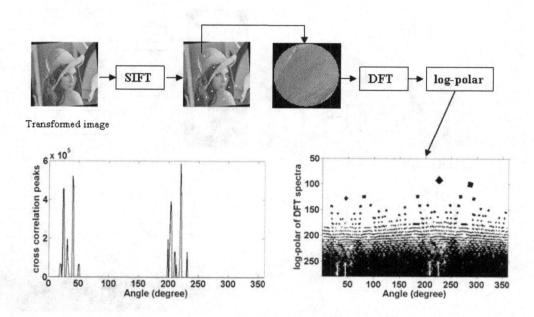

Here, the geometrical transformation which consists of rotation for 5° and scaling of 1.1x original image size is applied. Using the extraction procedure the peaks of cross correlation have been obtained (bottom left). First peak was found at 29° ($s_{n1} = 29$) and it corresponds to the embedded characteristic scale $s_0 = 34$ shifted for the actual rotation angle. The second peak was found at 40° ($s_{r1} = 40$), which corresponds to the $s_r = 45$. Firstly the parameter of rotation will be calculated from $rot = s_r - s_{r1} = 45° - 40° = 5°$. After that s_0 will be calculated as: $s_0 = s_{n1} + rot = 29 + 5 = 34$. Taking the ratio of s_n / s_0 , where $s_n = 47.6$ (calculated with SIFT detector) will give us the scaling parameter of 1.1.

Firstly, the feature points will be extracted from the original image using the SIFT detector. After that only the first 10 points with the largest characteristic scale are considered for embedding. The circular region around the selected feature point will be DFT transformed and log-polar mapped.

Two template structures will be embedded independently in the log-polar representation of DFT spectra: the first one containing the information about characteristic scale s_0 and second one randomly selected which will be used to detect the undergone rotation. The log-polar mapping is used because of property that each rotation and scaling will be transformed into translation. In other words, after rotation these two template structures will be only linearly shifted in log-polar representation of DFT spectra, for a shift that corresponds to the actual angle of rotation. The parameters of affine transformation can be correctly computed if these template structures are detected even from one image region. The peaks of cross-correlation function were used to detect the embedded templates. Experimental results have demonstrated that the parameters of affine transformation can be successfully computed if the compressions (JPEG, JPEG2000), spatial filtering, or various geometrical distortions, which consist of rotation, scaling, cropping, or combinations of them are applied.

IMAGE REGISTRATION TECHNIQUES

Image registration is the process of overlaying two or more images of the same scene taken at different times, from different viewpoints, and/or by different sensors. It geometrically aligns two images: the reference and sensed images. There are a lot of different image registration techniques in the open literature (Brown, 1992) that could be applied for watermarking (Caner, Tekalp, & Hainzelman, 2006; Kaewkamnerd & Rao, 2000; Yasein & Agathoklis, 2005).

The local image descriptors are mainly used for finding correspondences between the images. Many different techniques for describing local image regions have been developed. The simplest descriptor is a vector of image pixels. To compute a similarity score between two descriptors the cross-correlation can be used. Mikolajczyk and Schmid (2005) evaluate the performance of different local descriptors. It was concluded that SIFT-based descriptors perform best.

Here we will describe one simple technique (Terzija & Geisselhardt, 2005), which uses feature points extracted with the SIFT detector to align an original or watermarked image with a geometrical transformed original or watermarked image. When the correspondence between the two images is found the parameters of the undergone geometrical transformation can be estimated. From these parameters an inverse geometrical transformation can be calculated. This algorithm uses a SIFT descriptor.

The algorithm is performed in the following steps:

1. Detect the feature points using SIFT detector on both original and geometric transformed original image.
2. For every feature point, the corresponding SIFT descriptor is calculated. Array of SIFT descriptors calculated for original image is denoted by $SIFT_0$ and $SIFT_d$ for the geometrical transformed image, where $o = 1 \ldots n_1, d = 1 \ldots n_2$. n_1 and n_2 are the total numbers of feature points detected on original image and geometrical transformed image, respectively.
3. The comparison between each element of $SIFT_0$ and $SIFT_d$ is performed applying the correlation. The correlation coefficient between the $SIFT_0$ and $SIFT_d$, $o = 1 \ldots n_1, d = 1 \ldots n_2$ is computed (see Box 1). Where $\overline{SIFT_0}$ and $\overline{SIFT_d}$ are the mean values of $SIFT_0$ and $SIFT_d$. By this SIFT descriptor of every feature point is vector of 128 elements.
4. If the correlation coefficient is greater than a threshold thr the corresponding points are found. thr value is set to 0.9.

Now a few experiments will be performed in order to show ability of the method to register the image after geometric distortion. In the ex-

Box 1. Formula 14

$$corr(SIFT_0, SIFT_d) = \frac{\sum_{i=1}^{128}(SIFT_{0i} - \overline{SIFT_0})(SIFT_{di} - \overline{SIFT_d})}{\sqrt{\sum_{i=1}^{128}(SIFT_{0i} - \overline{SIFT_0})^2 \sum_{i=1}^{128}(SIFT_{di} - \overline{SIFT_d})^2}}$$

periments it is assumed that the original image is transformed by an affine transformation.

In order to determine the parameters of affine transformations it is enough to detect three corresponding points on an original and received image.

Six combined affine transformations are performed. These attacks consist of rotation, scaling, shearing, or a combination of them with the image cropping. These attacks are denoted as G1-G6 and the parameters of the affine transformations are given in the Table 2. G1 is the shearing attack with $Sh = 0.5$; G2 is the rotation attack with $\theta = 30°$;

G3 is the scaling attack with $S_{x_1} = S_{x_2} = 0.8$; G4 is the combination of rotation attack with $\theta = 20°$, scaling with $S_{x_1} = S_{x_2} = 1.2$ and cropping; G5 is combination of rotation with $\theta = 45°$, scaling with $S_{x_1} = 1.3$, $S_{x_2} = 0.9$; G6 is combination of rotation $\theta = 8°$ and scaling $S_{x_1} = S_{x_2} = 0.5$.

In Figures 9-14 the six geometrical attacks are presented: (a) is the original Lena image, (b) is geometrically transformed Lena image, and (c) is the reconstructed image after applying the inverse affine transformation. The corresponding feature points are presented on figures (a) and (b). It can be seen that for different distortion the different corresponding feature points are found.

Figure 9. (a) original Lena image. (b) Lena image after G1 attack; the corresponding feature points are presented on the both images (c) reconstructed image

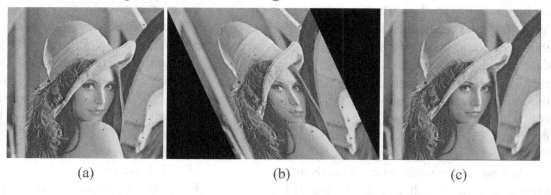

(a)　　　　　　　　(b)　　　　　　　　(c)

Figure 10. (a) original Lena image. (b) Lena image after G2 attack; the corresponding feature points are presented on the both images (c) reconstructed image

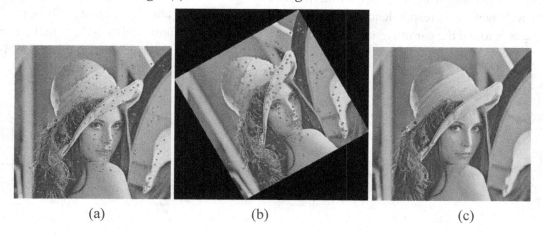

(a)　　　　　　　　(b)　　　　　　　　(c)

Figure 11. (a) original Lena image. (b) Lena image after G3 attack; the corresponding feature points are presented on the both images (c) reconstructed image

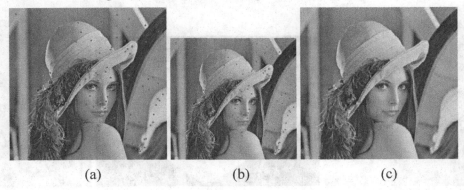

(a)   (b)   (c)

Figure 12. (a) original Lena image. (b) Lena image after G4 attack; the corresponding feature points are presented on the both images (c) reconstructed image

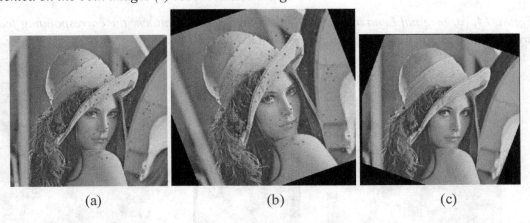

(a)   (b)   (c)

In Table 2 the following parameters are presented: the total number of feature points extracted from the original image ("fpo"); the total number of feature points extracted from transformed image ("fpt"); the size of the transformed image; the total number of corresponding points ("cp"); the parameters of applied affine transformation (a_{O11}, a_{O12}, a_{O21}, a_{O22}); and parameters of computed affine transformation $\mathbf{A}_{ffC}$ (a_{C11}, a_{C12}, a_{C21}, a_{C22}). The size of the original Lena image was 512×512.

In order to express the quality of the computed parameters the mean square error (MSE) was calculated. MSE value was $8.6 \cdot 10^{-7}$ which shows that the difference between the originally

applied parameters of affine transformation and computed parameters using this image registration technique is negligible.

The experiments showed that the image registration technique can successfully calculate the parameters of affine transformation. Using the correlation threshold above 0.9 to measure the similarity between the SIFT descriptors, only the corresponding and some nearly corresponding points will be extracted from original and transformed image. The percentage of nearly corresponding points is very low and it does not have influence on the computation of the affine parameters because a larger set of points is included in the computation of the affine parameters, than it is necessary.

Figure 13. (a) original Lena image. (b) Lena image after G5 attack; the corresponding feature points are presented on the both images (c) reconstructed image

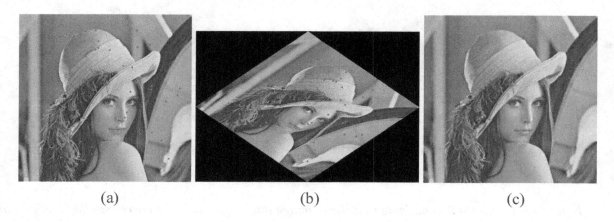

(a)   (b)   (c)

Figure 14. (a) original Lena image. (b) Lena image after G6 attack; the corresponding feature points are presented on the both images (c) reconstructed image

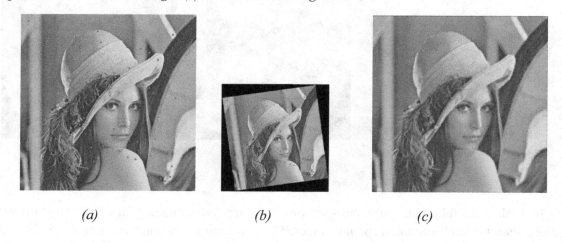

(a)   *(b)*   *(c)*

Table 2. The affine computation

	Fpo	fpt	size	cp	a_{O11}	a_{O12}	a_{O21}	a_{O22}	a_{C11}	a_{C12}	a_{C21}	a_{C22}
G1	515	550	512x768	37	1	0	0.5	1	1.002	0.0011	0.5002	1.0010
G2	515	582	701x701	340	0.867	-0.5	0.5	0.8666	0.866	-0.5004	0.5000	0.8655
G3	515	363	409x409	152	0.8	0	0	0.8	0.799	-0.0003	0.0001	0.7986
G4	515	778	614x614	187	1.127	0.41	-0.41	1.1276	1.127	-0.4097	0.4101	1.1272
G5	515	646	652x941	79	0.919	0.6364	-0.92	0.6354	0.918	0.6354	-0.92	0.6368
G6	515	166	293x293	49	0.495	0.0696	-0.06	0.4951	0.495	0.0695	-0.069	0.4945

CONCLUSION

In this chapter we gave an overview of different synchronization techniques that have been proposed in the literature during the last few years. Those techniques are generally classified into the two groups: image registration techniques and techniques that do not use the original image content. Several different strategies have been developed to achieve the synchronization without using the original image content and they can be categorized as exhaustive search, periodical sequences, techniques based on embedding the synchronization marks, and content-based techniques. It is shown that still none of those existing techniques can fully recover the synchronization after all kinds of geometrical distortions.

FUTURE RESEARCH DIRECTION

Synchronization is one of the most challenging elements of the watermarking scheme. However, a number of different approaches have been investigated and significant progress is being made. Some of the advantages of these approaches are discussed previously, but much interesting work remains to be done.

Handling geometric distortions without using the original image content remains a difficult problem. While many papers have illustrated the use of different synchronization strategies, there has been very little work on how to optimally fulfill imperceptibility and robustness constraints. Most of these techniques are computationally very expensive. We expect that development of the new techniques with reduced computational costs will become a fruitful area of research.

Random geometric distortion or Stirmark attack remains an open problem. A number of researchers have attempted to design a synchronization technique that is robust against Stirmark attack. However, a challenging task for many

researches would be still an estimation of the parameters of local geometric distortion.

We believe that synchronization techniques which are based on image content offer significant near-term improvements. Those techniques explore the robust image features for building of the reference system for watermark embedding and detection. A couple of different feature point detectors are used to extract the robust feature points. Among them a relatively new class of scale invariant feature point detectors provides a good potential which is not yet fully explored.

The research focus of the watermarking community in the last few years was the development of the watermarking and synchronization techniques that are invariant to general affine transformation. However, those techniques fail if a possibly watermarked image is corrupted with a projective transformation. Most of the proposed techniques that are invariant to projective transformation are also based on the robust feature points. Regrettably, the number of proposed techniques is still limited. We believe that development of the techniques that use the SIFT features that are invariant to projective transformations could possibly provide significant results and are therefore worth further study.

REFERENCES

Alghoniemy, M., & Tewfik, A. H. (1999). *Progressive quantized projection watermarking scheme*. Paper presented at the 7th ACM International Multimedia Conference, Orlando, FL.

Alghoniemy, M., & Tewfik, A. H. (2000). Geometric distortion correction through image normalization. *IEEE International Conference and Multimedia Expo, 3,* 1291-1294.

Antoine, J. P., Vandergheynst, P., & Murenzi, R. (1996). Two-dimensional directional wavelets in image processing. *International Journal of Imaging Systems and Technology, 7,* 152-165.

Bas, P., Chassery, J.-M., & Macq, B. (2002). Geometrically invariant watermarking using feature points. *IEEE Transactions on Image Processing, 11,* 1014-1028.

Brown, L. G. (1992). A survey of image registration techniques. *Journal of ACM Computing Surveys (CSUR), 24*(4), 325-376.

Caner, G., Tekalp, A. M., & Hainzelman, W. (2006). Local image registration by adaptive filtering. *IEEE Transactions on Image Processing, 15*(10), 3053-3065.

Cox, I. J., Miller, M. L., & Bloom, J. A. (2001*). Digital watermarking.* San Francisco: Morgan Kaufmann.

Deguillaume, F., Csurka, G., Ruanaidh, J. J. K. O., & Pun, T. (1999). Robust 3d dft video watermarking. *SPIE Electronic Imaging '99: Security and Watermarking of Multimedia Contents* (Vol. 3657, pp. 113-124).

Deguillaume, F., Voloshynovskiy, S., & Pun, T. (2002). A method for the estimation and recovering from general affine transforms in digital watermarking applications. *SPIE Electronic Imaging 2002, Security and Watermarking of Multimedia Contents IV* (Vol. 4675, pp. 313-322).

Delannay, D., & Macq, B. (2000). Generalized 2-d cyclic patterns for secret watermark generation. *IEEE International Conference on Image Processing* (Vol. 2, pp. 77-79).

Delannay, D., & Macq, B. (2002). Method for hiding synchronization marks in scale and rotation resilient watermarking schemes. *SPIE Security and Watermarking of Multimedia Contents IV* (Vol. 4675, pp. 520-529).

Harris, C., & Stephen, M. (1988). A combined corner and edge detector. *4th Alvey Vision Conference* (Vol. 1, pp 147-151).

Hartung, F., Su, J., & Girod, B. (1999). Spread-spectrum watermarking: Malicious attacks and counterattacks. *SPIE Security and Watermarking of multimedia contents* (Vol. 3657, pp. 147-158).

Herrigel, A., Ruanaidh, J. J. K. O., Petersen, H., Pereira, S., & Pun, T. (1998). Secure copyright protection techniques for digital images. *Second International Workshop IH'98* (LNCS 1525, pp. 169-190).

Herrigel, A., Voloshynovskiy, S., & Rytsar, Y. (2001). The watermark template attack. *SPIE Security and Watermarking of Multimedia Contents III* (Vol. 4314, pp. 394-405).

Kaewkamnerd, N., & Rao, K. R. (2000). Wavelet based watermarking detection using multiresolution image registration. *TENCON 2000* (Vol. 2, pp. 171-175).

Kalker, J. L. T., & Depovere, G. (1998). Modeling the false-alarm and missed detection rate for electronic watermarks. *Workshop on Information Hiding* (LNCS 1529, pp. 329-343).

Kutter, M. (1998). Watermarking resisting to translation, rotation and scaling. *SPIE Conference Multimedia Systems and Applications* (Vol. 3528, pp. 423-431).

Kutter, M., Bhattacharjee, S. K., & Ebrahimi, T. (1999). Toward second generation watermarking schemes. *IEEE International Conference on Image Processing* (Vol. 1, pp. 320-323).

Kutter, M., Jordan, F., & Bossen, F. (1997). Digital signature of colour images using amplitude modulation. *SPIE Storage and Retrieval for Image and Video Databases* (Vol. 3022, pp. 518-526).

Lee, H.-Y., Kim, H., & Lee, H.-K. (2006). Robust image watermarking using local invariant features. *Journal of Optical Engineering, 45*(3), 037002.

Lichtenauer, J., Setyawan, I., Kalker, T., & Lagendijk, R. (2003). Exhaustive geometrical search and false positive watermark detection probability. *SPIE Electronic Imaging 2002, Security and*

Watermarking of Multimedia Contents V (Vol. 5020, pp. 303-214).

Lin, C., Wu, M., Bloom, J. A., Cox, I., Miller, M., & Lui, Y. (2000). Rotation, scale, and translation resilient public watermarking for images. *SPIE Security and Watermarking of Multimedia Contents* (Vol. 3971, pp. 90-98).

Lin, C.-Y. (1999). *Public watermarking surviving general scaling and cropping: An application for print-and-scan process.* Paper presented at the Multimedia and Security Workshop at ACM Multimedia '99, Orlando, FL.

Lindeberg, T. (1998). Feature detection with automatic scale selection. *International Journal of Computer Vision, 30*(2), 79-116.

Lowe, D. (2004). Distinctive image features from scale invariant keypoints. *International Journal of Computer Vision, 2*(60), 91-110.

Maes, M., Kalker, T., Linnartz, J., Talstra, J., Depovere, G., & Haitsma, J. (2000). Digital watermarking for DVD video copy protection. *IEEE Signal Processing Magazine, 17*(5), 47-57.

Marr, D. (1982). *Vision.* San Francisco: Freeman.

Mikolajczyk, K., & Schmid, C. (2001). Indexing based on scale invariant interest points. *Proceedings of the 8th International Conference on Computer Vision* (Vol. 1, pp 525-531).

Mikolajczyk, K., & Schmid, C. (2004). Scale and affine invariant interest point detectors. *International Journal of Computer Vision, 1*(60), 63-86.

Mikolajczyk, K., & Schmid, C. (2005). A performance evaluation of local descriptors. *IEEE Transactions on Pattern Analysis and Machine Intelligence, 27,* 1615-1630.

Miller, M. L., & Bloom, J. A. (1999). Computing the probability of false watermark detection. *Third International Workshop on Information Hiding* (LNCS 1796, pp. 146-158).

Nikoladis, A., & Pitas, I. (1999). Region-based image watermarking. *IEEE Transaction on Image Processing, 1,* 320-333.

Pereira, S., & Pun, T. (1999, October). Fast robust template matching for affine resistant image watermarking. *International Workshop on Information Hiding* (LNCS 1768, pp. 200-210).

Pereira, S., & Pun, T. (2000). An iterative template matching algorithm using the chirp-z transform for digital image watermarking. *Pattern Recognition, 33*(1), 173-175.

Pereira, S., Ruanaidh, J. J. K. O., Deguillaume, F., Csurka, G., & Pun, T. (1999, June). Template based recovery of Fourier-based watermarks using logpolar and log-log maps. *IEEE Multimedia Systems 99, International Conference on Multimedia Computing and Systems* (Vol. 1, pp. 870-874).

Petitcolas, F. A. P. (2000). Watermarking schemes evaluation. *IEEE. Signal Processing, 17*(5), 58-64.

Petitcolas, F. A. P., Anderson, R. J., & Kuhn, M. G. (1998). Attacks on copyright marking systems. D. Aucsmith (Ed), *Information Hiding, Second International Workshop, IH'98* (LNCS 1525, pp. 219-239).

Ruanaidh, J. J. K. O., & Pun, T. (1998). Rotation, scale and translation invariant spread spectrum digital image watermarking. *Signal Processing, 66,* 303-318.

Solachidis, V., & Pitas, I. (1999). Circularly symmetric watermark embedding in 2-d dft domain. *ICASSP'99, 6*(1), 3469-3472.

Tang, C. W., & Hang, H.-M. (2003). A feature-based robust digital image watermarking scheme. *IEEE Transactions on Signal Processing, 51,* 950-959.

Tefas, A., & Pitas, I. (2000). Multi-bit image watermarking robust to geometric distortions. *IEEE International Conference on Image Processing* (Vol. 3, pp. 710-713).

Terzija, N., & Geisselhardt, W. (2003). Robust digital image watermarking method based on discrete Fourier transform. *5th IASTED International Conference on Signal and Image Processing* (Vol. 1, pp. 55-60).

Terzija, N., & Geisselhardt, W. (2005). *Robust digital image watermarking using feature point detectors.* Paper presented at the 9th WSEAS International Multiconference CSCC on Communication, Vouliagmeni Beach, Athens, Greece.

Terzija, N., & Geisselhardt, W. (2006). A novel synchronisation approach for digital image watermarking based on scale invariant feature point detector. *IEEE International Conference on Image Processing* (Vol. 1, pp. 2585-2588).

Tsekeridou, S., Nikoladis, N., Sidiropoulos, N., & Pitas, I. (2000). Copyright protection of still images using self-similar chaotic watermarks. *IEEE Conference on Image Processing* (Vol. 1, pp. 411-414).

Tsekeridou, S., & Pitas, I. (2000). Embedding self-similar watermarks in the wavelet domain. *IEEE International Conference Acoustic, Systems and Signal Processing (ICASSP'00)* (Vol. 4, pp. 1967-1970).

Voloshynovskiy, S., Deguillaume, F., & Pun, T. (2000). *Content adaptive watermarking based on a stochastic multiresolution image modeling.* Paper presented at the 10th European Signal Processing Conference (EUSIPCO'2000), Tampere, Finland.

Yasein, M. S., & Agathoklis, P. (2005). An improved algorithm for image registration using robust feature extraction. *Canadian Conference on Electrical and Computer Engineering* (Vol. 1, pp. 1927-1930).

ADDITIONAL READING

Alvarez-Rodriguez, M., & Perez-Gonzalez, F. (2002). Analysis of pilot-based synchronization algorithms for watermarking of still images. *Signal Processing: Image Communication, 17*(8), 633-661.

Barni, M. (2000). Geometric-invariant robust watermarking through constellation matching in the frequency domain. *IEEE International Conference on Image Processing* (Vol. 2, pp. 65-68).

Baudry, S., Nguyen, P., & Maitre, H. (2001). A soft decoding algorithm for watermark subjects to a jitter attack. *SPIE Applications of Digital Image Processing XXIV* (Vol. 4472, pp. 144-154).

Bauml, R. (2002). Channel model for desynchronization attacks on watermarks. *SPIE Security and Watermarking of Multimedia Contents IV* (Vol. 4675, pp. 281-292).

Chotikakamthorn, N., Pantuwong, N., & Wiyada, Y. (2005) Projective-invariant digital image watermarking technique using four co-planar feature points. *IEEE International Conference on Image Processing* (Vol. 1, pp. 1005-1008).

Cox, I. J., Kilian, J., Leighton, F. T., & Shamoon, T. (1997). Secure spread spectrum watermarking for multimedia. *IEEE Transactions on Image Processing, 6*(12), 1673-1687.

Cox, I. J., Miller, M. L., & Mckellips, A. (1999). Watermarking as communications with side information. *Proceedings of IEEE, 87*(7), 1127-1141.

Deguillaume, F., Voloshynovskiy, S., & Pun, T. (2002). Method for the estimation and recovering from general affine transforms in digital watermarking applications. *SPIE Electronic Imaging 2002, Security and Watermarking of Multimedia Contents IV* (Vol. 4675, pp. 313-322).

Delannay, D., & Macq, B. (2002). A method for hiding synchronization marks in scale and rotation resilient watermarking schemes. *SPIE Electronic Imaging 2002, Security and Watermarking of Multimedia Contents IV* (Vol. 4675, pp. 548-554).

Delannay, D., & Macq, B. (2004). Classification of watermarking schemes robust against loss of synchronization. *SPIE Security, Steganography, and Watermarking of Multimedia Contents VI* (Vol. 5306, pp. 581-591).

Delannay, D., Macq, B., & Barlaud, M. (2001). Compensation of geometrical deformations for watermark extraction in the digital cinema application. *SPIE: Electronic Imaging 2001, Security and Watermarking of Multimedia Contents III* (Vol. 4314, pp. 149-157).

Hartung, F., & Girod, B. (1998). Watermarking of uncompressed and compressed video. *Signal Processing, 66*, 283-301.

Joseph, J. K., Ruanaidh, O., & Pun, T. (1998). Rotation, scale and translation invariant spread spectrum digital image watermarking. *Signal Processing, 66*, 303-317.

Kundur, D., & Hatzinakos, D. (2004). Towards robust logo watermarking using multiresolution image fusion principles. *IEEE transactions on multimedia, 6*(1), 185-198.

Kutter, M., & Petitcolas, F. A. P. (1999). *A fair benchmark for image watermarking systems*. Paper presented at the 11th International Symposium on Electronic imaging, San Jose, CA.

Licks, V. (2003). The effect of the random jitter attack on the bit error rate performance of spatial domain image watermarking. *IEEE International Conference on Image Processing* (Vol. 2, pp. 455-458).

Loo, P., & Kingsbury, N. G. (2000). Watermarking using complex wavelets with resistance to geometric distortion. *Proceedings of the 10th European Signal Processing Conf (EUSIPCO 2000), European Assoc. for Signal, Speech, and Image Processing* (Vol. 3, pp. 1677-1680).

Moulin, P., & Ivanovic, A. (2001). The Fisher information game for optimal design of synchronization patterns in blind watermarking. *IEEE International Conference on Image Processing* (Vol. 1, pp. 550-553).

Nikolaidis, N., & Pitas, I. (1998). Robust image watermarking in the spatial domain. *Signal processing, 66*(3), 385-403.

Ozer, I. B., Ramkumar, M., & Akansu, A. N. (2000). A new method for detection of watermarks in geometrically distorted images. *IEEE International Conference on Acoustics, Speech, and Signal Processing* (Vol. 1, pp. 1963-1966).

Pereira, S., & Pun, T. (2000). Robust template matching for affine resistant image watermarks. *IEEE Transaction on Image Processing, 9*(6), 1123-1129.

Pereira, S., & Pun, T. (2000). An iterative template-matching algorithm using the Chirp-z transform for digital image watermarking. *Pattern Recognition, 33*(1), 173-175.

Petitcolas, F. A. P., Anderson, R. J., & Markus, G. K. (1999). Information hiding-a survey. *Proceeding of IEEE, 87*(7), 1062-1078.

Voyatzis, G., Nikolaidis, N., & Pitas, I. (1998). *Digital watermarking: An overview*. Paper presented at the EUSIPCO98.

Vassaus, B., Nguyen, P., & Baudry, S. (2002). A survey on attacks in image and video watermarking. *SPIE Applications of digital image processing XXV* (Vol. 4790, pp. 169-179).

Chapter VI
On the Necessity of Finding Content Before Watermark Retrieval:
Active Search Strategies for Localising Watermarked Media on the Internet

Martin Steinebach
Fraunhofer Institute for Secure Information Technology (SIT), Germany

Patrick Wolf
Fraunhofer Institute for Secure Information Technology (SIT), Germany

ABSTRACT

Digital watermarking promises to be a mechanism for copyright protection without being a technology for copy prevention. This sometimes makes it hard to convince content owners to use digital watermarking for protecting their content. It is only a passive technology adding information into the content to be protected. Therefore some active mechanism is required that completes the protection. This needs to be a search mechanism that localises potentially watermarked media on the Internet. Only then the passive information embedded in the content can help to fight illegal copies. We discuss strategies and approaches for retrieving watermarks from the Internet with the help of a media search framework. While various Internet domains like HTML pages (the Web), eBay, or FTP are discussed, the focus of this work is on content shared within peer-to-peer (P2P) networks.

INTRODUCTION

Digital watermarking has become an established media security mechanism and some see a trend towards an even wider use in the near future (Rosenblatt, 2007). Since the emergence of digital watermarking as an independent field of research more than 20 years ago (Anderson, 1996; Cox & Miller, 2002), a lot of progress has been made in imperceptibly embedding information (the *water-*

mark) into all kinds of digital media. There are algorithms for images, audio, and video but also text, 3D models, and even 3D surfaces (Belloni et al., 2006). The same holds true for retrieving (not extracting) the embedded information from watermarked media, which is naturally very closely connected to the embedding process.

All watermarking algorithms (or schemes) share basic properties like capacity, transparency, or robustness. Capacity describes how much information can be embedded. Transparency measures the (im-)perceptibility or fidelity, that is, how much (or less) does the watermark degrade the quality of the carrier medium. And robustness describes how much the embedded information changes when the carrier medium is altered (Cox, Miller, & Bloom, 2002). The type of information embedded plus the special properties of the watermarking scheme define possible application fields for the scheme.

An important field of application for digital watermarking is copyright protection. For this, information about the (copyright) owner of the medium to protect or, better, information about the receiver of the medium like customer or transaction IDs is embedded using robust watermarking schemes. The latter ensures that the source (or at least the buyer) of an illegally published medium can be identified. This is often called *transaction* or *forensic* watermarking (see also chapter XV, *Traitor Tracing for Multimedia Forensics*).

It might sound trivial, but in order to retrieve a watermark from any medium, one needs to have access to this medium, that is, the medium in question needs to be found first. This is a true challenge and this chapter discusses important issues when searching for watermarked content on the Internet.

This chapter is organised as follows: In the *Background* section, we discuss some fundamentals of the Internet and how currently copyright violations are dealt with. We will also see that watermarking is only a passive protection mechanism and needs an active component that completes the

protection. This active part can be fulfilled by a search mechanism for watermarked content on the Internet as described in the *Concept* section. There, a media search framework is introduced that structures such a search and delegates it to specialised components. We show in the *Media content distribution forensics* section, how such a search framework can concretely be used to search various networks and what strategies should be taken in order to reduce the number of files that need to be checked for watermarks. Finally, some future research directions will conclude the chapter.

BACKGROUND

While many media companies see the Internet as a promising market place of the future, currently most copies of their content are transferred without causing revenues (Andrews, 2005). Several technologies aim to reduce the stream of illegitimate copies, digital watermarking being only one of them. Classical digital rights management (DRM) tries to fully control what customers can do with the media they have access to. The media are encrypted using well established cryptographic methods. Rights customers have are described in licenses that are issued by license servers along with the keys for decryption (Rosenblatt, Trippe, & Mooney, 2001). DRM systems need to be present on the customers' hardware and often bury deep into the customers' operating system in order to establish their protection—sometimes even opening the customers' system to exploits (Electronic Frontier Foundation, 2007) or refusing play-back of legitimately acquired content (Halderman, 2002). This presence is necessary since they are providing an *active* protection. All active protection mechanisms shipwreck when the item under protection leaves the domain where it can be protected (Schneier, 2001). As we humans consume media in an analogue way through rendering devices, the media necessarily leave the protected digital domain at some point. This is called the *analogue gap*. The protection can be extended onto the rendering device—as it is done in DVI (Digital Display Working Group, 1999), but in principle the analogue gap cannot be securely bridged by active methods since human observers consuming a rendered media can always be replaced by recording devices creating an illegal and unprotected copy.

So, other forms of protection focus more on the media information. Content-sharing sites like YouTube, MySpace, or Flickr allow users to upload pieces of media and share them with the community. In order to prevent copyrighted material to be shared, some sites use robust hashing, which is sometimes also called (passive) fingerprinting (Allamanche et al., 2001; Haitsma, Kalker, & Oostveen, 2001; Venkatesan, Koon, Jakubowski, & Moulin, 2000). This technology *recognises* previously registered content by extracting certain characteristics based on the media information. The recognition is robust in the sense that slight changes to the media material will result in the same extracted characteristics. Robust hashing itself is a *passive* technology that is used to actively prevent uploads to particular sites. Such an approach also prevents propagation of content that was distributed without any protection like currently done with audio CDs. The success of this approach highly depends on the security of the robust hashing algorithms. Such systems inherently allow so-called *oracle* or *known-plain-text attacks* (Cayre, Fontaine, & Furon, 2005). A pirate can modify a piece of content in order to trick the robust hashing algorithm and try to upload it on such a network. If refused, the medium is again modified and uploaded until it is accepted. Sometimes this is also called *threshold attack*. Systems with a public detector are exposed to these kinds of attacks (Swaminathan, Mao, & Wu, 2006). Robust hashing does not work on open networks, where the content is not uploaded to a third party to be analysed. This is the way most file-sharing networks and other distribution channels work.

So therefore, additional protection is needed.

At this point, we see the major challenge the prevention of distributing illegal copies via the Internet faces: Active mechanisms like DRM or copy protection try to prevent the leakage of copyrighted material into the Internet, but due to various reasons like the huge number of attackers or the analogue gap regularly fail. Passive mechanisms like fingerprinting can be used to identify illegal content distribution. But as soon as they are used together with active measures like blocking such content are taken, attackers can try to develop strategies to circumvent the identification. Both strategies have one weakness in common: Attackers get an immediate feedback of the success or failure, but either gaining access to content or being able to distribute content via protected environments. Digital watermarking can circumvent this by being invisible to all outsiders and potential attackers. As long as watermarking is not used to block marked content or prevent copies of marked media files, an attacker has no feedback about the success or failure of his/her strategy to remove a watermark. The embedded information will stay imperceptible within the content until a detection algorithm together with the correct secret key reveals its presence. With this information, measures can be taken against copyright offenders. Therefore for digital watermarking the major challenge is to scan the Internet for potentially watermarked copies in a way no third party notices these activities. On the one hand, this allows legal file sharing activities to proceed unhindered; on the other hand, it allows tracing illegal activities without a chance of counterattacks.

While file-sharing networks (or P2P networks) may not be the biggest source of illegal copies (Biddle, England, Peinado, & Willman, 2003), currently they may be the most prominent. They consist of large distributed networks in which data is copied and shared without discriminating between legal and illegal copies. Some of them have been declared illegal because their aim was mainly seen in the distribution of copyright violations (e.g., Grokster). But this has not caused the phenomenon to stop. A multitude of new, and often more sophisticated networks are constantly introduced, allowing file-sharing enthusiasts to switch to a new and still legal network within a few hours.

The reaction of the content owners is twofold: Some try to use the same technology to provide a legal alternative to pirate networks (Schmucker & Ebinger, 2005). Others use various counter-measures ranging from technology to lobbying for more restrictive laws.

The most common methods include but are not limited to:

- Fake distribution to frustrate users
- Blocking of slots in order to slow down download
- Hacking and denial-of-service attacks against major servers or networks
- User identification through IP-addresses
- Legal measures to remove shut down servers

While some of the strategies, especially the legal measures, successfully removed a number of P2P networks from the Internet, the general advance of P2P technology and its illegal usage has not been stopped so far by any of these measures. Therefore any idea for copyright protection in P2P networks should not act against the networks, their users, or the enabling software. It should rather use the networks the same way common users would do: search for files and download them.

CONCEPT

The previous section suggests that effective measures for copyright protection are private, passive mechanisms that draw protection directly from the media information plus some active component completing the protection. Forensic watermarking that embeds transaction specific information into digital media can be used as the passive part (Craver, Wu, & Liu, 2001; Steinebach & Zmudzinski, 2004). This identifies the original buyer of the work. But before any retrieval of watermark information, *suspect* media that have been illegally published have to be found first. Since watermarking cannot help here, this is the task of an active component searching the Internet for such media.

This task could be described as very simple and impossible at the same time. Very simple, because the damage caused by illegally publishing a medium increases with number of people that have access to it—meaning the number of people who can find it. So the more damage is done, the easier to find such a medium should be for copyright holders (if and only if nothing distinguishes them from any other users). On the other hand, suspect media can appear everywhere on the Internet, which is surely impossible to search as a whole. The truth probably lies somewhere in between. The first part suggests that the problem of minimising damage done by copyright infringements is a well-conditioned problem, while the second part suggests a need for effective search strategies. In order to organise such a search, we have defined a media search framework.

This section describes how such a framework can be organised and structured. Principle steps are the definition of search criteria, conduction of a search in a subspace of the Internet, and finally processing of results—summarised as *mark, search, retrieve* (Figure 1).

Definition of Search Criteria

When the Internet is used as a distribution channel for media, any access technology will be created in such a way that it allows an effective search for content. Otherwise such an access technology would fail its purpose. Therefore a search for suspect media will be most effective if it is conducted in the same way as any user would perform this

Figure 1. The "mark, search, retrieve" concept

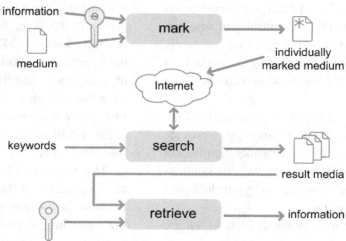

search. The information available to users about the media they search for is very rudimentary. It may be the title of the work or the name of an artist. Most of the time, it is also clear what type of medium (audio, video, etc.) they are searching for. All this is basically textual metadata. In addition, P2P networks work with cryptographic hashes uniquely identifying the medium as a whole or chunks thereof. This information forms the foundation of search criteria for the media search framework. Logical operators (and, or, not) are used to form more complex criteria. So, when searching for Harry Potter audio books, a search criterion could be ("Harry Potter audio book") or a combination of text and media type ("Harry Potter" AND MEDIA_TYPE="audio"). The definition and distribution of search criteria within the framework is coordinated by the *SearchManager*. After defining the search criteria, the Internet can be searched for matching media.

Searching Subspaces

The Internet is not one homogeneous network. It can be broken up into smaller spaces. The World Wide Web (WWW) is an example of such a sub-

space. All points in this subspace are interconnected through http. There are also subspaces within subspaces, like all points in the WWW that can be directly reached via Google. Other examples of subspaces are *file sharing networks* or *Gnutella*. Each of these subspaces can contain media and have their own special access methods to their media. An Internet-wide search needs to be able to take these specialties into account. An interesting fact is that some subspaces require other subspaces for accessing media. The most prominent example is the BitTorrent network where no search functionality for content is implemented. The network requires access to the WWW to browse Web pages providing a *catalogue* for content available within BitTorrent.

Even though a search criterion, as defined in the previous subsection, is generic and independent from any concrete subspace, the subspaces contain the media we are searching for and thus need to be utilised for the search. In terms of the mediasearch framework, we call components that deal with specific subspaces *NetworkConnectors*. Each NetworkConnector encapsulates the specific properties of a subspace and has the responsibility to search and access this subspace (Figure 2).

Figure 2. NetworkConnectors are ploughing subspaces of the Internet

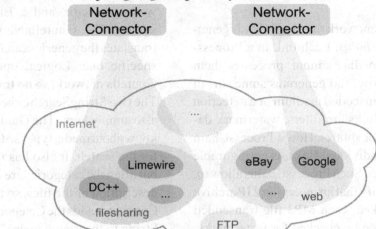

It receives a search criterion and has to output search results matching this criterion. In order to minimise overhead, this result set needs to be as small as possible. This is the major challenge for each NetworkConnector. Some strategies how to achieve this, are described in the next section.

It is important to note that the framework as such does not define an overall search strategy or search algorithm. This is only possible within a single subspace and is thus a task for individual NetworkConnectors. Even then, NetworkConnectors will not implement search algorithms for themselves but use search mechanisms that are available for the subspace (see Sample NetworkConnectors). This has two advantages: It mimics the usage of the subspace by other users and minimises the implementation work. So to summarise one can see the search framework as a control instance for a set of interfaces (the NetworkConnectors) to Internet subspaces trough which users can initiate and analyse parallel search queries for watermarked content.

NetworkConnectors can be nested just as subspaces can be nested. A "file sharing"-NetworkConnector could delegate search criteria to a Gnutella-and a BitTorrent-NetworkConnector. It can then consolidate search results from each of the sub-NetworkConnectors into an overall search result that is returned to the SearchManager.

So far, the results have not been analysed for watermarks. This is done in the following step.

Processing Search Results

After the NetworkConnectors return the result of their search, the media are ready to be checked for watermarks. Depending on the subspace, media are either directly available as streams or have to be at least partially downloaded first. On the Internet, especially in P2P networks, media are often not in the right format for watermark analysis. They might not even be in a multimedia format. ZIP-archives or ISO-images for burning CDs are common. Search results that return media in such a format need to be pre-processed before they can be checked for watermarks. Other complications include, but are not limited to, specific required input formats for the actual watermarking detection, demultiplexing of multimedia containers, or detection with several (different) watermark detectors. So, there is a need for flexibly handling the search results in order to be able to automate the system.

Within the framework this flexibility is generated by *ProcessChains*. Each link in a ProcessChain can take media as input, processes them in a predefined way, and generates some sort of output—like a transcoded medium or a detection result. Example links are filters, watermark detection modules, or splitter. How a ProcessChain is formed from individual links, is configurable through XML files. Such ProcessChains allow to, for example, specify that an incoming ZIP archive should be unpacked, each MP3 file transcoded into PCM and then be checked for watermarks; other file types in the archive should be ignored. This allows a very flexible handling of search results independent of format, file type, or other characteristics and allows concentrating on what exactly needs to be done to detect watermarks and not how this is specified.

Practical Example

Suppose an online shop wants to search for illegitimately published versions of its audio book hit *Harry Potter and the Deathly Hallows*. The sold audio books have been marked with a PCM transaction watermark and have been delivered in the MP3 format. The shop figures that audio books are most often shared within P2P networks rather then the Web. So it decides to search the Gnutella and the BitTorrent network. The shop is not interested in eBooks or movies related to the query subject.

The search query could look like this:

("Harry Potter and the Deathly Hallows" OR "Harry Potter 7") AND media_type="audio" AND category="audio book"

This query would be passed to the NetworkConnectorManager, which passes it on to its two registered NetworkConnectors, a GnutellaNetworkConnector, and a BittorrentNetworkConnector. The GnutellaNetworkConnector then translates the generic search query into a Gnutella specific one: Logical operators exist for the Gnutella network, so no translation is necessary. The two StringSearchCriteria (marked by "") are also simply kept. The Gnutella network does not know about media types so this criterion is ignored for the search. It also has no categories as such, but often the categories are included in the textual description of the files, so the GnutellaNetworkConnector adds the CategorySearchCriterion as a String to the search query. This translated query is now sent to the Gnutella network and yields results that are then downloaded. The BitTorrentConnector also translates the generic query into a specific one. There exists several Web sites where one can find .torrent files by issuing http requests. All these sites feature categories, so only trivial translation work is necessary. The resulting .torrent files point to the actual media files in the BitTorrent network that are then downloaded. In our example, this could be 40 MP3 files, 5 PDF files, 4 .iso CD images, 60 zip, and 80 rar files.

When the search results have been downloaded, they are passed to the ProcessChains. The target of each ProcessChain is to produce PCM output (wrapped in .wav) and then check this for watermarks—MP3 files can be decoded directly to PCM. The PDF files are ignored because they are of the wrong file type and cannot be further processed. Zip and rar files are extracted and the extracted files are again checked for their file type. If the zip file contained an MP3, it would be given to the MP3DecodeElement. If it contained a rar file, this would be unrared, and so forth. The .iso images are handled much like zipped content. The output of each ProcessChain is in any case a PCM file that is checked for watermarks by the corresponding algorithm that was used to embed the transaction watermark.

MEDIA CONTENT DISTRIBUTION FORENSICS

After introducing, on a more abstract level, how a media search framework organising an Internet-wide search could look like, this section will take a look at which concrete subspaces can currently be searched and what first strategies for reducing the number of unnecessarily downloaded and checked media are.

Sample NetworkConnectors

In the *Background* section, we motivated that a system searching the Internet for illegally published media should search using the same methods as other users looking for such content would. We will quickly introduce some representative NetworkConnectors, we have already implemented (Wolf, Steinebach, & Diener, 2007), that will make the principle clear how this can be achieved.

GoogleConnector

Web search engines like Google, usually do not yield good results when searching for larger continuous media like audio and video—especially not when looking for illegally published media. This is different for images since they are a native part of HTML pages. The GoogleConnector uses both Google Images as well as Google to search the Web for suspect images. Returned images are directly checked and returned Web sites are parsed for images—just like arbitrary users would view result pages. This technique also allows following links recursively on returned Web sites. It is clear that the depth of the recursion has a dramatic effect on the number of images to be checked. Filters that for example check image dimensions filter out images that are too small or otherwise too deformed to be of interest. Similar techniques are used by other systems that search for watermarked images—the Digimarc Marc-

Spider (Digimarc Cooperation, 2006) probably being the most prominent. In addition, Google's search algorithm can also be used to find links to, for example, .torrent files that can then be downloaded by other NetworkConnectors.

EbayConnector

eBay has become a large subspace of the Web and most parts are not accessible through Web search engines. Many auctions display images of the goods on sale and some images are used without permission of the copyright holder. The EbayConnector uses the built-in search of the eBay application program interface (API) to search for auctions with the help of keywords. From auctions the corresponding images plus metadata like size or format can be retrieved and also checked for watermarks. There is no difference (from the point of view of the auctioneer) in accessing auctions through eBay's Web interface like most users do and through the eBay API. Again, this makes the EbayConnector indistinguishable from other eBay users.

GnutellaConnector

The Gnutella network is one of the most popular file-sharing networks. It is fully decentralised featuring no central components. The GnutellaConnector connects to the network, accepts keyword-based search criteria, and translates them into Gnutella specific queries, which are sent to its neighbouring peers. Each query has its own globally unique identifier (GUID), identifying the query uniquely through the network and allowing peers to return query results to the GnutellaConnector—just like they would do to other clients.

BitTorrentConnector

BitTorrent does not describe a single network. It is rather a protocol that allows file exchange on a P2P basis with clients that serve and ask for content forming small P2P networks. Before a file can be shared, a metadata file called a torrent file is created, which contains information about the file to be shared and about the tracker, which coordinates the distribution of the file. Some implementations also work without trackers (or rather every peer is also a tracker) and rely on distributed hash tables to identify where a file can be found. The BitTorrentConnector is a two-layered NetworkConnector. In the first stage, it searches for torrent files on the Web. Here, other WebNetworkConnectors can also be used. In the second stage, it contacts the tracker responsible for a file and the tracker allows the BitTorrentConnector to contact peers offering portions of the file. The same arguments that make the GnutellaConnector indistinguishable also hold for the BitTorrentConnector.

Summarising, all NetworkConnectors presented use the networks they are responsible for in the same way other clients would. They search for media files and download them. They are thus indistinguishable from other clients. They also do not act against their network or its users (as a whole) or its shared content, which does not necessarily need to be illegally published. The watermark information the NetworkConnectors are helping to find only pinpoints the original buyers.

Since retrieving watermarks is a computationally costly operation, intelligent strategies need to be found that reduce the number of suspect media.

Gaining Relevant Search Results

A search for watermarked files on the Internet has two important cost factors: file download and watermark retrieval. Both should be minimised, while still maximising the number of successfully retrieved watermarks. For this, first of all, the search criteria need to be specific enough. How this can be achieved is probably a book chapter for itself and cannot be covered here. It is a question that is independent of media security questions and relates to automatic searches and recommender systems. In addition, this also depends on the actual watermark algorithms used. Some algorithms might be more suited for use in such a framework than others. We will not discuss specific watermarking algorithms here, but a problem that occurs even with the narrowest search criteria and all watermarking algorithms is the problem of duplicate media. Duplicate media mean that the same medium is returned more than once as a search result. It is important to understand that identification of duplicate media is not only important to circumvent multiple successful detections of watermarks within different copies of marked content. It is even more important to prevent multiple times trying to detect content from potentially marked copies that contain no watermark as scanning for a watermark without success often takes more computational power than successfully retrieving a watermark. The reason for this is that the scanning process in the latter case ends after the watermark is detected and after retrieval, the work with the media copy is finished. But in the former cases the detector aims to synchronise with the watermark trough the whole media file in some cases applying complex resynchronisation methods.

Duplicates can be recognised using, for example, cryptographic hashes. Web search engines usually do not supply any meta-information together with their results (aside from the file name). File-sharing networks work with cryptographic hashes to identify files and also supply some additional metadata. But different file-sharing networks use different hash algorithms. Since cryptographic hashes can of course not be converted into one another (that would break the hash), the file has to be downloaded first to gather additional information. After download various hashes can be computed. This is still less costly than trying to retrieve a watermark. In the media search framework, this can, for example, be described by a superordinated NetworkConnector

Figure 3. Filtering in the overall mediasearch framework workflow

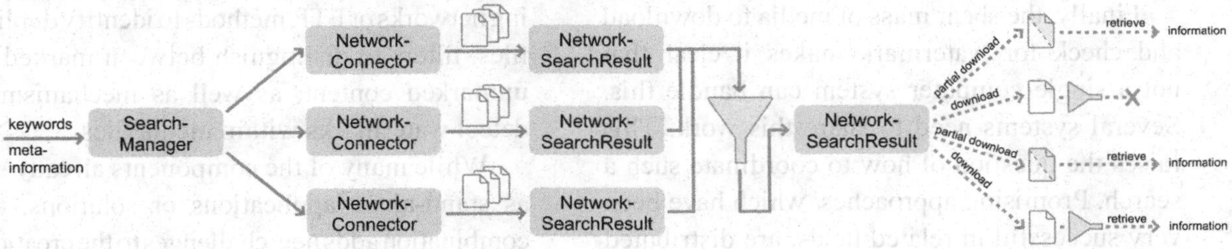

filtering search results from its sub connectors (Figure 3, middle part).

Cryptographic hashes change as soon as a single bit in the file changes. But the same medium (e.g., the same *song*) can appear in various disguises. For example the MP3 format allows the addition of textual metadata in the form of ID3 tags. Media players often also create metadata when ripping a CD—including information like "ripped by player XXX" or "ripped at DATE." This results in identical MP3 data (if the same bit rate etc. is used) but in different hash values. In order to find this kind of duplicates, a filter could strip the media files of meta-information and then hash it (rightmost part of Figure 3). Stripping is still a fast process in comparison to watermark detection. First experiments in this direction conducted by us suggest that the number of files that need to be searched for watermarks could drop by 50%: For a *Shakira* song that was at a top ten position in the charts at that time, roughly 100 hash different files where found in two file-sharing networks. After stripping, only around 50 remained. These experiments were not representative and many content uploaders might have ripped an unprotected audio CD, thus having the same base data, but still it at least justifies further investigation, especially when hashes are not the only meta-information available on the media. Even other analysis techniques may be used (see the *Future Research Directions* section).

Often media files are also found in formats the watermark detection cannot deal with and thus transcoding of the medium becomes necessary.

One could also compute hashes of transcoded files in order to reduce duplicates. Whether this is feasible or not depends on the watermarking algorithm and the formats in which typical media are found, so that no general statements can be made here.

Another approach to reduce costs for an Internet-wide search is not to download complete files (rightmost part of Figure 3). For continuous media like audio and video it is very common to periodically embed watermark information, so that the watermark can be detected even when only parts of the medium are published. This means that only a small part of the medium needs to be downloaded to find a watermark. This part needs to be continuous though. File-sharing clients usually do not download chunks in order and a single chunk is often too small. A Network Connector that acts as a file-sharing client could be programmed to download chunks in order or rather so that a large enough continuous portion of the medium is downloaded. But this is not standard behaviour of such clients and might thus be detected by other clients or the network itself.

A side effect of searching at least P2P-based, file-sharing networks is that any peer downloading a medium usually also shares this medium with other peers, thus publishing it. Peers observing file-sharing networks increase therefore the availability of illegally published media. This cannot be technically avoided except by a non-standard peer, which would reduce the investigative qualities of the search system. It is better if the operators of such search systems have contracts with the copyright holders that justify their activities.

Finally, the shear mass of media to download and check for watermark makes it clear that not a single computer system can handle this. Several systems need to share this work. This raises the question of how to coordinate such a search. Promising approaches, which have been very successful in related fields, are distributed computing as done in SETI@home (Anderson, Cobb, Korpela, Lebofsky, & Werthimer, 2002), grid computing (Vassiliadis, Fotopoulos, Xenos, & Skodras, 2004), or P2P approaches.

CONCLUSION

Fighting illegal copies can be done by many different means. There are active and passive approaches, countermeasures against networks, users, or files and technical as well as legal strategies. Until today, they all fail to offer a solution that on the one hand defends the rights of the copyright owners but on the other hand keeps up the open nature of the Internet and digital data.

Digital watermarking can provide a solution to this by embedding individual customer IDs within distributed content. In this way, users are free to handle the contents in any way they like, but need to do so in a fair way as with the help of the embedded watermarks occurring illegal copies can be traced back to them.

While this is a promising approach, one important aspect of digital watermarking has been neglected in many discussions: A watermark can only help to protect the rights of an owner if the media file it is embedded into is found in an illegal distribution channel. Only by advanced search mechanisms it is possible to monitor the appearance of such files in the various distribution channels of the Internet.

In this chapter we introduced a framework that provides such a mechanism and discussed the various components required to enable an efficient but exhaustive searching. This includes

connectors to distribution channels like file-sharing networks or FTP, methods to identify duplicate files, filters to distinguish between marked and unmarked content, as well as mechanisms to detect watermarks within media files.

While many of the components already exist as stand-alone applications or solutions, their combination adds new challenges to the creation of such a framework, inducing the need for a highly distributed network of peers with different tasks and an efficient communication protocol.

Therefore, we see this chapter as an overview to the approach of watermarking-based copyright protection, a conceptual description of requirements imposed by a framework needed to search actively for marked content to enable this and finally an overview of the current state of the art in this area.

FUTURE RESEARCH DIRECTIONS

Digital watermarking will become a common method to protect multimedia content in future distribution channels due to its passive and flexible nature. With the success of this technology, the amount of potentially watermarked content transferred via the Internet will increase. This includes legal but also illegal channels. More and more content in file-sharing networks and on pirate Web sites will need to be scanned for an embedded watermark. Therefore the need for efficient watermark detection will increase. A fast decision if a media file is marked or not is vital when dealing with a multitude of content to be scanned. This may lead to the common usage of meta-watermarks or templates (Pereira & Pun, 2000), which on the one hand increase the decision about the presence of a watermark, but on the other hand easily become the target of attacks against watermarking algorithms.

The development of presence watermarks allowing distinguishing between marked and unmarked content therefore will be an important future trend and challenge. Special attention will be placed on high robustness and security, while watermark payload is of no concern: The mark is the message.

An alternative to embedding a specific meta-watermark into the content can be to utilise the area of steganalysis (Fridrich & Goljan, 2002; Johnson & Jajodia, 1998; Ozer, Avcibas, Sankur, & Memon, 2003) where researchers aim at distinguishing between marked and unmarked content by scanning for typical artefacts or characteristics of watermarks embedded by a specific algorithm. While the current research has the security of embedding algorithms in focus and is used to identify hidden information channels, the results of this research can also be used to quickly determine if a media file is potentially marked by an algorithm the scanning party has a detector for. If this is the case, the file can be passed on to the detection algorithm. Of course, this approach is only applicable if the steganalysis process is faster than watermark detection (see chapter XII, *Steganalysis: Trends and Challenges* and chapter X, *Computational Aspects of Digital Steganography*). This is especially the case if the artefacts of an embedding process are easier to find than the embedded watermark.

A third and already mentioned technology to improve the decision speed of whether a media file is marked or not, is robust hashing. To circumvent the need to scan every media file for a watermark, any party using watermarking could submit a robust hash of marked content to a central database, building up an index of potentially marked content. For each media file found by a searching party its robust hash can then be checked for its presence in this index. Only if the check is positive, searching for an embedded watermark would be initiated. Similar to meta-watermarking, this approach would speed up the filtering process as robust hash calculation is usually faster than watermark detection. But attacks against the robust hash characteristics may also be possible masking marked content from the searching party.

REFERENCES

Allamanche, E., Herre, J., Helmuth, O., Fröba, B., Kasten, T., & Cremer, M. (2001). Content-based identification of audio material using MPEG-7 low level description. In *Electronic Proceedings of the International Symposium of Music Information Retrieval*.

Anderson, D. P., Cobb, J., Korpela, E., Lebofsky, M., & Werthimer, D. (2002, November). SETI@home: An experiment in public-resource computing. *Communications of the ACM, 45*(11), 56-61.

Andrews, R. (2005). Copyright infringement and the Internet: An economic analysis. *Journal of Science & Technology Law, 11*(2).

Anderson, R. J. (Ed.). (1996). *Proceedings of the First International Workshop on Information Hiding.* (LNCS 1174). London: Springer.

Belloni, S., Formaglio, A., Menegaz, G., Tan, H. Z., Prattichizzo, D., & Barni, M. (2006, February). Is haptic watermarking worth it? In B. E. Rogowitz, T. N. Pappas, & S. J. Daly (Eds.), *Proceedings of SPIE, 6057, Human Vision and Electronic Imaging XI.*

Biddle, P., England, P., Peinado, M., & Willman, B. (2003, January). The darknet and the future of content protection. *ACM Workshop on DRM* (LNCS 2696).

Cayre, F., Fontaine, C., & Furon, T. (2005, October). Watermarking security: Theory and practice. *IEEE Transactions on Signal Processing, 53*(10).

Cox I. J., & Miller, M. L. (2002). The first 50 years of electronic watermarking. *EURASIP Journal on Applied Signal Processing, 2*, 126-132.

Cox, I. J., Miller, M., & Bloom, J. (2002). *Digital watermarking.* San Diego, CA: Academic Press.

Craver, S. A., Wu, M., & Liu, B. (2001). What can we reasonably expect from watermarks? In *Proceedings of the IEEE Workshop on the Applications of Signal Processing to Audio and Acoustics* (pp. 223-226).

Digimarc Cooperation. (2006). *Digimarc digital image watermarking guide.* Retrieved March 21, from http://www.digimarc.com/comm/docs/WatermarkingGuide.pdf

Digital Display Working Group. (1999, April). *Digital visual interface, DVI.* Retrieved March 21, from http://www.ddwg.org/lib/dvi_10.pdf

Electronic Frontier Foundation. (2007). *EFF: Sony BMG litigation.* Retrieved March 21, from http://www.eff.org/IP/DRM/Sony-BMG/

Fridrich, J., & Goljan, M. (2002). Practical steganalysis—State of the art. In *Proceedings of the SPIE Symposium on Electronic Imaging*, San Jose, CA.

Haitsma, J., Kalker, T., & Oostveen, J. (2001). Robust audio hashing for content identification. In *Proceedings of the International Workshop on Content-Based Multimedia Indexing.*

Halderman, J. A. (2002). Evaluating new copy-prevention techniques for audio CDs. In *Proceedings of the ACM Workshop on Digital Rights Management.* New York: ACM Press.

Johnson, N., & Jajodia, S. (1998). Steganalysis: The investigation of hidden information. In *Proceedings of the IEEE Information Technology Conference.*

Ozer, H., Avcıbas, I., Sankur, B., & Memon, N. (2003, January). Steganalysis of audio based on audio quality metrics. *Security and Watermarking of Multimedia Contents V, 5020,* of Proceedings of SPIE55-66. Santa Clara, CA.

Pereira, S., & Pun, T. (2000). Robust template matching for affine resistant image watermarks. *IEEE Transactions on Image Processing, 9,* 1123-1129.

Rosenblatt, B. (2007, March). *Thomson moves watermarking into consumer devices.* Retrieved March 21, 2007, from http://www.drmwatch.com/drmtech/article.php/3667096

Rosenblatt, B., Trippe, B., & Mooney, S. (2001). *Digital rights management: Business and technology.* New York: Hungry Minds/John Wiley & Sons.

Schmucker, M., & Ebinger, P. (2005). Promotional and commercial content distribution based on a legal and trusted P2P framework. In *Proceedings of the Seventh IEEE International Conference on E-Commerce Technology* (CEC'05) (pp. 439-442).

Schneier, B. (2001). *The futility of digital copy prevention.* In CRYPTO-GRAM. Retrieved March 21, from http://cryptome.org/futile-cp.htm

Steinebach, M., & Zmudzinski, S. (2004). Complexity optimization of digital watermarking for music-on-demand services. In *Proceedings of Virtual Goods Workshop* 2004 (pp. 24-35). Illmenau, Germany.

Swaminathan, A., Mao, Y., & Wu, M. (2006). Robust and secure image hashing. *IEEE Transactions on Image Forensics and Security.*

Vassiliadis, B., Fotopoulos, V., Xenos, M., & Skodras, A. (2004, April). Could grid facilitate demanding media watermarking applications? In *Proceedings of the 4th International LeGE-WG Workshop*, Stuttgart, Germany

Venkatesan, R., Koon, S.-M., Jakubowski, M. H., & Moulin, P. (2000). Robust image hashing. In *Proceedings of the International Conference on Image Processing, 3.*

Wolf, P., Steinebach, M., & Diener, K. (2007). Complementing DRM with digital watermarking: Mark, search, retrieve. *Online Information Review, 31*(1), 10-21.

ADDITIONAL READING

Barni, M., & Bartolini, F. (2004). *Watermarking systems engineering: Enabling digital assets security and other applications.* Boca Raton, FL: CRC Press.

Cvejic, N., & Seppanen, T. (Eds.). (2007). *Digital audio watermarking techniques and technologies: Applications and benchmarks.* Hershey, PA: IGI Global.

Delaigle, J., Devleeschouwer, C., Macq, B., & Langendijk, L. (2002). Human visual system features enabling watermarking. *Proceedings of the IEEE International Conference on Multimedia and Expo, 2002. ICME '02, 2,* 489-492.

Gomez, E., Cano, P., De Gomes, L., Batlle, E., & Bonnet, M. (2002). Mixed watermarking-fingerprinting approach for integrity verification of audio recordings. In *Proceedings of IEEE International Telecommunications Symposium (ITS2002),* Natal, Brazil.

Herley, C. (2002). Why watermarking is nonsense. *IEEE Signal Processing Magazine, 19*(5), 10-11.

Johnson, N., Duric, Z., Jajodia, S., & Memon, N. (2000) *Information hiding: Steganography and watermarking—Attacks and countermeasures.* Norwell, MA: Kluwer Academic.

Moulin, P. (2003). Comments on "Why watermarking is nonsense." In *IEEE Signal Processing Magazine, 20*(6), 57-59.

Radhakrishnan, R., & Memon, N. (2002). Audio content authentication based on psycho-acoustic model. In *Proceedings of SPIE, Security and Watermarking of Multimedia Contents IV, 4675,* 110-117.

Steinebach, M., & Dittmann, J. (2003). Watermarking-based digital audio data authentication. *EURASIP Journal on Applied Signal Processing, 10,* 1001-1015.

Steinebach, M., Zmudzinski, S., & Bölke, T. (2005). Audio watermarking and partial encryption. In *Proceedings of SPIE—Volume 5681, Security, Steganography, and Watermarking of Multimedia Contents VII.*

Steinebach, M., Zmudzinski, S., & Neichtadt, S. (2006). Robust-audio-hash synchronized audio watermarking. In *Proceedings of the 4th International Workshop on Security in Information Systems* (WOSIS 2006) (pp. 58-66).

Yuan, S., & Huss, S. (2004). Audio watermarking algorithm for real-time speech integrity and authentication. In *MM&Sec '04: Proceedings of the 2004 multimedia and security workshop on Multimedia and security* (pp. 220-226). New York: ACM Press.

Zhu, B., Swanson, M., & Tewfik, A. (2004). When seeing isn't believing. *IEEE Signal Processing Magazine, 21*(2), 40-49.

Zmudzinski, S., & Steinebach, M. (2007). Robust message authentication code algorithm for digital audio recordings. In *Proceedings of SPIE Volume 6505 Security, Steganography, and Watermarking of Multimedia Contents IX, 650508, SPIE,* Bellingham, WA.

Chapter VII
Statistical Watermark Detection in the Transform Domain for Digital Images

Fouad Khelifi
The Institute of Electronics, Communications and Information Technology (ECIT),
Queen's University Belfast, UK

Fatih Kurugollu
The Institute of Electronics, Communications and Information Technology (ECIT),
Queen's University Belfast, UK

Ahmed Bouridane
The Institute of Electronics, Communications and Information Technology (ECIT),
Queen's University Belfast, UK

ABSTRACT

The problem of multiplicative watermark detection in digital images can be viewed as a binary decision where the observation is the possibility that watermarked samples can be thought of as a noisy environment in which a desirable signal, called watermark, may exist. In this chapter, we investigate the optimum watermark detection from the viewpoint of decision theory. Different transform domains are considered with generalized noise models. We study the effect of the watermark strength on both the detector performance and the imperceptibility of the host image. Also, the robustness issue is addressed while considering a number of commonly used attacks.

INTRODUCTION

Recently, we have seen an unprecedented advance in the use and distribution of digital multimedia data. However, illegal digital copying and forgery have become increasingly menacing as the duplication means are easy to use. This makes the protection of copyrighted original copies from illegal use and unrestricted broadcasting a very challenging task. These challenges and issues have involved the field of watermarking for the

Figure 1. Multi-bit watermark extraction system

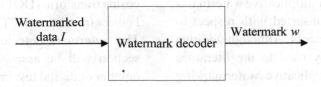

Watermarked data *I* → Watermark decoder → Watermark *w*

Figure 2. One-bit watermark detection system

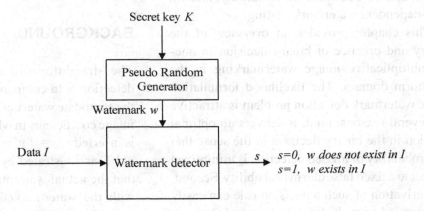

Secret key *K*

Pseudo Random Generator

Watermark *w*

Data *I* → Watermark detector → *s*

$s=0$, *w does not exist in I*
$s=1$, *w exists in I*

protection and security of digital data (Arnold, Schmucker, & Wolthusen, 2003).

Watermarking is the embedding of a hidden secondary data into the host data within an embedding distortion level. The robustness requires that the watermark information must be decoded/detected even if the watermarked data has undergone additional distortions. Existing systems are divided in two groups depending on the roles that watermarks play. In the first group, the watermarks are viewed as transmitted multi-bit information, where the decoder extracts the full version of the embedded message bit by bit. In such a case, the decoder already assumes that the input data is watermarked (Figure 1).

In the second group, known as one-bit watermarking, the watermarks serve as verification codes, as such a full decoding is not really necessary. It is used to decide whether or not a particular message or pattern is present in the host data (Figure 2).

In practice, the security of the entire one-bit watermarking systems is ensured by using a secret key, as commonly employed in communications, which is required to generate the watermark sequence. Only the legal owner of the watermarked data knows the key for the generation of that watermark and proves his/her ownership.

Depending on the embedding rule used in a watermarking system, the watermark is often additive or multiplicative (Langelaar, Setyawan, & Langendijk, 2000). To get better performances in terms of robustness and imperceptibility, both are used in the transform domain (Barni, Bartolini, Cappellini, & Piva, 1998; Cheng & Huang, 2001a). In fact, the energy compaction property exhibited in the transform domain suggests that the distortions introduced by a hidden data into a number of transform coefficients will be spread over all components in the spatial domain so as the change of the pixels values is less significant.

In additive watermarking, the watermark is simply added to a set of transformed coefficients with a scaling factor controlling the watermark strength. In the case of multiplicative watermarking, the watermark is inserted with respect to the transformed coefficients. Although additive watermarking is widely used in the literature for its simplicity, multiplicative watermarking exhibits a better exploitation of the characteristics of the human visual system (HVS) in digital images and, unlike additive watermarking, offers a data-dependent watermark casting.

This chapter provides an overview of the theory and practice of binary decision in one-bit multiplicative image watermarking in the transform domain. The likelihood formulation of the watermark detection problem is attractive for several reasons. First, it delivers an optimal solution in the binary decision in the sense that the probability of missed detection is minimized subject to a fixed false alarm probability. Second, the derivation of such a decision rule can easily be extended to multi-bit detection and thus can be used in the decoding of hidden data in multi-bit watermarking systems. Finally, it uses only few parameters to model the host data. These parameters are roughly unchanged even when the data holds the watermark and undergoes different attacks. Therefore, a fully blind detection can be used since the original data is not required. From a viewpoint of decision theory, the effect of multiplicative watermark strength on the visual quality of watermarked images and on the detection is investigated and different techniques proposed in the literature are reviewed in this chapter. The robustness issue is also addressed in this chapter while assessing a number of optimum detectors in the transform domain.

In the next section, we review different state-of-the-art watermark detection techniques proposed in the literature. Then, we describe the problem of watermark detection from a decision theory viewpoint in the third section. The fourth section describes two different generalized distributions to model the behavior of the host data in the transform domain. In particular, the discrete

wavelet transform (DWT) domain, the discrete cosine transform (DCT) domain, and the discrete Fourier transform (DFT) domain are considered. The watermark detectors derived in the fourth section will be assessed experimentally on a number of digital test images in the fifth section. Conclusions and further discussions are provided in the final two sections.

BACKGROUND

The straightforward approach for watermark detection is to compare the correlation between the candidate watermark $w^* = (w_1^*, \cdots, w_N^*)$ and image coefficients in which the actual watermark is inserted $y^* = (y_1^*, \cdots, y_N^*)$ with some threshold T as illustrated by Figure 3. This assumes that the actual watermark is strongly correlated with the watermarked samples and, thus, the correlation coefficient λ should be large to some extent (Cox, Kilian, Leighton, & Shamoon, 1997; Langelaar et al., 2000). However, such a correlation-based detection would be optimum only in the additive case under the assumption that the image coefficients follow a Gaussian distribution (Elmasry & Shi, 1999). This has been pointed out when formulating the watermark detection problem as a statistical hypothesis testing problem (Cheng & Huang, 2001a). In fact, the problem of watermark detection can be viewed as a binary decision where the observation is the possibly watermarked transformed coefficients, that is, this can be formulated as a problem of detecting a known signal in a noisy environment (Green & Swets, 1966) (Figure 4).

The statistical behavior of the transformed coefficients can be used to derive a decision rule that decides whether a candidate watermark presented to its input is actually embedded in the data (hypothesis H_1) or not (hypothesis H_0), thereby, conventional statistical signal detectors can be used. In additive watermarking, Hernandez, Amado, and Perez-Gonzalez (2000) used

Figure 3. Correlation-based watermark detector

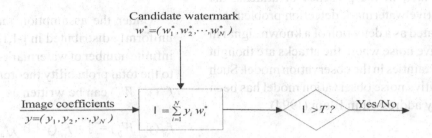

Figure 4. Block diagram illustrating the formulation of the problem of one-bit watermarking as a problem of signal detection in noisy observation.

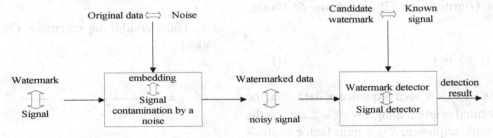

the generalized Gaussian (GG) distribution to statistically model the 8×8 DCT coefficients. The resulting detector structure has been shown to outperform a correlation based counterpart. In Cheng and Huang (2001a) the GG model was also adopted for DWT coefficients. In the multiplicative case, a generalized correlator based on the GG distribution has been derived and applied in the DWT domain (Cheng & Huang, 2001b). Such a detector is locally optimum in the sense that it approaches the optimality for weak signals[1] (Miller & Thomas, 1972). In the DFT domain, the Weibull distribution has been employed, based on which an optimum detector has been derived (Barni, Bartolini, De Rosa, & Piva, 2001). Likewise, the same distribution has been used to derive a locally optimum detector structure (Cheng & Huang, 2002). Kwon, Lee, Kwon, Kwon, and Lee (2002) have derived an optimum multiplicative detector based on the normal distribution. However,

although their proposed detector significantly outperforms the correlation-based detector for DWT-transformed images, such a distribution can not accurately model the host coefficients. In Ng and Grag (2005), the Laplacian model, which exhibits more accuracy, has been considered. Consequently, better performance in terms of detection has been achieved. It has also been used in Khelifi, Bouridane, and Kurugollu (2006) when investigating the problem of detector accuracy. Nevertheless, as many authors have pointed out, wavelet sub-bands can be modeled perfectly by a GG distribution (Calvagno, Ghirardi, Mian, & Rinaldo, 1997; Do & Vetterli, 2002). Thereby, the proposed detector in Ng and Grag (2004), using the GG model, has been proven to provide the best performance. In investigation on robust optimum detection of multiplicative watermarks, a class of locally optimum detectors has been developed based on the GG distribution for sub-band transformed domains (Cheng & Huang, 2003). In fact, in the presence of attacks, the multiplicative watermark detection problem can be formulated as a detection of a known signal in non-additive noise where the attacks are thought of as uncertainties in the observation model. Such a non-additive noise observation model has been extensively addressed in Blum (1994).

PROBLEM FORMULATION

The commonly used multiplicative embedding rule is (Barni et al., 2001; Cheng & Huang, 2003)

$$y_i = x_i \, (1 + \lambda \, w_i) \qquad (1)$$

where $x = (x_1,..., x_n)$ is a sequence of data from the transformed original image, $w = (w_1,...,w_N)$ is the watermark sequence, λ is a gain factor controlling the watermark strength, and $y = (y_1,...,y_N)$ is the sequence of watermarked data. By relying on decision theory, the observation variables are the vector y of possibly marked coefficients. The candidate watermark vector at the input of the detector is denoted by $w* = (w_1^*,..., w_N^*)$. Let us define two regions (classes) W_0 and W_I where $W_0 = \{w \mid w \neq w*\}$ (hypothesis H_0), including $w = 0$ that corresponds to the case where no watermark is embedded, and $W_I = \{w*\}$ (hypothesis H_I). The likelihood ratio $\ell(y)$ is

$$\ell(y) = \frac{f_y(y \mid W_1)}{f_y(y \mid W_0)} \qquad (2)$$

where $f_y(y \mid W)$ is the probability density function (pdf) of the vector y conditioned to W. In practice, y satisfies $f_y(y \mid W_0) > 0$ since the host samples have a non-zero occurrence probability. By relying on the fact that the components of y are independent of each other, we can write

$$f_y(y \mid W_0) = \prod_{i=1}^{N} f_y(y_i \mid W) \qquad (3)$$

Under the assumption that watermarks are uniformly distributed in [-1,1], W_0 consists of an infinite number of watermarks. Hence, according to the total probability theorem (Papoulis, 1991), $f_{yi}(y_i \mid W_0)$ can be written as

$$f_{yi}(y_i \mid W_0) = \int_{-1}^{1} f_{yi}(y_i \mid W) f_{wi}(w) \, dw \qquad (4)$$

where $f_{wi}(w)$ is the pdf of w_i. Therefore

$$f_{yi}(y_i \mid W_0) = \tfrac{1}{2} \int_{-1}^{1} f_{yi}(y_i \mid W) \, dw \qquad (5)$$

Thus, combining equations (2), (3), and (5) yields

$$\ell(y) = \frac{\prod_{i=1}^{N} f_{yi}(y_i \mid w_i^*)}{\frac{1}{2^N} \prod_{i=1}^{N} \int_{-1}^{1} f_{yi}(y_i \mid w) \, dw} \qquad (6)$$

By remembering the watermarking rule, the pdf $f_y(y \mid w)$ of a watermarked coefficient y conditioned to a watermark value w is

$$f_y(y \mid w) = \frac{1}{1+\lambda w} \, f_x\left(\frac{y}{1+\lambda w}\right) \qquad (7)$$

where $f_x(x)$ indicates the pdf of the original, non-watermarked coefficients.[2] Thus, equation (6) becomes

$$\ell(y) = \frac{\prod_{i=1}^{N} \frac{1}{1+\lambda w_i^*} f_{x_i}\left(\frac{y_i}{1+\lambda w_i^*}\right)}{\frac{1}{2^N} \prod_{i=1}^{N} \int_{-1}^{1} \frac{1}{1+\lambda w} f_{x_i}\left(\frac{y_i}{1+\lambda w}\right) \, dw} \qquad (8)$$

Under the assumption $\lambda \ll 1$, the following approximation is widely adopted in the literature[3] (Barni & Bartolini, 2004; Barni et al., 2001)

$$\frac{1}{2} \int_{-1}^{1} \frac{1}{1+\lambda w} f_x \left(\frac{y}{1+\lambda w} \right) dw \approx f_x(y) \quad (9)$$

More specifically, the derivation of the likelihood ratio relies on the assumption below

$$f_y(y \mid w_0) \approx f_y(y \mid 0) \qquad (10)$$

where by 0 the null watermark is meant. By evoking the approximation (9) and taking logarithm, the decision rule has the form (Barni & Bartolini, 2004)

$$\varphi(y) > T \boxtimes H_1$$
$$\quad < T \boxtimes H_0 \qquad (11)$$

where T is a properly chosen threshold, and

$$\phi(y) = \sum_{i=1}^{N} \left[ln \left(f_{x_i} \left(\frac{y_i}{1+\lambda w_i^*} \right) \right) - ln(f_{x_i}(y_i)) \right]$$

$$\varphi(y) = \sum_{i=1}^{N} v_i \qquad (12)$$

To obtain the threshold T, the Neyman-Pearson criterion is used in such a way that the missed detection probability is minimized, subject to a fixed false alarm probability (Ferguson, 1967).

$$P_{FA} = P(\phi(y) > T \mid W_0)$$

$$= \int_{T}^{+\infty} f_\phi(\alpha \mid W_0) \, d\alpha \qquad (13)$$

Note that the variable $\varphi(y)$ is a sum of statistically independent terms. Thus, by invoking the central limit theorem (Papoulis, 1991), its pdf can be assumed to be a normal one. Therefore, the mean and variance of $\varphi(y)$ are given by (Barni et al., 2001; Cheng & Huang, 2003)

$$\mu_\phi = \sum_{i=1}^{N} \mu_{v_i} \qquad (14)$$

$$\sigma_\phi^2 = \sum_{i=1}^{N} \sigma_{v_i}^2 \qquad (15)$$

where by μ_{v_i} and $\sigma_{v_i}^2$, it is meant the mean and the variance of v_i respectively. Under hypothesis $\prod_0$, in view of equation (10), we have

$$\mu_{v_i \mid y_i = x_i} = E \left[ln \left(f_{x_i} \left(\frac{x_i}{1+\lambda w_i^*} \right) \right) - ln(f_{x_i}(x_i)) \right] \qquad (16)$$

$$\sigma_{v_i \mid y_i = x_i}^2 = E \left[\left(ln \left(f_{x_i} \left(\frac{x_i}{1+\lambda w_i^*} \right) \right) - ln(f_{x_i}(x_i)) - \mu_{v_i} \right)^2 \right] \qquad (17)$$

Practically, the parameters of the pdf $f_{x_i}(\cdot)$ are not available (blind watermarking). Instead, the possibly marked coefficients are used. Finally, P_{FA} can be written as

$$P_{FA} = \int_{T}^{+\infty} \frac{1}{\sqrt{2\pi \sigma_\phi^2}} exp \left(- \left(\frac{\alpha - \mu_\phi}{2\sigma_\phi^2} \right)^2 \right) d\alpha$$

$$= \frac{1}{2} erfc \left(\frac{T - \mu_\phi}{\sqrt{2\sigma_\phi^2}} \right) \qquad (18)$$

where *erfc* is the complementary error function, given by

$$erfc(x) = \frac{2}{\pi} \int_{x}^{+\infty} e^{-t^2} dt \qquad (19)$$

Hence

$$T = erfc^{-1}(2\,P_{FA})\sqrt{2\sigma_\phi^2 + \mu_\phi}$$

(20)

APPLICATION

Watermark detector based on the GG model. The GG model is broadly used in the literature to describe some probability distributions of digital data in the transform domain. It basically provides a good understanding of the statistical behavior of those signals that are impulsive and heavy-tailed such as the wavelet sub-bands (Calvagno et al., 1997; Do & Vetterli, 2002) and non dc coefficients in the DCT transform domain (Birney & Fischer, 1995). The probability density function of a zero-mean GG distribution is

$$f_X(x) = A\,\exp\left(-|\beta\,x|^c\right), \quad c > 0$$

(21)

where $\beta = \frac{1}{\sigma}\sqrt{\left(\frac{\Gamma(3/c)}{\Gamma(1/c)}\right)}$, $A = \frac{\beta c}{2\Gamma(1/c)}$, σ is the standard deviation of the distribution, and $\Gamma(t) = \int_0^{+\infty} r^{t-1}\,e^{-r}\,dr$ is the Gamma function. It is worth mentioning that the GGD

contains the Gaussian and the Laplacian distributions as special cases, with $c = 2$ and $c = 1$, respectively. As depicted in Figures 5 and 6, when $c \to 0$, it approaches the Dirac function. When $c \to \infty$, it tends to the uniform distribution. Practically, c can be computed by solving (Mallat, 1989; Sharifi & Leon-Garcia, 1995)

$$c = F^{-1}\left(\frac{E[|x|]}{\sigma}\right)$$

(22)

where

$$F(z) = \frac{\Gamma(2/c)}{\Gamma(1/c)\Gamma(3/c)}$$

In Figure 7 we show the actual and estimated pdfs on a set of transformed coefficients in the DWT and DCT domains for 'Goldhill' 512×512 test image.

Obviously, the GG model fits the empirical distributions perfectly. By replacing the pdf of the GG model in equation (12), the detector can be expressed as (Cheng & Huang, 2003; Ng & Grag, 2004)

Figure 5. pdf of the generalized Gaussian distribution for small values of c with $\sigma = 15$

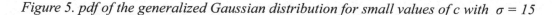

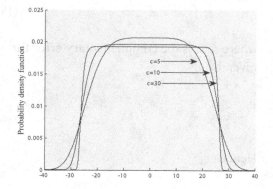
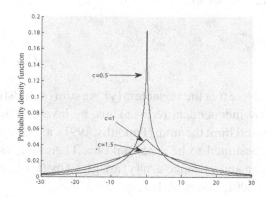

Figure 6. pdf of the generalized Gaussian distribution for large values of c with $\sigma = 15$

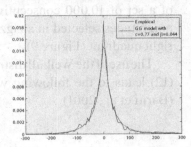 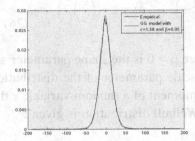

Figure 7. Fig. 7. Modeling of transformed coefficients for 'Goldhill' image. Left. DWT: third level sub-band HL3 coefficients using 9/7 biorthogonal filters. Right. DCT: a set of 12000 consecutive coefficients in a zigzag scan order of the whole DCT transformed image starting from sample 31000.

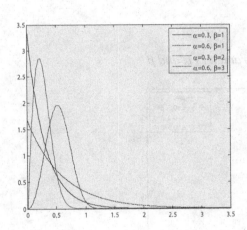 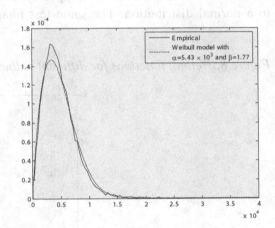

$$\phi(y) = \sum_{i=1}^{N} |\beta_i y_i|^{c_i} \left(1 - \frac{1}{(1+\lambda w_i^*)^{c_i}} \right) \quad (23)$$

$$\sigma_\phi^2 = \sum_{i=1}^{N} \frac{1}{c_i} \left(1 - \frac{1}{(1+\lambda w_i^*)^{c_i}} \right)^2 \quad (25)$$

The threshold T can be determined from equation (20) where,

$$\mu_\phi = \sum_{i=1}^{N} \frac{1}{c_i} \left(1 - \frac{1}{(1+\lambda w_i^*)^{c_i}} \right) \quad (24)$$

Watermark Detector Based on the Weibull Model

The Weibull distribution offers a good flexibility to describe the statistical characteristics of the coefficients magnitude in the DFT domain (Barni et al., 2001). It is defined as

$$f_X(x) = \frac{\beta}{\alpha}\left(\frac{x}{\alpha}\right)^{\beta-1} \exp\left(-\left(\frac{x}{\alpha}\right)^{\beta}\right) \tag{26}$$

for $x \geq 0$, where $\beta > 0$ is the shape parameter and $\alpha > 0$ is the scale parameter of the distribution. The nth raw moment of a random variable x that follows the Weibull distribution is given by

$$m_n = \alpha^n \Gamma\left(1 + \frac{n}{\beta}\right) \tag{27}$$

Figure 8 shows a number of Weibull functions with different parameters. When $\beta = 1$, the Weibull distribution reduces to the exponential distribution. When β increases, it appears similar to a normal distribution. The same test image

'Goldhill' is also used to show the model function of a set of 10,000 consecutive DFT coefficient magnitudes selected in a zigzag order of the top right quadrant (Figure 9).

The use of the Weibull distribution in equation (12) leads to the following watermark detector (Barni et al., 2001)

$$\phi(y) = \sum_{i=1}^{N} y_i^{\beta_i}\left(\frac{(1+\lambda\, w_i^*)^{\beta_i} - 1}{\alpha_i^{\beta_i}(1+\lambda w_i^*)^{\beta_i}}\right) \tag{28}$$

Equation (20) can be used to derive the threshold where,

Figure 8. Weibull functions for different values of parameters α and β

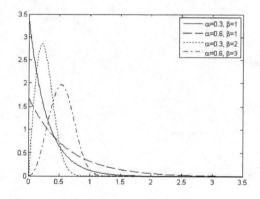

Figure 9. Modeling of DFT coefficients for 'Goldhill' image

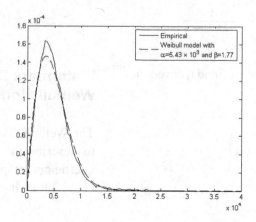

$$\mu_\phi = \sum_{i=1}^{N} \left(\frac{(1+\lambda\, w_i^*)^{\beta_i} - 1}{(1+\lambda w_i^*)^{\beta_i}} \right) \qquad (29)$$

$$\sigma_\phi^2 = \sum_{i=1}^{N} \left(\frac{(1+\lambda\, w_i^*)^{\beta_i} - 1}{(1+\lambda w_i^*)^{\beta_i}} \right)^2 \qquad (30)$$

EXPERIMENTAL ANALYSIS

In this section, we evaluate the performance of the detectors discussed earlier on six 512×512 grayscale standard images with different information content. At the detector side, the original image is assumed to be unavailable and therefore the statistical model parameters used to perform a decision are directly computed from the watermarked and possibly corrupted images. Three issues are considered here. First, the imperceptibility of the watermark which is assessed visually and quantitatively by using the peak signal-to-noise ratio (PSNR) as a fidelity measure. Second, the detection performance with respect to the probability of false alarm and the probability of missed detection. We use the receiver operating characteristic (ROC) curve which is widely adopted in the literature for interpreting the performance of communications systems. Eventually, the robustness of the watermark is addressed while considering a number of commonly used attacks.

Imperceptibility

It is worth mentioning that the watermark sequence consists of a sequence of 12,288 random real numbers uniformly distributed in[4] [-1,1]. The watermark casting procedure in the DFT and DCT domains is similar to that used in Barni et al. (1998, 2001), respectively. In Cox et al. (1997), a set of the largest coefficients in the DCT domain were selected to hold the watermark sequence. However, this would require the original image to determine those components which hide the watermark since the watermarked data may be

distorted. We have experimentally found that the approach used in Barni et al. (1998, 2001) to insert the watermark is more practical and brings comparable performance to that of Cox et al. (1997). This is justified by the fact that most of an image energy is packed into the low frequency components. Thus, the largest coefficients in the DCT and DFT domains are very likely to be found when scanning the image in a zigzag order starting from the first non-zero frequency coefficient. In the DWT domain, the watermark is embedded as suggested in Ng and Grag (2005). That is, all coefficients in the sub-bands of the third level, except the approximation sub-band, are used to insert the watermark sequence. In the DCT and DFT domains, the start point for embedding the watermark in a zigzag order has been selected in such a way the PSNRs obtained are close to those delivered in the DWT domain. In the experiments, the start point has been set to 1200 for the DFT and 4000 for the DCT. The PSNRs are plotted in Figures 10-12 for various test images.

In the evaluation of watermarking systems, two different types of imperceptibility assessment can be distinguished: *quality* and *fidelity* (Cox, Miller, & Bloom, 2002). Fidelity is a measure of the similarity between the watermarked data and the original one. The quality assessment, on the other hand, is concerned with obvious processing alterations without referring to the original data. In other words, only high quality of the watermarked data is targeted. In this chapter, fidelity is the perceptual measure of our concern.

From the first set of experiments, two relevant points arise when measuring the distortions by PSNRs. First, as pointed out in Jayant, Johnston, and Safranek (1993), although the automated fidelity test adopted here is often used in the literature, it does not reflect the true fidelity in some cases. Indeed, the visual imperceptibility also depends on the data content. The higher the frequency content exhibited in the image, the better the imperceptibility expected. Figure 13 shows an example of two test images with dif-

Figure 10. PSNR of watermarked images in the DWT domain

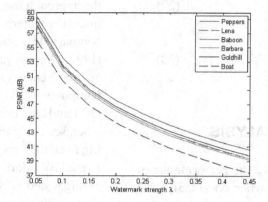

Figure 11. PSNR of watermarked images in the DFT domain

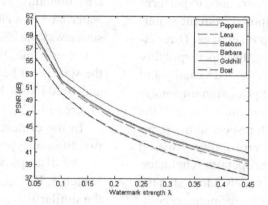

Figure 12. PSNR of watermarked images in the DCT domain

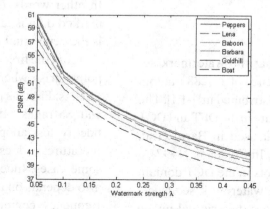

Figure 13. Illustration of a case in which PSNR cannot reflect the imperceptibility of the watermark. (a) Original Lena. (b) Watermarked Lena in the DFT domain PSNR=41.46 dB. (c) Original Baboon. (d) Watermarked Baboon in the DFT domain PSNR=39.62 dB.

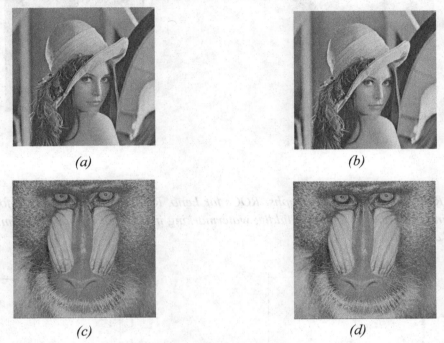

(a)   *(b)*

(c)   *(d)*

Figure 14. Visual effect of the watermark casting in different transform domains. (a) Watermarked Lena in the DWT domain PSNR=41.55. (b) Difference image with magnitudes multiplied by 20 in the DWT case. (c) Watermarked Lena in the DFT domain PSNR=41.46 dB. (d) Difference image with magnitudes multiplied by 20 in the DFT case.

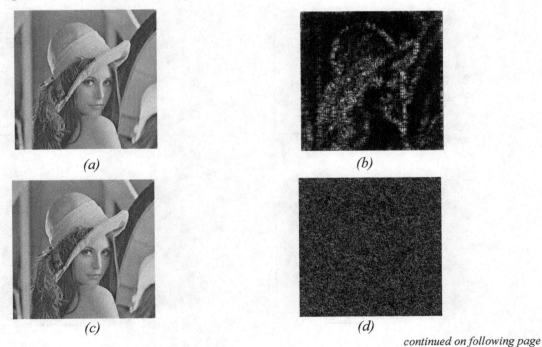

(a)   *(b)*

(c)   *(d)*

continued on following page

Figure 14. continued

(e)

(f)

Figure 15. ROC curves. Left side graphs: ROCs for Lena. Right side graphs: ROCs for Baboon. Top: watermarking in the DWT domain. Middle: watermarking in the DFT domain. Bottom: watermarking in the DCT domain.

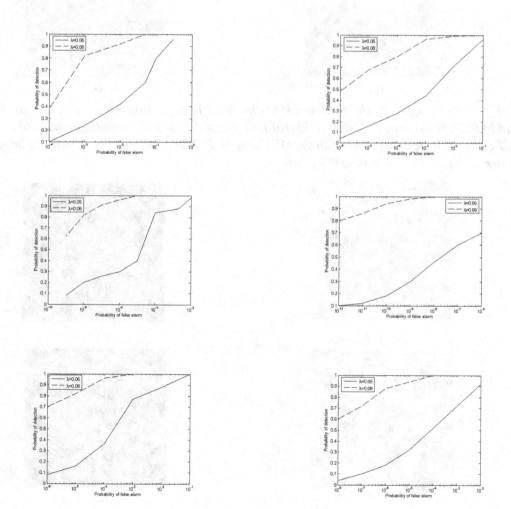

ferent frequency content. Obviously, PSNR, as a perceptual model, suggests that the watermarked version of 'Lena' should be perceptually better than the watermarked 'Baboon' image. However, the watermarked 'Lena' shows more visible distortions when compared to the original image. The second point that should be mentioned is that a wavelet transform offers the best imperceptibility of the embedded watermarks when compared to the other transforms. This transform actually provides an image-dependent distortion that is mostly concentrated at edges and detail regions. It is well known that the HVS is less sensitive to such regions compared to uniform and non-textured regions. Figure 14 illustrates an example of the 'Lena' image holding the same watermark in different transform domains. From this figure, it can be seen that the watermarked images in the DFT and the DCT domains show more noticeable distortions when compared against the watermarked image in the DWT domain. The difference image clearly shows the image dependency of the watermarking in the DWT domain. The distortion, which is similarly introduced in the DFT and DCT domains, appears like a noise independent of the host image.

Detection Performance

In order to gauge the performance of the detectors, a number of test images were watermarked using $\lambda=0.05$ and $\lambda=0.08$ in different transform domains. ROC curves were used to assess the watermark detection. These represent the variation of the probability of correct detection against the probability of false alarm. A perfect detection would yield a point at coordinate $(0,1)$ of the ROC space meaning that all actual watermarks were detected and no false alarms are found. Without loss of generality, the results on two sample images are plotted in Figure 15.

Obviously, the larger the watermark strength, the better detection performance is. In fact, from the standpoint of the signal detection theory,

the watermark strength can be thought of as the signal amplitude. Higher values for signal amplitude make the hypotheses H_0 and H_1 more distinguishable. Also, it can easily be seen that the 'Baboon' image, which carries more details and texture information than 'Lena', does offers an improved detection. This is justified by the fact that most of the transform coefficients that hold the watermark for 'Baboon' are larger. Indeed, since the watermark casting depends on the coefficients magnitude in the multiplicative case (see equation (1)), the coefficients with larger magnitude ensure significant presence of the watermark.

From the experiments, the performance of the Weibull model-based detector in the DFT domain is significantly better than that obtained with the DCT detector which, in turn, outperforms the DWT detector for all the test images. Indeed, at the same probability of detection, the DFT-based detector delivers the smallest probability of false alarm in comparison with the DWT- and DCT-based detectors. The DFT domain offers an effective solution to embed the watermark in the sense that it permits attractive ability of detection. However, in practical situations, this should be viewed in connection with the robustness of watermarks when the host data is altered with intentional or unintentional manipulations. The following section is devoted to analysis of the watermark robustness in the transform domain.

Robustness Analysis

In the set of experiments carried out, six various well known images were used. Namely, 'Peppers', 'Lena', 'Baboon', 'Barbara', 'Goldhill', and 'Boat'. As mentioned earlier with regard to the imperceptibility, and in order to make comparison as fair as possible, λ is set to 0.18 for the DCT and DFT domains. For the DWT domain $\lambda=0.2$. The robustness of embedded watermarks is measured against standard image processing and geometric manipulations. Given six different watermarks, each one of them is embedded

Table 1. Robustness of embedded watermarks in the transform domain. QF: Quality Factor. v : variance. W: Window size. P: Number of pixels the image is shifted up and left. C: size of the cropped image (center part) compared to the original one. a: rotation angle (in degrees).

Attack		DWT	DFT	DCT
JPEG compression	QF=90	1	1	1
	QF=75	0	1	1
	QF=10	0	1	1
	QF=5	0	0	0
Gaussian white Noise addition	v=500	1	1	1
	v=1000	0	1	1
	v=2000	0	1	1
	v=4000	0	0	1
	v=8000	0	0	1
	v=1600	0	0	0
Median filtering	W=3×3	1	1	1
	W=5×5	0	1	1
	W=7×7	0	1	1
	W=9×9	0	0	0
Shifting	P=5	0	1	1
	P=10	0	1	1
	P=50	0	1	1
	P=150	0	1	1
	P=200	0	0	0
Cropping	C=95 %	0	1	0
	C=90 %	0	1	0
	C=80 %	0	1	0
	C=70 %	0	1	0
	C=60 %	0	0	0
Rotation	a=0.1	1	1	1
	a=0.2	0	1	1
	a=0.5	0	1	1
	a=0.6	0	0	0

into a test image. For each image, a set of 1000 watermarks is presented to the detector. Among these watermarks, there is only one watermark sequence that is actually embedded in that image. For all the watermarked images, the detection is said to be accurate (denoted by 1) if none of the fake watermarks is detected while the actual one is correctly detected. Otherwise, the detection will be inaccurate (denoted by 0). The theoretical probability of false alarm P_{FA}, which is used to determine the decision threshold in equation (20), has been fixed at 10^{-6}. The results are summarized in Table 1.

From the results, it can clearly be seen that the detector operating in the DWT domain performs poorly when compared with those implemented in the DCT and DFT domains. Unlike the DCT and DFT, which are invariant to small rotational and translational manipulations,[1] the DWT does not exhibit such desirable properties. Therefore, the embedded watermarks in the DWT domain cannot be recovered even for those attacks of slight visual impact on the watermarked images. It can also be observed that the DFT shows attractive ability to detect the embedded watermarks in small sub-parts of the watermarked images. This cannot be achieved in the DWT and DCT domains although significant portions from the watermarked images were maintained in some experiments (95% of the watermarked images). Finally, it should be mentioned that the DCT detector provides the best robustness to noise addition attacks. Overall, the DCT and DFT detectors perform closely well and show significant superiority over the DWT detector.

CONCLUSION

This chapter discussed the problem of multiplicative watermark detection in the transform domain. The optimum watermark detection is based on the information theory and can be formulated as a detection of a known signal in noisy observation. In one-bit watermarking, the requirements on the robustness and imperceptibility are essential. Robustness refers to the ability to detect the watermark after common signal processing operations. The challenges in the design of such watermarking systems are that the requirements are generally conflicting with each other. Indeed, a perfect imperceptibility of the watermark can be obtained while reducing the watermark strength. However, such improvements come at the price of the robustness.

The transform domain yields better performances in terms of imperceptibility and robustness. We have focused on the watermark detection in three different transform domains that are widely used in the literature: DWT, DFT, and DCT. The GG and the Weibull models have been used to describe the statistical behavior of the transform coefficients in order to derive the decision rule.

The watermark imperceptibility in the transform domain has extensively been discussed through several experiments. The difficulty in measuring the visual perceptibility of the watermark lies in the fact that the automated evaluation is deceiving in some particular cases. Indeed, such a perceptual assessment treats changes in all regions of an image data equally. However, human perception mechanisms are not uniform.

The experimental results have shown that the DWT offers better visual fidelity with an image dependent watermark casting effect when compared against the DFT and DCT. That is, the distortions introduced affect the high activity regions in which the HVS is less sensitive. In the second set of experiments, we have studied the ability of detection in the transform domain without any attack. ROC curves have been used to assess the detection performance. It has been observed that the DFT detector considerably outperforms the DCT detector which, in turn, provides a better detection than that obtained with a DWT detector. The robustness of the watermark has also been addressed through different common intentional and unintentional manipulations. With a comparable visual fidelity of the embedded watermarks, the DFT and DCT detectors, though performing very closely, have shown to provide significant improvements over a detection in a DWT domain.

FUTURE RESEARCH DIRECTIONS

Several research trends attempt to adapt the watermark embedding procedure to the sensitivity of the HVS. For this purpose, a perceptual model can be used to select the best suited coefficients to hold the watermark in the transform domain. However, one should pay attention to the effect of image processing manipulations on the perceptual masking at the detector side. Indeed, a vulnerable perceptual model would certainly mislead the detection of an embedded watermark. The watermark strength can also be selected in an adaptive way depending on the reliability of transformed coefficients to increase the robustness of the watermark. It would be interesting to consider translation/rotation invariant transforms such as Fourier-Mellin transform which may provide an efficient way to tackle the robustness issue against geometric attacks. The modeling of the signal distortions due to commonly used image processing manipulations such as low pass filtering and compression could be useful to develop a robust detector that considers such alterations as uncertainties in the statistical model of the host image. Finally, as shown in this chapter, further investigation is required to develop an effective assessment measure of the imperceptibility of watermarks since there is no metric available in the literature so far that satisfies the need perfectly.

REFERENCES

Arnold, M., Schmucker, M., & Wolthusen, S. D. (2003). *Techniques and applications of digital watermarking and content protection.* Artech House Computer Security.

Barni, M., & Bartolini, F. (2004). *Watermarking systems engineering.* Marcel Dekker Inc.

Barni, M., Bartolini, F., Cappellini, V., & Piva, A. (1998). A DCT-domain system for robust image watermarking. *Signal Processing, 66,* 357-372.

Barni, M., Bartolini, F., De Rosa, A., & Piva, A. (2001). A new decoder for the optimum recovery of non additive watermarks. *IEEE Transactions on Image Processing, 10,* 755-765.

Birney, K. A., & Fischer, T. R. (1995). On the modeling of DCT and subband image data for compression. *IEEE Transactions on Image Processing, 4,* 186-193.

Blum, R. S. (1994). Asymptotically robust detection of known signals in non-additive noise. *IEEE Transactions on Information Theory, 40,* 1612-1619.

Calvagno, G., Ghirardi, C., Mian, G. A., & Rinaldo, R. (1997). Modeling of subband image data for buffer control. *IEEE Transactions on Circuits and Systems for Video Technology, 7,* 402-408.

Cheng, Q., & Huang, T. S. (2001a). An additive approach to transform-domain information hiding and optimum detection structure. *IEEE Transactions on Multimedia, 3,* 273-284.

Cheng, Q., & Huang, T. S. (2001b). Optimum detection of multiplicative watermarks using locally optimum decision rule. In *Proceedings of the IEEE International Conference Multimedia and Expo,* Tokyo, Japan.

Cheng, Q., & Huang, T. S. (2002). Optimum detection and decoding of multiplicative watermarks in DFT domain. In *Proceedings of the IEEE International Conference on Acoustic, Speech, and Signal Processing,* Orlando, FL.

Cheng, Q., & Huang, T. S. (2003). Robust optimum detection of transform domain multiplicative watermarks. *IEEE Transactions on Signal Processing, 51,* 906-924.

Cox, I. J., Kilian, J., Leighton, F. T., & Shamoon, T. (1997). Secure spread spectrum watermarking for multimedia. *IEEE Transactions on Image Processing, 6,* 1673-1687.

Cox, I. J., Miller, M. L., & Bloom, J. A. (2002). *Digital watermarking.* Academic Press.

Do, M. N., & Vetterli, M. (2002). Wavelet-based texture retrieval using generalized Gaussian density and Kullbackleibler distance. *IEEE Transactions on Image Processing, 11,* 146-158.

Elmasry, G. F., & Shi, Y. Q. (1999). Maximum likelihood sequence decoding of digital image watermarks. In *Proceedings of SPIE Security and Watermarking of Multimedia Contents* (pp. 425-436). San Jose, CA.

Ferguson, T. (1967). *Mathematical statistics: A decision theoretical approach.* Academic Press.

Green, D. M., & Swets, J. A. (1966). *Signal detection theory and psychophysics.* New York: Wiley.

Hernandez, J. R., Amado, M., & Perez-Gonzalez, F. (2000). DCT-domain watermarking techniques for still images: Detector performance analysis and a new structure. *IEEE Transactions on Image Processing, 9,* 55-68.

Jayant, N., Johnston, J., & Safranek, R. (1993). Signal compression based on models of human perception. *Proceedings of the IEEE, 81,* 1385-1422.

Khelifi, F., Bouridane, A., & Kurugollu, F. (2006). On the optimum multiplicative watermark detection in the transform domain. In *Proceedings of the IEEE International Conference on Image Processing.*

Kwon, S.-G., Lee, S.-H., Kwon, K.-K., Kwon, K.-R., & Lee, K. (2002). Watermark detection algorithm using statistical decision theory. In *Proceedings of the IEEE International Conference on Multimedia and Expo,* Lausanne, Switzerland.

Langelaar, G. C., Setyawan, I., & Langendijk, R. L. (2000). Watermarking digital image and video data. *IEEE Signal Processing Magazine, 17,* 20-46.

Mallat, S. G. (1989). A theory for multiresolution signal decomposition: The wavelet representation. *IEEE Transactions on Pattern Analysis and Machine Intelligence, 11,* 674-693.

Miller, J. H., & Thomas, J. B. (1972). Detectors for discrete-time signals in non-Gaussian noise. *IEEE Information Theory, 18,* 241-250.

Ng, T. M., & Grag, H. K. (2004). Wavelet domain watermarking using maximum likelihood detection. In *Proceedings of SPIE Conference on Security, Steganography, Watermarking Multimedia Contents, 5306,* San Jose, CA.

Ng, T. M., & Grag, H. K. (2005). Maximum likelihood detection in DWT domain image watermarking using Laplacian modeling. *IEEE Signal Processing Letters, 12,* 285-288.

Papoulis, A. (1991). *Probability, random variables, and stochastic processes.* McGraw-Hill.

Sharifi, K., & Leon-Garcia, A. (1995). Estimation of shape parameters for generalized Gaussian distributions in subband decomposition of video. *IEEE Transactions on Circuits and Systems for Video Technology, 5,* 52-56.

ADDITIONAL READING

Avciba, I., Sankur, B., & Sayood, K. (2002). Statistical evaluation of image quality measures. *Journal of Electronic Imaging, 11*(2), 206-223.

Barni, M., Bartolini, F., De Rosa, A., & Piva, A. (2003). Optimum decoding and detection of multiplicative watermarks. *IEEE Transactions on Signal Processing, 52*(4), 1118-1123.

Briassouli, A., & Strintzis, M. (2004). Optimal watermark detection under quantization in the transform domain. *IEEE Transactions on Circuits and Systems for Video Technology, 14*(12), 1308-1319.

Briassouli, M. A., & Strintzis, M. (2004). Locally optimum nonlinearities for DCT watermark detection. *IEEE Transactions on Image Processing, 13*(12), 604-1617.

Huang, X., & Zhang, B. (2007). Statistically robust detection of multiplicative spread-spectrum watermarks. *IEEE Transactions on Information Forensics and Security, 2*(1), 1-13.

Karybali, I. G., & Berberidis, K. (2006). Efficient spatial image watermarking via new perceptual masking and blind detection schemes. *IEEE Transactions on Information Forensics and Security, 1*(2), 256-274.

Khelifi, F., Bouridane, F., Kurugollu, F., & Thompson, A. I. (2005). An improved wavelet-based image watermarking technique. In *Proceedings of IEEE International Conference on Advanced Video and Signal Based Surveillance,* Italy.

Lu, C.-S. (2004). *Multimedia security: Steganography and digital watermarking techniques for protection of intellectual property.* Hershey, PA: Idea Group.

Noorkami, M., & Mersereau, R. M. (2007). A framework for robust watermarking of H.264-encoded video with controllable detection performance. *IEEE Transactions on Information Forensics and Security, 2*(1), 14-23.

ENDNOTES

[1] The DCT is actually the real part of the DFT. Approximately, it shares the same invariance properties with the DFT to small rotations and translations.

[2] To make the formulation of the detection problem as general as possible, the pdf is not specified.

[3] Taylor's series can be used up to the first order to approximate the expression in the integral about the point $\lambda \approx 0$.

Chapter VIII
On Noise, Steganography, and the Active Warden

Christopher B. Smith
Southwest Research Institute, USA

Sos S. Agaian
The University of Texas at San Antonio, USA

ABSTRACT

Modern digital steganography has evolved a number of techniques to embed information near invisibly into digital media. Many of the techniques for information hiding result in a set of changes to the cover image that appear, for all intents and purposes to be noise. This chapter presents information for the reader to understand how noise is intentionally and unintentionally used in information hiding. This chapter first reviews a series of noise-like steganography methods. From these techniques the problems faced by the active warden can be posed in a systematic way. Results of using advanced clean image estimation techniques for active warden based steganalysis are presented. This chapter is concluded with a discussion of the future of steganography.

INTRODUCTION

The *prisoner's problem* was introduced in 1982 by Gus Simmons (Simmons, 1984),

Two accomplices in a crime have been arrested and are about to be locked in widely separated cells. Their only means of communication after they are locked up will be the way of messages conveyed for them by trustees – who are known to be agents of the warden. The warden is willing to allow the prisoners to exchange messages in the hope that he can deceive at least one of them into accepting as a genuine communication from the other either a fraudulent message created by the warden himself or else a modification by him of a genuine message. However, since he has ev-

Figure 1. Prisoner's problem

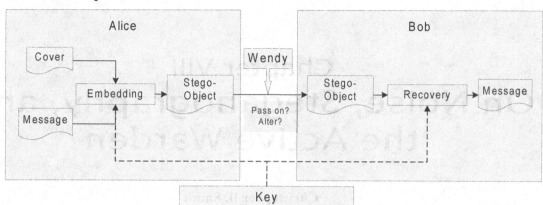

ery reason to suspect that the prisoners want to coordinate an escape plan, the warden will only permit the exchanges to occur if the information contained in the messages is completely open to him – and presumably innocuous. The prisoners, on the other hand, are willing to accept these conditions, i.e., to accept some risk of deception in order to be able to communicate at all, since they need to coordinate their plans. To do this they will have to deceive the warden finding a way of communicating secretly in the exchanges, i.e. establishing a "subliminal channel" between them in full view of the warden, even though the messages themselves contain no secret (to the warden) information. Since they anticipate that the warden will try to deceive them by introducing fraudulent messages they will only exchange messages if they are permitted to authenticate them.

Thus began the modern study of steganography. The two prisoners have since been named Alice and Bob, the warden is Wendy or Eve. Figure 1 shows an illustration of the basic scenario.

The modern warden, Wendy, has a challenge. Wendy's role is either to detect the presence of or to manipulate the message in order to prevent the undesirable escape of the two prisoners. Wendy practices the art and science of steganalysis.

The proliferation of electronic media has only increased the challenge of steganalysis.

In Wendy's more active role, the active warden scenario, she can modify each message that goes by. This can be based on a passive detection modifying only those messages that contain hidden data or by modifying all messages in a hope to prevent unknown hidden messages from making it through. The modification can be a simple attempt to scrambling any hidden messages, to prevent communication, or could include a sophisticated attempt to modify the message in the hopes of planting false messages to thwart the prisoner's escape plans.

This chapter explores the role of the active warden and how to exploit the noise-like properties of modern digital media. Here the focus is on image-based digital steganography. An overview of the topics covered appears in Figure 2. The next section discusses noise and the digital image. Including various types of noise and how steganography techniques can also appear as noise. The final section presents the active warden scenario from the perspective of removing artificial noise. This chapter is concluded with some discussion of the implications of noise and clean image estimation for steganalysis.

Figure 2. Topics in this chapter

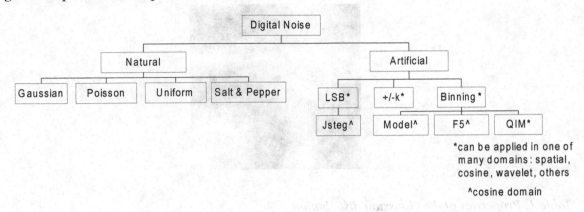

NATURAL NOISE IN DIGITAL MEDIA

Digital media include a rich set of information with much redundancy and many highly variable traits. Detecting artificially induced changes within a highly variable media is a challenge. In creating digital media, such as images or audio files, there are many sources of noise that may be present. Not the least of these is the noise introduced by the sensor sampling the real world, such as a charge coupled device (CCD) or an audio transducer. Many modern steganography techniques are designed to blend in with this naturally occurring noise. Their goal is to add the message in such a way as to be indistinguishable from the noise. To understand the effects of these techniques in digital images, here the properties of digital images and of statistical noise are reviewed.

As with any sensor, an imaging device is subject to noise. Imaging devices exhibit two basic types of noise: deterministic and stochastic. The first, deterministic noise includes two types of noise: dark noise and bias noise. The stochastic types of noise are generally attributed to two effects: first photon or Poisson noise, and second electronic noise or Gaussian noise. Each of these forms of noise are present in varying degrees in both CCD and complementary metal oxide semiconductor (CMOS) style photo sensors.

First, two deterministic effects are generated by the imaging device—dark noise and bias noise. Dark noise or dark current is an accumulation of heat-generated electrons within the photo sensor. Instead of only measuring photon induced electrons from the sensor, other electrons from the device itself are also measured. This effect is highly repeatable given a reasonably constant temperature over a similar period of time. Readout noise is generated by errors in reading electrons from the photon detector. This is largely a function of the amplifier design so is also highly repeatable. The constant nature of these effects has led to design improvements that measure and remove these fixed effects negating the need for an explicit model.

Two sources of random noise are also present in digital images. The first random effect is due to variations in electronic components. This effect is often attributed to thermal effects on the electronic components. In modern digital cameras, this effect is generally small and can be modeled as additive noise, independent of the image, following a Gaussian distribution.

The final source of noise is the stochastic nature of the photon. Photons do not arrive uni-

Figure 3. Clean image used in noise examples

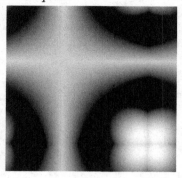

Table 1. Properties of the Gaussian distribution

$$\text{If } X \sim N\left(\mu_X, \sigma_X^2\right) \text{ and } Y \sim N\left(\mu_Y, \sigma_Y^2\right) \text{ then,}$$

$$aX + b \sim N\left(a\mu_X + b, \left(a\sigma_X\right)^2\right)$$

$$X + Y \sim N\left(\mu_X + \mu_Y, \sigma_X^2 + \sigma_Y^2\right)$$

$$X - Y \sim N\left(\mu_X - \mu_Y, \sigma_X^2 + \sigma_Y^2\right)$$

formly on any surface. This non-uniform spread of photons leads to small variations in intensity across an image. This effect follows a Poisson distribution and is most often multiplicative in nature, or correlated to the image.

The following sections present some forms of noise relevant to the analysis of steganography. These techniques are summarized in Exhibits 1 and 2. The clean image used for these charts is found in Figure 3. Figure 4 shows the bitplane decomposition of each of these types of noise, giving some intuition for the differences between the types.

Gaussian Noise

In many natural applications involving measurements, the bell-curve is an accurate model of the distribution of the measurements. The bell curve is a member of the family of distributions known as Gaussian distributions. These distributions are so common they are also known as *normal*

distributions. The probability density function (pdf) for the Gaussian random variable,

$$f_X\left(\mu_X, \sigma_X^2\right) = \frac{1}{\sigma_X \sqrt{2\pi}} e^{-\frac{(x - \sigma_X)^2}{2\sigma_X^2}},$$

is a continuous distribution with $X \in \mathbb{R}$. The Gaussian probability distribution is one of the central concepts in probability and statistics. The sum of an arbitrary set of random variables converges to the Gaussian random variable. This property is known as the *central limit theorem* and is the primary reason the Gaussian distribution is so prevalent in practical applications. For any known or unknown sources of variation, the distribution will tend toward the Gaussian distribution as the number of sources increases.

In imaging applications, noise is often approximated as a Gaussian component. This makes a convenient model for hiding steganography. Gaussian random variable is exceedingly easy to generate and is widely available in software libraries. The Gaussian distribution includes several interesting properties. Table 1 enumerates some of these.

Poisson Noise

Many natural problems can be formulated as a series of trials, with each trial having a probability of success or failure. As the number of trials approaches infinity, the probability of getting n successes follows the Poisson distribution. This limit is sometimes known as the *law of rare events*. This term is somewhat misleading as practical examples often involve very large numbers of events such as the number of telephone calls at a switchboard or the number of photons arriving at a surface.

In image-based media, an important form of noise follows the Poisson distribution. This component known as Poisson noise, or photon noise, is due to the random arrival of photons. This random arrival follows the Poisson distribution.

The pdf for the Poisson random variable,

$$f_X(k,\lambda) = \frac{e^{-\lambda}\lambda^k}{k!}.$$

The Poisson is a discrete distribution, where $X \in \mathbb{N}$. A common approximation of the Poisson uses a normal with a mean and variance of λ, this approximation is only justified if λ is large.

This form of noise is often heavily correlated with the image itself, giving rise to a multipli-

Exhibit 1.

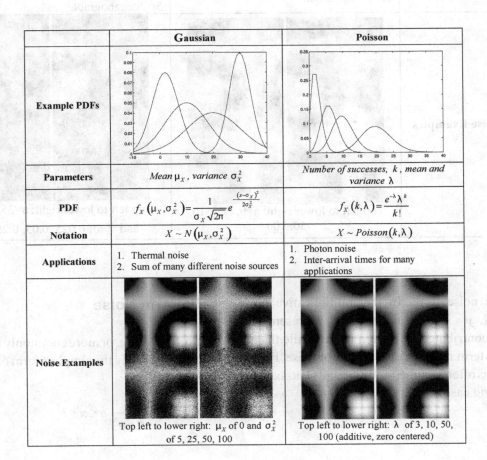

	Gaussian	Poisson
Example PDFs		
Parameters	*Mean* μ_X, *variance* σ_X^2	*Number of successes, k, mean and variance* λ
PDF	$f_X(\mu_X,\sigma_X^2) = \dfrac{1}{\sigma_X\sqrt{2\pi}}e^{-\frac{(x-\sigma_X)^2}{2\sigma_X^2}}$	$f_X(k,\lambda) = \dfrac{e^{-\lambda}\lambda^k}{k!}$
Notation	$X \sim N(\mu_X,\sigma_X^2)$	$X \sim Poisson(k,\lambda)$
Applications	1. Thermal noise 2. Sum of many different noise sources	1. Photon noise 2. Inter-arrival times for many applications
Noise Examples	Top left to lower right: μ_X of 0 and σ_X^2 of 5, 25, 50, 100	Top left to lower right: λ of 3, 10, 50, 100 (additive, zero centered)

Exhibit 2.

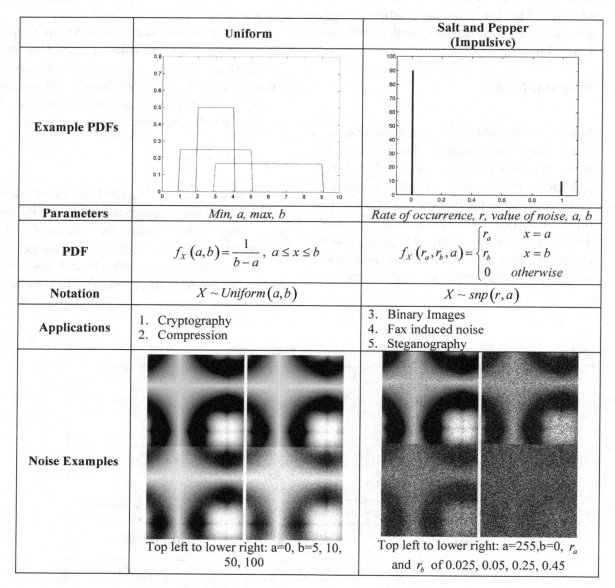

	Uniform	Salt and Pepper (Impulsive)
Example PDFs		
Parameters	*Min, a, max, b*	*Rate of occurrence, r, value of noise, a, b*
PDF	$f_X(a,b) = \dfrac{1}{b-a}, \ a \le x \le b$	$f_X(r_a, r_b, a) = \begin{cases} r_a & x = a \\ r_b & x = b \\ 0 & otherwise \end{cases}$
Notation	$X \sim Uniform(a,b)$	$X \sim snp(r,a)$
Applications	1. Cryptography 2. Compression	3. Binary Images 4. Fax induced noise 5. Steganography
Noise Examples	Top left to lower right: a=0, b=5, 10, 50, 100	Top left to lower right: a=255,b=0, r_a and r_b of 0.025, 0.05, 0.25, 0.45

cative noise term. In the multiplicative noise model, $y = n_p s + n_g$, the term n_p represents the term contributed by photon noise, while the additive term includes other forms of noise. Photon noise is often assumed additive and Gaussian, the limiting case.

Uniform Noise

Uniform noise, or more commonly random noise, is conceptually the simplest form of noise. Its pdf is as follows:

$$f_X(a,b) = \frac{1}{b-a}, \ a \le x \le b$$

Its values are evenly spread between two bounds. While conceptually simple, random noise is actually quite rare in physical phenomena. The reason for this is the reason why the Gaussian is so common. Given a source of pure random noise, the presence of a second source is enough to appear Gaussian. Two applications that generate random noise are compression and encryption. Both try

to remove all *predictable* information from a bit stream. What remains are the *unpredictable* bits, which approach a uniform distribution.

Salt-and-Pepper Noise

Salt-and-pepper noise is a form of noise commonly found in binary images. This form of noise in

Exhibit 3.

	Noisy Image				Noise Only			
	Bit 4	Bit 5	Bit 6	Bit 7	Bit 4	Bit 5	Bit 6	Bit 7
Clean								
	Bit 0	Bit 1	Bit 2	Bit 3	Bit 0	Bit 1	Bit 2	Bit 3
Gaussian $\sigma = 5$	Bit 4	Bit 5	Bit 6	Bit 7	Bit 4	Bit 5	Bit 6	Bit 7
	Bit 0	Bit 1	Bit 2	Bit 3	Bit 0	Bit 1	Bit 2	Bit 3
Uniform $b = 5$	Bit 4	Bit 5	Bit 6	Bit 7	Bit 4	Bit 5	Bit 6	Bit 7
	Bit 0	Bit 1	Bit 2	Bit 3	Bit 0	Bit 1	Bit 2	Bit 3
Poisson $\lambda = 5$	Bit 4	Bit 5	Bit 6	Bit 7	Bit 4	Bit 5	Bit 6	Bit 7
	Bit 0	Bit 1	Bit 2	Bit 3	Bit 0	Bit 1	Bit 2	Bit 3
Salt and Pepper $r = 0.25$	Bit 4	Bit 5	Bit 6	Bit 7	Bit 4	Bit 5	Bit 6	Bit 7
	Bit 0	Bit 1	Bit 2	Bit 3	Bit 0	Bit 1	Bit 2	Bit 3

images results in saturated pixels. Fax machines are a common application that is plagued by salt-and-pepper noise. The pdf for salt-and-pepper noise is as follows:

$$f_X\left(r_a, r_b, a\right) = \begin{cases} r_a & x = a \\ r_b & x = b \\ 0 & \textit{otherwise} \end{cases}$$

This pdf is a generalization of the physical effect of saturating a pixel, also known as *impulsive* noise. In this case, both the rate of occurrence and the value of the pixel are parameters of the model. The general form of salt-and-pepper noise shown in the noise table is a convenient model for many types of steganography.

ARTIFICIAL "STEGO"-NOISE

When the prisoner Alice wants to send a message to the prisoner Bob, the only means to send this message is through a channel that is monitored by the warden. In order to plot their escape, Alice must hide her message.

In the digital age, communication is dominated by the use of the Internet. In this media, one of the most prolific forms of communication is the digital image. There are a number of forms of

steganography for the digital image. Those that involve changing the image (not all of them do) to embed information generally fall into one of several forms. The simplest methods involve modification of some bits of the image itself. An example is found in Figure 5.

For the warden to learn how to detect this hidden information, it is important to understand the basic principles of each form of information hiding. This section introduces several methods.

Embedding Methods

The simplest image-based steganography technique is to replace the least significant information, the least significant bit (LSB), in the image with information from the secret message. Digital media, either image or audio, contains information at a precision that is beyond what a human can perceive. This extra precision is included simply due to the nature of the sampling devices and is often removed when undergoing lossy compression. If instead of removing the extra precision for lossy compression, these bits are replaced in a systematic way, many bits can be hidden within a single image.

The assumption of this technique is that the addition of this noise will not be noticeable to the observer, even an electronic observer. On average, only one-half of the LSBs in an image

Figure 5. Stego-embedding, left: Message, middle: Clean image, right: Stego-image containing both

Figure 6. First seven bit-planes of the glacier image available for use in +/- k embedding

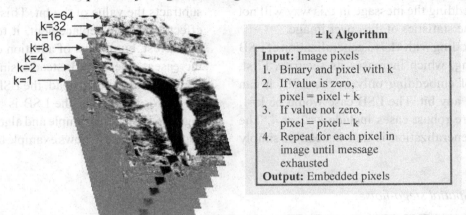

± k Algorithm

Input: Image pixels
1. Binary and pixel with k
2. If value is zero,
   pixel = pixel + k
3. If value not zero,
   pixel = pixel – k
4. Repeat for each pixel in image until message exhausted

Output: Embedded pixels

Figure 7. Color layers and bitplanes

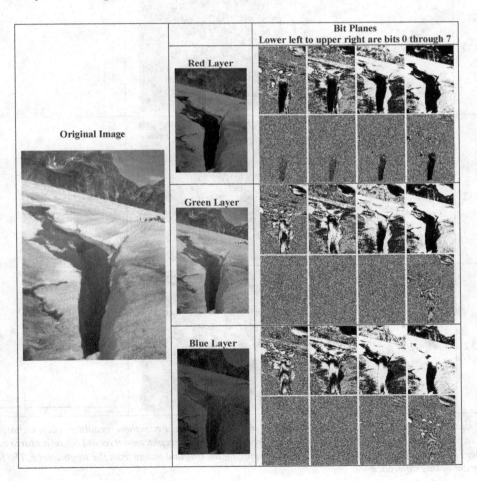

are changed by embedding and it is assumed that embedding the message in this way will not change the statistics of the cover image.

Embedding with ±k is a generalization of LSB embedding, which increases its security. First, instead of embedding only in the LSB, it can embed in any bit. The LSB case would be k=1, other more robust cases include k=2 or 4. The second generalization is that instead of simply

replacing the existing bit, the technique adds or subtracts the value of the bit. This has the same effect as simple replacement, it toggles the bit of interest, but the act of addition or subtraction increases the security. Instead of simply replacing the LSB with data, instead, the LSB is moved by ±k based on whether the LSB is a one or zero. Figure 6 shows an example and algorithm for this approach. Figure 7 shows example bitplanes from

Table 2. Spatial stego-noise

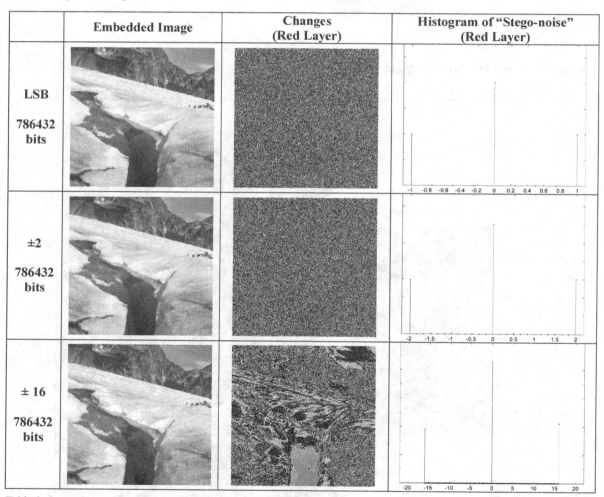

Table 2 shows the analysis of several different types of steganography. From these graphics, each technique embeds using a change in pixel value of ±1, or ±k. From a noise representation either replacement as in LSB or additive noise as ±k appears the same. The second column shows the residual of removing the original image from the stego-image. The third column shows a histogram of this difference.

each of the color layers. Examples of LSB, k=2, and k=16 are shown in Table 2.

The final fundamental approach to hiding information is *binning*. Binning is a trick used to quantize parts of the cover image in a way that itself delivers the information. An example could be developed using a JPEG compression. Bits could be represented by encoding different areas of an image at different quantization levels. Quantization quality of 90 could be one, 80 a zero. Choosing one of these two for each 8x8 block in a 512x512 image could effectively deliver 4096 bits. More subtle binning techniques include using a set of bit values to represent a binary zero or one. An example, a zero would be encoded by either 00 or 01, while a one is encoded as a 10 or 11. This approach can be used to guarantee a maximum number of changed bits. The F5 algorithm (Westfield, 2001) uses such an approach. The quantizer index modulation technique (QIM) (Chen & Wornell, 2001) is also a form of binning technique which has an implicit error correction component. These techniques have strong theoretical properties, and can be modeled as noise. Table 4 and Figure 8 show examples with F5.

Spatial vs. Transform Domain

Data formats that use lossy compression techniques, such as JPEGs or MP3s, dominate media on the Internet. The simple spatial domain embedding methods such as LSB or ±k require loss-less media, this makes embedding in the spatial domain less desirable. Instead, the most common image format on the Internet is JPEG. It stores information in the form of cosine transform coefficients. Directly embedding into these cosine domain coefficients is a simple approach that has led to the idea of transform domain steganography. These transform domain techniques have since grown to include domains other than cosine such as Fourier, wavelet, or other transformations.

Each of the basic embedding techniques can be applied in a number of different domains.

Often this significantly increases the security of the technique. Each domain has its advantages. In comparison with a spatial domain pixel, a single transform domain coefficient can generally be modified more than a single pixel without being human detectable. This is due to the property that a single coefficient will contribute to many pixels when reverted back to the spatial domain. The overall contribution of a single coefficient is spread over the entire image diluting the visual impact of the change. This spreading effect can be seen in Tables 3-5. What is very clearly small, salt-and-pepper type noise in the transform domain, is turned into a Gaussian-like distribution when viewed in the spatial domain—a very noise-like embedding.

Many practical codes have been developed using transform domain techniques. An example of this approach can be found in the classic Jsteg program (JPEG-JSteg-V4, n.d.). Jsteg is a ±k embedding technique, where k=1, applied to the cosine-domain JPEG coefficients. It has an additional feature of avoiding embedding in zero-value coefficients. An example can be seen in Table 3.

Other Tricks

On top of the raw embedding techniques, there are a number of tricks various authors have introduced to increase the security of the embedding. Two, more successful examples include spread spectrum techniques and model based techniques.

Spread spectrum methodologies use a technique from communications systems to modify the message bits prior to embedding in the image (Marvel, Boncelet, & Retter, 1999). Instead of simply changing one bit for one bit, this technique encodes a bit as the addition or subtraction of a randomly generated mask. This mask has the effect of spreading one bit across both frequency and space. The key to this technique is the use of orthogonal codes. The expanded bits do not each use the same encoding. Instead, they are

Figure 8. Embedded images, (left to right) Jsteg, F5, model-based

Table 3. Transform domain stego-noise using JSteg

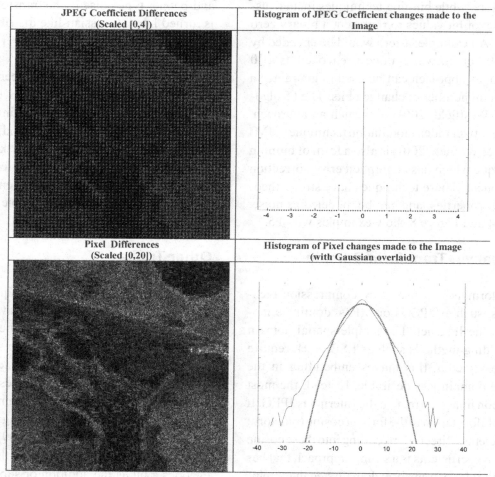

Table 4. Transform domain stego-noise using F5

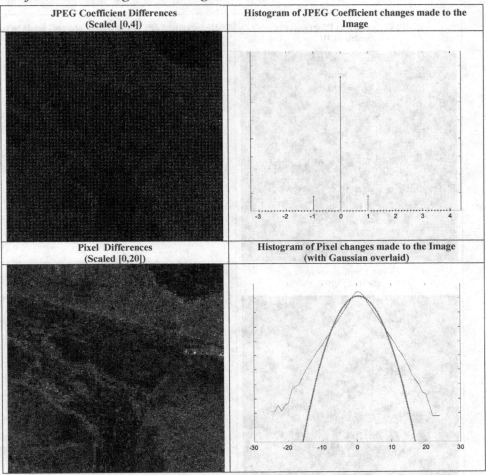

JPEG Coefficient Differences (Scaled [0,4])	Histogram of JPEG Coefficient changes made to the Image
Pixel Differences (Scaled [0,20])	Histogram of Pixel changes made to the Image (with Gaussian overlaid)

expanded to a set of orthogonal codes. When both the embedding and the image are Gaussian distributed, the optimal detector for a spread spectrum approach is a simple correlation with the embedded message.

Another powerful tool that can be used to hide the bits of the stego-message is to embed them in a way that is correlated to the image itself. The model-based approach uses a model of the image to avoid statistically altering it. In Sallee (2004) a technique is described that treats the embedded message as compressed data then *decompresses* it according to the statistics of the image. The resulting decompressed data are

then used to replace the JPEG coefficients. This approach results in a stego-image that is almost identical to the image itself, but introduces correlated noise that corresponds to the action of the encoder used. Again, viewing this sophisticated technique from the perspective of changes to the image, the actual change to the JPEG coefficients is a small salt-and-pepper distribution, but in the spatial domain, this again has a Gaussian-like distribution. Despite the sophistication of this approach, the results are still essentially small Gaussian noise. An example of this effect can be found in Table 5.

Table 5. Transform domain stego-noise using model based embedding

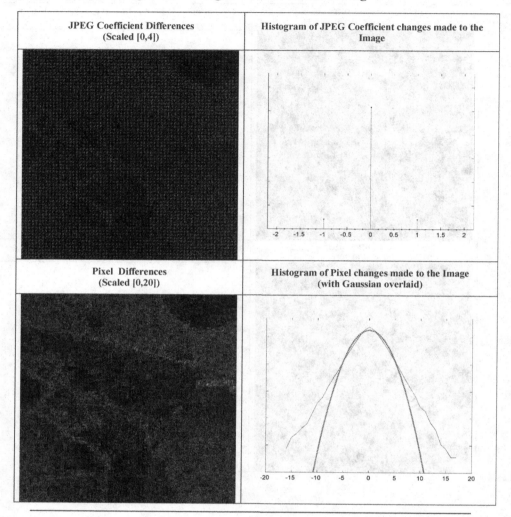

Tables 3-5 show the analysis of several different types of steganography. In each, the top left shows the residual of removing the original image from the stego-image in the JPEG domain. The top right shows a histogram of this difference, each technique embeds using a change in pixel value of ±1, or ±2. From this perspective, either replacement as in Model-based or additive noise as Jsteg appears the same. The bottom left shows the corresponding spatial domain differences. The bottom right shows a histogram of the spatial domain difference, in the spatial domain each embedding results in a Gaussian-like distribution.

THE ACTIVE WARDEN

In the general flow of steganography, when Wendy the warden modifies the information passing between Alice and Bob, she is called an *active warden* (Anderson & Petitcolas, 1998; Craver, 1998; Ettinger, 1998; Fisk, Fisk, Papadopoulos, & Neil, 2003). The active warden can take one of several forms:

1. Detecting steganography and complete deletion of any messages with stego-content
2. Detecting any hidden message and intelligently changing the stego-content

Figure 9. Bitplane original image with full histogram and histogram of bits [0,4]

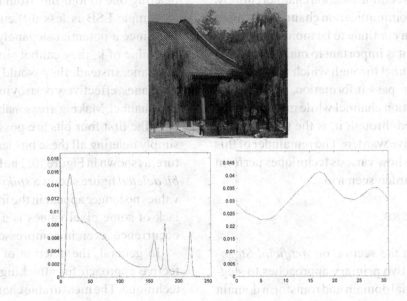

3. Inserting false stego-messages into the communication channel
4. Modifying all messages to disrupt any hidden communication

Each scenario requires a different level of knowledge about the information hiding system. Scenario 1 only requires the ability to detect and sort stego-messages from clean messages. Scenarios 2 and 3, each require complete knowledge including keys. While 4 only requires control of the communication channel.

Practically, scenarios 2 and 3 require more than can be taken for granted when combating steganography. In such situations, many options are open to the warden. The technical aspects of steganalysis are no longer the challenge. Instead, the challenge becomes how to construct a suitable message such that the prisoners will be fooled.

Scenario 1 is a logical extension of the passive warden scenario. The passive warden scenario is discussed in another chapter.

Scenario 4 presents a *likely* scenario, one that presents a challenge in how to render all hidden communication useless, without destroying the communication channel. Do methods exist that can be applied to all messages that will remove hidden content, *without* compromising the innocent information also passing through the channel?

For modern digital steganography, the sad truth is not only is it possible to modify the messages to remove the content, it is easy. Even so-called robust steganography techniques are extremely weak when attacked with simple operations such as filtering and shifting. For a simple example, take a simple linear filter operating on an image with LSB embedding. The linear filter, by definition, will change all the pixels in the image. Whether any of the least significant bits remain the same is random chance. This change is more than sufficient to corrupt the embedded message. Now a question that can be asked, can the intended recipient detect this change?

While it is easy to remove hidden data, the key for the warden to successfully defeat the prisoners' communication is to do so in a way that the prisoners cannot detect. If the prisoners suspect that they cannot reliably communicate through the channel, they will adjust tactics, possibly abandoning this communication channel entirely. As long as the communication channel continues to be used, it can continue to be monitored. Thus, for the warden, it is important to maintain a communication channel through which the prisoners believe they can pass information. Maintaining the communication channel while modifying the messages passed through it, is the true problem faced by the active warden. The remainder of this section presents how various techniques perform in the active warden scenario.

Simple Attacks

As discussed in the section on *Artificial Stego-Noise* there are two primary approaches to steganography: spatial domain and transform domain methods. The first includes techniques such as ±k and LSB that require the use of raw images. The second includes techniques such as F5 or JSteg, which require JPEG images. Each has a simple, intuitive method of attack, first the deletion of bits for spatial methods, and second, the re-compression of a JPEG image. In this section, we explore the ability to detect these methods and the effectiveness of each applied to four common steganography methods.

The two *spatial* methods of steganography introduced in the section on *Artificial Stego-Noise* are LSB and ±k. These methods are notoriously easy for an attacker to destroy. Simple deletion of bits is enough to destroy the message. The question remains, is deleting or shuffling a bit-plane a valid method of removing the hidden information while preserving the image? Can the recipient detect this modification?

Perceptually, a human cannot perceive the LSB in an 8-bit image. In fact, for a human observer, the deletion of any of the first 4-bit planes is not perceivable for many images. However, using even the simplest statistical techniques the deletion of a bitplane becomes easy to identify. Figure 10

shows the histograms and images resulting from deleting one to four bits from the image.

Simple LSB is less difficult to modify than ±k. Since a potential steganalyst does not know the value of k, they cannot simply delete the kth bit-plane. Instead, they would need to delete all bit-planes, effectively destroying the communication channel. Making a reasonable assumption that only the first four bits are possible hiding areas, simply deleting all these bits leaves a clear signature, as shown in Figure 10. The histograms of each *bit deleted* figure shows a *spiky* behavior as some values no longer appear in the image. This regular lack of some pixel values is a highly unnatural occurrence, even in compressed images.

In general, the deletion of bits is not an effective approach for attacking a steganography technique. The measurable change to the image is very distinct and sufficient to tip off Alice or Bob that messages are actively being changed. Once tipped off, they are free to adjust tactics to defeat this deletion. Beyond its detectability, the premise of deleting a bit-plane relies on knowing where all the embedded information will reside. This relies on knowing the embedding mechanism, which may or may not be a realistic assumption.

Another method of attacking a spatial embedding method is to shuffle the bits in the appropriate bit-plane, or inject randomized bits. This approach is equivalent to the original steganography problem, as embedding noise or shuffling bits is effectively hiding new information in the same image. The effectiveness of the technique applied to the active warden scenario depends on knowledge of the original embedding mechanism. Embedding the wrong bit-plane will not be an effective attack. While embedding in the correct bit-plane assumes a level of knowledge about the embedding mechanism that may not be realistic.

While spatial domain methods are important, JPEG-based media dominate the Internet. Three *transform domain* techniques were introduced in the section, *Artificial Stego-Noise*, both using JPEG-based methods. JSteg, F5, and model-based

Figure 10. Measuring the effects of bit deletion on the image, top to bottom, deleting bits 0 thru 4, left to right, the image, the full histogram, and the histogram of bits 0 through 4

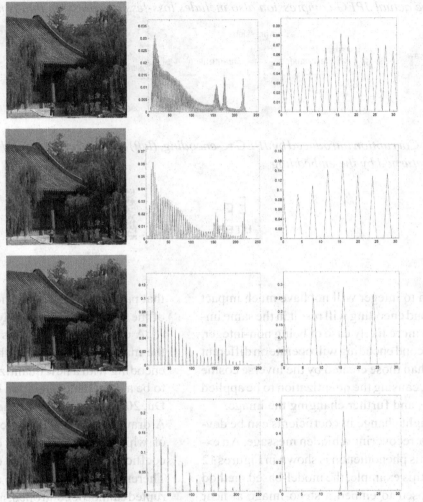

embedding are all techniques for hiding in the coefficients of the cosine domain.

While transform domain methods are generally considered more robust, since they should be less sensitive to the spatial LSB modifications discussed in the previous section. In both cases studied here, JSteg and model-based are extremely sensitive to changes to the JPEG coefficients. If the spatial domain changes enough to modify JPEG coefficients or the JPEG coefficients themselves are changed, the results are disastrous for the embedded data.

A simple method of changing JPEG coefficients is to re-encode the image. The process of JPEG compression is a lossy process. Passing a compressed image through compression a second time will not result in the same image. The reason can be seen in Figure 11. While the results of the two non-invertible processes shown will be the same if applied to the same raw image, applying a second time to a compressed image will *most likely* change the image further. This is dependent on the exact values produced by the inverse cosine transform. If these values are close to integers, the

Figure 11. Approximate JPEG compression and decompression algorithms, note passing the recovered image back through the same process (same quantization) will not likely result in the same compressed image. The actual JPEG compression also includes loss-less compression that is not shown here.

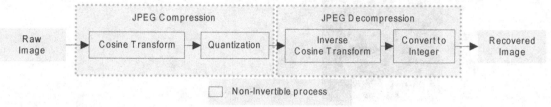

Figure 12. Corruption introduced by JPEG re-encoding, (left) encoded message and (right) the corrupted message returned by the embedding

conversion to integer will not have much impact so the second encoding will result in the same image. In the more likely case of being non-integer, then the second encoding will operate on different numbers than those created by the inverse cosine transform, causing the quantization to be applied differently, and further changing the image.

This slight change in coefficients can be devastating for recovering a hidden message. An example of this phenomenon is shown in Figures 12 and 13. In this example, the model-based method has been used to embed a stego-image at near maximum capacity. The stego-embedded image was read and re-encoded using the same quality, as well as the same quantization table. This resulted in changes to nearly half of the embedded bits. In the case of Figure 12, part of the message can be recovered, (the white area on the left of the image) while the rest is not recognizable. This highlights the fact that a change of ±1 in a single important JPEG coefficient is enough to throw the model-based stego-decoder off and corrupt all of the data received. Again, in Figure 12 the left portion of the message is correctly recovered, as no important JPEG coefficients are changed within

that part of the message. Though, the remainder of the message is completely lost.

A critical feature of this method of attack is the maintained quality of the image. While re-encoding with a new quantization table is known to be a detectable operation (Fridrich, Goljan, & Du, 2001), encoding with the same table has not. A drawback to this approach is the uncertainty of which coefficients will be changed. Which coefficients will be affected cannot be predicted. Therefore, which part of the message will be corrupted cannot be controlled, nor can it be predicted whether *any* of the message will be changed at all. It is even possible to design images insensitive to this attack.

Image Quality

An important aspect of the active warden for image-based steganography is the preservation of the quality of an image. Visual quality is a quantity that is difficult to define and measure. Many researchers have attempted to develop metrics to assess visual quality. These metrics include the mean square error (MSE), visual information

Figure 13. Corruption introduced by JPEG re-encoding, even using the same quantization table, left, original image, middle, the difference in the spatial domain and right the difference in JPEG coefficients of the red component of the image

Table 6. Measures of image quality

$$MSE\left(i,\hat{i}\right) = L_2\left(i,\hat{i}\right) = \frac{1}{K}\sum_{i=1}^{K}\left|i_i - \hat{i}_i\right|^2$$

$$SSIM(x,y) = \frac{\left(2\mu_x\mu_y + C_x\right)\left(2\sigma_{xy} + C_y\right)}{\left(\mu_x^2 + \mu_y^2 + C_x\right)\left(\mu_x^2 + \mu_y^2 + C_y\right)}$$

$$VIF\left(E,F\right) = \frac{\sum_{j \in subbands} I\left(C;F\mid s\right)}{\sum_{j \in subbands} I\left(C;E\mid s\right)}$$

fidelity (VIF) (Sheikh & Bovik, 2006), and the structural similarity index (SSIM) (Wang, Bovik, Sheikh, & Simoncelli, 2004).

A commonly referenced method of determining image quality is the MSE. This is a simple distance measure, also known as the L_2 norm, and has the advantage of being conceptually and computationally simple. This method has been shown to be of questionable value when applied to images due to the vast array of very different images that show similar MSE (Sheikh, Bovik, & De Veciana, 2005).

Two techniques that are more sophisticated are the SSIM and the VIF. The SSIM is a measure based on the idea that the human visual system appears to capture and use structural information more than other image features (Wang et al., 2004). The VIF uses a statistical model to determine if the amount of *human perceivable*

information present in an image deviates from the reference image (Sheikh & Bovik, 2006). These three criteria are shown in Table 6, where i and $\hat{i}$ are the reference and test images, μ is the mean, σ is the variance, C is the covariance E, and F are wavelet domain images.

Denoising for Message Removal

In the chapter XI, *On Steganalysis and Clean Image Estimation*, a number of denoising methods are introduced. Each technique has a much different impact on the image than simple bit deletion. Figure 14 shows the images and resulting histograms from eight denoising techniques, including those calibration techniques used in steganalysis by Ker and Farid.

From Figure 14, it is clear that the statistical effects of bit deletion are not present. Visually,

Figure 14. Images after denoising applied to the red component of the image found in Figure 9, (top left across to bottom right), original, mean filter, linear wavelet predictor, decimation through averaging, VisuShrink, BLS-GSM, Polynomial, non-local means

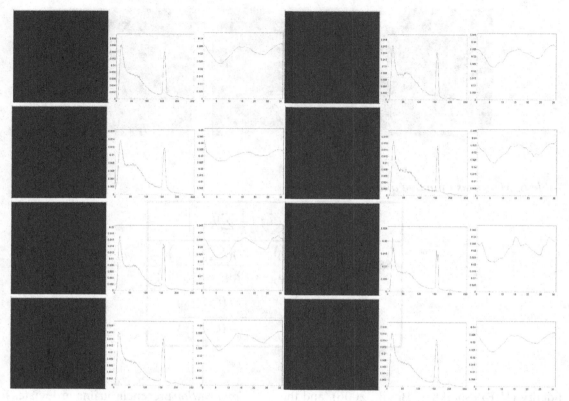

artifacts appear from using Farid's linear predictor, there is also a clear visual difference using Ker's technique that is not shown. Ker's decimation changes the size of the image so it is impractical for the active warden scenario, as Alice and Bob will eventually notice a consistent change in size. Of the other techniques, many appear roughly equivalent. The BLS-GSM technique tends to change the [0, 4] bit histogram the most, while *VisuShrink* has the most impact on the full histogram.

Since these denoising techniques all affect more than a single bitplane, it becomes important to ensure that the visual impact of the technique is not noticeable. Figures 15 and 16 show the visual impact of each of the five denoising techniques. Of these, the mean and Gaussian smoothers, *Visu-*

Shrink and BLS-GSM and all introduce different levels of blur, while the polynomial technique has less of an impact on the image. The NL-means method (not shown) performs poorly for low noise conditions. In the case of LSB embedding it does not alter the image making it useless for application as an active warden. (This feature is specifically designed into the NL-means implementation for use in texture synthesis where small details can be important.)

Tables 7 and 8 show the results from applying the denoising approaches to several embedding techniques. Sixty images were chosen randomly from a database of over 10,000. Each was embedded using each of four embedding methods, LSB, ±k, JSteg, and model-based embedding. The tables include three image quality metrics to

Figure 15. Image comparison of (top left to lower right), original stego-image, smoothed with spatial averaging, Gaussian smoothed, denoised via BLS-GSM, denoised with VisuShrink, and denoised with the polynomial threshold. The polynomial threshold appears to come closest to the original image.

Figure 16. Zoom-in comparison of (top left to lower right), original stego-image, smoothed with spatial averaging, Gaussian smoothed, denoised via BLS-GSM, denoised with VisuShrink, and denoised with the polynomial threshold

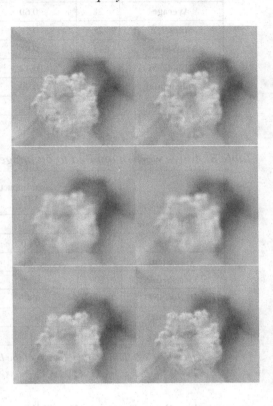

assess the impact of each denoising technique in its role as an active warden. From the tables, the denoising techniques each appear to have trade-offs. Non-local means preserves the image too well, not changing any bits. Polynomial threshold does better at making changes while preserving the image but also leaves more data. *VisuShrink* seems to be the best for changing all the bits at the cost of some image blurring, even out performing the more complex technique BLS-GSM.

CONCLUSION

In creating digital media, such as images or audio files, there are many possible sources of noise. Many modern steganography techniques can be modeled as an artificial version of these noise sources. These techniques generally affect the image in ways that mimic naturally occurring noise. For simple techniques such as LSB, this is intentional. More sophisticated techniques, such as the model-based approach, intentionally embed in information-containing regions of the

Table 7. Active warden applied to 60 images with message length of 2K bits

Operation	Visual Impact MSE	Visual Impact VIF	Visual Impact SSID	LSB BER	+- k BER	JSteg BER	Model BER	Execution Time (s)
Jpeg Re-encode	-	-	-	N/A	N/A	0.4	0	0
Average	28	0.60	0.94	0.5	0.5	0.5	0.5	0.2
Gaussian	28	0.58	0.92	0.5	0.5	0.5	0.5	0.2
VisuShrink	13	0.85	0.94	0.5	0.5	0.5	0.5	0.4
BLS-GSM	17	0.42	088	0.5	0.5	0.5	0.5	80
Polynomial	0.8	0.99	0.99	0.4	0.5	0.5	0	10
NL-Means	0	1	1	0	0	0.4	0	1500

Table 8. Active warden applied to 60 images with message length of 256K

Operation	Visual Impact MSE	Visual Impact VIF	Visual Impact SSID	LSB BER	+- k BER	JSteg BER	Model BER	Execution Time (s)
Jpeg Re-encode	-	-	-	N/A	N/A	*	*	0
Average	28	0.60	0.93	0.5	0.5	*	*	0.2
Gaussian	48	0.50	0.92	0.5	0.5	*	*	0.2
VisuShrink	10	0.54	0.94	0.5	0.5	*	*	0.4
BLS-GSM	17	0.42	0.87	0.5	0.5	*	*	80
Polynomial	0.4	0.98	0.99	0.3	0.3	*	*	10
NL-Means	0	1	1	0	0	*	*	1500

* recovered message less than half the length of the bits embedded

image rather than the noise. Regardless of the intent, most modern approaches affect the image in a very similar, noise-like manner.

This chapter has presented the importance of noise to steganography. Further, under the active warden, any modification to messages in the warden's communication channel must be made in a covert manner. If the prisoners believe they cannot reliably communicate through the channel, they will adjust tactics until communication becomes reliable. For the warden, the challenge is to consistently corrupt any passing messages without allowing the prisoners an opportunity to defeat his/her effort. With this goal in mind, the removal of the stego-message without corrupting the cover requires using very sophisticated methods.

Despite the connections between steganography and noise, the state of the art in image denoising approaches are not effective. They are simply not designed for the high quality, low noise images that are common in steganalysis. Much research remains in shaping this broad field for use in active or passive steganalysis.

FUTURE RESEARCH DIRECTIONS

The fields of steganography and steganalysis are in their infancy. The last 10 years have brought rapid improvements in the understanding of the field. The major challenge in digital image steganography is to model an image to identify changes that would be undetectable. The development of such an image model is the most important and most challenging research direction in the field. This leads toward a theoretically secure form of steganography.

Other challenges include exploring JPEG 2000-based media and raising the capacity of current steganographic approaches. Further, methods are needed to improve robustness to attack, including desynchronization, image compression, and sophisticated denoising-based attacks.

In addition, a re-evaluation of steganography from a cryptologic perspective may lead to new, unexplored directions.

REFERENCES

Agaian, S. (2005). Steganography & steganalysis: An overview of research & challenges. In *Network Security and Intrusion Detection, NATO Proceedings*.

Agaian, S., & Rodriguez, B. M. (2006). Basic steganalysis techniques for the digital media forensics examiner. In *Digital Crime and Forensic Science in Cyberspace* (pp. 175-225).

Anderson, R. J., & Petitcolas, F. A. P. (1998). On the limits of steganography. *IEEE Journal on Selected Areas in Communications, 16*(4), 474-481.

Avcibas, I., Memon, N., & Sankur, B. (2003). Steganalysis using image quality metrics. *IEEE Transactions on Image Processing, 12*(2), 221-229.

Cachin, C. (2004). An information-theoretic model for steganography. *Information and Computation, 192*(1), 41-56.

Chen, B., & Wornell, G. W. (2001). Quantization index modulation: A class of provably good methods for digital watermarking and information embedding. *IEEE Transactions on Information Theory, 47*(4), 1423-1443.

Cox, I. J., Miller, M., & Bloom, J. (2001). *Digital watermarking: Principles & practice* (1st ed.). San Francisco: Morgan Kaufmann.

Craver, S. (1998). On public-key steganography in the presence of an active warden. *Information Hiding, 1525*, 355-368.

Ettinger, J. M. (1998). Steganalysis and game equilibria. *Information Hiding, 1525*, 319-328.

Fisk, G., Fisk, M., Papadopoulos, C., & Neil, J. (2003, October 7-9). Eliminating steganography in Internet traffic with active wardens. In *Information Hiding: 5th International Workshop, IH 2002*, Noordwijkerhout, The Netherlands. *Revised Papers* (Vol. 2578, pp. 18-35). Berlin: Springer.

Fridrich, J., Goljan, M., & Du, R. (2001). *Steganalysis based on JPEG compatibility*. Paper presented at the Proceedings of SPIE Multimedia Systems and Applications IV, Denver, CO.

JPEG-JSteg-V4. (n.d.). Retrieved from http://www.funet.fi/pub/crypt/steganography/jpeg-jsteg-v4.diff.gz

Katzenbeisser, S., & Penticolas, F. A. P. (2000). *Information hiding techniques for steganography and digital watermarking*. Norwood, MA: Artech House.

Marvel, L. M., Boncelet, C. G., Jr., & Retter, C. T. (1999). Spread spectrum image steganography. *IEEE Transactions on Image Processing, 8*(8), 1075-1083.

Moulin, P., & Koetter, R. (2005). Data-hiding codes. *Proceedings of the IEEE, 93*(12), 2083-2126.

Provos, N., & Honeyman, P. (2001). *Detecting steganographic content on the Internet*. Ann Arbor, MI: University of Michigan, Center for Information Technology Integration.

Provos, N., & Honeyman, P. (2003). Hide and seek: An introduction to steganography. *IEEE Security and Privacy Magazine, 1*(3), 32-44.

Sallee, P. (2004). Model-based steganography. *Digital Watermarking, 2939*, 154-167.

Sheikh, H. R., & Bovik, A. C. (2006). Image information and visual quality. *IEEE Transactions on Image Processing, 15*(2), 430-444.

Sheikh, H. R., Bovik, A. C., & De Veciana, G. (2005). An information fidelity criterion for image quality assessment using natural scene statistics. *IEEE Transactions on Image Processing, 14*(12), 2117-2128.

Sheikh, H. R., Sabir, M. F., & Bovik, A. C. (2006). A statistical evaluation of recent full reference image quality assessment algorithms. *IEEE Transactions on Image Processing, 15*(11), 3440-3451.

Simmons, G. J. (1984). The prisoners' problem and the subliminal channel. In *Advances in Cryptology, Proceedings of CRYPTO '83* (pp. 51-67). New York: Plenum Press.

Wang, Z., Bovik, A. C., Sheikh, H. R., & Simoncelli, E. P. (2004). Image quality assessment: From error visibility to structural similarity. *IEEE Transactions on Image Processing, 13*(4), 600-612.

Wayner, P. (2002). *Disappearing cryptography—Information hiding: Steganography and Watermarking* (2nd ed.). San Francisco: Morgan Kaufmann.

Westfield, A. (2001). High capacity despite getter steganalysis (F5-A steganographic algorithm). In *Information Hiding: 4th International Workshop* (Vol. 2137, pp. 289-302). Springer-Verlag.

Zollner, J., Federrath, H., Klimant, H., Pfitzmann, A., Piotraschke, R., Westfeld, A., et al. (1998). Modeling the security of steganographic systems. *Information Hiding, 1525*, 344-354.

ADDITIONAL READING

A general introductory text to steganography and data hiding concepts can be found in *Disappearing Cryptography* (Wayner, 2002), or Katzenbeisser and Penticolas (2000), or the article by Provos and Honeyman (2003). A general introductory article for steganalysis can be found in Agaian and Rodriguez (2006), and for steganography Agaian (2005). See Cox, Miller, and Bloom (2001) for the watermarking perspective on data hiding.

For a theoretical introduction to data hiding, the work of Moulin in Moulin and Koetter (2005) is an excellent start. Then see Cachin (2004), Zollner et al. (1998), and Ettinger (1998) for different theoretical perspectives on the basic problem.

The paper by Sheikh, Sabir, and Bovik (2006) reviews a number of current image quality metrics. See Avcibas, Memon, and Sankur (2003) for a perspective on image quality in steganalysis.

See Provos and Honeyman (2001) and Fisk et al. (2003) for Internet implementation related issues and results.

Chapter IX
Visibility Control and Quality Assessment of Watermarking and Data Hiding Algorithms

Patrick Le Callet
Polytech'Nantes, University of Nantes, IRCCyN Lab, France

Florent Autrusseau
Polytech'Nantes, University of Nantes, IRCCyN Lab, France

Patrizio Campisi
Università degli Studi Roma TRE, Italy

ABSTRACT

In watermarking and data hiding context, it may be very useful to have methods checking the invisibility of the inserted data or at least, checking the objective quality after the mark embedding or after an attack on the watermarked media. Many works exist in the literature dealing with quality assessment mainly focused on compression application. Nevertheless, visual quality assessment should include special requirements that depend on the application context. This chapter presents an extended review of both subjective and objective quality assessment of images and video in the field of watermarking and data hiding applications.

INTRODUCTION

In the past few years, there has been an explosion in the use and distribution of digital multimedia data, essentially driven by the diffusion of the Internet. In this scenario, watermarking techniques have been devised to answer the ever-growing need to protect the intellectual property (copyright) of digital still images, video sequences, or audio from piracy attacks in a networked environment like the World Wide Web. Although copyright protection was the very first application of watermarking, different uses have been recently proposed in literature. Fingerprinting, copy control, broadcast monitoring, data authentication, multimedia indexing, content-based retrieval applications, medical imaging applications, covert communication (steganography), and error concealment, (Barni & Bartolini, 2004; Doerr & Dugelay, 2003; Kundur, Su, & Hatzinakos, 2004) are only a few of the new applications where watermarking can be usefully employed. Moreover, digital watermarking has been recently used for quality assessment purposes (Campisi, Carli, Giunta, & Neri, 2003; Ninassi, Le Callet, & Autrusseau, 2006), as well as for improved data compression (Campisi, Kundur, Hatzinakos, & Neri, 2002; Campisi & Piva, 2006).

Roughly speaking data hiding is the general process by which a discrete information stream is merged within media content. The general watermark embedding procedure consists of embedding a watermark sequence, which is usually binary, into host data by means of a key. In the detection/extraction phase, the key is used to verify either the presence of the embedded sequence or to extract the embedded mark. When considering a watermarking scheme, depending on its specific application, different requirements need to be achieved. One of them is the *perceptual invisibility* of the superimposed mark onto the host data. This implies that the alterations caused by the watermark embedding into the data should not degrade their perceptual quality. Moreover, when these techniques are used to preserve the copyright ownership with the purpose of avoiding unauthorized data duplications, the embedded watermark should be detectable. This is required even if malicious attacks or non-deliberate modifications (i.e., filtering, compression, etc.) affect the embedded watermark. This requirement is known as watermark *security*. When the watermark is required to be resistant only to non-malicious manipulations the watermarking techniques is referred to as *robust*. For some applications, when the robustness requirement is severely required, each attempt of removing the mark should result in irreversible data quality degradation. As

a consequence the quality of the image must noticeably decrease before the removal attempt succeeds. However in some applications the host data are intended to undergo a limited number of signal processing operations. Therefore we talk about *semi-fragile* watermarking when the watermark needs to be robust only to a limited number of set of manipulations, while leaving the perceived quality of the host data intact. On the contrary, when unwanted modifications of the watermarked data affect even the extracted watermark, the embedding scheme is known as *fragile*. Fragile watermarking can be used to obtain information about the tampering process. In fact, it indicates whether or not the data has been altered and supplies localization information as to where the data was altered. *Capacity* is another watermarking requirement, referring to the number of bits of information that can be embedded in the original data, which needs to be fulfilled, depending on the specific application. These requirements conflict each other. Therefore the optimal trade-off is strictly tied to the target application.

A comprehensive review of the different needed requirements depending on the intended application is given in Fridrich (1999) and they are summarized in Table 1 where a score from 1 to 7 indicating in increasing order the level of importance of the specific requirement is specified for a class of applications.

Because of the proliferation of watermarking algorithms and their applications, some benchmarks (Michiels & Macq, 2006; Pereira, Voloshynovskiy, Madueno, Marchand-Maillet, & Pun, 2001; Petitcolas, Anderson, & Kuhn, 1998) have been proposed in order to allow a fair comparison among watermarking algorithms in terms of robustness against various attacks. However, no equal attention has been devoted to the proposition of benchmarks tailored to assess the watermark perceptual transparency or, equivalently, to perform the watermarked image quality assessment. Thus, the mean square error (MSE) or the peak

Table 1. Requirements depending on the intended application (C stands for Capacity, R, stands for Robustness, I: Invisibility, S: Security, EC: Embedding Complexity, DC: Detection Complexity)

Requirements						Applications
C	R	I	S	EC	DC	
7	2	7	7	2	2	Covert Communication, Steganography
1	7	4	7	2	2	Copyright protection of images (authentication)
3	7	4	7	1	6	Fingerprinting (traitor-tracing)
4	5	4	1	2	7	Adding captions to images, additional information, …
2	6	5	7	7	2	Image integrity protection (fraud detection)
2	5	4	7	1	7	Copy control in DVD
2	6	4	7	1	7	Intelligent browsers, automatic copyright information, …

signal-to-noise ratio (PSNR) are commonly used by the watermarking community to assess the fidelity of embedding algorithms. However, the PSNR is not well suited to take into account the visual impairments present in an image, since it gives a measure of the statistical differences between an original image and a distorted version (marked one) and statistical differences do not represent visual impairments.

Quality assessment is achievable either through subjective tests or through objective metrics. Obviously, the best way to assess the visual quality of a watermarked image would be to run subjective experiments, according to standardized protocols, which are defined in order to obtain correct, universal, and reliable quality evaluations, in which several human observers are asked to judge the perceived image quality according to a predefined protocol and a defined quality scale. However, the use of subjective tests is a time-consuming approach. Furthermore, the analysis of the obtained results is not straightforward. Therefore, a great effort has been devoted by both the academic and the industrial community to develop objective metrics able to quantitatively evaluate the amount of degradation undergone by an image or a video sequence. Specifically the definition of perceptual objective metrics highly correlated with the subjective qual-

ity scores provided by observers would allow to reliably predict the perceived quality of images or videos thus leading to a great improvement in the quality assessment field.

Specifically, as for subjective quality assessment, several International Telecommunications Union (ITU) recommendations describe the environment, normalized conditions as well as the protocols needed to conduct experiments. Nevertheless, there is no clear statement about data hiding requirements. Moreover, as many labs involved in data hiding do not have the facilities to conduct subjective experiments and because subjective tests are time consuming and expensive, the use of objective assessment is strongly required. As mentioned before, several works about objective quality metrics have been published in the literature. However, it is important to highlight that most objective quality assessment metrics are specifically designed for coding algorithms covering a quality range going from excellent to very bad. No quality assessment metrics have ever been specifically proposed for watermarking applications and the design of an ad hoc tool is very challenging for the data hiding community.

The purpose of this chapter is mainly to give researchers working in the watermarking field, but not directly involved in quality assessment, the tools to test the imperceptibility requirement for watermarked images. Specifically, in the second section we briefly describe the benchmarking tools available in literature, which are mainly oriented towards robustness assessment and we address the invisibility issue in watermarking. In the third section we review subjective quality assessment as in the ITU-R-BT.500-11 recommendation (ITU, 2004a) and we provide a subjective protocol suited to watermarking quality assessment along with some experimental results for some tested watermarking algorithms. In the fourth section, state-of-the–art, general-purpose objective metrics are described. Their suitability for imperceptibility quality assessment of watermarking techniques is discussed in the fifth section where the correlation between the subjective evaluation and the objective assessment is evaluated and widely discussed for all the metrics taken into account and all the tested watermarking techniques. Future research issues and conclusions are drawn in the last two sections.

WATERMARKING QUALITATIVE ASSESSMENT

Benchmarking Watermarking Algorithm

As already pointed out in the Introduction, watermarking algorithms need to fulfill specific requirements, like robustness, perceptual imperceptibility/transparency, security, capacity, and so on according to the specific application. These requirements conflict with each other, therefore a compromise is always necessary. In order to automatically provide an evaluation of these watermarking algorithm characteristics some benchmarks have been proposed in the recent literature.

The first benchmarking suite, namely Stir-Mark, was proposed in Petitcolas et al. (1998) and made available online[1]. The StirMark tool performs a variety of both nonintentional and malicious attacks like cropping, signal enhancement, scaling, JPEG compression, line removal, median filtering, noise addition, affine transform, and random bilinear geometric distortions. After each attack has been performed by the StirMark tool, the watermarking algorithm detector verifies the presence of the mark. The percentage of the correctly detected watermarks is used as the performance score that is used to compare the efficiency of the watermarking algorithms. However, StirMark has some drawbacks that need to be addressed. In fact it does not take into account the embedding and detection time, the method's false alarm probability, moreover the scores obtained using different attacks are all combined with the same weight irrespectively of the probability of occurrence of the considered attack. These considerations have driven the necessity to devise new benchmarking tools overcoming the existing problems. The OptiMark benchmark was presented in Solachidis al. (2001) as an approach able to solve StirMark drawbacks and able to provide several statistical characteristics of an image watermarking scheme. The performance assessment is made by measuring the execution time and the robustness against attacks by means of the receiving operating characteristic (ROC). These figures of merit are then combined by taking into account the probability of occurrence of the considered attack in the considered scenario. An online version of OptiMark has been also made freely available[2]. A second generation benchmark for image watermarking that makes use of a priori information about the watermark and the watermarking algorithms has been proposed in Pereira et al. (2001) and Voloshynovskiy, Pereira, Iquise, and Pun (2001). The so proposed benchmarking tool, namely CheckMark,[3] employs tests like denoising attacks, wavelet compression, watermark copy attack, desyncronization, denoising and compression followed by perceptual remodulation, and random bending. Moreover, in contrast with StirMark where each attack has the same weight irrespective of the probability of occurrence, in CheckMark the performance evaluation is estimated by weighting the attack accordingly to its relevance to the considered application. The need to design a worldwide recognized standard benchmarking tool has also driven the European Community to start in May 2000 a project called Certimark[4] involving both academic and industrial partners, but the project outcome has not been provided to the scientific community.

Although these tools can provide relevant information about the performance of the water-marking method under analysis, they lack flexibility since they are tied to the employed operating system and/or to the used programming language. To allow a better interoperability among researchers thus overcoming the limitations deriving from the heterogeneity of the programming languages and of the operating systems some architectures for cooperative programming have been recently proposed: OpenWatermark[5] (Macq, Dittman, & Delp, 2004; Michiels & Macq, 2006) and Watermark Evaluation Testbed[6] (WET) (Hyung, Ogunleye, Guitar, & Delp, 2004). Specifically, OpenWatermark is a distributed application system where each user can upload a watermarking algorithm and test it. Java technology is used, thus guaranteeing the portability. Currently, both Windows and Linux C or C++ executables as well as Matlab or Python scripts are supported, but new operating systems and programming languages can be added through time. Many attacks are taken into account like geometrical distortions; attacks perpetrated by superimposing, either by adding or by multiplying; noise having different statistical properties like Gaussian, Laplacian, salt-and-pepper, and Poisson noise; format compression; common image processing applications; and malicious attacks; including the StirMark ones. The Watermark Evaluation Testbed is essentially composed by the front end module, the algorithm modules, and the image database. Six embedding algorithms have made available so far. The StirMark 3.1 suite is embedded in the

system. The performance are characterized by using the bit error rate and the ROC.

Therefore, although numerous benchmarking tools (Stirmark, Checkmark, Optimark, OpenWatermark, WET) have been provided since the late 1990's, it appears that special care has been taken more on robustness compared to invisibility/quality assessment. Furthermore, it is worth pointing out that these benchmarking tools use the PSNR, weighted PSNR (Pereira et al., 2001) or the Watson metric (Watson, 1993) to characterize the perceptual quality of the watermarked image. However, as shown in the following, such metrics are quite inappropriate for testing the mark transparency. Moreover, as previously seen in Table 1 the invisibility requirement is about as strong as the robustness one and invisibility, robustness, and capacity are very strongly linked to each others.

Invisibility and Quality Requirement for Data Hiding

In data hiding applications, invisibility is usually a strong requirement. However, it is crucial to distinguish between invisibility and quality. The term invisibility can also refer to the non-detectability. In psychophysics, detection is often checked by presenting at least a reference stimulus and another version including the target to detect. The change of the parameter's target, such as amplitude, affects its detection, for example, its visibility. Within this framework, the double presentation of the reference stimulus and the reference plus the target to the observer is mandatory to allow a target detection. In fact, if access to the reference stimulus is not granted, it is not possible to distinguish in the reference plus target stimulus what is due to the target and what is due to the host signal itself. This issue is more critical nearby visibility threshold or when the target content is spatially or temporally coherent with the reference signal.

When data hiding is the target application, the host media can be considered as the reference stimulus and the mark as the target. However, as for most watermarking applications, only the originator of the multimedia content will have access to the original data, only watermarked versions will be distributed, and therefore the invisibility property as previously defined is not strictly required because conditions to validate it are not fulfilled. Therefore, in this scenario the invisibility requirement is more related to the fact that the target should not introduce incoherence or any visual annoyance. Measuring visual annoyance corresponds to perform quality assessment accordingly to an impairment scale. In the framework of data hiding, we can state that an algorithm fulfills the invisibility requirement if it produces an invisible distortion in the best case and visible but not annoying distortions in the worst case.

Distortions Introduced by Watermarking Algorithms

It is worth pointing out that the distortions that can be introduced in an image by a watermarking algorithm depend on the embedding algorithm itself and on the data content. In order to get perceptual transparency, accordingly to the domain where the watermark is embedded, the mark insertion has to slightly modify the coefficients, which have a high impact on the perceptual appearance of the image. However, if robustness is required, the embedding strength has to be increased thus producing visible artifacts. In Figures 1a and 1b some visual examples of the possible distortions that can be introduced by the watermarking algorithms we have analyzed in this chapter (see Appendix A) and operating in the wavelet, Fourier, and discrete cosine transform (DCT) domain are given. Along with the watermarked image (left column), the error images, that is, the difference between the watermarked image and the original one are shown in the spatial domain (middle col-

umn), and the error Fourier spectra are displayed in the right column. As shown in Figures 1a and 1b, watermarking can introduce very different distortions on the watermarked images either in the spatial or in the frequency domain. Regarding spatial domain, several adaptive strategies seem to be used regarding local content categories (uniform areas, edges, textures, and so on). Common image processing techniques such as lossy coding schemes, introduce mainly distortions in high frequency. On the contrary, it is more difficult to identify such a common behavior for watermarking algorithms since, as it can be easily guessed from the error spectra, the watermarking process can have a spread spectrum, low pass, high pass, band pass behavior among the others.

Subjective vs. Objective Assessment

The following terminology is usually adopted:

- The term *subjective assessment* refers to the determination of the quality or impairment of pictures or video presented to a panel of human assessors in viewing sessions.
- The term *objective perceptual measurement* refers to the performance measurement of a picture or a video by the use of program-like pictures and objective (instrumental) measurement methods to get an indication that approximates the rating that would be obtained from a subjective assessment test. The word perceptual is often omitted even though it is important to distinguish such assessment from signal measurement. In the following, the terms objective measurement, objective metric, and objective assessment may be used interchangeably to refer to objective perceptual measurement.

Image and video processing designers produce new algorithms that raise quality of service considerations when humans are the end user of the service. In the case of data hiding, as pointed out in

Figure 1a. Left column: watermarked images. Middle column: difference in the spatial domain between the watermarked image and the original one (image equalized for display purposes). Right column: spectra of the error images (middle column) (image equalized for display purposes).

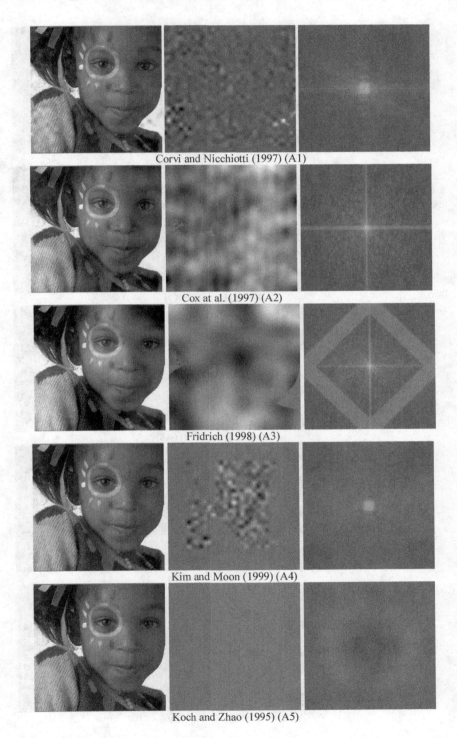

Corvi and Nicchiotti (1997) (A1)

Cox at al. (1997) (A2)

Fridrich (1998) (A3)

Kim and Moon (1999) (A4)

Koch and Zhao (1995) (A5)

Figure 1b. Left column: watermarked images. Middle column: difference in the spatial domain between the watermarked image and the original one (image equalized for display purposes). Right column: spectra of the error images (middle column) (image equalized for display purposes).

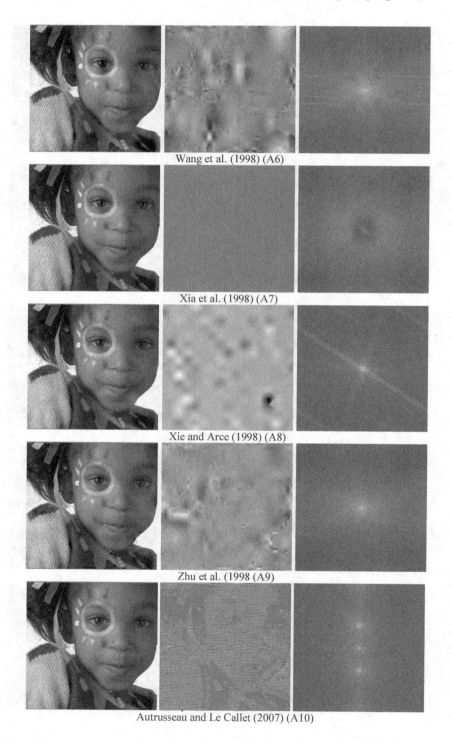

Wang et al. (1998) (A6)

Xia et al. (1998) (A7)

Xie and Arce (1998) (A8)

Zhu et al. (1998 (A9)

Autrusseau and Le Callet (2007) (A10)

the introduction of this chapter, quality of service is related to invisibility, capacity, and robustness. We must highlight that while objective measurements with good correlation to subjective quality assessment are desirable in order to reach an optimal quality of service, for example, the best trade-off between all requirements, objective measurements are not a direct replacement for subjective quality assessment. Subjective experiments are carefully designed procedures intended to determine the average opinion of human viewers to a specific set of contents (either pictures or videos) for a given application. Subjective quality assessments for a different application with different test conditions will still provide meaningful results. The results of such tests are valuable in basic system design and benchmark evaluations. It is worth pointing out that in order for objective measurements to be meaningful they have to be mapped into a subjective scale, which means that previous subjective assessment are required. Such mapping is dependent on the objective measurement itself, the application, and the subjective assessment methodology. Therefore objective measurements and subjective quality assessment are complementary rather than interchangeable.

As subjective assessment can be quite tedious, and time consuming, once an objective metric is correctly tuned to a given application, it might be used as an alternative with respect to the use of subjective assessment. However, this tuning work has been sparsely done for watermarking purposes. Such objective metrics would be useful to rank several watermarking algorithms in terms of perceived quality (Marini, Autrusseau, Le Callet, & Campisi, 2007), but also to choose the watermark weighting coefficient.

Most objective quality metrics existing in literature are actually fidelity metrics since they compare the similarity between a reference image and a distorted one. Regarding comments of the previous section on quality versus visibility, some objective metrics are possible candidates for data hiding invisibility requirement checking,

making the assumption that similarity between original image and watermarked image is linked with watermark visibility. Nevertheless, as pointed out in this section, this is not sufficient since the data hiding algorithm should carefully check the possible relevance of a given metric before using it.

SUBJECTIVE QUALITY ASSESSMENT

The most reliable technique to assess image or video perceptual quality is to set up subjective experiments. These experiments follow strictly defined procedures under normalized viewing conditions as those defined by the ITU recommendations. Since there is no explicit recommendation for data hiding context, the purpose of this section is to help the reader to be aware of the most commonly used methodologies for subjective assessment and therefore to use the most appropriate protocols for data hiding algorithms invisibility check. We first review ITU recommendations, then two protocols corresponding to quality assessment and visibility checking are presented and illustrated.

Review of ITU Recommendations for Subjective Quality Assessment

The ITU Radiocommunication assembly gives several recommendations concerning subjective quality assessment tests. Several methodologies are proposed depending on the application. We hereby restrict the review to video quality assessment presented on TV displays. Nevertheless, most of the protocols and principles still hold in other contexts. In the chosen framework, recommendation ITU-R-BT.500-11 (ITU, 2004a) provides suitable viewing conditions and methods. To conduct appropriate subjective assessments, it is first necessary to select from the different available options, those that best suit the objectives and circumstances of the assessment problem under examination. We briefly describe hereafter the main issues of this recommendation. Interested reader may refer to ITU-R-BT.500-11 (ITU, 2004a) for further details. Moreover, this description is not exhaustive since EBU recommendations as well as the SAMVIQ methodology (EBU-SAMVIQ, 2003) should be considered as well.

Environment

Two environments with different viewing conditions are described in the recommendation: The laboratory viewing environment is intended to provide critical conditions to check systems while the home viewing environment is intended to provide a mean to evaluate the quality at the consumer side of the TV chain even though the corresponding parameters define a slightly more critical environment than the typical home viewing situations. Viewing conditions include control of different parameters such as the ratio of inactive screen luminance to peak luminance, display brightness and contrast, maximum observation angle relative to the normal one, ratio of background luminance behind picture monitor to peak picture luminance, and screen size. The viewing distance and the screen sizes have to be selected in order to satisfy the preferred viewing distance (PVD) constraint.

Source and Content Selection, Anchoring

Source, for example, video used within a test session, should be selected depending on the assessment problem. In general, it is essential to include critical material, in order to get significant information when interpreting the results, not being possible to infer these data from non-critical material. Because most of the assessment methods are sensitive to contextual effects and specifically to variations in the range and distribution of conditions seen by observers, test sessions should include presentations that would fall at the extremes of the scales. These extreme cases may be represented as examples as most extreme (direct anchoring) or distributed throughout the session and not identified as most extreme (indirect anchoring).

Observers, Instructions, Session

Observers should be non-expert as for television picture/video quality assessment and they should not be experienced assessors. The observers should be screened before a session for (corrected-to-) normal visual acuity and for normal color vision using specially selected charts. The number of needed observers depends upon the sensitivity and reliability of the test procedure. Assessors should be carefully introduced to the assessment method, the types of impairment likely to occur, the grading scale, the sequence, and timing. Training sessions that demonstrate the range and the type of the impairments to be assessed should be performed using different contents with respect to the ones used during the test, but of comparable sensitivity. A session should last up to half an hour and a random order should be used for the images presentation.

Selection of Test Method

A wide variety of basic test methods is proposed in the recommendation. However, in practice, specific methods should be used to address specific assessment problems. In the case of data hiding, the following methods can be considered:

- The double stimulus impairment scale (DSIS) method is recommended to measure the robustness of systems (i.e., failure characteristics in terms of quality). With this method, the observer stares simultaneously at both the reference data (image or video) and the impaired data. Once this cycle is displayed, the assessor is asked to assess the quality of the impaired data compared to the reference (explicitly known) on a category impairment scale. The scale shown in Table 2 usually applies.

- The double stimulus continuous quality scale (DSCQS) method is recommended to measure the quality of systems relative to a reference. Contrary to the DSIS method, the assessor is not informed about the reference sequence. The assessor has to evaluate both presented contents according to a continuous quality scale.

- Threshold estimation by forced-choice method is recommended to establish the point at which an impairment becomes visible. An example of such method is presented in the next sub section.

Methodology for Invisibility Checking and Results

Concerning subjective experiments set up, among all the possible methodologies, the *two alternative forced choice* (2AFC) procedure with one presentation, may be appropriate for data hiding purposes, when invisibility, as defined in the second section, is of paramount importance for the considered application. This procedure is very useful in psychophysics in order to determine the visibility threshold, that is, when the target becomes visible. For data hiding purposes it may help to optimally tune the parameters of a given data hiding algorithm, while guaranteeing the invisibility of the embedded data. Practically, during a session, for each trial, a reference image (presented on a top panel), a copy of this one

(a hidden reference), and a modified version are displayed on the viewing monitor (on a bottom panel). Figure 2 represents a screenshot of such procedure. The modified image should be randomly presented in one of two positions A or B and the observer would be asked to identify the positions where it has occurred.

This test is commonly used since it gives the best precision for the target visibility thresholds, however, it is quite long and difficult for observers. Using several watermarked images computed with different watermarks strength, it is possible to find the optimal embedding strength. Since, observers must provide an answer at each trial, a good detection probability of 0.5 means that the observer answered randomly.

Usually, visibility threshold is measured for a probability of correct detection of 0.75, so one can set this same value to get the mark embedding strength at the mark visibility threshold. The 2AFC procedure was used in Autrusseau and Le Callet (2007), the results are shown in Figure 3, where each point represents a correct detection rate for eight observers with the "boats" and "goldhill" images according to different watermark strengths (on the X-axis). After fitting with a psychometric function it becomes possible to estimate the optimal watermark strength obtained leading to a 75% detection rate.

Methodology for Subjective Quality Assessment for Data Hiding, Applications and Results

As previously pointed out, invisibility requirement mostly refers to non-annoyance. As annoyance

Table 2. Assessment scale for DSIS

5	Imperceptible
4	Perceptible, but not annoying
3	Slightly annoying
2	Annoying
1	Very annoying

Figure 2. The 2AFC procedure

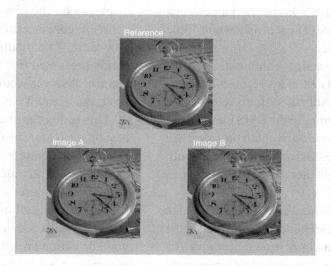

Figure 3. Detection rate plotted as a function of the embedding strength for the "boats" and "goldhill" images [reproduced from Figure 9 in, Autrusseau & Le Callet, 2007].

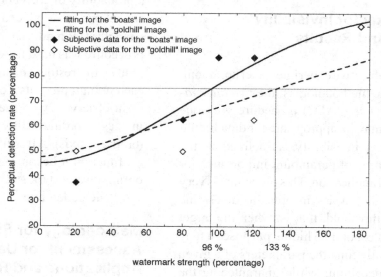

can be measured on an impairment scale, a DSIS protocol is preferable. Effectively, the watermark process can be considered as a source of distortions and therefore evaluate the corresponding annoyance.

However, it is worth noticing that the invisibility requirements can strongly differ depending on the specific data hiding application, and also that the display modalities of the watermarked image during subjective experiments can influence the human observer judgment. For example, if both the reference content and the marked one are successively displayed at the exact same position on the screen, the distortions will appear very clearly to the assessor, who will inevitably attribute a poor quality score to the marked image whereas if displayed by itself, this latter might not present such annoying artifacts.

Based on that statement, we have defined a subjective protocol suited to watermarking quality assessment purposes and we have run tests with human observers in a controlled environment defined accordingly to the ITU-R-BT.500-11 recommendation (ITU, 2004a).

In this protocol, the original and the watermarked images are presented explicitly to the observer, displayed side by side on the viewing monitor and the observers are asked to judge the quality of the marked image compared to the quality of the original (always displayed at the same position, on the left side). The observers have to rate the impairments on a scale of five categories according to Table 2. As previously stated, for watermarking applications, the expected quality score should be higher than 4.

Being the authors experienced with subjective quality assessment, as members of the Independent Lab Group (ILG) of the Video Quality Expert Group (VQEG), the aforementioned protocol has been applied to test some well-known watermarking algorithms in a silent room, which is compliant with the ITU-R-BT.500-11 recommendation (ITU, 2004a). Seventeen observers were enrolled, and their visual acuity was checked. Five different

contents (see Figure 4) have been watermarked by using 10 algorithms (see Appendix A) and two embedding strengths per algorithm (the default strengths and 1.5 times the default value). Finally the observers rated 100 images in a session of 20 minutes at an observation distance of 6 times the height of the displayed images.

For each image an average of the scores given by the observers were evaluated thus obtaining the mean opinion score (MOS) for the analyzed image. Then, in order to compare the algorithms quality in terms of the perceptual transparency of the embedded mark, we averaged the MOS values over the contents.

Figure 5 represents the averaged MOS for two different strengths (the default embedding strength (α), and a stronger one ($1.5 \times \alpha$)), as a function of the 10 tested watermarking algorithms (refer to Appendix A for further details on the ten algorithms). It can be seen that only four algorithms, whose embedding strengths are set to the default values (light gray bars) in their implementation, fulfill the requirement of a quality score greater than 4.

A rather important variation appears on the subjective scores plot, watermarks are spread from the *very annoying* score to the *imperceptible*.

Figure 4. The test images used during the subjective experiments

Figure 5. MOS per algorithm for two distinct strengths

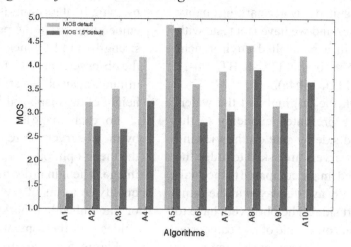

Subjective Quality with Respect to Frequency Properties of the Watermark

A frequency analysis of the watermarks' Fourier spectra can be performed in order to characterize the link between each watermarking algorithm and its impact on the visibility. The Fourier representations of the error images (Figure 1, right column) were split according to a human visual system (HVS) model decomposition (Figure 6b).

This frequency decomposition can be done using perceptual channels decomposition (PCD), which splits the Fourier domain in overlapping sub-bands, modeling the HVS behavior. From neurobiology there are evidences in the HVS that support the concept of receptive fields, which are tuned to given spatial frequencies and orientation. This can be emulated using a spatial frequency sub-band decomposition. In this work, we used the PCD detailed in Autrusseau and Le Callet (2007). The PCD uses a set of three band-pass radial frequency channels (crown III, IV, V) each being decomposed into angular sectors with an oriented selectivity of 45°, 30°, and 30° respectively. Interested readers may refer to Autrusseau

and Le Callet (2007) for further details on the decomposition.

The HVS's sensitivity varies according to spatial frequency. In order to take such property into account, the watermarks' Fourier spectra were weighted with a 2D-contrast sensitivity function (CSF) (the 2D-CSF is depicted in Figure 6c). Once this weighting function performed, the Fourier spectrum of each watermark was split according to the chosen HVS decomposition (Figure 6b) and the variance was computed independently for each sub-band of the PCD. Figure 6a represents for all 10 watermarking algorithms the variance as a function of the perceptual sub-bands. In this figure the 10 algorithms are separated into two sets; the solid lines represents the five algorithms presenting the worst perceived quality (see Figure 5 for subjective assessment of the algorithms), whereas the dashed lines represents the five best quality algorithms. It clearly appears on Figure 6a that the set of algorithms presenting the poorest quality presents a much higher variance within the most sensitive crown of the PCD (crown III). Furthermore, the algorithm providing the best visual quality (A5) according to Figure 5 presents a very flat distribution of the variance along the crowns of the PCD. Figure 6 shows that evidently, the embedding algorithms presenting the most

Figure 6. (a) Variance of the watermark within each perceptual sub-band of the Fourier decomposition for a given HVS model decomposition (b) weighted with a 2D-CSF (c)

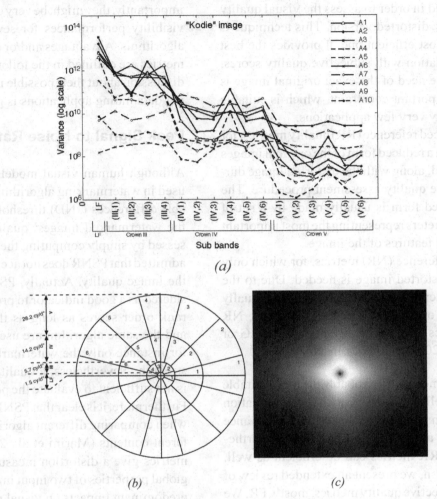

annoying artifacts strongly modify the Fourier spectrum where the HVS is the most sensitive (highest CSF values).

STATE OF THE ART OF OBJECTIVE QUALITY METRICS

As mentioned before, an objective metric is mainly designed for one given application and above all can be tuned using subjective assessment. Look-

ing for the right metric and knowing how to tune can be quite challenging for the non-expert. The goal of this section is to provide hints to interested reader to explore the literature on quality metrics. First of all, objective image and video quality metrics can be classified according to the availability of the distortion free image and video signal, which may be used as a reference to compare an original image or video signal against its distorted counterpart. Specifically, such metrics are usually of three kinds:

- Full reference (FR) quality assessment metrics for which the exact original image is needed in order to assess the visual quality of any distorted version. This technique is the most efficient one, it provides the best correlation with subjective quality scores, but the need of the exact original image is an important constraint, which is suitable in only very few applications.

- Reduced reference (RR) quality metrics, for which a reduced form of the original images is used, along with the distorted image during the quality assessment procedure. The reduced form is usually made by a set of parameters representing the most important visual features of the image.

- No reference (NR) metrics, for which only the distorted image is needed. Due to the complexity of such techniques, they usually focus on specific distortions, that is, NR metrics are specifically built for JPEG or JPEG2000 coding for instance.

The FR metrics are probably the more suitable to provide reliable assessment (the best correlation with human judgment) concerning annoyance induced by a data hiding algorithm. Nevertheless, some RR metrics can be efficient as well. In this section, we present an extended review of existing objective quality metrics, mostly FR. We particularly focus here on the inability of statistical metrics to efficiently evaluate the quality of a marked image. Concerning video, ITU standard related to digital television are presented. Concerning still images, there is no standard therefore we describe well-known metrics of the literature, SSIM (Wang, Bovik, Sheikh, & Simoncelli, 2004), RRIQA (Wang & Simoncelli, 2005), UQI (Wang & Bovik, 2002), C4 (Carnec, Le Callet, & Barba, 2003), Komparator (Barba & Le Callet, 2003). It is worth pointing out that these metrics have not specifically been designed to assess the watermark perceptual transparency. Nevertheless, although their performances for watermarking applications

might not be very competitive, they might give a good clue about the watermark visibility, and most importantly, they might be very useful to compare visibility performances for several embedding algorithms. Advantages and/or drawbacks of the metrics are outlined in the following as long as a discussion about their possible relevance regarding data hiding applications is given.

Peak Signal to Noise Ratio (PSNR)

Although human visual models are sometimes used in watermarking algorithms for just noticeable differences (JND) thresholds computation, the watermarked images' quality is mostly assessed by simply computing the PSNR. It is well admitted that PSNR does not accurately represent the image quality. Actually, PSNR can be considered as a good indicator to provide qualitative rank order scores as long as the same content and the same algorithm are used while varying for instance only the watermarking embedding strength. Nevertheless, a qualitative rank order is not sufficient to evaluate the perceived quality. Furthermore, it is clear that PSNR fails miserably when comparing different algorithms and/or different contents (Marini et al., 2007). Statistical metrics give a distortion measure based on the global properties of two input images. One of the predominant impacts on visual perception is the sensitivity to frequency components. Such sensitivity is not taken into account in the PSNR.

In Figure 7 some examples which show the questionable behavior of the PSNR are given. Specifically Figures 7a and 7b represent two different images watermarked with the same algorithm (Cox et al., 1997). Although it is evident that Figure 7a has been severely impaired by the watermarking process, the image in Figure 7a has a PSNR higher of 1 dB than the one in Figure 7b. On the contrary, in Figures 7c and 7d the same image watermarked with the algorithms (Xia et al., 1998) and (Corvi & Nicchiotti, 1997) are shown. As evident the quality of the two watermarked

Figure 7 Image watermarked using the same algorithm A2 (a): PSNR = 24,26 dB, MOS = 1.25, (b): PSNR = 23.36 dB, MOS = 3.94. (c): image watermarked using the A7 algorithm (PSNR = 31.05 dB). (d): image watermarked using the A1 algorithm (PSNR = 31.3 dB)

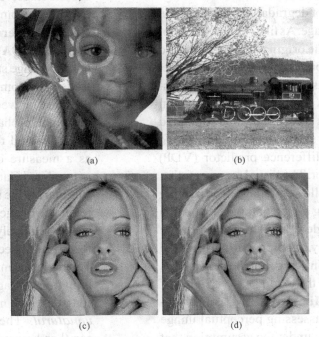

images is strongly different, but both images have a very close PSNR.

An extension of the PSNR has been provided in Pereira et al. (2001) where the weighted PSNR (wPSNR) has been defined. It weights each term of the PSNR by a local activity factor linked to the local variance.

Still Images Quality Metrics

We present in this subsection the most widely used objective metrics for still images, namely the Watson Metric (Watson, 1993), UQI (Wang & Bovik, 2002), Komparator (Barba & Le Callet, 2003), and SSIM (Wang et al., 2004), (FR metrics) as well as C4 (Carnec et al., 2003) and RRIQA (Wang & Simoncelli, 2005) (RR metrics). The metrics outputs are compared after mapping with subjective scores provided by observers and a comparison with the PSNR performances is

also given. A brief description of the aforementioned metrics is given hereafter. The softwares implementing the metrics can be found on the Internet[7].

- The **Watson metric** is widely used by the watermarking community to asses the quality of watermarked images. This metric is provided within the Checkmark benchmark tool (**Pereira et al., 2001**). It computes the perceptual error between two images in units of JND between a reference image and a test image.

- **Universal quality index (UQI)** is a universal objective image quality index, designed to model any image distortion as a combination of three factors: loss of correlation, luminance distortion, and contrast distortion. UQI is a mathematically defined metric such as the widely used root mean squared error (RMSE) or the PSNR.

- **Komparator** is an objective quality metric for color images based on HVS properties that does not need any a priori knowledge about the type of degradation introduced in the distorted image. As first step, a visual representation of the original and the distorted images is computed: in this stage a model based on results obtained by psychophysics experiments on color perception and on masking effects is used. The model adopted for early vision stages is inspired by the S. Daly's visual difference predictor (VDP) extended to color. The visual representation stage is then followed by an error pooling process merging all the obtained distortion maps into a single value. This stage is made up by a frequency, a component, and a spatial pooling taking into account the density and the structure of the error.

- **Structural SIMilarity (SSIM)** is an objective metric for assessing perceptual image quality, working under the assumption that human visual perception is highly adapted for extracting structural information from a scene. Quality evaluation is thus based on the degradation of this structural information assuming that error visibility should not be equated with loss of quality as some distortions may be clearly visible but not so annoying. Finally SSIM does not attempt to predict image quality by accumulating the errors associated with psychophysically understood simple patterns, but proposes to directly evaluate the structural changes between two complex-structured signals.

- **C4** is a metric based on the comparison between the structural information extracted from the distorted and the original images. What makes this metric interesting is that it uses reduced references containing perceptual structural information and exploiting an implementation of a rather elaborated model of the HVS. The full process can be decomposed into two phases. In the first step, perceptual representation is built for the original and the distorted images, then, in the second stage, representations are compared in order to compute a quality score.

- **Reduced reference image quality assessment (RRIQA)** is a RR metric, based on a natural image statistic model in the wavelet transform domain. The Kullback-Leibler distance between the wavelet coefficients marginal probability distributions of the reference and the distorted image is used as a measure of the image distortion. A generalized Gaussian model is employed to summarize the marginal distribution of the reference image wavelet coefficients, so that only a relatively small number of images' features are needed for quality evaluation. The basic assumption behind this approach is that most image distortions modify image statistics and make the distorted version *unnatural*. The measured unnaturalness can then be used to quantify image quality distortion.

Video: ITU Standards for Objective Quality Assessment

The VQEG, which reports to ITU-T Study Group 9 and ITU-R Study Group 6, is conducting studies on perceptual video quality measurements. One of the first tasks of VQEG was focused on the performance assessment of proposed full reference perceptual video quality measurement algorithms. VQEG first issued a comprehensive final draft report of its work in March 2000. Phase I did not provide sufficient evidence to identify a method to be recommended for objective assessment of perceptual video quality. A final report of the Phase II, pertaining Full Reference Television Test was issued in August of 2003. Results of this second phase indicate that four of the methods are appropriate for inclusion in the normative part of an ITU Recommendation.

The recommendation ITU-T-J.144 (ITU, 2004b) includes these methods or models, providing guidelines on the selection of ad hoc full reference perceptual video quality measurement equipment to be used in digital cable television assessment. The quality estimation methods are based on processing 8-bit digital component video as defined by recommendation ITU.R BT.601-5 (ITU, 1995) and they provide video quality estimations for television video classes (TV0-TV3) and multimedia video class (MM4) as defined in the Annex B of ITU-T recommendation ITU-T-P.911 (ITU, 1998). The applications of the quality estimation models concern the performance evaluation of a codec (encoder/decoder combination) or a concatenation of various coding methods and memory storage devices. This is mainly due to the fact that the models validation test material refers to degradations introduced by coding and that compression rates range 768 kbps to 5 Mbps, including different compression methods (e.g., MPEG, H.263, ...).

The predicted performance of the estimation models is not currently validated for all video systems and even less for a system that includes data impairments due to data hiding techniques. Moreover according to ITU-T-J.144 recommendation (ITU, 2004b) the correlation values between the results of the subjective experiment carried out in two different labs with the same modalities should provide values within the range 0.92 to 0.97. This implies that users of this recommendation should review the comparison of available subjective and objective results to gain an understanding of the range of video quality rating estimation errors. Nevertheless, the ITU-T-J.144 recommendation is so far, the most related to the perceptual quality requirements of data hiding techniques. Moreover, software tools implementing some of the recommendation methods are already available. Therefore, it could be as a first step and waiting for a complete validation an excellent alternative to usual PSNR for watermarked video quality assessment.

A major breakthrough brought by the recommendation compared to PSNR is related to correction for any offsets or gain differences and also temporal and spatial alignment processes. Consequently, the comparison between input and output signals is performed in two steps: first correction and alignment are applied, then the objective picture quality rating is computed, typically by applying a perceptual model of human vision. For instance, spatial alignment is designed to compensate for any vertical or horizontal picture shifts or cropping. Initially, this is required because most of the full reference methods, like PSNR, compare reference and processed pictures on what is effectively a pixel-by-pixel basis that can lead to strong impairment values while the effect of misalignment on perceptual quality is much lower. In the context of data hiding techniques assessment, realignment before objective quality rating is a real benefit since misalignment can be a consequence of the data embedding techniques without inducing effective perceived differences. Nevertheless, interpretation of the results of the objective metrics as they are should be done carefully. Ideally, prior subjective assessment experiments have to be conducted at least to map the models score into the subjective scale regarding the considered application.

So far, four methods have been recommended by VQEG to ITU. These are, as they appear in ITU-T-J.144 (ITU, 2004b):

- British Telecom (United Kingdom, VQEG Proponent D): BTFR algorithm
- Yonsei University/SK Telecom/Radio Research Laboratory (Republic of Korea, VQEG Proponent E): EPSNR algorithm
- CPqD (Federative Republic of Brazil, VQEG Proponent F): CPqD-IES algorithm
- NTIA (United States of America, VQEG Proponent H): General VQM algorithm

A short overview of each algorithm is presented next, where however temporal and spatial alignment and other compensation processes are not mentioned. Nevertheless, interested readers could find all the details in the recommendation.

- **The BTFR algorithm** consists in detection followed by integration. Detection involves the calculation of a set of perceptually meaningful detector parameters from the undistorted (reference) and distorted (degraded) video sequences. The choice of detectors and weighting factors are made using the knowledge of the spatial and temporal masking properties of the HVS and determined through calibration experiments. The set of detector parameters includes spatial frequency, edge and texture, and PSNR analysis. These parameters are then considered as input to the integrator, which produces an estimate of the perceived video quality by appropriate weighting: time averaging, and linear combination along averaged detector values.

- **Edge PSNR (EPSNR)** is taking into account the fact that humans are more sensitive to degradation around the edges while evaluating video quality. Therefore, the model provides an objective video quality measurement method that measures degradation around the edges. In the model, an edge detection algorithm is first applied to the source video sequence to locate the edge areas. Then, the degradation of the selected edge areas is measured by computing the MSE which is used to compute the edge PSNR.

- **The CPqD-IES (image evaluation based on segmentation) algorithm** is based on objective impairment measures, computed on plain, edge, and texture regions resulting from an image segmentation process. One objective measure is computed based on the difference between the corresponding frames of the reference and the processed video, for each of the three categories and for each image component Y, Cb, and Cr. Each objective measure produces a contextual impairment level based on its impairment estimation model. A video quality rate per frame is obtained by linear combination of the contextual impairment level. Finally, a temporal pooling along the frame is done applying a median filtering and a mean computation along time (e.g., frame).

- **The general NTIA-VQM** includes extraction of perception-based features, computation of video quality parameters, and calculation of the general model. The general model tracks the perceptual changes in quality due to distortions in any component of the digital video transmission system (e.g., encoder, digital channel, decoder). Actually, the method of measurement documented in the recommendation is based on high bandwidth reduced-reference parameters. These reduced-reference parameters utilize features extracted from spatio-temporal regions of the video sequence. The general model and its associated automatic calibration techniques have been completely implemented in user friendly software. This software is available to all interested parties via a no-cost evaluation license agreement (see www.its. bldrdoc.gov/n3/video/vqmsoftware.htm for more information).

VQEG reports provide complete insight on the work performed by VQEG concerning FR TV quality. Among the performance indicators, proponent models have been checked in terms of:

- Prediction accuracy (the model's ability to predict the subjective quality: RMS error),
- Prediction monotonicity (the degree to which the model's predictions agree with the rank ordering of subjective quality ratings: Pearson correlation).

Table 3. Model performance

Metric	BTFR	EPSNR	CpqD IES	General VQM	PSNR
Pearson correlation (525 data)	0.937	0.857	0.835	0.938	0.804
RMS error (525 data)	0.075	0.110	0.117	0.074	0.127
Spearman correlation (625 data)	0.779	0.870	0.898	0.886	0.733
RMS error (625 data)	0.113	0.089	0.079	0.083	0.122

Table 3 provides informative details on the models performances in the VQEG Phase II FRTV test. For the 525 line video data, models NTIA and BT performed statistically better than the other models and are statistically equivalent to each other. For the 625 line video data, three models—CPqD, NTIA, Yonsei/SKT/RRL—are statistically equivalent to each other and are statistically better than the other model. It is also noted that only the NTIA model statistically tied for top performances in both tests.

BENCHMARK OF STILL IMAGES QUALITY METRICS FOR WATERMARKING

Benchmark Specifications

In order to determine the relevance of the previously presented objective metrics, we have conducted a benchmark of six objective quality metrics (i.e., SSIM, C4, wPSNR, PSNR, Komparator, and Watson, see the *State of the art of Objective Quality Metrics* section) regarding data hiding applications. The basic idea of this benchmark is to specify if any of the considered metrics can be useful to determine whether a data hiding algorithm is better than another in terms of invisibility requirement. In other words, such benchmark should provide the best objective metric to perform invisibility assessment of data hiding algorithms. The benchmark of the quality metrics has to be robust regarding different contents, different data hiding algorithms, and

different corresponding strengths. After choosing content and data hiding algorithm, three steps are necessary and need to be specified: we first have to get subjective assessments as they represent the ground truth, then we have to map the objective metrics scores in the subjective scale, finally metrics performance must be defined and measured.

Content and Data Hiding Algorithm

Five different contents were selected regarding their spatio-frequency properties (refer to Figure 4 for presentation of the contents). Ten embedding algorithms have been used. For each employed watermarking technique two embedding strengths were tested. The chosen embedding algorithms are briefly summarized in Appendix A.

Subjective Assessment

Subjective experiments were conducted, as specified in the third section, following the DSIS procedure with 17 observers. The observers were asked to assess the quality of the five contents. Each content was independently watermarked using the 10 watermarking algorithms for two embedding strengths, the default embedding strength (α), and a stronger one ($1.5 \times \alpha$). Thus, we get 100 scores per observer, each score corresponding to a watermarked content at a given strength. The scores are averaged along observers to a MOS for each combination of content, algorithm, and strength.

MOS, MOSp, and Mapping

Considering the purpose of the benchmark (i.e., identify a quality metric for invisibility benchmarking of data hiding algorithm), we aggregate results along contents for each of the 10 watermarking algorithms, therefore both the MOS and the predicted MOS (MOSp) of the six objective metrics are averaged per embedding strength, as given by (1) and (2):

$$MOS = \frac{1}{N} \sum_{n=1}^{N} MOS_{(algo,s)}(n) \qquad (1)$$

$$MOSp = \frac{1}{N} \sum_{n=1}^{N} MOSp_{(algo,s)}(n) \qquad (2)$$

where *algo* represents the embedding algorithm under analysis, *s* stands for the embedding strength, and *N* represents the number of contents taken into account, which in our application is equal to five. Once all the objective measures are collected, for each of the metrics, MOSp are transformed into fitted MOSp by a mapping function. As previously explained, this mapping is necessary for the predicted MOS to be in correspondence with the subjective scale of the MOS. As depicted in Figure **8** the MOS and MOSp provided by Komparator are strongly correlated even if it is not obvious. Although the MOS provided by observers is in the range [1;5], the Komparator metric provides a measure of the differences between the two input images (original and watermarked one), thus, the smaller is the objective score, the most similar are the images. Moreover, the range of the Komparator measure is not well established, one could compare any watermarking algorithm with the 10 provided assessments, but it appears clearer when using the same scale as the subjective one. The mapping function is therefore necessary to easily link the MOS and fitted MOSp and to interpret the results. The main advantage of using a mapping function is the possibility to compute other factors besides correlation coefficient to qualify an objective metric performance. As for the considered benchmark, parameters estimation of the mapping function was performed, as recommended by the VQEG Multimedia TEST PLAN. Basically, it corresponds to a third order polynomial function.

Metric Performance

Finally, measures are computed between the fitted MOSp, for example, after mapping, and the actual MOS (correlation coefficient, RMSE, and rank correlation coefficient), in order to define the most appropriate objective metric for watermarking purpose. Those measures allow to qualify the

Figure 8. Relationship between the MOS (left panel) and predicted MOS (right panel) using the Komparator metric for all watermarking techniques

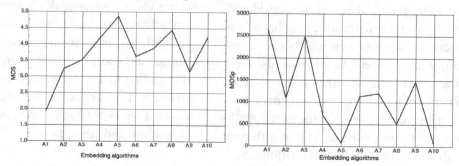

objective metrics in terms of prediction accuracy and monotonicity.

Results

This section is devoted to a comparison of the previously detailed objective metrics. Based on the benchmark specification, results concerning objective metrics performance after mapping are given in Table 4.

The correlation between two variables reflects the degree to which the variables are related. The most common measure of correlation is the Pearson Product Moment Correlation (called Pearson's correlation for short), which makes the assumption that values of the two variables are sampled from populations that follow a Gaussian distribution. Pearson's correlation reflects the degree of linear relationship between two variables. It ranges from -1 to +1. A correlation of +1 means that there is a perfect positive linear relationship between variables. Alternatively, the non-parametric Spearman correlation is based on ranking the two variables, and so makes no assumption about the distribution of the values. Spearman's correlation is a measure of monotonic association that is used when the distribution of the data make Pearson's correlation coefficient undesirable or misleading. It ranges also from -1 to +1. Table 4 clearly indicates the differences between objective metrics regarding correlation. Values of both Pearson and Spearman correlation are rather low for most quality metrics. Only Komparator metric is reasonably approaching 1 for both correlation values. However, when monotonicity is taken into

account, for example, Spearman correlation, the values are improved for all metrics. Nevertheless, the weaknesses of most metrics for watermarked images quality assessment are obvious. This statement highlights that the application of metrics to a framework for which they have not specifically designed should be done very carefully. RMSE values in Table 4 are related to the prediction accuracy of the objective metrics. The values are on the subjective scale ranking from 1 to 5. This means that a RMSE value of 0.4 in the table corresponds to 10% of the subjective scale, while 0.8 corresponds to 20%. Therefore, the RMSE between MOS and MOSp after mapping is between 11% and 18% of the subjective scale depending on the objective metric. An interpretation of these values should be done in comparison with the mean value of the interval of confidence (IC) at 95% on the MOS, that is, in the considered subjective assessment campaign around 0.5 on the subjective scale, for example, 12.5%. The use of a category scale introduces a quantization effect on the MOS that increases naturally the mean IC value. Therefore, an RMSE value below or close to 0.5 can be considered as satisfactory. Based on the results reported in Table 4, only C4 and Komparator fulfill this requirement.

An additional analysis of the results can be done by plotting the predicted objective scores, for the six tested metrics, after mapping, as a function of the MOS. Each panel of Figure 9 represents the predicted objective scores (for six tested metrics) as a function of the MOS, the results can be identified for the 10 analyzed watermarking algorithms. For each data hiding technique, two

Table 4. Objective metrics performances

Objective metrics	Watson	SSIM	wPSNR	PSNR	C4	Komparator
Pearson correlation	0.5458	0.5857	0.6560	0.6855	0.7917	0.8808
Spearman correlation	0.7158	0.7128	0.7444	0.7203	0.8541	0.8917
RMSE	0.7434	0.7114	0.6220	0.6385	0.5358	0.4398

Figure 9. Objective metrics scores as a function of the MOS

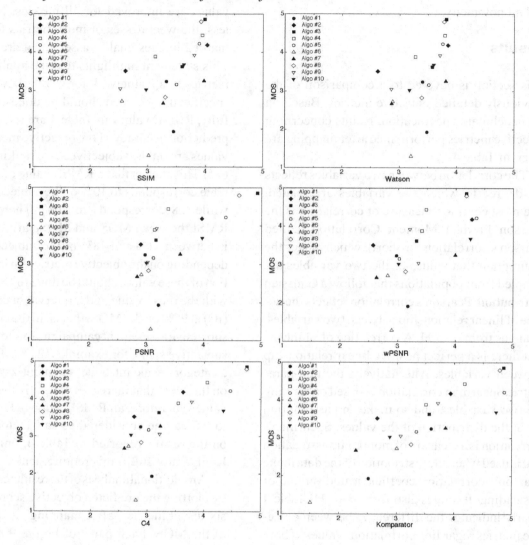

points are shown, representing the two embedding strengths. Evidently, the narrower is the point distribution, and the closest it is to y = x, the best is the prediction. In these plots, the mapping with subjective scores was performed.

It can be noticed that for most of the plots, the algorithms indexed as A1 and A6 are rather poorly assessed by the objective metrics. Effectively, for these two algorithms, the two embedding strengths are quite far away from the y = x line. The MOS and MOSp do not match. This is

probably caused by a quality overrating (MOSp) for the images marked with the strongest embedding parameter.

The Figure 10 shows for each of the 10 tested watermarking algorithms with the default strength, the obtained MOS (averaged over contents) along with the two best of the objective metrics predicted scores. Taking into account interval of confidence at 95% on the MOS, it appears that objective metrics perform well for most of the algorithms except for algorithms A1 and A3.

Figure 10. MOS averaged over contents for the set of 10 tested watermarking algorithms for the default embedding strength (reproduced from Figure 3. in Marini et al., 2007)

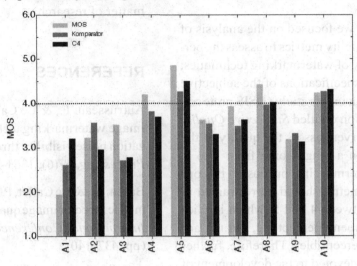

CONCLUSION

This work presents a preliminary study on quality assessment of watermarking algorithms, which first aim is to highlight the deficiencies of some metrics for data hiding purposes. A deep review of subjective experiment protocols has been carried out and both usual statistical metrics, and a few advanced objective metrics, have been detailed. A quality benchmark, which aim is to determine among several existing objective quality metrics, the one which would best predict the subjective scores has been presented. The widely used PSNR proves to poorly estimate the quality of water-marked images. Nonetheless, one objective metric has provided a rather good prediction of the MOS. However, although this metric has performed well when ranking algorithms altogether, it is important to notice that existing objective metrics may not yet be efficient enough to assess the quality of one single embedding technique for various contents or for different embedding strengths.

FUTURE RESEARCH DIRECTIONS

Within the framework of data hiding applications, quality metrics can be used for different purposes, like:

a. Quality assessment of the watermarking algorithm in terms of perceptual invisibility of the mark, which would allow to properly design the embedding strength for a given content and a given watermarking algorithm,

b. Quality assessment of attacked watermarked images to test the robustness of the used watermarking algorithm with respect of the amount of bearable distortion which can be introduced by the attack. In this scenario, the distortion that can be tolerated for an attack able to remove the embedded mark depends on the application. When a high quality image is required, like in cultural heritage applications, no perceptual distortion impairing the fruition of the master-piece is allowed, whereas in infotainment applications a higher level of distortion is allowed.

In this chapter we focused on the analysis of general purpose quality metrics to assess the perceptual invisibility of watermarking techniques. According to the specifications of the subjective experiments we ran in this study (DSIS protocol, as detailed in section entitled *Subjective Quality Assessment*), observers assess the quality of the distorted image on a range going from 1 to 5. However, for watermarking purposes, the optimum objective metric should be restrained to scores ranking between 4 and 5, which implies a watermark between "perceptible, but not annoying" and "imperceptible." Therefore, further research could be devoted to the development of an efficient quality metric within the aforementioned range.

Nevertheless, perceptual quality assessment of attacked watermarked images within the framework described in (b), which is a dual problem of the one presented in (a), is of interest as well since it poses the basic question of which metric can be used to assess the quality of a watermarked image when some malicious attacks have been perpetrated against it in order to remove the mark. Recently, a "watermarking contest"[8] has been organized challenging all participants to remove a watermark from some watermarked images while keeping the PSNR of the attacked image above 30 dB as a requirement to grant a sufficient quality of the attacked image effectively perceived by the final user. However, it is well known that the PSNR is not well suited to take into account the visual impairments present in an image. In fact PSNR is completely inefficient as long as geometric distortions are taken into account. For example, a simple 1° image rotation would absolutely not distort the image perceived quality, whereas its computed PSNR would be very strongly reduced. Therefore the design of a metric giving the right weight to perceptual ineffective geometric distortions is still a challenging matter of research.

REFERENCES

Autrusseau, F., & Le Callet, P. (2007). A robust image watermarking technique based on quantization noise visibility thresholds. *Elsevier Signal Processing, 87*(6), 1363-1383.

Barba, D., & Le Callet, P. (2003). A robust quality metric for color image quality assessment. In *IEEE International Conference on Image Processing* (pp. 437-440).

Barni, M., & Bartolini, F. (2004). *Watermarking systems engineering. Enabling Digital Assets Security and Other Applications*. New York: Marcel Dekker.

Campisi, P., Carli, M., Giunta, G., & Neri, A. (2003). Blind quality assessment system for multimedia communications. *IEEE Transactions on Signal Processing, Special issue on Signal Processing for Data Hiding in Digital Media & Secure Content Delivery, 51*(4), 996-1002.

Campisi, P., Kundur, D., Hatzinakos, D., & Neri, A. (2002). Compressive data hiding: An unconventional approach for improved color image coding. *EURASIP Journal on Applied Signal Processing, Special issue on Emerging Applications of Multimedia Data Hiding, 2002* (pp. 152-163).

Campisi, P., & Piva, A. (2006). Data hiding for image and video coding. In M. Barni & F. Bartolini (Eds.), *Document and image compression* (pp. 255-282). New York: Dekker.

Carnec, M., Le Callet, P. L., & Barba, D. (2003). An image quality assessment method based on perception of structural information. *IEEE Transactions on Image Processing, 3*, 185-188.

Corvi, M., & Nicchiotti, G. (1997). Wavelet based image watermarking for copyright protection. In *Scandinavian Conference on Image Analysis, SCIA* (p. 9705).

Cox, I., Kilian, J., Leighton, T., & Shamoon, T. (1997). Secure spread spectrum watermarking for multimedia. *Proceedings of the IEEE International Conference on Image Processing, 6,* 1673-1687.

Doerr, G., & Dugelay, J.-L. (2003). A guided tour to video watermarking. *Signal Processing: Image Communication, 18,* 263-282.

EBU-SAMVIQ. (2003). *Subjective assessment methodology for video quality report* (Tech. Rep. EBU BPN 056). EBU Project Group B/VIM (Video in Multimedia).

Fridrich, J. (1998, July 19-24). Combining low-frequency and spread spectrum watermarking. *Proceedings of the SPIE symposium on optical science, Engineering and Instrumentation* (Vol. 3456). San Diego, CA.

Fridrich, J. (1999). Applications of data hiding in digital images. *Tutorial for the ISSPA conference, Part I.*

Hyung, C. K., Ogunleye, H., Guitar, O., & Delp, E. J. (2004). The watermark evaluation testbed (WET). In E. J. Delp & P. W. Wong (Eds.), *Proceedings of SPIE, Security and Watermarking of Multimedia Contents VI* (pp. 236-247). San Jose, CA.

International Telecommunication Union (ITU). (1995). *Studio encoding parameters of digital television for standard 4:3 and wide-screen 16:9 aspect ratios* (Tech. Rep. No. ITU-R-BT.601-5).

International Telecommunication Union (ITU). (1998). *Subjective audiovisual quality assessment methods for multimedia applications* (Tech. Rep. No. ITU-T-P.911).

International Telecommunication Union (ITU).

(2004a). *Methodology for the subjective assessment of the quality of television pictures question ITU-R 211/11, g* (Tech. Rep. No. ITU-R-BT.500-11).

International Telecommunication Union (ITU). (2004b). *Objective perceptual video quality measurement techniques for digital cable television in the presence of a full reference* (Tech. Rep. No. ITU-T-J.144).

Kim, J., & Moon, Y. (1999). A robust wavelet based digital watermark using label adaptive thresholding. *Proceedings of the 6th IEEE International Conference on Image Processing* (pp. 202-205).

Koch, E., & Zhao, J. (1995). Towards robust and hidden image copyright labeling. *IEEE International Workshop on Nonlinear Signal and Image Processing* (pp. 452-455).

Kundur, D., Su, K., & Hatzinakos, D. (2004). Digital video watermarking: Techniques, technology and trends. In *Intelligent watermarking techniques* (pp. 265-314). World Scientific.

Macq, B., Dittman, J., & Delp, E. J. (2004). Benchmarking of image watermarking algorithms for digital rights management. *Proceedings of the IEEE, 92*(6), 971-984.

Marini, E., Autrusseau, F., Le Callet, P., & Campisi, P. (2007, January). Evaluation of standard watermarking techniques. *SPIE Electronic Imaging 2007, Security, Steganography, and Watermarking of Multimedia Contents IX,* San Jose, CA.

Meerwald, P. (2001, January). *Digital image watermarking in the wavelet transform domain.* Master's thesis, Department of Scientific Computing, University of Salzburg, Austria, Retrieved from http://www.cosy.sbg.ac.at/~pmeerw

Michiels, B., & Macq, B. (2006). Benchmarking image watermarking algorithms with openwatermark. In *14th European Signal Processing Conference, EUSIPCO06.*

Ninassi, A., Le Callet, P., & Autrusseau, F. (2006). Pseudo no reference image quality metric using perceptual data hiding. *SPIE Electronic Imaging, 6057,* 146-157.

Pereira, S., Voloshynovskiy, S., Madueno, M., Marchand-Maillet, S., & Pun, T. (2001). Second generation benchmarking and application oriented evaluation. In *Information Hiding Workshop III* (pp. 340-353).

Petitcolas, F. A., Anderson, R. J., & Kuhn, M. G. (1998). Attacks on copyright marking systems. *Second Workshop on information hiding, 1525,* 219-239.

Solachidis, V., Tefas, A., Nikoliaidis, N., Tsekeridou, S., Nikoliaidis, A., & Pitas, I. (2001). A benchmarking protocol for watermarking methods. In *IEEE International Conference on Image Processing* (pp. 1023-1026).

Voloshynovskiy, S., Pereira, S., Iquise, V., & Pun, T. (2001). Attack modeling: Towards a second generation watermarking benchmark. *Signal Processing, 81,* 1177-1214.

Wang, H.-J., Su, P.-C., & JayKuo, C. (1998). Wavelet based digital image watermarking. *Optic Express, 3,* 491-196.

Wang, Z., & Bovik, A. C. (2002). A universal image quality index. *IEEE Signal Processing Letters, 9*(3), 81-84.

Wang, Z., Bovik, A. C., Sheikh, H. R., & Simoncelli, E. P. (2004). Image quality assessment: From error visibility to structural similarity. *IEEE Transactions on Image Processing, 13*(4), 600-612.

Wang, Z., & Simoncelli, E. P. (2005). Reduced-reference image quality assessment using a wavelet-domain natural image statistic model. *SPIE Electronic Imaging X, 5666,* 149-159.

Watson, A. B. (1993). DCT quantization matrices visually optimized for individual images. *SPIE: Human vision, Visual Processing and Digital Display IV, 1913,* 202-216.

Xia, X.-G., Boncelet, C., & Arce, G. (1998). Wavelet transform based watermark for digital images. *Optic Express, 3,* 497-511.

Xie, L., & Arce, G. (1998). Joint wavelet compression and authentication watermarking. *Proceedings of the IEEE International Conference on Image Processing* (pp. 427-431).

Zhu, W., Xiong, Z., & Zhang, Y.-Q. (1998). Multiresolution watermarking for images and video: A unified approach. *Proceedings of the IEEE International Conference on Image Processing, 1,* 465-468.

ADDITIONAL READING

Avcibas, I., (2001). Image quality statistics and their use in steganalysis and compression. Unpublished PhD thesis, Bogazici University, Bebek, Istanbul.

Cox, I., Miller, M., & Bloom, J. (2001). *Digital watermarking.* San Francisco: Morgan Kaufmann.

Katzenbeisser, S., & Petitcolas, F. A. P. (1999). Information hiding techniques for steganography and digital watermarking. Norwood, MA: Artech House.

Wang, Z., & Bovik, A. (2006). *Modern image quality assessment.* Morgan & Claypool.

Wu, H. R., & Rao, K. R. (2005). *Digital video image quality and perceptual coding (signal processing and communications).* CRC Press.

ENDNOTES

[1]   http://www.*petitcolas*.net/fabien/watermarking/stirmark

2   http://poseidon.csd.auth.gr/optimark

3   http://watermarking.unige.ch/Checkmark/

4   http://vision.unige.ch/certimark

5   http://www.openwatermark.org

6   http://www.datahiding.com

7   SSIM:http://www.cns.nyu.edu/~lcv/ssim/
     RRIQA:http://www.cns.nyu.edu/~lcv/
     rriqa/

     UQI: http://www.cns.nyu.edu/~zwang/files/
     research/quality_index/demo.html
     C4:http://membres.lycos.fr/dcapplications/
     main.php
     wPSNR and Watson: http://watermarking.
     unige.ch/Checkmark/
     Komparator: http://autrusseau.florent.club.
     fr/Komparator/index.html

8   BOWS http://lci.det.unifit.it/BOWS

APPENDIX A

In this appendix the algorithms employed for our test are briefly sketched. The algorithms A1–A9 have been implemented using the code implementation proposed in Meerwald (2001).

A1: *Corvi and Nicchiotti (1997) method is a spread spectrum based watermarking algorithm operating in the wavelet domain.*

A2: *Cox et al. (1997) approach is a spread spectrum based watermarking algorithm operating in the DCT domain.*

A3: *Fridrich (1998) technique operates in the DCT domain by embedding different watermarks in distinct portions of the frequency space.*

A4: *Kim and Moon (1999) approach is a wavelet-based algorithm. Perceptually significant wavelet coefficients, selected using a level-adaptive thresholding approach, are watermarked using different scale factors according to the level of decomposition.*

A5: *Koch and Zhao (1995) method is based on the random generation of the locations where to insert a watermark and in the subsequent embedding in the DCT coefficients of the blocks, corresponding to the selected locations, of a binary generated watermark.*

A6: *Wang et al. (1998) algorithm is a perceptual watermarking scheme, operating in the wavelet domain, where the significant wavelet coefficients search is motivated by the principle for the design of the multi-threshold wavelet codec.*

A7: *Xia et al. (1998) approach is based on the watermark embedding in the large coefficients at the high and middle frequency bands of the discrete wavelet transform of the host image.*

A8: *Xie and Arce (1998) method is jointly designed together with a compression algorithm in order to prevent the watermark degradation after compression with the underlying assumption that coding is inevitably used during transmission. Specifically compression in the wavelet domain is taken into account.*

A9: *Zhu et al. (1998) algorithm embeds the watermark in high-pass bands in the wavelet domain.*

A10: *Autrusseau and Le Callet (2007) algorithm embeds a watermark in the Fourier domain, taking into account a weighting function defined by a perceptual mask.*

Chapter X
Computational Aspects of Digital Steganography*

Maciej Liśkiewicz
Institute of Theoretical Computer Science, University of Lübeck, Germany

Ulrich Wölfel
Federal Office for Information Security (BSI), Germany

ABSTRACT

This chapter provides an overview, based on current research, on theoretical aspects of digital steganography—a relatively new field of computer science that deals with hiding secret data in unsuspicious cover media. We focus on formal analysis of security of steganographic systems from a computational complexity point of view and provide models of secure systems that make realistic assumptions of limited computational resources of involved parties. This allows us to look at steganographic secrecy based on reasonable complexity assumptions similar to ones commonly accepted in modern cryptography. In this chapter we expand the analyses of stego-systems beyond security aspects, which practitioners find difficult to implement (if not impossible to realize), to the question why such systems are so difficult to implement and what makes these systems different from practically used ones.

INTRODUCTION

Digital steganography aims at hiding secret data in unsuspicious cover media. The field has been actively investigated since the early 1990s. In most cases, the cover media chosen are multimedia data, such as images, audio, or video. For this reason, many impulses in steganography research come from statistics, signal and image processing with a focus on heuristic algorithms for hiding, and experimental methods for detecting hidden information. In the early years of scientific investigations this focus caused a lack of theoretical analyses on fundamental properties of steganographic systems, namely capacity, security, and tractability.

Starting in the late 1990s, theoretical analyses of steganography began to be conducted, concerned primarily with security and capacity aspects, which unfortunately have mostly been neglected by practitioners in the field. This is in part due to unrealistic assumptions and simplifications that have been made in order to cope with the difficult problem of formal modeling of steganography. In the case of capacity—besides some superficial practical analyses—a good understanding from an information-theoretic point of view has been achieved (see e.g., the seminal paper by Moulin & O'Sullivan, 2003), but there is still a lack of some guiding theory describing any information-hiding system achieving maximum capacity. Moreover, the focus of the mentioned study was on active adversaries, a scenario that better suits digital watermarking more than steganography, where typically passive adversaries are considered. Because of this we view capacity as a topic that will have to receive renewed attention in the future and thus leave it out of our current study. Regarding security, the focus of theoretical investigations so far has been on the maximum achievable security in different attack scenarios, which has led to interesting insights, but not yet to more secure stego-systems, as practical implementations of such systems prove to be difficult, if not unfeasible, in terms of computational complexity. So the situation of steganography seems in some respects similar to that of cryptography some 50 years ago, where the existence of secure systems, such as the one-time pad, was known, but these could not be practically implemented.

When looking at stego-systems that have been practically implemented, however, one finds that the time span from announcement as the latest and greatest system to the first successful detection by steganalysis often lasts only some two or three years. Because this situation does not appear to change in spite of all efforts by the steganography community, the question arises whether bringing reliable security into real-life systems can be achieved at all. Using experience and methods from cryptography and theoretical computer science one can expect to find answers to the important question if the field of steganography can reach levels of security that are available today in cryptography.

This chapter provides an overview of previous work on theoretical analyses of steganography, in which the central question concerns the security of given systems. Several definitions of secure steganography have been proposed in the literature, but most of them make the rather unrealistic assumptions of unlimited computational power for the parties involved and complete knowledge of the cover and stego-text distributions. We focus on formal models of secure systems that make more realistic assumptions of limited computational resources and restricted access to cover-text distributions. This allows us to look at steganographic secrecy from a computational complexity point of view and to obtain provable security based on widely accepted complexity assumptions, as, for example, the existence of one-way functions. Such security evidence is commonly accepted in the field of cryptography.

We will additionally look at the tractability of secure stego-systems—a topic whose examination has only recently started (Hundt, Liśkiewicz, & Wölfel, 2006). For the tractability analysis we consider that not only the adversary, but also both parties that use steganography are restricted to working in polynomial time. This is an important assumption in the context of real-life stego-systems that is, unfortunately, often forgotten in theoretical constructions. In such systems the complexity of sampling typically plays a crucial role. Thus, the analysis of a stego-system's tractability is an important tool that complements theoretical security analyses and will likely be a major subject in future research. It also helps to divide known stego-systems into categories, yielding a more systematic view on the possibilities of different approaches to steganography. So, in this second part we will expand the analyses presented in this chapter beyond security analyses of stego-systems that practitioners find difficult (if not impossible) to implement to the question *why* such systems are so difficult to implement and what makes these systems different from practically used systems.

This chapter has the following organisation. In the second section we give the basic definitions of channels, sampling oracles, and their use in stego-systems. We will introduce in the third section the notion of steganographic security which is needed for the security analyses that follow in hte fourth section. Starting with a short overview of some early information-theoretic security approaches, we will detail some results on the cryptographic security of stego-systems by Hopper, Langford and Ahn (2002) and successive works. The tractability of stego-systems will be the subject of the fifth section. Finally, we summarise the chapter in sixth section and draw conclusions with an emphasis on practical implications of the results presented in the preceding sections. The chapter ends with a brief outlook on future research.

BASIC DEFINITIONS AND CONCEPTS

Before going into the details of security and tractability analyses of stego-systems, we give some basic definitions and fix the notation that will be used throughout this chapter.

Preliminaries

We call a function $\delta : N \to R$ negligible if for all $c > 0$ and for all sufficiently large $x, \delta(x) < 1/x^c$. Let Σ be a finite alphabet, Σ^l the set of strings of length l over Σ, and Σ^* the set of strings of finite length over Σ. We denote the length of a string u by $|u|$ and the concatenation of two strings u_1 and u_2 by $u_1 \| u_2$. We use the standard definition for the entropy $H(P) = -\sum_{x \in A} p(x) \log p(x)$ of a probability distribution P over a finite set A, where $p(x)$ means $\Pr_P[x]$, for short, the loga-

rithm base is 2, and by convention $0 \log 0 = 0$; the relative entropy (or Kullback-Leibler distance) between two probability distributions P and Q on the same (finite) space A is

$$D(P \| Q) = \sum_{x \in A} p(x) \log \frac{p(x)}{q(x)},$$

where $0 \log 0/q = 0$ and $p \log p/0 = \infty$; and the mutual information of random variables X and Y on A and B, respectively, is

$$I(X;Y) = \sum_{x \in A, y \in B} \Pr[X = x, Y = y] \log \frac{\Pr[X = x, Y = y]}{\Pr[X = x]\Pr[Y = y]}.$$

If P is a probability distribution with finite support A, we define the minimum entropy $H_\infty(P)$ of P as the value

$$H_\infty(P) = \min_{x \in A: p(x) > 0} (-\log p(x)).$$

The notion of minimum entropy provides a measure of the amount of randomness present in the distribution P. Informally speaking, if the minimum entropy of P is d, then the distribution P is at least as random as the uniform distribution on bit strings of length d. From the *entropy smoothing theorem* by Håstad, Impagliazzo, Levin, and Luby (1999) we can conclude even more—if $H_\infty(P)$ is at least d, then it is possible to construct from P an almost uniform distribution over almost all d bit strings, by hashing elements chosen according to P. This property is used extensively in stego-systems that work with rejection sampling, which will be discussed in the *Probably Secure Stego-Systems* section.

Channels and Sampling Oracles

Strings $u \in \Sigma^b$ of specific length b will be called documents and a finite concatenation of documents $u_1 \| u_2 \| \ldots \| u_l$ will be called the communication sequence (or string). Typically the document models a piece of data (e.g., a digital image or fragment of the image) while the communication sequence models the complete message send to the receiver in a single communication exchange.

Definition (Channel). *Let Σ be a finite alphabet. A channel C is a distribution on communication sequences on Σ, i.e. it is a distribution on $\left(\Sigma^b\right)^*$, where $b > 0$ denotes the length of documents.*

This is a very general definition of a communication channel that models dependencies between pieces of data (called documents in our setting) that are present in typical real-world communications. If C is a channel, then $c := EX_C()$ means that the communication sequence c is returned by an oracle EX modeling the communication according to the distribution C. Thus, if C is a real-world channel, then in a typical setting one can assume low cost for the sampling $EX_C()$. Interestingly, having only access to the sampler $EX_C()$ and no additional knowledge about C, there are no known efficient stego-systems that are provably secure. Below we characterise the types of samplers sufficient for secure steganography.

Definition (Sampling Oracle). *A sampling oracle for a channel C draws samples according to the channel distribution. We differentiate between the following three types, the first two of which work as black-box samplers, that is, it is not known what they do to access the channel. The third type is a white box sampler, that is, it is assumed that all parties involved in the steganographic communication exactly know the distribution C.*

- An *adaptive sampling oracle*, for a given context $u_{j_1}, u_{j_2}, \ldots, u_{j_l}$, returns a possible document u_j. There are many possibilities to define the context. Typically, an adaptive sampler is history-based, that is, it draws for a given history $h = u_1 \| u_2 \| \ldots \| u_{j-1}$ of previously drawn documents a sample

$u_j \in \Sigma^b$ according to the channel distribution conditioned on the full prior history h. We denote the conditional channel distribution by C_h and write $c := EX_{C_h}()$ for the sampling process, that is, when a document c is returned according to the distribution C_h.

- A *semi-adaptive sampling oracle* is queried with part of the prior history h, typically the last α documents of the entire history h, where α is a parameter of the sampling oracle. A sampler which ignores the complete history is called a non-adaptive or independent sampling oracle.

- An *algorithmic sampling oracle* contains an algorithm that is queried with a random string and produces a sample according to the channel distribution C. The algorithm assumes full knowledge of the distribution C.

To efficiently embed messages in cover-texts, it is reasonable to require that the channel is sufficiently random. In this chapter we will assume that cover-text channels have a sufficient minimum entropy and we will call such channels always informative (see Hopper et al., 2002 and Ahn & Hopper, 2004 for details).

Stego-Systems and Their Use of Sampling Oracles

In his seminal paper on hidden communications, Simmons (1984) was the first to use channels for his model of steganographic communications, exemplified in his now-famous *prisoners' problem*.

Alice and Bob are in jail. They are allowed to communicate, but all communication is monitored by Wendy, the warden. In order to hatch an escape plan, they have to communicate by means of messages that look normal and unsuspicious, but additionally contain some hidden information that can only be read by Alice and Bob.

Coming from a communications background, his *subliminal channel* models those parts of the cover-texts in which the steganographic message can be embedded. This channel plays an important role in analyses of the capacity of stego-systems, as capacity corresponds to the amount of data that can be embedded into cover-texts. Two other channels involved in the steganography are the **cover-text** and **stego-text** *channels* (alternately called cover-text, respectively stego-text distribution). The cover-text channel models a *normal*, non-steganographic communication between Alice and Bob using the cover medium into which the steganographic message will eventually be embedded, while the messages exchanged via the stego-text channel are cover-text messages that additionally contain steganographic messages. These two latter channels are important in the analysis of steganographic security, as the basic task of any passive warden is to decide which of the two channels is currently in use.

There is a distinction to be made between stego-systems that are specifically designed for a single given channel and those that are universal, that is, they are not limited to work with one specific cover-text channel. It is more realistic to assume universality for a stego-system, as in practice one rarely finds pure channels. Consider for example a stego-system that embeds into images. Unless there is a clearly defined source which these images come from, there will be a broad mixture of different types of images that have been taken with all sorts of imaging equipment under different conditions, so their characteristics will differ a lot. For our definition of steganography we thus concentrate on stego-systems that can be applied to any channel that fulfils some basic conditions.

Definition (Stego-system). *A stego-system for the message space* $\{0,1\}^n$ *consists of three probabilistic algorithms SK, SE, SD running in polynomial time, where:*

- *SK is the key generation procedure that on input of a parameter n (which denotes the length of the message) outputs a key k of length* κ*, where* κ *is the security parameter which is a function of n.*
- *SE is the encoding algorithm that takes a key* $k \in \{0,1\}^{\kappa}$*, a message* $m \in \{0,1\}^{n}$*, accesses the sampling oracle for a cover-text channel and returns a stego-text s.*
- *SD is the decoding algorithm that takes k and s and returns m.*

The time complexities of algorithms *SK, SE, SD* are functions with arguments *n*—the length of the message, and κ—the length of the key, which bound the number of steps made by the algorithms on any input message *m* of length *n* and working with the security parameter κ. We charge any oracle query by a unit cost. A stego-system (*SK, SE, SD*) is correct if for all messages $m \in \{0,1\}^{n}$ the probability that *SD* decodes incorrectly a message encoded by *SE*, that is,

$$\Pr\left[k \leftarrow SK(1^n) : SD\left(k, SE\left(k,m\right)\right) \neq m\right] \tag{1}$$

is negligible with respect to the security parameter κ. The maximum value of the probability (1) over all messages $m \in \{0,1\}^{n}$ is called *unreliability* of the stego-system.

We say that a stego-system (*SK, SE, SD*) is universal if the only information source to the algorithms *SE, SD* about the channel is the sampling oracle. Such systems will also be called black-box stego-systems.

STEGANOGRAPHIC SECURITY

In order to define steganographic security, we need to look at the types of attacks we want to defend against. For this reason, some scenarios for steganalysis have to be discussed. A first distinction in steganalysis is to be made between active and passive attacks. The notion of active attacks is for the most part connected with disrupting attacks that have the aim of destroying steganographic messages. Such attacks are commonly examined in digital watermarking and thus should not be considered here. Passive attacks that intend to distinguish between original and steganographic data by reading the public channel are the most common attacks against steganography and thus will be our main focus. We will also briefly cover active distinguishing attacks that play a role in public key steganography. In this setting, a public key cryptosystem is used instead of a symmetric cipher, so the communicating parties do not share a key and the attacker can mount attacks by writing to the public channel.

In this section we look at the security of stego-systems with an emphasis on the maximum achievable security in different scenarios. We start with a brief historic overview that will present the first security analyses of steganography, which were all based on an information-theoretic model. After this we move to some more recent results that we are going to put into context with the use of sampling oracles in steganography.

Early Information-Theoretic Results

In the first theoretic analysis of steganographic security, Klimant and Piotraschke (1997) and Zöllner et al. (1998) made use of information theory to measure security. Their model of steganography comprised sets of cover-texts C, stego-texts S, keys K and secret messages M. Interestingly, the proposed notion of *steganographic security* differs from all subsequent analyses in that the goal is that no information can be gained about M (i.e., the hidden message itself) or speaking formally, that the mutual information is zero:

$$I\big(M;(S,C)\big)= H\big(M\big)- H\big(M\big|(S,C)\big)=0.$$

Thus a stego-system is claimed to be secure if the additional knowledge about C and S does not decrease the entropy of secret messages:

$$H\big(M\big|(S,C)\big)= H\big(M\big).$$

Such a model actually does not quite fit the scenario of steganography, where the very *presence* of a hidden message is to be concealed.[1] Also, the lack of some probability distribution on the set of cover-texts and the application of information-theoretic tools on the cover-texts themselves (rather than their probability distribution), makes this model unsuitable, as—other than in watermarking—in steganography the specific cover-text is of no interest. It should be noted that a similar model has since been proposed by Mittelholzer (2000) for steganography and watermarking with active attacks.

A more appropriate information-theoretic model of steganography with passive attacks has been proposed by Cachin (1998, 2004), who uses a hypothesis-testing approach. He introduces the notion of cover-text and stego-text channels as probability distributions P_c and P_s, respectively, which leads him to the following definition of ε-*security*:

$$D\big(P_C\big\|P_S\big)\le \varepsilon,$$

with ε = 0 for *perfect security*. Thus, a stego-system is perfectly secure if the stego-text distribution P_s and the cover-text distribution P_c are identical. Cachin presents in his paper some examples of stego-systems that are secure by this definition, some of which will be discussed in the *Provably Secure Stego-systems* section.

Bounding the Power of the Warden

As in cryptography, the power of the warden plays a crucial role in the security of steganographic schemes. A fundamental distinction is being made between *unbounded adversaries*, as in the information-theoretic approach discussed in the previous section, and *computationally bounded adversaries*. In this setting, the adversary is a probabilistic polynomial-time algorithm and, speaking informally, a stego-system is *computationaly secure* if adversary's advantage is negligible in the security parameter κ. In this chapter we will focus mainly on computationally bounded adversaries, as these are also favoured in cryptography for being more realistic. Before we can start looking at the security of specific stego-systems, we need to review some attack scenarios, as these provide the setting in which a security analysis holds. These scenarios are inspired by attacks on cryptosystems and correspond to some of the attacks presented by Johnson (2000); however, the definitions presented here will be more formal.

The main attack used in this chapter considers a passive distinguishing adversary W who is allowed read access to the communication channel between Alice and Bob. Besides just reading cover-texts that may or may not contain hidden messages, W also has the power of influencing Alice to use a hidden message of his choice in case she is sending stego-texts. Thus, the only information he does not possess is the shared secret key k and the information, which messages contain steganography and which do not. Formally, this attack can be defined in the random oracle model (see Bellare & Rogaway, 1993) as follows.

Definition (Chosen Hiddentext Attack [CHA]). Let $S = SK, SE, SD$ be a stego-system and let C be a cover-text channel. In a CHA the warden W has access to two oracles:

- *A reference oracle $EX_C()$ that he can query for samples from the channel C and*
- *A challenge oracle CH that is either*
  - *OS- the oracle which for a randomly chosen key k and a given query message m draws a stego-text SE(k, m), or*
  - *OC- the oracle which for a randomly chosen key k and a given query message m draws a cover-text of length $\left| SE(k,m) \right|$ from the cover-text channel C.*

The task of the warden is to make a guess about the challenge oracle CH and to output 1 if it guesses the oracle is OS and 0 otherwise. We define W's advantage for a given cover-text channel C as

$$Adv_C(W) = \left| \Pr\left[W^{OS}(1^n) = 1 \right] - \Pr\left[W^{OC}(1^n) = 1 \right] \right|$$

where W^{OS} means that the challenge oracle is the oracle OS and W^{OC} means respectively, that the challenge oracle is OC.

The *insecurity* of a stego-system (SK, SE, SD) with respect to channel C is defined by

$$InSec_C(t,q,l,n) = \max_W \left\{ Adv_C(W) \right\}$$

where the maximum is taken over all wardens W working in time at most $t(n)$ and making at most $q(n)$ queries of total length of $l(n)$ bits to the challenge oracle CH. Stego-system (SK, SE, SD) is (t, q, l, ε) *steganographically secure against CHA* for the channel C if $InSec_C(t,q,l,n) \le \varepsilon$. Finally we say that (SK, SE, SD) is *universally steganographically secure against CHA* if for some polynomial p and negligible ε it is (p, q, l, ε) steganographically secure for every always informative channel C. In this chapter we call such systems also computationally secure, for short.

Note the similarity between CHAs in steganography and chosen plaintext attacks in cryptography. The former can be thought of as a generalisation of the latter with respect to a given cover-text channel distribution.

An example of an active distinguishing attack is the *chosen cover-text attack* (CCA) described by Backes and Cachin (2005). The idea behind this attack is that due to the use of public-key steganography, the attacker is able to use Alice's public-key and send stego-texts to her. Similar to the chosen ciphertext scenario in cryptography, Alice will decode the message and return the decoded message to the attacker. In a more formal modeling, Alice will be replaced by a decoding oracle *DE()* that the attacker can query with arbitrary cover-texts. There is one exception, the oracle refuses to decode challenge cover-texts from *CH()*. This attack is considered to be one of the strongest which public-key steganography can be made secure against.

PROVABLY SECURE STEGO-SYSTEMS

We classify stego-systems with respect to prior knowledge about the cover-text distribution. In case of partial knowledge, particularly if Alice has no information about the distribution at all, as in the black-box scenario, we consider different types of samplers to gain information about the distribution.

Adaptive Sampling

This section discusses stego-systems that use adaptive sampling, a powerful tool to generate appropriate cover-texts for any cover-text distribution. In this model the sampler is able to take an arbitrary history of documents as input and return a document distributed according to the cover-text distribution conditioned on the history. Such a sampling mechanism enables the construction of very strong systems—namely universal stego-systems—which can be made provably secure in the computational setting. The notion of computational security was formalised independently by Katzenbeisser and Petitcolas (2002) and Hopper et al. (2002); the latter of these also presented a proof of security for the following universal system based on adaptive sampling. The encoding algorithm uses the sampler in such

a way that for a given target bit x cover-text documents c are sampled until bit x is embedded in c or the number of samples exceeds the security bound *count*.

Procedure RS^F (*x, count, h*)
Input: Target bit x, iteration number *count*, history h
$i := 0$
repeat
$c := EX_{C_h}()$; $i := i + 1$
until $F(c) = x$ or $i = count$
Output: c

In the above procedure, the embedding function $F : \{0,1\}^b \to \{0,1\}$ is an appropriate pseudorandom function (recall that b denotes the length of documents c). Note that the sampling may fail, in which case we have $i = count$ and $F(c) \neq x$, so the selected sample c does not embed the requested bit x. The crucial property of the procedure RS is that if the channel C is sufficiently random, the output distribution generated by RS is statistically close to C_h.

For the stego-system (*SK, SE, SD*) based on the rejection sampler RS^F, we assume that Alice and Bob initially share a secret key k, chosen randomly by *SK*, and an initial value N of a synchronized counter used in order to communicate long messages. In the algorithms below, values N will be used to synchronise selection of a pseudorandom function family $F_k(N, \cdot)$ indexed by key k and synchronised by parameter N. To increase the correctness, the communicating parties use encoding and decoding algorithms with error correcting codes *Enc(m)* and *Dec(m)*, respectively. Next we show the complete algorithms for *SE* and *SD* (Construction 1, presented by Hopper et al., 2002). See Exhibit 1.

To guarantee that the output distribution generated by $RS^{F_k(N, \cdot)}$ is statistically close to C_h we call the procedure with the bound on the number of iterations in RS equal to 2. We can conclude

Exhibit 1.

Encoding *SE* (*k*,*m*)
Input: key *k*, message *m*, history *h*
$m' := Enc(m)$;
parse m' as $m_1 \| m_2 \| \ldots \| m_l$, where $|m_i| = 1$;
for $i = 1, \ldots, l$ do $c_i := RS^{F_k(N, \cdot)}(m_i, 2, h)$;
$h := h \| c_i$; $N := N + 1$;

Output: $c_1 \| c_2 \| \ldots \| c_l$

Decoding *SD* (*k*,*m*)
Input: key *k*, stegotext *s*
parse *s* as $s_1 \| s_2 \| \ldots \| s_l$, where $|s_i| = b$;
for $i = 1, \ldots, l$ do
$\quad m_i := F_k(N, s_i)$;
$\quad N := N + 1$;
$\quad m := m_1 \| m_2 \| \ldots \| m_l$;

Output: *Dec(m)*

that for all always informative channels *C* the following theorem is true.

Theorem (Hopper et al., 2002). *If* $F_k(\cdot, \cdot)$ *is pseudorandom, then the stego-system is universally secure against CHAs.*

The construction guarantees negligible insecurity for any channel. However, its capacity is very small—it transmits only one bit per document and because the rejecting sampling procedure *RS* samples the oracle at most twice, its reliability to correctly embed a bit *x* in a cover-text *c* is limited. In fact, one can prove that each bit *x* is embedded incorrectly with probability at least ¼. Thus, to improve the reliability of the stego-system, error-correcting codes are used. This, however, drastically decreases the transmission rate of the system. The transmission rate measures the number of bits per document of a given message *m* that the system can embed. In the *Limits of Universal Steganography* section we show an improvement of the previous stego-system, presented by Dedić et al. (2005).

Algorithmic Sampling

If Alice has full knowledge about the cover-text distribution, she can use a stego-system which does not need to use any sampler at all, besides maybe a general randomness resource, for example, a (pseudo-) random number generator. Note that such a stego-system is not universal any more. In this section we first discuss a provably secure stego-system that works correctly for some specific channels. This will be followed by systems that work securely for general stego-text distributions, assuming that Alice and Bob have full knowledge about this distribution. In the first case a perfectly secure stego-system will be presented; for an arbitrary distribution two systems will be discussed. The first of these guarantees statistical security and the second, which is more realistic, guarantees computational security.

First consider the uniform cover-text distribution. In this case, the following system based on the one-time pad makes a perfectly secure stego-system. The key generation procedure

$$SK\left(1^n\right) \text{ returns } k \xleftarrow{R} \{0,1\}^{\kappa}, \text{ with } \kappa = n.$$

Encoding *SE* (*k*,*m*)
Input: key *k*, message *m*
Output: stegotext $s := m \oplus k$

Decoding *SD(k,s)*
Input: key *k*, stegotext *s*
Output: message $m := s \oplus k$

Here, an n-bit secret key k is chosen with a uniform distribution; SE computes the bit-wise XOR of the n-bit message m and the key k, while SD uniquely decodes the message from the stego-text s by computing the bit-wise XOR of s and k.

Assume the cover-text C is uniformly distributed over $\{0,1\}^n$ and let Alice and Bob share an n-bit secret key k with uniform distribution. Then the resulting stego-text is also uniformly distributed over $\{0,1\}^n$. Thus, the cover-text and stego-text distributions are equal to each other, from which follows that the stego-system is perfectly secure. It is easy to see that the system has high capacity and is of small computational complexity. But the security property only holds for uniform distributions.

We now discuss a simple stego-system that is statistically secure, assuming that the a priori known cover-text distribution fulfils an appropriate property, which we show next. This system represents practical stego-systems for digital images that embed information by modifying the least significant bits of pixel values. For simplicity, the considered system embeds one-bit messages, but the extension to the encoding of more bits of information is a straightforward task. As usually, let C be the cover-text distribution on the support $\widetilde{C}$ and suppose $\left(\widetilde{C}_o, \widetilde{C}_1\right)$ is a partition of $\widetilde{C}$ such that the value

$$\delta = \left| \Pr\left[c \overset{R}{\leftarrow} C : c \in \tilde{C}_0\right] - \Pr\left[c \overset{R}{\leftarrow} C : c \in \tilde{C}_1\right] \right|$$

is minimal over all partitions of the support $\widetilde{C}$. Define C_0 to be the conditional distribution on $\widetilde{C}_0$: that is, let for any $c \in \widetilde{C}_0$ the probability

$$\Pr\left[x \overset{R}{\leftarrow} C_0 : x = c\right]$$

be equal to the conditional probability

$$\Pr\left[x \overset{R}{\leftarrow} C : x = c \,\middle|\, x \in \tilde{C}_0\right].$$

Analogously, we define the conditional distribution C_1 on $\widetilde{C}_1$. The following stego-system embeds a one-bit message m using a one-bit secret key k chosen uniformly by the key generation procedure presented previously.

Encoding *SE (k,m)*
Input: key k, 1-bit message m
$r := m \oplus k$;
$s := EX_{C_r}()$;
Output: stegotext s

Decoding *SD (k,s)*
Input: key k, stegotext s
if $s \in \widetilde{C}_0$ then $r := 0$ else $r := 1$;
$m := r \oplus k$;
Output: message m

This system works without errors; moreover, the encoding SE provides perfect secrecy for m and it is statistically secure. Note, however, that the system is not tractable. Finding the partition minimizing the value δ for a given distribution C is a hard combinatorial optimisation problem. More precisely, the corresponding decision problem is NP-complete.

Le and Kurosawa (2003) and Le (2004) have constructed a computationally secure compression-based stego-system that assumes both the sender and receiver exactly know the cover-text distribution. The quintessence of the solution are uniquely decodable variable length coding schemes $\Gamma = \left(\Gamma_e, \Gamma_d\right)$, called C-codes, with source alphabet $\{0,1\}$ and destination alphabet Σ such that if x is chosen randomly in $\{0,1\}^*$, then $\Gamma_e(x) \in \Sigma^*$ distributes according to C. Function Γ_d appropriately decodes the communication strings. The construction generalises an idea of Anderson and Petitcolas (1998) in which a perfect compression scheme on the cover-texts is used to obtain a perfectly secure steganographic system. Since such compression schemes do not exist in practice, the C-coding scheme heuristic by Le and Kurosawa (2003) and Le (2004) is based on non-perfect schemes, such as arithmetic compression. To construct the C-coding scheme Γ the algorithm uses as input a cumulative distribution function of the given cover-text distribution.

The resulting steganographic system achieves near optimal information rate and does not produce errors; for the coding scheme it is true that for all messages m we have $\Gamma_d\left(\Gamma_e\left(m\right)\right) = m$. To generate (pseudo)random bit strings the algorithms use a secure pseudorandom generator G and the secret key k is given as a seed to initialize G. The embedding and extracting operations are as follows (the encoding and decoding schemes Γ_e and Γ_d are initialized with an additional parameter z). See Exhibit 2.

Independently, Sallee (2004) implemented a compression-based stego-system for JPEG images that lets the sender and receiver estimate the cover-text distribution.

Semi-Adaptive Sampling

The crucial difficulty concerning adaptive sampling is that in the real world there are no known cover-text distributions that can be sampled adaptively. In the next section we will investigate algorithmic aspects of adaptive sampling and conclude that adaptive sampling from the distribution C_h can be hard even if sampling from the cover-text distribution C is feasible. Thus, the natural question arises if adaptive sampling is really necessary. Particularly, it is interesting to ask whether one can somehow restrict adaptive sampling, for example, by limiting access to the entire history

to make it more practical or feasible, but in such a way that the modified sampler preserves the initial distribution. In this section we will discuss this problem and reach the somewhat unsurprising conclusion that a universal (black-box) system has to use the accurate sampler.

Lysyanskaya and Meyerovich (2006) were the first who studied the security of stego-systems that have access to conditional samplers with a restricted history. In their work they examine whether accurate adaptive sampling is necessary and conclude that a stego-system can be broken if its sampler deviates from the cover-text sampler. In Lysyanskaya and Meyerovich (2006) the provably secure public key stego-system by Ahn and Hopper (2004) is analysed under the assumption that the sampler only considers the last documents of the history and it is shown how the inaccuracy in the sampler translates into insecurity in the stego-system. Basically, this system is built on Construction 2 by Hopper et al. (2002) which we present below. Let $F : \Sigma^b \rightarrow \{0,1\}$ be a public function.

Basic Encoding
Input: bits $m_1, \ldots, m_l$, history h, and
bound *count*
for $i := 1, \ldots, l$ do
$j := 0$
repeat
$c_i := EX_{C_h}(); j := j + 1$
until $F\left(c_i\right) = m_i$ or $j > count$
let $h := h \| c_i$;

Output: $c_1 \| c_2 \| \dots \| c_l$

Basic Decoding
Input: stegotext s
parse s as $s_1 \| s_2 \| \dots \| s_l$, where $|s_i| = b$;
for $i := 1, \dots, l$ do
$\quad m_i = F(c_i)$;
$m := m_1 \| m_2 \| \dots \| m_i$;
Output: m

The public-key stego-system initially encrypts a message m by means of a public-key cryptosystem. In a second step, the basic encoding is called with the encrypted message, current history and an appropriate bound *count* as inputs. The decoding works analogously. Let us denote the stego-system by S. Ahn and Hopper (2004) prove that if F is -biased then S is computationally secure.

To formally analyse scenarios where the sampler does not consider the entire history, one has to define the concept of an α-*memoryless distribution*. Such a distribution is computationally indistinguishable from some Markov process of order α. For a precise definition see Lysyanskaya and Meyerovich (2006), where it is also shown that for every cover-text distribution which is always informative but not α-memoryless, the following is true.

Theorem *If the stego-system S has access to the distribution via an oracle that only considers the last α documents of the history, then the system is not computationally secure.*

On the other hand, the system remains secure for cover-text distributions that are α-memoryless. Particularly, the following fully non-adaptive public-key stego-system based on the construction S is CHA-secure for every almost informative 0-memoryless cover-text distribution and ϵ-biased F. Below only the embedding algorithm SE will be presented and in the algorithm, $CE\,(pk, m)$ denotes a public-key encryption of message m using the key pk.

Encoding $SE(pk, m)$
Input: Public key pk, message m, and t cover-texts $c_1, \dots, c_t$
each of length $\left| CE(pk, m) \right|$
$m' := CE(pk, m)$
parse m' as $m_1 \| m_2 \| \dots \| m_l$, where $|m_i| = 1$;
parse every c_i as $c_{i,1} \| c_{i,2} \| \dots \| c_{i,l}$;
for $j := 1, \dots, l$ do
$i := 1$;
repeat
$s_j := c_{i,j}; i := i + 1$
until $F(s_j) = m_j$ or $i > t$;
end
Output: $s := s_1 \| s_2 \| \dots \| s_l$;

It is shown that the probability that the stego-system fails to encode m is negligible if the number t of cover-texts is chosen appropriately, and that the algorithm is secure if and only if the cover-text distribution is 0-memoryless. According to the definition, a 0-memoryless distribution is an independent, but not necessarily identically distributed sequence of random variables. This stego-system can be used with real world cover-text distributions since the real sampler (e.g., digital camera) can deliver the whole cover-texts c_i in a natural way.

Limits of Universal Steganography

If we ignore the complexity of the sampler in the sense that we charge any query of the stego-system with unit cost, there still remains another computational complexity aspect: How many queries are needed to construct an efficient stego-system? By an efficient stego-system we mean not only that both the encoding and decoding algorithms work fast using small space resources but also that the transmission rate of the stego-system is proportionally high. Recall that the transmission rate measures the number of hiddentext bits per document that the system can embed. Similarly, the query complexity of the stego-system measures how many times per document the encoding algorithm needs to query the sampler in order to create a stego-text document. For example, the secret-key system presented in the *Adaptive Sampling* section works with query complexity 2. The transmission rate, however, is not so obvious. To guarantee the correctness of the system, that is, that the probability in Equation 1, which describes the reliability of the system, is small, the encoding algorithm does not embed the bits of the message m directly; it uses an error correcting code generating the message m' and then embeds m' in the cover-text.[2] Hence the transmission rate depends on the error correcting encoding method and—as has been noted by Reyzin and Russell (2003)—the stego-system has to send 22 cover-text documents to reliably encode a single bit of the hiddentext.

In their paper, Dedić et al. (2005) systematically analyse the trade-off between transmission rate and query complexity. They provide strong evidence that black-box stego-systems with high transmission rates are very inefficient with respect to their query complexity. More specifically, a lower bound is demonstrated which states that a secure and reliable black-box stego-system

with a transmission rate of d bits per document requires that the encoder has to query the sampling oracle at least $a \cdot 2^d$ times per d bits sent, for some constant a. The value of a depends on security and reliability, and tends to $1/(2e)$ as insecurity and unreliability approach 0. This lower bound applies to secret-key as well as public-key stego-systems.

To prove the lower bound, a channel C is constructed with minimum entropy χ such that for any (black-box) stego-system S of insecurity $InSec_C$ and unreliability ρ, and for any pseudo-random function family $F(u)$, the probability that the encoder makes at most q queries to send a random message of length $n = ld$, is upper bounded by

$$\left(\frac{eq}{l2^d}\right)^l + \rho + R \cdot InSec_C + (R+1)\left(InSec_F^{PRF} + 2^{-u}\right)$$

where $InSec_F^{PRF}$ measures the insecurity of the pseudorandom function family F, and $R = 1/\left(1 - 2^x/\left|\Sigma^b\right|\right)$. The expected number of queries per document is at least

$$\frac{2^d}{e}\left(\frac{1}{2} - \rho - R \cdot InSec_C - (R+1)\left(InSec_F^{PRF} + 2^{-u}\right)\right).$$

Exhibit 3.

Encoding *SE (k, d, m, N)*
Input: Secret key k, message m, synchronised parameter N, and history h
parse message m as $m_1 \| m_2 \| \dots \| m_l$, where $|m_i| = d$;
for $i := 1, \dots, l$ do
    $j := 1; f := 0; N := N + 1$;
    repeat
        $j := j + 1$
        $s_{i,j} := EX_{C_h}()$;
        if $\exists j' < j$ s.t. $s_{i,j'} = s_{i,j}$ then
            $c \xleftarrow{R} \{0,1\}^d$; if $c = m_i$ then $f := 1$;
        else if $F_k\left(N, s_{i,j}\right) = m_i$ then $f := 1$;
until $f := 1$;
$s_i := s_{i,j}; h := h \| s_i$;
Output: $s := s_1 \| s_2 \| \dots \| s_l$;

Interestingly, this lower bound is tight. The following (stateful) black-box secret key stego-system by Dedić et al. (2005), which transmits d bits per document and needs 2^d samples per d bits, has unreliability of 2^{-x+d} per document, and negligible insecurity, which is independent of the channel. A very similar construction was independently given by Hopper (2004, Construction 6.10). See Exhibit 3.

TRACTABILITY OF STEGO-SYSTEMS

Algorithmic complexity and in particular the theory of NP-completeness helps to understand how easily a given problem can be solved in practice (for an introduction see Garey & Johnson, 1979). From cryptography it is known that certain problems that are considered difficult to solve practically can be used to provide security in cryptosystems, such as the trap-door functionality in public-key cryptosystems. As it is currently unknown how to make use of such problems for steganographic security, we will look at algorithmic complexity from a different perspective, namely the tractability of stego-systems and their requirements.

The analysis of steganography from a complexity theoretic perspective is still in its infancy with only few papers published so far. Chandramouli et al. (2004) discuss a problem that they call the "steganography problem," which models steganographic embedding by changes to the cover sample as an optimisation problem. The number of message bits that can be embedded is maximised subject to an upper bound of the distortion introduced to by the changes to the original. This problem is shown to be identical to the knapsack problem and thus it is NP-complete. It can be argued, however, if such a model of steganography really reflects the full problem of steganography. From the perspective of security, which Chandramouli et al. mention as the motivation for the distortion bound, the problem

of producing stego-texts that belong to the support of the cover-text channel is not addressed. Consider for example a cover-text channel that contains documents $r \| f$ composed of a random string r and some fixed string f. Any change of one single bit in the fixed string leads to the immediate detection of steganography, while the distortion bound is not reached. For this reason, the model of steganography used in Chandramouli et al. has to be considered unsuitable.

Hundt et al. (2006) analyse the computational complexity of adaptive sampling oracles. Such oracles are needed for secure stego-systems like the one described by Hopper et al. (2002). Therefore, the emphasis is not so much on the stego-system itself, but on the structure of the used channel and the construction of an oracle that adaptively samples it. The key requirement for such oracles is efficiency, defined as follows.

Definition (Efficient Sampling). A channel C can be sampled *efficiently* if there exists a probabilistic algorithm generating samples c with distribution C which runs in polynomial time and uses polynomial space.

The easiest way to sample a channel is to independently draw samples from it. If one assumes the existence of an efficient adaptive sampling oracle, it is trivial to obtain an efficient independent sampler from it. On the other hand, if only an independent sampler can be assumed to be available, it can be difficult to construct an adaptive sampling oracle from it. This difficulty is formulated in the following theorem.

Theorem (Hundt et al., 2006). *There exist channels C that can be efficiently sampled by an oracle $EX_c()$, but for which it is impossible to construct an oracle $EX_{Ch}()$ that efficiently samples the channel C_h, unless $P = NP$.*

For the proof of this theorem, a channel is used whose support is formed by the intersection of three simple context free grammars. It is shown that if there exists an efficient adaptive sampler for this channel, this sampler can be used to construct a deterministic algorithm that solves the NP-complete intersected context free language prefix (ICFLP) problem in polynomial time.

As Theorem 5.1 only concerns the existence of channels in which adaptive sampling is inefficient, the rest of the paper by Hundt et al. (2006) deals with a characterisation of the channels for which this type of sampling is hard and those for which it is not. It is shown that for every NP-complete problem a channel with hard adaptive sampling can be constructed. This means that for channels with a certain structural complexity the existence of efficient adaptive sampling oracles becomes unlikely. On the positive side, channels that have efficient independent sampling oracles running in polynomial time and using logarithmic space are shown to also have efficiently constructible adaptive samplers.

In summary, the results by Hundt et al. (2006) address the tractability of the most important building block in secure stego-systems that use adaptive sampling: the sampling oracle. Although examples of channels have been given which permit or prevent the construction of efficient samplers, it still remains an open task to give a full and precise characterisation of both categories of channels.

CONCLUSION

In this chapter we looked at aspects of security and tractability in digital steganography. The central questions in these areas concern the maximum achievable security for different steganography scenarios and the limitations in terms of time efficiency associated with stego-systems that achieve the highest levels of security.

One of the key aspects in such theoretic discussions is the access to different kinds of cover-text channels. We have presented three basic types of

sampling oracles that require distinct approaches to steganographic embedding. So far, only the most basic of these, namely independent sampling, has been practically implemented and used in stego-systems whose security has at best been tested against a few steganalysis algorithms, but without any formal security analysis. The vast majority of these stego-systems deals with multimedia data into which the hidden messages are embedded by changes to the sample being used. One of the big problems of this approach clearly is the creation of stego-text samples that are not in the support of the cover-text channel. All current steganalysis algorithms exploit this fact by trying to find anomalies that can be used to classify some sample as stego-text.

When looking beyond practically used systems, two additional types of sampling oracles appear, namely adaptive and algorithmic sampling. The first of these has been intensively investigated and stego-systems have been proposed that are secure against a number of strong attacks, such as chosen hiddentext attacks or chosen cover-text attacks. These results clearly answer our first question—it is possible to achieve steganographic security that is based on common assumptions from cryptography, concretely the existence of one-way functions. This conclusion is of high importance, as it directly relates the relatively young field of digital steganography to long-standing research in cryptography, from which the former benefits in terms of reliability and soundness of security results.

However, the mere existence of secure steganography does not directly lead to more security in practical implementations, as one might at first expect. The cause of this security gap between theory and practice lies in strong assumptions about the cover-text channel that are being made in the theoretic analyses of secure stego-systems. Availability of adaptive sampling oracles naturally is the key requirement for all stego-systems that depend on adaptive sampling, but the implementation of such oracles for many practically relevant cover-text channels, including digital multimedia data, leads to the necessity to solve NP-complete problems. It is this problem that prevents the otherwise attractive stego-system by Hopper et al. (2002) and its subsequent improvements from being implemented and deployed. Without the assumption of an adaptive sampling oracle, these stego-systems lose their appeal, as Dedić et al. (2005) could prove a lower bound for the number of draws from the cover-text channel that is exponential in the message length. In summary, all these theoretic results appear to show a fundamental dichotomy between insecure but practical stego-systems on the one side and theoretically secure but impractical stego-systems on the other side. However, when looking at the third possible sampling method, namely algorithmic sampling, we get a different perspective.

The results of Cachin (2004) on information-theoretically secure steganography show that under the assumption that cover-texts can be produced (approximately) according to the cover-text channel distribution using some random input, statistical security can be achieved. Although the knowledge needed to produce such cover-texts is difficult to obtain for some types of cover media, there are still many cover-text channels that could indeed be used for this type of steganography. One issue with all kinds of steganography and particularly this one is of non-technical nature: How plausible is the selected cover-text channel? If it was not for this additional constraint, a simple random bitstring would make a perfect cover. With the requirement of plausibility, however, it is always the task of the steganographer to ensure an unsuspicious way of communication to embed the hidden messages into.

All of the problems with steganography discussed previously essentially deal with the cover-text channel and different ways of making use of it. For this reason, we see it as an important future task in steganography research to look into these issues and analyse cover-text channels with respect to their suitability for steganography.

Finally, our distinction of steganography by their use of different types sampling oracles also has some implications for steganalysis. All currently known steganalysis methods work by detecting anomalies in the stego-texts, thus relying on the fact that most practically implemented steganography uses independent sampling oracles, embeds by actually changing cover-text samples, and produces with high probability stego-texts that are not in the support of the cover-text channel. Future stego-systems that might use adaptive sampling oracles will require very different steganalysis techniques that classify a cover-text as original or stego based on the probability of its appearance in a sequence of samples from the cover-text channel. The specification and implementation of such steganalysis schemes remains an open question.

FUTURE RESEARCH DIRECTIONS

Regarding the security of steganographic systems, there are two major goals that should be achieved by future research. One concerns the security of systems that embed messages by changing independently sampled cover-texts. A formal model that describes such systems is needed as well as new definitions of security that take into account the possibility that stego-texts outside the support of the cover-text channel might be produced. It will also be important to relate the maximum achievable security for such systems to the security levels achieved by stego-systems using adaptive sampling.

The other direction that should be considered is centred around alternatives to independent sampling steganography. The results on tractability of adaptive sampling steganography obtained by Hundt et al. (2006) are one step in a new direction that can potentially offer many new insights into the relationship between security and practicality in steganography. Also, the proposal and implementation of practically relevant and provably secure stego-systems that use algorithmic or adaptive sampling will be an important contribution that has some merits to offer. In this context, the properties of different cover-text channels and their suitability for secure steganography could be another topic that is worth pursuing further.

As a last interesting open question in this field we would like to point out that it is not known whether the security of a stego-system can be based entirely on some hard problem, such as the discrete logarithm or factorisation problems in public key cryptography.

NOTE

Supported by DFG research grant RE 672/5-1

REFERENCES

Ahn, L. V., & Hopper, N. J. (2004). Public-key steganography. In *Advances in Cryptology—Eurocrypt 2004* (LNCS 3027, pp. 323-341). Berlin: Springer.

Anderson, R. J., & Petitcolas, F. A. P. (1998). On the limits of steganography. *IEEE Journal of Selected Areas in Communications, 16*(4), 474-481.

Backes, M., & Cachin, C. (2005, February 10-12). Public-key steganography with active attacks. In J. Kilian (Ed.), *TCC 2005,* Cambridge, MA (LNCS 3378, pp. 210-226). Berlin: Springer.

Bellare, M., & Rogaway, P. (1993). Random oracles are practical: A paradigm for designing efficient protocols. In *First ACM Conference on Computer and Communications Security* (pp. 62-73). ACM Press.

Cachin, C. (1998). An information-theoretic model for steganography. In D. Aucsmith (Ed.), *Information Hiding, 2nd International Workshop* (LNCS 1525, pp. 306-318). Berlin: Springer.

Cachin, C. (2004). An information-theoretic model for steganography. *Information and Computation, 192*(1), 41-56.

Cachin, C. (2005). Digital steganography. In H. C. Van Tilborg (Ed.), *Encyclopedia of Cryptography and Security* (pp. 159-164). New York: Springer.

Chandramouli, R., Trivedi, S., & Uma, R. N. (2004). On the complexity and hardness of the steganography embedding problem. In E. J. Delp, III & P. W. Wong (Eds), Security, steganography, and watermarking of multimedia contents VI. *Proceedings of the SPIE, 5306, 496-500.*

Dedić, N., Itkis, G., Reyzin, L., & Russell, S. (2005). Upper and lower bounds on black-box steganography. In J. Kilian (Ed.), *Second Theory of Cryptography Conference, TCC 2005* (LNCS 3378, pp. 227-244). Berlin: Springer.

Garey, M. R., & Johnson, D. S. (1979). *Computers and intractability: A guide to the theory of NP-completeness.* New York: W. H. Freeman & Co.

Håstad, J., Impagliazzo, R., Levin, L., & Luby, M. (1999). Construction of a pseudo-random generator from any one-way function. *SIAM Journal on Computing, 28*(4), 1364-1396.

Hopper, N. J. (2004). *Toward a theory of steganography.* Unpublished PhD thesis, School of Computer Science, Carnegie Mellon University, Pittsburgh, PA.

Hopper, N. J., Langford, J., & Ahn, L. V. (2002). Provably secure steganography. In M. Yung (Ed.), *Advances in Cryptology—CRYPTO 2002* (LNCS 2442, pp. 77-92). Berlin: Springer.

Hundt, C., Liśkiewicz, M., & Wölfel, U. (2006). Provably secure steganography and the complexity of sampling. In T. Asano (Ed.), Proceedings of the *17th International Symposium on Algorithms and Computation (ISAAC 2006)* (LNCS 4288, pp. 754-763). Berlin: Springer.

Johnson, N. F. (2000). Steganalysis. In S. Katzenbeisser & F. A. P. Petitcolas (Eds), *Information hiding—Techniques for steganography and digital watermarking* (pp. 79-93). Boston: Artech House.

Katzenbeisser, S., & Petitcolas, F. A. P. (2002). Defining security in steganographic systems. In E. J. Delp, III & P. W. Wong (Eds.), Security and watermarking of multimedia contents IV. *Proceedings of the SPIE, 4675, 50-56.*

Klimant, H., & Piotraschke, R. (1997). Informationstheoretische Bewertung steganographischer Konzelationssysteme. In *Proceedings of the Verläßliche IT-Systeme (VIS'97)* (pp. 225-232). DuD Fachbeiträge, Vieweg.

Le, T. V. (2004). *Information hiding.* Unpublished PhD thesis, Florida State University, Tallahassee, College of Arts and Sciences.

Le, T. V., & Kurosawa, K. (2003). *Efficient public key steganography secure against adaptively chosen stegotext attacks* (Tech. Rep. No. 2003/244). IACR ePrint Archive.

Lysyanskaya, A., & Meyerovich, M. (2006). Provably secure steganography with imperfect sampling. In M. Yung, Y. Dodis, A. Kiayias, & T. Malkin (Eds), *Public Key Cryptography— PKC 2006* (LNCS 3958, pp. 123-139). Berlin: Springer.

Mittelholzer, T. (2000). An information-theoretic approach to steganography and watermarking. In A. Pfitzmann (Ed.), *Information Hiding, 3rd International Workshop (IH'99)* (LNCS 1768, pp. 1-16). Berlin: Springer.

Moulin, P., & O'Sullivan, J. A. (2003). Information-theoretic analysis of information hiding. *IEEE Transaction on Information Theory, 49*(3), 563-593.

Reyzin, L., & Russell, S. (2003). *More efficient provably secure steganography* (Tech. Rep. No. 2003/093). IACR ePrint Archive.

Sallee, P. (2004). Model-based steganography. In T. Kalker, Y. M. Ro, & I. J. Cox (Eds), *Digital Watermarking, Second International Workshop, IWDW 2003* (LNCS 2939, pp. 154-167). Berlin: Springer.

Simmons, G. J. (1984). The prisoner's problem and the subliminal channel. In D. Chaum (Ed.), *Advances in Cryptology: Proceedings of Crypto '83* (pp. 51-67). New York: Plenum Press.

Zöllner, J., Federrath, H., Klimant, H., Pfitzmann, A., Piotraschke, R., Westfeld, A., et al. (1998). Modeling the security of steganographic systems. In D. Aucsmith (Ed.), *2nd Information Hiding Workshop* (LNCS 1525, pp. 344-354). Berlin: Springer.

ADDITIONAL READING

Anderson, R. J., & Petitcolas, F. A. P. (1998). On the limits of steganography. *IEEE Journal of Selected Areas in Communications, 16*(4), 474-481.

Bleichenbacher, D. (1998). Chosen ciphertext attacks against protocols based on the RSA encryption standard PKCS #1. In H. Krawczyk (Ed.), *Advances in Cryptology—Crypto 1998* (LNCS 1462, pp. 1-12). Berlin: Springer.

Ettinger, J. M. (1998). Steganalysis and game equilibria. In D. Aucsmith (Ed.), *Information Hiding, 2nd International Workshop* (LNCS 1525, pp. 319-328). Berlin: Springer.

Goldreich, O., Goldwasser, S., & Micali, S. (1986). How to construct random functions. *Journal of the Association for Computing Machinery, 33*(4), 792-807.

Hopper, N. J. (2005). On steganographic chosen covertext security. In L. Caires, G. F. Italiano, L. Monteiro, C. Palamidessi, & M. Yung (Eds), *Automata, Languages and Programming, 32nd*

International Symposium, ICALP 2005 (LNCS 3580, pp. 311-323). Berlin: Springer.

Koblitz, N., & Menezes, A. J. (2007). Another look at "provable security." *Journal of Cryptology, 20*(1), 3-37.

Petitcolas, F. A. P., Anderson, R. J., & Kuhn, M. G. (1999). Information hiding—A survey. *Proceedings of the IEEE, Special Issue on Protection of Multimedia Content, 87*(7), 1062-1078.

Reyzin, L., & Russell, S. (2003). More efficient provably secure steganography (Tech. Rep. No. 2003/093). IACR ePrint Archive.

ENDNOTES

[1] Interestingly, Zöllner et al. (1998) state, "In our definition a steganographic system is insecure already if the detection of steganography is possible."

[2] The original stegosystem by Hopper et al. (2002) has a reliability that allows each individual bit of the message m to be incorrectly decoded with probability $1/3$. Thus the system requires only weak error correcting codes. However, for a stegosystem to be useful, a much higher reliability should be required, as we do in this chapter.

Chapter XI
On Steganalysis and Clean Image Estimation

Christopher B. Smith
Southwest Research Institute, USA

Sos S. Agaian
The University of Texas at San Antonio, USA

ABSTRACT

Steganalysis is the art and science of detecting hidden information. Modern digital steganography has created techniques to embed information near invisibly into digital media. This chapter explores the idea of exploiting the noise-like qualities of steganography. In particular, the art of steganalysis can be defined as detecting and/or removing a very particular type of noise. This chapter first reviews a series of steganalysis techniques including blind steganalysis and targeted steganalysis methods, and highlights how clean image estimation is vital to these techniques. Each technique either implicitly or explicitly uses a clean image model to begin the process of detection. This chapter includes a review of advanced methods of clean image estimation for use in steganalysis. From these ideas of clean image estimation, the problems faced by the passive warden can be posed in a systematic way. This chapter is concluded with a discussion of the future of passive warden steganalysis.

INTRODUCTION

The *prisoner's problem* was introduced in 1982 by Gus Simmons (Simmons, 1984),

Two accomplices in a crime have been arrested and are about to be locked in widely separated cells. Their only means of communication after they are locked up will be the way of messages conveyed for them by trustees—who are known to be agents of the warden. The warden is willing to allow the prisoners to exchange messages in the hope that he can deceive at least one of them into accepting as a genuine communication from

Figure 1. Prisoner's problem

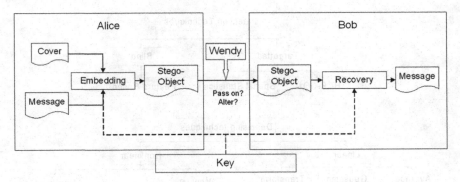

the other either a fraudulent message created by the warden himself or else a modification by him of a genuine message. However, since he has every reason to suspect that the prisoners want to coordinate an escape plan, the warden will only permit the exchanges to occur if the information contained in the messages is completely open to him—and presumably innocuous. The prisoners, on the other hand, are willing to accept these conditions, i.e., to accept some risk of deception in order to be able to communicate at all, since they need to coordinate their plans. To do this they will have to deceive the warden finding a way of communicating secretly in the exchanges, i.e. establishing a "subliminal channel" between them in full view of the warden, even though the messages themselves contain no secret (to the warden) information. Since they anticipate that the warden will try to deceive them by introducing fraudulent messages they will only exchange messages if they are permitted to authenticate them.

Thus began the modern study of steganography. The two prisoners have since been named Alice and Bob, the warden is Wendy or Eve. Figure 1 shows an illustration of the basic scenario.

The modern warden, Wendy, has a challenge. Wendy's role is either to detect the presence of or to manipulate the message in order to prevent the undesirable escape of the two prisoners. Wendy

practices the art and science of steganalysis. The proliferation of electronic media has only increased the challenge of steganalysis.

In Wendy's passive role, the passive warden, her primary goal is to detect the presence of steganography in a group of otherwise innocuous messages. In the modern scenario, the means of message conveyance now includes a wide array of electronic media such as the Internet and e-mail. All remain through *known agents of the warden*, that is, all messages are observable, but the number of messages and means of hiding due to the presence of electronic media has grown significantly. The sorting of legitimate messages from messages that would facilitate *an escape* remains a challenging problem. To do this Wendy must develop some basis for a *normal* message.

This chapter explores the role of the passive warden and how to exploit the noise-like properties of modern steganography for the purposes of steganalysis. Here the focus is on image-based digital steganography. An overview of the topics covered appears in Figure 2. The next section introduces various forms of steganalysis, highlighting how clean image estimation is currently used in each. The third section reviews several advanced techniques for image denoising. The final section shows how these approaches can be applied to the passive warden scenario. This chapter is concluded with some discussion of the

Figure 2. Topics in this chapter

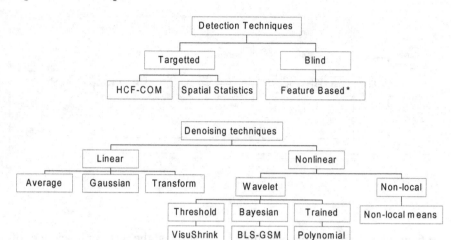

implications of noise and clean image estimation for steganalysis.

MODERN STEGANALYSIS

Steganalysis is the art and science of detecting messages hidden using steganography; directly analogous to cryptanalysis applied to cryptography. In the prisoner's problem, Wendy has the challenge of trying to prevent the escape of a pair of very clever prisoners. For modern digital steganography, the task is often one of statistical analysis and discrimination. Given a group of media, some clean and some stego-embedded, how can each file be classified into either the set of clean media or the set of stego-media.

Many techniques have been developed to classify clean from stego-embedded media. In most cases, this classifier has been developed with a specific steganography technique in mind. If a particular steganography technique hides stego by altering a feature of the media, then the steganalysis technique looks at that feature. An early example can be found in embedding data into audio files using echoes. Very slight echoes

in audio cannot be detected by the human ear, but are easily detectable using cepstral analysis (a technique developed for characterizing seismic echoes). The method of *decoding* the embedded data uses cepstral analysis. An effective steganalysis technique consists of the same process using cepstral analysis. The embedding can be easily discovered by simply *looking for echoes* around the optimal embedding delay, that is, the delay that allows the data to be recovered but still not audible (Anderson & Petitcolas, 1998).

As with any form of pattern recognition, steganalysis requires *a priori* information to establish the classifier. In the case of the echo hiding, this information is in the form of looking for echoes. For digital images, this information can be as simple as looking for echoes, but with a well-designed steganography technique a simple solution is often not possible. For a well-designed steganography technique, the problem of classifying clean and stego-embedded messages becomes much more difficult. For many image-based steganography techniques, the variability present in natural images is often much greater than the variability introduced by steganography.

To solve this problem of variability, a popular approach is to develop a reference from which to measure the feature. That reference reduces the natural variability to a relative quantity. The approach of developing this reference image is termed *clean image estimation*, or more generally *clean media estimation*.

An alternative approach taken by some researchers involves training the steganography system based on a *similar* class of images. The resulting approach would be to select a trained configuration based on some measure of image similarity. Images of class A must be classified using the training set A, images of class B use training set B, and so forth. Unfortunately, since it is unknown what statistics will be important for each steganography technique, it is difficult to define similarity in a meaningful manner. This does not necessarily invalidate this approach to steganography, but does make it difficult.

This section explores steganalysis and clean image estimation techniques as introduced by previous researchers.

Spatial Steganalysis

One example targeting the ±k embedding method is to treat the problem as a communication problem similar to a three level pulse amplitude modulation (PAM) signal. This is a well-studied communication problem, in which information is encoded in a series of signal pulses by modulating the amplitude of each pulse. In this scenario, the 3-level PAM is a series of +1, 0, and -1 *pulses* representing the hidden message, which is then corrupted by noise that is the clean image. This approach was explored byAgaian and Rodriguez (2006), as well as Soukal, Fridrich, and Goljan (2005), andHolotyak, Fridrich, and Soukal (2005). InHolotyak et al., this technique is explored in the context of a wavelet-based clean image estimation technique. In this approach, the clean image is estimated using a wavelet-based technique. By subtracting this estimate from the stego-image, the embedded message can be estimated, though it is still corrupted by the imperfect image esti-

mate. With this estimate of the image, a statistical technique such as a maximum likelihood (ML) estimator can be used to estimate the statistical parameters of the stego-message. A decision of the message length is then made using a simple threshold of the ML parameters. As an alternative, a maximum a posteriori (MAP) estimator can be used based on prior information of the message length. (For those unfamiliar with ML and MAP estimators, ML can be thought of as a sample average, while MAP is an average weighted by a ratio of the variance of a prior to the sample variance,

$$\frac{\sigma_P^2}{\sigma_P^2 + \sigma_S^2} .$$

This simplification is true only for normal data, but is useful for understanding.) The basic approach is shown in Figure 3.

In a similar paperSoukal et al. (2005), explores the use of a similar ML scheme based on using a high pass filter to directly estimate the stego-message. This spatial filter is applied in the place of the wavelet method. This approach is shown in Figure 4.

In either case, the basic approach is the same; estimate the stego-message then apply a statistical test.

HCF-COM

Harmsen and Pearlman (2003) developed a theory of steganalysis based on modeling steganography as a type of noise. They noted that this operation affects the histogram characteristic function (HCF), by shifting it slightly toward zero. They then measured this effect using the center of mass (COM), or geometric mean of the HCF.

For a color image, the addition of noise to the HCF has a well-defined behavior. While theoretically, this logic applies to a grayscale image, practically it is not very useful. The number of colors

Figure 3. Spatial steganalysis: Denoising estimator

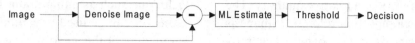

Figure 4. Spatial steganalysis: High pass filter

Figure 5. HCF-COM based steganalysis

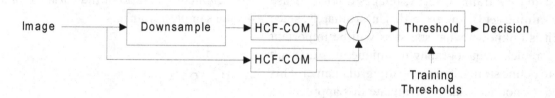

in a color image is actually very small compared to the number of possible colors. The addition of noise changes the number of colors present in an image to greater than what is naturally present, causing the HCF to shift from a *reasonable* value to an *unreasonable* one. In grayscale images, the number of grayscale tones used in the image is very large compared to the number of possible tones, in many natural images all grayscale tones can be used. Simply adding noise no longer shifts the HCF to a value beyond what is naturally found in clean images.

Ker (2005b) noted this and extended Harmsen and Pearlman's method by adding a "calibration" step. Instead of simply computing the COM of the HCF, Ker also computed the HCF-COM of a downsampled version of the image. This new COM is used to give a reference point from which to measure an *abnormal* deviation. By experiment, Ker showed that the noise added by steganography caused a bigger shift from the downsampled image than a non-stego-embedded image. This approach is shown in Figure 5, an example of the

downsampling technique is shown in Figure 6.

An interesting quality of the HCF-COM was that is was originally used for very noise-like spread spectrum embedding. It was later adapted to a different embedding method, LSB. This evolving use of the same basic principles leads logically toward developing a single, general method of steganalysis. The next section will discuss a more direct approach to developing a single, "universal" method of steganalysis.

Feature-Based High Order Statistics

The concept of blind or universal steganalysis is a powerful one. How can Wendy the warden detect a steganography method that she has not encountered before? Unlike targeted methods, there is no longer the ability to tailor the approach for a specific embedding method instead the goal must be to detect *any* embedding method, including those unknown.

One approach taken is to characterize some feature or set of features of the image that are sensitive to a generalized *embedding*. The key is

Feature Calculation 1. HCF-COM

Input: Image x

1. Calculate histogram of the image, $h = hist(x)$
2. Calculate the N-D FFT of the histogram, $hcf = H = FFT_N(h)$
3. Calculate the center of mass of the HCF, $com = \dfrac{\sum\limits_{i=1}^{n} i|hcf[i]|}{\sum\limits_{i=1}^{n} |hcf[i]|}$, where

   $n = \frac{1}{2} length(hcf)$
4. Repeat 2-3 for each dimension of the FFT
5. Downsample image $\hat{i}(x,y) = \left\lfloor \dfrac{1}{4}\sum\limits_{u=0}^{1}\sum\limits_{v=0}^{1} i(2x+u, 2y+v) \right\rfloor$
6. Calculate 1-4 on $\hat{i}$,
7. Calculate calibrated COM for each dimension of the FFT, $f = \dfrac{com(i)}{com(\hat{i})}$

Output: Feature f

Figure 6. Original image and Ker's "calibration" image, that is the image decimated by two through averaging

to select features such that all clean images appear to be similar, even those that are very different from one another. Steganographic content must appear different from this norm. The challenge becomes how to characterize a *normal* image in order to detect deviations from this norm.

Lyu and Farid (2006), Agaian and Cai (2005), and others have introduced methods of blindly characterizing images. Farid's approach to universal blind steganalysis is based on a wavelet-like multi-resolution decomposition; while Agaian's method is based on a cosine based multi-resolution decomposition. Based on either decomposition, a feature vector can be built using high order statistics (HOS) of the coefficients generated.

By itself, the variability present in natural images would be much too great to define a *normal* image. For these approaches, this is solved by calculating a linear predictor of the transform coefficients. This linear predictor is essentially a weighted spatial mask applied to the coefficients from two different decomposition levels. HOS are again calculated on the linear predicted coefficients, and then a difference is taken between the linear prediction and the actual coefficients.

Two possible linear predictors are shown next. In each a notation of *h*, *v*, and *d* are used for horizontal vertical and diagonal subbands of the wavelet transform. Using a 3-level wavelet decomposition (the sub-bands of each level out-

lined in black), Figure 9 shows the orientation of *h*, *v*, and *d*.

$$(x-1, y) + w_2 v_i(x+1, y) +$$
$$w_3 v_i(x, y-1) + ...$$
$$w_4 v_i(x, y+1) + w_5 v_{i+1}(\frac{x}{2}, \frac{y}{2}) + ...$$
$$w_6 d_i(x, y) + w_7 d_{i+1}(\frac{x}{2}, \frac{y}{2})$$

$$\hat{v}_i(x, y) = w_1 v_i(x-1, y) + w_2 v_i(x+1, y) +$$
$$w_3 v_i(x, y-1) + w_4 v_i(x, y+1) + ...$$
$$w_5 v_{i+1}(\frac{x}{2}, \frac{y}{2}) + w_6 h_{i+1}(\frac{x}{2}, \frac{y}{2}) + ...$$
$$w_7 d_{i+1}(\frac{x}{2}, \frac{y}{2}) + w_8 d_i(x, y) + w_9 h_i(x, y)$$

An alternative way of thinking about the linear predictor is as a filter applied to the multi-scale representation. This filter would look something like Exhibit 1, where v_i is the current sub-band, v_{i+1} is the next level of decomposition and $\otimes$ is a convolution. The multi-resolution decomposition at scale $i + 1$ is decimated by two, so v_{i+1} and d_{i+1} must be up sampled by two. This is an awkward representation, but it highlights the fact that the linear predictor is a simple method of estimating a clean image. Figure 10 shows the results of applying this linear predictor to an image.

The remainder of the blind steganalysis technique is to use one of several standard statistical discriminant analysis techniques. Different authors have explored the use of Fisher linear discriminant analysis (LDA) (Agaian & Cai, 2005;

Figure 7. Universal steganalysis

Figure 8. Universal steganalysis feature extraction, where ~ can be a number of combining operations such as subtraction, log(x)-log(y), division, or simple concatenation

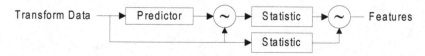

Table 1. High order statistics

Sample Mean	$\mu = \frac{1}{N}\sum\limits_{i=1}^{N} x_i$
Sample Variance	$\sigma^2 = \frac{1}{N}\sum\limits_{i=1}^{N}\left(x_i - \mu\right)^2$
m-th moment	$\gamma_m = \dfrac{\frac{1}{N}\sum\limits_{i=1}^{N}(x_i - \mu)^m}{\sigma^m}$

Figure 9. Three-level wavelet decomposition with coefficients needed for linear predictor of v_i highlighted for (left) Farid's linear predictor and (right) Agaian's linear predictor

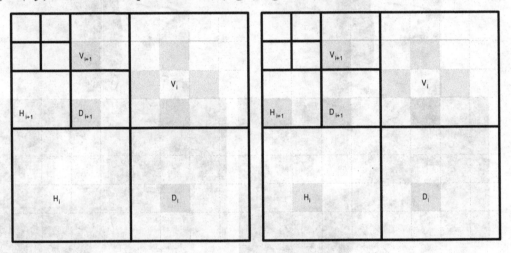

Exhibit 1.

$$\Delta v_i = \begin{bmatrix} 0 & w_4 & 0 \\ w_1 & 0 & w_2 \\ 0 & w_3 & 0 \end{bmatrix} \otimes v_i + \begin{bmatrix} 0 & 0 & 0 \\ 0 & w_5 & 0 \\ 0 & 0 & 0 \end{bmatrix} \otimes v_{i+1} + \begin{bmatrix} 0 & 0 & 0 \\ 0 & w_6 & 0 \\ 0 & 0 & 0 \end{bmatrix} \otimes d_i + \begin{bmatrix} 0 & 0 & 0 \\ 0 & w_5 & 0 \\ 0 & 0 & 0 \end{bmatrix} \otimes d_{i+1}$$

Farid, 2002; Fridrich, 2004) and support vector machines (SVM) (Lyu & Farid, 2003). Other classification techniques could be used as well.

Statistical classification (McLachlan, 2004) considers a set of observations x of an object or event, each of which has an inherent type y—clean or embedded. The classification problem is to find a predictor for the type y of any sample of the distribution given only an observation x.

LDA is related to principle component analysis (PCA). PCA has a geometric interpretation, in which the axes in an N-dimensional space are re-aligned such that the primary axis maximizes the variance of the observations. Figure 11 shows a simple two-dimensional example, in which the principle component lies along the axis of maximum variation. Unlike PCA, LDA does not capture the principle component, or the component with

Figure 10. Image with Farid's wavelet domain, linear predictor applied, left normal image, right after linear prediction

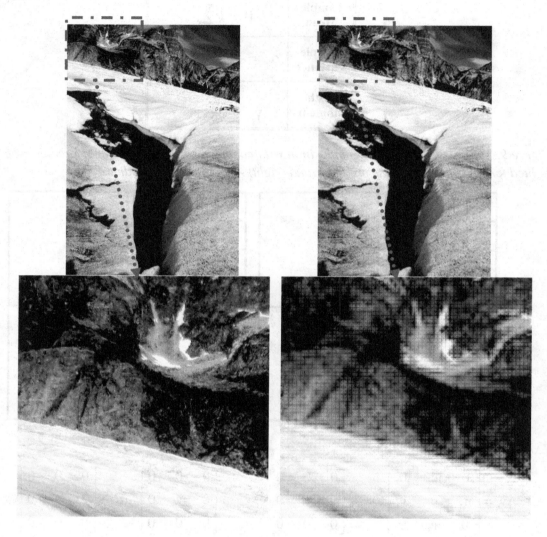

the greatest variance, rather it uses the component that best maximizes the between-set means and minimizes the within-set variance. An example appears in Figure 12. It does this based on the assumption of normality of the data.

This highlights the weakness of this basic approach, the requirement for a training set. Even though based on a general feature set, the detection method requires training. The diversity of the training set overall determines the *blindness* of the approach.

Feature Calculation 2. HOS

Input: Image

1. Transform image into wavelet space, $X = W(x)$

2. Calculate HOS of the horizontal, vertical, and diagonal wavelet subbands,

$$v = [\mu \; \sigma \; \gamma_3 \; \gamma_4 \; \gamma_5 \; \gamma_6 \; \gamma_7]$$

3. Calculate linear predictor for each wavelet coefficient,

$$\hat{X} = \left[\hat{v}_i(x,y) \; \hat{h}_i(x,y) \; \hat{d}_i(x,y) \right]$$

4. Calculate log error between predicted and original wavelet coefficients,

$$e = \log_2(X) - \log_2(\hat{X})$$

5. Calculate HOS of the log error of horizontal, vertical and diagonal wavelet subbands

$$\hat{v} = [\hat{\mu} \; \hat{\sigma} \; \hat{\gamma}_3 \; \hat{\gamma}_4 \; \hat{\gamma}_5 \; \hat{\gamma}_6 \; \hat{\gamma}_7]$$

6. Concatenate HOS vectors into a single feature vector

$$\mathbf{v} = [v \; \hat{v}]$$

Output: Feature vector **v**

Training Procedure 1

Input: Feature vectors for clean and embedded data set

1. Calculate features for two sets of images, clean and stego-embedded

2. Group clean and stego-images separately

3. Calculate eigen values and vectors of aggregate group

4. Find maximum eigen values, select corresponding vector as the separating component $\underline{c}$

5. Translate all feature vectors into component space by multiplying each feature vector by this component $\rho = \underline{c}v$, where ρ is a scalar

6. Search for threshold δ which best separates stego from non-stego values of ρ

Output: Separating component c, decision threshold δ

Detection Algorithm 1

Input: Image
1. Calculate features vector for image
2. Project feature vector into component space
3. Check if value is above or below threshold
Output: Decision

Figure 11. PCA example, highlighting the principle and secondary components of the multivariate space

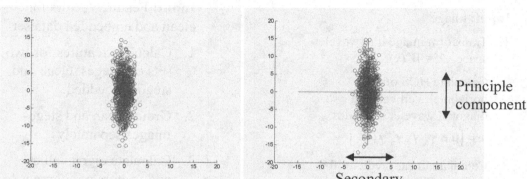

Figure 12. Data distribution showing the difference between the principle component using PCA, that is, the component with the highest variance, and the component with the best separation, which should be used for discrimination in LDA. The LDA discriminator is shown as a line, while the discriminator that an SVM would use is shown as an enclosing circle.

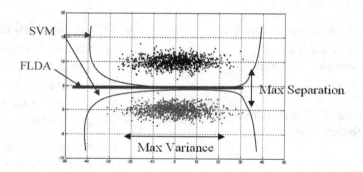

DENOISING OR CLEAN IMAGE ESTIMATION

Images are very difficult to model. The approaches taken by steganalysis researchers have for the most part been simple and somewhat effective in each case. A number of other approaches exist outside the information hiding literature. This section reviews the theory of noise removal and highlights several state-of-the-art approaches to image denoising.

To begin, the image itself can be modeled as a clean signal with a noise component,

$$y_i = s_i + n_i,$$

where y_i is a noisy image, s_i is a statistically deterministic, or information containing component of the image, and n_i is a noise component.

Spatial Mask

From the previous additive noise model, in many cases simple spatial filtering is all that is required

Exhibit 2. Summary

	Spatial	Transform Based	Blind
Example	• High pass filter based ML • Wavelet denoising based ML	• HCF-COM	• Wavelet w/FLD/SVD • Cosine w/FLD/SVD
Strengths	• Good targeted performance • Can estimate message length	• Fast • Only training is to determine a threshold • Generalizable to other techniques	• Uses *general* features to model image • Can detect unknown methods • Trainable
Weaknesses	• Targets a specific embedding method	• One feature may be insensitive to some embeddings	• Training is non-trivial
Selected Authors	• Holotyak, Soukal, Fridrich	• Harmsen and Pearlman (2003) • Ker	• Farid and Lyu • Agaian and Cai (2005)

to remove the noise component. In the case that both s_i and n_i follow Gaussian distributions, it has been shown that the Weiner filter is the optimal filter for removing n_i,

$$G = \frac{H^* P_i}{|H|^2 + \frac{P_N}{P_i}} = \frac{P_i}{P_i + \sigma_n^2},$$

where H is an arbitrary blurring function and P_i is the power spectrum of the image and σ_N^2 is the variance of the noise (Jain, 1989).

Unfortunately, for natural images, s_i has a decidedly non-Gaussian distribution (Simoncelli & Olshausen, 2001). This has led to the development of many other filtering techniques. Two commonly used spatial filters are the mean filter (Jain, 1989) and the Gaussian filter (Gonzalez & Woods, 2002),

$$\hat{i} = \begin{bmatrix} 1 & 1 & 1 \\ 1 & 1 & 1 \\ 1 & 1 & 1 \end{bmatrix} \otimes i \qquad \hat{i} = \begin{bmatrix} 2 & 4 & 5 & 4 & 2 \\ 4 & 9 & 12 & 9 & 4 \\ 5 & 12 & 15 & 12 & 5 \\ 4 & 9 & 12 & 9 & 4 \\ 2 & 4 & 5 & 4 & 2 \end{bmatrix} \otimes i$$

Both are effective low pass filters. These smoothing operators are used to blur images and remove detail as well as noise. While the mean filter is a true sample average of each pixel's neighborhood, the Gaussian outputs an average weighted by the Gaussian distribution.

While the mean filter has a fixed effect on an image based strictly on the width of the filter, for the Gaussian the degree of blur or smoothing introduced to an image is determined by the standard deviation of the Gaussian used. The larger standard deviations results in more smoothing and requires a larger spatial mask to approximate a Gaussian accurately.

As low pass filters, both filters attenuate high frequencies more than low frequencies, but the mean filter exhibits oscillations in its frequency response. This effect can be seen in Figure 13. The Gaussian on the other hand shows no oscillations. Unlike the mean filter, by choosing an appropriately sized Gaussian filter the range of spatial frequencies left in the image after filtering can be controlled.

Figure 13. Frequency domain characteristic function of (left) mean filter and (right) Gaussian filter

Figure 14. Left: Original image, center: first decomposition, right: full decomposition (note the peak in the upper left), the sparseness of the representation means the majority of coefficients are close to zero

Wavelets

The wavelet transform is an orthogonal transformation, based on one of many kernels that enjoy compact support in both time and frequency. This balance of time and frequency is suboptimal in a Heisenberg sense, but greatly improves over Fourier-based techniques. For applications, this property along with a fast algorithm implementation makes the wavelet a very useful tool (Gonzalez & Woods, 2002; Mallat, 1999; Vaidyanathan, 1992).

In the wavelet domain the additive noise model becomes, $Y = \theta + \varepsilon$, where Y, θ, and ε are wavelet domain representations of y, s, and n. $Y = W(y)$, $\theta = W(s)$, $\varepsilon = W(n)$, and $W(\cdot)$ is an orthogonal wavelet transformation. If the components of n are taken to be Gaussian of mean 0 and standard deviation of σ^2, then the orthogonality of W ensures that ε is the same Gaussian of mean 0 and standard deviation of σ^2.

For denoising, compact support leads to a sparse representation of smooth structures. This sparse representation allows for filtering to be accomplished through a process that is much simpler than classical Fourier-based techniques. An example wavelet transform is shown in Figure 14.

The sparse representation simplifies the model used to represent an image's information. Figure 15 shows the histogram of the full wavelet decomposition in Figure 14. Here a large number of zeros are present, while very few large values are present.

The sparse nature of the wavelet representation will compact the information present in the image

Figure 15. Example histogram of wavelet coefficients, note the large number of zeros and no other large peaks

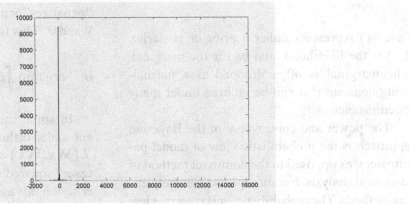

Exhibit 3. Wavelet based denoising procedure

1. Compute the wavelet transform of the data
2. Set all wavelet coefficients with value below a threshold δ to zero
3. Compute the inverse wavelet transform of the remaining coefficients.

into a relatively small number of large coefficients. The basic approach to wavelet-based denoising is to eliminate all but these large coefficients.

Or

$$T_\delta^h(x) = \begin{cases} x & |x| > \delta \\ 0 & |x| \leq \delta \end{cases}$$

An alternative approach, known as the soft threshold shrinks the wavelet coefficients toward zero instead of simply deleting,

$$T_\delta^s(x) = \begin{cases} x - \operatorname{sgn}(x)\delta & |x| > \delta \\ 0 & |x| \leq \delta \end{cases}$$

In this simple approach to removing noise, all that is needed for optimization is the selection of the threshold. Donoho and Johnstone (1995) proposed an effective solution, *VisuShrink*. This method is a simple threshold selection technique based on the number of data points n and the estimated standard deviation of the noise σ:

$$\delta = \sigma\sqrt{2\log(n)}$$

As with Fourier-based filtering, the simple elimination of coefficients is only optimal in an asymptotic sense. Since, other techniques have been developed that improve on the performance of these simple techniques. These include Bayesian and Polynomial methods.

Bayesian Wavelet Denoising

Bayesian statistics is a branch of statistics that deals with assuming prior information. This prior information (sometimes subjective) is used to condition measured data in an attempt to build a more accurate representation.

Bayes Law:

$$p(a|b) = \frac{p(b|a)p(a)}{p(b)} = \frac{p(a \cap b)p(a)}{p(b)},$$

is often written as

$$\pi\left(parameter\middle|data\right)=\frac{\ell\left(b\middle|a\right)\pi\left(a\right)}{m\left(b\right)}\propto\ell\left(b\middle|a\right)\pi\left(a\right)$$

here $\pi(\cdot)$ represents either a prior or posterior, $\ell\,(\cdot)$ is the likelihood, and $m(\cdot)$ is the marginal. The marginal is often dropped as a normalizing constant that can be ignored under many circumstances.

The power and controversy of the Bayesian approach is the probabilistic view of model parameters, as opposed to the dominant method of statistical analysis, commonly known as frequentist methods. The probabilistic, or Bayesian, view allows models to be constructed of each parameter, which then allow confidence intervals to directly represent the distribution of the parameter rather than the estimation system.

From the Bayesian perspective, the denoising problem is formulated in terms of a likelihood function with a prior for each of the model parameters. Assuming a Gaussian formulation as described inFigueiredo and Nowak (2001), in the observation domain, the likelihood is $y\mid s,\sigma^{2}\sim n\left(s,\sigma^{2}\right)$, while in the wavelet domain this has the form $\mathbf{Y}\mid\boldsymbol{\theta},\sigma^{2}\boldsymbol{\theta}=n\left(\ ,\sigma^{2}I\right)$.

From a Bayesian decision theory perspective, $\hat{\boldsymbol{\theta}}$ minimizes the posterior loss function,

$$\hat{x}=W^{-1}\arg\min_{\theta}E\left(L\left(\boldsymbol{\theta},\hat{\boldsymbol{\theta}}\right)\right)$$

$$=W^{-1}\arg\min_{\theta}\int L\left(\boldsymbol{\theta},\hat{\boldsymbol{\theta}}\right)p\left(\boldsymbol{\theta}\middle|Y\right)d\boldsymbol{\theta},$$

where $p\left(\theta\middle|Y\right)$, is the posterior probability function obtained from applying Bayes' theorem to the likelihood and priors. Where $L(\boldsymbol{\theta},\hat{\boldsymbol{\theta}})$ is the loss function which in Bayesian decision theory "penalizes" or measures the discrepancy between $\boldsymbol{\theta}$ and $\hat{\boldsymbol{\theta}}$. This is equivalent to

$$W^{-1}\arg\min_{\theta}\int L\left(\mathbf{Wx},\mathbf{W\hat{x}}\right)p\left(\mathbf{x}\middle|\mathbf{y}\right)d\mathbf{x}$$

In some cases, the loss function is invariant under orthogonal transformation, such that $L\left(\mathbf{Wx},\mathbf{W\hat{x}}\right)\propto L\left(\mathbf{x},\hat{\mathbf{x}}\right)$. Under two common cases, squared error and the 0/1 loss or MAP criterion this assumption does indeed hold. This is not the case in general.

Vidakovic (1998a) proposed a model for Bayesian estimation based on a Gaussian model of the wavelet coefficients.

$$Y\mid\theta,\sigma^{2}\sim N\left(\theta,\sigma^{2}\right)$$

For σ^{2} Vidakovic uses an exponential prior since the exponential "minimizes the Fisher information for all distributions with a fixed first moment supported on $[0,\ \infty)$"(Vidakovic, 1998b).

$$\sigma^{2}\sim\varepsilon\left(\lambda\right)$$

The marginal likelihood is then a double exponential,

$$Y\mid\theta\sim D\varepsilon\left(\theta,\frac{1}{\sqrt{2\lambda}}\right).$$

This follows from the fact that the double exponential distribution is a scale mixture of normal

Exhibit 4. Bayesian-wavelet denoising procedure

1.	Compute the wavelet transform of the data
2.	Obtain a Bayesian estimate $\hat{\boldsymbol{\theta}}$ given $\mathbf{Y}$,
3.	Compute the inverse wavelet transform of the estimate $\boldsymbol{\theta}$.

distributions. The prior on θ is a t-distribution with n degrees of freedom, location 0, and scale τ.

$$\theta \sim t_n(0,\tau)$$

This model results in an analytical solution for $\hat{\theta}$ given Y.

$$\delta(Y) = Y - \frac{\Pi'(\theta+d) - \Pi'(\theta-d)}{\Pi(\theta+d) + \Pi(\theta-d)},$$

Where $\Pi(.)$ is the Laplace operator on $\pi(.)$. An interesting special case of the Gaussian prior, is the case of a Gaussian assumption of θ with a mean of 0, or $\theta \sim n(0,\sigma^2)$, the resulting estimator takes a familiar form of

$$\theta \mid v = \frac{\sigma_\theta^2 v}{\sigma_\theta^2 + \sigma_n^2},$$

which is the Weiner filter.

The state of the art in Bayesian wavelet denoising uses a Gaussian scale-mixture as a prior for neighboring wavelet coefficients,

$$x = \sqrt{z}u,$$

where x is the local cluster of coefficients, u is a zero mean Gaussian vector with a covariance defined by x, and $\sqrt{z}$ is a *hidden* mixing multiplier. The techniques known as Bayesian least square, Gaussian scale mixture, BLS-GSM presented by Portilla, Simoncelli, et al. use this type of prior in (Portilla, Strela, Wainwright, & Simoncelli, 2003).

Polynomial Wavelet Denoising

In the case where the distribution of the priors cannot be modeled by a well-known distribution, another technique is needed to develop the wavelet shrinkage function. Smith, Akopian, and Agaian (2004) introduced the polynomial threshold that

can be adapted to a particular signal directly without a well-defined signal model.

The nonlinear thresholding operator $\mathbf{T}_\delta(\cdot)$ is defined as

$$\hat{\mathbf{s}} = \mathbf{W}^{-1}\mathbf{T}_\delta(\mathbf{W}\mathbf{y}),$$

representing the simple sequence of operations: (1) apply wavelet transform; (2) apply a threshold operator; (3) apply inverse wavelet transform.

The denoising problem is formulated as a search of threshold operators $\mathbf{T}_\delta(\mathbf{x})$ that minimize the error introduced. A solution to this is to use a parametric polynomial to represent the threshold operator. The polynomial threshold operator has the form,

$$T_{\delta,\mathbf{a}}(x) = \begin{cases} a_{N-1}x - a_N \operatorname{sgn}(x)\delta & |x| > \delta \\ \sum_{k=0}^{N-2} a_k x^{2k+1} & |x| \le \delta, \end{cases}$$

where $\mathbf{a} = [a_0,...,a_N]^T$ is an array of the coefficients for the polynomial. The polynomial threshold is a generalization of the hard and soft thresholds that can be obtained using the parameter selections:

$$T_{\delta,\mathbf{a}} = T_\delta^h : a_{N-1} = 1,$$
$$a_0 = a_1 = ... = a_{N-2} = a_N = 0$$

$$T_{\delta,\mathbf{a}} = T_\delta^s : a_N = a_{N-1} = 1,$$

$$a_0 = a_1 = ... = a_{N-2} = 0$$

Figure 16 shows a number of different realizations of the polynomial threshold. Provided a general form of the polynomial thresholding operator an optimization problem can be formulated as finding optimal set of the parameters, $\mathbf{a} = [a_0,...,a_N]^T$, which minimizes the error. One can equivalently define the proposed threshold operator in a matrix form

$$T_{\delta,a}(x) = \mathbf{f}(x)\mathbf{a},$$

where $\mathbf{f}(x) = \begin{bmatrix} f_0(x) & f_2(x) & ... & f_N(x) \end{bmatrix}$

where $\mathbf{f}(x)$ is the conditional

$$\begin{bmatrix} f_0(x) & f_2(x) & ... & f_N(x) \end{bmatrix} = \begin{cases} \mathbf{V}_1 & |x| > \delta \\ \mathbf{V}_2 & |x| \le \delta \end{cases}$$

and

$$\mathbf{V}_1 = \begin{bmatrix} 0 & 0 & ... & 0 & x & -\delta \operatorname{sgn}(x) \end{bmatrix}$$
$$\mathbf{V}_2 = \begin{bmatrix} x & x^3 & ... & x^{2N-3} & 0 & 0 \end{bmatrix}.$$

The polynomial-based system is its flexible parametric structure, allowing near arbitrary threshold operators to be developed. An optimum solution for the polynomial threshold can be constructed by solving the following optimization problem if the desired (training) signal $\mathbf{d}$, is available,

$$\mathbf{a}_{opt} = \arg\min_{\mathbf{a}} \left\| \mathbf{d} - \mathbf{W}^T \mathbf{f}(\mathbf{Y})\mathbf{a} \right\|.$$

For an energy-preserving transform such as orthogonal wavelets considered here, this can be simplified to

$$\mathbf{a}_{opt} = \arg\min \left\| \mathbf{D} - \mathbf{f}(\mathbf{Y})\mathbf{a} \right\|,$$

where $\mathbf{D}$ and $\mathbf{Y}$ are transformed versions of the desired and measured signals, $\mathbf{d}$, $\mathbf{y}$.

This optimization problem can be solved using two related techniques, first using linear least squares and second a minimum mean squared error (MMSE) approach. First using the technique of linear least squares (Press, Teukolsky, Vettering, & Flannery, 1992) $\mathbf{a}_{opt}$ can be calculated reversing the equation $\mathbf{a}^T \mathbf{f}^T(\mathbf{Y}) = \mathbf{D}^T$, to

$$\mathbf{a}_{opt} = (\mathbf{f}^T(\mathbf{Y})\mathbf{f}(\mathbf{Y}))^{-1}\mathbf{f}^T(\mathbf{Y})\mathbf{D}.$$

In the case of a square $\mathbf{f}(\mathbf{Y})$ this is a simple matrix inversion, for the non-square matrix a least squares approximation of $\mathbf{a}$ is found.

When considering a scenario with many observations, we can alternatively find the MMSE error across the observations using

$$\begin{aligned} MSE &= E\left((\mathbf{D}^T - \mathbf{a}^T \mathbf{f}^T(\mathbf{Y}))(\mathbf{D} - \mathbf{f}(\mathbf{Y})\mathbf{a}) \right) \\ &= E\left(\mathbf{D}^T\mathbf{D} - 2\mathbf{a}^T\mathbf{f}^T(\mathbf{Y})\mathbf{D} + \mathbf{a}^T\mathbf{f}^T(\mathbf{Y})\mathbf{f}(\mathbf{Y})\mathbf{a} \right) \\ &= E(\mathbf{D}^T\mathbf{D}) - 2\mathbf{a}^T E(\mathbf{f}^T(\mathbf{Y})\mathbf{D}) + \\ &\quad \mathbf{a}^T E(\mathbf{f}^T(\mathbf{Y})\mathbf{f}(\mathbf{Y}))\mathbf{a} \\ &= \mathbf{P}_d - 2\mathbf{a}^T\mathbf{p} + \mathbf{a}^T\mathbf{R}\mathbf{a} \end{aligned}$$

Figure 16. Realizations of the polynomial threshold, from (2.4) a) a_k=[0 1 0], *b)* a_k=[0 1 1], *c)* a_k=[A$_0$ 1 0.14163], *d)* a_k= [A$_0$ 1 0.5]

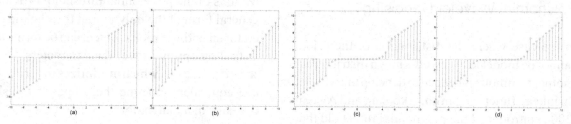

Exhibit 5. Polynomial Traning Procedure

Input: signal s

1. Create many noisy observations of signal **s** i.e.

   y = s + n

2. Compute the wavelet transform of each noisy observation

3. Concatenate the wavelet coefficients into a single vector

4. Compute the threshold δ estimate using any state-of-the-art method for soft and hard thresholding operators

5. Create the matrix **f**(x) of $T_{\delta,a}(x) = \mathbf{f}(x)\mathbf{a}$ using the transformed vector(s)

6. Calculate an optimal selection of **a** from the matrix **f**(x) using linear least squares

7. Calculate the results of $T_{\delta,a}$ from $\mathbf{T}_{\delta,a}(x) = \mathbf{f}(x)\mathbf{a}$

8. Calculate the MSE of the reconstructed signal, for orthogonal DWT it can be computed as the MSE between resulting wavelet coefficients and DWT coefficients of noise-free signal

Output: Denoising vector **a**

where

$$\mathbf{P}_d = E\left(\mathbf{D}^T\mathbf{D}\right), \mathbf{p} = E\left(\mathbf{f}^T(\mathbf{Y})\mathbf{D}\right),$$

$$\mathbf{R} = E\left(\mathbf{f}^T(\mathbf{Y})\mathbf{f}(\mathbf{Y})\right).$$

Then the optimal MMSE across the many observations is achieved at

$$\mathbf{a}_{opt} = \mathbf{R}^{-1}\mathbf{p} = E\left(\mathbf{f}^T(\mathbf{Y})\mathbf{f}(\mathbf{Y})\right)^{-1} E\left(\mathbf{f}^T(\mathbf{Y})\mathbf{D}\right)$$

The polynomial approach to developing a shrinkage function is complex compared to previous, threshold only techniques such as *VisuShrink*. An example of the training algorithm that uses the least squares optimization technique is shown in Exhibit 5.

Examples of trained thresholds appear in Figure 17, using four different artificial signals known as blocks, bumps, doppler, and spikes. These four signals have similar but slightly different optimal thresholds.

Non-Local Means

Many spatial and transform domain methods denoise an image by trading fine details for restoring the main geometry of the image. The assumption of local regularity allows many features such as fine structure and texture to be lost. The non-local

Exhibit 6. Polynomial wavelet based Denoising procedure

Input: signal s

1. Compute the DWT of the data

2. Apply $T_{\delta,a}(x)$ operator to wavelet coefficients

3. Compute the inverse wavelet transform of the new coefficients

Output: Denoised signal $\hat{s}$

Figure 17. Signals, (top left to right) blocks, bumps, doppler, spikes, and (bottom) their optimal threshold operators

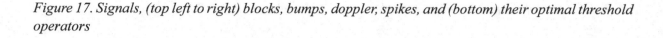

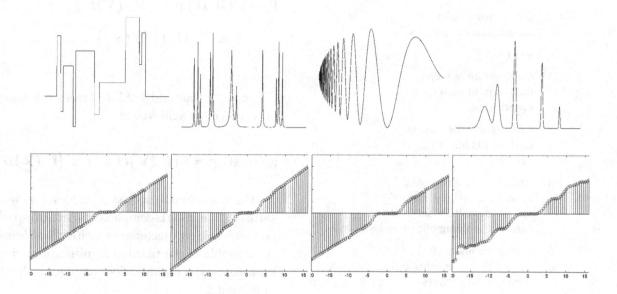

Figure 18. Similar image regions as utilized by NL-means

means algorithm takes advantage of the great redundancy present in a natural image. By exploiting similar features which appear in an image, but not necessarily close to one another, the non-local means algorithm learns from the image itself how to adapt to the images fine detail.

Non-local means is based on an averaging operation performed over many similar neighborhoods present in an image. An example appears in Figure 18.

Exhibit 7. Non-local means algorithm

Input: Image I, parameters w the dimension of the patch and h a constant controlling how similar a patch needs to be to effect a pixel

1. For each pixel i compute the patch N_i of the $2w + 1$ by $2w + 1$ pixels around it

2. Compute weights for each pixel

$$i, w(i, j) = \frac{1}{C_i} e^{-\frac{\|N_i - N_j\|_2^2}{h^2}},$$

where

$$C_i = \sum_j \exp\left(\frac{\|N_i - N_j\|_2^2}{h^2}\right)$$ is the

sum of all weights for i, and N_i, N_j are patches for pixels i and j, and $\|x - y\|_2^2$ is the L_2 distance

3. Replace each pixel in $\hat{I}$ with the weighted sum the other pixels

$$\hat{I}(i) = \sum_j w(i, j) I(j)$$

Output: Denoised image $\hat{I}$

THE PASSIVE WARDEN

The basic problem faced by Wendy the warden is to prevent the escape of the prisoners by monitoring and manipulating the communication channel. Any messages with overt plans to coordinate an escape will be immediately deleted from the communication channel. The challenge for Wendy is to determine when hidden messages are present. This detection of hidden information is known as the *passive warden*. This section discusses a

general form a steganography and the importance of clean image estimation.

While the prisoner's problem is an excellent description of steganography, it does not highlight a critical aspect of steganography. In the prisoner's problem, there is an assumption that the two prisoners will try to communicate. It must be secret and hidden, but the warden will not be surprised that it would occur. In other scenarios, the very act of communication or the desire to communicate would have serious consequences.

To pose a different scenario, imagine the consequences of discovering communication between a police officer and a drug dealer. Simple cryptography cannot mask the act of communication. The mere fact that the two parties are communicating is sufficient to raise an alarm. In this case the *new* Alice and Bob need to fundamentally hide the fact that any communication is occurring. For the warden, this becomes the same problem of trying to discover any hidden communication, but the warden has lost the ability to *target* her analysis. The definition of defeating the steganography is now simply the detection of the message.

The following section explores the use of clean image estimation in passive detection of steganography. First, a general framework for steganalysis is introduced highlighting the approaches of previous authors. Using this framework, the topic of clean image estimation is explored in a systematic manner, introducing the ideas of the stego-channel and stego-channel noise.

General Steganalysis

Steganalysis can be formulated as a three-stage process of *estimation, feature extraction, and classification* (the EFC formulation). Depending on the approach, the estimation stage could be clean image estimation or stego-estimation. These two approaches are a simple linear combination of one another,

Exhibit 7. Summary

	Spatial filter	Wavelet Threshold	Baysean Wavelet	Data Dependent Wavelet	Non-Local
Example	• Agerage or mean filter • Gaussian	• VisuShrink • SureShrink • MadShrink	• BayesShrink • BLS-GSM	• Polynomial threshold	• Non-local means
Strengths	• Simple • Fast	• Improved performance over spatial methods • Fast	• Some fast techniques • Good performance	• Trainable for unusual data or noise • Fast once trained	• Very good at recovering from high amounts of noise • No modeling assumptions or training sets needed
Weaknesses	• Blurring effects	• Varying degrees of blurring	• Fast techniques do not denoise well • Good performers are slow	• Selection of a training set is non-trivial	• Very slow
Authors	• Many	• Donoho and Johnstone (1995) • DeVore • Gao • Many others.	• Vidakovic • Chang • Portilla and Simoncelli • Many others.	• Smith, Akopian, and Agaian (2004)	• Buades, Coll, and Morel (2005)

Figure 19. Steganography: Wendy, Alice, and Bob

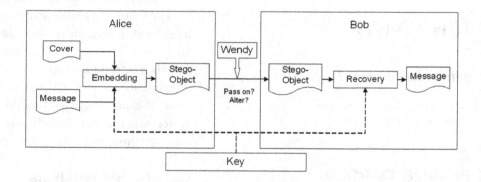

$image = stego\_estimate + clean\_image\_estimate$.

In the previous section *Modern Steganalysis*, a number of techniques for steganalysis were reviewed. These techniques each use calibration or clean image estimation methods to define a normal, non-embedded image. These steganalysis methods each include the three aspects of EFC.

For the high pass filter-based spatial approach from Soukal et al. (2005) and Figure 4.

The stego-message is estimated directly using a high pass filter. Feature extraction is in the form of an ML estimate of the message model parameters and pattern recognition is a training based threshold selection.

Figure 20. Common elements within steganalysis approaches including clean image estimation

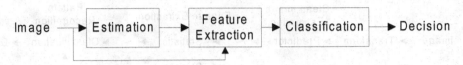

Figure 21. High pass filter-based spatial domain steganalysis

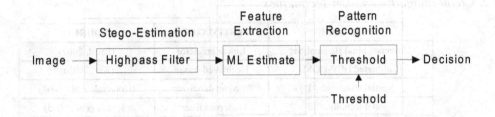

Figure 22. Denoising-based spatial domain steganalysis

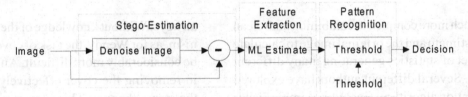

Figure 23. Calibrated HCF-COM-based steganalysis

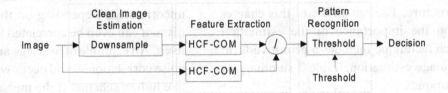

For the denoising approach from Holotyak et al. (2005) and Figure 3,the clean image is estimated using denoising. The stego-message is then estimated by subtraction. Similar to the previous, feature extraction is in the form of an ML estimate of the message model parameters and pattern recognition is just a training based threshold selection.

For the calibrated HCF-COM method from Ker (2005b) and Figure 5, the clean image is estimated

by down sampling, features are extracted using the HCF-COM algorithm from both the clean image estimate and the original image, and pattern recognition is again a simple threshold.

For the final approach, universal steganalysis originally from Farid (2002) and Figures 6 and 7, the strength and versatility of the EFC generalization becomes clear.

In this technique, the clean image is estimated using a linear predictor. Feature extraction has be-

Figure 24. Universal steganalysis

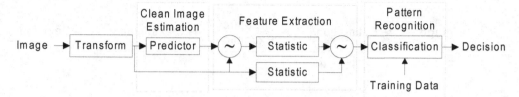

Table 2. Clean Image Estimation Techniques

TECHNIQUE	ESTIMATOR	SOURCE
Universal blind steganalysis	Linear predictor	(Farid, 2002)
Calibrated HCF-COM	Decimated image	(Ker, 2005a)
Spatial technique #1	Wavelet denoising	(Holotyak et al., 2005)
Spatial technique #2	High pass filter*	(Soukal et al., 2005)

*message estimator

come much more complex in combining both clean image estimate and the original image to calculate a large set of statistics generating many different features. Several different authors have explored classification algorithms, including simple Fisher LDA and support vector machines.

Each of these techniques applies different elements for the EFC stages, but each has the shared structure. The remainder of this chapter focuses on the importance of the estimation stage. Each technique includes a primitive form of clean image estimation. Table 2 summarizes these techniques.

The Stego-Channel

To analyze the effectiveness of clean image estimation for steganalysis, the concept of the stego-channel is introduced. The stego-channel is the channel the embedded stego-message must travel from sender to receiver—either the intended receiver Bob, or some eavesdropper, Wendy. The stego-message is embedded in cover media. In order to recover this message the cover must be removed. For the intended recipient (Bob), this task is aided by knowledge of the embedding type and

all keys. Without knowledge of the hiding mechanism, as for Wendy, the task of cover removal will be considerably more difficult. Any imperfection in removing the cover effectively adds noise to the stego-channel. This idea of a stego-channel with noise is shown in Figure 25.

Unlike traditional models of noise, stego-channel noise is often not white, Gaussian, or spatially uncorrelated. Depending on the hiding mechanism, it can even be correlated with the message itself. An example of message and stego-channel noise correlation would occur with a cover-adaptive hiding scheme. If the message is adaptively hidden inside the regions of the image that are most like the stego-message, as with the scheme from Agaian and Rodriguez(2006), the image removal techniques might treat these *similar regions* of the image as if they were stego-information; whether or not they are stego-information. This will tend to leave image residuals primarily in regions occupied by stego-information, resulting in a high correlation between the noise and stego-message.

In the field of communications the problem of removing complex noise and unusual signal corruptions can often be approached using knowledge

Figure 25. Stego-channel, Top full model, bottom effective model, here the only source of channel noise is the (in-)effectiveness of the cover removal

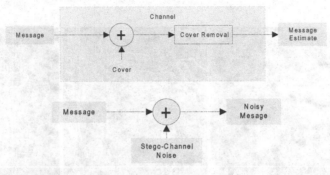

of the signal, such as in equalization or the use of matched filters (Haykin, 2001; Proakis, 2000). The steganalyst, in general, has no knowledge of the content of the stego-signal (the message), or even of its statistical distribution. Even the traditional simplifying assumption of normality cannot be used, as the *expected* case of an encrypted stego-message would follow a uniform distribution, not a Gaussian or normal distribution.

This lack of an exploitable embedded signal leaves the steganalyst with the problem of finding the *best* estimate of the clean image blindly. As discussed in the previous section this problem of blind denoising is very challenging.

Denoising and Stego-Channel Noise

To define how well a clean image estimation technique performs for steganalysis, only one metric matters—detection performance. This particular metric is also tied to the performance of all three aspects of the EFC system. If any aspect of the system is not correct or not performing well, detection performance will suffer. To better isolate the performance of the clean image estimation technique, a simpler metric can also be considered—minimizing stego-channel noise. To minimize stego-channel noise, a clean image estimation technique needs to remove only components of the steganographic message

hidden in the image, not portions of the actual image. The residual of the image and the denoised image can be analyzed to determine what portions of the image are affected by the estimation technique. For many denoising techniques, this residual will still look a great deal like the image itself. Examples can be found in Figure 26. This inclusion of energy from the actual image in the stego-message estimate changes the statistics of the message recovered, introducing stego-channel noise.

A number of efforts have been made to remove different types of noise from an image. The fundamental approach needed in steganography is similar to that which appears in the general image denoising literature—to develop a version of the image without any intervening corruptions.

Current image denoising techniques often simplify the problem by making assumptions about the noise. The most common of these is to assume a normal distribution, independent and identically distributed across the image. This model is of course not appropriate for steganographic noise. Thus using techniques that assume Gaussian noise results in the introduction of stego-channel noise. Figure 26 shows how a handful of denoising techniques perform when applied to a clean image. These techniques were explored in a previous section, including an average filter, a Gaussian filter, the BLS-GSM wavelet method,

Figure 26. Denoising effects on a clean image, Top left across to bottom right, Original image, residuals from using average filter, Gaussian filter, BLS-GSM, VisuShrink, polynomial threshold, scaled to the range [0,10]

Figure 27. Denoising effects on a JSteg embedded image. Top left across to bottom right, residual after removing clean image estimate using: original image, average filter, Gaussian filter, BLS-GSM, VisuShrink, polynomial threshold. Boxes show the area of greatest change in the JSteg-embedded image, note the polynomial threshold and VisuShrink are the only techniques to not induce structured changes in regions outside these boxes.

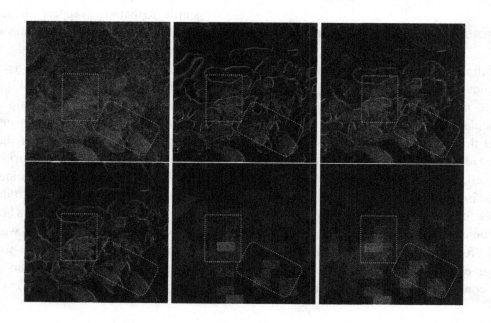

VisuShrink, polynomial threshold, and non-local means.

Figure 27 shows how the techniques performed at blindly denoising a clean high signal to noise ratio (SNR) image. The non-local means result is not shown, as it did not affect this very high SNR image. The images are scaled so black corresponds to a change of zero, while white is a change greater than or equal to 10. From this figure, the first three techniques remove *noise* that looks very much like the original image. These generally correspond to textures and edges of the image. The non-local means technique used (Peyré, 2007) preserved these features too well. The high SNR image was not changed by this approach. *VisuShrink* and polynomial threshold are applied to the image in blocks resulting in some blocking artifacts.

Figure 27, shows the application of the same techniques to a JSteg embedded image. The average filter, Gaussian filter, and BLS-GSM techniques introduce large amounts of stego-channel noise around the edges in the image. *VisuShrink* and polynomial threshold do not introduce nearly as much noise, but tend to miss part of the embedded message.

Denoising and Steganalysis

Using the current techniques, there is a trade-off between missing components of the message and introducing stego-channel noise. To analyze these results from a detection standpoint, a new concept is needed. From detection theory, a standard method of comparing the performance of two detection methods is the receiver operating characteristic (ROC) curve (Egan, 1975). The ROC generally displays the trade-off between the number of correctly and incorrectly identified observations, in this case, images. The actual curve is drawn by varying the parameters of the detection method, in this case a threshold. The ROC used here displays the probability of correctly identifying a stego-image, termed a *hit*, P_h,

and the probability of incorrectly calling a clean, non-stego-embedded image a stego-image, termed a *false alarm*, P_{fa}. An example ROC appears in Figure 28. The probability of a hit is important in identifying how many of a set of embedded images will be detected by the approach. For the stego-analyst in comparing steganalysis approaches this quantity is vital to identify how many images might be missed. Too low a probability of hits invalidates a detection method.

The probability of a false alarm defines the likelihood that a detection is actually incorrect. For the stego-analyst in comparing steganalysis approaches this quantity is vital to identify how many resources are going to be wasted pursuing images that are not actually embedded with stego-information. Too high a probability invalidates a technique.

Using the EFC approach, different denoising approaches can be applied to steganalysis. This approach results in varying performance depending on the effectiveness of the denoising technique applied. Figure 29 shows the performance using a universal-blind steganalysis approach. The spatial filters, average and Gaussian and the wavelet method BLS-GSM do not perform as well as the linear predictor, while the other denoising approaches all better this technique. Figure 30 shows the performance of the HCF-COM augmented with the different denoising approaches. Almost universally, each denoising approach slightly betters the original decimation approach.

Tables 3 and 4 summarize the performance of each technique at the point where a probability of hit is 50%, this is not the point of *best* trade-off between P_h and P_{fa}, but is a realistic metric for a real search, and provides a comparison point with other techniques. From Table 3, the technique using HOS, the generally best performing clean image estimation technique is the polynomial threshold, with *VisuShrink* also being very good. These techniques are highlighted in the table with a gray background.

Figure 28. Example ROC, points above the line of equal probability is better than randomly guessing, while points below are worse

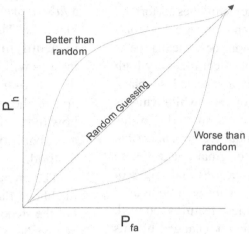

Table 3. Detection performance using HOS for a P_h of 50%

Detection technique HOS	F5 P_h	F5 P_{fa}	Jsteg P_h	Jsteg P_{fa}	LSB P_h	LSB P_{fa}	Model P_h	Model P_{fa}	±1 P_h	±1 P_{fa}	±2 P_h	±2 P_{fa}
Linear predictor	50.3	36.6	49.7	14.5	50.9	44.9	49.0	29.5	50.5	45.3	50.5	39.5
Average filter	49.7	40.3	50.4	39.6	50.0	45.9	50.7	44.9	50.4	45.5	50.3	36.7
Gaussian filter	50.5	42.6	50.1	37.4	50.0	43.1	49.8	40.4	49.6	43.5	49.3	37.8
VisuShrink	50.6	27.9	49.2	18.0	49.6	14.4	50.6	25.0	49.1	18.0	50.4	8.4
BLS-GSM	49.4	49.2	51.1	42.2	50.3	45.3	50.1	48.7	50.7	45.1	50.3	42.5
Polynomial threshold	49.5	6.0	50.1	11.2	50.3	30.9	50.5	16.6	49.6	28.9	50.9	16.2

Table 4. Detection performance using calibrated HCF-COM for a P_h of 50%

Detection technique HCF-COM	F5 P_h	F5 P_{fa}	Jsteg P_h	Jsteg P_{fa}	LSB P_h	LSB P_{fa}	Model P_h	Model P_{fa}	±1 P_h	±1 P_{fa}	±2 P_h	±2 P_{fa}
Decimation	49.7	37.4	50.3	28.1	49.9	25.8	50.5	31.1	49.7	31.5	49.9	49.7
Average filter	49.5	40.3	50.1	28.5	50.1	28.2	50.1	28.7	49.9	28.6	49.3	29.5
Gaussian filter	50.1	37.1	49.5	32.2	49.7	11.8	49.3	32.3	49.2	14.9	50.8	33.8
VisuShrink	50.2	25.7	49.5	29.1	49.6	31.4	49.8	26.2	50.1	25.4	50.0	29.0
BLS-GSM	49.9	39.9	49.8	40.4	49.3	40.6	50.2	43.0	50.0	42.9	49.9	45.5
Polynomial threshold	49.4	20.6	49.7	28.9	49.6	6.1	49.4	34.7	49.6	20.5	50.9	10.6

Figure 29. ROC curves comparing the performance of different denoising techniques applied to the feature-based HOS steganalysis algorithm, top left across to bottom right, original linear estimator, averaging filter of size 2, Gaussian filter, BLS-GSM, VisuShrink, polynomial threshold, the training set was 160 color images, the analysis set was 752 color images. Each technique embedded at, or close to, max capacity. VisuShrink and polynomial threshold make significant improvements over the original linear predictor for all embedding types, while the other techniques are significantly worse.

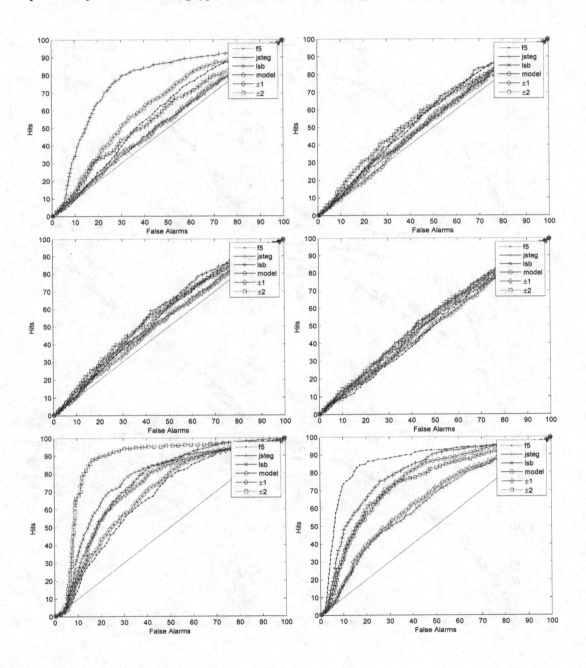

Figure 30. ROC curves comparing the performance of different denoising techniques applied to the calibrated HCF-COM steganalysis algorithm, top left across to bottom right, original linear estimator, averaging filter of size 2, Gaussian filter, BLS-GSM, VisuShrink, polynomial threshold, the training set was 160 color images, the analysis set was 752 color images. Each technique embedded at, or close to, max capacity. The Polynomial threshold and the Gaussian mask make slight improvements over the original linear predictor, while the other techniques are roughly equivalent.

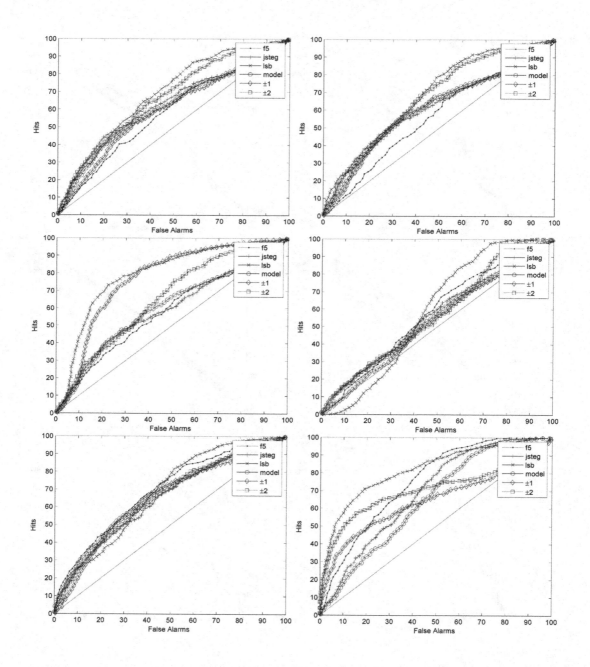

Figure 29, highlights how a *good* steganalysis technique can be either made significantly better or significantly worse by the choice of clean image estimation technique. The choice of technique is not intuitive as the most sophisticated and processor intensive techniques, the BLS-GSM and NL-Means do not perform well. The polynomial threshold is logically the best choice since it is tailored for odd noises, but

VisuShrink is, non-intuitively also a very good performer. Figure 30 confirms a similar performance using the calibrated HCF-COM technique. For this technique, the Gaussian mask is also a good choice for LSB and ±1 embedding techniques, a better choice than the original decimation approach.

CONCLUSION

Many modern steganography techniques can be modeled as an artificial source of noise. These techniques generally affect the image in ways that mimic naturally occurring noise. For simple techniques such as LSB, this is intentional. More sophisticated techniques, such as the model-based approach, intentionally embed in information containing regions of the image rather than the noise. Regardless of the intent, most modern approaches only make small changes to the image and consequently affect the image in a very similar, noise-like manner. This property hints at a common detection technique based on approaches to denoising, or clean image estimation.

This chapter has presented the importance of clean image estimation to steganalysis. Under the passive warden, a common approach to steganalysis was presented that underlies a number of current techniques, the EFC approach. For digital images, steganalysis is highly dependent on the effectiveness of the clean image estimation technique. A well-suited estimation technique will enhance the performance of a steganalysis technique, while an ill-suited estimator will cause

even a good steganalysis technique to fail. This chapter presented a systematic approach to evaluating a clean image estimation technique, based on stego-channel noise. The next generation of steganalysis techniques should pay close attention to the clean image estimator selected.

FUTURE RESEARCH DIRECTIONS

Steganalysis as a science is in its infancy. The last 10 years have brought rapidly increasing theoretical understanding of the field. In digital images, the major challenge is to model an image to such degree as to detect any changes. The development of an image model capable of such is the most important and most challenging research direction in the field.

In the absence of this highly detailed model, many possible efforts remain to derive *relative* image models. Image-denoising techniques are promising, and many methods remain unexplored. Further, denoising techniques have not developed along with steganography. Steganography-based noise breaks the assumptions of many image-denoising researchers. How to remove stego-noise is an important future research area.

The three basic components of steganalysis—clean image estimation, feature extraction, and pattern recognition—each contribute significantly to its overall success. Improvements in any single area will advance this multidisciplinary problem.

Other challenges include modeling artificial images and other high capacity media such as audio.

REFERENCES

Agaian, S. (2005). Steganography & steganalysis: An overview of research & challenges. *Network Security and Intrusion Detection, NATO Proceedings.*

Agaian, S., & Cai, H. (2005). *New multilevel DCT, feature vectors, and universal blind steganalysis.* Paper presented at the Security, Steganography, and Watermarking of Multimedia Contents VII.

Agaian, S., & Rodriguez, B. M. (2006). Basic steganalysis techniques for the digital media forensics examiner. In *Digital Crime and Forensic Science in Cyberspace* (pp. 175-225).

Anderson, R. J., & Petitcolas, F. A. P. (1998). On the limits of steganography. *IEEE Journal on Selected Areas in Communications, 16*(4), 474-481.

Antoniadis, A., Bigot, J., & Sapatinas, T. (2001). Wavelet estimators in nonparametric regression: A comparative simulation study. *Journal of Statistical Software, 6*(6).

Avcibas, I., Memon, N., & Sankur, B. (2003). Steganalysis using image quality metrics. *IEEE Transactions on Image Processing, 12*(2), 221-229.

Buades, A., Coll, B., & Morel, J. M. (2005). A review of image denoising algorithms, with a new one. *Multiscale Modeling & Simulation, 4*(2), 490-530.

Cachin, C. (2004). An information-theoretic model for steganography. *Information and Computation, 192*(1), 41-56.

Cox, I. J., Miller, M., & Bloom, J. (2001). *Digital watermarking: Principles & practice* (1st ed.). San Francisco: Morgan Kaufmann.

Donoho, D. L., & Johnstone, I. M. (1995). Adapting to unknown smoothness via wavelet shrinkage. *Journal of the American Statistical Association, 90*(432), 1200-1224.

Egan, J. P. (1975). *Signal detection theory and ROC analysis.* New York: Academic Press.

Ettinger, J. M. (1998). Steganalysis and game equilibria. *Information Hiding, 1525,* 319-328.

Farid, H. (2002). *Detecting hidden messages using higher-order statistical models.* Paper presented at the International Conference on Image Processing.

Figueiredo, M. A. T., & Nowak, R. D. (2001). Wavelet-based image estimation: An empirical Bayes approach using Jeffrey's noninformative prior. *IEEE Transactions on Image Processing, 10*(9), 1322-1331.

Fisk, G., Fisk, M., Papadopoulos, C., & Neil, J. (2003, October 7-9). Eliminating steganography in Internet traffic with active wardens. In *Information Hiding: 5th International Workshop, IH 2002,* Noordwijkerhout, The Netherlands, *Revised Papers* (Vol. 2578, pp. 18-35). Berlin, Germany: Springer.

Fridrich, J. (2004). Feature-based steganalysis for JPEG images and its implications for future design of steganographic schemes. *Information Hiding, 3200,* 67-81.

Gonzalez, R. C., & Woods, R. E. (2002). *Digital image processing* (2nd ed.). Prentice Hall.

Harmsen, J. J., & Pearlman, W. A. (2003). Steganalysis of additive noise modelable information hiding. *Proceedings of SPIE Electronic Imaging, 5022,* 21-24.

Haykin, S. (2001). *Adaptive filter theory* (4th ed.). Upper Saddle River, NJ: Prentice Hall.

Holotyak, T., Fridrich, J., & Soukal, S. (2005). *Stochastic approach to secret message length estimation in +/-K embedding steganography.* Paper presented at the Proceedings of SPIE, Electronic Imaging, Security, Steganography, and Watermarking of Multimedia Contents VII.

Jain, A. K. (1989). *Fundamentals of digital image processing.* Upper Saddle River, NJ: Prentice Hall.

Katzenbeisser, S., & Penticolas, F. A. P. (2000). *Information hiding techniques for steganography and digitial watermarking.* Artech House.

Ker, A. D. (2005a). A general framework for structural steganalysis of LSB replacement. *Information Hiding, 3727*, 296-311.

Ker, A. D. (2005b). Steganalysis of LSB matching in grayscale images. *IEEE Signal Processing Letters, 12*(6), 441-444.

Lyu, S., & Farid, H. (2003). Detecting hidden messages using higher-order statistics and support vector machines. *Information Hiding, 2578*, 340-354.

Lyu, S., & Farid, H. (2006). Steganalysis using higher-order image statistics. *IEEE Transactions on Information Forensics and Security, 1*(1), 111-119.

Mallat, S. (1999). *A wavelet tour of signal processing* (2nd ed.). Academic Press.

McLachlan, G. J. (2004). *Discriminant analysis and statistical pattern recognition* (Rev. ed.). Wiley.

Moulin, P., & Koetter, R. (2005). Data-hiding codes. *Proceedings of the IEEE, 93*(12), 2083-2126.

Peyré, G. (2007). *A toolbox for the non-local means algorithm.* Mathworks Matlab Central File Exchange.

Portilla, J., Strela, V., Wainwright, M. J., & Simoncelli, E. P. (2003). Image denoising using scale mixtures of Gaussians in the wavelet domain. *IEEE Transactions on Image Processing, 12*(11), 1338-1351.

Press, W. H., Teukolsky, S. A., Vettering, W. T., & Flannery, B. P. (1992). *Numerical recipes in C: The art of scientific computation* (2nd ed.). Cambridge University Press.

Proakis, J. G. (2000). *Digital communications* (4th ed.). McGraw-Hill Higher Education.

Provos, N., & Honeyman, P. (2001). *Detecting steganographic content on the Internet.* Center for Information Technology Integration, University of Michigano.

Provos, N., & Honeyman, P. (2003). Hide and seek: An introduction to steganography. *IEEE Security and Privacy Magazine, 1*(3), 32-44.

Sheikh, H. R., Sabir, M. F., & Bovik, A. C. (2006). A statistical evaluation of recent full reference image quality assessment algorithms. *IEEE Transactions on Image Processing, 15*(11), 3440-3451.

Simmons, G. J. (1984). The prisoners' problem and the subliminal channel. In *Advances in Cryptology, Proceedings of CRYPTO '83* (pp. 51-67). New York: Plenum Press.

Simoncelli, E. P., & Olshausen, B. A. (2001). Natural image statistics and neural representation. *Annual Review of Neuroscience, 24*, 1193-1216.

Smith, C. B., Akopian, D., & Agaian, S. (2004). *Least squares optimization of a polynomial threshold for wavelet domain denoising.* Paper presented at the 7th International Conference on Signal Processing Proceedings.

Soukal, D., Fridrich, J., & Goljan, M. (2005). *Maximum likelihood estimation of length of secret message embedded using +/-K steganography in spatial domain.* Paper presented at the Proceedings of SPIE, Electronic Imaging, Security, Steganography, and Watermarking of Multimedia Contents VII.

Vaidyanathan, P. P. (1992). *Multirate systems and filter banks.* Englewood Cliffs, NJ: Prentice Hall PTR.

Vidakovic, B. (1998a). Nonlinear wavelet shrinkage with Bayes rules and Bayes factors. *Journal of the American Statistical Association, 93*(441), 173-179.

Vidakovic, B. (1998b). Wavelet-based nonparametric bayes methods. In D. Dey, P. MÄuller, & D. Sinha (Eds.), *Practical nonparametric and semiparametric Bayesian statistics* (Vol. 133, pp. 133-155). Springer-Verlag.

Wayner, P. (2002). *Disappearing cryptography—Information hiding: Steganography and watermarking* (2nd ed.). San Francisco: Morgan Kaufmann.

Zollner, J., Federrath, H., Klimant, H., Pfitzmann, A., Piotraschke, R., Westfeld, A., et al. (1998). Modeling the security of steganographic systems. *Information Hiding, 1525*, 344-354.

ADDITIONAL READING

A general introductory text to steganography and data hiding concepts can be found in *Disappearing Cryptography* (Wayner, 2002), or Katzenbeisser and Penticolas (2000), or the article by Provos and Honeyman (2003). A general introductory article for steganalysis can be found in Agaian and Rodriguez (2006), and for steganography Agaian (2005). See Cox, Miller, and Bloom (2001) for the watermarking perspective on data hiding.

For a theoretical introduction to data hiding, the work of Moulin in Moulin and Koetter (2005) is an excellent start. Then see Cachin (2004), Zollner et al. (1998), and Ettinger (1998) for different theoretical perspectives on the basic problem.

For a review of image denoising techniques, many resources exist. Buades, Coll, and Morel (2005) is a recent paper which reviews this broad field, Antoniadis, Bigot, and Sapatinas (2001) is an aging review of wavelet based methods. The paper by Sheikh, Sabir, and Bovik (2006) reviews a number of current image quality metrics. See Avcibas, Memon, and Sankur (2003) for a perspective on image quality in steganalysis.

See Provos and Honeyman (2001) and Fisk, Fisk, Papadopoulos, and Neil (2003) for Internet implementation related issues and results.

Chapter XII
Steganalysis:
Trends and Challenges

Hafiz Malik
University of Michigan–Dearborn, USA

Rajarathnam Chandramouli
Stevens Institute of Technology, USA

K. P. Subbalakshmi
Stevens Institute of Technology, USA

ABSTRACT

In this chapter we provide a detailed overview of the state of the art in steganalysis. Performance of some steganalysis techniques are compared based on critical parameters such as the hidden message detection probability, accuracy of the estimated hidden message length and secret key, and so forth. We also provide an overview of some shareware/freeware steganographic tools. Some open problems in steganalysis are described.

INTRODUCTION

Steganography deals with hiding information into a cover (host or original) signal such that no one other than the intended recipient can detect or extract the hidden message. The steganographic encoder embeds a message into the cover signal using a secret key such that perceptual and other distortion constraints are satisfied. A statistical dissimilarity measure between the cover and the stego-signal is generally used to measure the security of a given steganographic method (Cachin, 1998; Chandramouli & Memon, 2003; Zollner et al., 1998).

Steganography can be modeled as a prisoner's problem (Simmons, 1984). For example, consider two prisoners, Alice and Bob, who want to secretly exchange information regarding their escape

Figure 1. Secret key steganography in the presence of a passive warden (top) and an active warden (bottom)

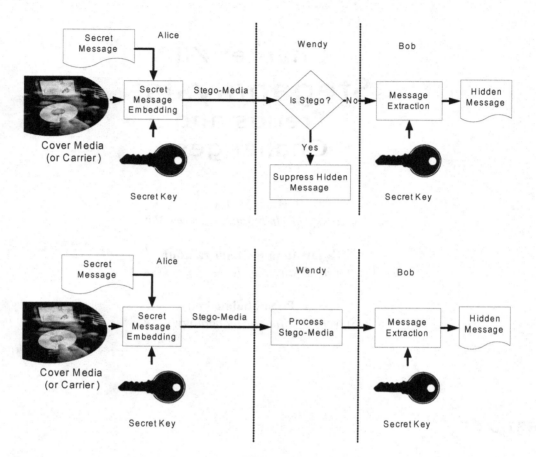

plan. However, the warden, Wendy, examines every communication between Alice and Bob and punishes them if steganographic covert communication is detected. In a standard steganographic framework, Alice sends a secrete message, *M*, to Bob by embedding her secret message into the cover signal, **S**, to obtain the stego-signal **X**. Alice then sends **X** to Bob using a public channel. The warden, who examines the communication channel between Alice and Bob, can be passive or active. A passive warden attempts only to detect a steganographic covert channel. An active warden, on the other hand, deliberately alters every

signal exchanged between Alice and Bob, to foil any covert communication between them. The allowable distortion the warden can introduce in the stego-signal depends on the underlying model and the cover signal used. Figure 1 illustrates secret key steganography for active and passive warden scenarios.

Clearly, Alice and Bob attempt to design the steganographic channel (encoder, secret key, and decoder) such that the warden is unable to distinguish in any sense (statistically as well as perceptually) between the cover signal and the stego-signal. On the other hand, Wendy tries to detect or estimate the hidden message, *M*, from the stego-signal, **X** by using one or several steganalysis algorithms. In general, steganalysis must not make any assumption about the underlying steganographic algorithm used to embed a secret message (Chandramouli, 2002).

Rapid proliferation of digital multimedia signals on the Internet makes them good candidates as cover signals. The simplest of the existing steganographic techniques is the least significant bit (LSB) steganography. Steganographic techniques based on LSB embedding exploit the fact that in general digital images/video are perceptually insensitive to the distortion introduced in the least significant bit plane. These techniques embed the secret message, *M*, in the cover signal by replacing the LSB plane of the cover signal in the spatial/time domain or in the transformed domain. Table 1 illustrates LSB embedding with an example. Here, an 8-bit secret message "01010011" is embedded into eight samples of the cover signal.

More than 250 steganographic (stego) software tools exist, commonly available on the Web, ranging from freeware to commercial products. Most of these software packages use some form of LSB embedding. For example, *Stegotif*,[1] *Blindside*,[2] *Hide*,[3] *Steganos*,[4] *S-Tools*,[5] and so forth embed a message in digital images using LSB replacement in the pixel domain. Software tools like *EzStego*,[6] *Hide and Seek*,[7] *Gifshuffle*,[8] *Gif-It-Up*,[9] and so forth embed a message in GIF images using LSB substitution of the color palette indices. Whereas *Jsteg*,[10] *OutGuess*,[11] *StegHide*,[12] *JP Hide and Seek*,[13] *Invisible Secrets*,[14] and so forth embed a secret message in JPEG images using LSB substitution of the quantized coefficients in discrete cosine transform (DCT) domain.

In contrast to the standard LSB embedding, steganographic tools such as *F5*,[15] *Hide*,[16] and so forth increment or decrement the sample/coefficient values to match the LSB plane of the cover to embed secret message, *M*. These methods can also be treated as LSB steganography.

Some steganographic techniques are robust to an active warden as well as statistical attacks. For example, Sallee (2003) and Fridrich and Goljan (2003) have proposed model based steganographic techniques which insert a secret message into

Table 1. LSB embedding

Input Sample Value		Message Bit	Output Sample Value	
Decimal	Binary (8 bit rep.)		Decimal	Binary (8 bit rep.)
149	10010101	*0*	148	10010100
12	00001100	*1*	13	10010101
201	11001001	*0*	200	10010100
203	11001011	*1*	203	11001011
150	10010110	*0*	150	10010110
15	00001111	*0*	14	00001110
159	10011111	*1*	159	10011111
32	00010000	*1*	33	00010001

Figure 2. Windmill cover (left) and the corresponding stego-image carrying 1.4 KB message and obtained using steganographic software Stego (right)

Figure 3. Least significant bit (LSB) plane of the cover (left) and the corresponding stego-image (right). Here black pixel stands for LSB = 0 and white for LSB = 1

 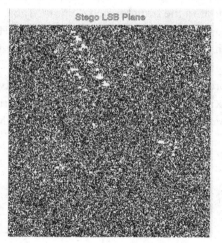

a cover image without perturbing the statistical features (e.g., probability density function) of the cover image significantly. Westfeld and Pfitzmann (1999) have shown that model based steganographic techniques are robust to statistical steganalysis attacks.

Quantization index modulation (QIM) based data hiding and its extensions (Chen & Wornell, 2000, 2001) have a high embedding capacity. They also allow the embedder to control the robustness of the hidden message to attacks and the corresponding embedding induced distortion. In addition, QIM-based data hiding can also be used for joint compression and message hiding applications.

Spread-spectrum-based steganographic techniques (Marvel, Boncelet, & Retter, 1999; Matsuoka, 2006) take advantage of the robustness of spread spectrum communications against anti-jamming and low probability of intercept, to embed a secret message into the cover signal. However, robustness of spread spectrum steganography against active warden attacks comes at the cost of low embedding capacity. It is worth mentioning that, in general, most steganographic techniques assume a passive warden scenario.

Data hiding also has several other applications such as copy right protection, ownership protection, fingerprinting, and so forth. Robustness against active warden attacks is desirable for some of these applications. In this chapter we focus on message embedding for covert communication only, that is, steganography robust to passive warden attacks. Therefore steganalysis techniques such as LSB embedding and QIM are consider here.

Steganalysis Techniques: State of the Art

Several approaches have been proposed for passive steganalysis. These techniques exploit embedding induced statistical anomalies to discriminate between the stego- and the cover signal. Next we describe some steganalysis approaches.

Visual Steganalysis

LSB embedding algorithms assume that the LSB plane of the luminance channel in digital images is completely random. However, Westfeld and Pfitzmann (1999) have shown that this assumption is not always true, especially for images containing reasonably large uniform areas (or low-texture images). For example, consider Figure 2 of the cover **Windmill** image (a low texture image) and the corresponding stego-image. The stego-image was obtained by embedding a 1.4 KB message using the steganographic software *Stego*. Figure 3 shows the LSB plane of these two images.

Similarly, LSB planes of the **Baboon** image (a rich-texture image) and the corresponding stego-image are shown in Figure 4. Here the stego-image was obtained by embedding 2.6 KB of data using the software tool *Stego*. Figure 3 shows that message embedding in low-texture images using LSB embedding methods introduce noticeable visual artifacts in the LSB plane of the corresponding stego-image. Therefore, visual inspection of the LSB plane of the test image can be used to distinguish between the cover and the stego-image. Westfeld and Pfitzmann (1999) have shown that visual attacks can successfully detect the stego-image obtained using software which embed a message in pixel domain, for example, *EzStego*, *Hide and Seek*, *Stego*, and *S-Tools*. We note that even though visual attacks are simple they are highly unreliable especially for rich-tex-

Figure 4. Baboon cover (left) and the corresponding stego-image (right) carrying a 2.6 KB message obtained using steganographic software Stego

Figure 5. LSB plane of the cover (left) and the corresponding stego-image (right)

Cover LSB Plane

Stego LSB Plane

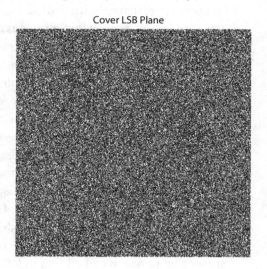
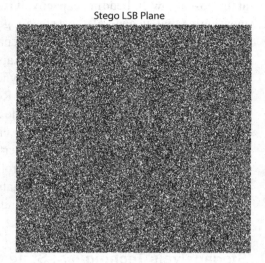

ture images. For example, Figure 5 shows that a visual attack will be unable to detect the hidden message by just inspecting the LSB plane of the stego-image. One reason for this is that for rich-texture images the LSB plane is pseudorandom (i.e., $Pr[x = 1] \approx Pr[x = 0] \approx \frac{1}{2}$, where x denotes that the values in the LSB plane).

Statistical Learning Based Steganalysis

Universal steganalysis techniques make no assumption about the statistical properties of the stego-signal. Instead statistics of some features are learned using a large training data set of cover and stego-signals. Some metric, which is a function of the feature statistics, is used to discriminate between cover and stego. Therefore, universal steganalysis techniques, in general, consist of two major stages:

1. Feature generation and feature selection stage to extract feature vectors from the training data set based on some feature selection criteria, and

2. Classification stage that uses the extracted feature vectors learn a classifier for cover-stego discrimination.

Some universal steganalysis techniques (Farid, 2001, 2002; Avcibas, Celik, Sharma, & Tekalp, 2004; Lyu & Farid, 2002, 2004, 2006) can detect steganographic tools such as *S-Tools*, *F5*, *Out-Guess*, *Hide*, *JP Hide and Seek*, *EzStego*, and so forth with reasonable accuracies.

Universal steganalysis techniques generally use supervised learning to train a statistical classifier. First, a *k*-dimensional feature vector is estimated from the training data set during the learning phase. Many of these techniques (Farid, 2001, 2002; Celik, Sharma, & Tekalp, 2004; Lyu & Farid, 2002, 2004, 2006) select this *k*-dimensional feature vector heuristically. Feature vectors that consist of higher-order statistics are widely used. The classifier then learns the best classification rule using the input feature vectors for each steganographic method. These techniques use sophisticated machine learning tools such as linear regression analysis based on Fisher linear discriminant (FLD), support vector machine (SVM), principal component analysis (PCA) (Duda & Hart, 1973), and so forth for the classification stage. Therefore, to design a universal steganalysis technique based on feature selection and classification involves independent problems: good feature selection and classifier design to obtain a low stego-classification rate. Obviously, choosing features capable of accurately capturing the statistical irregularities introduced by an embedding algorithm is critical. The chosen features must have a good prediction accuracy and a monotonic relationship with the embedded message size. Recently, Wang and Moulin (2006) have proposed a feature selection criterion for learning-based steganalysis.

Some learning-based steganalysis approaches include the following.

- Farid's (2001) steganalysis is an early work based on universal steganalysis. This technique uses a $24(n - 1)$-dimensional feature vector, where n is the number of muli-resolution decomposition scales. The feature vectors consist of first- and higher-order statistics and the transform coefficient prediction error of a multi-resolution decomposed natural image. It is shown that these features computed for natural images are relatively consistent. Steganographic tools such as *Jsteg*, *OutGuess*, *StegHide*, *JP Hide and Seek*, and *EzStego* have been found to affect these features in the discrete wavelet transform (DWT) domain. The $24(n - 1)$-dimensional feature vector consists of $12(n - 1)$-dimensional coefficient statistics and $12(n-1)$-dimensional linear prediction error statistics. The feature vector is then used to train a linear FLD classifier. Lyu and Farid (2002, 2004, 2006) and Farid (2002) later extended the learning-based steganalysis scheme using higher order image statistics. Advanced classifiers such as linear SVM, non-linear SVM, and one-

class SVM are used. For example, Lyu and Farid's (2006) proposed technique uses a 432-dimensional vector estimated from the four-level wavelet decomposition and three-level local angular harmonic decomposition (LAHD) of color images in the RGB color space. Feature vector used in Lyu and Farid (2006) consists of 108 magnitude statistics (e.g., mean, variance, skewness, and kurtosis), 108 error statistics, and 216 phase statistics. Comparisons of the detection performances of the proposed stegnalysis methods for linear SVM, non-linear SVM and one-class SVM, to detect steganographic tools such as *Jsteg*, *OutGuess*, *StegHide*, *JP Hide and Seek*, and *F*5 are presented. It is observed that a non-linear SVM classifier performs better than a linear SVM classifier for a given steganographic algorithm. In addition, one-class SVM classifier results in modest performance degradation while offering a simpler training stage. The results also indicate that at low embedding rates the detection performance deteriorates significantly irrespective of the underlying steganographic algorithm used for message embedding. It is interesting to notice that a larger feature space yields only a marginal improvement in the stego-detection rate.

- Celik et al. (2004) propose another supervised learning-based steganalysis technique to detect LSB embedding. A rate-distortion feature vector is used. They assume that the rate required to represent the seven most significant bits (MSB), R_{7MSB}, of a cover image, I_c, is approximately equal to the rate required to represent 7 MSB plus the LSB plane with all ones, $R_{7MSB}(I_c + 1)$, that is,

$$R_{7MSB}(I_c) \approx R_{7MSB}(I_c + 1) \qquad (1)$$

where **1** is a matrix of all ones. But, equation (1) may not necessarily hold for a stego-image I_S. In general,

$$R_{7MSB}(I_S) \le R_{7MSB}(I_S + 1) \qquad (2)$$

Therefore a normalized difference between these rates can be used as the distinguishing feature, that is, the feature is,

$$\Psi R(I_c) = \frac{\Delta R(I_c)}{\Delta R(\tilde{I}_c)} \qquad (3)$$

where $\Delta R I_c$ is defined as,

$$\Delta R I_c = |R_{7MSB}(I_c) - R_{7MSB}(I_c - 1)| \qquad (4)$$

Here, $\tilde{I}_c$ denotes the modified image obtained by randomizing the LSB plane of the test image to combat false positives due to under/over exposed regions in the cover image. The estimated feature vector is projected onto a low dimensional subspace using the Karhunen-Loeve (KL) transform. Feature vector in the subspace is then used to train a Bayes classifier. As observed from the simulation results presented in Celik et al. (2004) the detection performance of this technique depends on the embedding rate.

- Fridrich (2004) proposed learning-based steganalysis to detect JPEG stego-images. They use a 23-dimensional feature vector to train a linear LFD classifier. Feature vector used during the training phase consists of the following: (1) local and global first- and second-order statistics of DCT coefficients, (2) *blockiness* (or artifacts) in spatial domain, and (3) pairwise correlation in neighboring blocks (or *co-occurrence factor*) estimated from the difference between the stego-image and an estimate of cover image. The decompressed stego-image is cropped by four pixels from the top and left. The resulting cropped image is then recompressed using same JPEG quantization table to obtain an estimate of the cover image. It is seen that

the detection performance of this technique depends on the hidden message length.

- Sullivan, Bi, Madhow, Chandrasekaran, & Manjunath, 2004) have proposed supervised learning-based steganalysis technique to attack QIM steganography. Empirical probability mass function (PMF) estimated using a histogram with 300 bins from the test image in the DCT domain acts as a feature vector. However, details about the classifier are not presented in their paper. It is seen that the detection performance depends on:
  1. Quantization step-size used to embed the message using QIM steganography, and
  2. The embedding rate.

Model-Based Steganalysis

Model-based steganalysis generally assumes a suitable statistical non-parametric or parametric model for the cover and stego-signals. Detection statistic is then derived using these models (Fridrich & Goljan, 2002; Malik, Subbalakshami, & Chandramouli, in press-c). Statistical analysis based on first- and second-order statistics of the test image (i.e., mean and variance), Chi-square (χ^2) tests, and so forth are commonly used to distinguish between the stego- and the cover signals.

Some non-learning and parametric model-based steganalysis techniques can be found in Westfeld and Pfitzmann (1999); Fridrich, Goljan, Hogea, and Soukal (2003); Malik, Subbalakshami, and Chandramouli (in press-a); Malik et al. (in press-c); and Trivedi and Chandramouli (2005). A brief overview of some of these techniques is described as follows:

- Trivedi and Chandramouli (2003, 2004, 2005) propose a steganalysis technique to detect sequential steganography (Marvel et al.,

1999). They discuss a theoretical framework to detect abrupt changes in the stego-image statistics which can be used to distinguish between the cover and the stego- images. A locally most powerful (LMP) sequential hypothesis is designed to detect the secret key.

- Malik et al. (in press-a, in press-b, in press-c) address steganalysis of QIM-based embedding (Chen & Wornell, 2000, 2001). It is observed that the stego-image obtained using QIM embedding exhibits a higher degree of randomness than the corresponding quantized cover image (i.e., simply quantized without message embedding). This in turn increases the entropy of the stego-image. A non-parametric measure of randomness called the approximate entropy, *ApEn*, is then used to distinguish between the cover and stego-image.

Figure 6 shows the estimated *ApEn* of a quantized cover image and a QIM stego-image, in the DCT domain. These values are for the image number 47 of the uncompressed color image database (UCID).[17] For simplicity, this color image was first resized to 256x256 pixels and then transformed to a gray scale image. The gray-scale image, **S**,

was then used to generate the quantized cover and QIM stego-images. The quantized-cover image, $\mathbf{X}_q$, was obtained by quantizing 8x8, zig zag scanned DCT (AC) coefficients of the gray scale cover image, using quantization step-size, Δ. The corresponding QIM-stego image, $\mathbf{X}_{QIM}$, was obtained by embedding a 64 KB message using the same quantization step-size, Δ.

Following observations can be made from Figure 6:

1. The estimated *ApEn* from the cover image, **S**, remains approximately constant for all DCT coefficients, which implies that all DCT coefficient sequences exhibit approximately the same level of randomness.
2. On an average, *ApEn* for both $\mathbf{X}_q$ and $\mathbf{X}_{QIM}$ decreases from low to high frequency-coefficients. Here low and high frequency-coefficients correspond to DCT coefficients numbered from 2 to 32 and 32 to 64 respectively.
3. *ApEn* of $\mathbf{X}_q$ and $\mathbf{X}_{QIM}$ decreases at a higher rate for the low frequency-coefficients than the high frequency-coefficients.
4. *ApEn* of $\mathbf{X}_{QIM}$ has lower slope in both frequency regions than that of $\mathbf{X}_q$.

Figure 6. Estimated ApEn from the cover image, (S), quantized-cover, (Xq), and QIM-stego image, (XQIM)

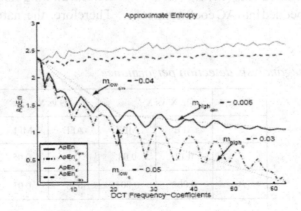

5. Let m_{low} and m_{high} denote slopes of the *ApEn* in low and high frequency-coefficients respectively, and define the change in the slope, δm, as,

$$\delta m = \frac{\left(m_{low} - m_{high}\right) \times 100}{m_{low}}$$

(5)

We observe that δm for the quantized-cover is well below 50% (36% to be exact) and it is well above 50% (85% to be exact) for the QIM-stego.

6. *ApEn* of QIM-stego is higher than that of the quantized-cover in the high frequency region, which implies that for high frequency-coefficients the QIM-stego is relatively more random than the corresponding quantized-cover. This higher *ApEn* value in the QIM-stego compared to the quantized-cover can be attributed to the randomness induced by the embedded message *M*.

The change in the slope, δm, from low to high frequency-coefficients can be used to differentiate a quantized-cover from QIM-stego. Consider two different message embedding scenarios:

1. **All frequency embedding** (AFE), that is, message M is embedded into every AC coefficient using QIM, and
2. **Mid-frequency embedding** (MFE), that is, message M is embedded into AC coefficients

5 to 32. MFE is commonly used to embed a message to lower embedding induced distortion without compromising robustness

Table 2 shows the false positive (P_{fp}) and false negative (P_{fn}) rates obtained from simulations using 1,000 images from the UCID database. We observe that *ApEn*-based steganalysis if reliable. The same method is also useful to distinguish between the cover, **S**, and the DM-stego, $\mathbf{X}_{DM}$.

Active steganalysis discussed in Malik et al. (in press-a, in press-c) estimates the hidden message. It is shown that accurate estimation of the hidden message length from a stego-image carrying a smaller message, an embedding rate, R, as low as 0.05 bits per pixel (bpp) is possible. It is also observed that the average steganalysis decoding bit error rate, P_e, depends on,

- The cover image statistics
- The embedding rate, R

Simulation results based on cover image statistics reveal that for any embedding rate $0 < R \leq 1$ and quantization step-size, Δ, low texture, QIM-stego images exhibit relatively higher P_e than rich-texture QIM-stego images. Higher decoding bit error, P_e, in the low texture, QIM-stego images can be attributed to what we call *natural binning*. That is, unquantized DCT coefficients are naturally rounded to the reconstruction grid points. Rich-texture images exhibit very little of natural binning compared to low textured images. Therefore, the naturally quantized coefficients

Table 2. ApEn-based steganalysis detection performance

Error	$\mathbf{X}_q$ vs $\mathbf{X}_{QIM}$		$\mathbf{S}$ vs $\mathbf{X}_{DM}$	
	AFE	MFE	AFE	MFE
P_{fp}	0.12	0.08	0.1	0.05
P_{fn}	0.002	0.001	0.07	0.01

Figure 7. Error in the estimated message location due to natural binning for different embedding rates: embedded message locations (first row), estimated message locations (second row), and error in the estimated message locations due to natural binning (bottom row)

Figure 8. Error in the estimated message location due to natural binning for different embedding rates: embedded message locations (first row), estimated message locations (second row), and error in the estimated message locations due to natural binning (bottom row)

contribute to the decoding bit error as the steganalysis decoder falsely identifies such coefficients as message carriers. Extensive simulation shows that the decoding error rate due to natural binning approaches 0 as R approaches 1 as illustrated in Figures 7 and 8.

In Figures 7 and 8 the first rows show the embedded message locations; second rows show the estimated message locations using active steganalysis technique presented in Malik et al. (in press-a), and the bottom rows show the errors in the estimated message. Here message embedding is done using 8x8 non-overlapping DCT blocks. It can be observed from the figures that the decoding bit error probability decreases monotonically as message embedding rate increases. We also observe that a low texture image such as the **Girl** image, exhibits higher decoding bit error rate than a rich-texture stego-image such as **Spring**. Plain areas (or low activity areas) in the stego-image are the main sources of decoding bit error in the estimated message. One possible way to mitigate these errors due natural binning is to use larger block sizes for plain areas of the cover image.

The effect of natural binning on the decoding error in the estimated message for two images: **Girl** (a low texture image) and **Spring** (a rich-texture image) is shown in Table 3. Embedding rate R = { 0.1, 0.3, 0.5}, Δ - 2 and 8x8 DCT block size were used to obtain Table 3.

These simulation results indicate that it is easier to steganalyze QIM-stego images that use one or all of the following:

- Larger block sizes, that is, block size + 8 x 8,
  ° Higher embedding rate, that is, R → 1, and
  ° Exclude zero from the quantization-grid used for QIM steganography.

- Amin and Subbalakshmi, 2007) propose a steganalysis technique to attack additive embedding. Their technique exploits the fact that the average power spectrum of natural images can be modeled as $1/f^a$ (Torralba & Olivia, 2003), where f is the spatial frequency and α is a decaying exponent. Decaying exponent is a positive real number and for all natural images it falls in the range $\alpha = [1.0, 2.0]$. This technique uses the estimated decaying exponent $\hat{\alpha}$ from the test image to distinguish between the cover and the stego-images. They estimate α as the slope of the *log-log* graph of spatial frequency, f, versus the amplitude of the test image. Simulation results shows that α for a stego-image is significantly higher than that for the corresponding cover image. Simulation results in Amin and Subbalakshmi are presented for stego-images obtained using additive embedding in spatial, DCT, DWT domain, and using the commercial image watermarking software *Digimarc*.[18] Also, images belonging to various categories, for example, skyscrapers, buildings, landscape,

Table 3. Decoding error due to natural binning

Image	Error in the Estimated Message		
	Embedding Rate R (bbp)		
	0.1	0.3	0.5
Girl	1.9×10^{-2}	5.5×10^{-3}	1.3×10^{-3}
Spring	5.9×10^{-3}	2.4×10^{-3}	4.6×10^{-4}

sky, forest, and so forth are also considered. However, this steganalysis method fails to detect the stego-image obtained by additive embedding in the DCT domain.

STEGANALYSIS SOFTWARE TOOLS

This section provides a brief overview of some of the available shareware/freeware tools for steganalysis.

Stegdetect[19] is a freeware steganalysis tool that is commonly used to detect JPEG stego-images obtained using steganographic tools such as *F5*, *JP Hide and Seek, Invisible Secrets*,[20] and *Jsteg*. This tool uses statistical analysis based on Chi-square (χ^2) test to distinguish between the cover and the stego-images in JPEG format. Figure 9 shows output of graphical user interface (GUI), *xsteg*, when stegdetect tool was applied to the **Lena**

image and the corresponding JPEG stego-image of **Lena**. Here stego-**Lena** image was obtained by embedding a 7KB message using *JP Hide and Seek* and *Invisible Secrets* steganographic tools.

It can be observed from Figure 9 that stegdetect tool has successfully detected the cover image (lena.jpg) and the corresponding stego-image (lenainvisible.jpg and lenaJPHS.jpg). In addition, it has also correctly detected the steganographic tool used. Detection performance of the stegdetect steganalysis tool depends on the length of the hidden message.

StegSpy[21] is also a freeware steganalysis tool which can be used to detect both the presence of the hidden message and the steganographic tool used. Latest StegSpy version can be used to attack steganographic tools such as *Hiderman, JP Hide and Seek, Masker,*[22] *JPegX,* and *Invisible Secrets*. Figure 10 shows an output of StegSpy GUI, when applied to gray-scale **Lena** image in

Figure 9. The output from xsteg GUI when steganalysis tool Stegdetect was applied to three JPEG images of Lena: original Lena image, Stego-Lena obtained using JP Hide and Seek, and Stego-Lena obtained using Invisible Secrets

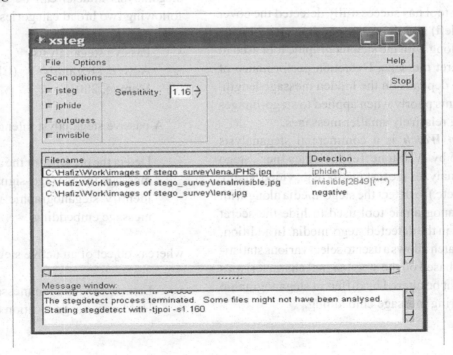

Figure 10. The output from StegSpy GUI when tested for two GIF images

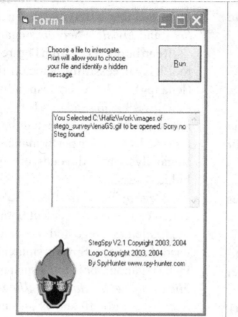
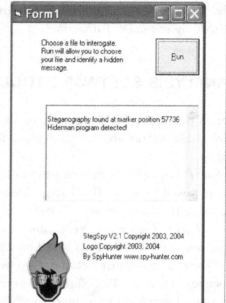

GIF format and its corresponding stego-image obtained by embedding a 7KB message using *Hiderman* steganographic tool.

It can be observed from Figure 10 that the StegSpy tool has successfully detected the cover image (left) and the corresponding stego-image (right) along with the steganographic tool used to hide secret message. Detection performance of StegSpy depends on the hidden message length. It performs poorly when applied to stego-images carrying relatively smaller messages.

Stego Watch is a commercial steganalysis software by WetStone Technologies Inc.[23] Stego Watch analyzes the test media (e.g., video, audio, images, etc.) to detect the stego-media along with the steganographic tool used to hide the secret message in the detected stego-media. In addition, Stego Watch allows a user to select various statistical tests based on the stego-signal characteristics that might be altered by different steganographic tools during message embedding.

STEGANALYSIS CLASSIFICATION

Based upon the objective of the steganalyst, steganalysis attacks can be classified into the following two broad categories:

- Passive steganalysis
- Active steganalysis (Chandramouli & Memon, 2003).

A passive steganalyst intends to:

- Detect the presence or the absence of hidden message in the stego-signal, and
- Identify steganographic method used for message embedding,

whereas object of an active steganalyst is to:

- Estimate the hidden message length,
- Hidden message location estimation,

- Embedding key estimation,
- Parameters of embedding algorithm,
- Extract the hidden message,
- Tamper (or modify) the hidden message.

Universal steganalysis techniques can only detect the presence or the absence of a hidden message, therefore belong to the passive steganalysis category. Whereas model-based steganalysis techniques can be used for steganalysis attacks such as hidden message detection, message extraction, secret key estimation, and so forth, therefore belonging to the active steganalysis category.

CRITICAL ANALYSIS OF STEGANALYSIS TECHNIQUES

We can analyze steganalysis techniques based on the underlying methodology employed for hidden message detection and/or extraction,

Supervised Learning-Based Steganalysis

Some salient features of supervised learning based steganalysis techniques include:

1. Reasonably accurate detection is achievable by training the underlying classifier for a given embedding algorithm. In addition, supervised learning-based steganalysis techniques do not require any prior statistical model about the cover and the stego-signal, as during training phase the classifier learns a classification rule which is averaged over a large data set.
2. Averaging over a large data set makes the averaged statistics robust to non-stationarity of multimedia objects (i.e., images, video, audio). Therefore non-stationeries do not limit the steganalysis detection performance.
3. Sophisticated machine learning and data analysis tools such as SVM, FLD, PCA,

independent component analysis (ICA), analysis of variance (ANOVA), and so forth can be readily used for classification.

On the other hand, supervised learning-based steganalysis techniques are limited by the following factors:

1. These methods require separate classifier training for each steganographic algorithm, which is a tedious and cumbersome task. In addition, these methods are unable to handle *zero-day attacks*[24] that is, they cannot differentiate between the stego- and the cover signal if the classifier is not trained for a given steganographic algorithm.
2. Detection performance of these methods critically depends on the selected feature space used to train the classifier. There is no systematic rule for feature selection to achieve desired detection performance, rather it is mostly heuristic or trial and error based.
3. Performance of these steganalysis methods depend on the structure of the underlying classifier used. Parameters such as the kernel type, classifier type (i.e., linear of non-linear), learning rate, maximum number of iterations, size of the training set, and so forth affect detection performance significantly. Once again, there is no systematic method to select these critical parameters.
4. Like other learning-based methods, these steganalysis methods are also sensitive to bias versus variance trade-off, that is, a classifier can be trained for very high accuracy for a given set of training data but its performance may deteriorate for diverse test data.
5. Steganalyst has no direct control over the achievable false alarm rate and miss probabilities.
6. Learning-based steganalysis methods usually produce a binary decision for a given

test signal, that is, whether a given test signal carries a hidden message or not. Therefore, such methods cannot be used to detect hidden message location or extract embedded information from the stego-signal.

7. Performance of these methods also depends on the embedding rate, that is, these techniques perform poorly for low embedding rates.

Model-Based Steganalysis

Performance of model-based steganalysis methods depend on the accuracy of the assumed statistical model and the amount of statistical information that is readily available. The amount of statistical information available to the steganalyst can be categorized as:

- **Completely known statistics:** This case is a direct implication of Kerchoff's security principle, that is, security of a given technique is determined by the security of the secret key alone. It is therefore reasonable to assume that complete statistics of the test signal is known to the steganalyst during the steganalysis process. In this case, the parametric model for the stego-signal and the cover signal are completely known. However this case is not very practical as in general steganalyst has no access to the cover signal.

- **Partially known statistics:** In this scenario, partial knowledge about the stego-algorithm is known to the steganalyst along with the cover and the stego-signal. Consider the case when the embedding algorithm is not known to the steganalyst but it is available to the steganalyst as a black box (for example, only an executable code of the embedding technique is available to the steganalyst). Under this scenario an approximate estimate of the test signal statistics may be obtained using an unprocessed large data set and the corresponding processed version of the data set obtained using the embedding technique available as a black box. The parametric probability models of the stego- and the cover signals may then be estimated using tools from estimation theory. Again this case is not very practical since in general a steganalyst has no access to the cover signal.

- **Completely unknown statistics:** This is perhaps the most practical. In this case Wendy, the warden, has access to the stego-signal only, that is, stego-signal is known to the steganalyst with no additional knowledge of the cover signal or the embedding algorithm (used to generate the corresponding stego-signal).

Some of the characteristics of these approaches are:

- Detection performance can be investigated using mathematical tools from the statistical detection theory.
- Steganalysis detection performance is completely specified by the receiver operating characteristic (ROC) curve. The ROC curve is the probability of detection (on y-axis) versus false alarm probability (on x-axis) plot. The ROC curve can be used to determine achievable error probabilities. In addition, it provides the steganalyst with a handle to operate the underlying detector at any point on the ROC curve.
- For a given error probability, closed-form solution for the optimal message detection threshold can be computed. In some cases, it may also be possible to specify constraints on the false alarm rate.
- Model-based techniques can also be used for secret key estimation, hidden message length estimation, hidden message extraction, and so forth.

But these techniques are limited by the following factors:

- Detection performance of model based steganalysis techniques depend on the accuracy of the assumed model.
- Detection performance of these methods deteriorates due to statistical nonstationarities in the multimedia signal (commonly used for covert communication).

CONCLUSION AND FUTURE RESEARCH DIRECTIONS

We observe that both learning- and model-based steganalysis techniques have their own set of pros and cons. A hybrid method based on decision-fusion, which combines decisions from several stegnalaysis methods for a final decision, can be used to improve performance. Designing these fusion rules for steganalysis has not received much attention.

The main goal of steganalysis is to develop techniques that can work effectively for almost all steganographic methods. But, this is a challenging task, especially for unknown steganographic techniques. Supervised learning-based universal steganalysis techniques achieve robustness at the cost of degradation in performance for a priori unknown embedding techniques. On the other hand, model-based steganalysis methods are generally embedding paradigm specific. These techniques generally have better detection performance for a given steganographic technique.

Computing steganographic capacity (Chandramouli, 2003) in the presence of a steganalysis detector is still an open problem. We note that capacity as defined for a digital watermarking system is not directly applicable to steganographic systems.

Currently there is no stegenalysis benchmarking framework to uniformly compare different steganalysis techniques. For example, there is a need to develop cover and stego data sets, design embedding rates, message lengths, and so forth for unbiased performance evaluation.

REFERENCES

Amin, P., & Subbalakshmi, K. (2007). Steganalysis using power spectra of digital images. In *IEEE International Conference on Image Processing*.

Anderson, R., & Petitcolas, F. (1998). On the limits of steganography. *IEEE Journal Selected Areas in Communications: Special Issue on Copyright and Privacy, 16*(5), 474-481.

Aura, T. (1997). Practical invisibility in digital communication. In *First International Workshop on Information Hiding* (Vol. 1174, pp. 51-67). Berlin/Heidelberg, Germany: Springer.

Cachin, C. (1998). Information-theoretic model for steganography. In *Second International Workshop on Information Hiding* (Vol. 1525, pp. 306-318). Berlin/Heidelberg, Germany: Springer.

Celik, M., Sharma, G., & Tekalp, A. (2004). Universal image steganalysis using rate-distortion curves. In *Security, Steganography, and Watermarking of Multimedia Content VI* (Vol. 5306, pp. 467-476). IS&T/SPIE.

Chandramouli, R. (2002). Mathematical theory for steganalysis. In *Security, Steganography, and Watermarking of Multimedia Contents IV* (Vol. 4675, pp. 14-25). IS&T/SPIE.

Chandramouli, R., Kharrazzi, M., & Memon, N. (2004). Image steganography and steganalysis: Concepts and practice. In *International Workshop on Digital Watermarking* (Vol. 2939, pp. 35-49). Berlin/Heidelberg, Germany: Springer.

Chandramouli, R., & Memon, N. (2001). Analysis of LSB based image steganography techniques. In *International Conference on image processing (ICIP'01)* (Vol. 3, pp. 1019-1022).

Chandramouli, R., & Memon, N. (2003). Steganography capacity: A steganalysis perspective. In *Security, Steganography, and Watermarking of Multimedia Contents V* (Vol. 5020, pp. 173-177). IS&T/SPIE.

Chang, C.-C., & Lin, C.-J. (2001). *Libsvm: A library for support vector machines.* Retrieved from http://www.csie.ntu.edu.tw/~cjlin/libsvm

Chen, B., & Wornell, G. (2000). Preprocessed and postprocessed quantization index modulation methods for digital watermarking. In *Security, Steganography, and Watermarking of Multimedia Contents III* (Vol. 3971). IS&T/SPIE.

Chen, B., & Wornell, G. (2001). Quantization index modulation: A class of provably good methods for digital watermarking and information embedding. *IEEE Transactions on Information Theory, 47*(4).

Duda, R., & Hart, P. (1973). *Pattern classification and scene analysis.* New York: John Wiley.

Dumitrescu, S., Wu, X., & Wang, Z. (2002). Detection of LSB steganography via sample pair analysis. In *5th International Workshop on Information Hiding* (Vol. 2578). Berlin/Heidelberg, Germany: Springer.

Farid, H. (2001). *Detecting steganographic messages in digital images* (Tech. Rep. No. TR2001-412). Department of Computer Science, Dartmouth College, Hanover, NH.

Farid, H. (2002). Detecting hidden messages using higher-order statistical models. In *International Conference on image processing (ICIP'02)* (Vol. 2, pp. 905-908).

Fridrich, J. (2004). Feature based steganalysis for jpeg images and its implications for future design of steganographic schemes. In *6th International Workshop on Information Hiding* (Vol. 3200). Berlin/Heidelberg, Germany: Springer.

Fridrich, J., Du, R., & Long, M. (2000). Steganalysis of LSB encoding in color images. In *International Conference on Multimedia and Expo (ICME'00)* (Vol. 3, pp. 1279-1282).

Fridrich, J., & Goljan, M. (2002). Practical steganalysis: state-of-the-art. In *Security, Steganography, and Watermarking of Multimedia Contents IV* (Vol. 4675, pp. 1-13). IS&T/SPIE.

Fridrich, J., & Goljan, M. (2003). Digital image steganography using stochastic modeling. In *Security, Steganography, and Watermarking of Multimedia Content V* (Vol. 5020, pp. 191-202).

Fridrich, J., Goljan, M., & Hogea, D. (2002a). Attacking the outguess. In *ACM Workshop on Multimedia and Security.*

Fridrich, J., Goljan, M., & Hogea, D. (2002b). Steganalysis of JPEG images: Breaking the F5 algorithm. In *5th International Workshop on Information Hiding* (Vol. 2578, pp. 310-323). Berlin/Heidelberg, Germany: Springer.

Fridrich, J., Goljan, M., & Hogea, D. (2003). New methodology for breaking steganographic techniques for JPEGS. In *Security, Steganography, and Watermarking of Multimedia Contents V* (Vol. 5020, p. 143-155). IS&T/SPIE.

Fridrich, J., Goljan, M., Hogea, D., & Soukal, D. (2003). Quantitative steganalysis of digital images: Estimation of the secret message length. *ACM Multimedia Systems Journal, 9.*

Fridrich, J., Holotyak, T. S., & Soukal, D. (2005). Maximum likelihood estimation of secret message length embedded using PMK steganography in spatial domain. In *Security, Steganography, and Watermarking of Multimedia Content VII* (Vol. 5681, pp. 595-606). IS&T/SPIE.

Fridrich, J., Soukal, D., & Goljan, M. (2005). Stochastic approach to secret message length estimation in +-k embedding steganography. In *Security, Steganography, and Watermarking of Multimedia Content VII* (Vol. 5681, pp. 673-684). IS&T/SPIE.

Harmsen, J., & Pearlman, W. (2003). Steganalysis of additive noise modelable information hiding. In *Security, Steganography, and Watermarking of Multimedia Content V* (Vol. 5020, pp. 131-142). IS&T/SPIE.

Holotyak, T., Fridrich, J., & Voloshynovskiy, S. (2005). Blind statistical steganalysis of additive steganography using wavelet higher order statistics. In *9th IFIP TC-6 TC-11 Conference on Communications and Multimedia Security*.

Johnson, N., & Jajodia, S. (1998a). Exploiting steganography: Seeing the unseen. *IEEE Computers, 31*(2), 26-34.

Johnson, N., & Jajodia, S. (1998b). Steganalysis of images created using current steganography software. In *Second International Workshop on Information Hiding* (Vol. 1525, pp. 273-279). Berlin/Heidelberg, Germany: Springer.

Kessler, G. (2004). An overview of steganography for the computer forensics examiner. *Forensics Science and Communications, 6*(3).

Kiayias, A., Raekow, Y., & Russell, A. (2005). E±cient steganography with provable security guarantees. In *7th International Workshop on Digital Watermarking* (Vol. 3727, pp. 118-130). Berlin/Heidelberg, Germany: Springer.

Lyu, S., & Farid, H. (2002). Detecting hidden messages using higher-order statistics and support vector machines. In *5th International Workshop on Information Hiding* (Vol. 2578, pp. 340-354). Berlin/Heidelberg, Germany: Springer.

Lyu, S., & Farid, H. (2004). Steganalysis using color wavelet statistics and one-class support vector machines. In *Security, Steganography, and Watermarking of Multimedia Contents VI* (Vol. 5306, pp. 35-45). IS&T/SPIE.

Lyu, S., & Farid, H. (2006). Steganalysis using higher-order image statistics. *IEEE Transactions on Information Forensics and Security, 1*(1), 111-119.

Malik, H., Subbalakshmi, K., & Chandramouli, R. (2007). Steganalysis of quantization index modulation based steganography using kernel density estimation. In *9th ACM Multimedia and Security Workshop*.

Malik, H., Subbalakshmi, K., & Chandramouli, R. (in press-a). Nonparametric steganalysis of quantization index modulation based steganography using approximate entropy. *IEEE Transactions on Information Forensics and Security*.

Malik, H., Subbalakshmi, K., & Chandramouli, R. (in press-b). Nonparametric steganalysis of quantization index modulation based steganography using kernel density estimaton. *IEEE Transactions on Information Forensics and Security*.

Malik, H., Subbalakshmi, K., & Chandramouli, R. (in press-c). Nonparametric steganalysis of quantization index modulation based steganography using approximate entropy. In *Security, Steganography, and Watermarking of Multimedia Contents IX*. IS&T/SPIE.

Marvel, L., Boncelet, C., & Retter, C. (1999). Spread spectrum image steganography. *IEEE Transactions on Image Processing, 8*(8), 1075-1083.

Matsuoka, H. (2006). Spread spectrum audio steganography using subband phase shifting. In *International Conference on Intelligent Information Hiding and Multimedia* (pp. 3-6).

Provos, N. (2001). Defending against statistical steganalysis. In *10th Usenix Security Symposium*.

Provos, N., & Honeyman, P. (2001). Detecting steganographic contents on the Internet (Tech. Rep. No. CITI 01-1a). Ann Arbor, MI: University of Michigan.

Provos, N., & Honeyman, P. (2003). Hide and seek: An introduction to steganography. *IEEE Security and Privacy Magazine, 1*(3), 32-44.

Sallee, P. (2003). Model-based steganography. In *6th International Workshop on Digital Watermarking* (Vol. 3929, pp. 154-167). Berlin/Heidelberg, Germany: Springer.

Simmons, G. J. (1984). "Prisoners" problem and subliminal channel. In *Crypto83-Advances in Cryptography* (pp. 51-67). New York: Plenum Press.

Sullivan, K., Bi, Z., Madhow, U., Chandrasekaran, S., & Manjunath, B. (2004). Steganalysis of quantization index modulation data hiding. In *International Conference on Image Processing (ICIP'04)* (Vol. 2, pp. 1165-1168).

Torralba, A., & Olivia, A. (2003). Statistics of natural image categories. IOP Network: *Computation in Neural Systems, 14,* 391-412.

Trivedi, S., & Chandramouli, R. (2003). Active steganalysis of sequential steganography. In *Security, Steganography, and Watermarking of Multimedia Contents V* (Vol. 5020, pp. 123-130). IS&T/SPIE.

Trivedi, S., & Chandramouli, R. (2004). Locally most powerful detector for secret key estimation in spread spectrum data hiding. In *Security, Steganography, and Watermarking of Multimedia Contents VI* (Vol. 5306, pp. 1-12). IS&T/SPIE.

Trivedi, S., & Chandramouli, R. (2005). Secret key estimation in sequential steganalysis. *IEEE Transactions on Signal Processing: Supplement on Secure Media, 53*(2), 746-757.

Wang, Y., & Moulin, P. (2006). Optimized feature extraction for learning-based image steganalysis. *IEEE Transactions on Information Forensics and Security, 1*(2), 31-45.

Westfeld, A. (2001). F5 -a steganographic algorithm high capacity despite better steganalysis. In *Fifth Information Hiding Workshop* (Vol. 2137, pp. 289-302). Berlin/Heidelberg, Germany: Springer.

Westfeld, A. (2002). Detecting low embedding rates. In *5th Information Hiding Workshop* (Vol. 2578, pp. 324-339). Berlin/Heidelberg, Germany: Springer.

Westfeld, A., & Pfitzmann. (1999). Attacks on steganographic systems. In *Third Information Hiding Workshop* (Vol. 1768, pp. 61-75). Berlin/Heidelberg, Germany: Springer.

Zollner, J., Federrath, H., Klimant, H., Pfitzmann, A., Piotraschke, R., Westfeld, A., et al. (1998). Modeling the security of steganographic systems. In *Second International Workshop on Information Hiding* (Vol. 1525, pp. 345-355). Berlin/Heidelberg, Germany: Springer.

NOTE

In this chapter we briefly reviewed current state-of-the-art in steganalysis. Further details on steganography and steganographic tools can be found on Neil F Johnson's Web page.[25] Johnson's Web page is a good a knowledge base for the steganographic and steganalysis tools till 1999. A recent article by Provos and Honeyman (2003) discusses key requirements of robust steganographic systems based on the existing steganalysis techniques. Anderson and Petitcolas' (1998) work provides analysis of existing of steganographic systems based on capacity and robustness. Information-theoretic analysis of steganographic systems can be found in Cachin (1998); Kiayias, Raekow, and Russell (2005); and Zollner et al. (1998), and Chandramouli and Memon's (2003) work provides analysis of steganographic systems based on a new measure of capacity. Steganography can also be used for illicit communication, details on using steganography for illicit applications and its forensic analysis based on the current existing steganographic and steganalysis tools can be found in an article by Kessler (2004). In addition, a paper by Chandramouli, Kharrazzi, and Memon (2004) provides theoretical analysis of steganalysis attacks under practical scenarios. Review of some steganalysis techniques and steganographic algorithms can be fond in Aura (1997); Provos and Honeyman (2001); Provos (2001); Sallee (2003); and Westfeld (2001).

ENDNOTES

1 Software available at http://www.demcom. com/deutsch/index.htm

2 Software available at http://www.cs.bath. ac.uk/~jpc/blindside/

3 Software Hide 2.1 available at http://www. sharpthoughts.org

4 Software available at http://www.demcom. com/deutsch/index.htm

5 Software available at ftp://idea.sec.dsi. unimi.it/pub/security/crypt/code/s-tools. zip

6 Software available at http://www.ezstego. com

7 Software available at http://linux01.gwdg. de/latham/sego

8 Software available at http://www.darkside. com.au/gifshuffle/

9 Software available at http://digitalforensics. champlain.edu/download/Gif-it-up.exe

10 Software available at ftp://ftp.funet.fi

11 Software available at http://steghide.source-forge.net/download.php

12 Software available at http://steghide.source-forge.net/download.php

13 Software available http://linux01.gwdg. de/\%7Ealatham/stego.html

14 Software available at http://www.invisibles-ecrets.com/

15 Software available at wwwwrn.inf.tu-dres-den.de/westfeld/f5

16 Software available at http:\\www.sharp-thoughts.org

17 Downloaded from http://www-users.aston. ac.uk/~schaefeg/datasets/UCID/ucid.html

18 Digimarc Corp. "My Picture Marc 2005 v1.0 adobe photoshope plugin" 2005. available at http://www.digimarc.com

19 Software available at http://digitalforen-sics.champlain.edu/download/stegdetect-0.4.zip

20 Software available at http://www.invisib-lesecrets.com/

21 Software available at http://www.spy-hunter. com/stegspydownload.htm

22 Software available at http://www.masker. de

23 http://www.wetstonetech.com/

24 http://en.wikipedia.org/wiki/Zero-Day_At-tack

25 http://www.jjtc.com/stegdoc/

Chapter XIII
Benchmarking Steganalysis

Andrew D. Ker
Oxford University Computing Laboratory, UK

ABSTRACT

This chapter discusses how to evaluate the effectiveness of steganalysis techniques. In the steganalysis literature, numerous different methods are used to measure detection accuracy, with different authors using incompatible benchmarks. Thus it is difficult to make a fair comparison of competing steganalysis methods. This chapter argues that some of the choices for steganalysis benchmarks are demonstrably poor, either in statistical foundation or by over-valuing irrelevant areas of the performance envelope. Good choices of benchmark are highlighted, and simple statistical techniques demonstrated for evaluating the significance of observed performance differences. It is hoped that this chapter will make practitioners and steganalysis researchers better able to evaluate the quality of steganography detection methods.

INTRODUCTION

Steganography is the study of the concealment of information. Typically this means embedding a covert payload in an item of digital media such as an image, audio file, or video, but steganographic methods have now been proposed for a wide range of cover objects. Successful steganography means that nobody other than the intended recipient can even detect the existence of the embedded payload, let alone decode it, in which case other information security measures are for naught.

This motivates the competing field of *steganalysis:* to determine whether digital media objects contain a covert payload or not. It seems that every steganographic embedding scheme is sooner or later followed by publication of steganalysis techniques for attacking it. It is then vital to evaluate the ability of these methods to meet their detection aims, and particularly to compare the efficacy of competing steganalysis algorithms. Unfortunately, although there is copious work proposing methods for steganalysis, the literature barely considers the question of how to measure their reliability; we observe poor practice and inconsistent benchmarks. We shall argue that some of the currently used benchmarks are statistically flawed, while others over-value detectors with weak practical detection power. Better choices exist. Furthermore, in the case of comparison of two steganalysis methods, there is rarely a consideration of the statistical significance of an observed difference: this could lead to flawed conclusions.

The chapter is not concerned with the creation of better steganalysis methods, nor with detailed benchmarking of current steganalysis methods, but with ways to measure steganalysis performance. It is aimed at practitioners who need to evaluate a particular steganalysis method and researchers who want to compare a new steganalysis proposal with those in competing literature. We will clarify the precise aims of steganalysis, separating those methods that detect payload from those that attempt to measure it, and survey some commonly used steganalysis benchmarks, pointing out weaknesses in some of the popular choices. We then suggest some good choices for benchmarks, and give simple statistical techniques to decide whether the evidence in a particular batch of experiments is sufficient to conclude a significant improvement. Throughout the chapter we will illustrate the techniques by comparing two competing steganalysis algorithms.

BACKGROUND

The terminology of steganography and steganalysis is now settled: the covert payload is embedded into a *cover object* producing a *stego-object*. Details of the *stego-system* (the embedding and extraction methods) are not relevant to this chapter, but it is generally assumed that the sender and recipient share knowledge of an embedding key, and that the recipient does not have access to the original cover object. The communicating parties' enemy is the *steganalyst* (often referred to as a *Warden*) and this is the role we are taking in this work, assuming that we are given *steganalysis* methods which try to determine whether an object is an innocent cover or a payload-carrying stego-object. Usually, different embedding methods and cover media types are attacked by specific steganalysis methods.

The literature contains a vast array of steganalysis techniques, for a range of embedding methods in a variety of cover media: the folklore method of replacing least significant bits (LSBs) in digital images is attacked in increasingly sophisticated ways in Westfeld and Pfitzmann (1999); Fridrich, Goljan, and Du (2001); Dumitrescu, Wu, and Wang (2003); Fridrich and Goljan (2004); Lu, Luo, Tang, and Shen (2004); and Ker (2005b, 2007a); replacement of multiple bit planes is attacked in Yu, Tan, and Wang (2005) and Ker (2007b); an alternative LSB method that avoids the previous steganalysis, described in Sharp (2001), is attacked in Harmsen and Pearlman (2003); Ker (2005a); and Fridrich, Goljan, and Holotyak (2006); the steganography software OutGuess embeds in JPEG images (Provos, 2001) and is attacked in Fridrich, Goljan, and Hogea (2002b); another popular JPEG embedding method is known as F5 (Westfeld, 2001) and this is detected by methods including Fridrich, Goljan, and Hogea (2002a); Harmsen and Pearlman (2004); Fridrich (2004); Shi, Chen, and Chen (in press); and Pevný and Fridrich (2007). Steganalysis is also possible in domains other than digital images: simple additive-noise embedding in video is attacked in Budhia, Kundur, and Zourntos (2006), and a method for embedding in MP3 audio files (Petitcolas, 1998) is attacked in Westfeld (2002). These references are not exhaustive and some others, including those proposing steganographic embedding schemes and those giving methods for their steganalysis, can be found under Additional Reading at the end of this chapter.

There does exist a concept of perfect, undetectable, steganography (Cachin, 2004) but it is difficult to practice in real cover media. Some schemes that attempt to do so are found in Moulin and Briassouli (2004) and Sallee (2005), but even they are subject to steganalysis as found in Wang and Moulin (2006) and Fridrich (2004), respectively. This apparent paradox is resolved by noting that the perfect security of these embedding methods is dependent on a certain model for the cover images, and the steganalysis methods are able to exploit a discrepancy between the idealized model and properties of genuine images. (We will argue that the fact that there exist only approximate or incomplete models for cover media is also significant for benchmarking.)

It is important to measure the ability of each steganalysis method to fulfil its aim of detecting payload, particularly if there are multiple algorithms attacking the same steganographic embedding scheme and we want to know which works the best. But the benchmarking of steganalysis methods, and particularly their comparison, is an area of distinct weakness in the literature. Many of the steganalysis papers cited previously use different performance benchmarks, making comparison difficult; further, some commonly used benchmarks are flawed in that they only represent performance in particular, sometimes quite unrealistic, applications. We will examine some of these benchmarks in the third section, and present some good—or less bad—options in the fourth section. In practice, because steganalysis is to take place on digital media objects, results must be obtained by experimentation with steganography and steganalysis performed on a set of genuine covers. But is the number of experiments sufficient to justify the conclusion that a performance difference is real, or might it be due to natural variation? This is the question of statistical *significance*, which almost no steganalysis literature addresses. We will suggest simple techniques for answering it in the fifth section.

Throughout, we will illustrate the concepts by testing and comparing two particular steganalysis methods: those known as sample pairs analysis (henceforth referred to as SPA) (Dumitrescu et al., 2003) and the least squares method (LSM) (Lu et al., 2004). Both methods are for the detection of LSB replacement steganography in digital images. These detectors have similar features, including analysis of LSB flipping in pairs of pixels, but their method of operation is irrelevant to the content of this chapter where we consider only their performance. (If the reader wishes to understand their operation, they should refer to the papers introducing them.) The two methods have been chosen because they are able to diagnose the presence or absence of LSB embedded payload, and to estimate its size, and therefore provide useful examples for all of the benchmarks we will consider. LSM is a variant of SPA which, treating the cover assumptions more generally, was touted as an improvement and we shall examine the extent to which this is true. For testing we have obtained two sets of covers: 1,000 1.5Mpixel grayscale never-compressed bitmap images, and 500 color 0.3Mpixel images that had previously been stored in a JPEG compressed format. It will be demonstrated that this number of covers, although apparently substantial, is not always sufficient to draw robust conclusions.

Before discussing steganalysis specifically, it is worthwhile to place the benchmarking of detectors into a historical context. The theory of *signal detection* dates back to early research in the fields of radar and psychology (Green & Swets, 1966; Marcum, 1948). For a thorough survey of the basics, see McNicol (1972). Signal detection literature describes ways to measure accuracy of classification, usually based on the receiver operating characteristic (ROC) curve. However the standard metrics found in the literature are usually influenced by implicit assumptions about the signal detection domain, for example, equivalence between false positive and false negative errors, which are not relevant to steganalysis. This is one negative influence on the development of steganalysis benchmarking.

BENCHMARKING IN THE STEGANALYSIS LITERATURE

Consider first the most common type of steganalysis: that which tries to diagnose payload embedded by a specific method. There are two distinct paradigms which have emerged in the literature. The natural type of detector is one that gives a positive or negative diagnosis of steganography in an object: we will call this *binary steganalysis* and it will be examined in the *Binary Classification* section. The alternative type provides an estimate of the size of hidden payload (possibly zero), and this has been termed *quantitative steganalysis*, and is examined in the *Payload Size Estimation* section. Of course, quantitative steganalysis can always be converted into binary steganalysis by setting a threshold and giving a positive diagnosis of steganography whenever the payload estimate exceeds the threshold. Indeed quantitative estimators are often also benchmarked as discriminators between the binary cases. (For a while, quantitative payload estimators were known as *threshold-free* steganalysis [Fridrich et al., 2002b] because their output is more nuanced than a simple yes or no, but if the eventual aim is a binary classification then a threshold will still have to be set.)

It may seem curious that so many steganalysis methods, which include Fridrich et al., (2001, 2002a); Dumitrescu et al. (2003); Fridrich and Goljan (2004); Lu et al. (2004); and Ker (2005a, 2007b) among many others, are presented as quantitative estimators of payload size rather than simple detectors. The reason is that a mathematical analysis of the effects of steganography will always include the payload size as an unknown parameter, and so it is quite natural for them to result in steganalysis methods that estimate that parameter. Nonetheless, it was demonstrated in Ker (2004b) that the binary steganalysis question could often be answered more accurately if the quantitative method was adapted to remove the payload estimation part.

Finally, we will briefly consider the more complex problem of *blind steganalysis*, which attempts to diagnose payload without knowledge of the embedding method, and *multi-class steganalysis*, which aims to determine the embedding method from a list of possibilities, in the *Multi-Class and Blind Detection* section.

Binary Classification

Binary steganalysis is a form of *hypothesis testing*. In the language of statistics, there is a *null hypothesis* that an object under examination is an innocent cover, and an *alternative hypothesis* that it is a stego-object containing a payload. A more precise alternative hypothesis is given by specifying the size of the payload. There are two ways in which a binary classifier can fail: rejecting the null hypothesis when it is true (this corresponds to a *false positive* diagnosis of steganography, known as a Type I error) or accepting the null hypothesis when it is false (this is a *false negative*, Type II error, or *missed detection*). The likelihood of these two errors, and their dependence on the payload size, forms the basis of benchmarks for any binary detector.

In principle one might hope to derive bounds on the probability of false positives and negatives, using statistical theory. For example, an optimal discriminator between simple hypotheses is given by the likelihood ratio statistic—this is the Neyman-Pearson Lemma (e.g., Rice, 1994)—and it is sometimes possible to derive exact probabilities of error for the likelihood ratio test. However this approach is almost invariably doomed for steganalysis, because of the lack of accurate statistical models for cover or stego-objects: one cannot even compute the likelihood functions, let alone reason about the likelihood ratio statistic. One must resort to empirical data.

Thus the simplest way to benchmark a classifier is to obtain a set of sample cover objects and run the classifier on them—the observed proportion of false positive classifications is an estimate of the false positive rate—and then embed a certain payload in each object and re-run the experiments to estimate the rate of false negatives. (We will discuss later the extent to which a set of sample covers could be considered representative of the wider class of all covers.) For classifiers with a canonical sensitivity parameter this is the natural choice of benchmark. Because false negative rates depend heavily on the size of embedded payload, it is usually necessary to repeat the experiment with different payloads. Such tests can be found in much steganalysis literature, including Lu et al. (2004); Shi et al. (in press); and Pevný and Fridrich (2007). Note that classifiers based on learning machines, which require training, must be trained and tested on separate sets of objects.

There is nothing wrong with this measurement but it represents only a fraction of the performance profile. Classification can almost always be made more or less sensitive: In the case of simple univariate (one-dimensional) features, including the use of quantitative estimators as binary discriminators, this amounts to moving a detection threshold; most multidimensional classifiers have corresponding parameters that can be adjusted. More sensitive detection leads to a lower rate of false negatives at the expense of a higher rate of false positives. The full performance profile of a binary classifier is therefore given by a ROC curve, a graph that shows how the false positive

and negative results trade off as sensitivity is adjusted. The experimentally observed ROC curve for a univariate classifier is obtained by counting, for each threshold, the proportion of cover objects exceeding the threshold and the proportion of stego-objects not exceeding the threshold; this can be done efficiently by one pass through a sorted list of all cover and stego-values. ROC curves are now a standard tool in classification benchmarking and we will not repeat standard material here; see Egan (1975) or the very helpful summary in Fawcett (2003) for more information. ROC curves are included in most modern binary steganalysis literature, including Fridrich and Goljan (2004); Ker (2004a, 2004b, 2005a, 2005b); Kharrazi, Sencar, and Memon (2005); Hogan, Hurley, Silvestre, Balado, and Whelan (2005); Draper et al. (2005); Fridrich et al. (2006); and Wang and Moulin (2007). Usually they are displayed with false positive rates (the complement of which is known as *specificity*) on the *x*-axis and true positive rates (also known as *sensitivity*, the complement of false negative rates) on the *y*-axis so that more accurate detectors have ROC curves nearer to the upper and left edges.

For a detector with fixed sensitivity the probability of false negative is dependent on the size of embedded payload. Therefore the full performance profile of a binary steganalysis method is a surface in three dimensions, showing how false

Figure 1. ROC curves observed in 500 color JPEG images

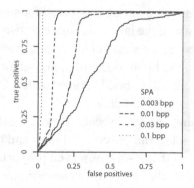
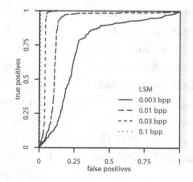
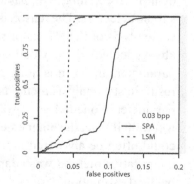

negative rates depend on false positive rates and payload size. Because of the difficulty in comparing three-dimensional surfaces visually, it is common to display plain ROC curves for a few embedding rates to illustrate a detector's performance. In Figure 1 we display ROC curves for four LSB replacement payload sizes. Payload size is measured in secret bits per cover pixel (bpp), which for this embedding method is equivalent to proportion of maximum payload. The payloads were embedded in our test set of 500 color JPEG covers and classified by the SPA and LSM steganalysis methods. (The raw methods produce payload size estimates, on which a threshold is set.) Comparing the first two graphs, it appears that LSM is the better detector, and a direct comparison of the two methods for only one payload is displayed in the third graph. It is common to restrict attention to the interesting range of false positives where the curves under consideration are not very close to 100% sensitivity, and in this case the x-axis runs only up to 20% false positives. The LSM method appears more sensitive than SPA, but whether the data support this conclusion will be examined later in later examples.

One difficulty with ROC curves is that it is difficult to make simple comparisons, particularly between two detectors whose curves cross, and authors have taken different views on how the dimensionality of the performance profile can be reduced. A number of popular measurements include the following. The *area under ROC (AUR or AUC)* is literally the area under the ROC curve, sometimes scaled for normalization; literature adopting this metric includes Fridrich (2004); Kharrazi et al. (2005); and Wang and Moulin (2007). Another popular measure is to fix a false positive rate, often 1% or 5%, and determine the corresponding false negative rate; literature adopting this metric includes Lyu and Farid (2002). Conversely, one can fix a false negative rate—a value of 50% was suggested in Ker (2004a) and is often adopted—and determine the corresponding false positive rate (Fridrich et al., 2006; Ker,

2005a; Westfeld, 2005). Finally, one can bound both false positive and false negative rates (5% and 50% are popular choices) and determine the lowest payload size at which detection meeting both these bounds is achieved (Ker, 2005b; Westfeld, 2005). This last metric reduces the three-dimensional performance curve into a single value, whereas the others are dependent on a particular payload size and should be computed for a range of payloads to explore the performance envelope fully.

Anything that reduces the dimensionality of the performance profile is discarding information, and there is no optimal metric. But there are two key features of steganalysis that our benchmarks ought to reflect, and some of the previous choices do not. First, in all conceivable steganalysis applications, there is an asymmetry between false positive and false negative results because we should assume that true positives are rare: the presence of steganography is the exception, not the rule. To avoid true positives being swamped by false positives, our focus should be on detectors with low false positive rates. Second, exactly how low the false positive rate needs to be depends heavily on the application: from *intelligence* on suspicious communications, where even 10% false positives might be acceptable, to automated scanning of an entire network, in which case even rates as low as 10^{-8} might cause a lot of false positive results.

The asymmetry between false positives and negatives makes AUR a poor benchmark. In some binary classification scenarios where true negatives and positives are equally likely it can be argued that AUR is an optimal measure, but for us it overvalues detectors with good sensitivity when the false positive rate is high: such detectors are likely to be worthless for steganalysis purposes. For similar reasons benchmarks that add up false positives and false negatives (sometimes called the *misclassification rate)*, for example in Harmsen and Pearlman (2004), or seek the position on the ROC curve to equalize false positives and false negatives, for example in Hogan, Silvestre, and

Hurley (2004) are giving too much weight to false negatives.

Fixing a false positive rate and measuring the false negative rate is an unsuitable benchmark unless we already know the application and the desired false positive rate. Because ROC curves of detectors are often steep, as those in Figure 1 are, fixing the false positive rate often gives little information about the overall performance of the detector since the observed false negative rate is near 0 or 1 for most false positive rates.

The aforementioned arguments are not to say that such benchmarks are worthless. Certainly if the aim is to demonstrate that a steganalysis method *works* then it suffices to illustrate its performance with a single point on the ROC curve or just about any performance summary. But benchmarking of steganalysis methods, and particularly comparison of two competing methods, asks us to align the metric more closely with potential applications.

Payload Size Estimation

Quantitative steganalysis is an example of statistical *estimation*, and the estimators are benchmarked by measuring their accuracy. Two difficulties particular to steganalysis payload estimators are that the standard measures of accuracy (mean and variance) can be unreliable, and that the accuracy can depend on a number of confounding factors.

One should first decide precisely what is being estimated: it could be the size of hidden payload (in bits or bytes) in a given object, or its size as a proportion of the maximum capacity of that object. The latter is most common in the literature and we will use it here too. Of course the two measures can be interconverted, but their benchmarks might differ inasmuch as one could be more sensitive to cover size than the other. When the covers are of uniform capacity (common in spatial-domain embedding methods if the covers are all the same size) then the two measures are equivalent.

Estimation error has two components: there might be a systematic *bias* (in statistical terminology, bias is additive error), and the estimator is subject to further random errors, which are commonly measured by variance. In initial investigations it is important to determine whether a payload estimator error has a bias component, not least because it might be possible to correct for it, but as long as the bias is small it is often appropriate to find a combined measure of (in)accuracy encompassing both bias and variance.

The obvious way to benchmark a quantitative steganalysis estimator is to take a set of cover objects and embed a certain payload in each, compute the estimates, and then use this sample to estimate the bias (by subtracting the true payload size from the observed sample mean) and variance (by computing the sample variance) or standard deviation. It is common for the steganalysis performance to depend heavily on the size of payload chosen, so the experiment should be repeated for a range of payloads and the performance displayed in a table or graph. Such benchmarks can be found in literature including Fridrich and Goljan (2004); Lu et al. (2004); Fridrich, Soukal, and Goljan (2005); and Holotyak, Fridrich, and Soukal (2005).

Typical charts are shown in Figure 2; embedding and payload estimation by both SPA and LSM methods was repeated in each of the 500 sample covers. On the *x*-axis is the payload size as a proportion of the maximum (which, in the case of LSB embedding, is the same as the number of secret bits per cover pixels). In each case the observed mean error and observed standard deviation are computed. These experiments show a particular pattern of behavior for near-maximal embedding rates, where both detectors lose their accuracy (this effect is explained in Ker, 2007b), but the errors take different forms for the two detectors. The SPA method suffers from a pattern of mostly positive bias whereas the LSM method sees bias gradually moving from small and positive to substantial and negative. Both methods have much wider distributional spread for near-maximal payloads. It is important to note that the same objects were used for each payload size, so there is likely to be a correlation of errors between different payload sizes.

However, sample mean and variance are not always good measures of location and spread. If the errors form a distribution with long tails (for example if the tails of the density function decay only as x^k for a small value of k) then sample mean and variance are not good estimators for population mean and variance (they might converge slowly or not at all) and indeed with extremely heavy-tailed distributions (such as the Cauchy distribution) the population mean and variance are not even defined, although there are other, well-defined, measures of location and spread (Taylor & Verbyla, 2004). This issue was first raised in Ker (2004a) and Böhme (2005) and investigated more carefully in Böhme and Ker (2006), where some payload estimators for LSB Replacement (including the two used for our examples in this chapter) are tested, with experimental results suggesting that they *do* have long tails. In such a case, robust estimators of location and spread should be used, and some will be suggested in the binary classification section.

Multi-Class and Blind Detection

This chapter is concerned mainly with steganalysis for a single steganographic embedding algorithm. There also exists so-called *blind* steganalysis methods, for example, Lyu and Farid (2002), which are not specialized to a single embedding method. They might work on as-yet unknown steganalysis methods, and their true aim is to detect anomalous objects rather than steganography per se. Related to this are the *multi-class* steganalysis methods, for example, Pevný and Fridrich (2007), which try to determine which steganography method has been used to embed a hidden message. We will not address their benchmark in detail, but highlight some of the additional challenges they present.

Multi-class detection is more difficult to benchmark, because the potential errors include classifying a stego-object as having payload embedded by the wrong method, as well as false positive and negative results. The analogue to a single false positive/negative point is known as the *confusion matrix*, which indicates how often each case (no embedding, and each different steganalysis method) is classified with each result, (see e.g., Pevný & Fridrich, 2007). Confidence intervals for elements of confusion matrices must be constructed carefully when the

Figure 2. Mean error, and standard deviation, of SPA and LSM payload estimators as true payload varies. Observed in 500 color JPEG images

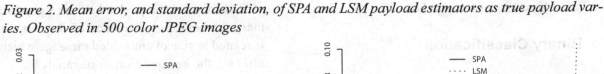

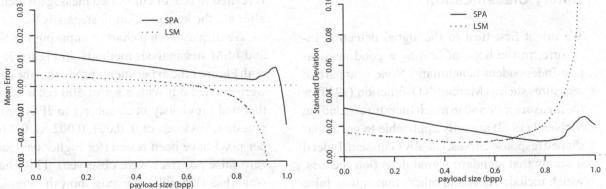

number of experiments on each case is not equal. One potential simplification is to equate incorrect classification of payload embedding method: although it is highly unlikely that false negatives and false positives errors are of equal cost, it may be reasonable to suppose equal costs for incorrectly diagnosing one payload type as another. This reduces to false negative, false positive, and false classification rates.

Blind steganalysis is even more difficult to benchmark fully. Certainly a blind method can be tested as if a standard binary method, but this is not a particularly fair measure of its value. It is hard to define a benchmark truly representing blind classification, because one cannot test against all possible embedding methods (including those not yet invented). In practice, the primary cause of false positives is misclassification of a certain type of covers (e.g., very noisy images) as stego-objects: we might never notice such covers unless the testing base is very wide. Indeed, it is not clear that the null and alternative hypotheses are properly defined in the blind case.

RECOMMENDED BENCHMARKS AND ILLUSTRATIONS

Having argued that, for binary and quantitative steganalysis, many of the methods found in the literature are inapt, we now suggest some sound (or at least less unsound) choices.

Binary Classification

We might first turn to the signal detection literature, in the hope of finding a good application-independent benchmark. None is apparent: measures such as Marcum's Q-function (1948) or the measure d' found in much literature including McNicol (1972) are only applicable to particular shaped response curves, usually Gaussian. Indeed it seems that standard signal detection metrics, which include AUR and others that equate false

positives and false negatives, are responsible for some of the poor steganalysis benchmarks chosen by steganalysis researchers.

Similarly, we could try making use of simple Bayesian techniques if we have prior knowledge about the likelihood of receiving cover or stego-objects; in the language of the *Benchmarking in the Steganalysis Literature* section this amounts to placing a suitable weight on false positives and false negatives. As with the methods discussed previously, this is only justifiable for particular applications and one cannot propose a sensible prior without making the benchmark specific to those applications.

If we do not know, at the benchmarking stage, what level of *evidence* we want our steganalysis method to give, it makes sense to try to measure that level of evidence rather than specify it in advance. In statistical terms, evidence is measured by *p-value,* which in our binary classification case is equivalent to the false positive rate on which threshold our observed data lies; the lower the false positive rate, the more evidence we have observed. It makes sense, therefore, to fix a false negative rate and find the corresponding false positive rate. We advocate that a fixed false negative rate of 50% is reasonable for many applications: at this rate a steganographer can only expect to escape detection an average of one time before being caught. Therefore a chart of how the false positive rate, corresponding to false negative rate of 50%, depends on payload size is a good summary. It shows how evidence of steganography is related to size of embedded message which is, after all, the key question in steganalysis.

We display such a chart, comparing the SPA and LSM steganalysis methods, in Figure 3. As with Figure 1 the experiments producing the chart were carried out with a set of 500 color covers that had previously been subject to JPEG compression. Payloads of 0, 0.001, 0.002,..., 0.2 bits per pixel have been tested (for higher payloads, zero false positives were observed). This chart, which has a logarithmic y-axis, shows how rapidly evidence increases as payload size increases, and also confirms that the LSM method has superior performance in these experiments.

If it is necessary to reduce each method to a single steganalysis benchmark, we advocate the metric of Ker (2004b), which fixes both false positive and false negative rate and then determines the lowest embedding rate for which the specified detector reliability is achieved. This metric has two drawbacks: it is computationally expensive to repeat all experiments with many different embedding rates, and of course the result depends heavily on the choice of false positive and false negative (the former, we have already commented, is highly application-dependent). But if a single benchmark is necessary it probably represents the least bad option for measuring sensitivity to payload. If we set bounds of 50% false negatives and 5% false positives and test all payloads at intervals of 0.001 bpp in the set of 500 covers, the SPA and LSM detectors achieve this performance for payloads over 0.065 bpp and 0.025 bpp, respectively.

The results we have presented in Figures 1-3 suggest that the LSM detector is superior to SPA in the binary steganalysis scenario. This is not the whole story. Our tests were carried out on color JPEG images, and work in Ker (2004a) shows that cover images previously subject to JPEG compression and used for spatial-domain embedding can have very different steganalysis performance: Some steganalysis methods gain and some lose sensitivity on such image types, and the *best* choice of detector can change depending on the type of cover. Furthermore, and perhaps contrary to intuition, if one takes large JPEG images and then reduces them in size, hoping to *wash out* the compression artifacts, the differences in steganalysis performance persist: even when the images are reduced by a factor of 5. Results in Ker (2005b, 2007a) confirm that differences also exist between grayscale and color covers. Moreover, none of these addresses directly the question of the size of covers or whether they consist of scanned images or digital photographs, or other potentially significant factors.

Figure 3. False positive rate when false negative is fixed at 50%, as payload size varies, observed in 500 color JPEG images

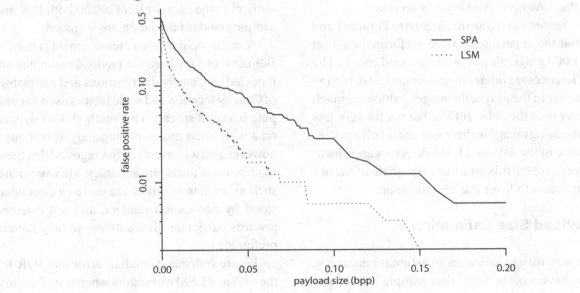

Figure 4. ROC curves observed in 1,000 grayscale images (compare with Figure 1)

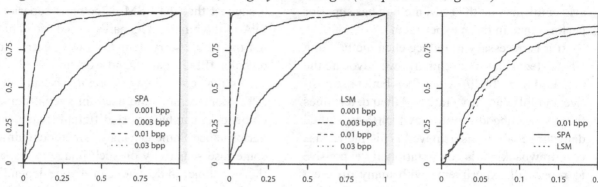

Therefore we might have to perform a large number of different experiments: only if one detector outperforms another on all image types, sizes, and sources can we start to suggest that it is always the better choice. It is tempting, then, to construct a single large set of covers that contains all types of images mixed together, and benchmark using that. Unfortunately that does not resolve the question, because the relative performance of the detectors might well be determined by the balance of the number of each type in the test set. There is little alternative to rigorous testing on many separate cover sets, although we will demonstrate one possible alternative approach in the *Advanced Benchmarks* section.

Figures 4 and 5 are analogous to Figures 1 and 3, but the experiments were performed on a set of 1,000 grayscale never-compressed covers. The differences are interesting: it seems that detection is easier in the grayscale images, which are much larger than the color JPEGs, but not for very low embedding rates. Furthermore, the relative performance of the SPA and LSM detectors appears to have changed: this time there is a small difference that seems to favor the SPA detector.

Payload Size Estimation

We now turn to measures of estimator accuracy. We have commented that sample mean and variance are not good measures of location and spread, when the sampled distributions have heavy tails, so we must find more widely applicable alternatives.

A convenient and robust measure of location is sample median. Spread is harder to estimate robustly and there is no optimal measure; one option is sample interquartile range (IQR), used in literature, including Böhme and Ker (2006) and Ker (2007a). One drawback is that it is not possible to justify the particular quartiles used (there is nothing optimal about using the 25% and 75% points as opposed to, for example, 10% and 90%) and that IQR is completely insensitive to outliers in the data. In Ker (2007a) both IQR and sample standard deviation are included.

A more sophisticated measurement is used in Böhme (2005), where the payload estimates are modeled as Cauchy distributions and estimators of Cauchy location and scale factors used to compute bias and spread. This method does depend on a well-fitted model of steganalysis response, however, and we have already suggested that these models are of uncertain accuracy. Measurements such as median and IQR are more easily understood by non-expert readers, and not oriented towards particular distributions, so may remain preferable.

Figure 6 displays median error and IQR for the SPA and LSM estimators when tested against

Figure 5. False positive rate when false negative is fixed at 50%, as payload size varies, observed in 1,000 grayscale images (compare with Figure 3)

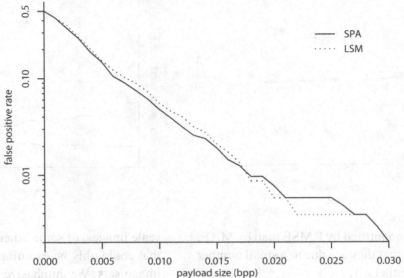

the set of 500 color JPEG images; these are robust measures of bias and spread as alternatives to those shown in Figure 2. The same general pattern emerges: poor performance for high payloads, and negative bias for the LSM estimator. But notice that the difference between SPA and LSM estimators, for high payloads, is more notable in the standard deviation chart in Figure 2 then the IQR chart in Figure 6, showing that the SPA method suffers from a large number of errors with moderate magnitude. On the other hand the LSM method suffers from distributional spread consisting of a relatively small number of large outliers (the standard deviation is more affected than IQR).

For an overall summary, it is attractive to combine bias and error spread into a single benchmark. In statistical literature the mean square error (MSE) is often used, computed from the observed sample statistics. An equivalent benchmark in the same units as the measurements is the square-root of this quantity (RMSE). But these statistics suffer from the same problem as sample variance: for long-tailed steganalysis error distributions they

might converge very slowly or not at all. Robust alternatives include median absolute error; this is very robust, but as with sample median, completely insensitive to outliers. We now advocate using the *mean* absolute error (MAE) as a reasonable benchmark, balancing robustness and sensitivity to outliers. Space permitting, it would be preferable to examine many measures—mean error, IQR, RMSE, MAE—to get a good picture of overall performance.

Figure 7 compares the SPA and LSM payload estimators using the RMSE and MAE benchmarks. The LSM method performs more accurately on low embedding rates (for near-zero rates the error magnitude is around half of that of the SPA method) but for high embedding rates the SPA method performs better. Both methods' overall estimation accuracy drops off considerably for near-maximal embedding, and further their performance dips for near-zero embedding. It seems that the LSM method is preferable for embedding rates below about 0.75. It is notable that the errors for near-zero embedding rates are

Figure 6. Median bias and interquartile range of payload estimators as true payload size varies. Data from 500 color JPEGs

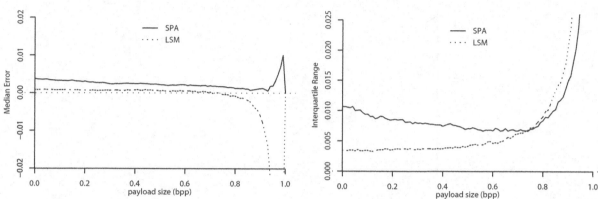

higher when quantified by RMSE than by MAE: this suggests that they are due to a small number of extreme outliers.

These results suggest that the LSM method should not be used for large payloads. Of course, if we already know the payload we do not need to apply quantitative steganalysis! One possibility, found in Ker (2005b), is first to perform the standard SPA estimate and only proceed to LSM if the SPA estimate is less than 0.75. Otherwise the plain SPA estimate is returned. This combined estimator concentrates the performance of each estimator where they are best.

Figure 8 shows the analogous comparison when the set of 1,000 never-compressed grayscale bitmaps are tested. Again we observe that the LSM method becomes unreliable for high embedding rates, but even for low embedding rates the SPA method seems to be slightly more accurate.

To summarize our example benchmarks: in the cover sets tested and regardless of benchmark, the LSM steganalysis method apparently outperforms the SPA method for classifying images which are color and had been subject to JPEG compression prior to embedding, but SPA very slightly outperforms the LSM method on grayscale bitmaps. Whether the difference in performance is due to the JPEG compression, the image size, the characteristics of color and gray-

scale images, or some other factor, is something that could only be examined with further cover image sets. We emphasize that our conclusions do not necessarily hold for all JPEG color covers or all grayscale bitmaps, only those classes of images of which our test set is representative. Furthermore, we will need to test these small differences for significance, which is the topic of the *Statistical Significance and Confidence Intervals* section.

Advanced Benchmarks

A new benchmarking metric is suggested in Ker (in press-b), for a different problem domain. Suppose that a steganalysis method detects payload in single objects, but is applied many times to the detection of payload in a large stream. This is a plausible situation, but benchmarks focusing on ability to detect payload in one object might not be the right way to measure ability to pool evidence, detecting payload spread over many objects. In order to formulate a benchmark we need some measure of steganographic capacity in this batch setting.

The *batch steganography* problem was presented in Ker (in press-a) and the capacity question addressed in Ker (2007d) with the conclusion that capacity (with respect to a quite general notion

Figure 7. Accuracy summaries: root mean square error and mean absolute error of payload estimators as true payload size varies. Data from 500 color JPEG images

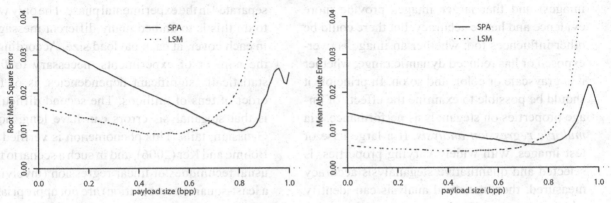

Figure 8. Accuracy summaries: root mean square error and mean absolute error of payload estimators as true payload size varies. Data from 1,000 grayscale bitmaps

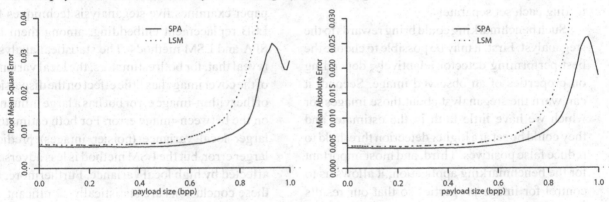

of security) is asymptotically proportional to the square root of the number of covers. The constant of proportionality is dependent on the detector and in the limit it represents a concise and practical measure of its detection power. It can be shown (Ker, in press-b) that under some regularity conditions this constant is determined by the *Fisher information* and therefore that a simple asymptotic benchmark of detection ability can be found by measuring Fisher information empirically: the larger the Fisher information, the smaller the payload which it is safe to embed, no matter what level of safety (in terms of false positives and negatives) is required.

Such a linear benchmark is attractive, particularly since it avoids having to consider different payload sizes, but there are some tricky aspects with the estimation of Fisher information from a sample. Further work is required to give robust answers and confidence intervals. We emphasize that it is, in any case, only an *asymptotic* measure of performance in a multiple-cover setting.

A quite different type of benchmark was proposed in Böhme (2005), and extended in Böhme and Ker (2006). The aim is to identify what properties of images make quantitative steganalysis more or less accurate. We might expect that steganography is harder to detect in images with a large local variance (e.g., noisy images) and that larger images provide more evidence and hence accuracy, but there could be other influences too: whether an image is over-exposed or has reduced dynamic range, whether it is grayscale or color, and so on. In principle it should be possible to examine the effects of image properties on steganalysis performance, via *multiple regression analysis*. If a large base of test images, with widely varying properties, is selected and quantitative steganalysis accuracy measured, then statistical analysis can identify which properties affect inaccuracy and determine whether such effects are statistically significant. This differs from the otherwise necessary practice of classifying images into different types and testing each set separately.

Such benchmarking could bring rewards to the steganalyst. First, it may be possible to choose the best-performing detector adaptively, depending on properties of an observed image. Second, it can warn the steganalyst about those images for which we have little faith in the estimate, and they could be set at a higher detection threshold to reduce false positives. Third, and most important for the benchmarking application, it allows us to control for image properties so that our results are not skewed by, for example, one detector's particular inaccuracy on a few noisy images in a test set.

Regression analysis is a standard technique, for example see Montgomery (2004), but the application to quantitative steganalysis presents a number of difficulties. First, Böhme and Ker (2006) note that most quantitative steganalysis methods have two separate sources of error: they make one assumption about cover images and another about the payload, neither of which will be exact. Inaccuracy in the first causes *between-image error*, which depends largely on the properties of the cover image itself, and inaccuracy in the second causes *within-image error* which depends on the payload. Because between- and

within-image errors are sometimes influenced differently by cover properties, they must be separated in the experimental phase. The only way to do this is to embed many different messages in each cover, at each payload size. Accordingly the number of experiments, necessary to find statistically significant dependencies, is of the order of tens of millions. The second difficulty is that steganalysis errors can have long, non-Gaussian, tails. This phenomenon is verified in Böhme and Ker (2006), and in such a scenario the usual techniques of linear regression (involving a least-squares computation) are not appropriate; more complex algorithms must be used.

As an example of the nature of results which can be obtained by these techniques, we extract a conclusion from Böhme and Ker (2006). The paper examines five steganalysis techniques for LSB replacement embedding, among them the SPA and LSM methods. The statistical analyses reveal that, for both estimators, the local variance of the cover image has little effect on the dispersion of the within-image error but has a large influence on the between-image error. For both estimators larger local variance (noisier images) predicts larger error, but the LSM method is less adversely affected by high local variance. Furthermore, all these conclusions are statistically significant, of which more in the next section.

STATISTICAL SIGNIFICANCE AND CONFIDENCE INTERVALS

Let us suppose that a set of test covers is deemed representative of some wider population (e.g., grayscale bitmaps of a certain size, or images from a particular class of digital camera). Even with this assumption granted, we cannot always deduce that experimental results for the test set are indicative of the population. As a very simple example, consider testing two steganalysis methods that actually have exactly the same accuracy in detection of steganography. Inevitably, because of randomness in the selection of covers tested, one of the methods will have performance *apparently* a bit better than the other, and if the test set is small then this difference might, by random chance, be quite large. One could be mislead into thinking that an experimentally observed difference is *significant*.

Thus there is a difference between an observation and a prediction: whatever benchmarks we use for steganalysis, we can always report what we observed. But if we want to place a margin of error on the observations—a *confidence interval*—or to claim that a difference in performance is significant, then we must use the tools of statistics.

When the benchmark is a single false positive/false negative rate the statistical analysis is straightforward: using the observed rates as an estimate of the population rates is a situation analogous to opinion polling. For rates not too close to 0% or 100% the Gaussian approximation to the binomial sampling distribution is appropriate, and 95% confidence intervals for the proportion are given by

$$\frac{x}{N} \pm 1.96\sqrt{x(N-x)/N} \, ,$$

where x is the number of incorrect (positive or negative) results and N the number of experiments. For rates near to 0% or 100% the Poisson approximation is more appropriate (even if 0% false positives are observed this does *not* allow the robust conclusion that there are 0% false positives in the population, only that the true rate is likely to be below a certain point), but we will not waste space considering such standard statistical material; see, for example pp. 203 and 220 of Spiegel and Stephens (1999).

However, in trying to compute confidence intervals for the other benchmarks—full ROC curves, particular false positive rates at fixed false negative, AUR, and so forth—we find immediate difficulties. For ROC curves it is *not* correct to apply the previous confidence intervals to each

false positive/false negative point on the curve. Theoretical determination of confidence intervals is difficult because, in almost all cases, we do not know the distribution of the features that underlie the classifier (the exception is Ker, 2007c, which begins to work out the distribution of the LSM payload estimate, but only for certain cases). Any model of steganalysis classifiers is likely to depend on a model of cover images, and we have already noted that inaccurate models of covers have been responsible for weaknesses in perfect steganography schemes. Therefore we should not put too much faith in such models.

There is one case in which finding a model fit is inescapable: if we want to estimate the false negative rate for a false positive rate less than $1/N$, where N is the number of experiments. For some applications this is the required benchmark, and there is then no alternative but to find a suitable model, but great care must be taken to check that the model does fit in the tails. Conclusions about very low false positive rates (as a rough guide any value below about $10/N$) are always to be treated with a certain level of suspicion, since there is not really sufficient experimental evidence to justify them.

In the absence of a population model we can determine confidence regions for binary classification accuracy using the statistical technique of *bootstrapping*. Here, the principle is to estimate the variability of an estimator by *resampling*, usually with replacement, from experimental data already obtained. The key is to use the observed distribution on which the estimator is based to approximate the true distribution, and then use (usually) Monte Carlo methods to deduce what this implies for the variability of the estimator. Chernick (1999) contains a survey of different bootstrap techniques; the one we use here is the simplest nonparametric bootstrap, known as the *percentile method*.

Suppose that every member of the population has a statistic s, and we have a sample of size N whose statistics are $s_1,...,s_N$. We have estimated some population parameter p from the sample statistics, giving estimate $\hat{p} = F(s_1,...,s_N)$. Now we want to know approximate confidence intervals for the true value of p. The bootstrap method is as follows:

1. Iterate many times (e.g., 10,000):
    a. Generate a sample of size N, $t_1,...,t_N$, picking uniformly *with replacement* from the values $s_1,...,s_N$.
    b. Compute $\hat{p}_i = F(t_1,...,t_N)$.
2. An approximate confidence interval for $\hat{p}$ of size α is obtained by taking an interval containing proportion α of the $\hat{p}_i$ (for example, an approximate 95% confidence interval is obtained by sorting the $\hat{p}_i$ and finding a region which includes the middle 95%).

If, instead of confidence intervals, we wish to conduct a hypothesis test to decide whether one steganalysis method has superior performance to another, we can use the bootstrap method to find a confidence interval for the difference of their benchmarks (in this case resampling is performed on both the cover and stego-object statistics). If the difference 0 lies outside the interval, there is a significant difference (although, as with all Monte Carlo procedures, the size of the significance test is only approximately accurate).

It might seem as if bootstrapping is getting "something for nothing" in re-using the original sample repeatedly, and indeed the technique was met with a certain amount of skepticism when developed in the statistics community, but it is now widely accepted. That is not to say that it is without dangers: There are a number of conditions for the bootstrap intervals to be asymptotically exact, but we do not wish to go into a discussion of the statistical minutiae. We will simply note that the original sample should not be very small (i.e., we need at least a few hundred experiments), and that bootstrapping is not appropriate for extreme order statistics such as sample quartiles very near 0% or 100%. Finally, we must decide

how many times to perform the resampling iteration; bootstrapping literature often mentions figures around 100-1,000. Because resampling is computationally cheap, out of an abundance of caution we have used 10,000 iterations in all of our experiments.

There now follow some examples of bootstrap confidence intervals for binary steganalysis. The first part of Figure 5 is identical to the third part of Figure 1, but we have added 95% confidence intervals for the false negative rate at each false positive rate. It is clear that the performance difference is indeed significant—it cannot be explained solely by natural variation in any finite set of experiments—and performing the bootstrap on the differences at each false positive point shows that LSM detects significantly more sensitively for false positive rates of approximately 5%-12%, which is the whole of the interesting range because outside it both detectors have close to either zero or perfect sensitivity. The second part of Figure 6 is identical to Figure 3, with 95% confidence bands. Because the bands do not overlap we can immediately conclude that the performance difference is significant at least for payloads of less than 10% (disjoint confidence intervals is a sufficient, but by no means necessary, condition for a significant difference). Above payloads of about 10% we should set no store by the results because they involve only a handful of false positives. Remember that bootstrapping is not appropriate for extreme order statistics, and that a few false positives are caused by the highest few observations amongst the cover objects.

We do not display confidence bands for the data in Figure 5, but simply comment that bootstraps indicate that none of the small observed differences are significant at any point. We must not conclude that the SPA method is a more reliable detector than LSM in grayscale never-compressed covers, without more evidence. And we emphasize that even a statistically significant result only allows us to generalize to the class of images of which our test set is representative (e.g., im-

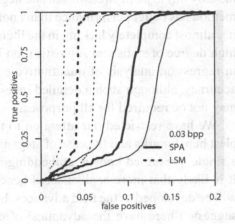 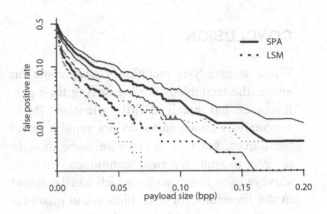

Figure 9. ROC curves (left), and false positive rate corresponding to 50% false negatives (right), observed in 500 color JPEG images, with 95% confidence regions obtained by bootstrapping

ages of a certain size from a certain source); for wider generalization one could try the advanced techniques discussed in *Advanced Benchmarks* section.

We also mention the results of bootstrap confidence intervals for AUR. Although we do not advocate AUR as a good performance summary, it is instructive to see how wide the margins of error should be: taking only the case of the gray-scale covers, an embedding rate of 2%, and the SPA method, we computed the ROC which has an observed AUR of 0.9877. Then, running the simple bootstrap, we find that an approximate 95% confidence interval for the population AUR runs from 0.9822 to 0.9926. Some authors have been observed to quote experimental AURs to four or more significant figures on an experimental base of around 1,000 images, and indeed it is accurate to report that such a value was *observed*. But as a *predictor* of population AUR, we have only two significant figures with 95% confidence. This is only a single example but we have observed similarly wide confidence intervals in many other situations, so the moral remains: one should not rely on experimentally obtained AUR for much accuracy unless bootstraps have been performed to verify the confidence intervals.

The same technology can be used to find approximate confidence intervals for quantitative benchmarks, and approximate levels of significance of differences between competing estimators: resampling from the observed data, with replacement, gives an estimate for the variability of an observed statistic.

Figure 10 compares the SPA and LSM detectors, using the MAE benchmark, on both the color JPEG and grayscale bitmap cover sets. Ninety-five percent confidence intervals, computed at each point on the *x*-axis using the simple bootstrap, are also displayed. For the JPEG covers it is clear that the differences are going to be significant, and a separate bootstrap for the difference between the MAE of SPA and LSM detectors gives the results seen in Exhibit 1.

For grayscale bitmap covers the confidence interval chart suggests that the SPA detector is uniformly more accurate. In fact a bootstrap for the difference in MAE is shown in Exhibit 2.

In order to conclude that SPA is uniformly more accurate than LSM on such covers we would need a few more experiments. This result is in contrast to that comparing the use of SPA and LSM for binary steganalysis; we showed that the latter was preferable for JPEG images but that the small observed differences in favor of SPA in grayscale images was not significant.

CONCLUSION

While steganalysis techniques have come on apace, the technology for measuring their performance has received little attention. Basic steganalysis benchmarks do not require novel techniques, but they do require some thought in order to apply the right techniques. We have surveyed the benchmarks which can be found in the literature, for both binary and quantitative steganalysis, and argued that some are poor choices: either overvaluing detectors with weak practical application, or using measurements that might unduly be influenced by a few outlier experiments. A pitfall is found in the application of standard benchmarks from other literature (AUR, estimator variance), which may be particularly ill-suited to steganalysis. Good alternatives have been suggested.

In the presence of multiple steganalysis methods for the same scenario, comparison becomes at least as important as absolute measurement. We have demonstrated how techniques, based on the simple bootstrap, can determine confidence intervals for performance and significance levels of performance difference. Such statistical rigor is the only way to justify a claim that one steganalysis method has better performance than another, but it is almost completely lacking in the literature. A high degree of statistical sophistication is found in regression analysis of quantitative estimator accuracy, although such a detailed investigation may not be required for all purposes.

We have restricted our attention to the simplest benchmarks and the case of steganalysis of a single, presumed known, embedding method. It is likely that more sophisticated benchmarks will be developed as the field advances, but those suggested here have the advantage of comprehensibility to non-specialist audiences. We hope that by informing the choice of benchmark and advocating measurement of statistical significance more rigorous practice can be introduced into steganalysis literature and applications.

FURTHER RESEARCH DIRECTIONS

One possible direction for future research is a wide-scale application of these benchmarks to many of the steganalysis methods in the literature, extending work such as Böhme and Ker (2006).

Figure 10. Mean absolute error of payload estimators in 500 color JPEG images (left) and 1,000 grayscale bitmaps (right), with 95% confidence regions obtained by bootstrapping

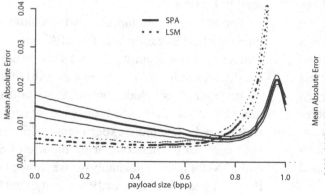
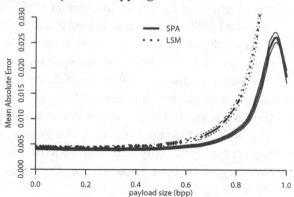

Exhibit 1. Bootstrap for the difference between the MAE of SPA and LSM detectors

Payload size	Conclusion
<66%	significantly* in favor of LSM
66-78%	difference not significant
>78%	significantly in favor of SPA
* at 95% significance level	

Exhibit 2. Bootstrap for the difference in MAE

Payload size	Conclusion
<4%	significantly in favor of SPA
4-16%	slightly but not significantly in favor of SPA (p-value between 0.05 and 0.1)
>16%	significantly in favor of SPA

Most large performance studies focus either on simple LSB Replacement (as does Böhme & Ker) or use limited benchmarks such as single false positive and false negative points (Fridrich, 2004; Pevný & Fridrich, 2007), so there is a clear need for a wide-ranging study using more appropriate benchmarks.

To widen the material presented here, one should also consider benchmarks for multi-class steganalysis. Perhaps one way forward is to return to the theory of decision making, and posit a *loss function* for the different types of misclassification and benchmark the minimum loss. Indeed, the same technique could be equally applied to binary classification. This is essentially an economic approach to benchmarking steganalysis: If we hypothesize a dollar cost for each bit successfully transmitted by the steganographer, and a dollar value for the detection of the steganographer, we can benchmark detectors by their expected value. There are many possible models (a particular question is whether it costs the steganographer to use more covers to spread their payload, or whether their available cover is fixed) and some interesting conclusions could result from their study.

However, as with fixed false-positive rates and related statistics, the benchmark produced will be heavily influenced by the parameters—in this case the ratio of losses associated with different types of error. A good steganalysis method with respect to one loss function may be poor with respect to another. Perhaps further research can identify some justifiable loss functions, but this problem is essentially unavoidable as it reflects the fact that some steganalysis methods are better in certain applications.

The *Advanced Benchmarks* section presents many opportunities for further research. Large-scale regression analysis of quantitative estimators presents challenges in both computing power (to create sufficient data) and analysis of results. The novel information-theoretic benchmark suggested in Ker (in press-b), which is in an asymptotic sense a truly application-independent measure, suggests many new avenues including efficient estimation and confidence intervals for Fisher information as well as further investigation into the crucial hypothesis (locally linear steganalysis response).

REFERENCES

Böhme, R. (2005). Assessment of steganalytic methods using multiple regression models. In M. Barni, J. Herrera-Joancomartí, S. Katzenbeisser,

& F. Pérez-González (Eds.), *Information Hiding, 7th International Workshop* (pp. 278-295). Berlin: Springer.

Böhme, R., & Ker, A. (2006). A two-factor error model for quantitative steganalysis. In E. J. Delp, III, & P. W. Wong (Eds.), *Security, steganography, and watermarking of multimedia contents VIII* (SPIE 6072, pp. 0601-0616). Bellingham, WA: SPIE.

Budhia, U., Kundur, D., & Zourntos, T. (2006). Digital video steganalysis exploiting statistical visibility in the temporal domain. *IEEE Transactions on Information Forensics and Security, 1*(4), 502-516.

Cachin, C. (2004). An information-theoretic model for steganography. *Information and Computation, 192*(1), 41-56.

Chernick, M. R. (1999). *Bootstrap methods: A practitioner's guide*. New York: Wiley.

Draper, S., Ishwar, P., Molnar, D., Prabhakaran, V., Ramchandran, K., Schonberg, D., et al. (2005). An analysis of empirical PMF based tests for least significant bit image steganography. In M. Barni, J. Herrera-Joancomartí, S. Katzenbeisser, & F. Pérez-González (Eds.), *Information Hiding, 7th International Workshop* (pp. 327-341). Berlin: Springer.

Dumitrescu, S., Wu, X., & Wang, Z. (2003). Detection of LSB steganography via sample pair analysis. *IEEE Transactions on Signal Processing, 51*(7), 1995-2007.

Egan, J. P. (1975). *Signal detection theory and ROC analysis*. New York: Academic Press.

Fawcett, T. (2003). *ROC graphs: Notes and practical considerations for data mining researchers* (Tech. Rep. No. HPL-2003-4). Palo Alto, CA: HP Labs.

Fridrich, J. (2004). Feature-based steganalysis for JPEG images and its implications for future designs of steganographic schemes. In J. Fridrich

(Ed.), *Information Hiding, 6th International Workshop* (pp. 67-81). Berlin: Springer.

Fridrich, J., & Goljan, M. (2004). On estimation of secret message length in LSB steganography in spatial domain. In E. J. Delp, III, & P. W. Wong (Eds.), *Security, steganography, and watermarking of multimedia contents VI* (SPIE 5306, pp. 23-34). Bellingham, WA: SPIE.

Fridrich, J., Goljan, M., & Du, R. (2001). Detecting LSB steganography in color and gray-scale images. *IEEE MultiMedia, Special Issue on Security, 8*(4), 22-28.

Fridrich, J., Goljan, M., & Hogea, D. (2002a). Steganalysis of JPEG images: Breaking the F5 algorithm. In F. A. P. Petitcolas (Ed.), *Information Hiding, 5th International Workshop* (pp. 310-323). Berlin: Springer.

Fridrich, J., Goljan, M., & Hogea, D. (2002b). Attacking the OutGuess. In *4th ACM Workshop on Multimedia and Security*. New York: ACM Press.

Fridrich, J., Goljan, M., & Holotyak, T. (2006). New blind steganalysis and its implications. In E. J. Delp, III, & P. W. Wong (Eds.), *Security, steganography, and watermarking of multimedia contents VIII* (SPIE 6072, pp. 0101-0113). Bellingham, WA: SPIE.

Fridrich, J., Soukal, D., & Goljan, M. (2005). Maximum likelihood estimation of length of secret message embedded using ±K steganography in spatial domain. In E. J. Delp, III, & P. W. Wong (Eds.), *Security, steganography, and watermarking of multimedia contents VII* (SPIE 5681, pp. 595-606). Bellingham, WA: SPIE.

Green, D. M., & Swets, J. A. (1966). *Signal detection theory and psychophysics*. New York: Wiley.

Harmsen, J. J., & Pearlman, W. A. (2003). Steganalysis of additive noise modelable information hiding. In E. J. Delp, III, & P. W. Wong (Eds.), *Security, steganography, and watermarking of multimedia contents V* (SPIE 5020). Bellingham, WA: SPIE.

Harmsen, J. J., & Pearlman, W. A. (2004). Kernel Fisher discriminant for steganalysis of JPEG hiding methods. In E. J. Delp, III, & P. W. Wong (Eds.), *Security, steganography, and watermarking of multimedia contents VI* (SPIE 5306, pp. 13-22). Bellingham, WA: SPIE.

Hogan, M. T., Hurley, N. J., Silvestre, G. C. M., Balado, F., & Whelan, K. M. (2005). ML detection of steganography. In E. J. Delp, III, & P. W. Wong (Eds.), *Security, steganography, and watermarking of multimedia contents VII* (SPIE 5681, pp. 16-27). Bellingham, WA: SPIE.

Hogan, M. T., Silvestre, G. C. M., & Hurley, N. J. (2004). Performance evaluation of blind steganalysis classifiers. In E. J. Delp, III, & P. W. Wong (Eds.), *Security, steganography, and watermarking of multimedia contents VI* (SPIE 5306, pp. 58-69). Bellingham, WA: SPIE.

Holotyak, T., Fridrich, J., & Soukal, D. (2005). Stochastic approach to secret message length estimation in ±K embedding steganography. In E. J. Delp, III, & P. W. Wong (Eds.), *Security, steganography, and watermarking of multimedia contents VII* (SPIE 5681, pp. 673-684). Bellingham, WA: SPIE.

Ker, A. D. (2004a). Quantitative evaluation of pairs and RS steganalysis. In E. J. Delp, III, & P. W. Wong (Eds.), *Security, steganography, and watermarking of multimedia contents VI* (SPIE 5306, pp. 83-97). Bellingham, WA: SPIE.

Ker, A. D. (2004b). Improved detection of LSB steganography in grayscale images. In J. Fridrich (Ed.), *Information Hiding, 6th International Workshop* (pp. 97-115). Berlin: Springer.

Ker, A. D. (2005a). Resampling and the detection of LSB matching in color bitmaps. In E. J. Delp, III, & P. W. Wong (Eds.), *Security, steganography, and watermarking of multimedia contents VII* (SPIE 5681, pp. 1-16). Bellingham, WA: SPIE.

Ker, A. D. (2005b). A general framework for structural steganalysis of LSB replacement. In M. Barni, J. Herrera-Joancomartí, S. Katzenbeisser, & F. Pérez-González (Eds.), *Information Hiding, 7th International Workshop* (pp. 296-311). Berlin: Springer.

Ker, A. D. (2007a). Optimally weighted least-squares steganalysis. In E. J. Delp, III, & P. W. Wong (Eds.), *Security, steganography, and watermarking of multimedia contents IX* (SPIE 6505, pp. 0601-0616). Bellingham, WA: SPIE.

Ker, A. D. (2007b). Steganalysis of embedding in two least-significant bits. *IEEE Transactions on Information Forensics and Security, 2*(1), 46-54.

Ker, A. D. (2007c). Derivation of error distribution in least squares steganalysis. *IEEE Transactions on Information Forensics and Security, 2*(2), 140-148.

Ker, A. D. (2007d). A capacity result for batch steganography. *IEEE Signal Processing Letters, 14*(8), 525-528.

Ker, A. D. (in press-a). Batch steganography and pooled steganalysis. *Information Hiding, 8th International Workshop.* Berlin: Springer.

Ker, A. D. (in press-b). The ultimate steganalysis benchmark? In *Proceedings of 9th ACM Multimedia and Security Workshop.* New York: ACM Press.

Kharrazi, M., Sencar, H. T., & Memon, N. (2005). Benchmarking steganographic and steganalysis techniques. In E. J. Delp, III, & P. W. Wong (Eds.), *Security, steganography, and watermarking of multimedia contents VII* (SPIE 5681, pp. 252-263). Bellingham, WA: SPIE.

Lu, P., Luo, X., Tang, Q., & Shen, L. (2004). An improved sample pairs method for detection of LSB embedding. In J. Fridrich (Ed.), *Information Hiding, 6th International Workshop* (pp. 116-127). Berlin: Springer.

Lyu, S., & Farid, H. (2002). Detecting hidden messages using higher-order statistics and support vector machines. In F. A. P. Petitcolas (Ed.), *Information Hiding, 5th International Workshop* (pp. 340-354). Berlin: Springer.

Marcum, J. I. (1948). A statistical theory of target detection by pulsed radar: Mathematical appendix. RAND Corporation Research Memorandum RM-753, 1948. Reprinted in *IRE Transactions on Information Theory, 6,* 59-267, 1960.

McNicol, D. (1972). *A primer of signal detection theory.* London: Allen and Unwin.

Montgomery, D. C. (2004). *Design and analysis of experiments* (6th ed.). New York: Wiley.

Moulin, P., & Briassouli, A. (2004). A stochastic QIM algorithm for robust, undetectable image watermarking. In *IEEE International Conference on Image Processing, ICIP 2004* (Vol. 2, pp. 1173-1176).

Petitcolas, F. A. P. (1998). *MP3Stego software, updated 2006.* Retrieved March 2007, from http://www.petitcolas.net/fabien/steganography/mp3stego/

Pevný, T., & Fridrich, J. (2007). Merging Markov and DCT features for multi-class JPEG steganalysis. In E. J. Delp, III, & P. W. Wong (Eds.), *Security, steganography, and watermarking of multimedia contents IX* (SPIE 6505, pp. 0301-0313). Bellingham, WA: SPIE.

Provos, N. (2001, August). *Defending against statistical steganalysis.* Paper presented at the 10th USENIX Security Symposium. Washington, DC.

Rice, J. A. (1994). *Mathematical statistics and data analysis* (2nd ed.). Pacific Grove, CA: Duxbury Press.

Sallee, P. (2005). Model-based methods for steganography and steganalysis. *International Journal of Image and Graphics, 5*(1), 167-189.

Sharp, T. (2001). An implementation of key-based digital signal steganography. In I. Moskowitz (Ed.), *Information Hiding, 4th International Workshop* (pp. 13-26). Berlin: Springer.

Shi, Y. Q., Chen, C., & Chen, W. (in press). A Markov process based approach to effective attacking JPEG steganography. *Information Hiding, 8th International Workshop.* Berlin: Springer.

Spiegel, M. R., & Stephens, L. J. (1999). *Schaum's outline of theory and problems of statistics.* Singapore: McGraw-Hill.

Taylor, J., & Verbyla, A. (2004). Joint modelling of location and scale parameters of the t distribution. *Statistical Modelling, 4*(2), 91-112.

Wang, Y., & Moulin, P. (2006). Statistical modelling and steganalysis of DFT-based image steganography. In E. J. Delp, III, & P. W. Wong (Eds.), *Security, steganography, and watermarking of multimedia contents VIII* (SPIE 6072, pp. 0201-0211). Bellingham, WA: SPIE.

Wang, Y., & Moulin, P. (2007). Optimized feature extraction for learning-based image steganalysis. *IEEE Transactions on Information Forensics and Security, 2*(1), 31-45.

Westfeld, A. (2001). F5—A steganographic algorithm: High capacity despite better steganalysis. In I. Moskowitz (Ed.), *Information Hiding, 4th International Workshop* (pp. 289-302). Berlin: Springer.

Westfeld, A. (2002). Detecting low embedding rates. In F. A. P. Petitcolas (Ed.), *Information Hiding, 5th International Workshop* (pp. 310-323). Berlin, Germany: Springer.

Westfeld, A. (2005). Space filling curves in steganalysis. In E. J. Delp, III, & P. W. Wong (Eds.), *Security, steganography, and watermarking of multimedia contents VII* (SPIE 5681, pp. 28-37). Bellingham, WA: SPIE.

Westfeld, A., & Pfitzmann, A. (1999). Attacks on steganographic systems. In A. Pfitzmann (Ed.), *Information Hiding, 3rd International Workshop* (pp. 61-76). Berlin: Springer.

Yu, X., Tan, T., & Wang, Y. (2005). Extended optimization method of LSB steganalysis. In *IEEE International Conference on Image Processing, ICIP 2005* (Vol 2., pp. 1102-1105).

ADDITIONAL READING

Anderson, R., & Petitcolas, F. A. P. (1998). On the limits of steganography. *IEEE Journal of Selected Areas in Communications, 16*(4), 474-481.

Bergmair, R. (2007). A comprehensive bibliography of linguistic steganography. In E. J. Delp, III, & P. W. Wong (Eds.), *Security, steganography, and watermarking of multimedia contents IX* (SPIE 6505, pp. 0W01-0W06). Bellingham, WA: SPIE.

Böhme, R., & Westfeld, A. (2004). Exploiting preserved statistics for steganalysis. In J. Fridrich (Ed.), *Information Hiding, 6th International Workshop* (pp. 82-96). Berlin: Springer.

Chandramouli, R., & Memon, N. D. (2003). Steganography capacity: A steganalysis perspective. In E. J. Delp, III, & P. W. Wong (Eds.), *Security, steganography, and watermarking of multimedia contents V* (SPIE 5020). Bellingham, WA: SPIE.

Cover, T. M., & Thomas, J. A. (1991). *Elements of information theory*. New York: Wiley.

Davison, A. C., & Hinkley, D. V. (1997). *Bootstrap methods and their applications*. Cambridge, UK: Cambridge University Press.

Dumitrescu, S., & Wu, X. (2005). A new framework of LSB steganalysis of digital media. *IEEE Transactions on Signal Processing, 53*(10), 3936-3947.

Franz, E. (2002). Steganography preserving statistical properties. In F. A. P. Petitcolas (Ed.), *Information Hiding, 5th International Workshop* (pp. 278-294). Berlin: Springer.

Fridrich, J., Goljan, M., Lisoněk, P., & Soukal, D. (2005). Writing on wet paper. *IEEE Transactions on Signal Processing, 53*(10), 3923-3935.

Fridrich, J., Goljan, M., & Soukal, D. (2003). Higher-order statistical steganalysis of palette images. In E. J. Delp, III, & P. W. Wong (Eds.), *Security, steganography, and watermarking of multimedia contents V* (SPIE 5020, pp. 178-190). Bellingham, WA: SPIE.

Fridrich, J., & Soukal, D. (2006). Matrix embedding for large payloads. *IEEE Transactions on Information Forensics and Security, 1*(3), 390-395.

Grimmett, G., & Welsh, D. (1986). *Probability: An introduction*. Oxford, UK: Oxford University Press.

Johnson, M. K., Lyu, S., & Farid, H. (2005). Steganalysis of recorded speech. In E. J. Delp, III, & P. W. Wong (Eds.), *Security, steganography, and watermarking of multimedia contents VII* (SPIE 5681, pp. 644-672). Bellingham, WA: SPIE.

Ker, A. D. (2005). Steganalysis of LSB matching in grayscale images. *IEEE Signal Processing Letters, 12*(6), 441-444.

Ker, A. D. (2006). Fourth-order structural steganalysis and analysis of cover assumptions. In E. J. Delp, III, & P. W. Wong (Eds.), *Security, steganography, and watermarking of multime-*

dia Contents VIII (SPIE 6072, pp. 0301-0314). Bellingham, WA: SPIE.

Kim, Y., Duric, Z., & Richards, D. (2006). Limited distortion in LSB steganography. In E. J. Delp, III, & P. W. Wong (Eds.), *Security, steganography, and watermarking of multimedia contents VIII* (SPIE 6072, pp. 0N1-0N9). Bellingham, WA: SPIE.

Kullback, S. (1968). *Information theory and statistics*. Mineola: Dover.

Lehmann, E. L. (1959). *Testing statistical hypotheses*. New York: Wiley.

Long, J. S. (1997). *Regression models for categorical and limited dependent variables*. Thousand Oaks, CA: Sage.

Lyu, S., & Farid, H. (2004). Steganalysis using color wavelet statistics and one-class support vector machines. In E. J. Delp, III, & P. W. Wong (Eds.), *Security, steganography, and watermarking of multimedia contents VI* (SPIE 5306, pp. 35-45). Bellingham, WA: SPIE.

Newman, R. E., Moskowitz, I. S., Chang, L., & Brahmadesam, M. M. (2002). A steganographic embedding undetectable by JPEG compatibility steganalysis. In F. A. P. Petitcolas (Ed.), *Information Hiding, 5th International Workshop* (pp. 258-277). Berlin: Springer.

Sullivan, K., Madhow, U., Chadrasekaran, S., & Manjunath, B. S. (2006). Steganalysis for Markov cover data with applications to images. *IEEE Transactions on Information Forensics and Security, 1*(2), 275-287.

Zhang, T., & Ping, X. (2003). A new approach to reliable detection of LSB steganography in natural images. *Signal Processing, 83*(10), 2085-2093.

Zhang, X., Wang, S., & Zhang, K. (2003). Steganography with least histogram abnormality. In *Second International Workshop on Mathematical Methods, Models, and Architectures for Computer Network Security, MMM-ACNS 2003* (pp. 395-406). Berlin: Springer.

Chapter XIV
Digital Camera Source Identification Through JPEG Quantisation

Matthew James Sorrell
University of Adelaide, Australia

ABSTRACT

We propose that the implementation of the JPEG compression algorithm represents a manufacturer and model-series specific means of identification of the source camera of a digital photographic image. Experimental results based on a database of over 5,000 photographs from 27 camera models by 10 brands shows that the choice of JPEG quantisation table, in particular, acts as an effective discriminator between model series with a high level of differentiation. Furthermore, we demonstrate that even after recompression of an image, residual artefacts of double quantisation continue to provide limited means of source camera identification, provided that certain conditions are met. Other common techniques for source camera identification are also introduced, and their strengths and weaknesses are discussed.

INTRODUCTION

In a forensic context, digital photographs are becoming more common as sources of evidence in criminal and civil matters. Questions that arise include identifying the make and model of a camera to assist in the gathering of physical evidence; matching photographs to a particular camera through the camera's unique characteristics; and determining the integrity of a digital image, including whether the image contains steganographic (hidden message) information.

From a digital file perspective, there is also the question of whether metadata has been deliberately modified to mislead the investigator, and in the case of multiple images, whether a timeline can be established from the various timestamps within the file, imposed by the operating system or determined by other image characteristics.

This chapter is concerned specifically with techniques to identify the make, model series, and particular source camera model given a digital image. We exploit particular characteristics of the camera's JPEG coder to demonstrate that such identification is possible, and that even when an image has subsequently been reprocessed, there are sufficient residual characteristics of the original coding to at least narrow down the possible camera models of interest in some cases.

BACKGROUND

In general, there are four sets of techniques for camera identification. The first uses information specifically embedded by the camera to identify itself (metadata). Metadata is usually specific to a make and model of camera, but not to a specific camera. The second set of techniques can be used to identify a specific camera, either by identifying specific characteristics of the camera (commonly referred to as bullet scratches or fingerprinting). These techniques generally require a candidate source camera for comparison. The third set of techniques relies on characteristics specific to a manufacturer and possibly a series of cameras, particularly the choice of coding parameters, interpolation, and filtering. These techniques are useful for checking consistency with other evidence and can aid the investigation when metadata has been removed. Finally, a wide range of steganographic (watermarking) techniques have been proposed, but these are really only useful for proving ownership of a copyright work and would almost certainly not be deliberately embedded in an image from a deliberately anonymous source. While watermarking might be introduced in a future generation of cameras, this is of no help in tracking the sources of the existing images of interest in the digital domain.

Metadata

The simplest technique for identifying the source camera is to use metadata embedded by the source camera, of which the Exif metadata standard, published by the Japan Electronics and Information Technology Industries Association (JEITA, 2002), is almost ubiquitously supported. In many

cases this is in fact sufficient because it is often beyond the skills of camera users to manipulate or remove the Exif metadata header. Two key forensic fields in the Exif metadata are the *make* and *model*. The metadata is easily extracted using a range of photography tools including recent versions of Adobe Photoshop and such shareware applications as IrfanView.

On the other hand, any savvy photographer who wishes to remove or modify Exif metadata will find a range of easy-to-use tools at their disposal on the Internet. Older versions of image manipulation software, such as early versions of Adobe Photoshop, do not recognise the Exif metadata standard and will strip such identification from the file. More sophisticated users can develop their own techniques to edit Exif. It should be noted in particular that Exif metadata is encoded in clear ASCII text and is both easy to read directly in the binary file, and easy to change.

For this reason, it is unreasonable to expect metadata to be present, and if it is present, to be a reliable indicator of the image source. It is true, however, that many photographers of interest are not aware of the existence of metadata, and the author's experience in criminal cases suggests that where metadata is not present this is more often due to inadvertent erasure rather than deliberate action.

Even if Exif metadata is present, other indicators of the source camera identity are useful to establish whether that metadata has been tampered with. For example, the image size should be consistent with the capabilities of the candidate camera. Also, many camera manufacturers define their own proprietary extensions to Exif, or use their own metadata protocol, which can also provide a level of confidence in the metadata present in the file.

Bullet Scratches

At the other end of the scale, techniques have been developed, particularly by Lukáš, Fridrich, and Goljan (2006) to use the unique noise signature of the charge coupled device (CCD) image sensor. The technique exploits the fact that each image sensor is different, even sensor arrays created on the same silicon wafer. This is due to small variations in doping levels and variations in surface area of each pixel. Unique identification is further aided by manufacturing variations from one otherwise identical camera to another, including lens positioning and defects on optical surfaces. In addition, this technique captures characteristic post-capture processing include de-mosaicing (interpolation) and filtering.

Briefly, this bullet scratch technique takes a set of photographs known to come from the candidate camera and creates a template by high pass filtering of each image. The filtered images are then averaged. The candidate photograph is then filtered in the same way and correlated with the template. A sufficiently high level of correlation indicates a match. Using a Neyman-Pearson detection formulation with probability of false alarm fixed at 10^{-3}, the authors claim probability of false rejection of significantly less than 10^{-3}.

This technique is useful when there is a specific candidate source camera but it requires multiple images to derive a fingerprint. Hence there remains a need to narrow down the range of candidate cameras to as small a list as possible.

Manufacturer Specific Techniques

A further interesting technique is to narrow down the source identity through the analysis of colour field array interpolation as described by Bayram, Sencar, Memon, and Avcibas (2005). This technique is of limited value as a discriminator particularly because the very small number of manufacturers of imaging sensors, and the small range of so-called *demosaicing* algorithms used in practice with a wide variety of parameters, means that the identification of the sensor might bring into consideration hundreds of candidate source cameras. Nevertheless, this approach serves as yet another identification and verification technique, and is particularly useful as the basis for detection of image tampering.

The technique presented in this chapter considers digital photographs that have been encoded as JPEG image files directly by the source camera. While there are a number of other coding options, notably a range of so-called *raw* formats, JPEG captures by far the vast majority of images taken, stored, transferred, and published by camera owners. Our general technique is to consider the choices made in the JPEG encoder of the candidate camera, with a particular focus on the choice of quantisation table. We argue and demonstrate that these choices are manufacturer specific. Although there are some overlaps between manufacturers, it is in fact possible to reduce the number of camera models under consideration from perhaps a thousand to a few tens of models. It is also possible to unambiguously exclude a wide range of models from consideration. Furthermore, we demonstrate that this discrimination technique can survive recompression of the image and discuss some practical applications.

ISSUES, CONTROVERSIES, PROBLEMS

We used multiple commercial online sources to identify as many camera brands and models as we could find as listed on January 1, 2007. We identified over 70 brands of cameras and mobile phones with built-in cameras, with a total of over 2,500 models as summarised in Table 1. We note that many camera models follow an obvious series within a particular brand and that some cameras are identical but have different model names depending on the market in which the cameras are released. In addition, we recognise that our list

Table 1. Summary of manufacturers and numbers of models on 1 January 2007

Manufacturer	Compact	SLR	Other*	Mobile Phone with Camera
Audiovox				20
BenQ / BenQ-Siemens / Siemens	35			48
Canon	109	21		
Casio	64	1	2	
Epson	15			
Fly	29			
Fujifilm	92	27		
HP	44	3		5
HTC				29
I-Mate				15
Innostream				14
Jenoptik				35
Kodak	78	25		
Konica / Konica-Minolta	48	19		
Kyocera	15	2		17
Leica	8	4		
LG				88
Minox	21			
Mitsubishi				12
Motorola				98
NEC				48
Nikon	60	17		
Nokia				105
O2				25
Olympus	142	29		
Panasonic	40	13		24
Pantech				17
Pentacon	33	2		
Pentax	53	9		
Philips				12
Polaroid	24			
Ricoh	39			
Rollei	31	6	1	
Samsung	71	4		171
Sanyo	41	1		24
Sharp	2			18
SiPix	11			
Sony / Sony-Ericsson	95	16		58
Toshiba	24	2		10
Vivitar	37	1	1	
Voigtlaender	14			

A further 23 manufacturers have 10 camera models or less

* Other includes unconventional packages such as binocular and watch cameras

is almost certainly incomplete and that some are branded versions of unbranded *original equipment manufacturer* (OEM) models.

Various market sources indicate that over 500 million digital cameras, and a similar number of mobile phones with in-built digital cameras, had been sold worldwide by the end of 2006. It is well known that digital photography has almost completely displaced conventional film photography in the consumer market, and it is common knowledge that digital photography bypasses the conventional censorship bottleneck available through a film development service.

A further challenge is that as film cameras are withdrawn from the market, crime scene forensic photography will be forced to move from film to digital equipment. The challenge is to establish the forensic chain of evidence in such a way that digital images (not to mention digital video) can meet the burden of proof in court. Thus, the development of digital camera forensic techniques is timely.

The number of camera models available actually suits forensic purposes quite well—small enough that a complete database of all cameras is technically and commercially viable, but large enough that identification of the make and model series of a candidate camera is of significant assistance in forensic investigation.

SOLUTIONS AND RECOMMENDATIONS

JPEG Image Compression

JPEG image compression is specified in the Joint Photographic Experts Group (JPEG) standard published by the International Telecommunications Union (ITU, 1993), and a useful introduction to the standard is given by Wallace (1991). We summarise the key steps here, noting potential forensic markers along the way.

Image Capture

The camera's image sensor captures light measurements on its array of light sensors. An array of sensor values is fed to the camera's microprocessor for post-processing and compression. The camera also uses the optical measurements to set parameters for the camera's optics, including aperture size and exposure time.

The image sensor is nominally uniformly sensitive over the entire sensor surface. In practice, there is a small amount of variation in the physical characteristics of the silicon sensor including the surface area of each picture element and the level of doping. In effect this means that there is some variation in inherent noise and sensitivity over the image area, which has been exploited by Lukáš et al. (2006) to derive a unique camera fingerprint that can be used to match a photograph uniquely to its camera source, provided that a candidate source camera can be found.

Colour Interpolation and Gamma Correction

The image sensor consists of a colour field array of photo detectors with red, green, and blue filters. As these sensors are adjacent to each other and not co-located, one of the first processing steps is to normalise the different colour sensivies and interpolate the red, green, and blue colour arrays onto a nominal co-located pixel grid. The interpolation algorithm, commonly known as demosaicing, varies according to the sensor and image settings and can also be used for limited forensic discrimination as described by Bayram et al. (2005).

Image Post-Processing

A modern digital camera will usually engage automatic brightness, contrast, sharpening, and other filters (such as red-eye reduction) before image compression. Automatic detection of the artefacts caused by such filters provides yet another opportunity to verify the identity of the source camera, although it is not clear whether this approach has been investigated in the literature.

JPEG Compression

The image is now presented to the JPEG compression algorithm as three arrays of co-located pixels representing red, green, and blue. The JPEG compression standard allows for significant choice in implementation, in the specific algorithms used for coding, the choice of parameters, and the specific construction of the JPEG image file. This means that there is a wide range of forensic discriminators, although some parameters always use default values in practice. Default values do in fact serve a useful purpose because their absence can indicate that an image has been tampered with.

Luminance/Chrominance Transform and Downsampling

The first step in JPEG compression is to transform the image from the [red, green, blue] representation to [luminance, chrominance$_{red}$, chrominance$_{blue}$]. This is a simple linear transformation that contains the same image information and is exactly the same representation that has long been used in colour television. The luminance plane contains a monochrome image that contains high resolution information to stimulate the high resolution rods in the human eye. The chrominance planes contain colour information to stimulate the low resolution cones, and because the eye is much less sensitive to changes in chrominance, these planes are usually downsampled (averaged). Usually, two horizontal values ("2h") and/or two vertical values ("2v") are averaged together, reducing the chrominance planes to one half or one quarter of the original size.

There is little to be gained from a forensic perspective at this point. All cameras tested in our

experiments performed 2h or 2v downsampling, or both. It would be possible, however, to test whether an image is downsampled according to the specifications of a candidate source camera as part of the source verification process.

Discrete Cosine Transformation and Rounding

In the second stage, JPEG treats the luminance and chrominance planes separately. Each plane is divided into microblocks of 8x8 pixels that undergo a discrete cosine transform (DCT) for representation in the spatial frequency domain, as shown in Figure 1.

The human eye and brain are more sensitive to overall changes than to specific details. The DCT stage neatly separates the image into coefficients representing broad detail, which must be kept with minimal losses, and into fine detail, which can be approximate or discarded. It is this discarding of detail that leads to both the effectiveness of JPEG as an image compression technique, and to a forensic identification opportunity.

Each microblock is divided (element-by-element) by a quantisation table that is specific to the JPEG encoder. An example is given in Figure 2.

Each microblock is now represented by approximate coefficients, many of which are zero. Such numbers can be coded efficiently, resulting in a compressed image file.

The choice of quantisation table is of great interest. No table is specified in the standard, although an example is given. In practice, our investigation found that the example is often used in preview (thumbnail) images but was not used by any camera for the primary image. In fact, we identified a wide range of quantisation tables with strong discrimination between manufacturers, as discussed in the *Quantisation Table as a Discriminator* section.

Figure 1. The discrete cosine transformation (DCT) represents a block of 8x8 pixels (top left figure) as spatial frequency coefficients (bottom table); the top left coefficient represents the average value of the pixels, while the bottom right represents the degree to which the pixels match a chess-board arrangement (as shown in the top right image)

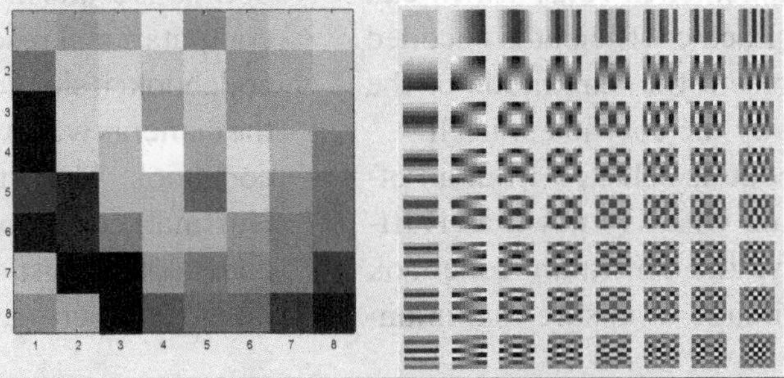

1440	-6	-13	-1	-2	1	-2	-5
19	-2	-1	-12	-5	-3	0	2
-3	6	10	8	7	0	-3	0
0	-5	0	1	5	8	6	1
1	1	1	0	-3	2	0	-6
2	-2	0	2	2	3	-3	-3
-1	-1	-1	-4	-2	-5	-1	2
-4	0	4	2	0	3	4	2

Figure 2. Quantisation leads to a representation which largely preserves broad details but discards fine detail; the division here is element-by-element, not a matrix division

DCT Coefficients

1440	-6	-13	-1	-2	1	-2	-5
19	-2	-1	-12	-5	-3	0	2
-3	6	10	8	7	0	-3	0
0	-5	0	1	5	8	6	1
1	1	1	0	-3	2	0	-6
2	-2	0	2	2	3	-3	-3
-1	-1	-1	-4	-2	-5	-1	2
-4	0	4	2	0	3	4	2

/

Quantization Table

8	7	7	7	8	9	11	13
7	7	7	7	8	9	11	14
7	7	8	8	9	11	13	16
7	7	8	10	12	14	16	20
8	8	9	12	15	18	22	26
9	9	11	14	18	23	29	36
11	11	13	16	22	29	38	49
13	14	16	20	26	36	49	65

=

180	-1	-2	0	0	0	0	0
3	0	0	-2	-1	0	0	0
0	1	1	1	1	0	0	0
0	-1	0	0	0	1	0	0
0	0	0	0	0	0	0	0
0	0	0	0	0	0	0	0
0	0	0	0	0	0	0	0
0	0	0	0	0	0	0	0

Efficient Coding

The final stage of the JPEG encoding process is the generation of the binary file. The file begins with various header information, including Exif meta-data, if it is used, along with parameters needed to decode the image. There is yet another forensic indicator here, because different encoders might order the parameters in different ways, although again it is not clear whether this has previously been investigated in the literature. The image coefficients are encoded by a process of ordering the coefficients in a zig-zag pattern so that the many zero coefficients in the bottom right hand corner are brought together in runs, which can be coded efficiently. Each coefficient is encoded using a code to represent the magnitude of the coefficient, followed by the coefficient itself.

The magnitude code is selected from an efficient codebook using what is known as Huffman coding. Ideally, the Huffman codebook is optimised to the image to ensure maximum compression. The JPEG standard describes how such optimisation can be achieved but also provides a non-binding example of a typical Huffman codebook which achieves good, but not optimal, results in practice. As it takes significant computational resources to generate the optimal codebook, it should come as no surprise that all of the cameras we investigated use only the example codebook. Thus, the only forensic value of the Huffman codebook is to note that a proprietary codebook almost certainly indicates subsequent image tampering. The standard also supports

Table 2. Sample images and number of quantisation tables by camera model in our dataset

Manufacturer	Camera Model	Images	Quantisation Tables Identified
Canon	Canon DIGITAL IXUS 400	2	1
	Canon DIGITAL IXUS 700	25	3
	Canon EOS 10D	14	1
	Canon EOS 300D DIGITAL	45	2
	Canon IXY DIGITAL 70	15	1
	Canon PowerShot A40	46	1
	Canon PowerShot A620	336	1
	Canon PowerShot G6	89	2
Casio	EX-Z40	311	63
Eastman Kodak Company	DC210 Zoom (V05.00)	165	1
	KODAK DC240 ZOOM DIGITAL CAMERA	37	1
Nikon	COOLPIX P2	27	14
	COOLPIX S3	34	8
	S1	9	8
Olympus	C760UZ	517	33
	FE100,X710	253	193
	C750UZ	82	27
Panasonic	DMC-FX8	1	1
	DMC-FZ7	104	19
PENTAX Corporation	PENTAX *ist DL	706	1
	PENTAX *ist DS	418	1
Samsung Techwin	U-CA 3 Digital Camera	30	2
SONY	CD MAVICA	322	9
	DCR-DVD803E	310	3
	DSC-P92	1363	19
	DSC-P93	207	6
(unknown OEM)	DigitalCam Pro	17	1

a slightly more efficient lossless compression algorithm known as algebraic compression, but this variation is rarely supported.

Quantisation Table as a Discriminator

The use of the quantisation table as a source discriminator has previously been mentioned by Lukáš et al. (2006) and considered in detail by Farid (2006). In that paper however, Farid investigated just one image each from over 300 cameras and concluded that there was insufficient discrimination to warrant further interest. Our investigation leads to quite a different interpretation.

We sourced 5,485 photographic images from friends and colleagues, each of whom provided a range of original images from their own digital camera. In all, images from 27 different camera types, from 10 brands, were obtained, as summarised in Table 2. We considered only the quantisation table for the luminance plane, but we note that the quantisation table or tables for the chrominance plane might in some cases offer an additional level of discrimination.

A total of 330 quantisation tables were extracted from our dataset of images, of which 42 were common to at least two camera models. A review of the common quantisation tables revealed obvious systematic commonality among similar

Table 3. Natural groupings of camera series by common quantisation tables

Camera Group	Included Models	Total Quantisation Tables	Total Quantisation Tables in Common
Canon IX+PS	Canon DIGITAL IXUS 400 Canon DIGITAL IXUS 700 Canon IXY DIGITAL 70 Canon PowerShot A40 Canon PowerShot A620 Canon PowerShot G6	3	2
Canon EOS	Canon EOS 10D Canon EOS 300D DIGITAL	2	2
Casio	EXZ40	63	n/a
Kodak	DC210 Zoom (V05.00) KODAK DC240 ZOOM DIGITAL CAMERA	1	1
Nikon	COOLPIX P2 COOLPIX S3 S1	20	8
Olympus C7	C760UZ C750UZ	33	27
Olympus F	FE100,X710	193	n/a/
Pentax	PENTAX *ist DL PENTAX *ist DS	1	1
Samsung	U-CA 3 Digital Camera	1	n/a
Sony DCR	DCR-DVD803E	3	n/a
Sony P9x	CD MAVICA DSC-P92 DSC-P93	21	10
OEM	DigitalCam Pro	1	n/a
Panasonic X	DMC-FX8	1	n/a
Panasonic Z	DMC-FZ7	19	n/a

Table 4. Showing the number of common quantisation tables between camera series

Camera Series	Nikon	Olympus C7	Sony P9X	Casio	Samsung	Canon EOS
OEM	1	1				
Nikon		19	5			
Olympus C7			7			
Sony P9X				3		1
Casio					1	1

cameras from the same manufacturer, as well as incidental commonality between unrelated cameras. The obvious camera groupings are given in Table 3.

It should be noted that the quantisation tables extracted for each camera are almost certainly not exhaustive. The only way to be sure of having an exhaustive list is to request such information from manufacturers or to reverse engineer the cameras' firmware. The grouping of cameras as shown in Table 3 is based primarily on the evidence of common quantisation tables as extracted in our experiment, but we have also considered the model series and in some cases reference to operation manuals to confirm membership of a series.

There is some commonality between camera series, which are for the most part coincidental, with one significant exception as shown in Table 4.

A total of 25 tables were found to be common to more than one camera series. Of particular note is that 19 tables (of a possible 20) are common to both Nikon and Olympus series, suggesting that both manufacturers are using the same JPEG encoder.

Discussion

The results of this experiment suggest that the quantisation table is a reasonable discriminator between model series, as over 92% of extracted tables were unique to one camera series.

From the tables extracted, it is also possible to infer a number of algorithms by which quantisation tables are computed.

- Some cameras, such as the Kodak and Pentax *IST series, use a single quantisation table for all images. This approach appears to be common both in older cameras (with limited processing capability) and in high-end cameras, for which image quality takes precedence over file size.
- Other cameras, notably the Sony DSC-P9X series, appear to have a single quantisation table, which is then scaled up or down to meet a particular file size requirement.
- Finally, we observed that some cameras, such as the Casio EXZ40 and the Olympus FE100, appear to use a much more sophisticated algorithm to choose an optimal quantisation table to suit the image.

One interesting point to note is that in most cases, the quantisation tables are asymmetric, so that the quantisation in the horizontal direction is different to the vertical direction. In our analysis we excluded images that had been rotated by 90 degrees to avoid double-counting of transposed quantisation matrices.

Our experiment merely demonstrates the merit of using the quantisation table as a forensic tool for identifying the make and model of a source camera. To be effective, an exhaustive database of all quantisation tables from all camera models would be required. Such a database would require constant updates as new camera models are introduced into the global market. Furthermore, we would stress that the only effective mechanism for such a database to operate is to rely on manufacturers to release complete specifications and parameters to the database manager. That is to say that the experimental technique we have used is not sufficiently reliable to ensure thorough coverage of all cameras.

Quantisation Tables Used by Popular Software

Images are commonly edited using popular software before being presented. We therefore considered the quantisation tables of two popular packages, namely Adobe Photoshop and Microsoft Photo Editor.

Adobe Photoshop allows 13 levels of JPEG image quality in integer steps from 0 to 12. One such quantisation table is shown in Table 5. It

is interesting to note that at low quality levels Photoshop quantises low frequency components particularly aggressively while retaining high frequency components. This behaviour is at odds with every other quantisation matrix we have identified, as well as the underlying psycho-visual theory behind JPEG compression (see for example Lohscheller, 1984). The observation helps to explain why JPEG images compressed by Photoshop at low quality show strong signs of blockiness, as the edges of the 8x8 pixel microblocks are readily apparent. A further anomaly in the Adobe Photoshop implementation is that the tables for quality levels 6 and 7 are in the wrong order, such that quality level 6 is actually higher quality than level 7. This is easily demonstrated by noting that saving an image at quality 6 results in a larger file than at quality 7.

Photoshop Version 4, and later versions, support Exif metadata and relevant tags are transferred to modified images. Photoshop identifies

Table 5. Representative quantisation tables used by Microsoft PhotoEditor and Adobe Photoshop

Microsoft PhotoEditor Quality Level 80%							
6	4	4	6	10	16	20	24
5	5	6	8	10	23	24	22
6	5	6	10	16	23	28	22
6	7	9	12	20	35	32	25
7	9	15	22	27	44	41	31
10	14	22	26	32	42	45	37
20	26	31	35	41	48	48	40
29	37	38	39	45	40	41	40
Adobe Photoshop Quality Level 8							
6	4	7	11	14	17	22	17
4	5	6	10	14	19	12	12
7	6	8	14	19	12	12	12
11	10	14	19	12	12	12	12
14	14	19	12	12	12	12	12
17	19	12	12	12	12	12	12
22	12	12	12	12	12	12	12
17	12	12	12	12	12	12	12

itself as the image editing software and modifies some tags to match the edited image in compliance with the Exif standard. Earlier versions of Photoshop do not support Exif metadata, ignore the Exif section of JPEG image files, and do not include Exif metadata in subsequent saved JPEG images.

Microsoft Photo Editor, on the other hand, offers 100 levels of JPEG image quality. Our analysis infers that Microsoft uses a single quantisation table that is scaled linearly according to the quality level and limited as necessary to the range [1...255]. Thus, quality level 100 uses no quantisation (all rounding coefficients equal to 1) while level 1 uses the coarsest possible quantisation (all rounding coefficients equal to 255). A representative quantisation table is given in Table 5. Unlike Photoshop, Photo Editor's quantisation tables are asymmetric, most likely recognising the physical layout of red, green, and blue pixels in conventional video displays.

Microsoft Photo Editor does not support Exif metadata and images saved by Photo Editor do not include any original metadata. Anomolously, Windows XP (which includes Photo Editor as a standard package) does use Exif metadata to identify certain image characteristics in the file browser.

Recompressed Images

A significant limitation of the experiment described in the *Quantisation Table as a Discriminator* section is that it assumes that an image is being investigated in its original form. This might in fact be the case in a range of applications, particularly to identify image tampering or to verify other identification information such as Exif metadata. More commonly however an image will undergo subsequent manipulation before being stored, transmitted, or posted on an Internet site. Examples of such manipulation include:

- Recompression, to reduce the size of the file
- Resizing of the image, reducing both the size of the file and making it more suited to display on a Web site
- Cropping, scaling, or rotation of the image
- Brightness, contrast, or colour adjustment• Modification of part of the image

Clearly, such manipulation will mask the original quantisation levels and so the technique described in 4.2 would not be possible. However, if we consider the situation in which the image is simply recompressed without scaling, cropping, or other adjustments, we can exploit the fact that such recompression leaves detectable artefacts from which the original image coefficients can be inferred. Anecdotal evidence provided in discussion with law enforcement personnel suggests that many images of interest are recompressed without resizing the image.

This technique was considered by Lukáš and Fridrich (2003), but the application to camera identification was not explicit, and the estimation techniques used were sub-optimal and ad hoc; similarly Neelamani, De Queiroz, Fan, Dash, and Baraniuk (2006) applied estimation techniques to determine compression history of JPEG images. Similarly, Popescu and Farid (2005) exploited double-compression artefacts to identify image tampering.

The Detection of Double Quantisation

Consider what happens when a coefficient is quantised to the nearest multiple of 2, and then to the nearest multiple of 3, as shown in Table 6. Direct quantisation rounds off three consecutive integers to a multiple of 3. Two-stage quantisation, however, results in four consecutive integers rounding off to odd multiples of 3, while two consecutive integers round off to multiples of 6.

The impact of this bias is that there is a periodic pattern in the distribution of coefficients after

Table 6. Rounding off by 2 and then 3, compared to direct rounding to 3

Original number n	1	2	3	4	5	6	7	8	9	10	11	12
Round off to 2	2	2	4	4	6	6	8	8	10	10	12	12
then round off to 3	3	3	3	3	6	6	9	9	9	9	12	12
Compare with direct round off to 3	0	3	3	3	6	6	6	9	9	9	12	12

Figure 3. Double rounding leads to a periodic pattern in the distribution of coefficients. The dotted line shows the distribution of the coefficients in the original image, rounded off to 2. The solid line shows the distribution after rounding off to 3. The periodic behaviour is starkly evident.

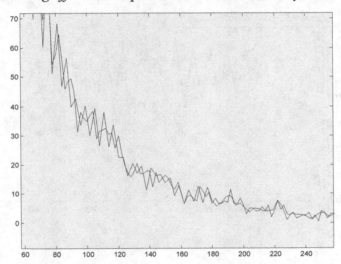

double quantisation, as demonstrated in Figure 3. Because we are interested in the periodic pattern of the coefficients, we apply a symmetric high pass filter to remove the underlying bell curve distribution:

$$\overline{x_k}(i) = \frac{2x_k(i) - x_{k-1}(i) - x_{k+1}(i)}{2}$$

Furthermore, we note that coefficients with value zero do not contribute to the periodic pattern of interest, and so these coefficients are explicitly removed by setting:

$$x_0(i) = \frac{x_{-1}(i) + x_1(i)}{2}$$

so that $\overline{x_0}(i) = 0$ and the impact of $x_0(i)$ on its immediate neighbours is reduced.

We then create a template for a given value of the original and secondary coefficients, $Q_1(i)$ and $Q_2(i)$ respectively, where i identifies one of the 64 coefficients of interest. A typical distribution and template is shown in Figure 4, for $Q_1(i)=2$ and $Q_2(i)=3$. The template $t(Q_1(i),Q_2(i))$ is created by generating a histogram from a uniform distribution of coefficients and then performing the same filtering as for $\overline{x}$. Both $\overline{x}$ and t are then normalised except for the special case when $Q_2(i)$ is divisible by $Q_1(i)$ as this will result in a flat template which is defined in this case as a zero vector.

The optimal test for each coefficient is to perform a matched filter correlation, that is:

Figure 4. The underlying bell-curve distribution of coefficients (top left) is filtered from the double-quantised coefficients, leaving periodic behaviour which may be matched with an appropriate template (dotted line). A further refinement is that zero coefficients are removed from consideration as these provide no differentiation between different quantisation values.

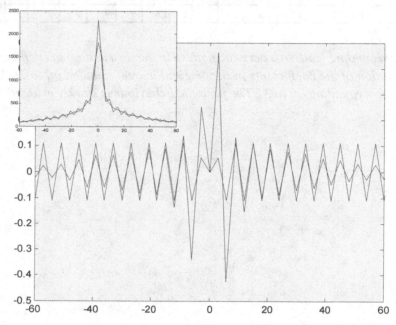

$$c(Q_1(i), Q_2(i)) = \sum_{k=-1023}^{1023} \overline{x_k} \cdot \overline{t_k}(Q_1(i), Q_2(i)).$$

A large and positive correlation indicates a good match with the template, whereas a small or negative correlation indicates a poor match.

Description of Classification Algorithm

The correlation filter described in the *Detection of Double Quantisation* section does not unambiguously identify a single possible original quantisation coefficient. For example, if $Q_2(i)=3$ and $Q_1(i)=2$, there will be strong correlation with 2, 4, 8, 10, 14, 16, and so forth as shown in Figure 5.

This observation means that it is not appropriate to estimate each quantisation coefficient independently or jointly, as there are too many valid options. Instead, we formulate the quantisation table detector as a multiple hypothesis test.

For each hypothetical quantisation table, we calculate a score based on the correlation coefficients for each individual table element. The score is then ranked so that the candidate quantisation table with the highest score is considered to be the best match.

The score function is the sum of the correlations for each DCT histogram, weighted by the number of non-zero coefficients:

$$S_j = \sum_{i=1}^{64} c(Q_j(i), Q_2(i)) \bullet N_{\bar{0}}(i)$$

where Q_j refers to the candidate quantisation table under hypothesis j and Q_2 similarly refers to the known secondary quantisation table; and $N_{\bar{0}}(i)$ refers to the number of non-zero coefficients in

Figure 5. If Q1(j)=2 and Q2(j)=3, there will be strong correlation for candidate values of Q1(j)=2, 4, 8, 10, 14, 16, etc.

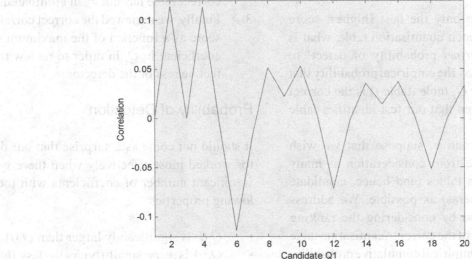

the histogram for coefficient *i*. Heuristically, it is easy to argue that the higher the positive correlation, and the higher the number of useful samples, the greater a particular coefficient component can contribute to the overall score.

The best match, assuming uniform prior probability, is then given by

$$J = \arg\max_j S_j$$

It should be noted that this is not the only form of detector that could be constructed using correlation of the 64 DCT coefficients, nor do we claim that this is an optimal detector. However, this detector is sufficient to demonstrate the efficacy of the approach.

Description of Experiment

We considered 4,500 photographs and the impact of requantisation by Adobe Photoshop (all 13 quality levels) and Microsoft Equation Editor (11 quality levels from 1% to 100%). Only the impact

of requantisation on the luminance plane was considered, primarily because both packages perform 2h2v downsampling in the chrominance plane which would have complicated our analysis.

The actual requantisation was performed by direct requantisation in our analysis software, although we verified that our requantisation algorithm mirrored the results from the original packages by testing several samples.

For each image, we considered 24 r-equantisation cases. In each case, we tested our correlation detector against 330 hypothetical quantisation tables, of which we knew that one would be the correct match. Of course, we were also able to keep track of the correct original quantisation table. We then ranked the scores for later analysis.

Results and Analysis

In order to analyse our results in a meaningful way, we chose to cluster original quantisation tables (Q_1) by the maximum of the 64 quantisation values. Although this is not an optimal clustering, it does at least bring together quantisation tables with generally similar characteristics.

We considered three questions in our analysis:

1. Considering only the best (highest score ranking) match quantisation table, what is the *a-posteriori* probability of detection, which is to say the empirical probability that a particular Q_1 table (table j) is the correct answer, given that our test identifies table j.

2. As an alternative, suppose that we wish to eliminate from consideration as many quantisation tables (and hence, candidate source cameras) as possible. We address this question by considering the ranking distribution of the correct quantisation table against the empirical cumulative probability of detection. This allows us to eliminate a proportion of candidate quantisation tables with, for example, 95% confidence that the correct table has not been eliminated.

3. Finally, we reviewed the correct correlation score as a function of the maximum value coefficient in Q_1 in order to review the effectiveness of the detector.

Probability of Detection

It should not come as a surprise that our detector worked most effectively when there were a significant number of coefficients with the following properties:

- $Q_1(i)$ is significantly larger than $Q_2(i)$
- $Q_2(i)$ is very small (typically less than or equal to 3)

Figure 6. A-posteriori probability of detection as a function of the maximum coefficient in Q1 for four representative secondary quantisations; the solid line shows the median empirical probability of detection while the dashed lines show the 90% confidence interval

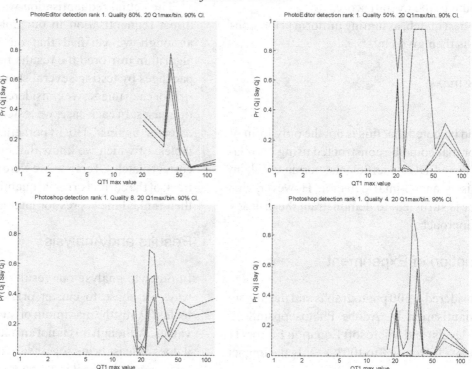

- In cases where $Q_2(i)$ is greater than $Q_1(i)$, $Q_2(i)$ is not divisible by $Q_1(i)$ to ensure residual periodic behaviour

Examples of our results are given in Figure 6 for four representative cases. These are representative of recompression at moderate and low image quality levels and are typical of the values used in requantised images for e-mail and Web applications. The quantisation tables are those given in Table 5.

It is interesting to note that in no case did the detector result in a match for a primary quantisation table maximum value of less than 18 in the examples given. The best results in fact were achieved with the highest quality settings of both software packages and even in this case results were unreliable for maximum primary quantisation less than 5.

This is in fact not surprising as small primary quantisation values are very likely to be divisors of secondary coefficients. In particular, because the highest frequency coefficients in most of Photoshop's quantisation tables is 12, it is very difficult to isolate 1, 2, 3, 4, 6, or 12 as a primary coefficient.

On the other hand, Photo Editor has such large quantisation values for high frequency coefficients that the number of non-zero elements is very small, leading to unreliable detection of primary quantisation values.

A similar argument explains why these graphs are not monotonic—there are certain combinations of values of primary and secondary quantisation tables that are simply difficult to detect because the primary is a divisor of the secondary.

Remembering that our detector is a 330-hypothesis test, a random guess would result in a probability of detection of 0.003. That a-posteriori detection rates in excess of 0.20 are routinely achieved is a strong indicator of the effectiveness of the detector.

We acknowledge however that our weighting functions in our detection score are heuristic,

and that further work is needed to improve the performance of the detector.

Ranking of Correct Match

Figure 7 shows the residual probability of miss as a function of rank order for the same four representative secondary quantisation cases. Three sets of primary coefficients were considered. These were grouped according to the maximum quantisation coefficient as follows:

1. Maximum primary coefficient in the range 2 to 6
2. Maximum primary coefficient in the range 7 to 23
3. Maximum primary coefficient greater than or equal to 24

It should be noted that the case where the primary quantisation table is all ones (that is, no quantisation) was excluded as this pathological case cannot be detected using this system.

Using these figures, Table 7 summarises the number of quantisation tables that cannot be excluded from the set of 330 used in our analysis, assuming a requirement for 95% confidence of non-exclusion.

With the exception of very high quality settings for secondary quantisation, these results, disappointingly, show that unless there is a strong initial probability of detection, very few quantisation tables can be excluded from consideration. The reason for this is clear—unless the correct primary quantisation table results in a high score due to large numbers of non-zero coefficients and strong periodic behaviour, it will not stand out from the alternative candidate tables and the result is little better than guessing.

Correlation Score

A deeper understanding of the detector performance can be gained from Figure 8, showing the

Figure 7. Residual probability of miss as a function of rank order for four representative secondary quantisations; the three cases in each graph represent small, medium and large values of primary quantisation

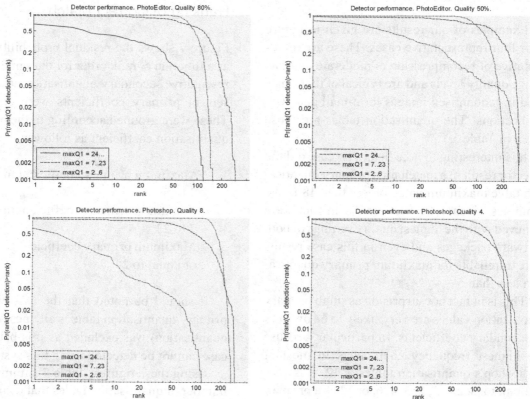

Table 7. From our experiment of detection of 330 candidate quantisation tables, this table shows the approximate size of the set of quantisation tables for 95% confidence of inclusion of the correct primary quantisation table; a small set size is desirable but as can be seen this is only achieved for high quality secondary quantisation (small quantisation values), particularly for high valued primary quantisation tables

Microsoft Photo Editor Quality Level	max Q1 [2..6]	max Q1 [7..23]	max Q1 [24..]
1%	250	250	250
10%	200	250	250
20%	250	250	250
30%	250	230	200
40%	200	250	250
50%	250	200	200
60%	250	200	70
70%	250	250	80
80%	180	250	100
90%	250	250	150
100%	2	1	1

continued on following page

Figure 7. continued

Adobe Photoshop Quality Level	max Q1 [2..6]	max Q1 [7..23]	max Q1 [24..]
0	200	250	200
1	200	250	250
2	200	250	200
3	200	250	200
4	250	250	200
5	150	250	180
7*	250	250	30
6*	200	220	180
8	250	250	30
9	200	250	60
10	150	180	18
11	250	200	1
12	30	2	1

* Note that Quality Level 6 of Adobe Photoshop uses smaller quantisation coefficients than quality level 7

Figure 8. Correlator performance as a function of the maximum coefficient in Q1 for four representative secondary quantisations

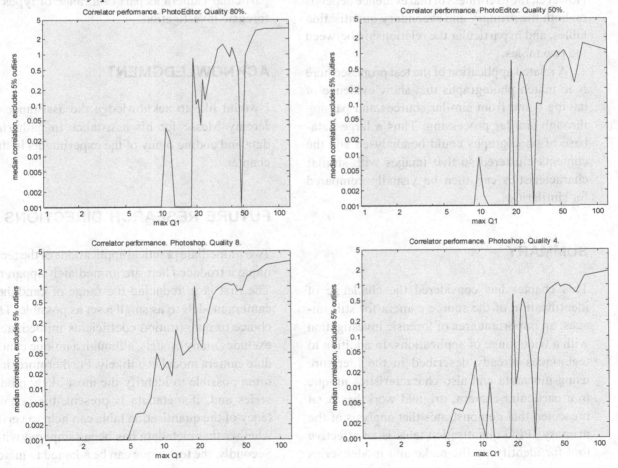

median score for the four representative quantisation cases. The performance is quite strong in all cases for primary quantisation tables with large coefficients, but particularly poor in cases where:

- The primary coefficients are small, due to the high probability of being a divisor of the secondary coefficient, and
- For primary coefficient values in the range of 10 to 20, which are likely to be equal to the secondary coefficient.

Discussion

The work presented here has demonstrated that some residual evidence remains of primary quantisation when a photographic image is requantised. However, the usefulness of that evidence depends on both the primary and secondary quantisation tables, and in particular the relationship between the two tables.

A related application of the test proposed here is to match photographs that show evidence of having come from similar sources and passing through similar processing. Thus a large database of photographs could be analysed and the contents clustered so that images with similar characteristics can then be visually compared for similarities.

SUMMARY

This chapter has considered the challenge of identification of the source camera for still images, an important area of forensic investigation with a wide range of applications. In addition to techniques already described in the literature using metadata and also characteristics unique to a particular camera, original work has been presented that demonstrates that analysis of the primary JPEG quantisation table is an effective tool for identifying the make and model series

of the source camera. Furthermore, it has been demonstrated that under some circumstances, it is still possible to identify the primary JPEG quantisation table after requantisation, meaning that identification of the camera series is often still possible after the image has been recoded.

In order to develop these techniques into a useful forensic tool, it would be necessary to develop and maintain an exhaustive database of all cameras on the global market. Such a database would require the infrastructure of a significant law enforcement agency or other similar agency and the cooperation of camera manufacturers. However the number of manufacturers and the range of cameras available, including new models introduced each year, suggests that such a database is technically and commercially feasible and would bring significant benefits in tying an image to a particular camera as part of a range of types of forensic investigation.

ACKNOWLEDGMENT

I would like to acknowledge the assistance of Jeremy Messé for his assistance in gathering data and coding many of the experiments in this chapter.

FUTURE RESEARCH DIRECTIONS

Two immediate practical applications of the technique introduced here are immediately apparent. The first is in reducing the range of candidate camera models to as small a set as possible. The choice of quantisation coefficients immediately excludes many models, although a unique candidate camera model is unlikely. Furthermore, it is often possible to identify the most likely model series and, if metadata is present, the consistency of the quantisation table can help to verify whether that metadata has been tampered with. Secondly, the technique can be adapted to match photographs in a database that have undergone the same primary and secondary quantisation. When dealing with a very larger number of photographs, particularly when the content is distressing, this is an important technique because it allows photographs with similar technical characteristics to be filtered for human analysis.

It became apparent in the images gathered for this experiment that newer high quality cameras are opting for higher quality images by using smaller valued quantisation tables. The justification for this design decision appears to be that memory cards are quickly increasing in size while becoming cheaper. For example, a camera from around 2002 would typically come with an 8MB memory card, a camera at a similar price in 2007 comes with a 512MB or 1GB memory card. This means that file size is quickly becoming less relevant and so images are being captured with minimal quantisation. We see no reason why this trend would not continue.

As a consequence, it is likely that identification of the primary quantisation matrix in a requantised image will not only get more difficult for new cameras, but such analysis will be of less value as cameras move towards un-quantised JPEG images.

On the other hand, the sale of mobile phones with inbuilt cameras is continuing strongly, and for these devices file size remains a key challenge for transmission. Hence larger valued quantisation tables are likely to continue to be used, and when considered in conjunction with the fact that mobile camera images are very often transmitted or shared directly with no editing, the techniques described in this chapter are likely to remain powerful tools in identifying the source of images for the foreseeable future.

It is likely that the performance of the detector presented here could be improved by reformulating our detection algorithm. It is also worth investigating a number of other variations, including:

- Incorporation of chrominance planes in the detector
- The impact of cropping and rescaling of the image
- The impact of other affine transforms, including rotation

The application of coding analysis to video brings new opportunities and challenges. On the one hand, quantisation tables are much less likely to vary across video camera devices, and in fact some early video standards have fixed quantisation.

However, it should also be noted that video coding typically uses a combination of *intra-frames*, that is, reference frames coded in a similar way to JPEG, and *inter-frames*, that is, frames that are constructed with reference to previous or future video frames. This is typically done using motion vectors that code a block of the frame as a spatial offset to the reference frame, adding detailed correction if necessary. Optimal calculation of motion vectors is computationally intensive and so sub-optimal techniques are normally used (see for example Al-Mualla, Canagarajah, & Bull, 2002) for a discussion on a range of sub-optimal strategies). By analysis of the video frames and motion vectors, it would be possible to identify the sub-optimal motion estimation strategy and hence link that evidence to a manufacturer and camera model series in a similar manner to that described here.

REFERENCES

Al-Mualla, M. E., Canagarajah, C. N., & Bull, D. R. (2002). *Video coding for mobile communications: Efficiency, complexity and resilience.* Boston: Academic Press.

Bayram, S., Sencar, H. T., Memon, N., & Avcibas, I. (2005, September 11-14). Source camera identification based on CFA interpolation. *Proceedings* of the IEEE International Conference on Image Processing 2005, ICIP 2005 (Vol. 3, pp. 69-72).

Farid, H. (2006). *Digital image ballistics from JPEG quantization* (Tech. Rep. No. TR2006-583). Hanover, NH: Dartmouth College, Department of Computer Science.

International Telecommunications Union (ITU). (1993). *CCITT T.81 information technology—Digital compression and coding of continuous-tone still images—Requirements and guidelines.* Author.

Japan Electronics and Information Technology Industries Association (JEITA). (2002). *JEITA CP-3451 Exchangeable image file format for digital still cameras: Exif Version 2.2.* Author.

Lohscheller, H. (1984). A subjectively adapted image communication system. *IEEE Transactions on Communications, 32*(12), 1316-1322.

Lukáš, J., & Fridrich, J. (2003, August). Estimation of primary quantization matrix in double compressed JPEG images. *Proceedings of Digital Forensic Research Workshop,* Cleveland, OH.

Lukáš, J., Fridrich, J., & Goljan, M. (2006). Digital camera identification from sensor pattern noise. *IEEE Transactions on Information Forensics and Security, 1*(2), 205-214.

Neelamani, R., De Queiroz, R., Fan, Z., Dash, S., & Baraniuk, R. (2006). JPEG compression history estimation for color images. *IEEE Transactions on Image Processing, 15*(6), 1365-1378.

Popescu, A. C., & Farid, H. (2005). Exposing digital forgeries by detecting traces of resampling. *IEEE Transactions on Signal Processing, 53*(2).

Wallace, G. K. (1991). The JPEG still picture compression standard. *Communications of the ACM, 34*(4), 30-44.

ADDITIONAL READING

In addition to the previous references, the following references related to camera source identification, image tampering, and JPEG parameter selection, particularly quantisation coefficients, may be useful. There is also a wide range of popular literature, especially on the Internet, on the topic of source camera identification, which is not listed here.

Ahmed, N., Natarajan, T., & Rao, K. R. (1974). Discrete cosine transform. *IEEE Transactions on Computers, C-23,* 90-93.

Alvarez, P. (2004). Using extended file information (EXIF) file headers in digital evidence analysis. *International Journal of Digital Evidence, 2*(3).

Chen, W. H., & Pratt, W. K. (1984). Scene adaptive coder. *IEEE Transactions on Communications, 32,* 225-232.

Fan, Z., & De Queiroz, R. (2000). Maximum likelihood estimation of JPEG quantization table in the identification of JPEG compression history. *Proceedings of the IEEE International Conference on Image Processing, ICIP,* Vancouver, Canada (Vol. I, pp. 948-951).

Fan, Z., & De Queiroz, R. (2003). Identification of bitmap compression history: JPEG detection and quantizer estimation. *IEEE Transactions on Image Processing, 12,* 230-235.

Farid, H. (2004). *Creating and detecting doctored and virtual images: Implications to the child pornography prevention act* (Tech. Rep. No. TR2004-518). Hanover, NH: Dartmouth College, Department of Computer Science.

Farid, H. (2006). *Exposing digital forgeries in scientific images.* ACM Multimedia and Security Workshop, Geneva, Switzerland.

Fridrich, J. (1998, November 4-6). Methods for detecting changes in digital images. *Proceedings of the 6th IEEE International Workshop on In-*

telligent Signal Processing and Communication Systems (ISPACS'98), Melbourne, Australia (pp. 173-177).

Fridrich, J., & Blythe, P. (2004, August 11-13). *Secure digital camera.* Paper presented at the Digital Forensic Research Workshop, Baltimore, MD.

Fridrich, J., Chen, M., & Goljan, M. (2007, January). *Digital imaging sensor identification (further study).* Proceedings of SPIE Electronic Imaging, Photonics West.

Fridrich, J., Chen, M., Goljan, M., & Lukáš, J. (2007, January). *Source digital camcorder identification using sensor photo-response non-uniformity.* Proceedings of SPIE Electronic Imaging, Photonics West.

Fridrich, J., Goljan, M., & Chen, M. (in press). *Identifying common source digital camera from image pairs.* Proceedings of ICIP, San Antonio, TX.

Fridrich, J., Soukal, D., & Lukáš, J. (2003, August 5-8). *Detection of copy-move forgery in digital images.* Proceedings of DFRWS 2003, Cleveland, OH.

Glanrath, D. J. (1981). The role of human visual models in image processing. *Proceedings of the IEEE, 67,* 552-561.

Johnson, M. K., & Farid, H. (2005). *Exposing digital forgeries by detecting inconsistencies in lighting.* ACM Multimedia and Security Workshop, New York.

Johnson, M. K., & Farid, H. (2006). *Exposing digital forgeries through chromatic aberration.* ACM Multimedia and Security Workshop, Geneva, Switzerland.

Lohscheller, H., & Franke, U. (1987). Colour picture coding—Algorithm optimization and technical realization. *Frequenze, 41,* 291-299.

Lyu, S. (2005). *Natural image statistics for digital image forensics.* Unpublished PhD dissertation, Hanover, NH: Dartmouth College, Department of Computer Science.

Lyu, S., Rockmore, D., & Farid, H. (2005). *Wavelet analysis for authentication.* Boulder, CO: University of Colorado, Art+Math=X.

Murdoch, S. J., & Dornseif, M. (2004). *Far more than you ever wanted to tell: Hidden data in Internet published documents, 21.* Chaos Communication Congress.

Peterson, H. A., et al. (1991). *Quantization of colour image components in the DCT domain.* SPIE/IS&T 1991 Symposium on Electronic Imaging Science and Technology.

Popescu, A. C. (2005). *Statistical tools for digital image forensics.* Unpublished PhD dissertation, Hanover, NH: Dartmouth College, Department of Computer Science.

Popescu, A. C., & Farid, H. (2004a). *Exposing digital forgeries by detecting duplicated image regions* (Tech. Rep. No. TR2004-515). Hanover, NH: Dartmouth College, Department of Computer Science.

Popescu, A. C., & Farid, H. (2004b). *Statistical tools for digital forensics.* 6th International Workshop on Information Hiding, Toronto, Canada.

Popescu, A. C., & Farid, H. (2005). Exposing digital forgeries in color filter array interpolated images. *IEEE Transactions on Signal Processing, 53*(10), 3948-3959.

Wang, W., & Farid, H. (2006). *Exposing digital forgeries in video by detecting double MPEG compression.* ACM Multimedia and Security Workshop, Geneva, Switzerland.

Chapter XV
Traitor Tracing for Multimedia Forensics

Hongxia Jin
IBM Almaden Research Center, USA

ABSTRACT

This chapter discusses the cryptographic traitor tracing technology that is used to defend against piracy in multimedia content distribution. It talks about different potential pirate attacks in a multimedia content distribution system. It discusses how traitor tracing technologies can be used to defend against those attacks by identifying the attackers involved in the piracy. While traitor tracing has been a long standing cryptographic problem that has attracted extensive research, the main purpose of this chapter is to show how to overcome many practical concerns in order to bring a theoretical solution to practice. Many of these practical concerns have been overlooked in academic research. The author brings first-hand experience on bringing this technology to practice in the context of new industry standards on content protection for next generation high-definition DVDs. The author also hopes to shed new insights on future research directions in this space.

INTRODUCTION

Today we live in a digital world. The advent of digital technologies has made the creation and manipulation of multimedia content simpler. It offers higher quality and a lot more convenience to consumers. For example, it allows one to make perfect copies.

Furthermore, the rapid advance of network technologies, cheaper storage, and larger bandwidth have enabled new business models on electronically distributing and delivering multimedia content, such as Disney's MovieBeam and Apple's iTune.

However, unauthorized music and movie copying are eating a big bite of the profit of the record industry and the movie studios. The success of these emerging business models hinges on the ability to only deliver the content to paying customers.

It is highly desirable to develop better techniques to protect the copyrighted material.

Content encryption solves part of the problem. It protects the content before and during delivery, but does not help after it has been decrypted. It is relatively easy for hackers to access the content after decryption. To protect the copyright of the content, one must also ensure that content is only consumed by authorized users.

Digital fingerprinting are unique labels/marks embedded in different copies of the same content. When an illegal copy of the post-delivery multimedia content is found, the embedded fingerprint can be used for tracing the illegal users who distributed that copy.

Of course there are different pirate attacks. The piracy may not be on content; it can also be on the decryption keys of the content. Fingerprinting technology usually does not apply to cryptographic keys.

The focus of this chapter is not on content fingerprinting, instead it is on *traitor tracing*.

Before we go on in this chapter, we need to first clarify the terminology traitor tracing.

People working on multimedia have been using the terminology traitor tracing meaning the function/capability that traces traitors. So one can say fingerprinting is a technology that can be used for traitor tracing. However, traitor tracing is also a terminology that has been actively appeared in cryptographic literatures. It refers to a class of key management schemes that can be used to trace pirated cryptographic keys, sometimes pirated content too. To this end, traitor tracing itself is a technology that can be used for forensics, including multimedia forensics. The focus of this chapter is on the latter cryptographic traitor tracing technology, which has been and still is a very active research area in cryptographic community.

In this chapter, we will describe different pirate attacks. We will survey the state of art and state of practice of the traitor tracing technologies for different pirate attacks. Different traitor tracing technologies are needed for different types of pirate attacks. The author and colleagues have been involved in this research area for many years. The technologies they developed have become the first large scale commercialization of traitor tracing technologies in the context of new industry content protection standard, the advanced access content system (AACS), for next generation high definition DVDs. In this chapter the author will describe their first hand experience on developing traitor tracing technologies that are practical enough for commercial use. The focus of this chapter is from a practical point of view looking at the problems and how researches can be done to make the technologies work in practice. It will give readers hands on knowledge on using traitor tracing technologies for multimedia forensics in different types of pirate attacks in real world. This chapter will also point out some of the issues that have been overlooked in years of academic researches.

BACKGROUND

A number of business models have emerged, whose success hinges on the ability to securely distribute digital content only to paying customers. Examples of these business models include pay-TV systems (Cable companies) or movie rental companies like Netflix, and massively distributing prerecorded and recordable media. These typical content protection applications imply a one-way broadcast nature. To ensure the content is only consumed by authorized users, broadcast encryption technologies are used.

A broadcast encryption system (Fiat & Naor, 1993) enables a broadcaster to encrypt the content so that only a privileged subset of users (devices, set up boxes) can decrypt the content and exclude another subset of users. In this system, each decoder box is assigned a unique set of decryption keys (called device keys). A key management algorithm is defined to assign keys to devices and encrypt the content that can guarantee that only compliant devices can decrypt the content, without requiring authentication of the device.

Broadcast encryption is currently being used for content protection of recordable and prerecorded media (CPRM/CPPM) and is implemented in consumer electronics devices ranging from highly portable audio players that use secure digital cards to top of the line DVD-audio players supporting multiple channels, higher sampling rates, and improved frequency response. The media, such as CD, DVD, or a flash memory card, typically contains in its header the encryption of the key K (called media key), which encrypts the content following the header. The media key is encrypted again and again using all the chosen device keys and forms a *media key block* (MKB), which is sent alongside the content when the content is distributed. The device keys used to encrypt the media key are chosen in a way as to cover all compliant boxes. It allows all compliant devices, each using their set of device keys, to calculate the same key K. But the non-compliant devices cannot calculate the correct key using their compromised keys. Thus the MKB enables system renewability. If a device is found to be non-compliant, a set of his/her device keys is compromised, an updated MKB can be released that causes a device with the compromised set of device keys to be unable to calculate the correct key K.

This effectively excludes the compromised device from accessing the future content. The compromised device keys are *revoked* by the updated MKB.

One of the biggest challenges of the design of a broadcast encryption system is the communication overhead, measured by the length of the cipher text message in order to revoke keys, in other words, the MKB size. A naive approach would encrypt the media key K using each compliant user's device key. In this approach, the size of the MKB is linear with the number of users. Of course this is only feasible when broadcasting to a very small set of users. When the set is large, this naive approach will explode in size. Therefore the research challenge is when the set is large, which is oftentimes true in reality, for example, DVD players can be over billions. In this case, the goal of the design is to make MKB size independent of the total number of users.

The best broadcast encryption system that uses for MKB is referred to as the subset-difference approach, or simply the NNL tree (Naor, Naor, & Lotspiech, 2001), named after the inventors. It achieves very concise MKBs. The algorithm is based on the principle of covering all non-revoked users by disjoint subsets from a predefined collection. It is tree-based and the subsets are derived from a virtual tree structure imposed on all devices in the system. The algorithm allows very efficient revocation of any combination of device key sets. It is used in the recently formed industry standard, AACS, on content protection for next generation high definition DVDs.

Another type of multimedia content distribution may not involve physical media. It is distributed through the communication channel. The cost shifts from manufacturing physical media to network bandwidth. For example, pay-TV systems and selling copyrighted music content through the Web. It is the *pay-per-view* type of system. A consumer device (e.g., a set-top box as a movie rental box) receives digital movies from some inexpensive source of data, usually some broadcast source or network download.

The content is bulk-encrypted and a content protection system needs to make sure that only paid customers can access the content.

Traitor tracing schemes are a class of key management schemes that are carefully designed to distribute the decryption keys to users so that they can identify the users (called traitors) who have been involved in the piracy when pirate evidences are found.

OVERVIEW ON ATTACKS

What are the security problems with the broadcast encryption systems described previously?

Here are the three major pirate attacks:

- Pirates disclose secret device keys by building a clone pirate decoder,
- Pirates disclose content encrypting key (media key): pirates stay anonymous, and
- Pirates disclose decrypted content: pirates stay anonymous.

The first pirate attack has been studied extensively. It is called *pirate decoder attack*.

A set of device owners attack their devices, extract device keys out of their devices, and use those keys collaboratively to build a clone pirate device that can decrypt the content. Of course this clone device does not have to be a physical device; it can be a software program. They can then sell it to illegitimate users for commercial interest. Any one owning the pirate decoder can extract the plaintext broadcasted by the broadcaster. For example, pirate decoders enable illegitimate users to watch pay-TV for free. The content protection scheme for DVDs called content scrambling system (CSS) was broken and the infamous software program De-CSS used for copying protected DVD discs is available anywhere on Internet. That is a typical example of this pirate decoder attack.

The goal of a traitor tracing scheme for this type of attack is to distribute the decryption keys to the devices in such a way so as to allow the identification of at least one key used in the pirate box or clone when a pirate device is found. Most existing broadcast encryption and traitor tracing schemes targeted on this type of pirate decoder attack.

Another possible attack, which is more popular in a business scenario like pay-per-view, is what we call *anonymous attack*. Some legitimate subscribers have instrumented their devices and resell the movies by redistributing the per-movie decryption keys or the decrypted movie itself. For example, in the aforementioned hybrid encryption-based broadcast encryption system, the attacker can simply redistribute the media key to stay anonymous and avoid being identified. Indeed, the attackers can set up a server that sells the per-movie keys (like media keys) on demand. To defend against these types of anonymous attacks, for different devices, the content needs to be differently encrypted. A traitor tracing scheme for this type of redistributing anonymous attack is to design a key management scheme that distributes the encryption/decryption keys in a way so that they allow one to identify the traitors when the pirated content/keys are found.

In rest of the chapter we will discuss in more detail traitor tracing technologies on each of the aforementioned attacks. We will mainly describe the technologies we have developed and have been adopted in the AACS content protection standard for next generation high definition DVDs. As mentioned earlier, traitor tracing is a long standing theoretical research topic in cryptographic literatures. We will talk about our first hand experience on bringing this long standing theoretical research topic to commercial use for Hollywood. Practicality was our number one focus.

TRAITOR TRACING FOR PIRATE DECODER ATTACK

A De-CSS type attack can end up with a clone decoder (or a software program) with built-in device keys. A traitor tracing scheme is designed to distribute the device keys in a way to allow the tracing and detection of at least one key that is used in the clone decoder.

Black-box tracing is usually used against this type of attack when a clone is found.

It assumes that only the outcome of the decoding box can be examined. It provides the black box with encrypted messages (e.g., MKB) and observes its output (the decrypted message, e.g., whether or not it can decrypt MKB correctly to get the media key to decrypt the content) trying to figure out who leaked the device keys. A pirate decoder is of interest only if it can correctly decode with probability bigger than some threshold.

While there has been a lot of work done for this type of attack, the state-of-art traitor tracing scheme for pirate decoder attack is seamlessly combined with the state-of-art broadcast encryption scheme, NNL scheme. After the tracing scheme identifies the compromised device keys, the distributor can revoke the pirate's device keys in the updated MKB in new released movies.

At a high level, a broadcast encryption system organizes the devices into overlapping subsets, with each subset associated with a key. Each device belongs to many different subsets and knows the key for every subset it is a member of. During broadcasting, the license agency picks subsets that cover all innocent devices but exclude all compromised devices. The MKB distributed together with the content contains the media key encrypted with all selected subset keys. In the broadcast encryption scheme shown in Naor et al. (2001), the devices are organized as the leaves of a tree. Each subtree in the tree becomes a subset, and each subtree is associated with a key. Each device belongs to many subtrees and knows all the keys associated with those subtrees.

The traitor tracing scheme shown in Naor et al. (2001) is called subset-based tracing. The subset tracing scheme is a black box tracing. The algorithm devises a series of carefully crafted cipher messages (queries) to feed into the decoder. These queries are called forensic MKBs. The scheme partitions the tree into subtrees (subsets). For a partition $S = S_{i1}, S_{i2},...S_{im}$, each subset S_{ij} is associated with a key. When building a forensic MKB, the algorithm carefully chooses to enable some keys and disable other keys. Enabling a key means encrypting the media key in the forensic MKB, and disabling a key means encrypting a random bit string (garbage) instead of the valid media key in the forensic MKB. As one can see, the

structure of these forensic MKBs is very similar to real production MKBs. But they choose keys to disable just for forensics purpose only, not for real revocation of users.

As the basic procedure of the tracing algorithm, a series of forensic MKBs are constructed using partition S and fed into the clone decoder. The clone either cannot decrypt MKB with probability greater than threshold q, or identify a subset S_{ij} such that S_{ij} contains a traitor. The paper by Naor et al. (2001) showed why this can be guaranteed in their tree structured broadcast encryption scheme. When a suspect subset is identified, it is split into two roughly equal size subsets and the next iteration continues with the new partition until it reaches a leaf node that identifies a guilty compromised device, that is, a traitor.

The efficiency of the tracing is mainly measured by how many forensic MKBs are needed in order to detect the traitors or disable a pirate decoder. The traitor tracing scheme shown in Naor et al. (2001) takes in total $T^3 \log T$ forensic MKBs where T is the number of traitors involved in constructing the pirate decoder.

What is Missing From Existing Approaches

The previous polynomial result seems to be satisfactory on paper. Theoretical research can happily stop here. Unfortunately we find it is not a completely practical solution for real use. The measures taken by the circumvention device might slow down the testing process. For example, each testing probe may take a minute or more. A circumvention device comprising 100 compromised keys (i.e., $t = 100$) may require over 100 millions of forensic MKB testings to determine the device keys the circumvention device has compromised. It is obvious this is not acceptable. In effect, such a circumvention device had defeated the content protection system. Therefore it is highly desirable to reduce the number of forensic MKBs needed.

New Approach

A more empirical approach (Zigoris & Jin, 2007) can be used to satisfy this need.

Similar to the original subset-based approach, the new approach picks a partition in a top down manner from the root of the tree. Given a partition S, for the set of keys associated with the partition S, it maintains a hypothesized model about the probabilities those keys are in the circumvention device. The hypothesized model is passed to the subset tracing procedure to identify which key is contained in the pirate device. When a suspect subset is identified and split into smaller subsets further down in the tree, the key associated with the suspect subset is removed from the MKB and replaced with one or more keys associated with the smaller subsets. The hypothesized model also gets updated with the keys added into the new forensic MKB.

The new approach also maintains a pirate device model, which models the behavior of the circumvention device in response to forensic MKB tests. This model can be based on prior knowledge or assuming the best strategy for attackers. It is conjectured that the best pirate decoder strategy is to decode the forensic MKB with one of its device keys chosen uniformly at random. If the key chosen is enabled then the decoder successfully plays the test; if it is disabled then it does not play.

When it receives the response from the pirate decoder after feeding a forensic MKB built on partition S, the algorithm updates the hypothesized model based on the response result and the pirate device model. Simply put, the update can be based on Bayes' theorem. When the guilty probability for a particular key in the hypothesized model is above some threshold, that key and its associated subset is identified. Moreover, one can quantify how informative a potential forensic MKB is, which can then be used to guide the tracing process. The algorithm always chooses the most informative forensic MKB as the next test.

The new approach is orders of magnitude more efficient than the original tracing scheme in Naor et al. (2001). It leverages the pirate device model as well as the clone's response to forensic MKBs to infer an explicit model of which keys have been compromised. It does not perform a simple significant test. Instead, it makes use of information gain and always chooses a forensic MKB that can give the most information to increase the belief on the guiltiness of the keys associated with the partition S. Moreover, since the new approach explicitly maintains the belief on guiltiness of each key, it essentially keeps the history. Overall, adaptively choosing the best forensic MKB at each step and continuously updating our beliefs about which keys are compromised allow one to substantially reduce the number of forensic MKBs needed to identify traitors. Readers refer to Zigoris and Jin (2007) for more details.

TRAITOR TRACING FOR ANONYMOUS ATTACK

As mentioned earlier, in an anonymous attack, attackers simply rebroadcast the per-movie encrypting keys or the content itself. They do this to avoid being caught, because typically the content encrypting key (media key) and the content are the same for every user. In a traitor tracing scheme for anonymous attack, different users must effectively playback content differently.

Unfortunately, it is oftentimes impossible to send a different version of the content to each user, because in this case the bandwidth usage is extremely poor. Hollywood only allows us to devote at most 10% of the extra disc space or bandwidth for forensics. Furthermore, for massively distributing physical DVDs, it only makes economical sense to prepare the content only once and distribute a copy as needed. In other words, each user should receive the same content (broadcasted or the physical media) but still play back the content differently to enable one to trace the pirates.

In the traitor tracing model for anonymous attack, one assumes that each piece of content (for example, a movie) is divided into multiple segments, among which n segments are chosen to have different variations. Each of these n segments has q possible variations. How to build variations are format specific. For example, there can be different ways to create the variations with HD-DVD and Blue-Ray discs. It is possible to use watermarks, different camera angles, or different play lists. It is outside of the scope of this chapter to discuss the approaches to create variations. Traitor tracing is a cryptographic technology that builds on top of these approaches. More importantly to traitor tracing, these variations must be differently encrypted.

Each device is assigned a unique set of tracing keys that enables it to decrypt exactly one variation at each point of the content during playback time. If the plain content or the actual variation encrypting keys get pirated and redistributed, a traitor tracing scheme can identify the original users who participated in the construction of the pirated copy of the content or content encrypting keys. The design of a traitor tracing scheme for anonymous attack is about how to assign the secret tracing keys to devices to enable tracing after piracy.

Pirate Model

There are two well-known models for how a pirated copy (be it the content or the key) can be generated:

- Given two variants v_1 and v_2 of a segment, the pirate can only use v_1 or v_2, not any other valid variant v_i.
- Given two variants v_1 and v_2 of a movie segment ($v_1 \neq v_2$), the pirate can generate any valid variant v_i out of v_1 and v_2.

In digital fingerprinting, there are similar pirate models. The first model is called narrow-case fingerprinting problem. The second model is called general or wide-case fingerprinting problem. As pointed out in Boneh and Shaw (1998), both models can be expanded by allowing generating something that is unreadable, or erased.

Schemes presented in Chor, Fiat, and Naor (1994); Chor, Fiat, Naor, and Pinkas (2000); Hollmann, Van Lint, Linnartz, and Tolhuizen (1998); Cohnen, Encheva, Litsyn, and Schaathun (2003) all used the first model. In Hollmann et al., it was also proved that for two colluders and $q \leq 3$, there exist codes that can provide exact identification of at least one traitor with exponentially many code words. In binary case, exact identification of even one traitor is generally impossible. So most of the works in this area (Barg, Blakely, & Kabatiansky, 2003; Tardos, 2003) allow some small error rate, in other words, they are probabilistic fingerprint codes.

Traitor tracing for anonymous attack is a similar area as fingerprinting but expands to cryptographic keys. Some cryptographic literature views traitor tracing as a fingerprinting problem on cryptographic keys. It is true that traitor tracing schemes also deal with pirated content, redistributing the plain content requires a lot of extra bandwidth.

It is oftentimes more convenient/economical to redistribute the content encrypting keys rather than the content itself. For example, it is more likely for the attackers to set up a server and sell pirated encrypting keys on demand. As one can imagine, when given two randomly chosen cryptographic keys, it is nearly impossible to come up with another valid cryptographic key. So, from the traitor tracing point of view, the so-called marking assumption is often made by traitor tracing schemes in the literature. It says it is hard to erase the mark, or come up with another valid mark. It is certainly true when we deal with cryptographic keys. Furthermore, as mentioned earlier, creating variation is format specific. Different approaches, with or without watermarking, can be used to create variations. Traitor tracing technology works on top of pirate models accepted by its applications. In our case, Hollywood accepts the first model. It is outside the scope of this chapter to discuss in depth why Hollywood accepts the first model.

Practicality Concerns

In this section, we will talk about the practical concerns we get from Hollywood to defend against anonymous attack in the real world, for example, to protect digital movies massively distributed in DVDs.

Of course, traceability is the basic functionality that a traitor tracing system offers. In turn, this has been the focus of most researches in literature. As one can imagine, traitors may collude. For anonymous attack, the traceability is measured by the number of pirated copies of content/keys needed to recover in order to identify traitors when there are T traitors in a coalition. In order to provide traceability, a traitor tracing scheme consists of two basic steps:

- **Assignment step:** Assign a version of the content to the device by assigning the playback path, that is, which variation to play for each augmented segment in the content.

- **Traitor/coalition detection step:** Based on the recovered pirated content/keys, trace back to the traitors.

The real world puts some restrictions on the design of a traitor tracing system.

The previous paragraphs already discussed one initial concern. It is not feasible to create and distribute a different version of the content and encrypt it differently for each different user. It has to prepare the content once and distribute a copy as needed.

A feasible model is to choose n segments from the content and create q variations for each segment. The variations are differently marked and encrypted. Each playing device receives the same disc with all the small variations at chosen segments in the content. However, each device plays back the movie through a different path, which effectively creates a different movie version.

As one can imagine, the variations takes extra space on the disc. A practical traitor tracing scheme on a prerecorded optical movie disc should take no more than 10% of the space on the disc to store the variations. For a normal 2-hour movie, it corresponds to 8 additional minutes (480 seconds) of video. This puts practical restriction on the number of variations one can put into a movie. The market for such discs is huge, involving literally a billion playing devices or more. This means a tracing scheme needs to be able to accommodate large numbers of devices. Of course, the traitor tracing system should provide reasonable traceability.

Unfortunately these requirements are inherently conflicting. Let us show some intuition on the conflicts between these parameters. Take a look at a code $[n,k,d]$, where n is the length of the code words, k is the source symbol size and d is the Hamming distance of the code, namely, the minimum number of symbols by which any two code words differ; q is the number of variations. There are mathematical connections between these parameters. For example, for a $[n,k,d]$ code, the number of code words is q^k; and Hamming distance satisfies the property that $d \leq n-k+1$. Furthermore, for a maximal difference separable (MDS) code, it satisfies $n \leq q$. For a traitor tracing system, the overhead, the number of users accommodated and the traceability depend on the choices of these parameters. The number of variations q decides the extra bandwidth needed for distributing the content.

The bigger q, the more overhead it incurs. So a practical system would prefer a small q. The Hamming distance d decides its traceability. The larger d means better traceability.

So we want a large d, in other words, a small k. Unfortunately, to accommodate a large number of devices, for example billions, either q or k or both have to be relatively big. The conflict between the parameters makes it inherently difficult to design a practical system to defend against collusion attack.

In summary, the reality puts the following practical requirements on the assignment and detection steps in a traitor tracing system when providing traceability:

- **Overhead:** The number of variations q for each movie cannot be big
- **Number of users:** The number of devices/ users must be big
- **Efficiency:** The number of movies necessary to detect a coalition of should be as small as possible

The first two requirements are on the assignment step, while the third requirement is on the actual coalition detection step. Furthermore, these requirements have to be satisfied in that order. When we started this work, there was not a solution satisfying all these requirements.

In addition to the previous requirements on a basic traitor tracing system, the real world has to take into consideration problems that arise throughout the lifetime of a system, as a result, in addition to basic traceability, it also demands the following two capabilities:

- **Revocation:** When traitors are identified, they can be excluded from access to future content.
- **Continuous traceability:** after revocation, the system can identify remaining or new traitors.

Indeed, the real world needs a trace-revoke-trace system to be actually useful. While there exists trace and revoke systems for pirate decoder attack, there does not exist a trace-revoke system

for anonymous attack. Moreover, the continuous traceability problem was overlooked.

What is Missing From Existing Approaches

Existing approaches on traitor tracing for anonymous attack used the same model as described previously. Each piece of content is divided into multiple segments and some segments are chosen to have multiple variations. They made the same marking assumptions as the first pirate model presented earlier. However existing approaches (Fiat & Tassa, 1999; Safavi-Naini, & Wang, 2003; Trung & Martirosyan, 2004) missed the following main points to be practically useful for Hollywood:

- Overhead is too big, much more than 10% of the extra space/bandwidth acceptable by Hollywood,
- Cannot accommodate large number of users, for example, a billion,
- Traceability is not good enough: take too many movies to trace traitors,
- Does not provide renewability to the traitor tracing system, and
- Does not consider/provide continuous traceability after revocation.

TRAITOR TRACING FOR ANONYMOUS ATTACK FOR AACS STANDARD

In following sections, we will provide our designs to address each of the requirements from Hollywood mentioned previously. Our system has been adopted by the content protection standard AACS for the next generation high definition optical discs and become the state of practice.

The *Key Assignment* section and the *Coalition Tracing* section consist of the first part of a trace-revoke-trace system, which is the basis of a traitor tracing system. The *Revoke After Tracing* section will show how to revoke compromised tracing keys after traitors are identified. The *Trace Again After Revocation* section will show how to continue tracing after revocation. Each of these sections shows our new solution to satisfy the practical requirements from Hollywood.

As mentioned earlier, a basic traitor tracing system consists of the assignment step and the actual detection step. The assignment step needs to satisfy the **overhead** and the **number of user** requirements; the detection step has to satisfy the **efficiency** requirement. It is very important to notice that much of the literature on traceability codes has taken the approach of fixing the number of colluders and the number of recovered movies and trying to find codes to support an optimal number of devices/users for a given number of variations of each movie. For example, the code shown in Trung and Martirosyan (2004) either has too few code words (accommodates a small number of devices) or the number of variations is too large (requires too much space on the disc). In reality, a traitor tracing scheme must first meet the two requirements on the overhead and the number of users, then its goal is to achieve high efficiency by minimizing the number of recovered pirated content/keys to detect a number of colluding traitors.

Key Assignment

Assume that each segment has q variations and that there are n segments. In our design, we use systematic assignment based on error correcting codes like Reed-Solomon code. This type of systematic assignment can guarantee some minimum number of differences between any two users' playback paths. As one can imagine, this difference is essential for tracing especially in the case that attackers collude to create the pirate copy.

In order to yield a practical scheme to meet the requirements on overhead and number of

users, we concatenate codes. For each movie, there is an *inner code* used to assign the different variations at the chosen points of the movie; it effectively creates different movie versions. For example, one can use a Reed-Solomon code for the inner code.

Suppose there are 16 variations created at each of the 15 points in the movie. Even though it can theoretically create 16^{15} number of versions, a Reed-Solomon code will create only $16^2 = 256$ code words (thus movie versions) but any two versions will differ at at least 14 points. Once the inner code creates the multiple movie versions (e.g., 256), over a sequence of movies, there is an *outer code* used to assign movie versions to different players. For example, each player is assigned one of the 256 versions for each movie in a sequence of 255 movies. A Reed-Solomon code can create 256^4 code words (thus players) with any two players differ at at least 252 movies. By concatenating the two levels of codes, the scheme managed to avoid having a big number of variations at any chosen point but can still accommodate the billions of devices. Suppose each segment is a 2-second clip, the extra video needed in this example is 450 seconds, within the 10% practical constraint. In fact, there is not a single level MDS code that can satisfy all the practical requirements. The two-level concatenated code is essential to meet the practical requirements.

During playback time, each device needs to decrypt exactly one variation for each segment. Using the previous parameters, a device needs to know 255 * 15 variation encrypting keys. If each key is 8 bytes, the storage requirement is 30.6KB. Needing to store 30.6KB securely is not easy. Furthermore, the set of keys are different for each device. It becomes a significant concern for the device manufacturers. In order to reduce the number of keys that need to be burned into the devices during manufacturing time, we used a level of indirection. For example, each device only stores 255 movie version keys corresponding to the 255 movies in the sequence. The assignment is based on the outer code. For each movie, the device can use its movie version key to unlock a table on the DVD disc that contains the actual variation encrypting keys for that movie. In other words, the variation encrypting keys that are assigned using the inner code are embedded on the DVD disc. These movie version keys that are assigned using outer side are burned into the devices during manufacture time. Those outer code keys are called *sequence keys* in AACS. So the space requirement now is only one-fifteenth of what was needed before. This not only reduces the space requirement, it also provides flexibility on the scheme during deployment. Only the outer code needs to be fixed and the sequence keys be assigned when the devices are manufactured. The inner code can be delayed at the content distribution time. The actual variant encrypting keys, contained in the 256 tables for the inner code, and even the inner code scheme itself, can all be flexible and varies movie by movie. The necessity of an inner code is also a movie-by-movie decision. For example, some unpopular movies may not need to be protected from piracy. Therefore no variations need to be created for the movie content. The table on the disc contains the same encrypting keys for every device.

The sequence keys for AACS are assigned from a large matrix. Each column corresponds to a movie. The number of columns corresponds to the number of movies considered in the sequence. The rows for each column correspond to multiple versions of the sequence keys for that movie. For example, if the variations for movie segments create 256 versions for each movie and we consider 255 movies in a sequence, then the matrix is 255 by 256. Each device is assigned a set of 255 keys, exactly one key from each column, corresponding to the 255 movies in the sequence. The key for each column has 256 versions. Many players will receive any given sequence key, but no two players will receive exactly the same set of 255 keys. Again, these sequence keys are placed in the players at manufacturing time. Figure 1 is an example of the matrix organization of the keys.

Coalition Tracing

Now that the assignment is done with the parameters satisfying the overhead and number of user requirements, keys are assigned and stored in each device. Content is augmented with different variations and distributed. Based on the pirate model we mentioned in the *Pirate Model* section, the attackers can collude and construct the pirate

Figure 1. Key assignment from a matrix

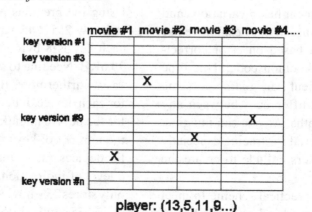

copy of the content/key based on the available versions to them. They can use whatever strategy to choose which version to use in the pirate copy. The strategy can be done at either the outer code level (movie-by-movie attack) or inner code level (mix-match attack) within the movie. When the license agency recovers pirated movies/keys, it tries to match the recovered movies/keys with the versions assigned to the devices to detect traitors. The coalition detection step is mainly concerned with the efficiency of tracing, measured by the number of recovered movies needed in order to detect traitors involved in a coalition.

In literature, this step always uses a straight forward, highest-score approach, where each player is scored based on the number of matchings between the recovered pirate movies and the versions assigned to the player, hoping the highest scored player is the guilty traitor. Furthermore, in the literature a traitor tracing scheme has been defined as a way to detect at least a traitor in the system when forensic evidence is recovered.

Therefore the goal of the traitor detection step, as well as the design of a traitor tracing scheme, is to identify a traitor. It is assumed that the identified traitor can be disconnected from the system and the tracing continues after that. Of course the ultimate security goal is to detect all traitors in the coalition. We believe using the one-by-one detection algorithm for anonymous attack is inefficient. Indeed, the efficiency of the detection of all traitors in the coalition was a bottleneck when bringing a traitor tracing scheme into practice.

The second motivation for a new coalition detection algorithm has to do with the fact that existing schemes assume a maximum number on the coalition size and hope to deterministically find a traitor when the coalition size is smaller than that maximum number. A t-traceability code enables one to decode to the nearest neighbor of a pirate code when the coalition size is at most t traitors and the nearest neighbor is deterministically a traitor.

Lemma 5.1. (Chor et al., 2000). Assume that a code C with length n and distance d is used to assign the symbols for variations to each user and that there are t traitors. If code C satisfies

$$d > (1 - 1/t^2) n \qquad (1)$$

then C is an t-traceability-code.

Based on the previous formula for traceability code, if using the parameters of choice for AACS, a simple Reed-Solomon assignment for both inner and outer code will allow one to deterministically identify a traitor after recovering 256 movies, if the coalition contains no more than nine traitors.

Unfortunately in reality the coalition size is usually unknown.

As pointed out in Jin, Lotspiech, and Nusser (2004), the tracing will have to be probabilistic. Indeed, the real world question is how to accurately detect traitors without knowing the coalition size and with what probabilities. Jin et al., 2006 showed the first traitor/coalition detection algorithm that tried to detect multiple traitors in the coalition together and also deduce the coalition size during tracing.

We believe it is easier to detect the multiple or entire coalition than detecting a single guilty individual one by one. It may seem counter-intuitive. After all, the number of coalitions is exponential compared to the number of individuals. For example, if there are a billion participants in the world, there are roughly 500 million billion pairs of participants. However, it is much easier to eliminate innocent coalitions than innocent individuals; because it is much less likely that coalitions appear by random chance than that the individual players randomly have a high score. An example can informally illustrate the underlying idea. Suppose there are four people involved in a colluding attack, and we have a random sequence of 20 recovered movies. Each movie originally has 256 variations of which a given player only plays one. The attackers wish to see that high scoring device can happen by chance. If the four attackers are using round robin, each guilty player will evenly score 5. Can we incriminate any player that share five movies with the recovered sequence? No, there will be about 15 completely innocent players scoring 5 or greater due to chance alone. What can you do then? You have to recover more movies before you can incriminate any player.

However, the previous four guilty players together can explain all the movies in the sequence. What is the chance that a coalition of size 4 might have all the variations in the sequence? The answer is roughly 0.04. In other words, while there are plenty of players that can explain five movies, it is unlikely that any four of them can *cover* all 20 movies. If we find four players that do cover the sequence, it is unlikely that this could have happened by chance. It is more likely that some devices in the coalition are indeed guilty.

The attackers could choose to use some player heavily and other players very lightly.

For this scapegoat strategy, the traditional approach can correctly identify him/her, but it is hard to find the lightly used player and the true coalition size. Our new tracing algorithm can nonetheless find the other members in the coalitions and find out the coalition size.

How did we get the previous answer 0.04? If there are N players, and a sequence of m movies are selected, each movie having one random variation out of q, the expected number of coalitions of size T are:

$$\binom{N}{T} * (1-(1-1/q)^T)^m \qquad (2)$$

If the expected number of coalitions is less than 1, this formula also gives an upper bound on the probability that a random sequence of m movie variations is covered by a coalition of size T.

If T is noticeably less than q, a simplification of this is a close upper bound:

$$\binom{N}{T} * (T/q)^m \qquad (3)$$

The problem of finding a coalition of players that covers a sequence of movies is equivalent to a well-known problem in computer science called *set cover*. It is NP hard. But in reality the calculation time is still reasonable, for the parameters that AACS is concerned with.

Once we have found a coalition using a set-cover algorithm, we cannot incriminate everybody in the coalition, so who in the coalition should we incriminate? What is the chance that some of the players in the purported coalition of size T might be actually innocent, being victimized by a scapegoat strategy that is hiding a few lightly used guilty players? This requires a filtering algorithm. For example, it can perform the following steps.

For each combination of T players:

- Temporarily assume that the players in the particular combination are guilty,
- If the number of players in this combination is c, subtract c from T,
- Temporarily subtract from the list of movies all the movies that can be explained by this combination of players, and
- Use formula 2 using the new number of movies m and T, to evaluate the probability that the remaining players are completely innocent. If the formula yields a number greater than 1, assume the probability is 1.

Our tracing algorithm assumes that the size of the coalition is unknown and proceeds to calculate both the size of the coalition as well as the actual players involved. If the size of the coalition is known from other sources, the answers may be exact; otherwise, the answer is always probabilistic. As we mentioned earlier, formula 2 gives one the false positive probability. We can make this probability arbitrarily small by just collecting more movies. From formula 2, one can calculate the number of recovered movies it takes to detect traitors in order to achieve a certain desired false positive rate.

When this procedure has ended, the license agency will only incriminate the players that seem guilty under all combinations. See Jin et al., 2006 for more details.

Figure 2 shows this relationship when the number of device is one billion. Interestingly, it takes almost the same number of movies (roughly $6T$) to achieve a super high confidence (below 0.0001%) as it does to achieve a moderately high confidence (below 0.1%) With the new tracing algorithm, our rule of thumb is it takes six recovered movies (or *effective movies* if the attack is mix-and-match) for each traitor in the coalition.

Revoke After Tracing

A traitor tracing scheme is defined to be finding at least a traitor even though there may exist a coalition. Indeed, all traitor tracing schemes (Fiat & Tassa, 1999; Jin et al., 2004; Safavi-Naini & Wang, 2003; Trung & Martirosyan, 2004) for anonymous attack stop when they detect a traitor. They assume this traitor can be disconnected in some way. In reality, how does one disconnect a traitor technically? It is by rendering the compromised keys no longer usable for future content. In other words, a traitor tracing system must also be able to revoke compromised keys to be actually useful in the real world.

Since many devices might share a single compromised key, revocation of a single key is impossible. However, we can revoke a unique set of keys owned by a traitor. Since no two devices have many keys in common, so even if the system has been heavily attacked, all innocent devices will have many columns in which they have uncompromised keys. Similar to using MKB to revoke device keys, we have designed a structure to revoke the keys assigned in our traitor tracing system. For AACS, that structure is called sequence key block (SKB) to revoke sequence keys.

The purpose of the SKB is to give all innocent devices a column they can use to calculate a correct answer, while at the same time preventing compromised devices (who have compromised keys in all columns) from getting to a correct answer. In MKB, a different device each using its device keys to process MKB differently but obtains the same valid key (media key). In an SKB there are actually many valid keys, one for each variation in the content.

As shown in Figure 3, the SKB begins with a first column, called the *unconditional* column. By *column*, we mean a column of sequence keys in the matrix will be indirectly used to encrypt the content. The first column will have an encryption of an output key (denoted 'K_1, K_2, ...' in the figure)

Figure 2. Traceability graph for q=256 with difference false positive rate

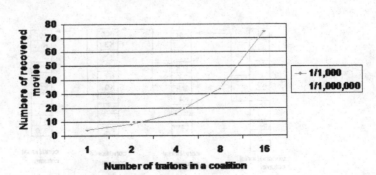

in every uncompromised sequence key's cell. Devices that do not have compromised keys in that column immediately decrypt a valid output key. Devices, both innocent and otherwise, that do have compromised keys instead decrypt a key called a link key that allows them to process a further column in the SKB. To process the further column they need both the link key and their sequence key in that column. Thus the subsequent columns are called *conditional* columns because they can only be processed by the device if it were given the necessary link key in a previous column.

The subsequent additional conditional columns are produced the same way as the first column: They will have an encryption of an output key in every uncompromised sequence key's cell. Devices with a compromised key will get a further link key to another column instead of the output key. However, after some number of columns depending on the actual number of compromised keys, the AACS licensing agency will know that only compromised devices would be getting the link key; all innocent devices would have found an output key in this column or in a previous column. At this point, rather than encrypting a link key, the agency encrypts a 0, and the SKB is complete. All innocent devices will have decrypted the output key, and all compromised devices have ended up decrypting 0.

Trace Again After Revocation

The previous solution provides a key management scheme that not only can trace traitors but also can revoke compromised keys. A real world traitor tracing system must be able to trace again after revocation. The challenge here is to make sure the newly released SKB can continue to provide tracing information to the license agency to enable continued tracing. Unfortunately that turns out to be non-trivial.

In Figure 3, each column in an SKB contains an encryption of an output key in every uncompromised sequence key's cell. The output key has multiple valid versions, each corresponds to one variation. For any content that goes to a disc, it comes with a selected set of variations. Notice the same set of valid variations (thus output keys) is encrypted in each column, although they are distributed differently in different columns. For a particular valid variation, it can be obtained from any column in the SKB. An uncompromised device will process SKB and obtain a correct key from the first column in SKB that it has a non-revoked key. However, when attackers collude and the system still has undetected attackers at large, the attacker can mix-and-match their revoked keys and non-revoked keys when processing SKB. In turn they have multiple ways to process SKB and

Figure 3. Sample SKB with one unconditional and multiple conditional columns

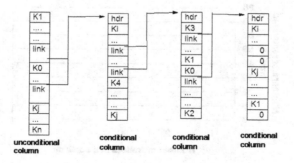

get a valid key to play back the content. They can choose in which column they want to use a non-revoked key to get a valid key.

When the licensing agency observes a pirate copy variation, since it can be obtained from any column, the licensing agency has no way to know which sequence key has been used in obtaining that valid variation. The entire path that the undetected traitors go through to process SKB can even look like one from an innocent device or from a path that was never assigned to any device, thus untraceable.

To force the undetected traitors to reveal the sequence keys they use when processing SKB, we must make sure each column gets different variations so that when recovering a key/variation, the scheme knows from which column it comes from. Only with that, the tracing scheme can continue tracing. Unfortunately that means the q variations have to be distributed among the columns contained in the SKB. Each column only effectively gets q/c variations where c is the number of columns in the SKB. It is clear that traceability degrades when the effective q decreases. When the number of columns c becomes big enough, the traceability degrades to so low that it basically becomes untraceable. The scheme is overwhelmed and broken in that case. As a result, that puts a limit on the revocation capability of the scheme.

An Improved Solution

In order to improve the previous scheme and lift the limit on revocation capability, we have designed a two-phase defense. In order to use this defense, the scheme assigns the sequence keys as shown in Figure 4 instead of Figure 1.

Basically we used a new concept called *slot*. Now the rows in the key matrix are grouped into clusters. A slot is defined to be an assignment of row clusters, one cluster for each column. At any given column, two slots are either identical or completely disjoint. Slots can be assigned to

individual manufacturers/models and the keys within the clusters are assigned to the devices made by the manufacturer/model. In effect, the outer code that is used to assign sequence keys to devices is now itself a two-level code.

The first level codes assign clusters to the manufacturer/models X and Y and the second level codes assign keys to players A, B within model X, and players C, D within model Y.

Model X gets the slot $(1,3,2,4...)$, which means it is assigned cluster #1 for movie #1, cluster #3 for movie #2, and so forth. Note that the second level code is the assignment inside the cluster. For example, player A gets $(3,1,3,3...)$ within the clusters assigned to model X, which makes its actual key assignment be $(3,9,7,15...)$ from the key matrix.

For example, we divide all the rows in each column to have 64 clusters. Using Reed-Solomon code, $q = 64$, it takes $k = 2$ to accommodate 64^2 slots. Suppose we have 4,096 keys in each column, there will be 64 keys in each cluster. Again using Reed-Solomon code, $q = 64$, it takes $k = 3$ to accommodate 64^3 devices within each slot.

The assignment can totally accommodate 64^5 devices. Each slot can be assigned to one manufacturer/model. A big manufacturer would, of course, overflow a single slot. He/she would just have more than one slot.

In the two-phase defense, when pirated movies/keys are found, the first SKBs would determine the slot used in the attack (or slots, but that is unlikely). Since the slot is assigned from the first level by using Reed-Solomon code $q = 64$, $k = 2$, there are only 64 variations needed per column in this case. Recall the inner code generates totally 256 variations for each movie. One can use four columns in the SKB and there is no problem with dividing the 256 variations across four columns. Each column would get 64 variations, which is all we need per column. By Reed-Solomon code's property, it takes only two ($k = 2$) movies to uniquely detect the slot.

Figure 4. New way for key assignment

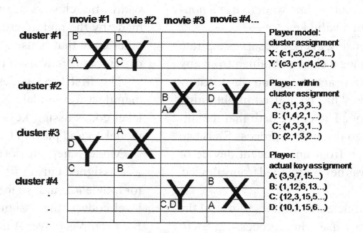

Once the licensing agency detects the slot, it can produce new SKBs that are only trying to detect the device within the slot. In the SKB, all other slots in the column(s) would go to a single variation that we would expect would never be recovered. We would use all the remaining variations within the single slot. We can get up to four columns and still have unique keys for each variation.

By using the two-phase defense, we reduce the population considered in each phase. The problem described previously is either completely eliminated or alleviated. However, it still puts a limit on how many devices the scheme can revoke before it is overwhelmed.

Revocation Capability and Traceability

More formally, the revocation capability is calculated by the following formula. Suppose the number of rows in the matrix is m; p is the acceptable maximum probability for an innocent device to be revoked when revoking the actual guilty devices; r is the number of guilty devices to be revoked in SKB; c is the number of columns in SKB.

The system still survives when the following holds:

$$(1-(1-1/m)^r)^c < p \qquad (4)$$

This formula can be used to determine how many columns c needed in a SKB when the licensing agency wants to revoke r devices.

We have performed preliminary simulation on how many columns the scheme needs in its SKB in terms of the number of devices that needs to be revoked. It confirms formula 4. We have also simulated the impact of deceased q on traceability. The traceability result is shown in the graph shown in Figure 5. It includes both the two-phase solution and the basic single-phase scheme. There is different traceability in the life of the system depending on how many devices are currently being revoked in the SKB. The more devices revoked the more columns it needs in SKB, the smaller the effective q is, the worse traceability. More details refer to Jin & Lotspiech, 2007.

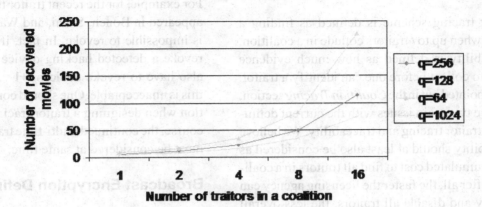

Figure 5. Traceability with different q with 1/1000000 false positive rate

CONCLUDING REMARKS

In this chapter, we have presented traitor tracing technologies for multimedia forensics. In particular, we are concerned with business scenarios that involve one-way digital content distribution, and the receiving user set is huge. In this type of scenario, usually hybrid encryption is used where the secret device keys encrypt a randomly chosen media key and put in the header, (called MKB); and the media key encrypts the actual content and puts it in the body. If a device is circumvented, its device keys can be revoked in the updated MKB in the newly released content.

Broadcast encryption system using MKB fits well in this type of scenario to distribute the content to a group of privileged users and exclude a set of revoking users. In this chapter we have shown different types of pirate attack. One type of piracy is for attackers to reverse engineer the device, extract secret keys from the device, and build a clone pirate decoder for profit. Another type of piracy is to pirate the content or the content encrypting key in order to stay anonymous. When forensic evidence like the pirate decoder or the pirated content/keys are found, traitor tracing technologies can identify the actual users

(traitors) who have involved in constructing the pirated decoder or content/key.

For both attacks, we have shown the insufficiency of existing systems from a practical point of view. We have presented our new approaches that become the new state of the art and practice for both types of attack. Our work not only provides better or more efficient approaches over existing approaches, we also addressed some of the overlooked issues in research communities so far. Here are the potential new research directions in this space.

FUTURE RESEARCH DIRECTIONS

From our own experience working on designing practical traitor tracing systems to defend against different pirate attacks for content protection, we learned some lessons and took a closer look at both broadcast encryption and traitor tracing. We believe academia research has overlooked some issues that we find actually very important. We highlight some of them hereafter as future directions on traitor tracing and broadcast encryption.

Traitor Tracing Definition

Traitor tracing scheme is defined as finding a traitor when up to t traitors collude in a coalition. Traceability is defined as how much evidence needs to collect before one can identify a traitor. As we pointed out in the *Coalition Tracing* section, we have two main issues with the current definition of traitor tracing and traceability. We believe traceability should at least also be considered as the accumulated cost to find all traitors in a coalition. After all, the faster the licensing agency can identify and disable all traitors, the less overall damage due to piracy. Second, the current tracing should not simply assume a maximum size of the coalition; it is much more desirable for a tracing scheme to be able to trace traitors as well as deducing coalition size.

Traitor Tracing Must be Combined with Revocation and Provide Continued Tracing

Again, traitor tracing scheme is defined as finding a traitor when up to t traitors collude in a coalition. They assume the traitor can be disabled in some way, and the same tracing can simply be repeated for the next traitor. As we see from the *Revoke After Tracing* section, it is not always easy to achieve the same traceability after revocation. This continued traceability issue was largely overlooked in literature. Trace-and-revoke systems are considered as optional. We believe this is due to the fact that academia research so far have considered traitor tracing and broadcast encryption as two separate and orthogonal problems. Revocation is inherently provided in broadcast encryption systems. A traitor tracing system does not have to provide revocation capability. But in reality, a traitor tracing system without revocation capability is practically useless. Because the current separation of considerations of broadcast encryption and traitor tracing in the state of the art, for some existing schemes, it is impossible to add revocation capability on top of tracing. For example, for the recent traitor tracing system appeared in Boneh, Sahai, and Waters (2006), it is impossible to revoke. In fact, if one needs to revoke a detected hacking device i, one would also have to revoke devices $i+1$ ...N. Of course this is unacceptable. One should consider revocation when designing a traitor tracing system. Of course, the continued multi-time tracing problem must be considered at same time.

Broadcast Encryption Definition

We also took a closer look at the security and soundness of a broadcast encryption system. Again, state-of-the-art researches have considered traitor tracing and broadcast encryption as two separate and orthogonal problems. Revocation is inherently provided in a broadcast encryption system; and traceability is provided by a traitor tracing system. Trace-and-revoke is optional. But we find a broadcast encryption system without traceability can be insecure and broken from practical point of view. As an example, for the broadcast encryption system recently presented in Boneh, Gentry, and Waters (2005), it does not provide traceability. However, it can be proven (Weng, Liu, & Chen, 2007) that attackers can construct a forged key to decrypt the encrypted content, and the forged key is untraceable even if it is retrieved. It is fine if one can revoke all the keys in a coalition that constructed that pirate key, assuming it effectively revokes the forged key. Unfortunately in this example, it can be proven that any subset S' of entire user set S, and $|S'| >$ 2 users may have colluded to forge that private key. The broadcast encryption scheme has no way to revoke this forged key. It can become a global secret and the broadcast encryption scheme is therefore broken. This broadcast encryption scheme is not sound regardless of the fact that the authors have proven its security against current security definition.

An interesting new research direction is to revise broadcast encryption definition. Current definition is not sufficient.

Equality of Broadcast Encryption and Traitor Tracing

As we pointed out here, it is not secure to design a broadcast encryption system without traceability, and on the other hand, a traitor tracing system also must provide broadcast revocation capability. Can we prove these two are equivalent problems, at least maybe in some cases? Or should we merge the definitions of broadcast encryption and traitor tracing into one problem?

Unified Solution for Different Pirate Attacks

As we have shown, different approaches have been taken to defend against different pirate attacks. Traitor tracing for pirate decoder attempts to identify the device keys; Traitor tracing for anonymous attacks attempts to identify the other set of keys (sequence keys). To build a content protection system to defend against different attacks, different sets of keys and different systems need to be deployed. This not only incurs more storage cost on the device, deploying different systems also incurs more management cost of the complicated system. Is it possible to make use of a same set of keys and build one unified system to defend against the different type of pirate attacks?

REFERENCES

Advanced Access Content System Licensing Administrator (AACS)-LA. (2006). *Sequence key block*. In *Pre-recorded video book*. Retrieved from, http://www.aacsla.com/specifications

Barg, A., Blakely, R., & Kabatiansky, G. (2003). Digital fingerprinting codes: Problem statements, constructions, identification of traitors. *IEEE Transactions on Information Theory, 49*(4), 852-865.

Boneh, D., Gentry, C., & Waters, B. (2005). Collusion resistant broadcast encryption with short ciphertexts and private keys. *Advance in Cryptography, Crypto* (LNCS 3621, pp. 258-275). Berlin, Heidelberg, New York: Springer-Verlag.

Boneh, D., Sahai, A., & Waters, B. (2006). Fully collusion resistant traitor tracing with short ciphertexts and private keys. *Advance in Cryptography, Eurocrypt* (LNCS, pp. 573-592). Berlin, Heidelberg, New York: Springer-Verlag.

Boneh, D., & Shaw, J. (1998). Collusion-secure fingerprinting for digital data. *IEEE Transactions on Information Theory, 44*(5), 1897-1905.

Chor, B., Fiat, A., & Naor, M. (1994). Tracing traitors. *Advance in Cryptography, Crypto* (LNCS 839, pp. 480-491). Berlin, Heidelberg, New York: Springer-Verlag.

Chor, B., Fiat, A., Naor, M., & Pinkas, B. (2000) Tracing traitors. *IEEE Transactions on Information Theory, 46*, 893-910.

Cohnen, G., Encheva, S., Litsyn, S., & Schaathun, H. G. (2003). Intersecting codes and separating codes. *Discrete Applied Mathematics, 128*(1), 75-83.

Cox, I., Killian, J., Leighton, T., & Shamoon, T. (1997). Secure spread spectrum watermarking for multimedia. *IEEE Transactions on Image Processing, 6*(12), 1673-1687.

Fiat, A., & Naor, M. (1993). Broadcast encryption. *Advance in Cryptography, Crypto* (LNCS 773, 480-491. Berlin, Heidelberg, New York: Springer-Verlag.

Fiat, A., & Tassa, T. (1999). Dynamic traitor tracing. *Advance in Cryptography, Crypto* (LNCS

1666, 354-371. Berlin, Heidelberg, New York: Springer-Verlag.

Hollmann, H. D., Van Lint, J. J., Linnartz, J. P., & Tolhuizen, L. M. (1998). On codes with the identifiable parent property. *Journal of Combinatorial Theory, series A, 82,* 121-133.

Jin, H., & Lotspiech, J. (2007). Renewable traitor tracing: a trace-revoke-trace system for anonymous attack. *European Symposium on Research on Computer Security* (pp. 563-577).

Jin, H., Lotspiech, J., & Nusser, S. (2004). Traitor tracing for prerecorded and recordable media. *ACM Digital Rights Management Workshop* (pp. 83-90). Washington DC: ACM Press.

Jin, H., Lotspiech, J. & Megiddo, N.(2006). *Efficient Traitor Tracing.* IBM research report, Computer Science, RJ10390.

Kiayias, A., & Yung, M. (2001). On crafty piates and foxy tracers. *ACM Digital Rights Management Workshop* (Vol. 2696, pp. 22-39). Washington DC: Springer-Verlag.

Naor, D., Naor, M., & Lotspiech, J. (2001). Revocation and tracing schemes for stateless receivers. *Advance in Cryptography, Crypto* (LNCS 2139, pp. 41-62). Berlin, Heidelberg, New York: Springer-Verlag.

Safavi-Naini, R., & Wang, Y. (2003). Sequential traitor tracing. *IEEE Transactions on Information Theory, 49*(5), 1319-1326.

Tardos, G. (2003, June 9-11). Optimal probabilistic fingerprint codes. In *Proceedings of the Theory of Computing* (pp. 116-125). San Diego, CA.

Trung, T., & Martirosyan, S. (2004). On a class of traceability codes. *Design, Code and Cryptography, 31,* 125-132.

Weng, J., Liu, S., & Chen, K. (2007). Pirate decoder for the broadcast encryption schemes. In *Series F: Information Science special issue on Information Security, 50*(3).

Zigoris, P., & Jin, H. (2007). Bayesian methods for practical traitor tracing. *Applied Cryptography and Network Security*(LNCS 4521, pp. 194-2006).

ADDITIONAL READINGS

Barg, A., Kabatiansky, G. (2004). A class of I.P.P. codes with efficient identification. *Journal of Complexity, 20*(2-3), 137-147.

Blakeley, R., & Kabatiansky, G. (2004). *Random coding technique for digital fingerprinting codes: Fighting two pirates revisited.* International Symposium on Information Theory, Chicago, IL.

Boneh, D., & Franklin, M. (1999). An efficient public key traitor tracing scheme. *Advance in Cryptography, Crypto* (LNCS 1666, pp. 338-353). Springer-Verlag.

Boneh, D., & Waters, B. (2006). A collusion resistant broadcast, trace and revoke system. *ACM conference on Communication and Computer Security* (pp. 211-220).

Chabanne, H., Phan, D. H., & Pointcheval, D. (2005). Public traceability in traitor tracing schemes. *Advance in Cryptography, Eurocrypt* (LNCS, pp. 542-558).

Gafni, E., Staddon, J., & Yin, L. (1999). Efficient methods for integrating traceability and broadcast encryption. *Advance in Cryptography, Crypto* (LNCS 1666, pp. 537-554).

Goodrich, M. T., Sun, J., & Tamassia, R. (2004). Efficient tree-based revocation in groups of low-state devices. *Advance in Cryptography, Crypto* (LNCS 3152, pp. 511-527).

Halevy, D., & Shamir, A. (2002). The LSD broadcast encryption scheme. *Advance in Cryptography, Crypto* (LNCS 2442, pp. 47-62).

Jin, H., & Blaum, M. (2007). Combinatorial properties of traceability codes using error correcting codes. *IEEE Transactions on Information Theory, 53*(2), 804-808.

Jin, H., & Lotspiech, J. (2005). Attacks and forensic analysis for multimedia content protection. *IEEE International Conference on Multimedia and Expo* (pp. 1392-1395).

Jin, H., & Lotspiech, J. (2006). Hybrid traitor tracing. *IEEE International Conference on Multimedia and Expo.*

Kurosawa, K., & Desmedt, Y. (1998). Optimum traitor tracing and asymmetric schemes. *Advance in Cryptography, EuroCrypt* (LNCS, pp. 145-157).

Lin, S., & Costello, D. J. (1983). *Error control coding: Fundamentals and applications.* Prentice Hall.

Naor, M., & Pinkas, B. (2000). Efficient trace and revoke schemes. *Financial Cryptography* (LNCS 1962, pp. 1-20). Spriner-Verlag.

Safavi-Naini, R., & Wang, Y. (2000). Sequential traitor tracing. *Advance in Cryptography, Crypto* (LNCS 1880, pp. 316-332). Berlin, Heidelberg, New York: Springer-Verlag.

Schaathun, H. G. (2003). Fighting two pirates, applied algebra, algebraic algorithms and error-correcting codes. *15th International Symposium, AAECC-15* (pp. 71 -78). Toulouse, France.

Staddon, J. N., Stinson, D. R., & Wei, R. (2001). Combinatorial properties of frameproof and traceability codes. *IEEE Transactions on Information Theory, 47,* 1042-1049.

Stinson, D. R., & Wei, R. (1998). Combinatorial properties and constructions of traceability schemes and frameproof codes. *SIAM Journal on Discrete Mathematics, 11,* 41-53.

Stinson, D. R., & Wei, R. (1998). Key preassigned traceability schemes for broadcast encryption. *ACM Symposium on Applied Computing* (LNCS 1556, pp. 144-156).

Trappe, W., Wu, M., Wang, Z., & Liu, R. (2003). Anti-collusion fingerprinting for multimedia. *IEEE Transactions on Signal Processing, 51,* 1069-1087.

Yacobi, Y. (2001). Improved Boneh-Shaw content fingerprinting. *RSA conference* (LNCS 2020, pp. 378-391). Berlin, Heidelberg: Springer-Verlag.

Zane, F. (2000). Efficient watermark detection and collusion security. *Financial Cryptography* (pp. 21-32).

Zeng, W., Yu, H., & Lin, C. (Eds.). (2006). *Multimedia security technologies for digital rights management.* Elsevier.

Chapter XVI
Efficient Transparent JPEG2000 Encryption

Dominik Engel
University of Salzburg, Austria

Thomas Stütz
University of Salzburg, Austria

Andreas Uhl
University of Salzburg, Austria

ABSTRACT

In this chapter we investigate two different techniques for transparent/perceptual encryption of JPEG2000 files or bitstreams in the context of digital rights management (DRM) schemes. These methods are efficient in the sense of minimizing the computational costs of encryption. A classical bitstream-based approach employing format-compliant encryption of packet body data is compared to a compression-integrated technique that uses the concept of secret transform domains, in our case a wavelet packet transform.

INTRODUCTION

Encryption schemes for multimedia data need to be specifically designed to protect multimedia content and fulfill the application requirements for a particular multimedia environment (Uhl & Pommer, 2005).

For example, real-time encryption of visual data using classical ciphers requires heavy com-putation due to the large amounts of data involved, but many multimedia applications require security on a much lower level (e.g., TV news broadcast-ing [Macq & Quisquater, 1995]). In this context, several selective or partial encryption schemes have been proposed recently which do not strive for maximum security, but trade off security for computational complexity by restricting the en-cryption to the perceptually most relevant parts of the data.

However, encryption may have an entirely different aim as opposed to pure confidentiality in the context of multimedia applications. Macq and Quisquater (1994, 1995) introduce the term *transparent encryption* mainly in the context of digital TV broadcasting: A broadcaster of pay TV does not always intend to prevent unauthorized viewers from receiving and watching his program, but rather intends to promote a contract with nonpaying watchers. This can be facilitated by providing a low quality version of the broadcasted program for everyone; only legitimate (paying) users get access to the full quality visual data. This is meant also by the term *try and buy* scenario. Therefore, privacy is not the primary concern in such an environment. The simplest approach to achieve this would be to simply distribute both versions, a low quality version to all potential viewers, and a high quality version only to paying viewers. However, this is mostly not desired due to the excessive demand of storage and bandwidth.

Transparent encryption usually transmits a high quality version of the visual data to all possible viewers but aims at protecting the details of the data which enable a pleasant viewing experience in an efficient manner. If these data are missing (i.e., are encrypted), the user is (hopefully) motivated to pay for the rest of the data which may be accessed upon transmission of the required key material by the broadcaster. Another application area of transparent encryption is preview images in image and video databases. Therefore, there are two major requirements that have to be met concurrently:

- To hide a specific amount of image information (security requirement)
- To show a specific amount of image information (quality requirement)

While the first requirement is a generalization of the confidentiality encryption approach—the condition of full encryption of all image infor-

mation is extended to a *specific amount*—the second requirement, namely to explicitly demand a certain image quality, is completely different from scenarios where confidentiality or privacy are the primary aims.

To implement transparent encryption, Macq and Quisquater (1995) propose using line permutations in the transform domain of a lossless multi-resolution transform. The permutations are only applied in the region of the transform domain corresponding to fine grained details of the data. Droogenbroeck and Benedett (2002) propose encrypting bitplanes of the binary representation of raw image data, in contrast to the privacy-focused approach they suggest to start with the LSB bitplane. With respect to JPEG encoded images, the authors suggest to encrypt sign and magnitude bits of medium and high frequency discrete cosine transform (DCT) coefficients (note that this is again exactly just the other way round as compared to encrypting low frequency coefficients only for privacy protection [Cheng & Li, 1996; Kunkelmann, 1998]). Droogenbroeck (2004) extends this latter idea to *multiple encryption* where different sets of DCT coefficients are encrypted by different content owners, and *over encryption*, where these sets do not have an empty intersection (i.e., coefficients are encrypted twice or even more often). Bodo, Laurent, & Dugelay (2003) propose a technique called *waterscrambling* where they embed a watermark into the motion vectors of an MPEG stream, thereby reducing the video quality significantly—only a legitimate user has access to the key and may descramble the motion vectors.

Transparent encryption may be implemented in the simplest way in the context of scalable or embedded bitstreams since parsing the file and searching for the data to be protected can be avoided to a large extent in this setting. Transparent encryption is achieved in this environment by simply encrypting the enhancement layer(s). This has been proposed by Kunkelmann and Horn using a scalable video codec based on a spatial resolution pyramid (Kunkelmann, 1998; Kunkelmann & Horn, 1998), by Dittmann and Steinmetz (1997a, 1997b) using an SNR scalable MPEG-2 encoder/decoder, and by Stütz and Uhl (2005) for the progressive JPEG variants (Fisch, Stögner, & Uhl, 2004). Yuan et al. (2003) propose using MPEG-4 FGS for transparent encryption, JPEG2000 transparent encryption is discussed in own earlier work (Uhl & Obermair, 2005).

In this chapter we systematically investigate JPEG2000 (Taubman & Marcellin, 2002) in the context of transparent encryption. In contrast to file formats like JPEG and MPEG, JPEG2000 is intrinsically scalable and can support progressiveness on a much finer granularity level than the other formats. The focus of this work is on efficient encryption schemes, that is, we aim at reducing the computational amount required for encryption to a minimum.

For JPEG2000 the concept of transparent encryption is often introduced as an application scenario for conditional access and access control. For example, in many publications (Apostolopoulos, Wee, Ebrahimi, Sun, & Zhang, 2006; Dufaux & Ebrahimi, 2003; Dufaux, Wee, Apostolopoulos, & Ebrahimi, 2004; Grosbois, Gerbelot, & Ebrahimi, 2001; Imaizumi, Watanabe, Fujiyoshi, & Kiya, 2005; Grangetto, Magli, & Olmo, 2006) it is proposed to employ conditional access to protect either the higher resolutions or higher quality layers of a JPEG2000 image. Lian, Sun, and Wang (2004) propose combining several known schemes, such as sign encryption of the wavelet coefficients, inter-block permutation and bitplane permutation. However, the quality requirement is not discussed in these contributions.

We have found that the necessity of meeting the security requirement in transparent encryption leads to the encryption of a large amount of data in case encryption proceeds from the end of the file to the beginning as done traditionally. However, since the last quality layers do not contribute much to the image quality, it may be more reasonable not to start encrypting at the end

of the data, but at a specific point in the bitstream according to the required image quality. This has been demonstrated in the context of progressive JPEG in previous work (Stütz & Uhl, 2006a).

We will show that the same functionality with respect to quality and security can be achieved by protecting data situated between base and enhancement layers while reducing the computational encryption effort significantly. The approach of applying encryption after compression on the compressed bitstream is called *bitstream-oriented encryption*.

An entirely different approach for providing transparent encryption is *compression-integrated encryption*. One possibility for compression-integrated encryption in JPEG2000 is to use key-dependent transform domains in the compression pipeline (as allowed in the standard part II) and to protect the key used for selecting the actual domain. We will discuss approaches based on wavelet packets (Engel & Uhl, 2006a, 2006b) where the amount of data required to be encrypted is limited to a few bytes only.

On the basis of experimental results, covering computational amount and image quality as well as security issues, we will discuss the suitability of the presented approaches for certain application scenarios.

BACKGROUND

JPEG2000

The discussed efficient transparent encryption schemes operate in the scope of the JPEG2000 standard. Its development started in 1997 with a call for contributions and the International Organization for Standardization (ISO) first published the new standard in December 2000. JPEG2000 has been designed to overcome some of the shortcomings of JPEG, such as no target bitrate specification, no lossless capability, loss of quality in case of recompression, and poor error resilience. Additionally to an improved compression efficiency (compared to JPEG) the main objective has been to create a new unified compression system that is suitable for many types of different images, for example, bi-level, grayscale (with different bit-depths), and multi-component images, and different source characteristics. The support of scalability has been a main objective as well. Furthermore region of interest coding (spatial regions of the image are coded with higher fidelity) has been an objective. Actually JPEG2000 can meet these requirements (at the cost of an increased computational complexity). It offers resolution and quality (SNR) scalability, region of interest coding, idempotent recompression, lossy and lossless compression, the support for single- to multi-component images with arbitrary bit-depth, a flexible bitstream, and an improved compression efficiency. Before each component is compressed independently, a component transform may be conducted, either reversibly (for lossless compression) or irreversibly (for lossy compression). Each component is compressed independently, its compressed data is multiplexed with the other components compressed data in the process of the final JPEG2000 bitstream generation (tier2 coding). Instead of discrete cosine transform (JPEG), JPEG2000 (Taubman & Marcellin, 2002) employs a wavelet

transform. The wavelet transform has several beneficial properties, such as energy compaction and multi-resolution capability. Furthermore it does not introduce blocking artifacts. Part I of the standard specifies a irreversible 9/7 and a reversible integer 5/3 wavelet transform and requires the application of classical pyramidal wavelet decomposition. The extensions of Part II allow employing custom wavelet transforms and different decomposition structures. After the wavelet transform the coefficients are quantized and encoded using the EBCOT scheme, which renders distortion scalability possible. The EBCOT scheme employs an arithmetic coder, namely the MQ-coder, to code the coefficients. Thereby the coefficients are grouped into codeblocks and these are encoded bitplane by bitplane, each with three coding passes (except the first bitplane). This process is also known as tier1 coding.

The coding passes may contribute to a certain quality layer. A packet body contains codeblock contribution to packet (CCPs) of codeblocks of a certain resolution, quality layer and precinct (a spatial inter-sub-band partitioning structure that contains one to several codeblocks), while the packet header contains the lengths of the CCPs, the number of leading zero bitplanes of a codeblock and several other information chunks that are necessary to decode the packet body

Figure 1. Restrictions within the CCPs

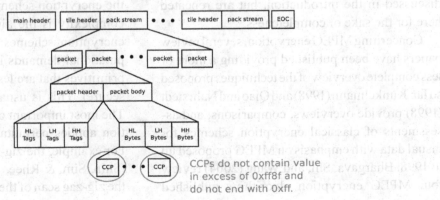

CCPs do not contain value in excess of 0xff8f and do not end with 0xff.

data correctly. The coding passes of a codeblock have to be assigned to a certain quality layer (rate distortion optimization is not standardized) and then the compressed data contributing to a specific quality layer of a several codeblocks (in the same precinct) are encoded in a packet. The coding of packets and the actual JPEG2000 bitstream formation (note the standard denotes the final JPEG2000 bitstream as codestream) are known as tier2 coding.

The JPEG2000 codestream consists of headers (main header, tile headers, tile part headers) and packets that consist of packet headers and packet bodies (cf. Figure 1). The compressed coefficient data is contained in the packet bodies. The packet header contains information about the CCPs of the codeblocks, for example, the number of coding passes and the CCP lengths. The packet header and the packet bodies must not contain any two byte sequence in excess of `0xff8f` nor end with a `0xff` byte (bitstream compliance).

Media Encryption

In this section we give a systematic overview of the different kinds of encryption schemes that exist in the area of media encryption and provide corresponding examples from the area of MPEG encryption. As the field is rather young, the nomenclature is not yet fully consistent. We will mention if different terms are used in parallel or if a term is used with different meanings in the following. Some of the terms have already been discussed in the introduction, but are repeated here for the sake of completeness.

Concerning MPEG encryption, several review papers have been published providing a more or less complete overview of the techniques proposed so far. Kunkelmann (1998) and Qiao and Nahrstedt (1998) provide overviews, comparisons, and assessments of classical encryption schemes for visual data with emphasis on MPEG proposed up to 1998. Bhargava, Shi, and Wang (2004) review four MPEG encryption algorithms published

by the authors themselves. More recent surveys are provided by Lu and Eskicioglu (2003), with focus on shortcomings of current schemes and future issues; But (2004), where the suitability of available MPEG-1 ciphers for streaming video is assessed); and Lookabaugh, Sicker, Keaton, Guo, and Vedula (2003), who focus on a cryptanalysis of MPEG-2 ciphers.

With regard to the provided level of security for multimedia content it is possible to distinguish different categories of encryption schemes. An encryption scheme can aim at full confidentiality (also: full privacy). In this case, no access to the plaintext, not even in parts or versions of lower quality is allowed without the (correct) key. In the case of visual content this means that no traces of the original plaintext may be discernible. Full confidentiality can be provided by using a classical strong cryptographic cipher for encrypting all of the multimedia bitstream. This option of full classical encryption gives the highest level of security. The DVD encryption scheme based on CSS was meant to provide this property; however, a weak cipher turned the scheme unintentionally into soft encryption (see later on). However, as mentioned previously, in multimedia applications other considerations may have precedence over achieving the highest level of security, like increased functionality or decreased computational demands. Such encryption schemes that do not provide the highest possible level of security are often termed lightweight. Depending on what security is traded in for, we can further distinguish the encryption schemes. If lower computational complexity is the aim, there are two kinds of encryption schemes: One way to lower computational demands is to employ cryptographic primitives that are less demanding (but also less secure). This is usually called soft encryption. The most important class of soft MPEG encryption applies permutations to parts of the data. For example, the zig-zag permutation algorithm (Shin, Sim, & Rhee, 1999; Tang, 1996) replaces the zig-zag scan of the DCT coefficients by a key-dependent permutation of the coefficients. Further examples apply permutations to bytes (Qiao & Nahrstedt, 1998), VLC codewords, blocks, and macroblocks (Kankanhalli & Hau, 2002; Wen, Severa, Zeng, Luttrell, & Jin, 2002; Zeng, Wen, & Severa, 2002).

Another way is to selectively encrypt only vital parts of the bitstream with a classical cipher. This is termed *partial/selective encryption*. Partial/selective MPEG encryption restricts the application of encryption primitives to low frequency DCT coefficients only (Cheng & Li, 1996; Kunkelmann, 1998; Kunkelmann & Reinema, 1997), to the sign bits of DCT coefficients (Bhargava et al., 2004; Shi & Bhargava, 1998; Zeng & Lei, 1999, 2003), or to I-frames thereby exploiting MPEG's GOP structure (Li, Chen, Tan, & Campbell, 1996; Spanos & Maples, 1995). If increased functionality is the aim, even more groups of encryption schemes can be distinguished.

Encryption schemes that seek to transfer some of the functionality of the original media bitstream to the encrypted bitstream are termed *format-compliant*. A format-compliantly encrypted bitstream can still be decoded with a standard decoder (although the resulting reconstruction will not be the original media plaintext). For scalable formats, for example, this means that tasks like rate adaptation can be performed directly on the encrypted media without the need for decoding. Format compliant MPEG encryption has been defined in the context of MPEG-4 IPMP (Wen, Severa, Zeng, Luttrell, & Jin, 2001; Wen et al., 2002) proposing compliant encryption of VLC codewords. Encryption of DCT coefficient sign bits (Bhargava et al., 2004; Shi & Bhargava, 1998) can also preserve bitstream compliance as does the zig-zag permutation algorithm. An example of highly non bitstream compliance preserving techniques are byte permutation (Qiao & Nahrstedt, 1998) and VEA (Qiao & Nahrstedt, 1997, 1998), which encrypts half of the bytes with a strong cipher and XORs the result with the other half of the bytes.

In the context of multimedia content, providing full privacy is often not required. For example, the possibility to decrypt a version of significantly lower quality than the retail version from the encrypted video bitstream is not a problem. Only the protection of the full quality retail version needs to be as high as possible. Depending on how the security and the quality requirement, which we discussed previously, are fulfilled, we can distinguish two categories: sufficient and transparent encryption. Encryption schemes that guarantee a minimum level of distortion for reconstructions from the encrypted bitstream are sometimes called *sufficient encryption schemes*. These schemes do not make any concessions about the quality of the reconstructions without the (correct) key other than that they will not exceed a specified quality. Note that in MPEG, encryption algorithms are seldom targeted towards sufficient encryption but result to be categorized into this class due to security flaws. Examples are many partial/selective schemes like I-frame encryption or partial encryption of low frequency DCT coefficients. For some applications, apart from the maximum quality, also a minimum quality for the decodable visual information is desired. Transparent encryption (also called perceptual encryption, predominantly in the area of audio encryption), as mentioned in the Introduction, aims at providing a version of the plaintext of lower quality that can be decoded from the encrypted bitstream without the (correct) key. Thereby the level of security for the full quality version should remain high, ideally as if it were encrypted with a strong cipher. Note that the use of the term *transparent encryption* is not always consistent in the literature. Often the quality requirement is not discussed for transparent encryption schemes; furthermore, the preview images are of such low quality that in the terminology introduced here these schemes would be termed sufficient rather than transparent. Explicit transparent MPEG encryption schemes have been proposed by Dittmann and Steinmetz (1997a, 1997b) and Yuan et al. (2003).

Another classification of encryption schemes, which we have already mentioned in the Introduction, relates to where encryption is applied: Whereas bitstream-oriented schemes apply encryption after compression, compression-integrated schemes apply encryption in the compression pipeline. Examples of bitstream-oriented MPEG encryption schemes are VEA or byte permutation, zig-zag permutation or secret Huffman tables (Wu & Kuo, 2000) are examples of compression-integrated MPEG encryption. In the fourth section we will discuss application scenarios for transparent encryption. We distinguish between online and off-line scenarios (Pommer & Uhl, 2002). In online applications data are available in unprocessed form for encryption. In off-line applications, the data have already been stored or compressed in some way before encryption. These two kinds of application scenarios differ from the notion of bitstream-oriented and compression-integrated, as we will discuss in detail in the fourth section.

JPSEC

In the context of JPEG2000 security JPSEC, or more precisely ISO/IEC 15444-8, (ISO/IEC, 2007), has to be discussed. The standardization process started with a call for proposals in March 2003 and since then quite a number of contributions have been made [46, 10, 43, 9, 4, 6, 3]. JPSEC is an open security framework for JPEG2000 that offers solutions for:

- Encryption
- Conditional access
- Secure scalable streaming
- Verification of data integrity
- Authentication

Encryption and conditional access overlap with the topic of this paper. The different approaches presented in this paper can be implemented within the JPSEC standard, which is an extensible framework for the specification of security processes. The JPSEC framework offers a syntax for the definition of JPEG2000 security services. To that end a new marker segment (SEC) is defined which is placed in the main header. The SEC marker segment defines which security service (encryption, authentication, ...) is applied, where it is applied, and how it is applied. Currently security services are grouped into three types of tools, namely template, registration authority, and user-defined tools. Template tools are defined by the normative part of the standard, registration authority tools are registered with and defined by the JPSEC registration authority, and user-defined tools can be freely defined by users or applications. The registration authority and the user-defined tools enable the application of custom and proprietary encryption methods, which leads to a flexible framework. Services include encryption, authentication, and integrity verification.

A security service operates on a user- or application-defined portion of the JPEG2000 bitstream. This portion is defined by the zone of influence (ZOI). The ZOI can be specified either by image-related parameters (resolution, image area, tile index, quality layer, or color component) or by non-image-related parameters, such as byte ranges or packet indices.

Further, template and processing parameters can be specified, for example, the use of AES in CBC mode. However, JPSEC rather defines a syntax than actual encryption schemes.

TRANSPARENT BITSTREAM-BASED JPEG2000 ENCRYPTION

The simplest solution to achieve the goals of transparent encryption is to simply distribute an encrypted high-quality version and a public low-quality version of the visual data. This approach wastes storage and bandwidth while the computational effort remains very high, making real-time usage (e.g., streaming) difficult. Hence efficient solutions for transparent encryption are strongly needed. The scheme proposed by Uhl and Obermair (2005) solves the problem of unnecessary bandwidth and storage consumption for JPEG2000 compressed images, but still remains computationally complex since most of the data has to be encrypted. The requirements of transparent encryption can only be met to a certain extent, which is improved by the encryption scheme proposed by Stütz and Uhl (in press), which uses an encryption window approach.

This window encryption approach preserves the excellent compression performance of JPEG2000 and reduces the encryption complexity compared to the complexity of encrypting the entire file (compressed with no target rate and therefore nearly losslessly compressed). Therefore this scheme is optimally fitted for mobile and wireless environments where both bandwidth consumption and computational complexity play decisive roles. The encryption window approach produces format-compliant JPEG2000 files, which enable the approach to be deployed without the distribution of any additional software. In order to implement bitstream-based transparent encryption schemes, encryption methods that preserve the format compliance of the JPEG2000 files are needed. These are briefly discussed next, followed by a presentation of the encryption window approach and related experimental results.

Encryption of JPEG2000 Bitstreams

Format-compliant encryption schemes for JPEG2000 usually encrypt the packet body data, which contain the compressed coefficient data (Dufaux et al., 2004; Fang & Sun, 2006; Kiya, Imaizumi, & Watanabe, 2003; Wu & Ma, 2004). Thereby care must be taken because the CCPs and the packet body must not contain any two byte sequence in excess of $0xff8f$ (delimiting markers) nor end with $0xff$.

Hence encryption schemes that avoid the

generation of these markers have to be employed (Dufaux et al., 2004; Fang & Sun, 2006; Kiya et al., 2003; Wu & Ma, 2004).

While the schemes of Kiya et al., (2003) Wu and Ma (2004), and Dufaux et al. (2004) are comparably simple, the scheme of Fang and Sun (2006) is rather sophisticated. Kiya et al. propose encrypting only the four least significant bits of a packet body byte and only if the byte is below $0xf0$. Thus no new $0xff$ bytes are generated and bytes that are not in excess of $0xff8f$ are kept in this range. The encryption algorithm of Wu and Ma is a significant improvement as it is capable of encrypting more of the packet data. All packet body bytes, except those two bytes sequences that start with a $0xff$, are encrypted modulo $0xff$. More precisely, the bytes of the keystream are added modulo $0xff$ to the packet body bytes. Obviously this algorithm encrypts a higher percentage of packet body data than the one proposed by Kiya et al. The generation of delimiting markers is avoided as no new $0xff$ bytes are generated in the ciphertext. It has to be noted that the keystream must not contain any $0xff$ bytes, because otherwise a strong bias in the encryption is introduced (the preservation of a plaintext byte in the ciphertext is twice as probable as every other byte). A further minor improvement is proposed in Dufaux et al.: Only the $0xff$ are preserved and the next plaintext byte is encrypted modulo $0x90$ (again addition with a pseudorandom keystream byte modulo $0x90$). All other bytes are encrypted in the same way as in the algorithm of Wu and Ma.

There are, however, more sophisticated schemes, such as the algorithm proposed in Fang and Sun (2006) or a scheme roughly sketched in the FDIS of the JPSEC standard (more details about this scheme can be found in Engel et al., in press-c). A thorough discussion of these schemes is not possible within the scope of this paper, the main advantage of the two schemes is that no packet body byte is preserved, which is of great importance if the identification of the ciphertext with a given plaintext must not be possible (i.e., if full confidentiality is desired). Their computational complexity is similar and only slightly higher.

In the case of transparent encryption full confidentiality is no objective, as a low quality version is desired to be publicly available. Hence the identification of a transparently encrypted image and the plaintext image is always possible.

Efficient Bitstream-Based Transparent Encryption

The traditional approach to implement transparent encryption on top of scalable multimedia data is to successively encrypt all enhancement layers until the desired quality is achieved (Stütz & Uhl, 2006b; Uhl & Obermair, 2005).

For the approach proposed by Uhl and Obermair (2005), most of the JPEG2000 file has to be encrypted in order to obtain a suitable low quality version. There is, however, a gap between the image qualities obtained by a direct reconstruction (the encrypted file is regularly decompressed) and by a possible attack. This gap has to be as small as possible, because otherwise an attacker can retrieve a quality that is too high or possible customers a quality that is too low.

The approach of window encryption format-compliantly encrypts only a small amount (Stütz & Uhl (in press) of the packet body data at a certain position in the file. Note that the optimal position depends on the desired low quality and can be easily determined for every image.

Stütz and Uhl (in press) point out that an attacker may identify the encrypted parts and replace them, thereby enhancing the image quality. They present two known attacks: the concealment and the truncation attack.

The **concealment attack** has been proposed by Norcen and Uhl (2003) and employs the JPEG2000 built-in error concealment mechanisms. The basic idea is that an attacker has to identify the encrypted parts and replace them in order to obtain the best

possible recoverable image quality. To mimic these attacks JPEG200 error concealment strategies can be employed. The encryption of packet body data is not likely to accidentally produce correct error concealment information. Hence the encrypted parts are identified as erroneous and therefore discarded.

At the end of every bitplane an additional symbol (0xa) is encoded; if it is not decoded correctly, the coding pass and all successive ones are discarded. It is invoked by the `-Cseg _ symbol` on option of the JJ2000 (a Java reference implementation) encoder. Note that only the error detection is defined within the standard, the actual error concealment is a decoder choice. In Stütz and Uhl (in press) it is noted that the error concealment in the JJ2000 reference software is not working well and therefore we also present results based on an improved and corrected error concealment. Additionally to the usage of the segmentation symbol, predictive termination can be employed for error concealment. Thereby in average 3.5 bit of error concealment information are embedded in the spare least significant bits of a coding pass.

The **truncation attack** consists of simply truncating the encrypted parts of the codestream; in the case of the traditional approach of Uhl and Obermair (2005) this is basically the best recoverable image quality, disregarding standard image enhancement processing and the information contained in the JPEG2000 packet headers.

Good results for efficient transparent encryption (with the encryption window approach) are obtained with layer progression and a small codeblock size, for example, 16x16 (a detailed analysis of the impact of compression parameters on the traditional approach can be found in Engel et al. (in press-c). The encryption window scheme makes it possible to realize transparent encryption very efficiently and securely. The security against known attacks remains the same as for the traditional approach. The gap between the known attacks and the direct reconstruction is decreased as compared to the traditional approach and the

Figure 2. Results for layer progression and 16×16 codeblocks

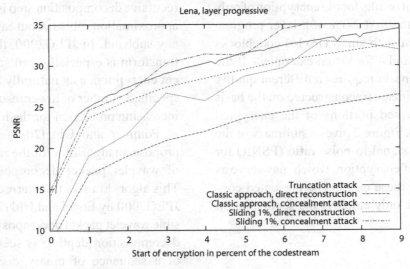

Lena, layer progressive

Figure 3. Truncation attacks for layer progression

2%: PSNR 26.9dB, ESS 0.18

3%: PSNR 28.4dB, ESS 0.69

Figure 4. Direct reconstruction for layer progression 16×16 codeblocks and encryption at 2%

SlidW: *PSNR 1.4dB, ESS 0.39*

Trad: *PSNR 18.6dB, ESS 0.30*

computational complexity is greatly reduced as well. We present results for the encryption of only 1% located at the first 2-3% of a layer progressive codestream with small (16x16) codeblocks (see Figures 3 and 4 for visual examples). If the application scenario requires a different quality of the preview image (reconstructed on the basis of the unencrypted portions of the encrypted JPEG2000 file), Figure 2 gives a summary of the achieved peak signal-to-noise ratio (PSNR) for various starts of encryption, which may serve as a guideline for these cases. The presented concealment attack only employs the segmentation symbol.

TRANSPARENT ENCRYPTION WITH WAVELET PACKETS

There are a number of suggestions for performing compression-integrated encryption with key-dependent transform domains, some of which are given in the section on Additional Reading. The basic idea for using a key-dependent transform domain for encryption is to select a basis to be used for encoding based on a secret key. Without the knowledge of the secret key, the transform coefficients, which are transmitted in plaintext, cannot be interpreted correctly and the visual data cannot be accessed. In a way, this procedure can be seen as an extreme form of header encryption, as only the information pertaining to the secret transform domain needs to be encrypted. An advantage of such an approach is the fact that due to the extremely small amount of data that needs to be encrypted it can directly be used in public-key systems and benefit from their superior key management. Furthermore, for some transform domains, transparent encryption can be provided naturally.

For wavelet-based coding systems, such as JPEG2000, the wavelet packet transform is a likely candidate to be used for compression-integrated encryption. The wavelet packet transform is a

generalization of the pyramidal transform. The recursive decomposition step is not limited to the approximation subband, but can be performed on any subband. In JPEG2000, the wavelet packet transform is especially well suited for transparent encryption, as it naturally allows access to a specified number of lower resolutions and offers increasing protection for the higher resolutions.

Pommer and Uhl (2003) were the first to propose an algorithm for the random generation of wavelet packet decomposition structures. This algorithm was transferred to the domain of JPEG2000 by Engel and Uhl (2006b). Each possible wavelet packet decomposition of maximum decomposition depth g is seen as the outcome of a sequence of binary decisions. For each sub-band, a random number is generated. This random number is evaluated within the context of parameters that allow favoring deeper or more shallow decompositions. If the random number is below a parameterized threshold, the current sub-band is left at its present decomposition depth and is not decomposed further. Otherwise, if the current sub-band has not already reached the maximum decomposition depth, the sub-band is decomposed and the decision process is applied to each of the resulting children.

Transparent encryption is inherently possible as the lowest resolution is the same as for a conventional pyramidal decomposition. This resolution only contains the approximation sub-band, hence it can be decoded with any codec compliant to JPEG2000 part I. A preview image of higher resolution can be incorporated by the encoder by using the pyramidal wavelet decompositions for the target resolution and all resolutions below it. All resolutions higher than the target preview resolution are protected by the use of wavelet packets. Figure 5 shows two preview images for Lena for resolution 1 and resolution 2 respectively.

The pyramidal wavelet transform has favorable properties for the compaction of energy in the transform domain of natural images. When using the wavelet packet transform, we have to expect

Figure 5. Preview images for wavelet packet encryption

Resolution 1

Resolution 2

some loss of energy compaction and therefore some loss of compression performance. We need to limit the loss in compression performance as far as possible, while still retaining a high number of possible bases. If the number of possible bases is too small, an attack would become easy. On the other hand, if many bases are possible, which do not perform well at compression, the scheme becomes useless. A number of parameters for the encryption scheme have been evaluated in the context of JPEG2000 (Engel & Uhl, 2006a). Because the approximation sub-band contains the most energy, it needs to be decomposed a minimum number of times to facilitate energy compaction. Furthermore, the overall number of possible decompositions needs to be restricted, because otherwise the great number of sub-bands in the detail trees produce too much overhead in the bitstream. With sensible settings of these parameters the loss in compression performance seems acceptable. For the test images used by Engel and Uhl (2006a) of size 512 times 512 pixels, and with the minimum decomposition of the approximation sub-band set to 3, and the overall maximum decomposition also set to 5, the average PSNR performance at a rate of 0.25 drops

less than 1 dB. For images with more energy in the higher frequencies the drop is only around 0.2 dB on average.

In recent work (Engel & Uhl, 2006b, 2007) the wavelet packet approach is extended to use anisotropic wavelet packets. For the anisotropic wavelet packet transform, the vertical and horizontal decomposition steps need not be applied in pairs. The basic considerations regarding compression performance, complexity, and security also apply to anisotropic wavelet packets. The main motivation to introduce anisotropic wavelet packets in the context of lightweight encryption is a significant increase in keyspace size: The keyspace is not only determined by the decision whether a specific sub-band is decomposed or not, but also by the dimension of the decomposition. This makes a larger library of bases available for equivalent decomposition depths.

Security

The number of possible wavelet packet bases up to level n is equivalent to the number of quadtrees of up to level n. For a maximum overall decomposition depth of 5 this number is 2^{261}. So theoretically, a brute-force attack trying all different wavelet packet decompositions is above the complexity of a brute-force attack on a 256-bit-key AES encryption. Brute-force only gives an upper bound on security, and in the following we investigate the security properties of the wavelet packet approach in more detail.

Two basic possibilities exist for an attacker: finding a way to obtain the correct wavelet packet decomposition structure, or finding a way to reconstruct the transformed data without knowing the correct decomposition structure. For the latter attack, success is gradual: any quality that can be obtained that is better than the preview image is a certain success for the attacker, up to the point where an image of full or nearly full quality is obtained, which amounts to a total break.

An attacker who wants to obtain the sub-band structure will first turn to the JPEG2000 header information and look for parts in the header that might leak information on the subband structure. The main header, the tile header, and the tile-part header do not contain any information related to the sub-band structure (apart from the explicit description of the used subband structure, which in our case is encrypted). The packet headers contain the inclusion information for each codeblock in the packet's precinct, coded by the use of so-called tag trees (Taubman & Marcellin, 2002). As the number and sequencing of the codeblocks is unavailable if the sub-band structure is unknown, the inclusion information cannot be interpreted by an attacker. Especially for the higher resolution there is an abundant amount of possibilities. So theoretically, the sub-band structure is not leaked by the inclusion information. However, there is a caveat: the first packet of a resolution needs to contain an output of the tag tree of each sub-band in the resolution (assuming no precinct partitioning is used). As the higher resolution levels will in practice not be significant in the first layer, the attacker can obtain the number of sub-bands in the resolution by counting zeros in the beginning of the packet. Knowing the number of sub-bands

in a resolution diminishes the keyspace drastically and opens the opportunity for an attacker to iteratively search for the correct sub-band structure (e.g., by comparing the reconstruction to the preview image and iteratively minimizing the MSE). Of course, the attacker will first have to identify the packet borders and distinguish packet headers from packet bodies, which might be cumbersome, but usually will be possible. To prevent an attacker from using the information leakage in the inclusion information, we propose encrypting the relevant portions in the packet headers. For a format-compliant packet header encryption scheme, see Engel, Stütz, and Uhl (in press-c).

Partial reconstruction without the knowledge of the sub-band structure is not feasible in JPEG2000. Without the sub-band structure, the transform coefficient data is not accessible. As an attacker does not know which codeblocks a CCP is intended for, he/she cannot associate the body data of a packet with the correct coefficients. In other codecs, access to the coefficients may be possible. In this case, the attacker can try to impose different subband structures on the coefficient data. The visual quality of this attack will depend on how similar the two sub-band structures are, especially if the approximation subband is of the same size in both structures. Figures 6 and 7 give examples of the visual quality when two differing sub-band structures are used. For Figure 6 the sizes of the approximation sub-bands are the same, for Figure 7 they differ. Because of the large size of the space of possible bases, two randomly generated sub-band structures will almost never be similar enough to produce reconstruction results that are comparable to the full quality version of the visual data. Engel and Uhl (2007) investigate the expected distance between two randomly generated sub-band structures in detail for the anisotropic case.

Combined with header encryption, the wavelet packet scheme successfully secures the coefficient data from access. However, it has to be noted that

Figure 6. Imposing subband structure on transform coefficients: same size of approximation subband

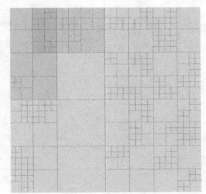

WP structure for encoding

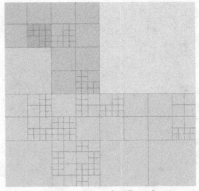

WP structure for decoding

Results of reconstruction (PSNR 22.28dB, ESS 0.47)

as the entire coefficient information is available in plaintext, all sorts of statistical analyses may be conducted by attackers, potentially allowing them to identify an image in encrypted form.

Complexity

Wavelet packets bring an increase in complexity as compared to the pyramidal wavelet decomposition: The order of complexity for a level *l* full wavelet packet decomposition of an image of size N^2 is

$$O(\sum_{i=1}^{l} 2^{2(i-1)} \frac{N^2}{2^{2(i-1)}})$$

compared to

$$O(\sum_{i=1}^{l} \frac{N^2}{2^{2(i-1)}})$$

for the pyramidal decomposition, with the randomized wavelet packet decompositions ranging in between. With the parameters used in our empirical tests the average time needed for the transform stage increased by 45% as compared to the pyramidal transform. The average time needed for the whole compression pipeline increased by 25%.

For the wavelet packet approach, there are two possibilities of how to secure the sub-band structure. First, the seed and the parameters for random generation can be included in the header in encrypted form. And second, the sub-band structure as such can be included in encrypted

Figure 7.

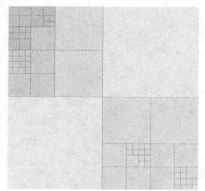

WP structure for encoding

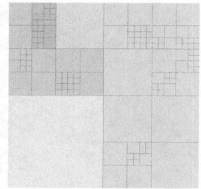

WP structure for decoding

Results of reconstruction (PSNR 11.84dB, ESS 0.25)

form. A straightforward representation format is a sequence of binary decisions, for example, in depth-first scanning order. The former possibility is the one where the smallest amount of data has to be encrypted. The seed and the parameters typically do not take up more than a couple of bytes. The size of the latter depends on the depth of the sub-band structure. If the straightforward representation is used, then for a pyramidal decomposition of level 5, 20 bits have to be spent. This corresponds to 0.0023% of the whole bitstream for Lena with no target bitrate (i.e., nearly lossless). For a full wavelet packet decomposition this number goes up to 1,365 bits (corresponding to 0.16% of the whole bitstream), with the randomized wavelet packet structures ranging in between. Of course, the representation

could be improved, but generally we can again observe a trade-off between the amount of data to be encrypted and computational complexity: If the parameters are encrypted, then the decoder needs to build the whole wavelet packet structure before decoding. If the sub-band structure as such is encrypted, this means slightly more data has to be protected, but the decoder does not have to run through the process of quadtree generation (which mainly consists of producing the decomposition decisions).

The anisotropic wavelet packet transform does not increase complexity compared to the isotropic case. As more bases can be constructed with lower decomposition depths, the use of the anisotropic wavelet packet transform lowers the computational demands of the scheme.

In general, wavelet packets dramatically reduce the effort for encryption compared to full encryption and other partial or selective encryption schemes. This circumstance makes encryption with a public key scheme feasible, which reduces the effort for key management considerably.

However, the considerable computational complexity that is introduced for the transform step needs to be taken into account for potential application scenarios. For some application scenarios the decrease of complexity in the encryption stage might not suffice the increase of complexity in the compression stage.

APPLICATION SCENARIOS

Application scenarios for the employment of encryption technology in multimedia environments can be divided into two categories (Pommer & Uhl, 2002): we distinguish whether the data is given as plain image data (i.e., not compressed) or in form of a bitstream resulting from prior compression. In applications where the data is acquired before being further processed the plain image data may be accessed directly for encryption after being captured by a digitizer. We denote such applications as *online*. Examples for this scenario are video conferencing and online surveillance. On the other hand, as soon as visual data has been stored or transmitted once, it has usually been compressed in some way. Applications where compressed bitstreams are handled or encrypted are denoted *offline*. Examples are video on demand and retrieval of medical images from a database.

There are many application scenarios for transparent encryption for which both, bitstream-oriented and compression-integrated approaches can be used. An example is TV broadcasting: a preview video is available for all users, but the full-quality version remains exclusive to the paying subscribers. Also in image databases, the availability of a thumbnail is of advantage as an incentive for buying the full-quality version. The same is true for online video databases, of course.

For video surveillance it is sometimes desirable to show the video feed in order to discourage theft. However, privacy should be protected. A possible solution is to only show the poor quality as a deterrent. If an incident should occur then the full quality version can be accessed by security personnel.

The main difference between compression-integrated and bitstream-oriented approaches is the fact that bitstream-oriented approaches can be used for online and off-line scenarios, whereas compression-integrated approaches are mainly restricted to online scenarios (because if compression has already been done, transcoding would become necessary to apply the encryption in this case). This makes bitstream-oriented approaches more flexible in comparison. On the other hand, compression-integrated encryption also offers some advantages: (a) only very little data has to be encrypted even compared to selective encryption schemes (of course this comes at the cost of increased complexity in the compression pipeline), (b) format-compliance comes naturally and does not need to be taken care of explicitly (as it is the case for bitstream oriented approaches), and (c) signal processing is to some extent possible in the encrypted domain, which allows secure watermarking and intrinsic fingerprinting, as discussed below.

It should be noted for (c) that signal processing in the encrypted domain is also possible for partial bitstream-oriented encryption to some extent, because only small amounts of data are encrypted and even the encrypted data can be processed on a packet or even CCP basis, for example, enabling efficient transcoding and cropping. The advantage of the compression-integrated approach is that the full transform coefficients are available for signal processing. In the case of JPEG2000, for example, key-dependent wavelet packet subband structures allow direct access to the transform coefficients and with a part II compliant codec all features of JPSearch can be used.

In the context of key-dependent wavelet packet subband structures in JPEG2000, the fact that a part II compliant decoder is needed to access the full quality version can be seen as another advantage: Even if a key is compromised, the visual data is only accessible with such a decoder (if no transcoding is performed of course), which might hinder dispersion of the full quality version. A traitor-tracing scheme can be employed that uses the unique wavelet packet structure to determine the source of pirated visual data. This works in the second and third scenario and is discussed later on.

For both compression-oriented and bitstream-oriented approaches we can combine symmetric transparent encryption with public key encryption to facilitate distribution and key management. For the bitstream-oriented approach the visual data is first encrypted symmetrically (using one of the schemes discussed previously). Then the key of the symmetric encryption scheme is encrypted with a public-key scheme and sent to the (paying) user. In the case of the compression-integrated approach, the visual data is first encoded with a randomly selected basis. For a paying user, the description of this basis is then encrypted with the user's public key and sent to the user. This basically amounts to a hybrid encryption scenario with combined symmetric and asymmetric encryption: The description of the basis used for encoding is the key to the symmetric encryption scheme, key management and distribution is realized by classical public key encryption. Both kinds of approaches can be used for protection on three different levels: (a) individual protection for each image (or groups of images) regardless of the associated user, (b) individual protection for each user (for all images associated with the user) or

(c) individual protection for each image and each user. We use wavelet packets in the following discussion as a representative of compression-integrated encryption, but it should be noted that the reflections are valid for other key-dependent transform domains as well.

Protection for Each Image

This approach presents a pay-per-item implementation. Each image (e.g., in a database) is encrypted with an individual key or decomposed with a unique wavelet packet sub-band structure respectively. Any non-paying subscriber can get a preview image.

If we allow more than one image to share the same symmetric key (or the same sub-band structure), then a channel-based subscription service can be implemented: if, for example, all sports pictures share the same symmetric key, a person paying for the sports key can access all of the pictures in this group.

For compression-integrated encryption, the unique frequency domain of each image allows copy-tracing. For example, a crawler could be employed to search for images with a particular sub-band structure. This can be done by matching the coefficients in the transform domain, or by reconstructing the image and matching in the spatial domain. Even if transcoding is employed, there can be some traces of the sub-band structure left, as outlined in the following scenario.

Protection for Each User

In this scenario, a unique symmetric key (or sub-band structure) is assigned to each user. In an image database with personal albums, for example, this key would be used for each item the user uploads.

A nice feature of key-dependent transform domains in this context is that the transform domain can be used to trace the user's data if it gets redistributed. A crawler could, for example, look for images coded in a particular user's sub-band structure. Even if transcoding was used, for example, if the JPEG2000 image has been transformed to a JPEG image, due to quantization there could be traces left in the visual data that allow the linking to the sub-band structure of a particular user. To make the tracing scheme more reliable, a watermark can be embedded in the wavelet packet domain (Dietl & Uhl, 2003).

Another feature provided by the use of user-dependent wavelet packet structures is secure annotation watermarks. As these watermarks can be embedded in the wavelet packet domain to enhance security, only a person knowing the sub-band structure can extract the contained information (Dietl & Uhl, 2004). Any person lacking the sub-band structure can only access the preview image, but not the annotations. As the secret transform domain is already available, apart from embedding no additional computational costs are introduced.

Protection for Each User and Each Image

This scenario is similar to the previous scenario, but a new symmetric key is created for each of the user's images. This is important if one or some of the images get sold and access should not be given to the other images. This is especially interesting for personalized visual data, for example, personalized greeting cards. Each personalized card is encrypted using a unique symmetric key, only the user who ordered the card may access the full quality version. Another example is blueprints, which an architect creates for a specific customer. The customer can get a preview image, but to access the blueprints in full detail, he/she has to obtain the symmetric key. A different key is used for the next set of blueprints from a different order, even if it is the same customer.

Also in this scenario the possibilities of copy-tracing and secure annotation watermarks come

for free with the use of key-dependent transform domains.

CONCLUSION

Both techniques investigated succeed in reducing the computational demand for encryption significantly as compared to traditional transparent encryption methods. While the bitstream-based window encryption technique is more flexible and thereby allows a wider range of application scenarios to be supported, the secret wavelet packet approach requires a much lower data amount to be encrypted (which has to be paid for with a higher complexity in the compression pipeline) and does not have to obey any restrictions imposed by the requirement for format compliance as required for bitstream packet data encryption. Therefore, for specific application scenarios, for example, such that require public-key cryptography to be applied (where a minimal data amount subjected to encryption is a must and bitstream compliance is harder to achieve), the compression integrated wavelet packet technique is an interesting alternative to bitstream-based transparent encryption.

FUTURE RESEARCH DIRECTIONS

Multimedia data has made its way into everybody's everyday life and it is unlikely that this (r)evolution will be reversed or even slowed down. Hence so-called DRM solutions will be a topic for the next years. However, current DRM systems largely tend to annoy paying customers, while the commercial black market is highly unaffected by these measures. Thus the content providers will face the decision to make their system more consumer friendly (transparently useable media files even in low quality are a step in this direction) or even completely dropping the deployment of these systems (only recently EMI announced that they will offer DRM free music content[1]).

In the context of JPEG2000 encryption flexible encryption schemes that can be adapted to the needs of an application will become more important. Engel, Stütz, and Uhl (in press-a) point out that the encryption of JPEG2000 packet bodies alone, that is, leaving the packet headers in plaintext is not secure for applications that require full confidentiality. A scheme for packet header encryption is proposed. The usability of this scheme for transparent encryption is discussed in Engel, Stütz, and Uhl (in press-b).

From the practical point of view, the detailed investigation of application scenarios in which transparent encryption is employed is still missing. Applications like digital libraries (there are propositions to use JPEG2000, e.g., for Google Books, see Langley & Bloomberg, 2007) are likely to profit from transparent encryption techniques. JPEG2000 as a standard for scalable still image coding is a promising starting point in this context.

The Digital Cinema Initiative (DCI), an entity created by seven major motion picture studios, has published a specification for a unified Digital Cinema System (DCI, 2007), which uses JPEG2000 for compression. Their document also extensively discusses security issues. The proposed encryption techniques, however, remain rather conventional.

The techniques discussed here can be transferred and adapted to video encryption in general. There has been a lot of research in the area of scalable video coding recently. Therefore, a promising research area will be the development of reliable bitstream-oriented approaches for the scalable extension of H.264/AVC (Schwarz, Marpe, & Wiegand, 2006). The use of secret transform domains for video encryption should be assessed in the context of wavelet-based scalable video coding (Ohm, 2005).

Media encryption is a young and thriving topic with many possible directions for future research, of which we have only mentioned a small selection. Many more research directions will come up in the future. They will on the one hand entail the continued investigations of specialized topics, while on the other hand they will have to look at the bigger picture and research the integration and the interplay of different areas of security, for example, encryption, watermarking, perceptual hashing, and fingerprinting, in practical systems.

REFERENCES

Apostolopoulos, J. S., Wee, F. D., Ebrahimi, T., Sun, Q., & Zhang, Z. (2006, May). The emerging JPEG2000 security (JPSEC) standard. *IEEE Proceedings of the International Symposium on Circuits and Systems (ISCAS)*.

Bhargava, B., Shi, C., & Wang, Y. (2004). MPEG video encryption algorithms. *Multimedia Tools and Applications, 24*(1), 57-79.

Bodo, Y., Laurent, N., & Dugelay, J.-L. (2003, December). A scrambling method based on disturbance of motion vector. *Proceedings of ACM Multimedia 2002* (pp. 89-90). Juan Le Pins, France.

But, J. (2004, April). *Limitations of existing MPEG-1 ciphers for streaming video* (Tech. Rep. No. CAIA 040429A). Swinburne University, Australia.

Cheng, H., & Li, X. (1996, September). On the application of image decomposition to image compression and encryption. In P. Horster (Ed.), *Communications and Multimedia Security II, IFIP TC6/TC11 Second Joint Working Conference on Communications and Multimedia Security, CMS '96* (pp. 116-127). Essen, Germany: Chapman & Hall.

Dietl, W., & Uhl, A. (2003, October). Watermark security via secret wavelet packet subband structures. In A. Lioy & D. Mazzocchi (Eds.), *Communications and Multimedia Security. Proceedings of the Seventh IFIP TC-6 TC-11 Conference on Communications and Multimedia Security* (LNCS 2828, pp. 214-225). Turin, Italy: Springer-Verlag.

Dietl, W. M., & Uhl, A. (2004, June). Robustness against unauthorized watermark removal attacks via key-dependent wavelet packet subband structures. *Proceedings of the IEEE International Conference on Multimedia and Expo, ICME '04.* Taipei, Taiwan.

Digital Cinema Initiatives (DCI). (2007). *Digital Cinema System Specification, v1.1.* Retrieved April 12, 2007, from http://www.dcimovies.com/

Dittmann, J., & Steinmetz, R. (1997a, July). Enabling technology for the trading of MPEG-encoded video. *Information Security and Privacy: Second Australasian Conference, ACISP '97* (Vol. 1270, pp. 314-324).

Dittmann, J., & Steinmetz, R. (1997b, September). A technical approach to the transparent encryption of MPEG-2 video. In S. K. Katsikas (Ed.), *Communications and Multimedia Security, IFIP TC6/TC11 Third Joint Working Conference, CMS '97* (pp. 215-226). Athens, Greece: Chapman and Hall.

Droogenbroeck, M. V. (2004, April). Partial encryption of images for real-time applications. *Proceedings of the 4th 2004 Benelux Signal Processing Symposium* (pp. 11-15). Hilvarenbeek, The Netherlands.

Droogenbroeck, M. V., & Benedett, R. (2002, September). Techniques for a selective encryption of uncompressed and compressed images. *Proceedings of ACIVS (Advanced Concepts for Intelligent Vision Systems)* (pp. 90-97). Ghent University, Belgium.

Dufaux, F., & Ebrahimi, T. (2003). Securing JPEG2000 compressed images. In A. G. Tescher (Ed.), *Applications of Digital Image Processing XXVI* (SPIE 5203, pp. 397-406).

Dufaux, F., Wee, S., Apostolopoulos, J., & Ebrahimi, T. (2004, August). JPSEC for secure imaging in JPEG2000. *Proceedings of SPIE* (SPIE 5558, pp. 319-330).

Engel, D., & Uhl, A. (2006a, May). Secret wavelet packet decompositions for JPEG2000 lightweight encryption. *Proceedings of 31st International Conference on Acoustics, Speech, and Signal Processing, ICASSP '06* (Vol. V, pp. 465-468). Toulouse, France.

Engel, D., & Uhl, A. (2006b, July). Lightweight JPEG2000 encryption with anisotropic wavelet packets. *Proceedings of International Conference on Multimedia & Expo, ICME '06* (pp. 2177-2180). Toronto, Canada.

Engel, D., & Uhl, A. (2007, January). An evaluation of lightweight JPEG2000 encryption with anisotropic wavelet packets. In E. J. Delp & P. W. Wong (Eds.), *Security, Steganography, and Watermarking of Multimedia Contents IX* (SPIE, pp. 65051S1-65051S10). San Jose, CA: SPIE.

Engel, D., Stütz, T., & Uhl, A. (2007a, September). Format-compliant JPEG2000 encryption with combined packet header and packet body protection. *Proceedings of the ACM Multimedia and Security Workshop (MM-SEC '07),* (pp. 87-95). Houston, TX.

Engel, D., Stütz, T., & Uhl, A. (2007b, November). Efficient JPEG2000 transparent encryption with format-compliant header protection. *Proceedings of the IEEE International Conference on Signal Processing and Communications (ICSPC '07)* (pp. 1067-1070). Dubai, UAE.

Engel, D., Stütz, T., & Uhl, A. (in press-c). *Format-compliant JPEG2000 encryption in JPSEC: Security, applicability and the impact of compression parameters.* DOI: 10.1155/2007/94565, article ID# 94565.

Fang, J., & Sun, J. (2006). Compliant encryption scheme for JPEG2000 image code streams. *Journal of Electronic Imaging, 15*(4), 043013.

Fisch, M. M., Stögner, H., & Uhl, A. (2004, September). Layered encryption techniques for DCT-coded visual data (paper cr1361). *Proceedings (CD-ROM) of the European Signal Processing Conference, EUSIPCO '04*. Vienna, Austria.

Grangetto, M., Magli, E., & Olmo, G. (2006). Multimedia selective encryption by means of randomized arithmetic coding. *IEEE Transactions on Multimedia, 8*(5), 905-917.

Grosbois, R., Gerbelot, P., & Ebrahimi, T. (2001, July). Authentication and access control in the JPEG2000 compressed domain. In A. Tescher (Ed.), *Applications of Digital Image Processing XXIV* (SPIE 4472, pp. 95-104). San Diego, CA.

Imaizumi, S., Watanabe, O., Fujiyoshi, M., & Kiya, H. (2005, September). Generalized hierarchical encryption of JPEG2000 codestreams for access control. *Proceedings of the IEEE International Conference on Image Processing (ICIP'05)* (Vol. 2).

International Organization for Standardization (ISO)/IEC. (2007, April). *Information technology—JPEG2000 image coding system, Part 8: Secure JPEG2000* (ISO/IEC 15444-8). Author.

Kankanhalli, M. S., & Hau, K. F. (2002). Watermarking of electronic text documents. *Electronic Commerce Research, 2*(1), 169-187.

Kiya, H., Imaizumi, D., & Watanabe, O. (2003, September). Partial scrambling of image encoded using JPEG2000 without generating marker codes. *Proceedings of the IEEE International Conference on Image Processing (ICIP'03)* (Vol. III, pp. 205-208). Barcelona, Spain.

Kunkelmann, T. (1998, September). Applying encryption to video communication. *Proceedings of the Multimedia and Security Workshop at ACM Multimedia '98* (pp. 41-47). Bristol, England.

Kunkelmann, T., & Horn, U. (1998). Partial video encryption based on scalable coding. *5th International Workshop on Systems, Signals and Image Processing (IWSSIP'98)* (pp. 215-218). Zagreb, Croatia.

Langley, A., & Bloomberg, D. S. (2007, January). Google books: Making the public domain universally accessible. *Proceedings of SPIE, Document Recognition and Retrieval XIV* (paper 65000H). San Jose, CA.

Li, Y., Chen, Z., Tan, S.-M., & Campbell, R. H. (1996). Security enhanced MPEG player. In *Proceedings of IEEE first international workshop on multimedia software development (mmsd'96)* (pp. 169-175). Berlin, Germany.

Lian, S., Sun, J., & Wang, Z. (2004, September). Perceptual cryptography on JPEG2000 compressed images or videos. *4th International Conference on Computer and Information Technology*. Wuhan, China: IEEE.

Lookabaugh, T. D., Sicker, D. C., Keaton, D. M., Guo, W. Y., & Vedula, I. (2003, September). Security analysis of selectiveley encrypted MPEG-2 streams. In *Multimedia systems and applications vi* (Vol. 5241, pp. 10-21).

Lu, X., & Eskicioglu, A. M. (2003, November). Selective encryption of multimedia content in distribution networks: Challenges and new directions. In *Proceedings of the IASTED international conference on on communications, internet and information technology (CIIT 2003)*. Scottsdale, AZ.

Macq, B., & Quisquater, J. (1994). Digital images multiresolution encryption. *The Journal of the Interactive Multimedia Association Intellectual Property Project, 1*(1), 179-206.

Macq, B. M., & Quisquater, J.-J. (1995). Cryptology for digital TV broadcasting. *Proceedings of the IEEE, 83*(6), 944-957.

Norcen, R., & Uhl, A. (2003, October). Selective encryption of the JPEG2000 bitstream. In A. Lioy & D. Mazzocchi (Eds.), *Communications and Multimedia Security. Proceedings of the IFIP TC6/TC11 Sixth Joint Working Conference on Communications and Multimedia Security, CMS '03* (LNCS 2828, pp. 194-204). Turin, Italy: Springer-Verlag.

Ohm, J.-R. (2005). Advances in scalable video coding. *Proceedings of the IEEE, 93*(1), 42-56.

Pommer, A., & Uhl, A. (2002, December). Application scenarios for selective encryption of visual data. In J. Dittmann, J. Fridrich, & P. Wohlmacher (Eds.), *Multimedia and Security Workshop, ACM Multimedia* (pp. 71-74). Juan-les-Pins, France.

Pommer, A., & Uhl, A. (2003). Selective encryption of wavelet-packet encoded image data—Efficiency and security. *ACM Multimedia Systems (Special issue on Multimedia Security), 9*(3), 279-287.

Qiao, L., & Nahrstedt, K. (1997, June). A new algorithm for MPEG video encryption. In *Proceedings of the international conference on imaging science, systems, and technology, CISST '97* (pp. 21- 29). Las Vegas, NV.

Qiao, L., & Nahrstedt, K. (1998). Comparison of MPEG encryption algorithms. *International Journal on Computers and Graphics, Special Issue on Data Security in Image Communication and Networks, 22*(3), 437-444.

Schwarz, H., Marpe, D., & Wiegand, T. (2006, October). Overview of the scalable H.264/MPEG4-AVC extension. *Proceedings of the IEEE International Conference on Image Processing (ICIP '06)*. Atlanta, GA.

Shi, C., & Bhargava, B. (1998, September). A fast MPEG video encryption algorithm. In *Proceedings of the sixth ACM international multimedia conference* (pp. 81-88). Bristol, UK.

Shin, S., Sim, K., & Rhee, K. (1999, November). A secrecy scheme for MPEG video data using the joint of compression and encryption. In *Proceedings of the 1999 information security workshop (ISW'99)* (Vol. 1729, pp. 191-201). Kuala Lumpur: Springer-Verlag.

Spanos, G., & Maples, T. (1995). Performance study of a selective encryption scheme for the security of networked real-time video. In *Proceedings of the 4th international conference on computer communications and networks (ICCCN'95)*. Las Vegas, NV.

Stütz, T., & Uhl, A. (2005, December). Image confidentiality using progressive JPEG. *Proceedings of Fifth International Conference on Information, Communication and Signal Processing (ICICS '05)* (pp. 1107-1111). Bangkok, Thailand.

Stütz, T., & Uhl, A. (2007, September). On efficient transparent encryption of JPEG2000. In *Proceedings of the ACM Multimedia and Security Workshop, MM-Sec '07* (pp. 97-108). Houston, Tx.

Stütz, T., & Uhl, A. (2006a, September). Transparent image encryption using progressive JPEG. In S. Katsikas et al. (Eds.), *Information Security. Proceedings of the 9th Information Security Conference (ISC'06)* (LNCS 4176, pp. 286-298). Springer-Verlag.

Stütz, T., & Uhl, A. (2006b). On format-compliant iterative encryption of JPEG2000. *Proceedings of the Eighth IEEE International Symposium on Multimedia (ISM'06)* (pp. 985-990). Los Alamitos, CA: IEEE Computer Society.

Stütz, T., & Uhl A. (in press). Efficient transparent encryption of JPEG2000. *Proceedings of the ACM Multimedia and Security Workshop (MM-SEC '07)*. Houston, TX.

Tang, L. (1996, November). Methods for encrypting and decrypting MPEG video data efficiently.

In *Proceedings of the ACM multimedia 1996* (pp. 219-229). Boston.

Taubman, D., & Marcellin, M. (2002). *JPEG2000— Image compression fundamentals, standards and practice.* Kluwer Academic.

Uhl, A., & Obermair, C. (2005). Transparent encryption of JPEG2000 bitstreams. In P. Podhradsky et al. (Eds.), *Proceedings EC-SIP-M 2005 (5th EURASIP Conference focused on Speech and Image Processing, Multimedia Communications and Services)* (pp. 322-327). Smolenice, Slovak Republic.

Uhl, A., & Pommer, A. (2005). *Image and video encryption. from digital rights management to secured personal communication:* Vol. 15. *Advances in Information Security.* Springer-Verlag.

Wen, J., Severa, M., Zeng, W., Luttrell, M., & Jin, W. (2001, October). A format-compliant configurable encryption framework for access control of multimedia. In *Proceedings of the IEEE workshop on multimedia signal processing, MMSP '01* (pp. 435-440). Cannes, France.

Wen, J., Severa, M., Zeng, W., Luttrell, M., & Jin, W. (2002, June). A format-compliant configurable encryption framework for access control of video. *IEEE Transactions on Circuits and Systems for Video Technology, 12*(6), 545-557.

Wu, C.-P., & Kuo, C.-C. J. (2000, November). Fast encryption methods for audiovisual data confidentiality. In *SPIE Photonics East—Symposium on Voice, Video, and Data Communications* (Vol. 4209, pp. 284-295). Boston.

Wu, H., & Ma, D. (2004, May). Efficient and secure encryption schemes for JPEG2000. In *Proceedings of the 2004 International Conference on Acoustics, Speech and Signal Processing (ICASSP 2004)* (pp. 869-872).

Yuan, C., Zhu, B. B., Su, M., Wang, Y., Li, S., & Zhong, Y. (2003, September). Layered access control for MPEG-4 FGS. *Proceedings of the IEEE International Conference on Image Processing (ICIP'03).* Barcelona, Spain.

Zeng, W., & Lei, S. (1999, November). Efficient frequency domain video scrambling for content access control. In *Proceedings of the seventh ACM international multimedia conference 1999* (pp. 285-293). Orlando, FL.

Zeng, W., & Lei, S. (2003, March). Efficient frequency domain selective scrambling of digital video. *IEEE Transactions on Multimedia, 5*(1), 118-129.

Zeng, W., Wen, J., & Severa, M. (2002, September). Fast selfsynchronous content scrambling by spatially shuffling codewords of compressed bitstreams. In *Proceedings of the IEEE international conference on image processing (ICIP'02).*

ADDITIONAL READING

Acharya, T., & Ray, A. K. (2006). *JPEG2000 standard for image compression: Concepts, algorithms and VLSI architectures.* NJ: Wiley.

Apostolopoulos, J. S., Wee, F. D., Ebrahimi, T., Sun, Q., & Zhang, Z. (2006, May). The emerging JPEG2000 security (JPSEC) standard. *IEEE Proceedings International Symposium on Circuits and Systems (ISCAS).* IEEE.

Fridrich, J., Baldoza, A. C., & Simard, R. J. (1998, April). Robust digital watermarking based on key-dependent basis functions. In D. Aucsmith (Ed.), *Information Hiding: Second International Workshop,* Portland, OR (LNCS 1525, pp. 143-157). Berlin, Germany: Springer–Verlag.

Furht, B., & Kirovski, D. (Eds.). (2005). *Multimedia security handbook.* Boca Raton, FL: CRC Press.

Furht, B., Muharemagic, E., & Socek, D. (2005). *Multimedia encryption and watermarking:* Vol.

28. *Multimedia Systems and Applications*. Berlin, Heidelberg, New York, Tokyo: Springer-Verlag.

Stütz, T., & Uhl, A. (2006). On format-compliant iterative encryption of JPEG2000. *Proceedings of the Eighth IEEE International Symposium on Multimedia (ISM'06)* (pp. 985-990). Los Alamitos, CA: IEEE Computer Society.

Taubman, D., & Marcellin, M. (2002). *JPEG2000— Image compression fundamentals, standards and practice*. Kluwer Academic.

Uhl, A., & Pommer, A. (2005). *Image and video encryption. from digital rights management to secured personal communication:* Vol. 15. *Advances in Information Security*. Springer-Verlag.

Zeng, W., Yu, H. H., & Lin, C.-Y. (2006). *Multimedia security technologies for digital rights management*. Amsterdam: Elsevier.

ENDNOTE

[1]   http://arstechnica.com/news.ars/post/20070401-emi-to-announced-drm-free-plans-tomorrow-reports.html

Compilation of References

Advanced Access Content System Licensing Administrator (AACS)-LA. (2006). *Sequence key block.* In *Pre-recorded video book.* Retrieved from, http://www.aacsla.com/specifications

Agaian, S. (2005). Steganography & steganalysis: An overview of research & challenges. In *Network Security and Intrusion Detection, NATO Proceedings.*

Agaian, S., & Cai, H. (2005). *New multilevel DCT, feature vectors, and universal blind steganalysis.* Paper presented at the Security, Steganography, and Watermarking of Multimedia Contents VII.

Agaian, S., & Rodriguez, B. M. (2006). Basic steganalysis techniques for the digital media forensics examiner. In *Digital Crime and Forensic Science in Cyberspace* (pp. 175-225).

Ahn, J., Shim, H., Jeon, B., & Choi, I. (2004). Digital video scrambling method using intra prediction mode. In *PCM2004* (LNCS 3333, pp. 386-393). Springer.

Ahn, L. V., & Hopper, N. J. (2004). Public-key steganography. In *Advances in Cryptology—Eurocrypt 2004* (LNCS 3027, pp. 323-341). Berlin: Springer.

Alghoniemy, M., & Tewfik, A. H. (1999). *Progressive quantized projection watermarking scheme.* Paper presented at the 7th ACM International Multimedia Conference, Orlando, FL.

Alghoniemy, M., & Tewfik, A. H. (2000). Geometric distortion correction through image normalization. *IEEE International Conference and Multimedia Expo, 3,* 1291-1294.

Allamanche, E., Herre, J., Helmuth, O., Fröba, B., Kasten, T., & Cremer, M. (2001). Content-based identification of audio material using MPEG-7 low level description. In *Electronic Proceedings of the International Symposium of Music Information Retrieval.*

Al-Mualla, M. E., Canagarajah, C. N., & Bull, D. R. (2002). *Video coding for mobile communications: Efficiency, complexity and resilience.* Boston: Academic Press.

Amin, P., & Subbalakshmi, K. (2007). Steganalysis using power spectra of digital images. In *IEEE International Conference on Image Processing.*

Anderson, D. P., Cobb, J., Korpela, E., Lebofsky, M., & Werthimer, D. (2002, November). SETI@home: An experiment in public-resource computing. *Communications of the ACM, 45*(11), 56-61.

Anderson, R. J. (Ed.). (1996). *Proceedings of the First International Workshop on Information Hiding.* (LNCS 1174). London: Springer.

Anderson, R. J., & Petitcolas, F. A. P. (1998). On the limits of steganography. *IEEE Journal on Selected Areas in Communications, 16*(4), 474-481.

Anderson, R., & Manifavas, C. (1997). Chameleon—A new kind of stream cipher. In *Fast Software Encryption* (LNCS, pp. 107-113). Springer-Verlag.

Andrews, H. C., & Patterson, C. (1976). Singular value decomposition (SVD) image coding. *IEEE Transactions on Communications, 24*(4), 425-432.

Andrews, R. (2005). Copyright infringement and the Internet: An economic analysis. *Journal of Science & Technology Law, 11*(2).

Antoine, J. P., Vandergheynst, P., & Murenzi, R. (1996). Two-dimensional directional wavelets in image processing. *International Journal of Imaging Systems and Technology, 7,* 152-165.

Antoniadis, A., Bigot, J., & Sapatinas, T. (2001). Wavelet estimators in nonparametric regression: A comparative simulation study. *Journal of Statistical Software, 6*(6).

Apostolopoulos, J. S., Wee, F. D., Ebrahimi, T., Sun, Q., & Zhang, Z. (2006, May). The emerging JPEG2000 security (JPSEC) standard. *IEEE Proceedings of the International Symposium on Circuits and Systems (ISCAS).*

Arnold, M., Schmucker, M., & Wolthusen, S. D. (2003). *Techniques and applications of digital watermarking and content protection.* Artech House Computer Security.

Aura, T. (1997). Practical invisibility in digital communication. In *First International Workshop on Information Hiding* (Vol. 1174, pp. 51-67). Berlin/Heidelberg, Germany: Springer.

Autrusseau, F., & Le Callet, P. (2007). A robust image watermarking technique based on quantization noise visibility thresholds. *Elsevier Signal Processing, 87*(6), 1363-1383.

Avcibas, I., Memon, N., & Sankur, B. (2003). Steganalysis using image quality metrics. *IEEE Transactions on Image Processing, 12*(2), 221-229.

Awrangjeb, M., & Kankanhalli, M. S. (2004). Lossless watermarking considering the human visual system. *International Workshop on Digital Watermarking 2003* (LNCS 2939, pp. 581-592).

Backes, M., & Cachin, C. (2005, February 10-12). Public-key steganography with active attacks. In J. Kilian (Ed.), *TCC 2005,* Cambridge, MA (LNCS 3378, pp. 210-226). Berlin: Springer.

Barba, D., & Le Callet, P. (2003). A robust quality metric for color image quality assessment. In *IEEE International Conference on Image Processing* (pp. 437-440).

Barg, A., Blakely, R., & Kabatiansky, G. (2003). Digital fingerprinting codes: Problem statements, constructions, identification of traitors. *IEEE Transactions on Information Theory, 49*(4), 852-865.

Barni, M., & Bartolini, F. (2004). Watermarking systems engineering: Enabling digital assets security and other applications. *Signal processing and communications, 21.* New York: Marcel Dekker.

Barni, M., & Bartolini, F. (2004a). Data hiding for fighting piracy. *IEEE Signal Processing Magazine, 21*(2), 28-39.

Barni, M., Bartolini, F., & Furon, T. (2003). A general framework for robust watermarking security. *Signal Processing, 83*(10), 2069-2084.

Barni, M., Bartolini, F., Cappellini, V., & Piva, A. (1998). A DCT-domain system for robust image watermarking. *Signal Processing, 66,* 357-372.

Barni, M., Bartolini, F., De Rosa, A., & Piva, A. (2001). A new decoder for the optimum recovery of non additive watermarks. *IEEE Transactions on Image Processing, 10,* 755-765.

Barreto, P. S. L. M., & Kim, H. Y. (1999). Pitfalls in public key watermarking. In *Proceedings of the Brazilian Symposium on Computer Graphics and Image Processing* (pp. 241-242).

Barreto, P. S. L. M., Kim, H. Y., & Rijmen, V. (2002). Toward a secure public-key blockwise fragile authentication watermarking. *IEE Proceedings Vision, Image and Signal Processing, 149*(2), 57-62.

Bas, P., Chassery, J.-M., & Macq, B. (2002). Geometrically invariant watermarking using feature points. *IEEE Transactions on Image Processing, 11,* 1014-1028.

Bayram, S., Sencar, H. T., Memon, N., & Avcibas, I. (2005, September 11-14). Source camera identification based on CFA interpolation. *Proceedings of the IEEE International Conference on Image Processing 2005, ICIP 2005* (Vol. 3, pp. 69-72).

Bellare, M., & Rogaway, P. (1993). Random oracles are practical: A paradigm for designing efficient protocols.

In *First ACM Conference on Computer and Communications Security* (pp. 62-73). ACM Press.

Belloni, S., Formaglio, A., Menegaz, G., Tan, H. Z., Prattichizzo, D., & Barni, M. (2006, February). Is haptic watermarking worth it? In B. E. Rogowitz, T. N. Pappas, & S. J. Daly (Eds.), *Proceedings of SPIE, 6057, Human Vision and Electronic Imaging XI.*

Bhargava, B., Shi, C., & Wang, Y. (2004). MPEG video encryption algorithms. *Multimedia Tools and Applications, 24*(1), 57-79.

Bhattacharjya, A. K., & Ancin, H. (1999). Data embedding in text for a copier system. *International Conference on Image Processing, 2,* 245-249.

Biddle, P., England, P., Peinado, M., & Willman, B. (2003, January). The darknet and the future of content protection. *ACM Workshop on DRM* (LNCS 2696).

Birney, K. A., & Fischer, T. R. (1995). On the modeling of DCT and subband image data for compression. *IEEE Transactions on Image Processing, 4,* 186-193.

Bloom, J. (2003). Security and rights management in digital cinema. *Proceedings of IEEE International Conference on Acoustic, Speech and Signal Processing, 4,* 712-715.

Bloom, J. A., Cox, I. J., Kalker, T., Linnartz, J. P., Miller, M. L., & Traw, C. B. (1999). Copy protection for digital video. *Proceedings of IEEE, Special Issue on Identification and Protection of Multimedia Information, 87*(7), 1267-1276.

Blum, R. S. (1994). Asymptotically robust detection of known signals in non-additive noise. *IEEE Transactions on Information Theory, 40,* 1612-1619.

Bodo, Y., Laurent, N., & Dugelay, J.-L. (2003, December). A scrambling method based on disturbance of motion vector. *Proceedings of ACM Multimedia 2002* (pp. 89-90). Juan Le Pins, France.

Böhme, R. (2005). Assessment of steganalytic methods using multiple regression models. In M. Barni, J. Herrera-Joancomartí, S. Katzenbeisser, & F. Pérez-González (Eds.), *Information Hiding, 7th International Workshop* (pp. 278-295). Berlin: Springer.

Böhme, R., & Ker, A. (2006). A two-factor error model for quantitative steganalysis. In E. J. Delp, III, & P. W. Wong (Eds.), *Security, steganography, and watermarking of multimedia contents VIII* (SPIE 6072, pp. 0601-0616). Bellingham, WA: SPIE.

Boneh, D., & Shaw, J. (1998). Collusion-secure fingerprinting for digital data. *IEEE Transactions on Information Theory, 44*(5), 1897-1905.

Boneh, D., Gentry, C., & Waters, B. (2005). Collusion resistant broadcast encryption with short ciphertexts and private keys. *Advance in Cryptography, Crypto* (LNCS 3621, pp. 258-275). Berlin, Heidelberg, New York: Springer-Verlag.

Boneh, D., Lynn, B., & Shacham, H. (2002). Short signatures from the weil pairing. *Advances in Cryptology—Asiacrypt'2001* (LNCS 2248, pp. 514-532).

Boneh, D., Sahai, A., & Waters, B. (2006). Fully collusion resistant traitor tracing with short ciphertexts and private keys. *Advance in Cryptography, Eurocrypt* (LNCS, pp. 573-592). Berlin, Heidelberg, New York: Springer-Verlag.

Borges, P. V. K., & Mayer, J. (2007). Text luminance modulation for hardcopy watermarking. *Signal Processing, 87*(7), 1754-1771.

Brassil, J. T., Low, S., & Maxemchuk, N. F. (1999, July). Copyright protection for the electronic distribution of text docu-ments. *Proceedings of IEEE, 87*(7), 1181-1196.

Brown, I., Perkins, C., & Crowcroft, J. (1999). Watercasting: Distributed watermarking of multicast media. In *Proceedings of International Workshop on Networked Group Communication* (LNCS 1736). Springer-Verlag.

Brown, L. G. (1992). A survey of image registration techniques. *Journal of ACM Computing Surveys (CSUR), 24*(4), 325-376.

Buades, A., Coll, B., & Morel, J. M. (2005). A review of image denoising algorithms, with a new one. *Multiscale Modeling & Simulation, 4*(2), 490-530.

Budhia, U., Kundur, D., & Zourntos, T. (2006). Digital video steganalysis exploiting statistical visibility in the temporal domain. *IEEE Transactions on Information Forensics and Security, 1*(4), 502-516.

But, J. (2004, April). *Limitations of existing MPEG-1 ciphers for streaming video* (Tech. Rep. No. CAIA 040429A). Swinburne University, Australia.

Byun, S.-C., Lee, S.-K., Tewfik, H., & Ahn, B.-A. (2002). A SVD-based fragile watermarking scheme for image authentication. In F. A. P. Petitcolas & H. J. Kim (Eds.), *International Workshop on Digital Watermarking* (IWDW '02), Seoul, Korea (pp. 170-178). Berlin/Heidelberg, Germany: Springer.

Cachin, C. (1998). An information-theoretic model for steganography. In D. Aucsmith (Ed.), *Information Hiding, 2nd International Workshop* (LNCS 1525, pp. 306-318). Berlin: Springer.

Cachin, C. (1998). Information-theoretic model for steganography. In *Second International Workshop on Information Hiding* (Vol. 1525, pp. 306-318). Berlin/Heidelberg, Germany: Springer.

Cachin, C. (2004). An information-theoretic model for steganography. *Information and Computation, 192*(1), 41-56.

Cachin, C. (2005). Digital steganography. In H. C. Van Tilborg (Ed.), *Encyclopedia of Cryptography and Security* (pp. 159-164). New York: Springer.

Cai, L., & Du, S. (2004). Rotation, scale and translation invariant image watermarking using radon transform and Fourier transform. In *Proceedings of the Circuits and Systems Symposium on Emerging Technologies: Frontiers of Mobile and Wireless Communication* (pp. 281-284). IEEE.

Calagna, M., & Mancini, L. V. (2005). A blind method for digital watermarking attacks. In M. H. Hamza (Ed.), *International Conference on Internet and Multimedia Systems and Applications* (EuroIMSA '05), Grindelwald, Switzerland (pp. 265-270). Calgary, AB, Canada: IASTED/ACTA Press.

Calagna, M., & Mancini, L. V. (2007). Information hiding for spatial and geographical data. In A. Belussi, B. Catania, E. Clementini, & E. Ferrari (Eds.), *Spatial data on the Web—Modeling and management*. Springer.

Calagna, M., Guo, H., Mancini, L. V., & Jajodia, S. (2006). A robust watermarking system based on SVD compression. In *Proceedings of the Symposium on Applied Computing* (SAC '06) Dijon, France (pp. 1341-1347). New York: ACM Press.

Caldelli, R., Piva, A., Barni, M., & Carboni, A. (2005). Effectiveness of ST-DM watermarking against intra-video collusion. In *Proceedings of 4th International Workshop on Digital Watermarking, IWDW 2005*, Siena, Italy (LNCS 3710, pp. 158-170).

Calvagno, G., Ghirardi, C., Mian, G. A., & Rinaldo, R. (1997). Modeling of subband image data for buffer control. *IEEE Transactions on Circuits and Systems for Video Technology, 7*, 402-408.

Campisi, P., & Piva, A. (2006). Data hiding for image and video coding. In M. Barni & F. Bartolini (Eds.), *Document and image compression* (pp. 255-282). New York: Dekker.

Campisi, P., Carli, M., Giunta, G., & Neri, A. (2003). Blind quality assessment system for multimedia communications. *IEEE Transactions on Signal Processing, Special issue on Signal Processing for Data Hiding in Digital Media & Secure Content Delivery, 51*(4), 996-1002.

Campisi, P., Kundur, D., Hatzinakos, D., & Neri, A. (2002). Compressive data hiding: An unconventional approach for improved color image coding. *EURASIP Journal on Applied Signal Processing, Special issue on Emerging Applications of Multimedia Data Hiding, 2002* (pp. 152-163).

Caner, G., Tekalp, A. M., & Hainzelman, W. (2006). Local image registration by adaptive filtering. *IEEE Transactions on Image Processing, 15*(10), 3053-3065.

Carnec, M., Le Callet, P. L., & Barba, D. (2003). An image quality assessment method based on perception of structural information. *IEEE Transactions on Image Processing, 3*, 185-188.

Cayre, F., Fontaine, C., & Furon, T. (2005). Watermarking security: Theory and practice. *IEEE Transactions on Signal Processing, 53*(10), 3976-3987.

Celik, M. U., Sharma, G., & Tekalp, A. M. (2005). Collusion-resilient fingerprinting by random pre-warping. *IEEE Signal Processing Letters,* Preprint.

Celik, M. U., Sharma, G., Saber, E., & Tekalp, A. M. (2002b). Hierarchical watermarking for secure image authentication with localization. *IEEE Transactions on Image Processing, 11*(6), 585-595.

Celik, M. U., Sharma, G., Tekalp, A. M., & Saber, E. (2002a). Reversible data hiding. *IEEE International Conference on Image Processing* (Vol. 2, pp. 157-160).

Celik, M. U., Sharma, G., Tekalp, A. M., & Saber, E. (2005). Lossless generalized-LSB data embedding. *IEEE Transactions on Image Processing, 14*(2), 253-266.

Celik, M., Sharma, G., & Tekalp, A. (2004). Universal image steganalysis using rate-distortion curves. In *Security, Steganography, and Watermarking of Multimedia Content VI* (Vol. 5306, pp. 467-476). IS&T/SPIE.

Chandramouli, R. (2002). Mathematical theory for steganalysis. In *Security, Steganography, and Watermarking of Multimedia Contents IV* (Vol. 4675, pp. 14-25). IS&T/SPIE.

Chandramouli, R., & Memon, N. (2001). Analysis of LSB based image steganography techniques. In *International Conference on image processing (ICIP'01)* (Vol. 3, pp. 1019-1022).

Chandramouli, R., & Memon, N. (2003). Steganography capacity: A steganalysis perspective. In *Security, Steganography, and Watermarking of Multimedia Contents V* (Vol. 5020, pp. 173-177). IS&T/SPIE.

Chandramouli, R., Kharrazzi, M., & Memon, N. (2004). Image steganography and steganalysis: Concepts and practice. In *International Workshop on Digital Watermarking* (Vol. 2939, pp. 35-49). Berlin/Heidelberg, Germany: Springer.

Chandramouli, R., Trivedi, S., & Uma, R. N. (2004). On the complexity and hardness of the steganography

embedding problem. In E. J. Delp, III & P. W. Wong (Eds), Security, steganography, and watermarking of multimedia contents VI. *Proceedings of the SPIE, 5306, 496-500.*

Chang, C.-C., & Lin, C.-J. (2001). *Libsvm: A library for support vector machines.* Retrieved from http://www.csie.ntu.edu.tw/~cjlin/libsvm

Chang, C.-C., Tseng, C.-S., & Lin, C.-C. (2005). Hiding data in binary images (LNCS 3439, pp. 338-349).

Chen, B., & Wornell, G. (2000). Preprocessed and postprocessed quantization index modulation methods for digital watermarking. In *Security, Steganography, and Watermarking of Multimedia Contents III* (Vol. 3971). IS&T/SPIE.

Chen, B., & Wornell, G. W. (2001). Quantization index modulation: A class of provably good methods for digital watermarking and information embedding. *IEEE Transactions on Information Theory, 47*(4), 1423-1443.

Cheng, H., & Li, X. (1996, September). On the application of image decomposition to image compression and encryption. In P. Horster (Ed.), *Communications and Multimedia Security II, IFIP TC6/TC11 Second Joint Working Conference on Communications and Multimedia Security, CMS '96* (pp. 116-127). Essen, Germany: Chapman & Hall.

Cheng, Q., & Huang, T. S. (2001a). An additive approach to transform-domain information hiding and optimum detection structure. *IEEE Transactions on Multimedia, 3,* 273-284.

Cheng, Q., & Huang, T. S. (2001b). Optimum detection of multiplicative watermarks using locally optimum decision rule. In *Proceedings of the IEEE International Conference Multimedia and Expo,* Tokyo, Japan.

Cheng, Q., & Huang, T. S. (2002). Optimum detection and decoding of multiplicative watermarks in DFT domain. In *Proceedings of the IEEE International Conference on Acoustic, Speech, and Signal Processing,* Orlando, FL.

Cheng, Q., & Huang, T. S. (2003). Robust optimum detection of transform domain multiplicative watermarks. *IEEE Transactions on Signal Processing, 51*, 906-924.

Chernick, M. R. (1999). *Bootstrap methods: A practitioner's guide.* New York: Wiley.

Chor, B., Fiat, A., & Naor, M. (1994). Tracing traitors. *Advance in Cryptography, Crypto* (LNCS 839, pp. 480-491). Berlin, Heidelberg, New York: Springer-Verlag.

Chor, B., Fiat, A., Naor, M., & Pinkas, B. (2000) Tracing traitors. *IEEE Transactions on Information Theory, 46*, 893-910.

Chun, I. G., & Ha, S. H. (2004). A robust printed image watermarking based on iterative halftoning method. *International Workshop on Digital Watermarking 2003* (LNCS 2939, pp. 200-211).

Chung, K.-L., Shen, C.-H., & Chang, L.-C. (2001). A novel SVD-and VQ-based image hiding scheme. *Pattern Recognition Letters, 22*, 1051-1058.

Cohen, H., Frey, G., Avanzi, R. M., Doche, C., Lange, T., Nguyen, K., et al. (2005). *Handbook of elliptic and hyperelliptic curve cryptography.* Chapman & Hall/CRC.

Cohnen, G., Encheva, S., Litsyn, S., & Schaathun, H. G. (2003). Intersecting codes and separating codes. *Discrete Applied Mathematics, 128*(1), 75-83.

Corvi, M., & Nicchiotti, G. (1997). Wavelet based image watermarking for copyright protection. In *Scandinavian Conference on Image Analysis, SCIA* (p. 9705).

Cox I. J., & Miller, M. L. (2002). The first 50 years of electronic watermarking. *EURASIP Journal on Applied Signal Processing, 2*, 126-132.

Cox, I. J., Kilian, J., Leighton, F. T., & Shamoon, T. (1997). Secure spread spectrum watermarking for multimedia. *IEEE Transactions on Image Processing, 6*, 1673-1687.

Cox, I. J., Miller, M. L., & Bloom, J. A. (2002). *Digital watermarking.* San Francisco: Morgan Kaufmann.

Cox, I. J., Miller, M., & Bloom, J. (2001). *Digital watermarking: Principles & practice* (1st ed.). San Francisco: Morgan Kaufmann.

Craver, S. (1998). On public-key steganography in the presence of an active warden. *Information Hiding, 1525*, 355-368.

Craver, S. A., Wu, M., & Liu, B. (2001). What can we reasonably expect from watermarks? In *Proceedings of the IEEE Workshop on the Applications of Signal Processing to Audio and Acoustics* (pp. 223-226).

Craver, S., Memon, N., Yeo, B., & Yeung, M. (1998). Resolving rightful ownerships with invisible watermarking techniques: Limitations, attacks, and implications. *IEEE Journal on Selected Areas in Communications, 16*(4), 573-586.

Dedić, N., Itkis, G., Reyzin, L., & Russell, S. (2005). Upper and lower bounds on black-box steganography. In J. Kilian (Ed.), *Second Theory of Cryptography Conference, TCC 2005* (LNCS 3378, pp. 227-244). Berlin: Springer.

Deguillaume, F., Csurka, G., Ruanaidh, J. J. K. O., & Pun, T. (1999). Robust 3d dft video watermarking. *SPIE Electronic Imaging '99: Security and Watermarking of Multimedia Contents* (Vol. 3657, pp. 113-124).

Deguillaume, F., Voloshynovskiy, S., & Pun, T. (2002). A method for the estimation and recovering from general affine transforms in digital watermarking applications. *SPIE Electronic Imaging 2002, Security and Watermarking of Multimedia Contents IV* (Vol. 4675, pp. 313-322).

Delannay, D., & Macq, B. (2000). Generalized 2-d cyclic patterns for secret watermark generation. *IEEE International Conference on Image Processing* (Vol. 2, pp. 77-79).

Delannay, D., & Macq, B. (2002). Method for hiding synchronization marks in scale and rotation resilient watermarking schemes. *SPIE Security and Watermarking of Multimedia Contents IV* (Vol. 4675, pp. 520-529).

Dietl, W. M., & Uhl, A. (2004, June). Robustness against unauthorized watermark removal attacks via key-dependent wavelet packet subband structures. *Proceedings of the IEEE International Conference on Multimedia and Expo, ICME '04*. Taipei, Taiwan.

Dietl, W., & Uhl, A. (2003, October). Watermark security via secret wavelet packet subband structures. In A. Lioy & D. Mazzocchi (Eds.), *Communications and Multimedia Security. Proceedings of the Seventh IFIP TC-6 TC-11 Conference on Communications and Multimedia Security* (LNCS 2828, pp. 214-225). Turin, Italy: Springer-Verlag.

Digimarc Cooperation. (2006). *Digimarc digital image watermarking guide*. Retrieved March 21, from http://www.digimarc.com/comm/docs/Watermarking-Guide.pdf

Digital Cinema Initiatives (DCI). (2007). *Digital Cinema System Specification, v1.1*. Retrieved April 12, 2007, from http://www.dcimovies.com/

Digital Display Working Group. (1999, April). *Digital visual interface, DVI*. Retrieved March 21, from http://www.ddwg.org/lib/dvi_10.pdf

Dinitz, J. H., & Stinson, D. R. (1992). *Contemporary design theory: A collection of surveys*. New York: Wiley.

Dittmann, J., & Steinmetz, R. (1997a, July). Enabling technology for the trading of MPEG-encoded video. *Information Security and Privacy: Second Australasian Conference, ACISP '97* (Vol. 1270, pp. 314-324).

Dittmann, J., & Steinmetz, R. (1997b, September). A technical approach to the transparent encryption of MPEG-2 video. In S. K. Katsikas (Ed.), *Communications and Multimedia Security, IFIP TC6/TC11 Third Joint Working Conference, CMS '97* (pp. 215-226). Athens, Greece: Chapman and Hall.

Dittmann, J., Katzenbeisser, S., Schallhart, C., & Veith, H. (2004). *Provably secure authentication of digital media through invertible watermarks. Cryptology ePrint Archive: Report 2004/293*. Retrieved from http://eprint.iacr.org/2004/293

Do, M. N., & Vetterli, M. (2002). Wavelet-based texture retrieval using generalized Gaussian density and Kullbackleibler distance. *IEEE Transactions on Image Processing, 11*, 146-158.

Doerr, G., & Dugelay, J. L. (2003b). New intra-video collusion attack using mosaicing. In *Proceedings of IEEE International Conference Multimedia Expo*. (Vol. II, pp. 505-508).

Doerr, G., & Dugelay, J. L. (2004). Security pitfalls of frame-by-frame approaches to video watermarking. *IEEE Transactions on Signal Processing, 52*, 2955-2964.

Doerr, G., & Dugelay, J.-L. (2003). A guided tour to video watermarking. *Signal Processing: Image Communication, 18*, 263-282.

Doerr, G., & Dugelay, J.-L. (2003a). A guide tour of video watermarking. *Signal Processing: Image Communication, Special Issue on Technologies for Image Security, 18*(4), 263-282.

Donoho, D. L., & Johnstone, I. M. (1995). Adapting to unknown smoothness via wavelet shrinkage. *Journal of the American Statistical Association, 90*(432), 1200-1224.

Draper, S., Ishwar, P., Molnar, D., Prabhakaran, V., Ramchandran, K., Schonberg, D., et al. (2005). An analysis of empirical PMF based tests for least significant bit image steganography. In M. Barni, J. Herrera-Joancomartí, S. Katzenbeisser, & F. Pérez-González (Eds.), *Information Hiding, 7th International Workshop* (pp. 327-341). Berlin: Springer.

Droogenbroeck, M. V. (2004, April). Partial encryption of images for real-time applications. *Proceedings of the 4th 2004 Benelux Signal Processing Symposium* (pp. 11-15). Hilvarenbeek, The Netherlands.

Droogenbroeck, M. V., & Benedett, R. (2002, September). Techniques for a selective encryption of uncompressed and compressed images. *Proceedings of ACIVS (Advanced Concepts for Intelligent Vision Systems)* (pp. 90-97). Ghent University, Belgium.

Duda, R., & Hart, P. (1973). *Pattern classification and scene analysis.* New York: John Wiley.

Dufaux, F., & Ebrahimi, T. (2003). Securing JPEG2000 compressed images. In A. G. Tescher (Ed.), *Applications of Digital Image Processing XXVI* (SPIE 5203, pp. 397-406).

Dufaux, F., Wee, S., Apostolopoulos, J., & Ebrahimi, T. (2004, August). JPSEC for secure imaging in JPEG2000. *Proceedings of SPIE* (SPIE 5558, pp. 319-330).

Dumitrescu, S., Wu, X., & Wang, Z. (2002). Detection of LSB steganography via sample pair analysis. In *5th International Workshop on Information Hiding* (Vol. 2578). Berlin/Heidelberg, Germany: Springer.

Dumitrescu, S., Wu, X., & Wang, Z. (2003). Detection of LSB steganography via sample pair analysis. *IEEE Transactions on Signal Processing, 51*(7), 1995-2007.

EBU-SAMVIQ. (2003). *Subjective assessment methodology for video quality report* (Tech. Rep. EBU BPN 056). EBU Project Group B/VIM (Video in Multimedia).

Edfors, O., Sandell, M., Van de Beek, J.-J., Wilson, S. K., & Borjesson, P. O. (1998). OFDM channel estimation by singular value decomposition. *IEEE Transactions on Communications, 46*(7), 931-939.

Egan, J. P. (1975). *Signal detection theory and ROC analysis.* New York: Academic Press.

Eggers, J. J., & Girod, B. (2001). Blind watermarking applied to image authentication. *ICASSP'2001: International Conference on Acoustics, Speech and Signal Processing.* Salt Lake City, UT.

Ekici, O., Sankur, B., & Akcay, M. (2004). A comparative evaluation of semi-fragile watermarking algorithms. *Journal of Electronic Imaging, 13*(1), 209-219.

Electronic Frontier Foundation. (2007). *EFF: Sony BMG litigation.* Retrieved March 21, from http://www.eff.org/IP/DRM/Sony-BMG/

Elmasry, G. F., & Shi, Y. Q. (1999). Maximum likelihood sequence decoding of digital image watermarks.

In *Proceedings of SPIE Security and Watermarking of Multimedia Contents* (pp. 425-436). San Jose, CA.

Engel, D., & Uhl, A. (2006a, May). Secret wavelet packet decompositions for JPEG2000 lightweight encryption. *Proceedings of 31st International Conference on Acoustics, Speech, and Signal Processing, ICASSP '06* (Vol. V, pp. 465-468). Toulouse, France.

Engel, D., & Uhl, A. (2006b, July). Lightweight JPEG2000 encryption with anisotropic wavelet packets. *Proceedings of International Conference on Multimedia & Expo, ICME '06* (pp. 2177-2180). Toronto, Canada.

Engel, D., & Uhl, A. (2007, January). An evaluation of lightweight JPEG2000 encryption with anisotropic wavelet packets. In E. J. Delp & P. W. Wong (Eds.), *Security, Steganography, and Watermarking of Multimedia Contents IX* (SPIE, pp. 65051S1-65051S10). San Jose, CA: SPIE.

Engel, D., Stütz, T., & Uhl, A. (in press-a). Format-compliant JPEG2000 encryption with combined packet header and packet body protection. *Proceedings of the ACM Multimedia and Security Workshop (MM-SEC '07).* Houston, TX.

Engel, D., Stütz, T., & Uhl, A. (in press-b). Efficient JPEG2000 transparent encryption with format-compliant header protection. *Proceedings of the IEEE International Conference on Signal Processing and Communications (ICSPC '07).* Houston, TX.

Ettinger, J. M. (1998). Steganalysis and game equilibria. *Information Hiding, 1525,* 319-328.

Fang, J., & Sun, J. (2006). Compliant encryption scheme for JPEG2000 image code streams. *Journal of Electronic Imaging, 15*(4), 043013.

Farid, H. (2001). *Detecting steganographic messages in digital images* (Tech. Rep. No. TR2001-412). Department of Computer Science, Dartmouth College, Hanover, NH.

Farid, H. (2002). Detecting hidden messages using higher-order statistical models. In *International Conference on image processing (ICIP'02)* (Vol. 2, pp. 905-908).

Farid, H. (2006). *Digital image ballistics from JPEG quantization* (Tech. Rep. No. TR2006-583). Hanover, NH: Dartmouth College, Department of Computer Science.

Fawcett, T. (2003). *ROC graphs: Notes and practical considerations for data mining researchers* (Tech. Rep. No. HPL-2003-4). Palo Alto, CA: HP Labs.

Ferguson, T. (1967). *Mathematical statistics: A decision theoretical approach*. Academic Press.

Fiat, A., & Naor, M. (1993). Broadcast encryption. *Advance in Cryptography, Crypto* (LNCS 773, 480-491). Berlin, Heidelberg, New York: Springer-Verlag.

Fiat, A., & Tassa, T. (1999). Dynamic traitor tracing. *Advance in Cryptography, Crypto* (LNCS 1666, 354-371. Berlin, Heidelberg, New York: Springer-Verlag.

Figueiredo, M. A. T., & Nowak, R. D. (2001). Wavelet-based image estimation: An empirical Bayes approach using Jeffrey's noninformative prior. *IEEE Transactions on Image Processing, 10*(9), 1322-1331.

Fisch, M. M., Stögner, H., & Uhl, A. (2004, September). Layered encryption techniques for DCT-coded visual data (paper cr1361). *Proceedings (CD-ROM) of the European Signal Processing Conference, EUSIPCO '04*. Vienna, Austria.

Fisk, G., Fisk, M., Papadopoulos, C., & Neil, J. (2003, October 7-9). Eliminating steganography in Internet traffic with active wardens. In *Information Hiding: 5th International Workshop, IH 2002,* Noordwijkerhout, The Netherlands. *Revised Papers* (Vol. 2578, pp. 18-35). Berlin: Springer.

Fridrich, J. (1998, July 19-24). Combining low-frequency and spread spectrum watermarking. *Proceedings of the SPIE symposium on optical science, Engineering and Instrumentation* (Vol. 3456). San Diego, CA.

Fridrich, J. (1999). Applications of data hiding in digital images. *Tutorial for the ISSPA conference, Part I.*

Fridrich, J. (1999). Methods for tamper detection in digital images. In *Proceedings of the ACM Workshop on Multimedia and Security* (pp. 19-23).

Fridrich, J. (2004). Feature-based steganalysis for JPEG images and its implications for future design of steganographic schemes. *Information Hiding, 3200,* 67-81.

Fridrich, J., & Goljan, M. (2002). Practical steganalysis: state-of-the-art. In *Security, Steganography, and Watermarking of Multimedia Contents IV* (Vol. 4675, pp. 1-13). IS&T/SPIE.

Fridrich, J., & Goljan, M. (2003). Digital image steganography using stochastic modeling. In *Security, Steganography, and Watermarking of Multimedia Content V* (Vol. 5020, pp. 191-202).

Fridrich, J., & Goljan, M. (2004). On estimation of secret message length in LSB steganography in spatial domain. In E. J. Delp, III, & P. W. Wong (Eds.), *Security, steganography, and watermarking of multimedia contents VI* (SPIE 5306, pp. 23-34). Bellingham, WA: SPIE.

Fridrich, J., Du, R., & Long, M. (2000). Steganalysis of LSB encoding in color images. In *International Conference on Multimedia and Expo (ICME'00)* (Vol. 3, pp. 1279-1282).

Fridrich, J., Goljan, M., & Du, R. (2001). Detecting LSB steganography in color and gray-scale images. *IEEE MultiMedia, Special Issue on Security, 8*(4), 22-28.

Fridrich, J., Goljan, M., & Du, R. (2001). Invertible authentication. *Proceedings of SPIE Security and Watermarking of Multimedia Contents III* San Jose, CA (Vol. 3971, pp. 197-208).

Fridrich, J., Goljan, M., & Du, R. (2001). *Steganalysis based on JPEG compatibility*. Paper presented at the Proceedings of SPIE Multimedia Systems and Applications IV, Denver, CO.

Fridrich, J., Goljan, M., & Du, R. (2002). Lossless data embedding—New paradigm in digitalwatermarking. *EURASIP Journal on Applied Signal Processing, 2,* 185-196.

Fridrich, J., Goljan, M., & Hogea, D. (2002a). Steganalysis of JPEG images: Breaking the F5 algorithm. In F. A. P. Petitcolas (Ed.), *Information Hiding, 5th International Workshop* (pp. 310-323). Berlin: Springer.

Fridrich, J., Goljan, M., & Hogea, D. (2002b). Attacking the OutGuess. In *4th ACM Workshop on Multimedia and Security*. New York: ACM Press.

Fridrich, J., Goljan, M., & Hogea, D. (2003). New methodology for breaking steganographic techniques for JPEGS. In *Security, Steganography, and Watermarking of Multimedia Contents V* (Vol. 5020, p. 143-155). IS&T/SPIE.

Fridrich, J., Goljan, M., & Holotyak, T. (2006). New blind steganalysis and its implications. In E. J. Delp, III, & P. W. Wong (Eds.), *Security, steganography, and watermarking of multimedia contents VIII* (SPIE 6072, pp. 0101-0113). Bellingham, WA: SPIE.

Fridrich, J., Goljan, M., Hogea, D., & Soukal, D. (2003). Quantitative steganalysis of digital images: Estimation of the secret message length. *ACM Multimedia Systems Journal, 9*.

Fridrich, J., Soukal, D., & Goljan, M. (2005). Maximum likelihood estimation of length of secret message embedded using ±K steganography in spatial domain. In E. J. Delp, III, & P. W. Wong (Eds.), *Security, steganography, and watermarking of multimedia contents VII* (SPIE 5681, pp. 595-606). Bellingham, WA: SPIE.

Fridrich, J., Soukal, D., & Goljan, M. (2005). Stochastic approach to secret message length estimation in +-k embedding steganography. In *Security, Steganography, and Watermarking of Multimedia Content VII* (Vol. 5681, pp. 673-684). IS&T/SPIE.

Friedman, G. L. (1993). The trustworthy digital camera: Restoring credibility to the photographic image. *IEEE Transactions on Consumer Electronics, 39*(4), 905-910.

Fu, M. S., & Au, A. C. (2004). Joint visual cryptography and watermarking. In *Proceedings of the International Conference on Multimedia and Expro (ICME2004)* (pp. 975-978).

Fu, M. S., & Au, O. C. (2000). Data hiding by smart pair toggling for halftone images. *IEEE International Conference on Acoustics Speech and Signal Processing* (Vol. 4, pp. 2318-2321).

Ganic, E., & Eskicioglu, A. M. (2004). Robust DWT-SVD domain image watermarking: Embedding data in all frequencies. In *Proceedings of the Multimedia and Security workshop* (MM&Sec '04), Magdeburg, Germany (pp. 167-174). New York: ACM Press.

Ganic, E., Zubair, N., & Eskicioglu, A. M. (2003). An optimal watermarking scheme based on singular value decomposition. In M. H. Hamza (Ed.), *International Conference on Communication, Network and Information Security* (CNIS '03), Uniondale, NY (pp. 85-90). Calgary, AB, Canada: IASTED/ACTA Press.

Ganz, A., Park, S. H., & Ganz, Z. (1999). Experimental measurements and design guidelines for real-time software encryption in multimedia wireless LANs. *Cluster Computing, 2*(1), 35-43.

Garey, M. R., & Johnson, D. S. (1979). *Computers and intractability: A guide to the theory of NP-completeness.* New York: W. H. Freeman & Co.

Golomb, S. W. (1966). Run-length encodings. *IEEE Transactions on Information Theory, 12*, 399-401.

Golub, G. H., & Van Loan, C. F. (1996). *Matrix computations* (3rd ed.). Baltimore, MD: Johns Hopkins University Press.

Gonzalez, R. C., & Woods, R. E. (2002). *Digital image processing* (2nd ed.). Prentice Hall.

Gorodetski, V. I., Popyack, L. J., Samoilov, V., & Skormin, V. A. (2001). SVD-based approach to transparent embedding data into digital images. In V. I. Gorodetski, V. A. Skormin, & L. J. Popyack (Eds.), *Workshop on information assurance in computer networks: Methods, models, and architectures for network security* (MMM-ACNS '01), St. Petersburg, Russia (LNCS 2052, pp. 263-274). London: Springer-Verlag.

Grangetto, M., Magli, E., & Olmo, G. (2006). Multimedia selective encryption by means of randomized arithmetic coding. *IEEE Transactions on Multimedia, 8*(5), 905-917.

Green, D. M., & Swets, J. A. (1966). *Signal detection theory and psychophysics.* New York: Wiley.

Grosbois, R., Gerbelot, P., & Ebrahimi, T. (2001, July). Authentication and access control in the JPEG2000 compressed domain. In A. Tescher (Ed.), *Applications of Digital Image Processing XXIV* (SPIE 4472, pp. 95-104). San Diego, CA.

Haitsma, J., Kalker, T., & Oostveen, J. (2001). Robust audio hashing for content identification. In *Proceedings of the International Workshop on Content-Based Multimedia Indexing*.

Halderman, J. A. (2002). Evaluating new copy-prevention techniques for audio CDs. In *Proceedings of the ACM Workshop on Digital Rights Management*. New York: ACM Press.

Harmsen, J. J., & Pearlman, W. A. (2003). Steganalysis of additive noise modelable information hiding. In E. J. Delp, III, & P. W. Wong (Eds.), *Security, steganography, and watermarking of multimedia contents V* (SPIE 5020). Bellingham, WA: SPIE.

Harmsen, J. J., & Pearlman, W. A. (2004). Kernel Fisher discriminant for steganalysis of JPEG hiding methods. In E. J. Delp, III, & P. W. Wong (Eds.), *Security, steganography, and watermarking of multimedia contents VI* (SPIE 5306, pp. 13-22). Bellingham, WA: SPIE.

Harris, C., & Stephen, M. (1988). A combined corner and edge detector. *4th Alvey Vision Conference* (Vol. 1, pp 147-151).

Hartung, F., & Girod, B. (1997). Digital watermarking of MPEG-2 coded video in the bitstream domain. *Proceedings of the International Conference on Acoustics, Speech and Signal Processing, 4,* 2621-2624.

Hartung, F., Su, J., & Girod, B. (1999). Spread-spectrum watermarking: Malicious attacks and counterattacks. *SPIE Security and Watermarking of multimedia contents* (Vol. 3657, pp. 147-158).

Håstad, J., Impagliazzo, R., Levin, L., & Luby, M. (1999). Construction of a pseudo-random generator from any one-way function. *SIAM Journal on Computing, 28*(4), 1364-1396.

Hauer, E., & Thiemert, S. (2004). Synchronization techniques to detect MPEG video frames for watermarking retrieval. *Proceedings of the SPIE, Security and Watermarking of Multimedia Contents IV, 5306,* 315-324.

Haykin, S. (2001). *Adaptive filter theory* (4th ed.). Upper Saddle River, NJ: Prentice Hall.

Hernandez, J. R., Amado, M., & Perez-Gonzalez, F. (2000). DCT-domain watermarking techniques for still images: Detector performance analysis and a new structure. *IEEE Transactions on Image Processing, 9,* 55-68.

Herrigel, A., Oruanaidh, J., Petersen, H., Pereira, S., & Pun, T. (1998). Secure copyright protection techniques for digital images. In *Second Information Hiding Workshop (IHW)* (LNCS 1525). Springer-Verlag.

Herrigel, A., Voloshynovskiy, S., & Rytsar, Y. (2001). The watermark template attack. *SPIE Security and Watermarking of Multimedia Contents III* (Vol. 4314, pp. 394-405).

Hogan, M. T., Hurley, N. J., Silvestre, G. C. M., Balado, F., & Whelan, K. M. (2005). ML detection of steganography. In E. J. Delp, III, & P. W. Wong (Eds.), *Security, steganography, and watermarking of multimedia contents VII* (SPIE 5681, pp. 16-27). Bellingham, WA: SPIE.

Hogan, M. T., Silvestre, G. C. M., & Hurley, N. J. (2004). Performance evaluation of blind steganalysis classifiers. In E. J. Delp, III, & P. W. Wong (Eds.), *Security, steganography, and watermarking of multimedia contents VI* (SPIE 5306, pp. 58-69). Bellingham, WA: SPIE.

Holliman, M., & Memon, N. (2000). Counterfeiting attacks on oblivious block-wise independent invisible watermarking schemes. *IEEE Transactions on Image Processing, 9*(3), 432-441.

Hollmann, H. D., Van Lint, J. J., Linnartz, J. P., & Tolhuizen, L. M. (1998). On codes with the identifiable parent property. *Journal of Combinatorial Theory, series A, 82,* 121-133.

Holotyak, T., Fridrich, J., & Soukal, D. (2005). Stochastic approach to secret message length estimation in ±K embedding steganography. In E. J. Delp, III, & P. W. Wong (Eds.), *Security, steganography, and watermarking of multimedia contents VII* (SPIE 5681, pp. 673-684). Bellingham, WA: SPIE.

Holotyak, T., Fridrich, J., & Voloshynovskiy, S. (2005). Blind statistical steganalysis of additive steganography using wavelet higher order statistics. In *9th IFIP TC-6 TC-11 Conference on Communications and Multimedia Security*.

Honsinger, C. W., Jones, P. W., Rabbani, M., & Stoffel, J. C. (2001). Lossless recovery of an original image containing embedded data (US Patent #6,278,791).

Hopper, N. J. (2004). *Toward a theory of steganography.* Unpublished PhD thesis, School of Computer Science, Carnegie Mellon University, Pittsburgh, PA.

Hopper, N. J., Langford, J., & Ahn, L. V. (2002). Provably secure steganography. In M. Yung (Ed.), *Advances in Cryptology—CRYPTO 2002* (LNCS 2442, pp. 77-92). Berlin: Springer.

Howard, P. G., Kossentini, F., Martins, B., Forchhammer, S., & Rucklidge, W. J. (1998). The emerging JBIG2 Standard. *IEEE Transactions on Circuit Systems of Video Technology, 8*(7), 838-848.

Hundt, C., Liśkiewicz, M., & Wölfel, U. (2006). Provably secure steganography and the complexity of sampling. In T. Asano (Ed.), Proceedings of the *17th International Symposium on Algorithms and Computation (ISAAC 2006)* (LNCS 4288, pp. 754-763). Berlin: Springer.

Hyung, C. K., Ogunleye, H., Guitar, O., & Delp, E. J. (2004). The watermark evaluation testbed (WET). In E. J. Delp & P. W. Wong (Eds.), *Proceedings of SPIE, Security and Watermarking of Multimedia Contents VI* (pp. 236-247). San Jose, CA.

Imaizumi, S., Watanabe, O., Fujiyoshi, M., & Kiya, H. (2005, September). Generalized hierarchical encryption of JPEG2000 codestreams for access control. *Proceedings of the IEEE International Conference on Image Processing (ICIP'05)* (Vol. 2).

International Organization for Standardization (ISO). (1999). *Information technology—Coded representation of picture and audio information—Lossy/lossless coding of bi-level images.* Retrieved from http://www.jpeg.org/public/fcd14492.pdf

International Organization for Standardization (ISO)/ IEC. (2007, April). *Information technology—JPEG2000 image coding system, Part 8: Secure JPEG2000* (ISO/IEC 15444-8). Author.

International Telecommunication Union (ITU). (1995). *Studio encoding parameters of digital television for standard 4:3 and wide-screen 16:9 aspect ratios* (Tech. Rep. No. ITU-R-BT.601-5). Author.

International Telecommunication Union (ITU). (1998). *Subjective audiovisual quality assessment methods for multimedia applications* (Tech. Rep. No. ITU-T-P.911). Author.

International Telecommunication Union (ITU). (2004a). *Methodology for the subjective assessment of the quality of television pictures question ITU-R 211/11, g* (Tech. Rep. No. ITU-R-BT.500-11). Author.

International Telecommunication Union (ITU). (2004b). *Objective perceptual video quality measurement techniques for digital cable television in the presence of a full reference* (Tech. Rep. No. ITU-T-J.144). Author.

International Telecommunications Union (ITU). (1993). *CCITT T.81 information technology—Digital compression and coding of continuous-tone still images—Requirements and guidelines.* Author.

Jain, A. K. (1989). *Fundamentals of digital image processing.* Upper Saddle River, NJ: Prentice Hall.

Japan Electronics and Information Technology Industries Association (JEITA). (2002). *JEITA CP-3451 Exchangeable image file format for digital still cameras: Exif Version 2.2.* Author.

Jayant, N., Johnston, J., & Safranek, R. (1993). Signal compression based on models of human perception. *Proceedings of the IEEE, 81,* 1385-1422.

Jin, H., & Lotspiech, J. (2007). Renewable traitor tracing: a trace-revoke-trace system for anonymous attack. *European Symposium on Research on Computer Security* (pp. 563-577).

Jin, H., Lotspiech, J., & Nusser, S. (2004). Traitor tracing for prerecorded and recordable media. *ACM Digital Rights Management Workshop* (pp. 83-90). Washington DC: ACM Press.

Johnson, N. F. (2000). Steganalysis. In S. Katzenbeisser & F. A. P. Petitcolas (Eds), *Information hiding—Techniques for steganography and digital watermarking* (pp. 79-93). Boston: Artech House.

Johnson, N., & Jajodia, S. (1998). Steganalysis: The investigation of hidden information. In *Proceedings of the IEEE Information Technology Conference*.

Johnson, N., & Jajodia, S. (1998a). Exploiting steganography: Seeing the unseen. *IEEE Computers, 31*(2), 26-34.

Johnson, N., & Jajodia, S. (1998b). Steganalysis of images created using current steganography software. In *Second International Workshop on Information Hiding* (Vol. 1525, pp. 273-279). Berlin/Heidelberg, Germany: Springer.

JPEG-JSteg-V4. (n.d.). Retrieved from http://www.funet.fi/pub/crypt/steganography/jpeg-jsteg-v4.diff.gz

Judge, P., & Ammar, M. (2000, June). WHIM: Watermarking multicast video with a hierarchy of intermediaries. In *Proceedings of NOSSDAV 2000*. Chapel Hill, NC.

Kaewkamnerd, N., & Rao, K. R. (2000). Wavelet based watermarking detection using multiresolution image registration. *TENCON 2000* (Vol. 2, pp. 171-175).

Kalker, J. L. T., & Depovere, G. (1998). Modeling the false-alarm and missed detection rate for electronic watermarks. *Workshop on Information Hiding* (LNCS 1529, pp. 329-343).

Kalker, T. (2001). Considerations on watermarking security. In *Proceedings of the IEEE Multimedia Signal Processing MMSP'01 Workshop,* Cannes, France (pp. 201-206).

Kankanhalli, M. S., & Guan, T. T. (2002). Compressed-domain scrambler/descrambler for digital video. *IEEE Transactions on Consumer Electronics, 48*(2), 356-365.

Kankanhalli, M. S., & Hau, K. F. (2002). Watermarking of electronic text documents. *Electronic Commerce Research, 2*(1), 169-187.

Karthik, K., & Hatzinakos, D. (2007). Decryption key design for joint fingerprinting and decryption in the sign bit plane for multicast content protection. *International Journal of Network Security, 4*(3), 254-265.

Katzenbeisser, S., & Penticolas, F. A. P. (2000). *Information hiding techniques for steganography and digital watermarking.* Norwood, MA: Artech House.

Katzenbeisser, S., & Petitcolas, F. A. P. (2002). Defining security in steganographic systems. In E. J. Delp, III & P. W. Wong (Eds.), Security and watermarking of multimedia contents IV. *Proceedings of the SPIE, 4675, 50-56.*

Ker, A. D. (2004a). Quantitative evaluation of pairs and RS steganalysis. In E. J. Delp, III, & P. W. Wong (Eds.), *Security, steganography, and watermarking of multimedia contents VI* (SPIE 5306, pp. 83-97). Bellingham, WA: SPIE.

Ker, A. D. (2004b). Improved detection of LSB steganography in grayscale images. In J. Fridrich (Ed.), *Information Hiding, 6th International Workshop* (pp. 97-115). Berlin: Springer.

Ker, A. D. (2005). A general framework for structural steganalysis of LSB replacement. *Information Hiding, 3727,* 296-311.

Ker, A. D. (2005a). Resampling and the detection of LSB matching in color bitmaps. In E. J. Delp, III, & P. W. Wong (Eds.), *Security, steganography, and watermarking of multimedia contents VII* (SPIE 5681, pp. 1-16). Bellingham, WA: SPIE.

Ker, A. D. (2005). Steganalysis of LSB matching in grayscale images. *IEEE Signal Processing Letters, 12*(6), 441-444.

Ker, A. D. (2007). Optimally weighted least-squares steganalysis. In E. J. Delp, III, & P. W. Wong (Eds.), *Security, steganography, and watermarking of multimedia contents IX* (SPIE 6505, pp. 0601-0616). Bellingham, WA: SPIE.

Ker, A. D. (2007). Steganalysis of embedding in two least-significant bits. *IEEE Transactions on Information Forensics and Security, 2*(1), 46-54.

Ker, A. D. (2007). Derivation of error distribution in least squares steganalysis. *IEEE Transactions on Information Forensics and Security, 2*(2), 140-148.

Ker, A. D. (2007d). A capacity result for batch steganography. *IEEE Signal Processing Letters, 14*(8), 525-528.

Ker, A. D. (in press). Batch steganography and pooled steganalysis. *Information Hiding, 8th International Workshop.* Berlin: Springer.

Ker, A. D. (in press). The ultimate steganalysis benchmark? In *Proceedings of 9th ACM Multimedia and Security Workshop.* New York: ACM Press.

Kerckhoffs, A. (1883). La cryptographie militaire. *Journal des sciences militaires, IX,* 5-83.

Kessler, G. (2004). An overview of steganography for the computer forensics examiner. *Forensics Science and Communications, 6*(3).

Kharrazi, M., Sencar, H. T., & Memon, N. (2005). Benchmarking steganographic and steganalysis techniques. In E. J. Delp, III, & P. W. Wong (Eds.), *Security, steganography, and watermarking of multimedia contents VII* (SPIE 5681, pp. 252-263). Bellingham, WA: SPIE.

Khelifi, F., Bouridane, A., & Kurugollu, F. (2006). On the optimum multiplicative watermark detection in the transform domain. In *Proceedings of the IEEE International Conference on Image Processing.*

Kiayias, A., & Yung, M. (2001). On crafty piates and foxy tracers. *ACM Digital Rights Management Workshop* (Vol. 2696, pp. 22-39). Washington DC: Springer-Verlag.

Kiayias, A., Raekow, Y., & Russell, A. (2005). E±cient steganography with provable security guarantees. In

7th International Workshop on Digital Watermarking (Vol. 3727, pp. 118-130). Berlin/Heidelberg, Germany: Springer.

Kim, H. Y. (2005). A new public-key authentication watermarking for binary document images resistant to parity attacks. *IEEE International Conference on Image Processing, 2,* 1074-1077.

Kim, H. Y., & Afif, A. (2004). Secure authentication watermarking for halftone and binary images. *International Journal of Imaging Systems and Technology, 14*(4), 147-152.

Kim, H. Y., & De Queiroz, R. L. (2004). Alteration-locating authentication watermarking for binary images. *International Workshop on Digital Watermarking 2004, (Seoul)* (LNCS 3304, pp. 125-136).

Kim, H. Y., & Mayer, J. (in press). Data hiding for binary documents robust to print-scan, photocopy and geometric Distortions. *Proceedings of the Simpósio Bras. Comp. Gráfica e Proc. Imagens.*

Kim, J., & Moon, Y. (1999). A robust wavelet based digital watermark using label adaptive thresholding. *Proceedings of the 6th IEEE International Conference on Image Processing* (pp. 202-205).

Kiya, H., Imaizumi, D., & Watanabe, O. (2003, September). Partial scrambling of image encoded using JPEG2000 without generating marker codes. *Proceedings of the IEEE International Conference on Image Processing (ICIP'03)* (Vol. III, pp. 205-208). Barcelona, Spain.

Klimant, H., & Piotraschke, R. (1997). Informationstheoretische Bewertung steganographischer Konzelationssysteme. In *Proceedings of the Verläßliche IT-Systeme (VIS'97)* (pp. 225-232). DuD Fachbeiträge, Vieweg.

Knuth, D. E. (1987). Digital halftones by dot diffusion. *ACM Transactions Graph., 6*(4).

Koch, E., & Zhao, J. (1995). Towards robust and hidden image copyright labeling. *IEEE International Workshop on Nonlinear Signal and Image Processing* (pp. 452-455).

Kundur, D., & Hatzinakos, D. (1998). Towards a telltale watermarking technique for tamper-proofing. *Proceedings of the IEEE International Conference on Image Processing* (Vol. 2, pp. 409-413).

Kundur, D., & Karthik, K. (2004). Video fingerprinting and encryption principles for digital rights management. *Proceedings of the IEEE, 92*(6), 918-932.

Kundur, D., Su, K., & Hatzinakos, D. (2004). Digital video watermarking: Techniques, technology and trends. In *Intelligent watermarking techniques* (pp. 265-314). World Scientific.

Kunkelmann, T. (1998, September). Applying encryption to video communication. *Proceedings of the Multimedia and Security Workshop at ACM Multimedia '98* (pp. 41-47). Bristol, England.

Kunkelmann, T., & Horn, U. (1998). Partial video encryption based on scalable coding. *5th International Workshop on Systems, Signals and Image Processing (IWSSIP '98)* (pp. 215-218). Zagreb, Croatia.

Kutter, M. (1998). Watermarking resisting to translation, rotation and scaling. *SPIE Conference Multimedia Systems and Applications* (Vol. 3528, pp. 423-431).

Kutter, M., Bhattacharjee, S. K., & Ebrahimi, T. (1999). Toward second generation watermarking schemes. *IEEE International Conference on Image Processing* (Vol. 1, pp. 320-323).

Kutter, M., Jordan, F., & Bossen, F. (1997). Digital signature of colour images using amplitude modulation. *SPIE Storage and Retrieval for Image and Video Databases* (Vol. 3022, pp. 518-526).

Kwon, S.-G., Lee, S.-H., Kwon, K.-K., Kwon, K.-R., & Lee, K. (2002). Watermark detection algorithm using statistical decision theory. In *Proceedings of the IEEE International Conference on Multimedia and Expo,* Lausanne, Switzerland.

Lan, T. H., Mansour, M. F., & Tewfik, A. H. (2001). Robust high capacity data embedding. *IEEE International Conference on Acoustics Speech and Signal Processing, 1,* 581-584.

Langelaar, G. C., Setyawan, I., & Langendijk, R. L. (2000). Watermarking digital image and video data. *IEEE Signal Processing Magazine, 17,* 20-46.

Langley, A., & Bloomberg, D. S. (2007, January). Google books: Making the public domain universally accessible. *Proceedings of SPIE, Document Recognition and Retrieval XIV* (paper 65000H). San Jose, CA.

Le, T. V. (2004). *Information hiding.* Unpublished PhD thesis, Florida State University, Tallahassee, College of Arts and Sciences.

Le, T. V., & Kurosawa, K. (2003). *Efficient public key steganography secure against adaptively chosen stego-text attacks* (Tech. Rep. No. 2003/244). IACR ePrint Archive.

Lee, H.-Y., Kim, H., & Lee, H.-K. (2006). Robust image watermarking using local invariant features. *Journal of Optical Engineering, 45*(3), 037002.

Lemma, A. N., Katzenbeisser, S., Celik, M. U., & Veen, M. V. (2006). Secure watermark embedding through partial encryption. In *Proceedings of International Workshop on Digital Watermarking (IWDW 2006)* (LNCS 4283, pp. 433-445). Springer.

Li, C. T., Lou, D. C., & Chen, T. H. (2000). Image authentication and integrity verification via content-based watermarks and a public key cryptosystem. *IEEE International Conference on Image Processing* (Vol. 3, pp. 694-697).

Li, Y., Chen, Z., Tan, S.-M., & Campbell, R. H. (1996). Security enhanced MPEG player. In *Proceedings of IEEE first international workshop on multimedia software development (mmsd'96)* (pp. 169-175). Berlin, Germany.

Lian, S., Liu, Z., Ren, Z., & Wang, H. (2006). Secure distribution scheme for compressed data streams. In *2006 IEEE Conference on Image Processing (ICIP 2006).*

Lian, S., Liu, Z., Ren, Z., & Wang, Z. (2005). Selective video encryption based on advanced video coding. In *2005 Pacific-Rim Conference on Multimedia (PCM2005)* (LNCS 3768, pp. 281-290).

Lian, S., Sun, J., & Wang, Z. (2004). A novel image encryption scheme based-on JPEG encoding. In *Proceedings of the Eighth International Conference on Information Visualization (IV)* (pp. 217-220). London.

Lian, S., Sun, J., & Wang, Z. (2004c). Perceptual cryptography on SPIHT compressed images or videos. *The IEEE International Conference on Multimedia and Expro (I) (ICME2004), Taiwan, 3*, 2195-2198.

Lian, S., Sun, J., & Wang, Z. (2004d). Perceptual cryptography on JPEG2000 compressed images or videos. In *The International Conference on Computer and Information Technology (CIT2004)* (pp. 78-83). Wuhan, China.

Lian, S., Sun, J., & Wang, Z. (2005). Security analysis of a chaos-based image encryption algorithm. *Physica A: Statistical and Theoretical Physics, 351*(2-4), 645-661.

Lian, S., Sun, J., & Wang, Z. (2005). A block cipher based on a suitable use of the chaotic standard map. *International Journal of Chaos, Solitons and Fractals, 26*(1), 117-129.

Lian, S., Sun, J., Zhang, D., & Wang, Z. (2004a). A selective image encryption scheme based on JPEG2000 codec. In *The 2004 Pacific-Rim Conference on Multimedia (PCM2004)* (LNCS 3332, pp. 65-72). Springer.

Lichtenauer, J., Setyawan, I., Kalker, T., & Lagendijk, R. (2003). Exhaustive geometrical search and false positive watermark detection probability. *SPIE Electronic Imaging 2002, Security and Watermarking of Multimedia Contents V* (Vol. 5020, pp. 303-214).

Lin, C. Y., Wu, M., Bloom, J. A., Cox, I. J., Miller, M. L., & Lui, Y. M. (2001). Rotation, scale, and translation resilient watermarking for images. *IEEE Transactions on Image Processing, 10*(5), 767-782.

Lin, C.-Y. (1999). *Public watermarking surviving general scaling and cropping: An application for print-and-scan process*. Paper presented at the Multimedia and Security Workshop at ACM Multimedia '99, Orlando, FL.

Lin, C.-Y., & Chang, S.-F. (2000). Semi-fragile watermarking for authenticating JPEG visual content. *Proc. SPIE Int. Soc. Opt. Eng, 3971,* 140-151.

Lin, C.-Y., & Chang, S.-F. (2001). A robust image authentication method distinguishing JPEG compression from malicious manipulation. *IEEE Transactions on Circuits and Systems of Video Technology, 11*(2), 153-168.

Lin, E. I., Eskicioglu, A. M., Lagendijk, R. L., & Delp, E. J. (2005). Advances in digital video content protection. *Proceedings of the IEEE, 93*(1), 171-183.

Lin, E., Podilchuk, C., & Delp, E. (2000b). Detection of image alterations using semi-fragile watermarks. *Proceedings of the SPIE International Conference on Security and Watermarking of Multimedia Contents II, 3971.*

Lindeberg, T. (1998). Feature detection with automatic scale selection. *International Journal of Computer Vision, 30*(2), 79-116.

Liu, R., & Tan, T. (2002). An SVD-based watermarking scheme for protecting rightful ownership. *IEEE Transactions on Multimedia, 4*(1), 121-128.

Lohscheller, H. (1984). A subjectively adapted image communication system. *IEEE Transactions on Communications, 32*(12), 1316-1322.

Lookabaugh, T. D., Sicker, D. C., Keaton, D. M., Guo, W. Y., & Vedula, I. (2003, September). Security analysis of selectiveleyencrypted MPEG-2 streams. In *Multimedia systems and applications vi* (Vol. 5241, pp. 10-21).

Lowe, D. (2004). Distinctive image features from scale invariant keypoints. *International Journal of Computer Vision, 2*(60), 91-110.

Lu, C.-S., & Hsu, C.-Y. (2005). Geometric distortion-resilient image hashing scheme and its applications on copy detection and authentication. *Multimedia Systems, 11*(2), 159-173.

Lu, P., Luo, X., Tang, Q., & Shen, L. (2004). An improved sample pairs method for detection of LSB embedding. In J. Fridrich (Ed.), *Information Hiding, 6th International Workshop* (pp. 116-127). Berlin: Springer.

Lu, X., & Eskicioglu, A. M. (2003, November). Selective encryption of multimedia content in distribution networks: Challenges and new directions. In *Proceed-*

ings of the IASTED international conference on on communications, internet and information technology (CIIT 2003). Scottsdale, AZ.

Lukáš, J., & Fridrich, J. (2003, August). Estimation of primary quantization matrix in double compressed JPEG images. *Proceedings of Digital Forensic Research Workshop,* Cleveland, OH.

Lukáš, J., Fridrich, J., & Goljan, M. (2006). Digital camera identification from sensor pattern noise. *IEEE Transactions on Information Forensics and Security, 1*(2), 205-214.

Lysyanskaya, A., & Meyerovich, M. (2006). Provably secure steganography with imperfect sampling. In M. Yung, Y. Dodis, A. Kiayias, & T. Malkin (Eds), *Public Key Cryptography—PKC 2006* (LNCS 3958, pp. 123-139). Berlin: Springer.

Lyu, S., & Farid, H. (2002). Detecting hidden messages using higher-order statistics and support vector machines. In *5th International Workshop on Information Hiding* (Vol. 2578, pp. 340-354). Berlin/Heidelberg, Germany: Springer.

Lyu, S., & Farid, H. (2003). Detecting hidden messages using higher-order statistics and support vector machines. *Information Hiding, 2578*, 340-354.

Lyu, S., & Farid, H. (2004). Steganalysis using color wavelet statistics and one-class support vector machines. In *Security, Steganography, and Watermarking of Multimedia Contents VI* (Vol. 5306, pp. 35-45). IS&T/SPIE.

Lyu, S., & Farid, H. (2006). Steganalysis using higher-order image statistics. *IEEE Transactions on Information Forensics and Security, 1*(1), 111-119.

Macq, B. M., & Quisquater, J.-J. (1995). Cryptology for digital TV broadcasting. *Proceedings of the IEEE, 83*(6), 944-957.

Macq, B., & Quisquater, J. (1994). Digital images multiresolution encryption. *The Journal of the Interactive Multimedia Association Intellectual Property Project, 1*(1), 179-206.

Macq, B., Dittman, J., & Delp, E. J. (2004). Benchmarking of image watermarking algorithms for digital rights management. *Proceedings of the IEEE, 92*(6), 971-984.

Maes, M., Kalker, T., Linnartz, J., Talstra, J., Depovere, G., & Haitsma, J. (2000). Digital watermarking for DVD video copy protection. *IEEE Signal Processing Magazine, 17*(5), 47-57.

Malik, H., Subbalakshmi, K., & Chandramouli, R. (2007). Steganalysis of quantization index modulation based steganography using kernel density estimation. In *9th ACM Multimedia and Security Workshop.*

Malik, H., Subbalakshmi, K., & Chandramouli, R. (in press). Nonparametric steganalysis of quantization index modulation based steganography using approximate entropy. *IEEE Transactions on Information Forensics and Security.*

Malik, H., Subbalakshmi, K., & Chandramouli, R. (in press). Nonparametric steganalysis of quantization index modulation based steganography using kernel density estimaton. *IEEE Transactions on Information Forensics and Security.*

Mallat, S. (1999). *A wavelet tour of signal processing* (2nd ed.). Academic Press.

Mallat, S. G. (1989). A theory for multiresolution signal decomposition: The wavelet representation. *IEEE Transactions on Pattern Analysis and Machine Intelligence, 11,* 674-693.

Maniccam, S. S., & Nikolaos, G. B. (2004). Image and video encryption using SCAN patterns. *Pattern Recognition, 37*(4), 725-737.

Mao, Y., & Mihcak, M. K. (2005). Collusion-resistant international de-synchronization for digital video fingerprinting. In *IEEE Conference on Image Processing.*

Marcum, J. I. (1948). A statistical theory of target detection by pulsed radar: Mathematical appendix. RAND Corporation Research Memorandum RM-753, 1948. Reprinted in *IRE Transactions on Information Theory, 6,* 59-267, 1960.

Marini, E., Autrusseau, F., Le Callet, P., & Campisi, P. (2007, January). Evaluation of standard watermarking techniques. *SPIE Electronic Imaging 2007, Security, Steganography, and Watermarking of Multimedia Contents IX,* San Jose, CA.

Marr, D. (1982). *Vision.* San Francisco: Freeman.

Marvel, L. M., Boncelet, C. G., Jr., & Retter, C. T. (1999). Spread spectrum image steganography. *IEEE Transactions on Image Processing, 8*(8), 1075-1083.

Marvel, L. M., Hartwig, G. W., Jr., & Boncelet, C., Jr. (2000). Compression compatible fragile and semifragile tamper detection. *Proceedings of the SPIE International Conference on Security and Watermarking of Multimedia Contents II* (Vol. 3971).

Matsuoka, H. (2006). Spread spectrum audio steganography using subband phase shifting. In *International Conference on Intelligent Information Hiding and Multimedia* (pp. 3-6).

Maxemchuk, N. F., & Low, S. (1997). Marking text documents. *IEEE International Conference on Image Processing* (Vol. 3, pp. 13-17).

McGrew, D. A., & Viega, J. (2005). *The Galois/counter mode of operation (GCM)* (NIST Draft Special Publication 800-38D). Retrieved from http://csrc.nist.gov/CryptoToolkit/modes/proposed-modes/gcm/gcm-revised-spec.pdf

McLachlan, G. J. (2004). *Discriminant analysis and statistical pattern recognition* (Rev. ed.). Wiley.

McNicol, D. (1972). *A primer of signal detection theory.* London: Allen and Unwin.

Meerwald, P. (2001, January). *Digital image watermarking in the wavelet transform domain.* Master's thesis, Department of Scientific Computing, University of Salzburg, Austria, Retrieved from http://www.cosy.sbg.ac.at/~pmeerw

Mei, Q., Wong, E. K., & Memon, N. (2001). Data hiding in binary text documents. *Proceedings of SPIE* (Vol. 4314, pp. 369-375).

Michiels, B., & Macq, B. (2006). Benchmarking image watermarking algorithms with openwatermark. In *14th European Signal Processing Conference, EU-SIPCO06.*

Mikolajczyk, K., & Schmid, C. (2001). Indexing based on scale invariant interest points. *Proceedings of the 8th International Conference on Computer Vision* (Vol. 1, pp 525-531).

Mikolajczyk, K., & Schmid, C. (2004). Scale and affine invariant interest point detectors. *International Journal of Computer Vision, 1*(60), 63-86.

Mikolajczyk, K., & Schmid, C. (2005). A performance evaluation of local descriptors. *IEEE Transactions on Pattern Analysis and Machine Intelligence, 27,* 1615-1630.

Miller, J. H., & Thomas, J. B. (1972). Detectors for discrete-time signals in non-Gaussian noise. *IEEE Information Theory, 18,* 241-250.

Miller, M. L., & Bloom, J. A. (1999). Computing the probability of false watermark detection. *Third International Workshop on Information Hiding* (**LNCS 1796**, pp. 146-158).

Mittelholzer, T. (2000). An information-theoretic approach to steganography and watermarking. In A. Pfitzmann (Ed.), *Information Hiding, 3rd International Workshop (IH'99)* (LNCS 1768, pp. 1-16). Berlin: Springer.

Miyaji, A., Nakabayashi, M., & Takano, S. (2001). New explicit conditions of elliptic curve traces for FR-reduction. *IEICE Transactions on Fundamentals, E84-A*(5), 1234-1243.

Mollin, R. A. (2006). *An introduction to cryptography.* CRC Press.

Montgomery, D. C. (2004). *Design and analysis of experiments* (6th ed.). New York: Wiley.

Moulin, P., & Briassouli, A. (2004). A stochastic QIM algorithm for robust, undetectable image watermarking. In *IEEE International Conference on Image Processing, ICIP 2004* (Vol. 2, pp. 1173-1176).

Moulin, P., & Koetter, R. (2005). Data-hiding codes. *Proceedings of the IEEE, 93*(12), 2083-2126.

Moulin, P., & O'Sullivan, J. A. (2003). Information-theoretic analysis of information hiding. *IEEE Transaction on Information Theory, 49*(3), 563-593.

Muti, D., Bourennane, S., & Guillaume, M. (2004). SVD-based image filtering improvement by means of image rotation. In *Proceedings of the International Conference on Acoustics, Speech and Signal Processing* (ICASSP '04), Montreal, Quebec, Canada (pp. 289-292). IEEE Press.

Nakajima, N., & Yamaguchi, Y. (2004). Enhancing registration tolerance of extended visual cryptography for natural images. *Journal of Electronics Imaging, 13*(3), 654-662.

Naor, D., Naor, M., & Lotspiech, J. (2001). Revocation and tracing schemes for stateless receivers. *Advance in Cryptography, Crypto* (LNCS 2139, pp. 41-62). Berlin, Heidelberg, New York: Springer-Verlag.

Naor, M., & Shamir, A. (1994). Visual cryptography. In A. De Santis (Ed.), *Advances in Cryptology-Eurocrypt '94* (LNCS 950, pp. 1-12). Berlin, Germany: Springer-Verlag.

National Institute of Standards and Technology (NIST). (2005). *Recommendation for block cipher modes of operation: The CMAC mode for authentication* (Special Publication 800-38B). Retrieved from http://csrc.nist.gov/CryptoToolkit/modes/800-38_Series_Publications/SP800-38B.pdf

Neelamani, R., De Queiroz, R., Fan, Z., Dash, S., & Baraniuk, R. (2006). JPEG compression history estimation for color images. *IEEE Transactions on Image Processing, 15*(6), 1365-1378.

Ng, T. M., & Grag, H. K. (2004). Wavelet domain watermarking using maximum likelihood detection. In *Proceedings of SPIE Conference on Security, Steganography, Watermarking Multimedia Contents, 5306*, San Jose, CA.

Ng, T. M., & Grag, H. K. (2005). Maximum likelihood detection in DWT domain image watermarking using Laplacian modeling. *IEEE Signal Processing Letters, 12*, 285-288.

Ni, Z. C., Shi, Y. Q., Ansari, N., Su, W., Sun, Q. B., & Lin, X. (2004). Robust lossless image data hiding. *IEEE International Conference and Multimedia and Expo 2004* (pp. 2199-2202).

Nikoladis, A., & Pitas, I. (1999). Region-based image watermarking. *IEEE Transaction on Image Processing, 1*, 320-333.

Ninassi, A., Le Callet, P., & Autrusseau, F. (2006). Pseudo no reference image quality metric using perceptual data hiding. *SPIE Electronic Imaging, 6057*, 146-157.

Norcen, R., & Uhl, A. (2003, October). Selective encryption of the JPEG2000 bitstream. In A. Lioy & D. Mazzocchi (Eds.), *Communications and Multimedia Security. Proceedings of the IFIP TC6/TC11 Sixth Joint Working Conference on Communications and Multimedia Security, CMS '03* (LNCS 2828, pp. 194-204). Turin, Italy: Springer-Verlag.

Ohm, J.-R. (2005). Advances in scalable video coding. *Proceedings of the IEEE, 93*(1), 42-56.

Ozer, H., Avcibas, I., Sankur, B., & Memon, N. (2003, January). Steganalysis of audio based on audio quality metrics. *Security and Watermarking of Multimedia Contents V, 5020*, of Proceedings of SPIE55-66. Santa Clara, CA.

Ozer, H., Sankur, B., & Memon, N. (2005). An SVD-based audio watermarking technique. In *Proceedings of the Workshop on Multimedia and Security* (MM&Sec '05), New York (pp. 51-56). New York: ACM Press.

Pamboukian, S. V. D., & Kim, H. Y. (2005). New public-key authentication watermarking for JBIG2 resistant to parity attacks. *International Workshop on Digital Watermarking 2005, (Siena)* (LNCS 3710, pp. 286-298).

Pamboukian, S. V. D., & Kim, H. Y. (2006). *Reversible data hiding and reversible authentication watermarking for binary images.* Retrieved from http://www.lps.usp. br/~hae/sbseg2006-rdtc.pdf

Papoulis, A. (1991). *Probability, random variables, and stochastic processes.* McGraw-Hill.

Parnes, R., & Parviainen, R. (2001). Large scale distributed watermarking of multicast media through encryption. In *Proceedings of the IFIP International Conference on Communications and Multimedia Security Issues of the New Century.*

Pereira, S., & Pun, T. (1999, October). Fast robust template matching for affine resistant image watermarking. *International Workshop on Information Hiding* (LNCS 1768, pp. 200-210).

Pereira, S., & Pun, T. (2000). An iterative template matching algorithm using the chirp-z transform for digital image watermarking. *Pattern Recognition, 33*(1), 173-175.

Pereira, S., & Pun, T. (2000). Robust template matching for affine resistant image watermarks. *IEEE Transactions on Image Processing, 9,* 1123-1129.

Pereira, S., Ruanaidh, J. J. K. O., Deguillaume, F., Csurka, G., & Pun, T. (1999, June). Template based recovery of Fourier-based watermarks using logpolar and log-log maps. *IEEE Multimedia Systems 99, International Conference on Multimedia Computing and Systems* (Vol. 1, pp. 870-874).

Pereira, S., Voloshynovskiy, S., Madueo, M., Marchand-Maillet, S., & Pun, T. (2001). Second generation benchmarking and application oriented evaluation. In I. S. Moskowitz (Ed.), International *Workshop on Information Hiding* (IWIH '01), Pittsburgh, PA (LNCS 2137, pp. 340-353). London: Springer-Verlag.

Petitcolas, F. A. P. (1998). *MP3Stego software, updated 2006.* Retrieved March 2007, from http://www.petitcolas. net/fabien/steganography/mp3stego/

Petitcolas, F. A. P. (2000). Watermarking schemes evaluation. *IEEE. Signal Processing, 17*(5), 58-64.

Petitcolas, F. A. P., Anderson, R. J., & Kuhn, M. G. (1998). Attacks on copyright marking systems. D. Aucsmith (Ed),

Information Hiding, Second International Workshop, IH'98 (LNCS 1525, pp. 219-239).

Pevný, T., & Fridrich, J. (2007). Merging Markov and DCT features for multi-class JPEG steganalysis. In E. J. Delp, III, & P. W. Wong (Eds.), *Security, steganography, and watermarking of multimedia contents IX* (SPIE 6505, pp. 0301-0313). Bellingham, WA: SPIE.

Peyré, G. (2007). *A toolbox for the non-local means algorithm.* Mathworks Matlab Central File Exchange.

Phillips, C. L., & Parr, J. M. (1999). *Signals, systems, and transforms.* Prentice Hall.

Pommer, A., & Uhl, A. (2002, December). Application scenarios for selective encryption of visual data. In J. Dittmann, J. Fridrich, & P. Wohlmacher (Eds.), *Multimedia and Security Workshop, ACM Multimedia* (pp. 71-74). Juan-les-Pins, France.

Pommer, A., & Uhl, A. (2003). Selective encryption of wavelet-packet encoded image data—Efficiency and security. *ACM Multimedia Systems (Special issue on Multimedia Security), 9*(3), 279-287.

Popescu, A. C., & Farid, H. (2005). Exposing digital forgeries by detecting traces of resampling. *IEEE Transactions on Signal Processing, 53*(2).

Portilla, J., Strela, V., Wainwright, M. J., & Simoncelli, E. P. (2003). Image denoising using scale mixtures of Gaussians in the wavelet domain. *IEEE Transactions on Image Processing, 12*(11), 1338-1351.

Press, W. H., Teukolsky, S. A., Vettering, W. T., & Flannery, B. P. (1992). *Numerical recipes in C: The art of scientific computation* (2nd ed.). Cambridge University Press.

Proakis, J. G. (2000). *Digital communications* (4th ed.). McGraw-Hill Higher Education.

Provos, N., & Honeyman, P. (2001). Detecting steganographic contents on the Internet (Tech. Rep. No. CITI 01-1a). Ann Arbor, MI: University of Michigan.

Provos, N., & Honeyman, P. (2003). Hide and seek: An introduction to steganography. *IEEE Security and Privacy Magazine, 1*(3), 32-44.

Qiao, L., & Nahrstedt, K. (1997, June). A new algorithm for MPEG video encryption. In *Proceedings of the international conference on imaging science, systems, and technology, CISST '97* (pp. 21- 29). Las Vegas, NV.

Qiao, L., & Nahrstedt, K. (1998). Comparison of MPEG encryption algorithms. *International Journal on Computers and Graphics, Special Issue on Data Security in Image Communication and Networks, 22*(3), 437-444.

Reyzin, L., & Russell, S. (2003). *More efficient provably secure steganography* (Tech. Rep. No. 2003/093). IACR ePrint Archive.

Rice, J. A. (1994). *Mathematical statistics and data analysis* (2nd ed.). Pacific Grove, CA: Duxbury Press.

Roetling, P., & Loce, R. (1994). Digital halftoning. In E. Dougherty (Ed.), *Digital image processing methods.* New York: Marcel Dekker.

Rosenblatt, B. (2007, March). *Thomson moves watermarking into consumer devices.* Retrieved March 21, 2007, from http://www.drmwatch.com/drmtech/article.php/3667096

Rosenblatt, B., Trippe, B., & Mooney, S. (2001). *Digital rights management: Business and technology.* New York: Hungry Minds/John Wiley & Sons.

Ruanaidh, J. J. K. O., & Pun, T. (1998). Rotation, scale and translation invariant spread spectrum digital image watermarking. *Signal Processing, 66,* 303-318.

Safavi-Naini, R., & Wang, Y. (2003). Sequential traitor tracing. *IEEE Transactions on Information Theory, 49*(5), 1319-1326.

Sallee, P. (2003). Model-based steganography. In *6th International Workshop on Digital Watermarking* (Vol. 3929, pp. 154-167). Berlin/Heidelberg, Germany: Springer.

Sallee, P. (2004). Model-based steganography. In T. Kalker, Y. M. Ro, & I. J. Cox (Eds), *Digital Watermarking, Second International Workshop, IWDW 2003* (LNCS 2939, pp. 154-167). Berlin: Springer.

Sallee, P. (2005). Model-based methods for steganography and steganalysis. *International Journal of Image and Graphics, 5*(1), 167-189.

Salomon, D. (2004). *Data compression: The complete reference* (3rd ed.). Springer.

Schmucker, M., & Ebinger, P. (2005). Promotional and commercial content distribution based on a legal and trusted P2P framework. In *Proceedings of the Seventh IEEE International Conference on E-Commerce Technology* (CEC'05) (pp. 439-442).

Schneider, M., & Chang, S.-F. (1996). A robust content based digital signature for image authentication. *IEEE International Conference on Image Processing* (Vol. 3, pp. 227-230).

Schneier, B. (1996). *Applied cryptography* (2nd ed.). John Wiley & Sons.

Schneier, B. (2001). *The futility of digital copy prevention.* In CRYPTO-GRAM. Retrieved March 21, from http://cryptome.org/futile-cp.htm

Schnorr, C. P. (1991). Efficient signature generation for smart cards. *Journal of Cryptology, 4*(3), 161-174.

Schwarz, H., Marpe, D., & Wiegand, T. (2006, October). Overview of the scalable H.264/MPEG4-AVC extension. *Proceedings of the IEEE International Conference on Image Processing (ICIP '06).* Atlanta, GA.

Sharifi, K., & Leon-Garcia, A. (1995). Estimation of shape parameters for generalized Gaussian distributions in subband decomposition of video. *IEEE Transactions on Circuits and Systems for Video Technology, 5,* 52-56.

Sharp, T. (2001). An implementation of key-based digital signal steganography. In I. Moskowitz (Ed.), *Information Hiding, 4th International Workshop* (pp. 13-26). Berlin: Springer.

Sheikh, H. R., & Bovik, A. C. (2006). Image information and visual quality. *IEEE Transactions on Image Processing, 15*(2), 430-444.

Sheikh, H. R., Bovik, A. C., & De Veciana, G. (2005). An information fidelity criterion for image quality assessment using natural scene statistics. *IEEE Transactions on Image Processing, 14*(12), 2117-2128.

Sheikh, H. R., Sabir, M. F., & Bovik, A. C. (2006). A statistical evaluation of recent full reference image quality assessment algorithms. *IEEE Transactions on Image Processing, 15*(11), 3440-3451.

Shi, C., & Bhargava, B. (1998, September). A fast MPEG video encryption algorithm. In *Proceedings of the sixth ACM international multimedia conference* (pp. 81-88). Bristol, UK.

Shi, T., King, B., & Salama, P. (2006). Selective encryption for H.264/AVC video coding. *Proceedings of SPIE, Security, Steganography, and Watermarking of Multimedia Contents VIII, 6072, 607217.*

Shi, Y. Q. (2004). Reversible data hiding. *International Workshop on Digital Watermarking 2004, (Seoul)* (LNCS 3304, pp. 1-13).

Shi, Y. Q., Chen, C., & Chen, W. (in press). A Markov process based approach to effective attacking JPEG steganography. *Information Hiding, 8th International Workshop.* Berlin: Springer.

Shin, S., Sim, K., & Rhee, K. (1999, November). A secrecy scheme for MPEG video data using the joint of compression and encryption. In *Proceedings of the 1999 information security workshop (ISW'99)* (Vol. 1729, pp. 191-201). Kuala Lumpur: Springer-Verlag.

Si, H., & Li, C. (2004). Fragile watermarking scheme based on the block-wise dependence in the wavelet domain. In *Proceedings of the Workshop on Multimedia and Security* (MM&Sec '04), Magdeburg, Germany (pp. 214-219). New York: ACM Press.

Simitopoulos, D., Zissis, N., Georgiadis, P., Emmanouilidis, V., & Strintzis, M. G. (2003). Encryption and watermarking for the secure distribution of copyrighted MPEG video on DVD. *ACM Multimedia Systems Journal, Special Issue on Multimedia Security, 9*(3), 217-227.

Simmons, G. J. (1984). The prisoners' problem and the subliminal channel. In *Advances in Cryptology,* *Proceedings of CRYPTO '83* (pp. 51-67). New York: Plenum Press.

Simoncelli, E. P., & Olshausen, B. A. (2001). Natural image statistics and neural representation. *Annual Review of Neuroscience, 24,* 1193-1216.

Smith, C. B., Akopian, D., & Agaian, S. (2004). *Least squares optimization of a polynomial threshold for wavelet domain denoising.* Paper presented at the 7th International Conference on Signal Processing Proceedings.

Solachidis, V., & Pitas, I. (1999). Circularly symmetric watermark embedding in 2-d dft domain. *ICASSP '99, 6*(1), 3469-3472.

Solachidis, V., & Pitas, I. (2004). Watermarking polygonal lines using Fourier descriptors. *Computer Graphics and Applications, 24*(3), 44-51.

Solachidis, V., Tefas, A., Nikoliaidis, N., Tsekeridou, S., Nikoliaidis, A., & Pitas, I. (2001). A benchmarking protocol for watermarking methods. In *IEEE International Conference on Image Processing* (pp. 1023-1026).

Soukal, D., Fridrich, J., & Goljan, M. (2005). *Maximum likelihood estimation of length of secret message embedded using +/-K steganography in spatial domain.* Paper presented at the Proceedings of SPIE, Electronic Imaging, Security, Steganography, and Watermarking of Multimedia Contents VII.

Spanos, G., & Maples, T. (1995). Performance study of a selective encryption scheme for the security of networked real-time video. In *Proceedings of the 4th international conference on computer communications and networks (ICCCN'95).* Las Vegas, NV.

Spiegel, M. R., & Stephens, L. J. (1999). *Schaum's outline of theory and problems of statistics.* Singapore: McGraw-Hill.

Steinebach, M., & Zmudzinski, S. (2004). Complexity optimization of digital watermarking for music-on-demand services. In *Proceedings of Virtual Goods Workshop 2004* (pp. 24-35). Illmenau, Germany.

Stinson, D. (2002). *Cryptography: Theory and practice* (2nd ed.). Chapman & Hall/CRC.

Stütz, T., & Uhl A. (in press). Efficient transparent encryption of JPEG2000. *Proceedings of the ACM Multimedia and Security Workshop (MM-SEC '07)*. Houston, TX.

Stütz, T., & Uhl, A. (2005, December). Image confidentiality using progressive JPEG. *Proceedings of Fifth International Conference on Information, Communication and Signal Processing (ICICS '05)* (pp. 1107-1111). Bangkok, Thailand.

Stütz, T., & Uhl, A. (2006, September). Transparent image encryption using progressive JPEG. In S. Katsikas et al. (Eds.), *Information Security. Proceedings of the 9th Information Security Conference (ISC'06)* (LNCS 4176, pp. 286-298). Springer-Verlag.

Stütz, T., & Uhl, A. (2006). On format-compliant iterative encryption of JPEG2000. *Proceedings of the Eighth IEEE International Symposium on Multimedia (ISM'06)* (pp. 985-990). Los Alamitos, CA: IEEE Computer Society.

Su, K., Kundur, D., & Hatzinakos, D. (2005a). Spatially localized image-dependent watermarking for statistical invisibility and collusion resistance. *IEEE Transactions on Multimedia, 7,* 52-56.

Su, K., Kundur, D., & Hatzinakos, D. (2005b). Statistical invisibility for collusion-resistant digital video watermarking. *IEEE Transactions on Multimedia, 7,* 43-51.

Sullivan, K., Bi, Z., Madhow, U., Chandrasekaran, S., & Manjunath, B. (2004). Steganalysis of quantization index modulation data hiding. In *International Conference on Image Processing (ICIP'04)* (Vol. 2, pp. 1165-1168).

Swaminathan, A., Mao, Y., & Wu, M. (2006). Robust and secure image hashing. *IEEE Transactions on Image Forensics and Security.*

Tang, C. W., & Hang, H.-M. (2003). A feature-based robust digital image watermarking scheme. *IEEE Transactions on Signal Processing, 51,* 950-959.

Tang, L. (1996, November). Methods for encrypting and decrypting MPEG video data efficiently. In *Proceedings of the ACM multimedia 1996* (pp. 219-229). Boston.

Tardos, G. (2003, June 9-11). Optimal probabilistic fingerprint codes. In *Proceedings of the Theory of Computing* (pp. 116-125). San Diego, CA.

Taubman, D., & Marcellin, M. (2002). *JPEG2000—Image compression fundamentals, standards and practice.* Kluwer Academic.

Taylor, J., & Verbyla, A. (2004). Joint modelling of location and scale parameters of the t distribution. *Statistical Modelling, 4*(2), 91-112.

Tefas, A., & Pitas, I. (2000). Multi-bit image watermarking robust to geometric distortions. *IEEE International Conference on Image Processing* (Vol. 3, pp. 710-713).

Terzija, N., & Geisselhardt, W. (2003). Robust digital image watermarking method based on discrete Fourier transform. *5th IASTED International Conference on Signal and Image Processing* (Vol. 1, pp. 55-60).

Terzija, N., & Geisselhardt, W. (2005). *Robust digital image watermarking using feature point detectors.* Paper presented at the 9th WSEAS International Multiconference CSCC on Communication, Vouliagmeni Beach, Athens, Greece.

Terzija, N., & Geisselhardt, W. (2006). A novel synchronisation approach for digital image watermarking based on scale invariant feature point detector. *IEEE International Conference on Image Processing* (Vol. 1, pp. 2585-2588).

Tian, J. (2002). Wavelet-based reversible watermarking for authentication. *Proceedings of the SPIE Security and Watermarking of Multimedia Contents IV* (Vol. 4675, pp. 679-690).

Tian, J. (2003). Reversible data embedding using difference expansion. *IEEE Transactions on Circuits Systems and Video Technology, 13*(8), 890-896.

Tikkanen, K., Hannikainen, M., Hamalainen, T., & Saarinen, J. (2000). Hardware implementation of the improved WEP and RC4 encryption algorithms for wireless terminals. In *Proceedings of the European Signal Processing Conference* (pp. 2289-2292).

Torralba, A., & Olivia, A. (2003). Statistics of natural image categories. IOP Network: *Computation in Neural Systems, 14*, 391-412.

Torrubia, A., & Mora, F. (2002). Perceptual cryptography on MPEG Layer III bit-streams. *IEEE Transactions on Consumer Electronics, 48*(4), 1046-1050.

Tosum, A. S., & Feng, W. (2000). Efficient multi-layer coding and encryption of MPEG video streams. *IEEE International Conference on Multimedia and Expo (I)*, 119-122.

Trappe, W., Wu, M., Wang, Z. J., & Liu, K. J. R. (2003). Anti-collusion fingerprinting for multimedia. *IEEE Transactions on Signal Processing, 51*, 1069-1087.

Trivedi, S., & Chandramouli, R. (2003). Active steganalysis of sequential steganography. In *Security, Steganography, and Watermarking of Multimedia Contents V* (Vol. 5020, pp. 123-130). IS&T/SPIE.

Trivedi, S., & Chandramouli, R. (2004). Locally most powerful detector for secret key estimation in spread spectrum data hiding. In *Security, Steganography, and Watermarking of Multimedia Contents VI* (Vol. 5306, pp. 1-12). IS&T/SPIE.

Trivedi, S., & Chandramouli, R. (2005). Secret key estimation in sequential steganalysis. *IEEE Transactions on Signal Processing: Supplement on Secure Media, 53*(2), 746-757.

Trung, T., & Martirosyan, S. (2004). On a class of traceability codes. *Design, Code and Cryptography, 31*, 125-132.

Tsekeridou, S., & Pitas, I. (2000). Embedding self-similar watermarks in the wavelet domain. *IEEE International Conference Acoustic, Systems and Signal Processing (ICASSP'00)* (Vol. 4, pp. 1967-1970).

Tsekeridou, S., Nikoladis, N., Sidiropoulos, N., & Pitas, I. (2000). Copyright protection of still images using self-similar chaotic watermarks. *IEEE Conference on Image Processing* (Vol. 1, pp. 411-414).

Tseng, Y. C., Chen, Y. Y., & Pan, H. K. (2002). A secure data hiding scheme for binary images. *IEEE Transactions on Communications, 50*(8), 1227-1231.

Uhl, A., & Obermair, C. (2005). Transparent encryption of JPEG2000 bitstreams. In P. Podhradsky et al. (Eds.), *Proceedings EC-SIP-M 2005 (5th EURASIP Conference focused on Speech and Image Processing, Multimedia Communications and Services)* (pp. 322-327). Smolenice, Slovak Republic.

Uhl, A., & Pommer, A. (2005). *Image and video encryption. from digital rights management to secured personal communication: Vol. 15. Advances in Information Security.* Springer-Verlag.

Ulichney, R. (1987). *Digital halftoning.* Cambridge, MA: MIT Press.

Vaidyanathan, P. P. (1992). *Multirate systems and filter banks.* Englewood Cliffs, NJ: Prentice Hall PTR.

Vassiliadis, B., Fotopoulos, V., Xenos, M., & Skodras, A. (2004, April). Could grid facilitate demanding media watermarking applications? In *Proceedings of the 4th International LeGE-WG Workshop*, Stuttgart, Germany

Venkatesan, R., Koon, S.-M., Jakubowski, M. H., & Moulin, P. (2000). Robust image hashing. In *Proceedings of the International Conference on Image Processing, 3.*

Vidakovic, B. (1998a). Nonlinear wavelet shrinkage with Bayes rules and Bayes factors. *Journal of the American Statistical Association, 93*(441), 173-179.

Vidakovic, B. (1998b). Wavelet-based nonparametric bayes methods. In D. Dey, P. MÄuller, & D. Sinha (Eds.), *Practical nonparametric and semiparametric Bayesian statistics* (Vol. 133, pp. 133-155). Springer-Verlag.

Vinod, P., & Bora, P. (2006). Motion-compensated inter-frame collusion attack on video watermarking and a countermeasure. *Information Security, IEE Proceedings, 153*, 61-73.

Vleeschouwer, C. D., Delaigle, J. E., & Macq, B. (2001, October). Circular interpretation of histogram for reversible watermarking. In *Proceedings of the IEEE*

4th Workshop on Multimedia Signal Processing (pp. 345-350). France.

Voloshynovskiy, S., Deguillaume, F., & Pun, T. (2000). *Content adaptive watermarking based on a stochastic multiresolution image modeling.* Paper presented at the 10th European Signal Processing Conference (EU-SIPCO'2000), Tampere, Finland.

Voloshynovskiy, S., Pereira, S., Iquise, V., & Pun, T. (2001). Attack modeling: Towards a second generation watermarking benchmark. *Signal Processing, 81,* 1177-1214.

Wallace, G. K. (1991). The JPEG still picture compression standard. *Communications of the ACM, 34*(4), 30-44.

Wang, H.-J., Su, P.-C., & JayKuo, C. (1998). Wavelet based digital image watermarking. *Optic Express, 3,* 491-196.

Wang, Y., & Moulin, P. (2006). Optimized feature extraction for learning-based image steganalysis. *IEEE Transactions on Information Forensics and Security, 1*(2), 31-45.

Wang, Y., & Moulin, P. (2006). Statistical modelling and steganalysis of DFT-based image steganography. In E. J. Delp, III, & P. W. Wong (Eds.), *Security, steganography, and watermarking of multimedia contents VIII* (SPIE 6072, pp. 0201-0211). Bellingham, WA: SPIE.

Wang, Y., & Moulin, P. (2007). Optimized feature extraction for learning-based image steganalysis. *IEEE Transactions on Information Forensics and Security, 2*(1), 31-45.

Wang, Z. J., Wu, M., Trappe, W., & Liu, K. J. R. (2005). Group-oriented fingerprinting for multimedia forensics. Preprint.

Wang, Z., & Bovik, A. C. (2002). A universal image quality index. *IEEE Signal Processing Letters, 9*(3), 81-84.

Wang, Z., & Simoncelli, E. P. (2005). Reduced-reference image quality assessment using a wavelet-domain natural image statistic model. *SPIE Electronic Imaging X, 5666,* 149-159.

Wang, Z., Bovik, A. C., Sheikh, H. R., & Simoncelli, E. P. (2004). Image quality assessment: From error visibility to structural similarity. *IEEE Transactions on Image Processing, 13*(4), 600-612.

Watson, A. B. (1993). DCT quantization matrices visually optimized for individual images. *SPIE: Human vision, Visual Processing and Digital Display IV, 1913,* 202-216.

Wayner, P. (2002). *Disappearing cryptography—Information hiding: Steganography and Watermarking* (2nd ed.). San Francisco: Morgan Kaufmann.

Wen, J., Severa, M., Zeng, W., Luttrell, M., & Jin, W. (2001, October). A format-compliant configurable encryption framework for access control of multimedia. In *Proceedings of the IEEE workshop on multimedia signal processing, MMSP '01* (pp. 435-440). Cannes, France.

Wen, J., Severa, M., Zeng, W., Luttrell, M., & Jin, W. (2002, June). A format-compliant configurable encryption framework for access control of video. *IEEE Transactions on Circuits and Systems for Video Technology, 12*(6), 545-557.

Weng, J., Liu, S., & Chen, K. (2007). Pirate decoder for the broadcast encryption schemes. In *Series F: Information Science special issue on Information Security, 50*(3).

Westfeld, A. (2001). F5—A steganographic algorithm: High capacity despite better steganalysis. In I. Moskowitz (Ed.), *Information Hiding, 4th International Workshop* (pp. 289-302). Berlin: Springer.

Westfeld, A. (2002). Detecting low embedding rates. In *5th Information Hiding Workshop* (Vol. 2578, pp. 324-339). Berlin/Heidelberg, Germany: Springer.

Westfeld, A. (2005). Space filling curves in steganalysis. In E. J. Delp, III, & P. W. Wong (Eds.), *Security, steganography, and watermarking of multimedia contents VII* (SPIE 5681, pp. 28-37). Bellingham, WA: SPIE.

Westfeld, A., & Pfitzmann, A. (1999). Attacks on steganographic systems. In A. Pfitzmann (Ed.), *Information Hiding, 3rd International Workshop* (pp. 61-76). Berlin: Springer.

Westfield, A. (2001). High capacity despite getter stega-nalysis (F5-A steganographic algorithm). In *Information Hiding: 4th International Workshop* (Vol. 2137, pp. 289-302). Springer-Verlag.

Wolf, P., Steinebach, M., & Diener, K. (2007). Comple-menting DRM with digital watermarking: Mark, search, retrieve. *Online Information Review, 31*(1), 10-21.

Wong, P. W. (1998). A public key watermark for image verification and authentication. *IEEE International Con-ference on Image Processing* (Vol. 1, pp. 455-459).

Wu, C., & Kuo, J. C. C. (2000). Fast encryption methods for audiovisual data confidentiality. *Proceedings of SPIE, SPIE International Symposia on Information Technolo-gies 2000, 4209,* 284-295.

Wu, C., & Kuo, J. C. C. (2001). Efficient multimedia encryption via entropy codec design. *Proceedings of SPIE, SPIE International Symposium on Electronic Imaging 2001, 4314,* 128-138.

Wu, H., & Ma, D. (2004, May). Efficient and secure en-cryption schemes for JPEG2000. In *Proceedings of the 2004 International Conference on Acoustics, Speech and Signal Processing (ICASSP 2004)* (pp. 869-872).

Wu, M., & Liu, B. (2004). Data hiding in binary image for authentication and annotation. *IEEE Transactions on Multimedia, 6*(4), 528-538.

Wu, M., Trappe, W., Wang, Z. J., & Liu, R. (2004). Col-lusion-resistant fingerprinting for multimedia. *IEEE Signal Processing Magazine,* 15-27.

Wu, Y. (2005, March 18-23). Linear combination col-lusion attack and its application on an anti-collusion fingerprinting. IEEE International Conference on Acous-tics, Speech, and Signal Processing, 2005. *Proceedings. (ICASSP '05), 2,* 13-16.

Xia, X.-G., Boncelet, C., & Arce, G. (1998). Wavelet transform based watermark for digital images. *Optic Express, 3,* 497-511.

Xie, L., & Arce, G. (1998). Joint wavelet compression and authentication watermarking. *Proceedings of the IEEE International Conference on Image Processing* (pp. 427-431).

Yang, J.-F., & Lu, C.-L. (1995). Combined techniques of singular value decomposition and vector quantization for image coding. *IEEE Transactions on Image Processing, 4*(8), 1141-1146.

Yasein, M. S., & Agathoklis, P. (2005). An improved algorithm for image registration using robust feature extraction. *Canadian Conference on Electrical and Computer Engineering* (Vol. 1, pp. 1927-1930).

Yeung, M. M., & Mintzer, F. (1997). An invisible watermarking technique for image verification. *IEEE International Conference on Image Processing* (Vol. 1, pp. 680-683).

Yi, X., Tan, C. H., Siew, C. K., & Rahman, S. M. (2001). Fast encryption for multimedia. *IEEE Transactions on Consumer Electronics, 47*(1), 101-107.

Yu, G. J., Lu, C. S., & Liao, H. Y. M. (2001). Mean-quan-tization-based fragile watermarking for image authentica-tion. *Optical Engineering, 40*(7), 1396-1408.

Yu, X., Tan, T., & Wang, Y. (2005). Extended optimiza-tion method of LSB steganalysis. In *IEEE International Conference on Image Processing, ICIP 2005* (Vol 2., pp. 1102-1105).

Yuan, C., Zhu, B. B., Su, M., Wang, Y., Li, S., & Zhong, Y. (2003, September). Layered access control for MPEG-4 FGS. *Proceedings of the IEEE International Conference on Image Processing (ICIP'03).* Barcelona, Spain.

Zamiri-Jafarian, H., & Gulak, G. (2005). *Iterative MIMO channel SVD estimation. International Conference on Communications* (ICC '05) (pp. 1157-1161). IEEE Press.

Zeng, W., & Lei, S. (1999, November). Efficient frequency domain video scrambling for content access control. In *Proceedings of the seventh ACM international multime-dia conference 1999* (pp. 285-293). Orlando, FL.

Zeng, W., & Lei, S. (2003). Efficient frequency domain selective scrambling of digital video. *IEEE Transactions on Multimedia, 5*(1), 118-129.

Zeng, W., Wen, J., & Severa, M. (2002, September). Fast selfsynchronous content scrambling by spatially shuffling codewords of compressed bitstreams. In *Proceedings of the IEEE international conference on image processing (ICIP'02)*.

Zhang, F., Safavi-Naini, R., & Susilo, W. (2004). An efficient signature scheme from bilinear pairings and its applications. *Practice and Theory in Public Key Cryptography—PKC'2004* (LNCS 2947, pp. 277-290).

Zhang, X.-P., & Li, K. (2005). Comments on "An SVD-based watermarking scheme for protecting rightful ownership." *IEEE Transactions on Multimedia: Correspondence, 7*(1).

Zhao, H. V., Liu, K. J. R. (2006). Fingerprint multicast in secure video streaming. *IEEE Transactions on Image Processing, 15*(1), 12-29.

Zhao, J., & Koch, E. (1995). Embedding robust labels into images for copyright protection. *International Congress on Intellectual Property Rights, Knowl*

Zhu, W., Xiong, Z., & Zhang, Y.-Q. (1998). Multiresolution watermarking for images and video: A unified approach. *Proceedings of the IEEE International Conference on Image Processing, 1*, 465-468.

Zigoris, P., & Jin, H. (2007). Bayesian methods for practical traitor tracing. *Applied Cryptography and Network Security*(LNCS 4521, pp. 194-2006).

Zöllner, J., Federrath, H., Klimant, H., Pfitzmann, A., Piotraschke, R., Westfeld, A., et al. (1998). Modeling the security of steganographic systems. In D. Aucsmith (Ed.), *2nd Information Hiding Workshop* (LNCS 1525, pp. 344-354). Berlin: Springer.

About the Contributors

Sos Agaian is the Peter T. Flawn Distinguished Professor of Electrical Engineering at the University of Texas at San Antonio, he is the director of the Electrical and Computer Engineering PhD Program and head of the Multimedia and Mobile Signal Processing Laboratory. Additionally, he is chair of the Electrical Engineering Graduate Studies Committee, and is a professor at the University of Texas Health Science Center in San Antonio. He has received numerous honors and awards and authored more than 300 scientific publications, 5 books, and established 12 patents.

Florent Autrusseau received an MS degree in electronic systems and image processing from the University of Nantes in 1999 and a PhD degree in signal and image processing from the IRESTE institute, IRCCyN lab, University of Nantes, in 2002. He was a research associate in the University of Chicago in 2003. He is currently a research engineer at Polytech'Nantes, IRCCyN Lab, University of Nantes since 2004. His research interests include digital watermarking, human visual system models, quality assessment, cryptography, biometrics, and lossless image compression.

Paulo S. L. M. Barreto (born 1965) is a Brazilian cryptographer. He graduated with a BSc in physics from the University of São Paulo in 1987, and received his PhD degree in engineering at the Escola Politécnica of the same university in 2003. He has authored or co-authored over 50 research works on design and analysis of block ciphers, cryptographic hash functions, elliptic curve cryptography, and pairing-based cryptography. These works have received some 400 references in the literature; the Web of Science records over 150 of them, with an h-level of 6. In 2005, the Essential Science Indicators recognized one of Barreto's papers as both "Hot Paper" (by virtue of being among the top 0.1% most cited computer science papers) and "Fast Breaking Paper" (for having the largest percentage increase in citations among the 1% most cited papers in its category). Currently Barreto is assistant professor in the Department of Computer and Digital Systems Engineering, Escola Politécnica, University of São Paulo.

Ahmed Bouridane received the Ingenieur d'Etat degree in electronics from Ecole Nationale Polytechnque of Algiers (ENPA), Algeria, in 1982, the MPhil degree in electrical engineering (VLSI design for signal processing) from the University of Newcastle-Upon-Tyne, UK, in 1988, and a PhD in electrical engineering (computer vision) from the University of Nottingham, UK, in 1992. From 1992 to 1994, he worked as a research developer in telesurveillance and access control applications. In 1994, he joined Queen's University Belfast, Belfast, UK, initially as lecturer in computer architecture and image processing. He is now a reader in computer science, and his research interests are in imaging for forensics and security, biometrics, homeland security, image/video watermarking, and cryptography. He has authored and co-authored more than 180 publications. Bouridane is a senior member of IEEE.

Maria Calagna received the Laurea degree in computer engineering in April 2002 from University of Palermo (Italy) with a thesis about 3D object recognition in robotics. In February 2007, she received a PhD in computer science from University La Sapienza (Roma, Italy). Her research interests are security techniques about intellectual property protection, especially watermarking, steganography, and digital rights management. In 2002-2003 she collaborated with CASPUR (Rome) on a project about controlled nuclear fusion, promoted by ENEA. Currently, she works for the Agenzia delle Entrate (Italian Revenues Agency) as an internal auditor.

Roberto Caldelli graduated cum laude in electronic engineering from the University of Florence in 1997, where he also received a PhD in computer science and telecommunications engineering in 2001. He received a 4-year research grant (2001-2005) from the University of Florence to research digital watermarking techniques for protection of images and videos. He is now an assistant professor in the Department of Electronics and Telecommunications of the University of Florence. He is a member of CNIT. His main research activities, witnessed by several publications, include digital image sequence processing, image and video digital watermarking, multimedia applications, and MPEG-1/2/4.

Patrick Le Callet holds a PhD in image processing from the University of Nantes. Engineer in electronic and informatics, he was also student at the Ecole Normale Superieure de Cachan. He received his aggregation degree in electronics in 1996. He is currently the head of the image and videocommunication group at CNRS IRCCyN lab. He is mostly engaged in research dealing with the application of human vision modeling in image processing. His current centers of interest are image and video quality assessment, watermarking techniques, and visual attention modeling and applications.

Patrizio Campisi is currently an associate professor with the Department of Applied Electronics, University of Rome, Roma TRE, Italy. He received a PhD in electronic engineering from the University of Rome, Roma TRE. He was a visiting researcher at the University of Toronto, Canada, at the Beckman Institute, University of Illinois at Urbana-Champaign, USA, and at the Ecole Polytechnique de L'Université de Nantes, IRRCyN, France. His research interests have been focused on digital signal and image processing with applications to multimedia. Specifically, he has been working on image deconvolution, image restoration, image analysis, texture coding, texture classification, gray scale, color, and video texture synthesis, watermarking, data hiding, and biometrics. He is co-editor of the book *Blind Image Deconvolution: Theory and Applications*. He is co-recipient of an ICIP 2006 best student paper award for the paper titled "Contour Detection by Multiresolution Surround Inhibition." He is a member of SPIE and of the IEEE Communications and Signal Processing Society and the Italian Professional Engineers Association.

Rajarathnam Chandramouli is the Thomas E. Hattrick Chair Associate Professor of Information Systems in the Electrical and Computer Engineering (ECE) Department at Stevens Institute of Technology. His research in wireless networking and security, cognitive networks, steganography/steganalysis, and applied probability is funded by the NSF, U.S. AFRL, U.S. Army, ONR, and other agencies. Currently, he is the founding chair of the IEEE COMSOC technical subcommittee on cognitive networks, and management board member of IEEE SCC 41 standards committee. Further information about his research can be found at http://www.ece.stevens-tech.edu/~mouli

Dominik Engel studied computer science at the University of Salzburg (Austria), where he focussed on image processing and graduated in 2002. As a research assistant in the Department of Computer Sciences of Salzburg University, he is currently finishing his PhD in the area of multimedia security. He is also a lecturer at the Salzburg University of Applied Sciences.

Anthony TS Ho obtained his BSc(Hons) in physical electronics from the University of Northumbria, UK in 1979, his MSc in applied optics from Imperial College in 1980, and his PhD in digital image processing from King's College, University of London in 1983. He is a fellow of the Institution of Engineering and Technology (FIET). He joined the Department of Computing, School of Electronics and Physical Sciences, University of Surrey in 2006 and holds a personal chair in multimedia security. He was an associate professor at Nanyang Technological University (NTU), Singapore from 1994 to 2005. Prior to that, he spent 11 years in industry in the UK and Canada specializing in signal and image processing projects. Ho has been working on digital watermarking and steganography since 1997 and co-founded DataMark Technologies in 1998, one of the first companies in the Asia-Pacific region, specializing in the research and commercialization of digital watermarking technologies. He continues to serve as a non-executive director and consultant to the company. Ho led the research and development team that invented a number of novel watermarking algorithms that resulted in three international patents granted including the US patent (6,983,057 B1).

Hongxia Jin obtained her PhD in computer science from Johns Hopkins University in 1999 and has worked as a research staff member for IBM research ever since. She is currently at the IBM Almaden Research Center, where she is the leading researcher working on key management, broadcast encryption, and traitor tracing technologies. The key management and forensic technologies she developed have been chosen as the core technologies by AACS, a new content protection industry standards for managing content stored on the next generation of prerecorded and recorded optical media for consumer use with PCs and consumer electronic devices. She has filed a dozen patents in this area. She also published numerous papers and a couple invited book chapters.Her research interests include digital rights managements; content protection; multimedia security; software security; security measurement; and information security in general. She particularly enjoys bringing technologies from theory to practice.

Andrew D. Ker received a BA in mathematics and computer science from Oxford University in 1997, and a DPhil in computer science from the same institution in 2001. His doctoral thesis was on the theoretical foundations of computer science, but he now studies information hiding, steganography, and steganalysis. He is presently a Royal Society University Research Fellow at Oxford University Computing Laboratory, and a fellow of University College, Oxford. Ker is a member of the IEEE and SPIE.

Fouad Khelifi received the Ingenieur d'Etat in electrical engineering from the University of Jijel, Algeria, in 2000, the Magistere degree in electronics from the University of Annaba, Algeria, in 2003. From 2003 to 2004, he worked as a lecturer at the University of Jijel, Algeria. Since 2004, he has been pursuing a PhD at the school of electronics, electrical engineering, and computer science, Queen's University of Belfast, UK. His research interests include image coding; image watermarking; digital signal and image processing; statistical signal and image processing; artificial intelligence; and pattern recognition and classification. He is a reviewer for a number of international conferences and Journals. He is also a member of EURASIP and IEEE.

Hae Yong Kim was born in Korea in 1964 and migrated to Brazil in 1975. He received the best rating in the university ingressing examination for computer science, Universidade de São Paulo (USP), Brazil, and graduated with the best average marks in 1988. He received an MSc in applied mathematics (1992) and a PhD in electrical engineering (1997) from USP. Since 1989 he has been teaching at USP, and currently he is an associate professor with the Department of Electronic Systems Engineering, USP. Since 2002, the National Council for Scientific and Technological Development (CNPq) has granted him a "research productivity award" scholarship. His research interests include the general area of image and video processing and analysis, authentication watermarking, machine learning, and medical image processing.

Fatih Kurugollu received a BSc, an MSc, and a PhD in computer engineering from the Istanbul Technical University, Istanbul, Turkey in 1989, 1994, and 2000, respectively. From 1991 to 2000, he was a research fellow in Marmara Research Center, Kocaeli, Turkey. In 2000, he joined the School of Computer Science, Queen's University, Belfast, UK, as a postdoctoral research assistant. He was appointed as a lecturer in the same department in 2003. His research interest includes multimedia watermarking, soft computing for image and video segmentation, visual surveillance, hardware architectures for image and video applications.

Shiguo Lian, member of IEEE, SPIE, EURASIP, and Chinese Association of Images & Graphics, received his PhD in multimedia security from Nanjing University of Science & Technology in July 2005. He was a research assistant in City University of Hong Kong in 2004. He has being with France Telecom R&D Beijing since July 2005, focusing on multimedia content protection, including digital rights management, multimedia encryption, watermarking and authentication, and so forth. He received the nomination prize of 2006 Innovation Prize in France Telecom. He is author or co-author of 3 books, 50 international journal or conference papers, 8 book chapters, and 6 patents.

Maciej Liśkiewicz received his PhD in 1990 and Habilitation in 2000, both from the University of Wroclaw, Poland. Currently, he is an associate professor with the Faculty of Technical and Natural Sciences, University of Lübeck, teaching theoretical computer science. His current research interests include computational complexity, privacy and security, information hiding, efficient algorithms, and parallel processing. From 1981 he worked for the Institute of Informatics, University of Wroclaw. From 1991 to 1993 he was with the Institute of Theoretical Computer Science, Technical University Darmstadt, Germany, as an Alexander von Humboldt Research Fellow. He was a visiting scientist at International Computer Science Institute (ICSI), Berkeley, California from 1995 to 1996, and 1998-1999 he was a visiting scientist at Wilhelm-Schickard Institute of Informatics, Eberhard-Karls-University of Tübingen, Germany.

Hafiz Malik is an assistant professor in the Electrical and Computer Engineering Department at Stevens Institute of Technology. He received his BE in electrical and communication engineering from the University of Engineering and Technology Lahore, in 1999 and a PhD in electrical and computer engineering from the University of Illinois at Chicago, in 2006. Malik has served as the session chair for 2nd *Secure Knowledge Management Workshop* 2006; organizer for special track on *Doctoral Dissertation in Multimedia, IEEE International Symposium on Multimedia* (*ISM*) 2006; member Technical Program Committee, *IEEE CCNC* 2007, 2008, *IEEE ICC* 2007, and *IEEE FITs* 2004, 2005. His research interests lie in information security, digital rights management, multimedia systems, digital signal processing, and digital forensic analysis. Further information about his research can be found at http://multimedia.ece.uic.edu/hafiz

Sergio Vicente Denser Pamboukian was born in Brazil in 1965. He received a BSc in civil engineering (1988); an MSc in electrical engineering (1998) from the Universidade Presbiteriana Mackenzie (UPM), Brazil; and a PhD in electrical engineering (2007) from the Universidade de São Paulo, Brazil. He is an assistant professor with the Department of Electrical Engineering at UPM, since 1989. He is the author of many books about programming languages like C++ and Delphi. His research interests include authentication watermarking, image processing, software engineering, programming languages and techniques, object orientation, educational software, and electronic data acquisition.

Alessandro Piva obtained a PhD in computer science and telecommunications engineering from the University of Florence in 1999. From 2002 until 2004 he was a research scientist at CNIT. He is currently an assistant professor at the University of Florence. His main research interests are: technologies for multimedia content security; image processing techniques for cultural heritage applications; video processing techniques; and multimedia applications in the cultural heritage field. He is co-author of more than 90 papers published in international journals and conference proceedings. He holds three Italian patents and one international patent regarding watermarking techniques.

Christopher B. Smith has been an engineer in security related fields since 1999. He received his PhD and MS degrees in electrical engineering from the University of Texas at San Antonio. He has undergraduate degrees in electrical engineering and computer science from Texas Tech University. He is an adjunct professor in the Department of Electrical Engineering at the University of Texas at San Antonio, and a licensed professional engineer working at Southwest Research Institute in San Antonio.

Matthew J. Sorell is a lecturer in telecommunications and multimedia engineering in the School of Electrical and Electronic Engineering at the University of Adelaide, South Australia. He is general chair of e-Forensics—the International Conference on Forensic Applications and Techniques in Telecommunications, Information and Multimedia. His research interests include a range of commercially relevant telecommunications topics, public policy relating to regulation of multimedia entertainment, and forensic investigative techniques in multimedia. He holds a BSc in physics, a BE in computer systems (with first class honours), a graduate certificate in management from the University of Adelaide, and a PhD in information technology from George Mason University (Virginia, USA).

Martin Steinebach is a researcher at the Fraunhofer Institute for Secure Information Technology (SIT) in Darmstadt, Germany and head of its media security group. In 2003, he received his PhD from the University of Technology Darmstadt for his work on digital audio watermarking. His main research interest is digital audio watermarking especially algorithms for mp2, MIDI, and PCM data watermarking, content fragile watermarking, and invertible audio watermarking. He is a member of the Ecrypt European Union Network of Excellence for cryptography and digital watermarking and the speaker of the steganography and digital watermarking working group of the security unit of Gesellschaft für Informatik (GI).

Thomas Stütz graduated from the University of Salzburg in 2006, where he is currently employed as research assistant in the Department of Computer Science. He is working on his PhD, which focuses on secure transmission of scalable video. Multimedia security and image processing are his main research interests.

K.P. Subbalakshmi (Suba) is an associate professor in electrical and computer engineering. Her research interests lie in information and network security, cognitive radio networks, and wireless and multimedia networking and coding. Suba is the chair of the Special Interest Group in Multimedia Security, IEEE Technical Committee on Multimedia Communications (MMTC), IEEE COMSOC and also serves as the Secretary of the MMTC. She is a recipient of the Stevens Technogenesis Award for research technology contributions in 2007. She has served/is serving as guest/associate editors for several journals as well as the program co-chair of several conferences.

Nataša Terzija received the Dipl.-Ing. degree from Faculty of Electrical Engineering of the University of Belgrade, Belgrade, Serbia in 2000. Her academic career started in 2001 when she joined the Institute of Information Technology of the University Duisburg-Essen, Duisburg, Germany as an associate teaching and research assistant. She completed her PhD in the field of digital image watermarking in 2006 from the University Duisburg-Essen, Germany. In January 2007, Terzija joined the School of Electrical and Electronic Engineering at the University of Manchester as a research associate. Her current research is focused on data analysis and image reconstruction techniques for chemically selective optical tomography.

Andreas Uhl is an associate professor of the Computer Science Department of Salzburg University (Austria) where he leads the Multimedia Signal Processing and Security Lab. He is also lecturer at the Carinthia Tech Institute and the Salzburg University of Applied Sciences. His research interests include image and video processing, wavelets, multimedia security, biometrics, parallel algorithms, and numbertheoretical numerics.

Patrick Wolf has studied mathematics and philosophy at Johannes Gutenberg-University, Mainz, Germany and since his return from IBM Research in Hawthorne, New York, Wolf is a research associate at Fraunhofer Gesellschaft, currently working for the Fraunhofer Institute for Secure Information Technology (SIT) in Darmstadt, Germany. His research interests encompass generic watermarking and integration of watermarking in multimedia information systems.

Ulrich Wölfel received his diploma in computer science in 2004 from the University of Lübeck, Germany, where he is currently working on his PhD thesis. From 2005 to 2007 he was with the Federal Office for Information Security in Bonn, Germany. His research interests include steganography, steganalysis, and cryptography.

Index

Symbols

2D-contrast sensitivity function (CSF) 176

A

Active Steganalysis 258
active warden 139
active warden, the 152
advanced access content system (AACS) 315
advanced benchmarks 278
advanced birthday attacks 13
All frequency embedding 254
artificial "stego"-noise 146
authentication watermarking (AW) 1
authentication watermarking, for binary images 8
authentication watermarking by self-toggling (AWST) 8
authentication watermarking by template ranking (AWTR), and parity atacks 9
authentication watermarking derived from Chang, Tseng and Lin's data hiding (AWCTL) 11
AW by template ranking with symmetrical central pixels (AWTC) 9

B

batch steganography 278
Bayesian wavelet denoising 225
benchmarking, in the steganalysis literature 269
benchmarks 266
bias noise 141
binary classification 274
binary images, classifications of 2
binary steganalysis 269

bitstreams 336
BitTorrentConnector 113
Blindside 247
blind steganalysis 273
blokiness 252
BLS signatures 12
broadcast encryption systems, security problems with 317
broadcasting encryption 30
bullet scratch technique 293

C

C4 metric 180
camera identification, four sets of techniques 292
center of mass (COM) 215
central limit theorem 142
Chameleon method 31
Chang, Tseng, and Lin's data hiding (DHCTL, block-wise) 7
charge coupled device (CCD) 141
charge coupled device (CCD) image sensor 293
Chi-square tests 252
clone decoder 317
CMAC message authentication code 12
coalition tracing 324
coded fingerprinting 28
collusion attack 67
collusion attack, definitionof 73
colour interpolation, and gamma correction 295
complementary metal oxide semiconductor (CMOS) 141
Completely Known Statistics 260
Completely Unknown Statistics 260